# Trinidad & Tobago

written and researched by

## Dominique De-Light and Polly Thomas

this edition updated by
### Lesley Rose and Ross Velton

ROUGH
GUIDES

NEW YORK • LONDON • DELHI
www.roughguides.com

▲ Coconut grove, Manzanilla

## Introduction to

# Trinidad & Tobago

**Just off the coast of the South American mainland they were once part of, the twin islands of Trinidad and Tobago (usually shortened to T&T) form one republic at the southernmost islands of the Lesser Antilles chain and are the most exciting and underexplored of Caribbean islands. A cultural pacemaker best known as the home and heart of West Indian Carnival, the nation also boasts the region's most diverse and absorbing culture.**

Trinidad and Tobago manage to be relatively inexpensive and well suited for independent travellers without being full-fledged tourist resorts. The republic has been able to remain largely unfettered by the more noxious elements of the Caribbean tourist trade due to its economic independence, based mostly on natural reserves of gas and oil. Visitors are generally not corralled in all-inclusives or holed-up on private beaches and – though you could easily spend two weeks just exploring seashores, which range from palm-lined white sand fringed by limpid waters to secluded, wave-whipped outcrops – you'll find there's far more to T&T than suntans and snorkelling.

You'd be hard pressed to find a Caribbean location that offers such a variety of wildlife and habitats in such a compact area (Trinidad covers less than 5000 square kilometres, Tobago just 300), making T&T one of the richest destinations in the region for **eco-tourism**. In **Trinidad**, there are tropical rainforests with towering canopies of mahogany and teak, wetlands harbouring all manner of exotic wildlife, and remote beaches where leatherback turtles lay their eggs, not to mention opportunities for birdwatching, which

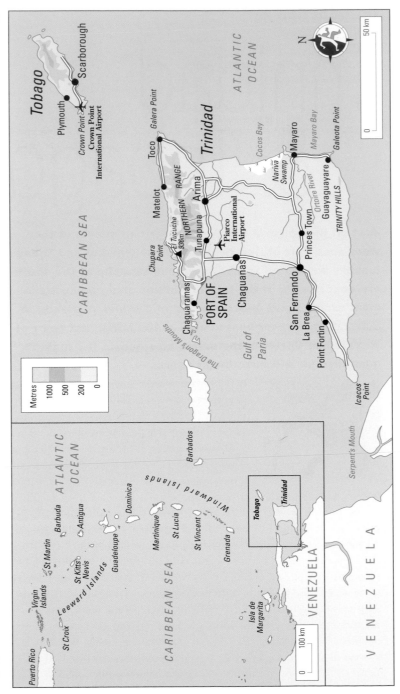

## Street food

In a land that takes its culinary traditions so seriously, it's no surprise that the ubiquitous street food in T&T is so delicious; you can get your fix from the ever-present roadside stalls by regularly inspected, hygiene-badge-wearing vendors. One of the more common delicacies is the double: flat, fried bara breads filled with a runny channa (chickpea) curry and served with spicy kucheela chutney. Equally easy to find is corn soup, a thick and fortifying blend of split peas, vegetables, chadon beni and chunks of corn on the cob – excellent for soaking up an excess of beer and rum. Other specialities to look out for include pholourie (spiced split-pea doughballs served with sweet and spicy tamarind sauce), and accra (peppery saltfish fritters). The hands-down king of street food, however, is the roti: an Indian bread wrap or "skin" (either a split pea-filled paratha, a shredded buss-up-

shut or a floury, griddled sada), filled with channa or potato curry, plus any combination of chicken, mutton, pumpkin, bodi (green) beans or bhaji (spinach-like greens), and finished off with a dollop of pepper sauce and kucheela. A "beastly cold" Carib beer is, of course, the perfect accompaniment to Trinbagonian dining al fresco.

– with more than 430 brilliantly hued species – is among the world's best. **Tobago** is best known for its glorious beaches and stunning coral reefs, favoured by manta rays and shoals of brightly-coloured tropical fish.

Equally engaging are T&T's crowded and dynamic **towns and cities**, where barrack-house complexes and fretworked townhouses sit side by side with temples, mosques, Catholic cathedrals and Anglican churches. The different **ethnic groups** brought to labour in the islands after the slaves were freed in 1834 have given rise to a remarkably varied populace, hailing from India, China, Portugal and Syria as well as Africa, England, France and Spain. Though racial tensions are inevitably present, Trinbagonians (as they're collectively known) generally coexist with good humour, and are proud of the multiculturalism that has so enriched the life of the nation.

Trinbagonians have a less harrowing past to contend with than many of their Caribbean neighbours. Neglected by the Spanish for most of their three centuries of rule, Trinidad experienced full-scale slavery for only fifty years, while the Dutch, French and English were too busy fighting over Tobago to dedicate it to the demands of King Sugar. Consequently, the national psyche is characterized by a strong sense of identity and a laid-back enjoyment of the good things in life, the latter best displayed in the local propensity for liming – taking time out to meet friends, talk and sink a Carib beer or some rum. Feeding off this attitude is an electrifying **music scene**

## Fact file

- Standing at about 1.3 million, Trinidad and Tobago's population is around 40 percent Indian, 39.5 percent black, 18.4 percent mixed-race, and 0.6 percent white.

- With 29.4 percent of its population Roman Catholic, 23.8 percent Hindu, 10.9 percent Anglican, 5.8 percent Muslim and 3.4 percent Presbyterian, T&T is the most theologically diverse nation of the Caribbean.

- The islands boast one of the highest literacy rates in the Western Hemisphere, at 98.6 percent.

- The Trinidad and Tobago economy is the most diversified and industrialized in the English-speaking Caribbean. As well as exporting fruit, vegetables and sugar cane, T&T produces 120 thousand barrels of oil and 1.462 billion cubic feet of natural gas per day.

- The Pitch Lake, at La Brea on Trinidad's southwestern coast, is the world's largest natural reservoir of asphalt.

- As the southernmost islands in the Caribbean chain, T&T lie outside the region's hurricane belt, and haven't suffered a big blast since Flora in 1963. The closest thing to a thrilling natural phenomenon here are the rather underwhelming mud volcanoes – a 1997 eruption in Piparo, Trinidad, saw mud flying 150 feet into the sky.

▲ Baptist prayer flags at Toco, Trinidad

that rivals even that of Jamaica, having spawned the influential calypso and soca genres. The islands' thirteen public holidays and numerous local festivals are mere limbering up for the republic's most famous party, the annual pre-Lenten **Carnival**. During this unique and explosive event, the no-holds-barred debauchery of opening night Jouvert celebrations is followed by two days of pure joy as 5000-strong bands of intricately costumed revellers take to the streets in a celebration of life.

# Where to go

B ound together for the convenience of the British empire, Trinidad and Tobago share little more than their status as a republic. **Trinidad** offers culture, ethnic diversity, music, clubs, great food and a wealth of gorgeous beaches and pristine rainforest. A more conventional holiday destination, **Tobago** boasts archetypal Caribbean beaches thronged by hotels of every budget. It's impossible to get a full picture of all the republic has to offer without visiting both islands, but regular plane and ferry service make it possible to see the best of each even during a short stay.

A visit to Trinidad will inevitably begin in **Port of Spain**, the vibrant, bustling capital and centre of **Carnival**. With the island's best selection of restaurants, local music and accommodation, this urbane metropolis is a natural base from which to explore the rest of the country. **Chaguaramas** to the west is the capital's playground, a national park with a string of open-air clubs providing lively, sophisticated nightlife. For the ultimate escape, however, it's not far to the rocky, wooded islands of the **Bocas**.

A sweeping curve of powdery sand and powerful waves, **Maracas Bay** is the first of many lovely beaches along the north coast. Between **Blanchisseuse** and **Matelot** runs a long stretch of completely undeveloped coastline – thirty kilometres of footprint-free sand and total seclusion – while the coastline further east is spectacularly rugged. Dominated by the densely forested peaks of the **Northern Range**, the northern interior offers excellent hiking and superb birdwatching opportunities. South of the hills, the traffic-choked **Eastern Main Road** links the capital with the sizeable town of **Arima**

## The great outdoors

Blessed with an incredible richness in fauna and flora, as well as pristine rainforest and miles of undeveloped coastline, T&T is perhaps the best place in the Caribbean to drag yourself away from the resorts. Trinidad in particular has endless opportunities for adventure, especially in the Northern Range, where you can hike through steamy rainforest in search of secluded waterfalls or rise to the challenge of squeezing and swimming your way through the Guanapo Gorge. Birdwatching trips into the hinterland are equally rewarding, and it's hard to forget your first sight of a toucan peering down through the foliage, or the jewel-like flash of a hummingbird whirring past your nose. Animal life is similarly absorbing, from reclusive ocelots, oposums and armadillos to the howler monkeys or manatees, and the leatherback turtles which lay their eggs on T&T's beaches. With a few brilliant small-scale operators offering regular hikes, bush camps and birdwatching alongside anything from dawn kayaking in search of manatees to batcave visits or mountain-biking, experiencing T&T's wild side couldn't be easier.

vii

▶ Jelly coconut van

and provides access to swimmable rivers and waterfalls, caves, and the oldest Benedictine monastery in the Caribbean, from which you get an awesome view of the unravelling plateau below.

Dominated by flat agricultural plains, **central Trinidad** provides a fascinating contrast to the north; from the ethereal **Waterloo Temple** to the busy market town of **Chaguanas**, Indian culture predominates here. Just forty minutes from Port of Spain lies the mangrove labyrinth of **Caroni Swamp**, home of the striking national bird, the scarlet ibis. On the east coast, the protected wetlands at **Nariva** are the habitat of endangered manatees and giant anacondas, while four kilometres of fine brown sand lined by groves of coconut palms make **Manzanilla** a favourite spot to recover from the rigours of Carnival. The burgeoning city of **San Fernando** is a friendly base from which to explore the largely unvisited "deep south", where modern oil towns such as **Fyzabad** contrast with the picturesque fishing villages and calm, deserted beaches of **Cedros** and **Erin**, and **Mayaro Bay** on the southeast coast.

Most people travelling to **Tobago** head for the translucent waters, coral reefs and excellent facilities of the island's low-lying southwestern tip around **Crown Point**, staying in one of the multitudinous hotels slung along the coastline. The vibrant capital, **Scarborough**, with its market and historic fort, offers a more genuine picture of local life, while the rugged **windward**, or Atlantic, coast is best known for the spectacular waterfall at **Argyll** and the island's most dazzling scuba diving at **Speyside**. The **leeward**, or Caribbean, coast – popular with day-trippers – is lined by a precipitous snake of tarmac that passes superb beaches at **Castara** and **Englishman's Bay**, while in the northwest, **Charlotteville** is a picturesque fishing village overlooking a couple of gorgeous horseshoe beaches.

# When to go

Though T&T's temperatures remain tropical year-round, most people visit between January and March, when **Carnival** explodes into life; the trees are in bloom and the climate is at its most forgiving: the sun shines, rain is rare and the nights are cool. By May, however, the lack of rain has parched the formerly lush landscape: greens turn to yellow, dust clouds put the views into soft focus and bush fires rage through the hills. The only relief from the aridity takes the form of brief, sudden tropical rain-storms. At the end of May, the **rainy season** sets in, and the skies open up with dramatic deluges. The rainy season often continues into December, but there's usually a respite from the

▲ Manzanilla beach

downpours in September, a period of hot sunshine and blue skies known as the **petit carem**. It's an excellent time to visit, with flights at low season rates, though you'll find the resorts a little quiet. Only Tobago hoteliers generally charge higher rates during the **high season** (Dec 15–April 15), while many smaller hotels charge the same all year round in both islands. Many hotels in and around Port of Spain, however, boost prices during Carnival week.

## Average temperatures and rainfall in Port of Spain

|  | temperature (°C) | | temperature (°F) | | rainfall | |
|---|---|---|---|---|---|---|
|  | max / min | | max / min | | mm / in | |
| January | 31 | 21 | 87 | 69 | 69 | 2.7 |
| February | 31 | 20 | 88 | 68 | 41 | 1.6 |
| March | 32 | 20 | 89 | 68 | 46 | 1.8 |
| April | 32 | 21 | 90 | 69 | 53 | 2.1 |
| May | 32 | 22 | 90 | 71 | 94 | 3.7 |
| June | 32 | 22 | 89 | 71 | 193 | 7.6 |
| July | 31 | 22 | 88 | 71 | 218 | 8.6 |
| August | 31 | 22 | 88 | 71 | 246 | 9.7 |
| September | 32 | 22 | 89 | 71 | 193 | 7.6 |
| October | 32 | 22 | 89 | 71 | 170 | 6.7 |
| November | 32 | 22 | 89 | 71 | 183 | 7.2 |
| December | 31 | 21 | 88 | 69 | 125 | 4.9 |

# 25

## things not to miss

*It's not possible to see everything that Trinidad and Tobago have to offer in one trip - and we don't suggest you try. What follows is a selective sampling of the country's highlights: gorgeous beaches, thrilling nightlife, fine food and exotic wildlife. It's arranged in five colour-coded categories, so that you can browse through to find the very best things to see, do and experience. All highlights have a page reference to take you into the guide, where you can find out more.*

x

**01 Maracas beach** Page **134** • Enclosed by forested hills and whipped by Atlantic waves, Maracas offers Trinidad's best beach scene.

**02** **Hiking in the north-ern range** Page **162** • The beautiful, forested mountains in Trinidad's north are perfect for long, adventurous treks.

**03** **Chaguaramas nightlife** Page **60** • From exuberant pre-Carnival fetes to danceclubs under the palm trees, you'll rarely want to go to bed early in this nightlife hotspot.

**04** **Roti** Page **36** • T&T's ultimate fast food, rotis are filling, inexpensive, delicious and extremely addictive; be sure to try all the different combinations.

**05** **Turtle-watching** Page **166** • Viewing the slow journey of the leatherback turtles as they lay their eggs is an oddly enjoyable and emotional experience.

**06 Diving and snorkelling** Page **248** • With its intricate reefs patrolled by shoals of colourful fish, the Tobago coast provides a beguiling alternative to mere sun and sand.

**09 Marianne River** Page **143** • Take a natural jacuzzi under the pounding cascades at the waterfalls along this river.

**07 Panyards** Page **101** • Take a pre-Carnival tour of Port of Spain's panyards and judge for yourself which band might take the coveted Panorama prize.

**08 Jouvert morning** Page **109** • This pre-Carnival, bacchanalian street party sees mud- and paint-coated revellers chipping through the streets before crossing the savannah stage at dawn.

**10 Carnival** Page **108** • Whether you're just taking in the parade or becoming part of it by joining a mas band, Carnival is T&T's ultimate party.

**11** **Grande Riviere** Page **171** • You'll have a hard time finding a more ideal or unspoiled place than this remote coastal village.

**12** **St James lime** Page **96** • St James comes alive after dark, its parade of bars and low-key clubs perfect for learning the art of liming.

**14** **Tobago coastal cruise** Page **247** • A catamaran cruise along the Caribbean coast provides a spectacularly different perspective of Tobago's scenery and the chance to moor up at a deserted cove for a spot of lunch by the water.

**13** **Castara** Page **296** • With its crop of funky guesthouses and decidedly laid-back feel, Castara is the spot for some of Tobago's most absorbing beach scene.

**15 North coast drive** Page 131 • The drive along Trinidad's spectacular northern coastline provides tantalizing glimpses of innumerable tiny coves and rainforest-smothered headlands.

**16 Old Mas, Victoria Square** Page **109** • This small-scale parade of traditional characters – old-fashioned sailors, pipe-smoking firemen or menacing devils – provides a stirring introduction to the true essence of Carnival.

**17 Blanchisseuse-Paria hike** Page **145** • This gentle trek along one of Trinidad's last-remaining stretches of undeveloped coastline promises deserted beaches, stunning scenery and a dip in a rainforest waterfall.

**18 Englishman's Bay** Page **298** • A deliciously remote arc of white sand licked by gin-clear Caribbean sea and featuring a wonderful offshore reef for snorkelling, this is beach life at its best.

**19 Caroni swamp trip** Page 183 • Climb aboard a pirogue and putter through the tunnel-like channels of one of Trinidad's richest wetland areas to spot caimans, snakes, anteaters and dazzlingly coloured flocks of scarlet ibis.

**20 Indian festivals** Page 186 • From the paint-spattered antics of Phagwa to the stirring drumming of Hosay, Trinidad's Muslim and Hindu communities stage several annual festivals that are open for all to enjoy.

**21 Breakfast Shed** Page 104 • This hangar-like dockside building in Port of Spain offers delicious, no-nonsense Creole food.

**22 Pirate's Bay** Page 315 • This secluded horseshoe of white sand is one of Tobago's finest, with great snorkelling and abundant peace and quiet.

**23** **Mayoro-Manzanilla road drive** Page **200** • With its forests of swaying palms and roadside mangrove swamps, this east coast drive offers some of Trinidad's most lovely scenery.

**24** **Birdwatching** Page **148** • T&T promises the chance to see up close an astonishing number of brightly coloured tropical birds, most especially at the Asa Wright Nature Centre. The well-tended grounds of this luxurious, 800,000 square-metre, nonprofit retreat in northern Trinidad provide the opportunity to see up to 40 species a day.

**25** **Waterloo Temple** Page **190** • Trinidad's most unusually located Hindu temple is an arresting symbol of the island's Indian culture.

# Contents

# Using this Rough Guide

We've tried to make this Rough Guide a good read and easy to use. The book is divided into five main sections, and you should be able to find whatever you want in one of them.

## Front section

The front colour section offers a quick tour of Trinidad & Tobago. The **introduction** aims to give you a feel for the place, with suggestions on where to go. We also tell you what the weather is like and include a basic country fact file. Next, our authors round up their favourite aspects of T&T in the **things not to miss** section – whether it's great food, amazing sights or a special hotel. Right after this comes the Rough Guide's full **contents** list.

## Basics

You've decided to go and the Basics section covers all the **pre-departure** nitty-gritty to help you plan your trip. This is where to find out which airlines fly to your destination, what paperwork you'll need, what to do about money and insurance, about Internet access, food, security, public transport, car rental – in fact just about every piece of **general practical information** you might need.

## Guide

This is the heart of the Rough Guide, divided into user-friendly chapters, each of which covers a specific region. Every chapter starts with a list of **highlights** and an **introduction** that

helps you to decide where to go, depending on your time and budget. Likewise, introductions to the various towns and smaller regions within each chapter should help you plan your itinerary. We start most town accounts with information on arrival and accommodation, followed by a tour of the sights, and finally reviews of places to eat and drink, and details of nightlife. Longer accounts also have a directory of practical listings. Each chapter concludes with **public transport** details for that region.

## Contexts

Read Contexts to get a deeper understanding of how T&T ticks. We include a brief **history**, an A–Z of mythology, articles about **wildlife** and **music**, together with a detailed further-reading section that reviews dozens of **books** relating to the country.

## Small print + index

Apart from a **full index**, which includes maps as well as places, this section covers publishing information, credits and acknowledgements, and also has our contact details in case you want to send in updates and corrections to the book – or suggestions as to how we might improve it.

# Chapter list and map

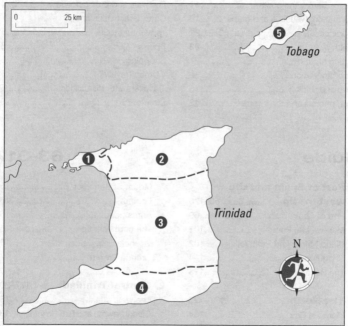

# Contents

# Contexts                    319–364

# Language                    365–371

# Small print and index      389–400

# Basics

# Basics

# Getting there

Unless you're arriving by cruise ship, your only option is to fly to Trinidad and Tobago. The number of regular flights to both islands has increased in recent years, meaning prices have stabilised for the most part. However, you can still find good charter deals in the wet season (August to December) and it can be difficult to find an inexpensive flight during the summer holidays, at Christmas and, of course, during Carnival. It is worth remembering that both Trinidad and Tobago experience an Indian summer known as the "petite careme" during the rainy season in September, offering two to four weeks of hot, dry weather at a time when air fares are usually a steal.

You can often cut costs by going through a **specialist flight agent** – either a consolidator, who buys up blocks of tickets from the airlines and sells them at a discount, or a **discount agent**, who in addition to dealing with discounted flights may also offer special student and youth fares and a range of other travel-related services such as travel insurance, rail passes, car rentals, tours and the like. Some agents specialize in **charter flights**, which may be cheaper than anything available on a scheduled flight, but again departure dates are fixed and withdrawal penalties are high.

If you're planning to spend your whole holiday based in one spot in Tobago, booking a **package holiday** might be your best option. There are legions of specialist companies who can arrange flights, airport transfers and accommodation, often at a significantly lower rate than you'd get independently. You can book all grades of villas and hotels, as well as meal plans, all-inclusive deals (where all meals are included in the room rate) or self-catering apartments. As Trinidad is less geared toward tourists, there are fewer deals available beyond birdwatching trips or Carnival packages; Tobago-oriented companies often offer a few days in Trinidad in conjunction with a Tobago trip. Alternatively, the companies listed in this section can arrange meet-and-greet services, airport transfers, car rental and accommodation booking.

A further possibility is to see if you can arrange a **courier flight**, although you'll need a flexible schedule, and preferably be traveling alone with very little luggage. In return for shepherding a parcel through customs, you can expect to get a deeply discounted ticket. You'll probably also be restricted in the duration of your stay.

If the Caribbean is only one stop on a longer journey, you might want to consider buying a **Round-the-World** (RTW) ticket. Some travel agents can sell you an "off-the-shelf" RTW ticket that will have you touching down in about half a dozen cities; others will have to assemble one for you, which can be tailored to your needs but is apt to be more expensive.

Several Caribbean airlines offer **air passes** which can be used for **island-hopping** around the region: available for purchase in conjunction with any international carrier, these allow unlimited stopovers within a thirty-day period, and prices start from £281/US$399/A$555/NZ$600. Passes are valid only within the Caribbean region and usually have to be purchased prior to your visit. However, inter-island flights are cheap and frequent enough to make the passes unnecessary.

## Booking flights online

Many airlines and discount travel websites offer you the opportunity to book your tickets online, cutting out the costs of agents and middlemen. Good deals can often be found through discount or auction sites, as well as through the airlines' own websites.

## Online booking agents and general travel sites

ⓦ**www.cheapflights.com** Flight deals, travel agents, plus links to associated sites serving Canada, the UK, Australia and more.

ⓦ**www.cheaptickets.com** Discount flight specialists (US only). Also at ☎1-888/922-8849.

ⓦ**www.deckchair.com** Bob Geldof's online travel booking venture, drawing on a wide range of airlines.

ⓦ**www.ebookers.com**. Efficient, easy to use flight finder, with competitive fares.

ⓦ**www.etn.nl** A hub of consolidator and discount agent web links.

ⓦ**www.expedia.com** Discount airfares, all-airline search engine and daily deals, associated sites serving the UK and Canada.

ⓦ**www.flyaow.com** Air travel info and reservations site.

ⓦ**www.gaytravel.com** Online travel agent for gay travellers, concentrating mostly on accommodation and cruises.

ⓦ**www.geocities.com/Thavery2000/** Has an extensive list of airline toll-free numbers and websites.

ⓦ**www.hotwire.com** Bookings from the US only. Last-minute savings of up to 40 percent on regular published fares. Travellers must be at least 18 and there are no refunds, transfers or changes allowed. Log-in required.

ⓦ**www.kelkoo.co.uk** Useful UK-only price comparison site which checks several sources to find low cost flights.

ⓦ**www.opodo.co.uk** Popular and reliable source of low UK fares, run in conjunction with nine major European airlines.

ⓦ**www.priceline.com** Name-your-own-price website that has deals at around 40 percent off standard fares. You cannot specify flight times (although you do specify dates) and the tickets are nonrefundable, nontransferable and nonchangeable.Now has links to associated sites in Hong Kong and the UK, but this side only offer booking from the US.

ⓦ**www.site59.com** (US). Offers good last-minute holiday package and flight-only deals.

ⓦ**www.skyauction.com** Bookings from the US only. Auctions tickets and travel packages using a "second bid" scheme. The best strategy is to bid the maximum you're willing to pay, since if you win you'll pay just enough to beat the runner-up regardless of your maximum bid.

ⓦ**www.travelocity.com** Destination guides, web fares and best deals for car hire, accommodation & lodging as well as fares.

ⓦ**www.travelshop.com.au** Australian website offering discounted flights, packages, insurance and online bookings.

ⓦ**www.uniquetravel.com.au** Australian site with a good range of packages and good value flights.

ⓦ**http://travel.yahoo.com** Incorporates a lot of Rough Guide material in its coverage of destination countries and cities across the world, with information about places to eat and sleep, etc.

# Flights from the USA and Canada

Cheap flights to Trinidad and Tobago from the **United States** and **Canada** are scarce, although flights from the East Coast are considerably less expensive than from the West Coast. Barring special offers, the least expensive of the airlines' published fares is usually an advance purchase excursion, or **APEX** ticket, although this will carry certain restrictions: you have to book – and pay – at least 21 days before departure, spend at least seven days abroad (maximum stay three months), and you tend to get penalized if you change your schedule.

Round-trip APEX **fares,** outside of the peak periods to Piarco Airport, Trinidad from New York and Boston start from US$550, US$400 from Miami, US$650 from Chicago and CAN$850 from Toronto. Fares from San Francisco and Los Angeles start from US$760, Vancouver from CAN$1150. **During peak times,** you can add $50–100 to US fares, CAN$100–200 to Canadian fares. Flights to Crown Point Airport in Tobago cost roughly the same amount, although few direct flights are available; you will most likely have to change planes in San Juan, Barbados, St Kitts, Grenada or Trinidad.

**Continental Airlines** and **American Airlines** fly most frequently to the islands from North America, with daily flights to Tobago and Trinidad from most US and Canadian cities connecting through Miami and San Juan. **Air Canada** flies direct to Trinidad from Toronto three times a week. You can also buy an Air Canada ticket from Toronto to Tobago, but you'll have to switch to LIAT Airlines in Barbados (weekends only).

The Trinidadian airline **BWIA International** offers daily flights at competitive prices from New York and Miami in addition to a 30-day air pass, valid for travel around the Caribbean and available in the US. See below for contact details.

## Airlines

**Air Canada** ☎1-888/247-2262, ⓦwww.aircanada.ca.
**American Airlines** ☎1-800/433-7300, ⓦwww.aa.com.
**BWIA International** ☎1-800/538-2942, ⓦwww.bwee.com.
**Continental** ☎1-800/523-FARE, ⓦwww.continental.com.
**Dutch Caribbean Airlines** Trinidad ☎1-868/623 8201, Canada ☎1-800/325-1705, US ☎1-800/327 7230, ⓦwww.flydca.net.

## Courier flights

**Air Courier Association** ☎1-800/280-5973, ⓦwww.aircourier.org. Courier flight broker. Membership (1 year $24, lifetime $100) also entitles you to a 20-percent discount on travel insurance and name-your-own-price noncourier flights. Can arrange flights to San Juan, Puerto Rico and the Bahamas, but you'll need to find a local flight from there.

## Discount travel companies

**Air Brokers International** ☎1-800/883-3273 or 415/397-1383, ⓦwww.airbrokers.com. Consolidator and specialist in RTW tickets.
**Airhitch** ☎1-800/326-2009 or 212/219-7000, ⓦwww.airhitch.org. Standby-seat broker: for a set price, they guarantee to get you on a flight as close to your preferred destination as possible, within a week. Costs are currently $165 (plus taxes and a $29 processing fee) from or to the east coast region of the US; $233 (plus tax & $29 reg. fee) from/to the west coast or (when available) the Pacific northwest; $199 (plus tax & $29 reg. fee) from/to the midwest; and $177 (plus tax & $29 reg. fee) from/to the southeast. (Taxes for all Europe itineraries are $16 eastbound and $46 westbound.) Note that while they're unlikely to get you all the way to Trinidad and Tobago, Airhitch is nevertheless a good option for looking for the first leg of a trip if you're planning on finding a connection from Miami or San Juan.
**Airtech** ☎212/219-7000, ⓦwww.airtech.com. Standby seat broker; also deals in consolidator fares and courier flights for flights from the US, including seats to Trinidad for $250 from the West Coast.
**Airtreks** ☎1-877/AIRTREKS, ⓦwww.airtreks.com. RTW tickets. The website features an interactive database that lets you build and price your own RTW itinerary.
**Long Haul Travel** ☎1 866/548-4548 or 416/360 7711, ⓦwww.longhaultravel.com. Canadian company specializing in RTW trips and adventure travel. Partnered with Airtreks.
**STA Travel** ☎1-800/781-4040, ⓦwww.statravel.com. Worldwide specialists in independent travel; also student IDs, travel insurance, car rental, rail passes, etc. Website does not offer flights to the Caribbean, but these can be arranged over the phone.
**Travel Avenue** ☎1-800/333-3335, ⓦwww.travelavenue.com. Full-service travel agent that offers discounts in the form of rebates. Can help with booking cruises.
**Travel Cuts in Canada** Canada ☎1-800/667 2887; US ☎416/979 2406. Canadian student-travel organization.
**Travelers Advantage** ☎1-877/259-2691, ⓦwww.travelersadvantage.com. Discount travel club; annual membership fee required (currently $1 for 3 months trial) $90 a year. Services include booking cruises.

## Tour operators

Although contact information for tour operators is provided here, you're better off making **tour reservations** through your local travel agent. An agent will make all the phone calls, sort out the snafus and arrange flights, insurance and the like – all at no extra cost to you.
**Alken Tours** ☎1-800/221-6686 or 718/282-1152, ⓦwww.alkentours.com. Tailor-made air and accommodation packages.
**American Airlines Vacations** ☎1-800/321-2121, ⓦwww.aavacations.com. Three-day all-inclusive packages in Tobago starting at $344, plus airfare.
**BWIA Vacations** ☎1-877/FUN-BWIA, ⓦwww.bwee.com. Discounted accommodation with airline bookings.
**Island Resort Tours** ☎1-800/351-5656, ⓦwww.Islandresorttours.com. Accommodation bookings, discounted airfares and flexible packages.
**Tour Host International** ☎1-866/729-4678 or 212/953-7910, ⓦwww.tourhost.com. Air, cruise and accommodation services in all price ranges. From $380 for 3 nights, without airfare, in Tobago, or $320 in Trinidad.
**TourScan Inc** ☎1-800/962 2080 or 203/655 8091, ⓦwww.tourscan.com. Tailor-made and all-inclusive packages. 7-nights all-inclusive in Tobago start at $1469, with airfare from New York included.

## A Caribbean cruise

The archetypal luxury vacation – a **Caribbean cruise** – is relatively accessible in North America. Prices on a luxury liner can scale the heights of silliness, although if you're willing to bunk in the "lower-class" rooms you can usually cut the price somewhat. Of the scores of shipping companies that peddle all-inclusive cruises, however, only a few include Trinidad and Tobago on their itineraries, and each line routes only a couple of ships per year through Trinidad and Tobago, so be prepared for inflexible travel dates. Another downside of choosing a cruise is that you only get to see the tourist ports, and for just a few hours at that; the ocean liners listed below stop only in Port of Spain.

**Cruise operators**
The fares quoted are for single person/double occupancy "inside" (no ocean views) cabins, and are exclusive of port charges, which add an extra US$100–150. Ports of call vary from season to season, depending on the deals the ports offer. For up to date information, check ⓦ www.caribbean-cruises-vacations.com.
**Holland America** ☏ 1-800/426-0327 or 206/281-3535,
ⓦ www.hollandamerica.com. Eleven-day cruises from Fort Lauderdale, Florida, from $1500.
**WindJammer** ☏ 1-800/327-2601, ⓦ www.windjammer.com. Thirteen-day cruises leaving from Freeport, Bahamas, for $1475.

**Travel Impressions** ☏ 1-800/284-0044, ⓦ www.travelimpressions.com. Flights, accommodation bookings and packages in Trinidad and Tobago. 8-nights all-inclusive package in Trinidad starting at $1000.

## Flights from the UK and Ireland

The vast majority of **British and Irish** residents visiting Trinidad and Tobago are on some form of package tour which includes a **charter flight** direct to Tobago. This is certainly the simplest way of going about things, and even if you plan to travel independently, a seat on a charter is normally the cheapest way to get there. But charters do have their drawbacks, especially if your plans don't exactly fit into their usual two-week straitjacket. That said, some companies do offer relatively flexible packages allowing you to vary where you stay; it's worth asking to find out.

There are an increasing number of **direct flights** to both Trinidad and Tobago, but you still have a somewhat limited choice. Virgin Atlantic and British Airways fly direct to Tobago from the UK, departing from London, Gatwick, and only BWIA flies to Trinidad (from Heathrow). While there are no direct flights **from Ireland**, there are good connections via London or, on Aer Lingus or Delta, via New York or Miami.

**British Airways** flies to Tobago twice a week, on Thursdays and Saturdays. Fares begin from around £400. Once again, shop around – it's possible to reduce these figures through last-minute deals and by buying advance purchase tickets.

**Virgin Atlantic** flies to Tobago on Mondays, and their tickets are generally more expensive, starting from £550 and increasing during Britain's high season, July and August.

**BWIA** is the West Indies' own airline. Although its pricing classification is very complicated, the general price range is similar to BA's. There are daily flights from London Heathrow to Piarco, Trinidad; transfers to Tobago on frequent daily BWIA flights can be arranged, and are included in the fare. Prices start at £450, but vary according to the season.

### Airlines

**Aer Lingus** UK ☏ 0845/084 4444, Republic of Ireland ☏ 0818/365 000, ⓦ www.aerlingus.ie.
**British Airways** UK ☏ 0845/773 3377, ⓦ www.britishairways.com; Republic of Ireland ☏ 0141/2222345.
**BWIA** ☏ 020/7745 1100, ⓦ www.bwee.com.

**Delta** UK ☎0800/414 767, Republic of Ireland
☎1800/768 080 or 01/407 3165,
🌐www.delta.com.
**Virgin Atlantic** ☎01293/450-150,
🌐www.virgin-atlantic.com.

## Courier flights

**Ben's Travel** ☎020/7462 0022,
🌐www.benstravel.co.uk.
**International Association of Air Travel
Couriers** ☎0800 0746 481 or 01305/216 920,
🌐www.aircourier.co.uk. Agent for lots of
companies.

## Flight and travel agents

As well as the agents listed below, check the
Sunday papers and free weeklies, *Time Out*
and the *Evening Standard* in London. Look
for last-minute deals on the Internet or in
Caribbean-oriented newspapers such as the
*Voice*, the *Gleaner* and the *Caribbean Times*.
**Chartered Flight Centre** ☎020 7845 8434,
🌐http://Caribbean.charterflights.co.uk. A good
source for charter deals.
**Co-op Travel Care** ☎0870/112 0085
🌐www.travelcareonline.com. Flights and holidays
around the world from the UK's largest independent
travel agent. Non-partisan and informed.
**ebookers** UK ☎0870/010 7000,
🌐www.ebookers.com; Republic of Ireland
☎01/241 5689, 🌐www.ebookers.ie. Low fares on
an extensive selection of scheduled flights and
package holidays.
**Flynow.com** 125a Gloucester Rd, London SW7
4SF ☎020/7835 2000; 597 Cheetham Hill Rd,
Manchester M8 5EJ ☎0161/721 4000;
🌐www.flynow.com. Large range of discounted
tickets.
**North South Travel** Moulsham Mill Centre,
Parkway, Chelmsford, Essex CM2 7PX
☎/🖷01245/608 291,
🌐www.northsouthtravel.co.uk. Friendly,
competitive travel agency, offering discounted fares
worldwide – profits are used to support projects in
the developing world, especially the promotion of
sustainable tourism.
**STA Travel** ☎0870/1600 599,
🌐www.statravel.co.uk. Worldwide specialists in
low-cost flights and tours for students and under-
26s, though other customers welcome.
**Top Deck** ☎020 887 96789,
🌐www.topdecktravel.co.uk. Long-established
agent dealing in discount flights and tours.

**Trailfinders** 1 Threadneedle St, London EC2R 8JX
☎020/7628 7628; 4 5 Dawson St, Dublin 2
☎01/677 7888; plus branches nationwide;
🌐www.trailfinders.com. One of the best-informed
and most efficient agents for independent travellers;
they also produce a very useful quarterly magazine
worth scrutinizing for round-the-world routes.
**USIT Now** Belfast ☎028/9032 7111, Dublin
☎01/602 1777 or 677 8117, Cork ☎021/270
900, Derry ☎028/7137 1888, 🌐www.usitnow.ie.
Student and youth specialists for flights.

## Tour operators

**Caribbean Journeys** 22 Stephenson Way,
London NW1 2HD ☎020/7388 9292,
🌐www.wwj.uk.com. Tailor-made hotel and villa
holidays (Tobago only), concentrating on more
upmarket properties with a few guesthouses on the
books.
**Caribtours** Kiln House, 210 New Kings Rd,
London SW6 4NZ ☎020/7751 0660, 🖷7751
9030, 🌐www.caribtours.co.uk. Reliable group
offering luxurious packages to Tobago.
**Classic Connection** Concorde House, Canal St,
Chester CH1 4EJ ☎020/7344 3000,
📧lindafrance@itc-uk.com. Flights and hotel
packages and discounted Carnival trips.
**The Destination Group** 14 Greville St, London
EC1N 8SB ☎020/7400 7037. All types of package
or tailor-made holidays to Tobago, including eco-
tours and all-inclusives.
**Holiday in Tobago** Carlyn Lodge, 43 Carnbee No
1 Trace, Carnbee, Tobago ☎868 631 0266,
🌐www.holidayintobago.com. Small company, run
by an ex-pat couple living in Tobago, which will help
organise your Tobagonian holiday.
**JMC Holidays** 2–4 Godwin Street, Bradford BD7
2ST ☎0870 607 5085, 🌐www.jmc.com.
Specializes in inexpensive package tours to Tobago.
**Just Tobago** The Barns, Woodlands End, Mells,
Frome, Somerset, BA11 3QD ☎01373/814234
🌐www.justtobago.co.uk. Specialist company
offering flexible packages to Tobago with a range of
prices.
**Kuoni Worldwide** Kuoni House, Dorking, Surrey
RH5 4AZ ☎01306/742 222; 2a Barton Square (off
St Ann's Square), Manchester M2 7LW
☎0161/832 0667; plus branches elsewhere in
London, Manchester and Surrey;
🌐www.kuoni.co.uk. Flexible package holidays and
good family deals.
**Owners' Syndicate** 6 Port House, Plantation
Wharf, Battersea, London SW11 3TY ☎020/7801
9801, 📧caribbean@ownersyndicate.com. Good
value for villa holidays in Tobago, as well as a few

13

small properties.

**Regal Holidays** 22 High St, Sutton, Ely, Cambridgeshire CB6 2RB ☎0870/220 1777, ℻01353/777897, ⊛www.regal-diving.co.uk. Specializes in diving packages, including eco-friendly packages. Prices start at £919 for five days at a B&B with two dives a day.

**Trips Worldwide** 9 Byron Place, Clifton, Bristol BS8 1JT ☎0117/987 2626, ℻0117/3311 4401, ⊛www.tripsworldwide.co.uk. Eco-tours and tailor-made holidays to T&T, in collaboration with Trinidad's Wildways tour company. Knowledgeable staff organize flights, accommodation, transport and tour guides for holidays starting from £800.

**Villa Connections** 27 Park Lane, Poynton, Cheshire SK12 1RD ☎01625/858158, ⊛www.villaconnnections.co.uk. Customized villa and small hotel holidays in Tobago, excursions to Trinidad, Carnival packages and flights and car rental arrangements.

**Wildlife Worldwide** 170 Selsdon Rd, South Croydon, Surrey CR2 6PJ ☎020/8667 9158, ℻020/8667 1960, ⊛www.wildlifeworldwide.com. Nature-oriented holidays based at Trinidad's Asa Wright Nature Centre (see p.148) and birdwatching or diving tours in Tobago.

**Wildwings** 577–579 Fishponds Rd, Bristol BS16 3AF ☎0117/965 8333, ℻0111/937 5681, ⊛www.wildwings.co.uk. Birdwatching and eco-tours packages staying at guesthouses.

**Worldwide Fishing Safaris** 21 Station Rd, Thorney, Peterborough PE6 0QE ☎01733/271123, ℻01733/271125, ⊛www.worldwidefishingsafaris.co.uk. Deep-sea and fly-fishing holidays to Tobago including flights and accommodation.

## Flights from Australia and New Zealand

The Caribbean is no bargain destination from Australasia. There are no direct flights **from Australia or New Zealand** to Trinidad and Tobago, so you'll have to fly to one of the main US/Canada gateway airports, and pick up onward connections from there.

The best option is Air Canada who offer a through fare to Port of Spain via **Honolulu** and **Toronto**. Prices vary greatly, but in the low season, expect to pay upwards of AS$2700. A flight from Port of Spain to Tobago on Tobago Express will cost about AS$50 return and can be purchased in Australia before departure or from the airport, but plan in advance if you are travelling around Carnival.

You can also go via **New York**, from where there are regular flights to both Trinidad and Tobago, or **Miami**, which has frequent flights to Trinidad (see p.10 for full details of routes from North America).

Air New Zealand, United and Qantas have regular services to Los Angeles, with connecting flights to New York or Miami on American Airlines or United: return fares to Miami start from around A$2500. From Miami to Trinidad, return flights with American Airlines cost A$370. **From New Zealand**, Air New Zealand, Qantas and United fly to Los Angeles, with connections on to Miami or New York. Through fares to New York start from NZ$3000, and the return to Piaro or Crown Point will add another NZ$500 or so.

**Package holidays** from Australia and New Zealand to Trinidad and Tobago are few and far between, and many specialists simply act as **agents** for US-based operators, tagging a return flight from Australasia onto the total cost. Your best bet is to look for hotels that offer the deals you want, book directly and buy a flight separately. **Cruises** (see p.12), most of which depart from Miami, account for the largest sector.

The luxury end of the market is also catered for by Caribbean Destinations who offer **resort-** and **villa-based** holidays as well as cruises, with a choice of accommodation on Trinidad and a limited range on Tobago. Prices start at around A$3500 for 14 days (based on twin-share accommodation and low-season airfares from Australia), but really the sky's the limit.

None of the adventure-tour operators based in Australasia venture to Trinidad and Tobago; for **independent travellers**, the cheapest way to visit the Caribbean is as part of a round-the-world or American holiday, making creative use of airpasses – see p.15.

### Airlines

**Air Canada** Australia ☎1300/656 232 or 02/9232 5222, New Zealand ☎09/377 8833, ⊛www.aircanada.ca.
**Air New Zealand** Australia ☎13 24 76, New Zealand ☎0800/737 000 or 09/357 3000, ⊛www.airnz.com.
**American Airlines** Australia ☎1300/650 747,

New Zealand ☏ 09/309 0735 or 0800/887 997, ⓦ www.aa.com.
**BWIA International Airways** Australia ☏ 02/9285 6811, ⓦ www.bwee.com.
**Qantas** Australia ☏ 13/13 13, New Zealand ☏ 09/357 8900 or 0800/808 767; ⓦ www.qantas.com.au.
**United Airlines** Australia ☏ 13/17 77, New Zealand ☏ 09/379 3800, ⓦ www.united.com.

## Travel agents

**Budget Travel**, New Zealand ☏ 09/366 0061 or 0800/808 040, ⓦ www.budgettravel.com.
**Destinations Unlimited**, New Zealand ☏ 09/373 4033, ⓦ www.travel-nz.com.
**ecruising** Australia ☏ 1300/369 848 or 02/9249 6060, ⓦ www.ecruising.com.au. Searchable fare database of cruises worldwide.
**Flight Centres**, Australia ☏ 02/9235 3522 or for nearest branch ☏ 13 16 00, New Zealand ☏ 09/358 4310, ⓦ www.flightcentre.com.au.
**Holiday Shoppe** New Zealand ☏ 0800/808 480, ⓦ www.holidayshoppe.co.nz. Great deals on flights, hotels and holidays.
**Northern Gateway** Australia ☏ 08/8941 1394, ⓦ www.norgate.com.au.
**OTC** Australia ☏ 1300/855 118, ⓦ www.otctravel.com.au Deals on flights, hotels and holidays.
**STA Travel** Australia ☏ 13 17 76 or 1300/360 960, New Zealand ☏ 09/309 0458 or 09/366 6673, ⓦ www.statravel.com.au.
**Student Uni Travel** Australia ☏ 02/9232 8444, Ⓔ Australia@backpackers.net, ⓦ www.stut.com.au.
**Trailfinders** Australia ☏ 02/9247 7666, ⓦ www.trailfinders.com.au. One of the best-informed and most efficient agents for independent travellers.

## Specialist agents and tour operators

**Caribbean Destinations**, 4/115 Pitt St, Sydney; 38/525 Collins St, Melbourne ☏ 1800/816 717, ⓦ www.caribbeanislands.com.au. Comprehensive range of tailor-made Caribbean holidays, including a choice of accommodation packages.

# Flights from other Caribbean islands

Four **airlines** fly between Trinidad and Tobago and other Caribbean islands and nearby destinations. BWIA (☏ 627 2942, ⓦ www.bwee.com) flies to Trinidad from Barbados (average of 4 flights daily), Antigua (1–2 daily), Jamaica (1 daily), Cuba (2 weekly), Dominican Republic (2 weekly), Grenada (2 daily), St Maarten (2 weekly), St Lucia (2 weekly), Costa Rica (2 weekly), Guyana (4 daily), Suriname (2 weekly) and Caracas (1 daily). LIAT (☏ 627 6274, ⓦ www.liat airline.com) flies to Trinidad (6 flights daily) and Tobago (2 daily) from all islands in the eastern Caribbean, linking up with various connecting flights. Caribbean Star, (☏ 268/461 7827 or 625 0710, ⓦ www .flycaribbeanstar.com) flies from Antigua (3 flights daily), Barbados (3 daily), Dominica (1 daily), Grenada (3 daily), St Kitts (1 daily), St Lucia (3 daily), St Vincent (4 daily) and Tortola (1 daily) to Trinidad. And Dutch Caribbean Airlines (☏ 623 6522) flies five times a week from Curacao.

BWIA and LIAT both sell **Caribbean air passes** that allow for multiple trips around the Caribbean on their airline only. LIAT charges US$75 plus taxes for each island visited, three to six islands allowed, within 21 days. Possible destinations include Puerto Rico, Dominican Republic, St Thomas, St Croix, Tortola, St Kitts, Anguilla, Nevis, St Martin, Antigua, Guadeloupe, Dominica, Martinique, St Lucia, Barbados, St Vincent, Grenada and T&T. The pass can only be bought in Europe in conjunction with a long-distance air ticket to the Caribbean. Another Liat pass, the Caribbean Super Explorer, allows unlimited travel for 30 days throughout the airline's entire network and costs US$425 or US$399 (off-peak). BWIA's thirty-day air pass costs US$350 (if bought in Europe or Australia), US$450 or US$550 and covers fewer islands. Contact the airlines for more information.

As with everything in the Caribbean, airlines are more informal than their European and American counterparts. Flights are cancelled at the last minute and planes do not necessarily leave on time. Always ring ahead to check your departure time, and be prepared to alter your plans.

# Red tape and visas

Citizens of European Union countries (as well as Switzerland and Norway), the US and Canada do not require a visa for stays of less than three months. Nationals of Australia, New Zealand and South Africa all need visas before entering the country. You can apply for visas through the offices listed below or else have your travel agent obtain one on your behalf. On arrival, you will have to provide an address where you will be staying (hotels and guesthouses are acceptable), and occasionally proof that you have adequate finances for the length of your stay and a return or onward ticket. Your passport must be valid for six months beyond the period of your proposed visit. Even if you are entitled to stay for up to three months, the immigration officer may stamp your passport for exactly the length of time that you state that you will be staying in the country. It is a good idea, therefore, to exaggerate the length of your stay to avoid going through the hassle of getting a visa extension should your travel plans change.

If you intend to travel between Trinidad and Venezuela using the ferry service at *Pier One* in Chaguaramas (see p.117), you must have a **Yellow Fever Vaccination Certificate**.

**Visa extensions** are usually for an extra three months, but this depends on your reasons for wanting to stay; they are issued by the **Immigration Office**, 67 Frederick St, Port of Spain ☎625-3571 (Mon–Thurs 7am–4pm, Fri 7am–3.45pm). You must first make an appointment to see an immigration officer; a one-week wait is typical. Bring your passport and, if you have one, a return ticket (the latter is only sometimes asked for), as well as the TT$50 fee. Note that the policy regarding visa extensions is subject to change, and a lot can depend on the individual officer dealing with your case.

Applications for **work permits**, which are required for certain types of paid and unpaid employment, can be made at the **Ministry of National Security**, Temple Court, 31–33 Abercromby St, Port of Spain, ☎623 2441.

> Trinidad and Tobago embassies, high commissions, consulate generals and honorary consuls abroad

### UK

**High Commission** 42 Belgrave Square, London SW1X 8TNT ☎020/7245 9351, ℻823 1065, ⓦhttp://trinidad.embassyhomepage.com.

### US

**Embassy** 1708 Massachusetts Ave, NW, Washington, DC 20036-1975 ☎202/467 6490 or 6491 or 6492 or 6493, ℻785 3130, ⓦwww.bordeglobal.com/ttembassy.
**Consulate General** 733 Third Ave, Suite 1716, New York, NY 10017-3204 ☎212/682 7272 or 7273 or 7274, ℻986 2146, Ⓔttconsulateny@np1.net; 1000 Brickell Ave, Suite 800, Miami, FL 33131-3047 ☎305/374 2199, ℻374-3199, Ⓔttmiami@worldnet.att.net.

### Canada

**High Commission** 200 First Ave, Ottawa, Ontario K1S 2G6 ☎613/232 2418 or 2419, ℻232 4349, ⓦwww.ttmissions.com.
**Consulate General** 2005 Sheppard Ave E, Suite 303, Willowdale, Ontario M2J 5B4 ☎416/495-9442, ℻495-6934, ttcontor@idirect.com.

### Australia

**Honorary Consul** PO Box 109, Rose Bay, New South Wales 2029 ☎02/9327 8468, ℻9327 8469, Ⓔconsgentt@aol.com.

### New Zealand

**Honorary Consul** Level 26, NZI House, 151 Queen St, Auckland ☎09/302 1860, ℻302 1863, Ⓔwjfalcon@xtra.co.nz.

# Money, banks and costs

Trinidad and Tobago is undoubtedly one of the cheapest Caribbean destinations due to its low profile on the tourist market. If you are prepared to take the least expensive accommodation, eat at budget cafés and street stalls and limit your travel to public transport, you can get by on £20/US$35 a day. If, however, you opt for tourist accommodation and eat at more formal restaurants, you will need at least £40/US$70 a day. Renting a car is obviously an added expense – expect around £20–40/US$35–70 per day.

**Costs** vary around T&T – Tobago is generally more costly than Trinidad as a result of its greater tourist trade. **Accommodation** is cheaper outside Port of Spain, San Fernando and Tobago's Crown Point area. **Restaurants** vary greatly in price: fine dining establishments, recognizable by their plush decor, charge US$25 and up per meal; the more basic restaurants, with plastic tables and buffet-style service, offer huge meals for less than US$5.

During **Carnival season** all accommodation rates in Port of Spain jump by anywhere from 10 to over 100 percent, depending on the hotel. Carnival season often sees increases in other prices, such as drinks, taxi fares and club covers. And then there are the all-inclusive Carnival fetes (parties), which can set you back around £30/US$50 a time. Therefore if you intend to enjoy yourself during Carnival season, budget for £80/US$140 a day and up.

The **minimum wage** in T&T is currently TT$8/US$1.33 an hour, and the average wage is between TT$250–500/US$42–83 per week. Bear this fact in mind when negotiating taxi fares to off-route destinations and prices for other goods and services. A dollar will almost always be worth more to a Trinbagonian than it is to you.

## Currency

The local currency is the **Trinidad and Tobago dollar**. This is usually abbreviated to **TT$**, and is divided into one hundred cents. Coins start at 1 cent and range up through 5, 10 and 25 cents. Notes start at 1 dollar and are in denominations of 5, 10, 20 and 100. It is best to keep some of your cash in small denominations: supermarkets and bars can usually exchange TT$100, but taxis and street vendors often can't and should be paid with TT$20 or less.

## Travellers' cheques and credit and debit cards

Take along a mixture of **cash**, **credit cards** and **travellers' cheques** to cover all eventualities. Travellers' cheques and credit cards are accepted in most restaurants, malls, high-class shops and hotels. In smaller establishments and rural areas they are unlikely to take anything but local currency. **Personal cheques** are not usually accepted in hotels, and if you stay in a host home you may find they do not have the facilities for payment by credit card.

The usual fee for buying travellers' cheques is one or two percent, though this fee may be waived if you buy the cheques through a bank where you have an account. It pays to get a selection of denominations; and cheques in US dollars or pounds sterling are good for T&T. Make sure to keep the purchase agreement and a record of cheque serial numbers safe and separate from the cheques themselves. In the event that cheques are lost or stolen, the issuing company will expect you to report the loss forthwith to their office in T&T; most companies claim to replace lost or stolen cheques within 24 hours.

**Visa TravelMoney** is a pre-paid debit card with a personal identification number (PIN) which works in all ATM machines which accept Visa cards. You load up your account with funds before leaving home, and when they run out, you simply throw the card away. You can buy up to nine cards to access the same funds – useful for couples or families travelling together – and it's a good idea to purchase at least one extra card as a back-up in case of loss or theft. The card is available in most countries from branches of Travelex and AAA, and also from ☎877/394-2247. For more information, check the Visa TravelMoney website at ⓦusa.visa.com/personal/cards/visa_travel_money.

## Exchange, ATMS and banks

It is best to buy only a small amount of TT$ abroad, as the **exchange rate** is much more favourable in the country – you may gain as much as 5–10 percent on the transaction. The exchange rate at the time of publication was around TT$6 to US$1 and TT$10.5 to £1. There is a 24-hour bureau de change and a First Citizen bank at **Piarco International Airport**, and a Republic Bank at **Crown Point Airport** in Tobago. Exchange rates at these locations are more or less the same as elsewhere, although you may have to pay a small commission (about US$1).

T&T **banks** will exchange most major currencies and travellers' cheques. Commission varies; some banks charge nothing for American Express or Visa cheques, while others impose a mandatory charge of around US$1–2. You'll always receive a lower rate for exchanging cash than for travellers' cheques. There is often a separate exchange counter, so ask before joining the main queue which can be very long, especially during lunch hour (noon–2pm) and on Fridays. While all the cities and most towns in **Trinidad** have banks, in **Tobago** there is only one bank outside Scarborough, at Crown Point Airport, so bear this in mind before heading off to remoter regions.

Most banks have **ATM** machines which generally accept the following credit and debit cards: Visa, MasterCard, Linx, Plus and Cirrus. American Express cards are less useful for ATM withdrawals. Remember that all cash advances on credit cards are treated as loans, with interest accruing daily from the date of withdrawal; there may be a transaction fee on top of this.

**Banking hours** vary slightly depending on the bank, but are usually Monday to Thursday from 8am to 3pm. Opening hours on Fridays are 8am to 1pm, and 3pm to 5pm. Most banks in Trinidad's larger malls open and close later (10am–6pm) with no break.

Outside banking hours, money can be exchanged in the larger hotels and in some shops in Port of Spain, though at a less advantageous rate. Most shops and vendors will accept **American dollars** for purchases – pay in small denominations and be prepared to receive your change in local currency.

## Wiring money

**Wiring money** is a fast, efficient but expensive way to send and receive money abroad, and should be considered only as a last resort. The money wired is available for collection, in local currency, from a variety of outlets, including the local Hi-Lo supermarket chain, within a few minutes of being sent via Western Union (☎0800/833 833 in the UK or ☎623 6000 in T&T) or Moneygram (☎0800/6663 9472 in the UK or ☎627 2000 in T&T); both charge on a sliding scale, so sending larger amounts of cash is better value. It's also possible to have money wired directly from a bank in your home country to a bank in T&T, although this is somewhat less reliable because it involves two separate institutions. If you go this route, your home bank will need the address of the branch bank where you want to pick up the money and the address and telex number of the head office in Port of Spain, which will act as the clearing house; money wired this way normally takes two working days to arrive, and costs around £25/US$45 per transaction. Check with your bank before travelling to see if they have reciprocal arrangements with any Trinidadian banks.

# Information, websites and maps

Local TIDCO (Tourism and Industrial Development Company of Trinidad and Tobago) offices and their foreign representatives send out standard information packs on request, which include some general background information and sometimes a road map.

Though they're few and far between, it's worth visiting the **local TIDCO offices** once you've arrived; they dole out advice on hotels, transport and activities, not to mention free maps and flyers. Their single most useful publication is the annually updated *Trinidad & Tobago Destination Handbook*, which covers most aspects of a visit to the islands. TIDCO's main office is in Port of Spain, but the information booths at Crown Point and Piarco airports are actually more accessible and better equipped to deal with the public.

Other sources of local information are the **radio** and **national press**, which advertise upcoming events (especially during Carnival season) and several free **tourist-oriented publications**. Written by locals and updated annually, the fact-filled *Discover Trinidad and Tobago* (ⓦ www.discovertrinidad.com) includes features on subjects such as Carnival and eco-tourism, suggested touring schedules, and hotel, restaurant and tour operator listings. The monthly *Tobago Today* newspaper (available in Tobago only; ⓦ www.tobagotoday.com) carries Tobago listings and topical features such as goat racing for the Easter issue, as well as Tobagonian recipes and hints on etiquette. First published in 2000, *The Ins and Outs of Trinidad and Tobago* is a glossy annual publication which deals with Trinidad and Tobago separately, and has sections on Carnival, shopping, art and craft, eco-tourism and business, along with accommodation, eating and nightlife listings for both islands. All of these publications are available at hotels, tourist offices and other places frequented by foreigners.

## Tourist offices in Trinidad and Tobago

### Trinidad

**TIDCO information office** Piarco International Airport ☎ 669 5196.
**TIDCO main office** 10–14 Philipps St, Port of Spain ☎ 623 1932, ⓕ 623 3848, ⓦ www.visittnt.com.

### Tobago

**TIDCO information office** Crown Point Airport ☎ 639 0509.
**TIDCO main office** Unit 12, TIDCO Mall, Sangster's Hill, Scarborough ☎ 639 4333, ⓕ 639 4514.
**Tobago House of Assembly Department of Tourism** Doretta's Court, 197 Mt Marie, Scarborough ☎ 639 2125, ⓕ 639 3566, ⓦ www.visittobago.gov.tt.

## TIDCO representatives abroad

### Canada

**The RMR Group Inc** Taurus House, 512 Duplex Ave, Toronto MR4 2E3 ☎ 416/485-7827 or 1-888/535-5617, ⓕ 485-8256, ⓔ assoc@thermrgroup.ca.

### Germany

**Basic Service Group** Bahnhofsplatz 4, 55116 Mainz ☎ 06131/73337, ⓕ 73307, ⓔ tnt@bsg-net.de.

### UK

**Morris Kevan International Ltd** Mitre House, 66 Abbey Rd, Bush Hill Park, Enfield, Middlesex EN1 2QE ☎ 020/8350 1009, ⓕ 020/8350 1011, ⓔ mki@ttg.co.uk.

### USA

**Cheryl Andrews Marketing Inc** 311 Almeria Ave, Coral Gables, Florida 33134 ☎ 305/444-4033, ⓕ 447-0415, ⓔ cheryl@cherylandrewsmarketing.com.

## Websites

There are hundreds of T&T-oriented **web-sites**, which differ hugely in style and content – and the number of sites grows all the time. Hotels are lining up to market their establishments online (we list websites in the Guide accommodation sections), and it's often a convenient, hassle-free way to find a place to stay. The listings below are for sites with high-quality general content and lots of useful links, as well as a selection of more specific sites.

ⓦ **www.carnaval.com** The best T&T Carnival site, with features on everything from mas camps and panyards to music, accommodation and restaurants. Pretty good for visits to Port of Spain, too. Also has coverage of other major Carnivals around the world.

ⓦ **www.homeviewtnt.com** Slick site with extensive content, from live feeds to WE FM and other stations, sports, news, music, Carnival, history, listings, loads of Trini titbits and a chatroom. A good place to start.

ⓦ **www.lanic.utexas.edu/la/cb/tt** Huge directory of T&T links organized by category, from academic research and arts and culture to business, the economy and environment.

ⓦ **www.pantrinbago.com** The official website of Pan Trinbago, T&T's steel pan governing body, with lots of background on the genre as well as info on pan competitions.

ⓦ **www.search.co.tt** Exhaustive directory of T&T-related sites. Essential and non-essential stuff.

ⓦ **www.seetobago.com/trinidad/pan/bands_tt .htm** Everything you ever wanted to know (and probably some stuff you didn't) about steel pan in T&T.

ⓦ **www.tntisland.com** One of the best of the many personal websites devoted to T&T; an exhaustive collection of pages on everything from Trinbagonian beauty queens to places to do your laundry.

ⓦ **www.trinibase.com** Fact-heavy site with local statistics and links to all things Carnival and Trinbagonian. You must register (for free) in order to access the site.

ⓦ **www.trinimusic.com** Good potted descriptions of T&T's different musical styles and instruments, along with up-to-date chart info and album reviews.

ⓦ **www.triniweb.com** Listen to continuous soca on Radio Triniweb's online radio station or download popular soca songs for US$1 a track.

ⓦ **www.visittnt.com** Maintained by TIDCO, this is the best all-round website on the islands, with country details, attraction listings, flight information and feature pages on Carnival, soca and calypso, as well as links to lots of other pertinent sites.

## Maps

For a good **map** of the islands, try the *Rough Guide Map to Trinidad and Tobago* (£4.99) – the waterproof paper will last through the worst rainstorm and all the major (and most minor) towns and roads are clearly marked. TIDCO produces a free map of both Trinidad and Tobago, showing main roads, beaches and tourist attractions, which is adequate for mainstream exploration. A good alternative for those who want to get off the beaten track and drive the minor roads is the 1:150,000 **road map** of Trinidad and the 1:50,000 map of Tobago, both issued by the Land and Surveys Division. Although the print quality of the photos on the reverse of these maps is appalling and the last updates were in 1990 and 1991, respectively, they are still the most detailed and useful sources available. The Land and Surveys Division is also responsible for the most comprehensive plan of Port of Spain and its suburbs, a 1:10,000 map published in 2001. All of the Land and Surveys Division maps are increasingly hard to find outside of T&T; they – and a good selection of other maps – are available at Nigel R. Khan Bookseller, Ellerslie Plaza, Maraval ☎672 8128.

### Map and travel book suppliers

As well as over-the-counter sales, most of the outlets listed below allow you to order and pay for maps and books by mail, over the phone and often via the Internet.

#### UK and Ireland

**Stanfords** 12–14 Long Acre, London WC2E 9LP ☎020/7836 1321, ⓦ www.stanfords.co.uk. Also at 39 Spring Gardens, Manchester ☎0161/831 0250. Maps by mail or phone order are available on this number and via ⓔ sales@stanfords.co.uk. Other branches within British Railway offices at 156 Regent St, London W1R 5TA ☎020/7434 4744 and 29 Corn St, Bristol ☎0117/929 9966.

**Blackwell's Map Centre** 50 Broad St, Oxford OX1 3BQ ☎01865/793 550, ⓦ maps.blackwell.co.uk. Branches in Bristol, Cambridge, Cardiff, Leeds, Liverpool, Newcastle, Reading & Sheffield.

**The Map Shop** 30a Belvoir St, Leicester, LE1 6QH ☎0116/247 1400, ⓦ www.mapshopleicester.co.uk.

National Map Centre 22–24 Caxton St, London SW1H 0QU ☎020/7222 2466, ⓦwww.mapsnmc.co.uk.
National Map Centre Ireland 34 Aungier St, Dublin ☎01/476 0471, ⓦwww.mapcentre.ie.
The Travel Bookshop 13–15 Blenheim Crescent, London W11 2EE ☎020/7229 5260, ⓦwww.thetravelbookshop.co.uk.
Traveller 55 Grey St, Newcastle-upon-Tyne NE1 6EF ☎0191/261 5622, ⓦwww.newtraveller.co.

## USA and Canada

110 North Latitude US ☎336/369-4171, ⓦwww.110nlatitude.com.
Book Passage 51 Tamal Vista Blvd, Corte Madera, CA 94925, and in the San Francisco Ferry Building ☎1-800/999-7909 or 415/927-0960, ⓦwww.bookpassage.com.
Distant Lands 56 S Raymond Ave, Pasadena, CA 91105 ☎1-800/310-3220, ⓦwww.distantlands.com.
Globe Corner Bookstore 28 Church St, Cambridge, MA 02138 ☎1-800/358-6013, ⓦwww.globecorner.com.
Longitude Books 115 W 30th St #1206, New York, NY 10001 ☎1-800/342-2164,

ⓦwww.longitudebooks.com.
Map Town 400 5 Ave SW #100, Calgary, AB, T2P 0L6 ☎1-877/921-6277 or 403/266-2241, ⓦwww.maptown.com.
Travel Dug Bookstore 3065 W Broadway, Vancouver, BC, V6K 2G9 ☎604/737-1122, ⓦwww.travelbugbooks.ca.
World of Maps 1235 Wellington St, Ottawa, ON, K1Y 3A3 ☎1-800/214-8524 or 613/724-6776, ⓦwww.worldofmaps.com.

## Australia and New Zealand

Map Centre ⓦwww.mapcentre.co.nz.
Mapland 372 Little Bourke St, Melbourne ☎03/9670 4383, ⓦwww.mapland.com.au.
Map Shop 6–10 Peel St, Adelaide ☎08/8231 2033, ⓦwww.mapshop.net.au.
Map World (Australia) 371 Pitt St, Sydney ☎02/9261 3601, ⓦwww.mapworld.net.au. Also at 900 Hay St, Perth ☎08/9322 5733; Jolimont Centre, Canberra ☎02/6230 4097; and 1981 Logan Road, Brisbane ☎07/3349 6633.
Map World (New Zealand)173 Gloucester St, Christchurch ☎0800/627 967, ⓦwww.mapworld.co.nz.

# Insurance

Trinidad and Tobago has only the most basic public health system; consequently if you fall ill while visiting the country, it is advisable to go to a private doctor or hospital (see p.23). Medical treatment is expensive; it is therefore essential that you take out travel insurance before entering the country.

Before paying for a **new policy**, however, it's worth checking whether you are already covered: some all-risks home insurance policies may cover your possessions when overseas, and many private medical schemes include cover when abroad. In Canada, provincial health plans usually provide partial cover for medical mishaps overseas, while holders of official student/teacher/youth cards in Canada and the US are entitled to meagre accident coverage and hospital in-patient benefits. Students will often find that their student health coverage extends during the vacations and for one term beyond the date of last enrollment.

After exhausting the possibilities above, you might want to contact a **specialist travel insurance company**, or consider the travel insurance deal we offer (see box, overleaf). A typical travel insurance policy usually provides cover for the loss of baggage, tickets and – up to a certain limit – cash or cheques, as well as cancellation or curtailment of your journey. Most of them exclude so-called dangerous sports unless an extra premium is paid: in Trinidad and Tobago this can mean scuba-diving, windsurfing and trekking, though probably not kayaking. Read the small print and benefits tables of prospective policies carefully; coverage can

## Rough Guides travel insurance

Rough Guides Ltd offers a low-cost **travel insurance** policy, especially customized for our statistically low-risk readers by a leading British broker, provided by the American International Group (AIG) and registered with the British regulatory body, GISC (the General Insurance Standards Council). There are five main Rough Guides insurance plans: **No Frills** for the bare minimum for secure travel; **Essential**, which provides decent all-round cover; **Premier** for comprehensive cover with a wide range of benefits; **Extended Stay** for cover lasting four months to a year; and **Annual Multi-Trip**, a cost-effective way of getting Premier cover if you travel more than once a year. Premier, Annual Multi-Trip and Extended Stay policies can be supplemented by a "Hazardous Pursuits Extension" if you plan to indulge in sports considered dangerous, such as scuba-diving or trekking.

For a **policy quote**, call the Rough Guide Insurance Line: toll-free in the UK ☎0800/015 09 06 or ☎+44 1392 314 665 from elsewhere. Alternatively, get an online quote at ⓦwww.roughguides.com/insurance.

vary wildly for roughly similar premiums. Many policies can be chopped and changed to exclude coverage you don't need – for example, sickness and accident benefits can often be excluded or included at will. Flights paid for with a major credit card frequently offer some automatic cover, but usually only while travelling to and from your destination.

If you do purchase medical coverage, ascertain whether benefits will be paid as treatment proceeds or only after your return home, and whether there is a **24-hour medical emergency number**. When securing baggage cover, make sure that the per-article limit – typically under £500/US$890 and sometimes as little as £250/US$445 – will cover your most valuable possessions. If you need to make a claim, you should keep receipts for medicines and medical treatment, and in the event you have anything stolen, you must obtain an official statement from the police. Keep photocopies of everything you send to the insurer and don't allow months to elapse before contacting them – most insurance policies require that you inform them of a loss within a specific time.

# Health

Travelling around Trinidad and Tobago carries little risk to your health: the islands are nonmalarial, there are no mandatory immunizations (though some are recommended; see below) and the chlorinated tap water is safe to drink. The most likely hazards are overexposure to the sun, too much rum and the inevitable minor stomach upsets that come with unfamiliar food and water. If you do find yourself in need of minor medical attention, remember that most insurance policies require you to pay up initially and retain the receipts for the claim you'll submit once you get home.

The main **hospitals** in **Trinidad** are Port of Spain General and the Mount Hope complex in St Augustine; there are also small, poorly equipped regional hospitals in all the main towns, as well as the more efficient private establishments such as St Clair Medical Centre in Port of Spain (see below). **Tobago's** sole public hospital is in Scarborough, next to the Fort complex. You won't have to pay for treatment at public hospitals, but will be charged a fee at Mount Hope and all others listed. The long waits and severely stretched facilities at public hospitals make it more sensible to plump for a private option straight away, particularly as your insurance should eventually cover costs in any case.

Though we have recommended reliable doctors and medical centres throughout the guide, it's also wise to enquire at your hotel if you need attention. Many have a resident nurse or can recommend someone who'll be there quickly. In Trinidad, you can call a Red Cross **ambulance** on ☎627 8214. In Tobago, call ☎639 2781. For an ambulance from a public hospital, call ☎990.

Many pharmacies stock a modest range of herbal remedies and other **alternative medicines**, while most doctors should be able to refer you to a reputable alternative health practitioner. Trinidad's best **homeopath** is Harry Ramnarine, an ex-surgeon turned alternative practitioner. His practice is at 403 Rodney Rd, Chaguanas (☎665 8041), but as his waiting lists are extremely long, it's best to make appointments as early as possible. In Tobago, you can get advice on herbal treatments, and buy medicinal herbs and alternative health products, from E&F

Health Foods, Scarborough Mall, Carrington St, Scarborough (☎639 3992).

## Hospitals

### Trinidad

**Arima District Hospital** Queen Mary Ave, Arima ☎667 4714.
**Community Hospital** Western Main Rd, Cocorite, Port of Spain ☎622 1191.
**Mount Hope Hospital (Eric Williams Medical Sciences Complex)** Eastern Main Rd, St Augustine ☎645 4673.
**Port of Spain General Hospital** 169 Charlotte St, Port of Spain ☎623 2951 or 2952.
**San Fernando General Hospital** Independence Ave, San Fernando ☎652 3581 or 3580.
**St Clair Medical Centre** 18 Elizabeth St, St Clair, Port of Spain ☎628 1451 or 8615.

### Tobago

**Tobago County Hospital** Calder Hall Rd, Scarborough ☎639 2551 or 2552.

## Before you go

Though you should ensure that you're up to date with polio and tetanus vaccines, no **inoculations** are needed to enter Trinidad and Tobago – unless you're travelling from a country where smallpox vaccinations are required or you intend to use the ferry between Trinidad and Venezuela, in which case you'll need a Yellow Fever Vaccination Certificate. Along with yellow fever, immunizations for typhoid and hepatitis A are worth considering if you think you'll be spending a lot of time off the beaten track. Take precautions to ensure that you're as healthy as possible before you travel; have a **dental check-up** and bring supplies of any **prescription medicines** that you use regularly, as well as the generic name of the product in case you need more after you've arrived.

## Heat and sun problems

**Heat** and **humidity** make cuts and grazes slower to heal and more vulnerable to infection than in temperate climates; clean all wounds scrupulously, apply iodine or antiseptic spray or powder (cream just keeps a cut wet and slows down healing) and try to keep the wound dry. You can use rum to clean wounds if nothing else is available. Seawater is said to help a cut heal quickly, but as most of the ocean carries plenty of bacteria along with the salt, you may be risking infection.

The benign but unsightly fungal skin disease **pityriasis** – known locally as *lota* – is common; it appears on white skin as circular, crispy patches and as lighter patches of discoloration on black skin. It's passed on through body contact, and can be hard to avoid if you're susceptible. Though there are a thousand "bush remedies", the best treatment is to apply an anti-fungal cream, sulphur-based lotions or anti-dandruff shampoo. Failing to dry your feet properly and

### Travel medical kit

There are many **pharmacies** all over T&T which stock most, if not all, of the items listed below. This said, you might find it more convenient and reassuring to assemble a kit before you leave home:

• Band-Aids
• Scissors
• Bandages and sterile gauze
• Antiseptic spray or iodine liquid
• Antiseptic wipes
• Painkillers/aspirin
• Diarrhoea remedy
• Calamine lotion or any bite-soothing remedy
• Medicated talcum powder
• Thrush and cystitis remedies
• Anti-fungal cream

constantly wearing trainers or boots provide the perfect conditions for the **athlete's foot** fungus to flourish – treat it with anti-fungal cream, stick to open sandals as much as possible and wear flip-flops in communal showers and around the pool.

Be stringent about personal hygiene. If you live in a cool climate, your skin will need to adjust to the heat; sweat ducts take a little while to open sufficiently, and blocked ducts can cause an itchy prickly **heat rash**. To treat or avoid it, wear loose cotton clothes and take frequent cold showers without soap, dusting with medicated talcum powder afterwards. Avoid applying sunscreen or moisturizer to affected areas and try to spend some time in an air-conditioned room if it gets really bad.

T&T's hot and humid climate puts you at risk of **dehydration**, heat exhaustion and sunstroke – symptoms of all these are light-headedness, headache, fatigue and nausea. If affected, rest in a cool place, drink lots of water (especially nutritious, easy-to-find coconut water) and take regular doses of a rehydration solution (see "stomach problems", below). Avoid **sunburn** by restricting your sunbathing to no more than half an hour per day to begin with, getting some shade between 11am and 2pm, and always using a good quality, high-factor cream – remember that sunscreen loses its effectiveness over time, so make sure your supply is less than a year old. Bear in mind that you will be especially vulnerable to sunburn on boat trips, and that UV rays can penetrate even on cloudy days. If you do get burnt, liberally apply after-sun cream, fresh aloe vera or a weak vinegar solution. Sunscreen and after-sun are widely available in T&T.

## Stomach problems

Though serious dysentery-type **stomach bugs** are very rare, taking common-sense precautions lessens the chances of a bout of "traveller's tummy". For instance, wash and peel fresh fruit and vegetables and clean your hands well before you eat. If you do fall victim to **diarrhoea**, try to rest and drink plenty of fluid: water, herbal tea, fruit juice, clear soup and especially nutritious, vitamin-packed coconut water, rather than fizzy drinks or beer. After every bowel movement

## Aloe vera

The thick, spiky stems of **aloe vera** grow profusely throughout T&T, and in Tobago it's common for hawkers to sell them on the beaches. A staple of local healing and skin care, the plant is a veritable cure-all – drunk as a purgative, used as a conditioning rinse and applied to cuts, grazes and burns to draw out infection. It's an excellent remedy for sunburn, heat rash and insect bites, and is even distilled into aloes wine.

To extract fresh aloe gel from the stem, cut off a section and pare away the spiky edges. Slice in half and wipe the vaguely mauve gel onto the affected areas, scratching the surface to release more jelly as needed and being careful not to get it on clothing, since it leaves a stubborn purple stain.

and once an hour, drink a glass of water mixed with a teaspoon of sugar and half a teaspoon of salt to make up for lost minerals, and eat small quantities of bland foods such as rice or bread; avoid fruit, fatty foods and dairy products. See a doctor (we've listed these in the Guide) should symptoms persist for more than three days. You may be tempted to take a commercial anti-diarrhoea remedy, but this will merely prevent the body from flushing out whatever is troubling the system; use these only if you cannot get to a toilet, or before a long journey.

Though it's generally heavily chlorinated and safe (if a bit unpalatable), **tap water** can sometimes become slightly contaminated after heavy rain, particularly in rural areas. It's probably best to stick to cheap and widely available bottled water during short stays, unless you've got the constitution of an ox.

## Animal and plant hazards

Though there are no deadly **snakes** in Tobago, Trinidad's forests nevertheless harbour four venomous varieties; the fer-de-lance and the bushmaster or pit viper (both known as mapepire, pronounced "mah-pee-pee"), and two species of brightly coloured coral snake (for more detailed information on T&T's snakes, see "Fauna and flora", p.353). It's best to wear long trousers, shoes or boots and socks when walking in the bush, and to refrain from investigating rock crevices with your bare hands. If you do encounter a snake, simply move it gently out of the way with a long stick. In the event of a **bite**, keep calm; death from a snake bite is almost unheard of in these parts, and your

worst enemy is panic, since violent activity causes the venom to spread more rapidly through the system. When caring for someone who has been bitten, reassure the victim and keep them immobilized. Bandage the affected area tightly (if the bite is on a limb, tie a tourniquet above it), note down all that you can about what the snake looks like (but on no account try to capture it), and seek medical help immediately; all local hospitals have stocks of the relevant antidote.

The commonality of **rabies** among cattle, cats and dogs, spread by the feeding activities of **vampire bats**, means it's best not to disturb sleeping bats, and to avoid petting stray animals; many have mange in any case. Be wary of cats or dogs behaving strangely, and report such incidences to the police. Seek medical attention immediately should you be bitten by any type of animal.

## Insect and arachnid bites

**Insect bites** can be a real nuisance, particularly when visiting during the wet season (June–Dec). **Mosquitoes** and **sand flies** (the latter deliver a small but incredibly itchy and long-lasting bite) are at their most aggressive at sundown, especially around standing water. Cover your arms and legs at dusk and use plenty of strong insect repellent. If you dislike using chemicals, try citronella or lavender oils. Once you've been bitten (and no matter how thorough your precautions, you will be), do not scratch the bites at any cost. Applying soothing creams or sprays may help – homeopathic pyrethrum is particularly good – but one of the best remedies is a coating of fresh aloe vera gel (see box, above).

Large, hornet-like **wasps** (known as jackspaniards) are common throughout both islands and deliver a nasty sting; keep well away, especially if they seem to be building a nest. **African bees** – distinguishable by their brown-black head and thorax and black-tipped orange abdomen – made the journey from Venezuela in the late 1970s and are now common throughout Trinidad. They are extremely aggressive if disturbed, so keep out of their way; do not wear strong perfume in the bush and avoid brushing leaves and branches, where hives are often hidden. If you disturb a nest and the bees swarm, stand still, and don't try the old trick of plunging into water – the bees will simply wait for you to surface. Never kill a bee after having been stung, as this will cause it to emit a pheromone which attracts even more bees.

There are a number of creepy-crawlies to watch out for in forested areas. **Scorpions**, found on both islands, are particularly fond of dead wood. Though their sting is painful, it is not usually serious; the severity of the effect varies with individual susceptibility, but you should consult a doctor if worried – you might want to avoid the local remedy of eating the offender. Some **centipedes** can also deliver a painful bite. To minimize chances of a nip or sting from either, step over rotting wood while walking in the bush rather than treading on it, and in rustic surroundings shake shoes before putting them on and check under toilet seats prior to using them.

## Marine animals

Given the local predilection for consuming **shark**, you could be forgiven for believing that the waters of Trinidad and Tobago are swarming with voracious great whites; however, this is far from the truth. Death-by-jaws is unheard of on the beaches and you are only likely to encounter a shark (usually of the rather benign nurse variety) when snorkelling or scuba diving around their reef feeding-grounds or in very deep offshore water; as many species rest in the day and hunt at night, they're unlikely to be aggressive.

Endowed with sharp teeth and a bit of an attitude if cornered, **barracuda** are best admired from a distance, as are moray eels. Don't stick your hand into rock crevices when diving or snorkelling, and never touch **coral**; quite apart from killing the organism with a caress, you'll probably come away with an unattractive, slow healing rash, particularly if you touch fire coral. A far more likely encounter is with one of the many spiny black **sea urchins** that inhabit reefs and bays; if you tread on one, remove as much of the spine as possible, douse the area in vinegar (or even urine) and see a doctor; washing with vinegar is also the best way to treat **jellyfish** stings. Most common are the globular, 4–5cm "wasp" variety which occasionally swarm onto beaches – their sting is no worse than a bee's. Take care, though, to avoid the long trailing tendrils of the purple **Portuguese man-of-war**, fairly common in the waters around Trinidad; seek medical help if you think you've been stung by one of these, and don't touch specimens that have washed up on the beach, as they remain harmful for weeks.

## Manchineel trees

Take care to avoid the poisonous **manchineel trees**. They are easy to identify: they grow to around 12 metres, with a wide, spreading crown of small, dark green leaves on long stalks and innocuous-looking green flowers. The milky sap, however, causes severe skin blisters. Do not touch any part of the tree, and don't even shelter under the boughs when it's raining. Although manchineels have been removed from many popular beaches and warning signs put up where they've been allowed to remain, some still grow unnoticed in wilder coastal areas, and the round, green and incredibly poisonous fruit occasionally wash up on other stretches of sand, so take care if you're beachcombing.

# Sexual health

As cases of **sexually transmitted diseases** such as gonorrhoea and even syphilis – not to mention HIV – are on the increase, casual sex in T&T is a pretty reckless pastime.

The latest World Health Organization (WHO) estimates are that the national HIV

For advice on **HIV/AIDS**, call the National Aids Hotline (T625 2437).

prevalence is at least one percent in twelve countries in the Caribbean Basin, including Trinidad and Tobago. T&T is also one of six countries where HIV prevalence among pregnant women reaches or exceeds two percent. There could be as many as 39,000 cases of HIV infection in Trinidad and Tobago. Bringing **condoms** – and using them – obviously makes sense. Following strenuous government health campaigns, safe sex awareness is fairly good, and condoms are widely available. If you use the **contraceptive pill**, bring more supplies with you than necessary, as vomiting or diarrhoea may lessen its effectiveness.

## Women's health

Time in the tropics creates the perfect conditions for a bout of **thrush** – come equipped with bifidum acidophilus capsules, and take them daily to balance yeasts. Also carry plenty of Canesten cream or pessaries, keep heavily perfumed products and soap away from the vagina and always wear cotton underwear if you know you're susceptible.

Dehydration and the stress of travel can encourage **cystitis**; to avoid it, drink copious amounts of water and be rigorous about vaginal hygiene. Regular sufferers should also bring sachets of acidifying remedies which contain potassium citrate. You should have a good supply of sanitary protection, since your favourite brand will be more expensive in T&T; and bear in mind that flushing towels or tampons down the toilet will often send them straight to the sea.

# Getting around

Travelling around Trinidad and Tobago can at first seem chaotic and unpredictable. However, once you've got the hang of the different forms of public transportation on offer, getting around these two compact islands is relatively straightforward.

There are four types of transport available: **buses**, **maxi taxis**, **route taxis** and **private taxis**. Between them, you can get to most places mentioned in the Guide. This said, a few of the more rural areas are only accessible with your own transportation, which makes **renting a car** something to consider. Having your own wheels is also useful if you're planning to go out late at night; **public transport** runs all night – albeit infrequently – in Port of Spain and San Fernando, but elsewhere it peters out after midnight. Whatever form of transport you are using, avoid travelling at **peak hours** (6–8am, 3–6pm), when the roads are clogged and maxis and taxis heave with people.

## Buses

The **Public Transport Service Corporation (PTSC)** operates a small network of **public buses** on both islands. The introduction of a rural bus service in Trinidad and an expansion of services in Tobago in recent years have greatly improved bus travel, making it a viable option for the independent traveller, where previously it was an exercise in frustration. Even so, the maxis and route taxis (see below) are still by far the most practical forms of public transport, with PTSC buses best for quick, cheap and comfortable travel between Trinidad's main urban centres (Port of Spain, San Fernando, Arima and Chaguanas). Journeys by bus between Port of Spain and Arima are especially quick due to the **Priority Bus Route**, reserved for

## PTSC "Know Your Country Tours"

In addition to its standard bus services, PTSC offers tours to some of Trinidad's most popular attractions. The **"Know Your Country Tours"** are designed for locals as much as tourists, and only include transportation to the various destinations on the selected itinerary (entrance fees and meals are your responsibility). However, for those without their own transport, this is an excellent and very cheap way of getting to some of the more inaccessible parts of the island.

Current tours, all departing from **City Gate** in Port of Spain, visit Los Iros (stopping at Penal and Siparia), Maracas, Blanchisseuse (stopping at the Asa Wright Nature Centre and passing through Morne La Croix and Brasso Seco), Mayaro (stopping at Manzanilla Beach) and Granville (stooping at the Pitch Lake). Tour **prices** range from TT$40 to TT$80 per person. For more information, call ☏624 9839.

buses and maxis and running parallel to the Eastern Main Road along **Trinidad**'s east-west corridor, the former course of the railway.

**Bus stops** are often small concrete shelters on the side of the road; sometimes just a sign on a telephone pole. **Tickets** must be bought in advance, either from the main terminus in Port of Spain, the Scarborough bus terminal or from small general stores around the country – you cannot simply board a bus and buy your fare from the driver. Weekly and monthly tickets are available from the main bus stations.

There are two types of buses **in Trinidad**: the blue **transit** buses – known as "Super Express" – and the red, white and black **ECS** buses. Despite its nickname, the transit bus is the slower option, and also has no air conditioning or music. You can sit or stand on these – during rush hour they become very sweaty and crowded. The slightly pricier ECS buses (Mon–Fri 6am–9pm, Sat 7am–7pm) are quicker and run every ten to fifteen minutes during peak time (7–8am, 4–6pm), and every twenty minutes during off-peak hours. They are also air-conditioned, play music and allow only seated passengers.

All buses in Trinidad leave and terminate at **City Gate** – sometimes referred to as **South Quay** in official literature – in Port of Spain, the country's main transportation hub (this is also the main terminus for maxi taxis that travel across the country). Examples of ECS **fares** from Port of Spain are TT$4 to Arima, Chaguanas or Piarco airport and TT$6 to San Fernando. Super Express transit costs around 50 cents less and runs every half-

hour or hour from 4am to 10pm. Other destinations served by either ECS, transit or the so-called "rural" services include: Chaguaramas, Tunapuna, Sangre Grande, Blanchisseuse, Toco, Princes Town, Point Fortin, Siparia and Guayaguayare.

In **Tobago**, all buses leave from the Greenside Street terminal in Scarborough. The vehicles are blue-striped minibuses and services tend to be more frequent during peak hours. The timetable varies and though some information has been included in the appropriate sections, it is always wise to check before setting out. Officially the buses run from Scarborough to Crown Point (TT$3), Plymouth (TT$3) and Black Rock (TT$2).

**Information** on bus services in Trinidad can be obtained from the helpful Customer Care Centre next to the San Fernando ECS stand in City Gate, or by ringing ☏623 7872. For information on buses in Tobago, call ☏639 2293.

## Maxi taxis

**Maxi taxis** are minibuses containing ten to twenty people – privately owned but formed into associations with set routes and standardized fares. In the past they were famed for their loud music, which made the maxi a sort of travelling disco, but a law – passed to assuage worries that children were grooving aboard their favourite "party maxi" after school – now requires drivers to pay for a license if they wish to play music in their vehicles.

A ride in a maxi can still be an entertaining experience, however. The interior often reflects the tastes of the owner, and may declare anything from religious faith to a devotion to love, money and good times. More ornate maxis have padded ceilings, photographs of favourite personalities and hand-painted interiors. Many have a recognizable slogan across their front windshield: the nickname of the driver, perhaps ("Mister Painter", "Young Adult" or "Black Man Redemption"), or their personal motto.

The maxis are **organized by region** and have **colour-coded** stripes relating to the area in which they work. Each area has a main meeting point for maxis in the nearest large town. In Trinidad, **yellow-striped** vehicles work from in and around Port of Spain to the Western Tip; **red stripes** in the east; **green stripes** in the centre and south of the island; **black stripes** in and around Princes Town; and **brown stripes** from San Fernando to the southwest peninsula. **Blue-striped** maxis operate in Tobago; there is only one set route, from Scarborough to Charlotteville, and the rest are used mainly to ferry schoolchildren or as private charters for tourists.

Maxis adhere to **no fixed timetable**. There are more of them around during busy periods (every five minutes between 6–10am and 3–8pm). The later it gets, the fewer there are; after 8pm you can expect a ten-to twenty-minute wait. Some maxis do run throughout the night, albeit intermittently, serving areas with fetes and concerts, and commuting between the major towns.

Maxi **routes** radiate out from the main centres, which means that to get from one small town to another you may have to travel twice the distance. They can be hailed anywhere along their route – just stick out your hand and if they have space they will pick you up – but it is often quicker to go to the main stand; since maxis wait until they are full before leaving, they may not have free seats until they reach their destination. Once you are aboard, the maxis will let you off at any point; press the buzzers by the windows to stop the bus. **Off-route drops** may also be made, though this depends on the driver's good will and the destination requested.

**Fares** are fixed, going up only when the price of petrol does, and only occasionally displayed (on a laminated sheet stuck somewhere inside the maxi), as it is presumed that everyone knows their fare. Where possible these prices have been listed in the Guide. Fares usually range between TT\$2 and TT\$6; from Port of Spain, for example, it costs TT\$4 to Chaguanas, TT\$5 to Arima and TT\$6 to San Fernando. Travelling longer distances to out-of-the-way places works out to be more expensive as you will probably have to take more than one maxi.

## Route taxis and private taxis

**Route taxis** follow similar rules to maxis, but they rarely have a main meeting point, with stands scattered around the towns and cities. They can hold **four to five passengers** in addition to the driver and, apart from their **H number plates**, they are indistinguishable from private cars (which have P number plates – although note that some P licensed cars also operate as route taxis). They come in various states of repair: some are brand new and air-conditioned, but the majority are old but functional cars. Route taxis will not leave their stand until they are full, which means you may have to wait while the driver cries out, "one to go". However, they are usually quicker (and slightly more expensive) than maxis as they have fewer passengers and therefore stop less frequently.

To stop a taxi en route, hail it with your hand. There is a widely accepted code of **hand signals**; point left or right to indicate which direction you want to take at the next major turn-off. When entering the car it is normal to greet the other passengers with a "good morning" or a "good afternoon". To stop the taxi tell your driver you want to get off as you approach your destination – in Trini speak, "nex corner drive".

**Private taxis** take you directly to your destination, with you as the only passenger. As with route taxis, they have an H number plate. They are **unmetered,** so a price must be agreed beforehand, and they can work out to be just as expensive as a cab in Britain or the US. If you want to be taken door to door, they are the only official option, although it is often possible – and more economical – to bargain with a route taxi driver to drop you where you want. Phone-A-Taxi (☎628 TAXI) offers the cheapest 24-hour, island-wide service in Trinidad.

## Driving

Driving in T&T requires **patience** and constant **alertness**; you simply cannot take your eyes off the road for one moment, and the packed streets of Port of Spain with their complicated one-way systems can be a nightmare at first. Throughout the islands, drivers will habitually stop at short notice, turn without indicating and happily block traffic to stop and chat with a friend. The best thing to do is accept it; beeping your horn out of irritation will just get you withering stares; horns are more frequently used as a thank-you gesture and as an indication of an intention to overtake.

Trinbago drivers seem to have a sixth sense that enables them to judge when taxis and maxis will brake sharply in front of them or when cars might overtake (often on corners) despite oncoming traffic; you probably don't possess such a sense, so stay aware of the position of taxis and maxis, expecting them to brake at any moment, and always drive **defensively**. Trinbago drivers are generally courteous, especially when confronted with a rental car, often stopping to allow you to pull out or shouting advice whether you need it or not. Some, however, take to the road at night with only one headlight or taillight, and being dazzled by full-beam headlights is often the norm. Flash once to alert the other driver; if they don't dip, reduce speed and keep your eyes to the left verge of the road. Another puzzling practice is the use of **hand signals**, an art which route taxi drivers have perfected and one often appropriated by those gesturing in the middle of a heated in-car debate. In general, an up-and-down movement indicates that the driver in front is about to stop, though it can be an instruction to stop due to a hazard ahead. Whatever the motivation, slow down if faced with a hand signal.

Though the wide lanes and fast flow are actually less of a problem than traffic- and pedestrian-choked city streets, driving on **highways** can feel initially hair-raising – a favourite Trinbago habit is a high-speed weaving technique which looks as though it ought to cause a multiple pile-up, but rarely does. In such cases, take extra care, especially behind taxis and in the **tropical rains**.

Local **traffic lights** can be confusing. There are usually three, each relating to the relevant lanes; left for left-hand turns, middle for straight on, right for right-hand turns. In Tobago, you'll see drivers breaking red lights to make a left-hand turn; this is entirely legal so long as you come to a full stop at the line and check that the coast is clear before moving off. In Trinidad, you'll see flashing red or yellow lights at major road junctions; both mean "proceed with caution"; yellow means it's primarily your right of way, red that it's someone else's.

A widespread disrespect for authority, and the idea that "we don't drive fast enough to have an accident", mean that many traffic regulations are cheerfully ignored. The wearing of **seat belts** is compulsory, but not always practised or enforced. **Drinking and driving** is also illegal, though the attitude toward it is more laid back in T&T than in some other countries; many people will go to the beach at the weekend, have a few drinks and drive home. The law also demands that drivers be properly attired; it's possible to be charged for "driving bareback", so always keep a T-shirt handy.

You'll find **Tobago's** roads much quieter than those in Trinidad; the main hazards are blind corners on tiny roads (sound your horn if you can't see), the occasional monumental pothole, and cows put out to graze by the road. Both Tobagonians and their animals tend to take their time when moving out of the way or crossing the road; drive slowly, particularly if you have to cross an animal's tethering rope.

**Road signs** are based on the English system (although distances and speed limits are in kilometres), and you must drive on the left. The speed limit is **80kph** on highways and **55kph** on main roads in built-up areas. Tobago's speed limit is **50kph**.

**Petrol stations** are scarce outside urban areas – in Tobago, those in Scarborough stay open until 11pm or midnight, but others shut up shop by 9pm (and most are only open for a few hours on Sunday). It is therefore wise to keep the tank full, especially if you're planning to make long journeys.

### Driving licence

A valid international **driving licence** or one issued in the US, Canada, UK, Germany or the Bahamas is required for driving both cars and motorcycles for up to ninety days. Apply to the Licensing Division on Wrightson Road, Port of Spain (☎625 1031) if you intend to stay longer.

## Car rental

Of the major **international car rental chains**, only Thrifty (🖝www.thrifty.com) and Hertz (🖝www.hertz.com) have offices in Trinidad and Tobago, though Holiday Autos works through the many **local firms** (see below). All companies require you to be **25 or over** and hold a valid driving licence. Almost all firms ask for a deposit, which often must be guaranteed by a credit card imprint. Some of the smaller firms, especially in Tobago, will accept a cash deposit of around US$170. You may be offered a **collision damage waiver** at extra cost (usually US$5–15 per day); without one, you may be liable for damage. If your car is stolen and you don't have the keys, you will have to pay the car's replacement costs, so never leave keys in a parked car. **Prices** vary according to the time of year and the availability of promotional rates or frequent-flyer discounts, so shop around; they tend to start at around US$35 per day in Trinidad for the smallest vehicle, inclusive of third-party insurance and unlimited kilometres. Larger companies can usually rent you **baby car-seats** on request.

### Car rental firms in Trinidad

**Auto Rentals** Piarco Airport ☎669 2277. One of Trinidad's largest car rental firms, with eight branches around the islands.
**Convenient** Tropical Marine, Western Main Rd, Chaguaramas ☎/📠634 4017, 📧crl@carib-link.net. Reasonable rates and excellent personalized service.
**Econo-Car** 191–193 Western Main Rd, Cocorite ☎622 8072; Piarco Airport ☎669 1119. One of the cheapest firms around.
**Hertz** 17 St Helena Village, ☎800 3131 (toll-free). Well-known international chain.
**Kalloo's** 31 French St, Port of Spain ☎622 9073, 🖝www.kalloos.com. Friendly and efficient, with branches throughout Trinidad and Tobago, including the airport.
**Signal** Chaguaramas Hotel and Convention Centre, Western Main Rd, Chaguaramas ☎800 2277 (toll-free). Excellent rates, with airport pickups/dropoffs.

**Singh's** 7–9 Wrightson Rd, Port of Spain ☎623 0150, 📠627 8476. Huge, spanking-new fleet, reasonable rates, 24hr call-out service and three additional branches islandwide, including Piarco.

### Car rental firms in Tobago

**Auto Rentals** Crown Point ☎639 0644. Located next to the airport building, this firm has branches on both islands.
**Baird's** Scarborough ☎639 2528. Rents jeeps, buses, motorbikes and scooters at reasonable rates.
**Rattan's** Crown Point ☎639 8271. Has a branch close to the airport. Helpful service.
**Rollocks** Crown Point ☎639 0328. Small local firm based near the airport renting jeeps and cars.
**Sherman's** Lambeau ☎639 2292, 📠639 3084. Extremely efficient and helpful service; will deliver car to your hotel or meet you at the airport. Free day of car rental with every seven days rented.
**Singh's** *Grafton Beach Resort*, Black Rock ☎639 0624. Large fleet, reasonable rates and a 24hr call-out service; with three branches in Trinidad.
**Thrifty** Crown Point and *Turtle Beach* hotel ☎639 8507 or 8062. Friendly, reliable service based at the airport.

## Motorcycle and bicycle rental

### Motorcycles

**Baird's** Scarborough, Tobago ☎639 2528. Reliable local firm with reasonable rates.
**Greene's General Cycle Ltd** Skinner St, at Eastern Main Rd, Arouca, Trinidad ☎646 2453 or 646 7433. Trinidad's only motorcycle and scooter rental service.

### Bicycles

**Bay Sports** Williams Bay, Chaguaramas, Trinidad ☎687 0566 or 681 8887. Mountain bike rentals plus guided rides in the Chaguaramas National Park.
**Glorious Ride** Crown Point, Tobago ☎639 7124. Cheap and cheerful service.
**Marco Polo Tourism** Mount Irvine Beach car park, Tobago ☎639 7420. Offers bike rentals, as well as tours and sports activities.

## Travelling between Trinidad and Tobago

There are two options available if you wish to travel **between the islands** – the **ferry**, slow but inexpensive, and the **plane**, quick but pricier. It is far easier to go by air, though if you have spare time, the sea crossing can be a romantic starlit experience.

### By ferry

Travelling from Trinidad to Tobago, boats (*MF Panorama* and *MV Beauport*) leave Monday to Friday at 2pm and 11pm, and Saturday and Sunday at 11am, from the Government Shipping Passenger Service opposite the Twin Towers on Wrightson Road in Port of Spain. This journey takes five to six hours and can be rough – take **seasickness tablets**, as strong currents in the Bocas can make even the staunchest stomach queasy. The crossing from Tobago to Trinidad is usually calmer; the boat leaves at 11am and 11pm Monday to Friday, and 11pm on Saturday and Sunday, from the Scarborough docks on Carrington Street.

**Tickets** cost TT$50–60 return for a seat, while a cabin for two is TT$160. These should be bought in advance, unless you're prepared to join the queue at least three hours before the boat leaves. The ticket office at the Government Shipping Passenger Service in Port of Spain is open Mon–Thurs 7.15am–3pm, 4.15–6pm & 7–10.30pm, Fri 7.15am–3pm. In Scarborough, you can buy tickets at the ferry terminal on Carrington Street. For further information, call ☏625 4906 in Trinidad, ☏639 2416 in Tobago.

### By plane

The main **inter-island airline** is Tobago Express (☏627 5160, ⊛www.tobago express.com), a BWIA affiliate which flies between Trinidad and Tobago fourteen times a day (TT$100 one way and TT$200 return). LIAT (☏627 6274) also makes a daily flight between the islands (TT$300 return). For general enquiries on flight arrivals and departures, ring Piarco International Airport (☏669 8048) or Crown Point International Airport (☏639 8547).

# Accommodation

Although Trinidad and Tobago are not the most tourist-oriented islands in the Caribbean, this doesn't mean that there's any shortage of places to stay. In Trinidad, there is plenty of accommodation in Port of Spain — due mostly to the annual Carnival invasion and the flow of business travellers and visitors from other Caribbean islands – as well as guesthouses and hotels on or near most of the better beaches, especially along the north coast. The situation in the island's centre and south, however, is rather less promising; with the exception of Mayaro Bay in the southeast, what hotels there are cater to oil workers and are expensive. Tobago, meanwhile, with its relatively high number of tourists, has every category of room in the Crown Point area, and plenty of options throughout the island.

While it's always reassuring to have pre-arranged somewhere to stay for the first couple of nights, if you haven't booked a room in advance you should have no problem finding **suitable accommodation** once you've arrived. The staff at the TIDCO desks at Piarco and Crown Point airports (see p.19) can direct you to a place that suits your plans and budget. Many hotels, particularly in Tobago, also offer free airport pick-ups as an extra incentive.

Accommodation in T&T is cheaper than you might expect for a Caribbean destination – ranging from as little as US$20 per night for a basic room with a fan in Port of Spain to US$50–70 for an a/c unit with satellite TV – but it's still likely to be your major **expense**. Rates at most hotels and guesthouses in Trinidad change only at Carnival time, but properties in Tobago tend

## Accommodation price codes

All accommodation listed in this guide has been graded according to the following **price categories**:

- ❶ under US$10
- ❷ US$10–20
- ❸ US$20–35
- ❹ US$35–50
- ❺ US$50–70
- ❻ US$70–100
- ❼ US$100–150
- ❽ US$150–200
- ❾ US$200 and above

Rates are for the cheapest double or twin rooms, including 10 percent tax and 10 percent service charge where applicable. In Tobago, rates quoted are those used during the high season, normally mid December to mid April. During low season (mid April–mid December) rates are liable to fall by up to 25 percent. There are no high and low seasons in Trinidad, but rates may rise by over 100 percent during Carnival (where applicable we've given two rates separated by a slash, the higher one being the Carnival rate). Many hotels give rates in US dollars – we have followed suit in determining our price codes; however, payment can be made in either US or TT currency.

to have two rates; one for the summer **low season** (mid-April to mid-Dec) and another for the winter **high season** (mid-Dec to mid-April). However, many local hoteliers are perfectly open to a bit of **haggling**, particularly in summer. You may also get a discount if you arrange to stay for more than a couple of weeks. Don't be surprised if the Trini in front of you at check-in gets the same room at a lower rate; this is normal practice, and ensures that local people get as much from their resorts as the tourists.

There are a couple of hidden extras to watch out for: **room tax** (10 percent) and **service charge** (10 percent) are added to quoted room rates at the more upmarket hotels, though sometimes not at the guesthouses. Throughout the Guide, we have taken the tax and service charge into account when giving price codes, but it's worth checking whether these charges have been included each time you rent a room.

Whatever level of accommodation you choose, you can pretty much guarantee that it will be **clean**; West Indian hygiene standards tend to be high, and even the most basic of rooms will usually be spotless.

## Hotels, guesthouses and camping

Most of T&T's **resort-type hotels** cluster around Tobago's better beaches; here you'll find everything from expansive, landscaped enclaves with hundreds of rooms, high walls and private beaches to "eco-hotels" and holistic havens. In between these are no-nonsense concrete monoliths dedicated to the needs of the package tourist, and

## Carnival rates

**Carnival**, and the few days preceding it, is the one time of year when you simply cannot count on getting a room in Trinidad. This is the biggest event in the local calendar, and rooms must be booked months in advance – even the grottiest of box-cupboards are in demand, and Carnival regulars don't leave Trinidad without reserving a room for the following year. Most hotels, guesthouses and host homes offer special Carnival packages for the Friday before Carnival to Ash Wednesday; expect to pay between US$70–100 per night for a basic room, and anything up to US$250 in the smarter hotels. If you arrive on spec and without digs, check the local newspaper classified columns (the *Express*, *Newsday* and *Trinidad Guardian* classifieds are available online; see p.44) or ask around to see if any locals have a spare room to rent – many people open up their homes to make a little cash at this time of year and you'll probably pay less than at an established hotel or guesthouse.

legions of eight- to-twelve-room properties with pastel decor, loud bedspreads and a pool. Thankfully, the **all-inclusive** trend that's swept through the rest of the Caribbean has not yet caught on here. At many resorts, however, you may be offered the option of a "meal plan" – the most common are CP (Continental; room and breakfast), MAP (Modified American; room, breakfast and dinner) or FAP (Full American; room and all meals including snacks and tea, etc).

In Trinidad, large-scale hotels meet international standards; a/c, TV (usually satellite or cable), telephone, jacks for Internet access, private bathroom with hot water and maybe a balcony, as well as restaurants, bar and sometimes a pool on site. However, most of the smarter hotels cater largely to business travellers, so you won't find much in the way of organised entertainment or a holiday atmosphere.

A **guesthouse** can be anything from a couple of rooms tacked on to a private home to a smoothly run nine-room establishment. Whatever form they take, guesthouses are generally small-scale properties with less in the way of facilities than you would expect at a hotel; don't expect a pool, and you could get a fan instead of air conditioning. There may also be no hot water, a shared bathroom, homelier decor and more of a personal touch. Prices at the more basic guesthouses are lower than at the hotels, although the more upmarket guesthouses can often cost as much as a hotel.

Budget-minded travellers should note that a disproportionately high number of T&T hotel and guesthouse rooms include a **kitchen** or kitchenette (the latter usually consists of a hot plate, fridge and sometimes a microwave) for roughly the same rate as a standard room. Most provide utensils; make sure that an inventory is taken in your presence to ensure that you are not held liable for breakages that occurred before you arrived.

Although **camping** is a popular activity for Trinidadian families during holiday weekends, it's not recommended on either island unless you are with a local group or can be sure that someone will stay awake to provide security. The beach is the most common spot to pitch a tent and some stretches of sand, such as Vessigny in Trinidad and

Canoe Bay in Tobago, have their own dedicated camping grounds. For more information about camping and permission for beach camping, contact the Forestry Division of the Ministry of Agriculture (☎622 4521 or 7476). Hike Seekers (see p.53) lead regular group camps to some of Trinidad's most beautiful, unspoiled areas.

## Host homes and bed and breakfasts

Private **host homes** and **bed and breakfasts** are excellent and inexpensive accommodation options; neither charge room tax or VAT, and you may get more insight into local lifestyles and attitudes than you'd experience in a regular hotel or guesthouse. Both host homes and B&Bs are monitored and inspected by TIDCO, which also produces a list of registered establishments on both islands. Host homes consist of little more than a spare room in someone's house. They normally rent at around US$20–35 per room, though owners are often open to a bit of bargaining, especially if you plan an extended stay.

B&Bs – basically the same deal as a host home but with your morning meal included in the room rate – are best arranged through the oversight associations. In Trinidad, write to or email the Trinidad and Tobago Bed and Breakfast Co-Operative, 108A Juniper Road, Maracas, St Joseph (☎/🖷663 4413, Ⓔla-belle@tstt.net.tt); in Tobago, contact Ms Miriam Edwards, c/o Federal Villa, 1–3 Crooks River, Scarborough (☎639 3926).

What you get for your money varies enormously in both host homes and B&Bs; from air conditioning and a private bathroom with hot water to a bed, a fan and a shower at the end of the corridor.

## Villas, beach houses and long-term rentals

Most **holiday villas** rented to tourists are in Tobago and tend to have full staff and facilities such as a kitchen and pool. Though you might expect a villa to break the bank, they can actually be quite cost effective if you're travelling in a group; plan on paying US$150 per week for the most basic villa to as much as US$4000 for something in the lap of luxury. Most are privately owned, but represented by **agencies**; in Tobago, contact Island Investments, 30 Shirvan Rd, Scarborough (℡639 0929, ℻639 9050, ℯislreal@ tstt.net.tt.) In the UK, try The Owners' Syndicate, 3 Calico Row, Plantation Wharf, Battersea, London SW11 3YH (℡020/7801 9801, ℻801 9800, ⓦwww.ownerssyndi-cate.com), where prices start from £900 per week.

In Trinidad, there are **beach houses** in resort areas such as Mayaro and the Toco coast. These are generally geared to locals on a weekend break (you'll often have to bring your own towels, linen and kitchen utensils), and you can get some real bar-gains by scanning the local papers. Bear in mind though, that (as with hotels) there are often two rates; one for Trinidadians and another (more expensive) for foreigners. Just

turning up and expecting to rent a beach house on the spot is a risky business, since the owners will often only be there if they know that someone is coming.

If you are planning to stay in Trinidad for a month or more, it's well worth considering a **furnished apartment**. The best place to start looking is the newspaper classified pages, particularly in the *Trinidad Guardian*. One-bedroom apartments in and around Port of Spain rent at around US$130–250 per month; good deals can be hard to find and you'll probably see loads of rooms before you find one to suit you. Ads for "tourist" or "vacation" accommodation often mean higher rates, though you might get a more palatial apartment for the extra money and you'll probably ultimately pay less than you would at a hotel.

 # Food and drink

One of the highlights of visiting Trinidad and Tobago is the chance to sample the islands' fantastic cuisine, a unique and addictive blend of African, Indian, Chinese, European and Latin American influences. It's hard to overemphasize the centrality of food to Trinbagonian culture; a true Trini would never lime with-out a full stomach, and many leisure activities revolve around the preparation of food. It's rare to visit a private home without being offered something to eat, and you may be regarded as rude if you refuse, but as the local cuisine is so good, it's not very likely that you'll do so.

## Trinbagonian cuisine

Although T&T's larger hotels often offer insipid tourist-oriented fare, you're much more likely to be offered dishes from the vast variety of **local cuisine**. Due to the islands' diverse heritage, "local" can mean anything from **Indian curry** and **roti** to **Creole coocoo** and **oil down** (see p.36), or Spanish and **South American**-style **pastelles** and **arepas** (Christmas cornflour patties filled with ground meat, olives and raisins and cooked wrapped in a banana leaf).

### Spices

Cooks in T&T have a far lighter hand with **hot peppers** than you might expect, preferring to allow the delicate flavours of fresh herbs such as the ubiquitous coriander-like **chadon beni** to come through. Heat is usually added later at the table, in liberal dashes of fiery **hot pep-per sauce**, often home-made by the islands' more serious cooks. If you don't like things too hot, remember to say so when eating out, or your meal may be automatically smothered with pepper sauce and a gloopy conglomer-ate of tomato ketchup and mustard; if you like things a bit spicy, ask for "slight pepper".

## Creole cooking

In culinary terms, **Creole** refers to African-style cooking which has picked up many other influences along the way. Usually served with a slice of **zaboca** (avocado), **pelau** is a classically Creole chicken dish, utilizing the "browning down" tradition of caramelizing meat in nearly burnt brown sugar. Rice, pigeon peas, garlic, onions and vegetables are then added and cooked in coconut milk.

Caramelizing is also used to make the traditional Sunday **baked chicken**, usually accompanied by cheesy macaroni pie and potato or green fig salad. Another Creole staple is **callaloo**: chopped dasheen leaves cooked with okra coconut milk, and occasionally crab meat, into a glutinous, pleasantly slimy mixture that's sometimes pureed into a soup. It's often served with **coocoo**, a kind of cornmeal polenta flavoured with okra. Other Creole main meals, almost always backed up by a hearty rearguard of ground provisions (see "Fruit and vegetables", opposite), include spicy **oxtail** (cow tails stewed with vegetables and butter beans or split peas), and **curry goat** (tender goat, and sometimes mutton, cooked in a curry sauce). Two dishes not for the squeamish are **black pudding**, a highly spiced pigs' blood sausage, and **souse**, pigs' or chickens' feet marinated in lime juice and peppers, served cold. A classic accompaniment to main meals is **oil-down**: vegetables (particularly breadfruit or cassava) stewed in coconut milk.

Though increasingly rare these days, "**wild meat**" such as agouti, lappe, manicou, tattoo, quenk and even iguana end up in the pot where available; these days, the best place to taste wild meat is in rural communities; it's also a staple of Tobago's harvest festivals. If you see any of these on a menu, before ordering bear in mind that many of these animals are now endangered.

Creole **soups** include **san coche**, a lentil soup cooked with pig's tail for flavouring, and **cowheel soup**, thick with split peas and slowly cooked meat which should fall off the bone. Many feature seafood; **fish broth** is a watery and delicious fortifying soup padded out with boiled green bananas and dumplings, while **pacro water** is similar but substitutes pacro (a small mollusc known as **chip-chip** in Trinidad) for fish. Reputed to be a strong aphrodisiac, it's sometimes called "Man Water". You'll also see Cajun-style seafood chowder on many restaurant menus.

**Seafood** in general is extremely popular in Creole cooking; you'll often be offered thick steaks of dense and delicious kingfish, shark, grouper, tuna, cavalli, carite, barracuda and dolphin (the fish also known as "dorado", not the mammal), as well as smaller fillets of "red fish": moonshine, snapper, parrotfish, flying fish and fresh-water tilapia. Creole-style fish is usually fried or stewed in a peppery tomato-based marinade of onion, sweet and hot peppers and garlic, while **curry crab and dumplin'** (crab cooked in its shell with a coconut curry and sauce served with bland boiled dumplings) is a marvellous Tobago speciality. Though you'll mostly see it on the menus of smarter restaurants, local **lobster** is doused in the classic butter of lemon, garlic or herbs and sometimes curried, while the slightly chewy and extremely nutritious **conch** (lambie) is curried, steamed, made into chowder, or, occasionally, marinated in lime and served raw in a ceviche salad.

## Indian cooking

Though the obvious staple of **Trinidadian Indian cooking** is **curry**, the T&T version is somewhat different to that served in India, using fresh hot peppers rather than chilli paste and a blend of curry powder that's peculiar to the islands. One of the most popular curry dishes is **duck**, which forms the centrepiece of a "curry duck lime".

One of the mainstays of Trinidadian Indian cookery is the vast array of **chutneys** and **relishes**, ranging from super-sweet to tart or pepper hot. The recipes are too numerous to list, but look out for sweetly curried mango on the seed, peppery **anchar** and **kucheela**, a hot mango pickle that's universally plopped into rotis, doubles (see p.39) and aloo pies.

### Roti

The unofficial national dish, **roti** is made practically everywhere and eaten by just about everyone as a convenient lunch or evening snack. A stretchy flat bread (called a skin) is used to wrap curried meat, vegetables or fish, a style of preparation that originated in Trinidad but is now popular across the Caribbean. There are several variations of roti skins including **dhalpourri** (with seasoned, ground split peas layered into the dough), **sada** (cooked on a hot griddle and usually cooked in the early morning only, and served with delicious fresh tomato "choka") and **buss-up-shut**, a thin, tasty shredded skin that resembles a torn cloth shirt and is usually used to spoon up mouthfuls of curry. Paratha is a plain roti skin.

Roti **fillings** range from curried chicken and beef to conch, goat and shrimp. Common vegetarian fillings (also used to complement the meats) are **channa** (curried chickpeas), **aloo** (curried potato), **pumpkin** (usually very sweet), **bodi** (green beans) and **bhaji** (spinach-like greens). In a restaurant, you may be offered a bowl of thin and peppery lentil **dahl** as an accompaniment to your roti. Many vendors include meat on the bone in their roti – if you don't fancy sucking out the marrow as the locals do, ask for no bones.

## Fruit and vegetables

Local **fruit and vegetables** are plentiful and relatively cheap, particularly if you buy from large markets rather than supermarkets, which charge quite a lot more for their wilting specimens. You'll see some unfamiliar fruits alongside the more recognizable items.

Super-sweet and extremely popular, the **sapodilla** is grey and globular with gritty, sweet pulp, while cherry-sized **chenets** have smooth green skin and a large seed surrounded by a thin covering of sweet, slightly acidic flesh. The knobbly green and brown skin of the **soursop** surrounds a delectable milky white pulp that is often made into ice cream or drinks; its smaller cousin the **sweetsop** is less common. The round **pomme cythere** (called pomsitae) is sweet and yellow when ripe, but is often eaten green with salt and pepper as "chow", as is the star-shaped **carambola** (five finger) and unripe mango.

Green-skinned with a soft, aromatic, orange flesh, **pawpaw** (papaya) is a staple of hotel fruit plates, as are bananas (these are often called **figs** – look out for the exceptionally tasty, tiny finger variety or young green bananas boiled and eaten as a savoury), **watermelon** and **pineapples**; the local fruits are powerfully perfumed and very sweet. **Passion fruit** (granadilla) and **guava** are often blended into drinks. **Citrus fruit** is ever-popular; you'll see lemons, limes, oranges and grapefruit (the latter two sweeter than in cooler climates), while **portugals** are easy-peel, thick-skinned mandarins with lots of pips and juice.

The king of the island fruits, though, are the many varieties of **mango** which grow so profusely in rural areas that whole communities are perfumed with the distinctive aroma of rotting fruit during the season (roughly April to August). The most popular (and most expensive) type is the rosy, medium-sized julie, while the long stringy mango is best avoided unless you have dental floss handy.

The most frequent **vegetables** seen on the Creole dinner plate are the Caribbean staples known locally as **blue food** or **ground provisions**; these include boiled root vegetables such as the many varieties of **yam**, as well as chewy, purple-tinted **dasheen** and **tannia**, the softer, white-coloured **eddoe**, **cassava**, **sweet potato** and regular potatoes. Dasheen leaves are also hugely popular, cooked up with **okra** (ladies' fingers) to make callaloo (see opposite). You'll also see aubergine (locally called **melongene**), **christophenes** – pear-shaped and light green with a bland, watery taste similar to marrow – as well as pumpkin, green **bodi** string beans and **breadfruit** (pembois), green and thick-skinned with clothy white flesh that can be baked, boiled or fried. Popular accompaniments to most meals are slices of avocado (**zaboca**) and fried, pounded or boiled **plantain**, a larger, denser but still sweet member of the banana family.

Thanks to the Indian influence, **pulses** (referred to as peas) are widely used; you'll see red lentils cooked into dahl, green lentils cooked with vegetables in a coconut oil-down sauce, chickpeas curried into channa, and pigeon or gungo peas and black-eye peas cooked with rice, seasoning and coconut milk to make the Caribbean classic of rice and peas.

## Eating out

In **Trinidad**, where the tourism industry is just beginning to develop and most people still prefer to eat at home, a serious **restaurant culture** is barely starting to develop. However, there are some splendid and stylish places to eat Indian, Creole, Chinese and international cuisine in and around Port of Spain. You'll also find a huge lunchtime variety in Port of Spain's shopping mall food courts, but the majority of eateries are no-nonsense places where decor and ambience come second to the food, which is invariably inexpensive and delicious: curries, roti, Chinese staples, macaroni pie and lentils, potato or green fig salad, Creole-style fish and chicken or the ubiquitous pelau.

When Trinidadians do eat out, it's often to fill up on the marvellous array of **street food.** Almost every city corner is an impromptu trading post for some kind of food, particularly brown paper bags of salted (or "ital") **freshly roasted peanuts**. Western Main Road in Port of Spain's St James district offers particularly rich pickings, with food available throughout the night. All vendors are subject to stringent regular hygiene checks; a clean bill provides an official badge, so eating on the hop rarely constitutes a health risk.

In **Tobago**, you'll see more variety in the restaurants, many of which are decidedly upscale and aimed at the tourist market, with prices to match. Local seafood, curries, Creole sauces and roti do feature, but you'll also encounter plenty of dishes like imported US steak or fish and chips. With fewer office workers and late-night revellers to fuel the trade, street food is far less widely available, and the best place to sample typical Tobagonian dishes such as **crab and dumplin** is probably the *Blue Crab* restaurant (see p.293) in Scarborough or the tiny cookshops in the market.

On both islands, **breakfast** is traditionally a hearty meal, ideally taken with a steaming mug of **chocolate tea**: hot chocolate made with fresh cocoa rolled into an oily ball with nutmeg, cinnamon and sugar, which is grated and mixed with condensed milk and water. Designed to stand you in good stead for a hard day's work, a local breakfast may consist of smoked mackerel or herring cooked up with onions and hot peppers, fried fish or the classic semi-salad **buljol**, an extremely tasty blend of soaked, boiled and flaked saltfish, fresh onions, tomatoes, lime juice and hot peppers, usually eaten with avocado and a couple of light, airy rolls called **hops**. Other popular breakfast breads include banana bread or fried **bakes**, non-yeast rolls of variable shape that are sometimes sweetened or flavoured with grated coconut to make the classic **coconut bake**. If you don't fancy eating heavily in the morning, most hotels offer a "continental" option of toast, juice, fruit and coffee or tea.

## Tax and tipping

One important point to note is the addition of a **tax** (up to 15 percent) and a **service charge** (usually 10 percent) to your bill; these extras are not usually included in prices given for individual dishes, and can make what seems a moderately priced meal considerably more expensive. If the service charge is included, you don't need to leave a tip.

## Fast food and street food

Though the international **fast-food** chains – *Pizza Hut*, *Kentucky Fried Chicken* and *McDonald's* – are now a part of the scenery, local outlets still manage to draw the crowds. The best T&T chain for chicken is *Royal Castle*, which uses a tasty blend of spices and herbs in the batter and serves flying-fish sandwiches and veggie burgers; there's a delicious dollop of chadon beni-laced, not-too-hot pepper sauce on everything as well. *Mario's* or *Pizza Boys* are good options for pizza, and all branches deliver, while the *Donut Boys* chain does a nice line in fancy cakes, filled croissants and doughnuts. *Roti Boys* serve up a range of hearty rotis at reasonable prices.

However, Trinidad's **street food** is by far the best option if you're after a bite to eat on the go, with everything from halal meat or fish sandwiches to fried chicken and, of course, **roti**. You're guaranteed to find something tasty if you head for the vendors along Western Main Road in St James, Port of Spain. Other good shops include *Patraj* in

Tragarete Road, *The Hott Shoppe* on Mucurapo or Maraval roads, the *Home Restaurant* in St James and Arima and *Ali's* on Back Chain Street, San Juan.

The other popular Indian snack is **doubles**, two pieces of soft, fried **bara** bread sandwiching a runny channa curry and spiced up with cucumber pepper sauce and kucheela mango chutney. Curried potato wrapped in *bara* bread and fried **aloo pies** are another popular snack, as are cheese, beef or fish pies sold from large wicker baskets in the streets or hole-in-the-wall shops; there's usually more pastry than filling, though. A little less substantial are the selection of seasoned breads such as the incredibly addictive **pholouri** (split-pea balls served with tart and tasty tamarind sauce) or **sahina**, a ground channa and dasheen leaf fritter.

Port of Spain's Savannah and most junctions along the Eastern Main Road are flanked by vendors selling small local **oysters**. Said to revive flagging libidos, they're served with a peppery, vinegary tomato sauce and slurped from a cup. However, fears of contamination by industrial pollution and the threat of cholera have led to periodic government bans; buy only from vendors who have a queue.

Creole street delicacies include the staple **corn soup**, a thick and satisfying split-pea broth with vegetables, chunks of young sweet corn and mini dumplings – a favourite hangover cure; pick a vendor with a queue as quality can vary. **Accra** is a peppery salt fish fritter, while the ubiquitous **bake and shark** is best consumed on the sand at Maracas beach, where vendors compete to produce the tastiest version of this sandwich of a slab of shark meat between pieces of fried bread. Jamaican **jerk chicken** and pork – spiced up in a tasty pimento-based marinade and cooked over a wood fire – is very popular in Trinidad, with stalls dotted all over the city; it's often served with **festival**, a sweetish fried dumpling.

Another popular choice is the food of Trinidadian Rastafarians, **ital** cooking, which (strictly speaking) refers to fresh vegetables, fruits and pulses prepared with no salt or additives. However, though Trini ital food stalls haven't managed to relinquish salt, the cooking remains some of the most wholesome you'll find, with beautifully seasoned soya mince, black-eye peas, split-peas, rice, macaroni pie and mixed vegetables served in a carton under the wonderful moniker "food" or in a roti skin; check the truck near to *KFC* in Independence Square, Port of Spain (Wed–Sat), or *Chinkies Night Beat* (Tues–Sun), opposite *Smokey and Bunty* in St James or at the croisee in San Juan.

## Desserts and sweets

With so much locally grown cane sugar and raw cocoa, it's not surprising that there's plenty to choose from on both islands for those with for a sweet tooth. **Desserts** like **paimie**, a delectable coconut, cornmeal and pumpkin pudding boiled in a banana leaf (or plastic wrap these days) and **pone**, a wet cake made with cassava, and sometimes sweet potato, spiced with nutmeg, or the classic **black cake** – a ridiculously rich, rum-soaked Christmas speciality – are sublime. Home-made fruit **ice cream**, sold everywhere from street stalls, is particularly good, as is the Guinness-flavoured variety.

**Sweets** come in numerous varieties. In Tobago, look out for **benet**, a tooth-crunching ball of sesame seeds and sugar, and **coconut cake**, a slab of shredded coconut boiled in sugar syrup and pink food colouring. **Tamarind balls** take a little getting used to, combining the tart taste of tamarind with sugar and salt, as do **salt prunes** (seasoned, sweet-and-sour prunes rolled in a dusty red colouring, often dropped into white rum for flavour) and **red mango**, which is green mango, well-seasoned with spices and sugar and doused in bright red colouring. Other candies include **toolum**, a sticky ball of grated coconut, molasses and ginger, **pawpaw** balls (shredded green papaya boiled in sweet syrup and rolled in sugar) and an amazingly sugary **fudge**, while the often sickly sugared and fried **Indian sweets** come in hundreds of varieties. Among them, **kurma** (sweet fried dough balls sold everywhere in plastic bags) is probably the most popular.

## Drinking

Given the local capacity for consuming huge amounts of **beer**, it's hardly surprising that the national brews go down extremely smoothly. The market leader, **Carib**, is a light, golden lager, while its close competitor, **Stag**, is a little sweeter and marketed as "a man's beer". Both taste better drunk out of the bottle. Newer locally brewed lagers such as **Samba**, or the Guyanese **Polar**, have yet to make an impact on local drinkers.

## The Angostura saga

Producing T&T's favourite rum is honour enough, but having cricket supremo Brian Lara as figurehead and being main sponsor for the steel pan competition Panorama ensures that **Angostura** enjoys the highest profile of any Trinbago company. Trinbagonians stick by Angostura with a nationalistic zeal, declaring its rum the best in the world and adding a dash of its **aromatic bitters** to everything from drinks to marinades, soups and puddings, as well as swearing by the mixture as a cure for almost any ailment.

### Company history
Angostura was founded by **J.G.B. Siegert**, a German surgeon who left his homeland to join Simon Bolivar in the fight for Venezuelan independence from Spain. Alarmed at the debilitating stomach ailments which plagued Bolivar's troops, Siegert began experimenting with South American herbs and spices to concoct a remedy. He succeeded in 1824, creating the secret blend of botanicals that still make up the bitters today. He named his tonic after the Venezuelan town where Bolivar's movement was based.

Popularized by sailors who brought wind of its curative powers to England, the mixture was first exported six years later, and demand increased rapidly. Production was shifted to the more economically and politically stable Trinidad, and the George Street plant soon dominated the small town of Port of Spain. After Siegert died in 1870, the company was taken over by his sons. The founder's great grandson Robert Siegert, who took the helm in 1928, steered Angostura to greater heights, establishing the Caribbean's most modern distillery in 1949 and exporting Trinidad's beloved product all over the world.

As the company became more valuable, so foreign investors began to make increasingly generous takeover bids. By now, however, Angostura had become so entrenched in the psyche (and the economy) of Trinidad that the government stepped in, taking control of the company in the mid-1950s, and returning it to Siegert Holdings, who offered cut-price shares to employees and affirmed Angostura as the "people's distiller".

Despite its bitters being voted the world's worst displayed product by the British Advertising Council in 1995 (the packaging has changed little since 1824), Angostura has gone from strength to strength, buying out other local distillers, establishing a shiny new factory on the outskirts of Laventille and winning scores of awards; no less than seven monarchs, including Britain's Queen Elizabeth, have given bitters the royal stamp.

### Angostura today
The company continues to take its traditions seriously, and the **secret recipe** for bitters remains cloaked in mystery. None of the five people who have memorized a section of the recipe are allowed to enter the blending room (or even travel) together. After mixing the ingredients, each sends their part of the blend down a chute to the same percolating container that's been used since the company began trading in Trinidad, where the herbs and spices are "shampooed" in alcohol for twenty hours before fermentation and bottling.

**Tours** of the Laventille factory are well worth taking in – they cover the history of the company as well as a look around the distilling areas and a chance to sample some of the products; to find out how to get on one of the regular tours call ☏ 623 1841 or check out ⓦ www.angostura.com.

**Guinness** is brewed in Trinidad but, though bitter and refreshing, it bears little similarity to the draught or bottled versions produced elsewhere. The sweeter **Royal Extra** or **Mackeson** stouts are excellent local alternatives.

Both dark (or "red") and white **rum** are downed with equal enthusiasm, the white tending to be less abrasively strong than the overproof brands of other islands; regular T&T rums are 43 percent alcohol. The most popular brands are **Old Oak** and **Vat 19** white and gold rums, and **Black Label** red rum. **Royal Oak** and **Angostura Premium White** are a little higher in quality. Though it's illegal to produce and possess, home-produced cane spirit – called **bush rum**, **babash** or **mountain dew** – is eternally popular, with a distinctive engine-oil aroma, a strangely pleasant taste and a wicked kick (it's rumoured to be strong enough to make ice sink to the bottom of the glass), but take care to ensure that it's been distilled cleanly, or to be safe, avoid it. Many drink their rum straight or with water, but Coke, tonic and coconut water are all excellent mixers, often with a splash of **Angostura bitters** (see box, opposite). Trinidadian **rum punch** is delicious, using blended fruits, syrup, bitters and a generous topping of ground nutmeg.

Sweet and strong homemade **wines** – cashew, banana, aloes, hibiscus, etc – are also excellent if you can get your hands on them; imported wine is widely available, though it's usually fairly expensive. Brand-name **spirits** are expensive and much sought after, but various local alternatives (**Angos Dry** gin, **Molotoff** vodka) are more than acceptable. Imported Jamaican coconut rum is a favourite tipple, and locally produced **Mokatika** coffee liqueur is a worthy after-dinner drink, often mixed with milk.

Of the available **soft drinks** beyond Coca-Cola and Sprite, there's energy-boosting **Ginseng-Up**, delicious **Carib Shandy**, in sorrel and ginger varieties, and **Bentley**, a refreshing bitter lemon soda. The best thing to drink in the heat, however, is vitamin and mineral-packed fresh **coconut water**, sold in water or jelly varieties; the contents of one nut will keep you going for ages. Vendors – grouped around Port of Spain's Savannah and busy junctions – chop off the outer husk with a machete to expose a drinking hole (ask for a straw as the juice and husk stains clothing), and then hack the nut in two so you can scoop out the jelly using a portion of the husk as a spoon.

Made from boiled tree bark, cloves and aniseed, reddish-brown (and sometimes yellow) **mauby** is wonderfully bitter, but a bit of an acquired taste. Other unusual drinks include tart, bright pink **sorrel**, usually enjoyed at Christmas with a dash of rum, as is the strong **poncha crema**, an eggnog boosted with plenty of rum. **Sea moss**, a white and glutinous preparation made from sea moss and milk, is widely believed to enhance sexual performance; other stamina-inducing potions are the **bomb**, a blended concoction of Guinness, nutmeg and condensed milk or a carton of Supligen energy drink. Cinnamon- and nutmeg-infused **carrot juice** and **peanut punch**, blended with condensed and fresh milk, are a meal in themselves and are sold from stalls all over the island. The best place for delicious blended juice drinks are *Hardline Vegetarian* and *Mother Nature* in Port of Spain (see p.104); aside from wonderful fig, pineapple or beetroot and cane juice blends, they also sell channa, okra and male or female "sex" punches.

# Post, phones and the Internet

There is no need to be out of touch when you are in Trinidad and Tobago. There are public payphones – most of which can be used to make international calls – all over the country, the postal service is trustworthy and you can get online at numerous Internet cafés.

## Mail

The country's postal service, snappily known as TT Post, is reliable and inexpensive. Outgoing and incoming **post** travels reasonably quickly (one to two weeks to Europe and the US, three to Australia). The closer you are to the capital, the sooner your letters will be delivered.

If receiving your post is a matter of urgency, it is best to arrange a **private box** at the general post office in the capital (see p.112); you can then have your letters sent poste restante to any post office in T&T. They will keep your mail for up to two weeks – to collect you must bring ID such as a passport or a driving license. If items are valuable, it is better to have them sent by registered mail.

Most towns and villages have a **post office**; these are generally open Monday to Friday from 7am to 5pm and Saturday from 8am to noon. **Post boxes** on the street are small, red, quite rare and easily missed; many still bear the insignia of the British postal service, a remnant of the colonial era. **Stamps** are sold at post offices. Letters and postcards weighing up to 20 grams cost TT$3.75 to the US and Canada, TT$4.50 to Europe and TT$5.25 to the rest of the world. Beautiful aerogrammes, decorated with scarlet ibises and available at any post office, can be sent worldwide for TT$2.

## Phones

Using the **telephone** in T&T is simple. Public phones take twenty-five cent coins for local calls; you'll need to put in at least a dollar's worth if you're calling a cellular phone. The alternative to using coins is to purchase a **Companion phonecard**, issued by the Telecommunication Service of T&T (TSTT) and available in newsagents, pharmacies, supermarkets and TSTT offices. These cards come in denominations of TT$10, TT$30, TT$60 and TT$100 (exclusive of VAT). Each has a security number (you scratch off the security strip to find it), which you punch in after dialling ☎888 2273 from any public or private phone.

Companion cards can also be used to make **international calls**, although the cheaper option is the **Talk Fuh So phonecard**, which comes in just one denomination (TT$20, excluding VAT) and allows you to talk for TT$1.09 per minute to Europe, the US and Canada. Hotels and guesthouses offer a telephone service, but the rates are usually a lot higher than using either a Companion or Talk Fuh So card. Another way of reducing international call charges without using a card is to take advantage of **Night Saver Rates** by making your overseas calls between 11pm and 7am.

## Mobile phones

You can **rent a mobile phone** from Caribel (☎652 4982, ⓦwww.caribel.com) for around US$35 per week plus call charges; rentals can be arranged online with the phones then delivered anywhere in Trinidad. Bear in mind that you'll pay for both incoming and outgoing calls.

As TSTT has a monopoly, your **mobile phone** will not work on the islands unless you register with them on the number below; that's unless you have a world-roaming GSM tri-band unit (the frequency in T&T is 1800MHz). Phones must be TDMA and digital compatible. The company offers two options. The prepaid card service requires that you purchase a SIM card (TT$100) and

## Useful numbers

Area code for Trinidad and Tobago
☎868
Local and international operator ☎0
Directory enquiries ☎6411

### Phoning abroad from Trinidad and Tobago

**To the UK** dial ☎011, then 44 then
the area code (without the first zero)
and number. Cost TT$4.50 per min.
**To the US and Canada** dial ☎1,
then the area code and number.
Cost TT$4 per min.
**To Australia** dial ☎011, then 61,
then area code and number. Cost
TT$6.85 per min.
**To New Zealand** dial ☎011, then
64. Cost TT$6.85 per min.

pay an activation fee (TT$150). After that,
you can buy cards worth TT$30, TT$75,
TT$100 or TT$200 (excluding VAT); calls are
charged at TT$1.29 off-peak, TT$2.39 peak.
The "roamer" service will activate your phone
every time you come to T&T and costs
TT$100 to license, with a TT$1000 deposit
billed to a credit card for international calls.

For more information on using mobile
phones in T&T, call ☎824 8788 (toll-free).

## Internet

There are various ways of getting online in
Trinidad and Tobago. Some of the more
upmarket hotels and guesthouses, especially those catering to a business clientele,
either have their own computers with
**Internet access** for their guests' use or provide data ports where you can get online
using your own computer. In the former
case, Internet access may be free or
charged at an hourly rate; in the latter case,
you will normally have to pay the applicable
hotel telephone rates for the time you spend
online.

The much easier – and cheaper – option is
to visit an **Internet café**. There are several of
these in Port of Spain, a couple in San
Fernando and smattering of others in urban
centres around Trinidad, while in more
touristy Tobago the choice is proportionally
greater. Nowadays, most of these cafés
have the latest computers and high-speed
Internet access. Prices range from TT$5 to
around TT$12 per hour. Meanwhile, **free
Internet access** is available at the main
libraries in Port of Spain and San Fernando.

# The media

Dipping into the local media is an excellent way to acclimatize yourself to the nation's cultural and political life. From the outspoken columnists and scurrilous headlines of the daily papers to the many local programmes on TV, the media offer a fascinating picture of Trini society – especially during Carnival, when TV shows preview costumes, road march songs and fetes, and the papers hotly debate the merits of the year's calypsos.

## Newspapers and magazines

Trinidad's main **daily newspaper** is the *Trinidad Guardian* (ⓦwww.guardian.co.tt), a high-brow paper with a somewhat conservative attitude. The other well-established dailies are the tabloids *Trinidad and Tobago Express* (ⓦwww.trinidadexpress.com) and *Newsday* (ⓦwww.newsday.co.tt); these are picture-dominated with plenty of space for their sometimes outspoken **columnists** – look out especially for Kevin Baldeosingh's writing in *Newsday*. All of the dailies have fat weekend editions with extended music, lifestyle and kiddies' features, but the selection of salacious weekend scandal rags – *The Bomb*, *Blast*, *Heat*, *TnT Mirror* and particularly *Sunday Punch* – are incredibly popular. All carry hysterical headlines and plenty of bikini-clad women, as well as some wicked political satire and thinly disguised attacks on public figures. **Tobago** boasts only one paper, *Tobago News* (ⓦwww.the tobagonews.com), which is published on Fridays and concentrates on local events.

Sold at Piarco and Crown Point airports, supermarkets and book stores, **foreign magazines** – *Time*, *Newsweek*, *Cosmopolitan*, etc – are easy to find, but newspapers – except for *USA Today* – are practically nonexistent; try the airports. Of the **local glossies**, the lifestyle and culture magazine *Ibis* and women's magazine *Esse* are both worth a look, while Carnival souvenir magazines from previous years provide a good insight into T&T's biggest festival; all magazines are sold in pharmacies and supermarkets. Local newspapers are sold at petrol stations, supermarkets, pharmacies and by vendors trading at busy corners.

## TV and radio

Trinidad and Tobago have three **terrestrial TV** stations: TV6, TIC and government-owned TTT. These stations tend to occupy the fist channels on the cable or satellite selection, and all show American soaps, sitcoms and game shows alongside educational and home-grown programmes. The main local news (including some international stories) is shown on TV6 at 7pm with another slot at 10pm, while TTT has news headlines at 6pm and 9pm. **Cable TV** is universally available in T&T; many hotels also have **satellite TV**.

**Radio** is hugely popular in Trinidad and Tobago (see below for a list of stations and frequencies). As well as keeping the nation tapping its collective feet, the radio is a good source of information on upcoming events and parties. Talk shows give insight into local culture and attitudes, while music programmes reflect Trinidad's kaleidoscopic musical styles. From November until Ash Wednesday, most stations are entirely devoted to soca and calypso, but after Carnival the mood switches abruptly and you'll hear reggae, R&B, hip-hop, rock and the inevitable "slow jams". The best stations for contemporary local music are **Yes FM**, **POWER 102**, **The Vibe** (Comedy Tempo) and **WEFM** (With Energy For Music). Daily newspapers carry listings of radio programmes.

### Radio stations and frequencies

**Radio 90.5** 90.5 FM. Indian music.
**Swar Milan** 91.1 FM. Indian music, religious programming and community announcements.
**Hott 93** 93.1 & 93.5. Comedy, local music and chat.

**Love FM** 94.1 FM. Gospel music and religious programming.

**The Rock** 95.1 FM. Nonstop "alternative" music (mostly soft rock) for the more mature listener.

**WEFM** 96.1 FM. Pumping local music, a good breakfast show with Nikki Crosby (6–9am) and reggae, hip-hop and R&B from Rodney "Fireball" King (9pm–1am).

**Radio 97** 97 FM. Dated hits from the 1970s, 80s, and 90s, interrupted only by news and sports reports.

**YES FM** 98.9 FM. Lively and firmly music-based, with soca, reggae and hip-hop.

**100 FM** News and easy-listening music.

**Masala** 101.1 FM. Indian music, chutney and chat.

**Power 102** 102 FM. Soca and reggae, interspersed with lighthearted chat.

**103 FM** Music and talk with an Indian flavour.

**104 FM** News, business and sports reports, comedy and talk shows.

**The Vibe (Comedy Tempo)** 105 FM. Comedy, news and music, with the excellent Jenelle Phillips breakfast show (5–9am).

**Sangeet Radio** 106.1 FM. Indian film music and chutney.

**Radio Trinidad** 730 AM. Magazine programmes, government info slots and music.

# Safety and drugs

**Visiting Trinidad and Tobago poses few security risks. Most islanders are generally more interested in going about their business than in harassing you or one another, and though downtown Port of Spain can feel a bit hairy at night, it's hardly a den of iniquity with a criminal on every corner.**

In **Port of Spain**, the area east of Charlotte Street around the market is the most raucous part of downtown, while there is more **crime** – some of it violent – further east in the hillside suburb of Laventille than in any other part of the country. Another part of Port of Spain that can feel a bit dodgy at night is the bottom of St Ann's Road next to the *Trinidad Hilton*, where dubious characters mill around the bridge waiting to hustle passers-by for a few dollars; this area is made a lot safer in the week or two preceding Carnival by the presence of a Mobile Police Station. In **Tobago**, recent media reports suggest that the Old Grange District, including Buccoo and Mount Irvine, is one of the fastest growing crime areas in Tobago, even if crime levels on the island are still generally low. In any case, non-violent muggings on the beach still pose the greatest risk.

If you use your common sense, however, and take the same **precautions** you would in any strange environment, you should find that the prospect of trouble is minimal wherever you are in T&T. Avoid walking alone or in small groups late at night or on deserted beaches and forest trails, keep flashy jewellery to a minimum (especially during Carnival), think twice before accepting lifts from strangers and don't go telling everyone where you're staying – or letting new acquaintances into your hotel room. Carry only as much cash as you need, get small bills when changing money so that you don't have to pull out wads of hundreds and never leave belongings unattended on a beach or in a car. Have your valuables locked in a hotel safe or use the security deposit box, if one is available.

In **rural areas** of both islands, you have little to fear – many Tobagonian doors are still sometimes left unlocked – but as a foreigner you may be a target. If you're unlucky enough to be the victim of theft or other offences, report the incident immediately, as you'll need a police report to make any insurance claim. Local officers are generally pleasant and happy to help, though things may take a little longer than you're used to.

> To call the police in an emergency, dial ☎999; for emergency services (fire and ambulance), it's ☎990.

Trinidadians are far more likely to avoid tourists than hassle them; even in the more touristy Tobago, **harassment** hasn't reached anything like the proportions you'd encounter in more established Caribbean destinations. Many locals make their living from foreign visitors; you will likely be approached on the beach by vendors selling crafts or aloe vera, but most are extremely polite and rarely pushy.

## Drugs

Visitors to the Caribbean tend to assume that all West Indians move around in a permanent haze of marijuana smoke. Though many islanders do of course indulge, this stereotype is hardly the reality. **Cannabis** (also weed, herb, ganja) is illegal to grow, sell or possess in Trinidad and Tobago, and penalties are severe. Tourists caught in possession are highly likely to be deported without a moment's notice, and jail sentences and fines are frequently imposed; the excuse that "it's OK at home to carry a little marijuana for personal use" is not acceptable. Local people who choose to smoke do so with extreme caution, shutting windows and doors and lighting plenty of incense. You probably will be offered weed (sometimes sold ready-rolled), particularly in Tobago. If you don't want it, refuse politely and firmly; if you do, be extremely careful about who you buy from, and equally cautious when smoking. Don't light up in the street, bars, nightclubs and popular beaches, and never leave the associated paraphernalia lying around your hotel room.

Marijuana is not the only illegal drug with a local following; powder and, particularly, **crack cocaine** have become common in T&T. Geographically well placed as a convenient trans-shipment point from South America, both Trinidad and Tobago have been badly affected; narcotics police regularly patrol stretches of the coastline, and there are "crack blocks" in every large town. However, you are more likely to be offered the drug in Tobago, where some visitors' taste for cocaine has provided a lucrative market. The same rules apply as with marijuana; if you are offered cocaine or crack cocaine, refuse calmly and politely. Also remember that where there are drugs, there is also **drug-related crime**, including robberies and muggings; be wary walking around late at night, check the security of your hotel room and beware of putting too much trust in new-found friends. Finally, do not consider taking drugs in or out of the country under any circumstances; customs officers have seen all the methods of concealment before and the chances are that you will be caught.

# Festivals and public holidays

Trinbagonians have a well-deserved reputation for partying. With thirteen public holidays there are plenty of occasions to celebrate, and no religious event passes without some festivity. On holidays, banks and workplaces close and many take the opportunity to enjoy the country's beaches. Concerts are organized, shops have holiday sales and the newspapers are full of events and articles relating to the celebrations.

**Public holidays** embody T&T's cultural and ethnic diversity: there are holidays acknowledging Hindus, Muslims, Baptists, Roman Catholics, trade unions, and those of African and Indian descent. Every year there is a debate whether the Chinese should be given a day for Chinese New Year. There is frequent debate, too, as to whether the country has too many days off, but each festival is avidly defended by its own lobbying group, and no politician is likely to risk offending a sector of the community.

There are other celebrations that, for all intents and purposes, are public holidays though they are not officially recognized as such. The most famous is **Carnival**, held on the Monday and Tuesday before Lent. In Trinidad, especially in Port of Spain, everything shuts down for these two days, and often for Ash Wednesday as well, while people recover from the festivities.

Most celebrations are local events based on African and Indian traditions, which entail audience participation, such as dancing, singing along to songs and eating. **Street festivals** feature local artists, good street-stall food and lots of music. Makeshift bands, with instruments ranging from a bottle and spoon to steel drums, drive around in the back of pick-up trucks entertaining spectators.

Many **religious days** are also celebrated in small ways, even by those who are not followers of the religion – many Trinbagonians will light a *deya* for the Hindu festival **Diwali**, then the next week light a candle for the Roman Catholic celebration of **All Souls'** day.

For the latest information on festival events, contact TIDCO at ☎868/623 6022; see also p.19.

## Festival calendar

### January

**New Year's Day** A quiet day, usually spent recovering from the festivities of "Old Year's Night" as New Year's Eve is known in T&T. This public holiday signals the opening of Port of Spain's calypso tents, where calypsonians compete with each other in a battle of wit and satire in the run-up to February's Calypso Monarch Competition (for more on this competition, see p.109).

### February

**Carnival Monday and Tuesday** The country's most famous festival, celebrated nationwide with costumed street processions and lots of music. Carnival will fall on March 7–8, 2005, February 27-28 2006; February 19–20 2007; February 4–5 2008 (for a detailed description of Carnival events, see p.108). Ash Wednesday is known as "Carnival cool-down", with revellers heading to Maracas and Manzanilla for huge beach parties in Trinidad and Store Bay to chill out in Tobago.

**Crate Races** These take place three to four times a year, in February, March, August and October, at Chaguaramas in Trinidad's Northwest Tip. The participants build makeshift sailing craft – no motors or real boats are allowed.

### March

**Phagwah** Celebrated nationwide in late March or early April, this festival is best seen in central Trinidad. It's not a public holiday, but many Trinis of all backgrounds participate. Based on the Indian tradition – known as Holi – that celebrates the arrival of spring, it has grown in popularity over the years to become the Hindu equivalent of Carnival. (See p.186 for more on this festival.)

**Good Friday** and **Easter Monday** are public holidays in T&T and are days when people make

47

enormous meals, visit relatives and head to the beach. On the Tuesday after Easter in Buccoo on Tobago, crab and goat races are held. These bizarre spectacles are entertaining to watch (see the box on p.276 for more).

**Shouter Baptist Liberation Day** Held on March 30, this is a relatively new public holiday in recognition of the African-based religion that suffered persecution in colonial Trinidad (for more information on Shouter (or Spiritual) Baptists see p.336).

**Crate Race** (see February).

## April

**Festival of Rapso and the Oral Traditions** Usually starting after Easter and featuring lots of concerts by new and old Rapso artists (for more on Rapso see p.347), this festival also has workshops for aspiring Rapso singers and culminates in the "Breaking New Ground" concert in Port of Spain.

**La Divina Pastora** Held on the third Sunday after Easter in Siparia in southern Trinidad. The Black Virgin statue is carried in a procession through the streets of the town, while locals, decked out in new clothes, celebrate the event with general feasting and merrymaking (see p.220).

## May

**Pan Ramajay** A month-long steel-band festival held all over T&T. Small-pan ensembles play a wide range of music including classical and jazz, with a large dose of improvisation.

**Angostura Yachting Week Regatta** (Ⓦ www.sailweek.com) Most of the events in this regatta – which draws yachties from all over the Caribbean – are held around Pigeon Point, Mount Irvine and Stone Haven bays in Tobago in the middle of the month.

**Ganga Dashara** A Hindu river festival held on May 17 in Blanchisseuse.

**Indian Arrival Day** Held on May 30, this public holiday commemorates the 1845 arrival of the first indentured Indian labourers in Trinidad (for more background on this holiday, see p.323).

## June

**Hosay** This Islamic festival changes date every year, moving between May and June. Originally a procession of mourning commemorating the martyrdom of Hussein and his brother Hassan, grandsons of the prophet Mohammed, in Trinidad the event has become carnivalesque, with a spectacular procession of handmade tombs and excellent tassa drumming. The biggest display of tombs and drumming takes place in the Port of Spain suburb St James, though it is also celebrated in Curepe,

Tunapuna, Couva and Cedros. (For more on this festival see p.96).

**Corpus Christi** A Roman Catholic public holiday on June 10. Some small villages celebrate it with processions but in urban areas it tends to be a quiet day.

**Labour Day** This public holiday is held on June 19 in recognition of the trade unions and workers in T&T. It is most publicly celebrated in Fyzabad in southern Trinidad, the town at the centre of the establishment of the powerful Oil Workers' Union (see p.221 for more information).

**St Peter's Day** Celebrated on June 29 (or the nearest weekend) in fishing communities throughout T&T, with huge fishermen's fetes on the beaches, where pots of fish broth sustain dancing to the strains of pumping sound systems. The main celebrations are at the Charlotteville Fisherman's Fete, held on Man O' War Bay beach, Tobago – a wild, all-night beach party.

## July

**Tobago Heritage Festival** Held in the last two weeks of July all over the island. Festivities include a traditional calypso competition, an "old-time" Tobago wedding ceremony and sports events.

## August

**Emancipation Day** Every August 1 the islands commemorate the 1834 abolition of slavery with a procession through Port of Spain. Tobago celebrates Emancipation Day with the Great Race, in which speedboats navigate the dangerous currents of the Dragon's Mouth in a race from Trinidad to Tobago. It starts from Chaguaramas in the morning, but the festivities take place at the finishing line at Store Bay in Tobago in the afternoon. Celebrations were originally called Columbus' Discovery Day but were replaced by Emancipation Day in 1985; diehards of the older festival still celebrate it in Moruga in southern Trinidad (see p.230).

**Santa Rosa Festival** Held the last week in August in Arima in the north part of central Trinidad. Celebrating the culture and tradition of the first Trinbago people, the Amerindians, it has musical and acrobatic performances as well as the obligatory feasting and street parties.

**Independence Day** Every August 31, locals celebrate their independence from Britain in 1962. Flags and bunting decorate all public buildings, banks and large institutions, while fetes and street parties feature performances by local soca and dub artists.

**Crate Race** (see February).

## September

A quiet month, September begins with **Cycling Classic Festival,** when cars make way for the hordes of cyclists that take up the roads in this furious race under the tropical sun. The **Royal Oak Derby** brings out horse race enthusiasts in late September, while **Republic Day** on the 24th is a national holiday.

## October

**Best Village Competition (aka National Folk Festival)** A nationwide event where villages send their best dancing troupes, musicians, actors, playwrights, handicrafts and cooks to contests in Port of Spain. The competition begins in the middle of October and lasts until the beginning of the next month when the Prime Minister announces the winner.

**T&T Awards** The island's equivalent of the Grammys, this event sees the Trinbagonian elite come out in glitzy outfits to congratulate successful musicians from all aspects of the country's music scene.

**World Steel Band Festival** Concerts hosted in venues around Trinidad feature the best steel bands displaying their skills by playing everything from classical music to the latest calypso tunes plus a specially composed piece for the competition.

**Diwali** An end-of-month festival that honours Mother Lakshmi, the Hindu goddess of light and spiritual wealth. The National Council of Indian Culture celebrates Diwali with nine days of shows, stalls and events (for more information see p.185).

**Crate Race** (see February).

## November

**Pan Jazz Festival** An international event celebrating the diversity of the steel drum with open-air concerts given by pan ensembles from around the world. These events can be expensive, but there is usually a free night of entertainment down on Brian Lara Promenade in Port of Spain. The festival usually occurs every year, though lack of finances has led to cancellations in recent years.

**Eid-ul-Fitr** This festival has no fixed date as it signals the beginning of the Islamic New Year and is determined by the position of the moon. A relatively private and subdued affair, it marks the end of Ramadan and a month of fasting for Muslims with ritual songs sung in mosques around the country. Donations are given to the poor and gifts exchanged.

## December

**Parang** A tradition of nativity songs sung in Spanish with a mix of French patois dating from colonial days; performed mostly in December. Parang groups perform in many bars and nightclubs during this time; local groups go from door to door, filling the streets with the rich, haunting music. Hearing these songs you could be forgiven for thinking you were in South America – until you detect the deep Trinbago accents of the singers. (For more on parang, see p.340).

**Christmas Day** Celebrated in typical Trinbago fashion with large social gatherings and plenty of food and drink. People visit friends and relatives during the day and eat the obligatory Christmas fare; ham, pastelles (see p.35) and the rich and fruity black cake. In the evening the festivities continue in bars, clubs, fetes and parties.

**Boxing Day** The public holiday that marks the start of the Carnival season on December 26. Radio stations start to play continuous soca and calypso music, and fetes and parties are advertised with increasing frequency.

# Outdoor activities and adventure tours

A far cry from your average sun-sand-and-sea Caribbean destination, T&T offers plenty to do beyond the beach, and the hugely rich natural environment affords many opportunities for outdoor activities such as birdwatching and hiking, while offshore pursuits include a wide range of watersports.

## Birdwatching

**Birdwatching** is a popular pastime among tourists and locals alike, which is not surprising as Trinidad and Tobago rank among the world's top ten countries in terms of bird species per square kilometre, boasting a diversity unmatched in the Caribbean: more than **430 recorded species** and around 250 known to breed. Migrant species from South America are most common between May and September, while birds from North America visit between October and March. The **dry months** (January to March or April) are traditionally the most popular time for birders to visit; during the wet season, however, birds tend to grab whatever chance they can to feed between the showers, so you'll still see a lot of activity.

The best place to start in Trinidad is in the middle of the Northern Range at the acclaimed **Asa Wright Nature Centre** (☎667 4655, ⓦwww.asawright.org, see p.148); workers there assert that even on a relatively short visit you can see as many as 150 species. Other essential stops include the **Caroni Bird Sanctuary** (see p.183), south of Port of Spain, where you can take an afternoon boat tour to see the flocks of **scarlet ibis**, the national bird and most arresting of the 156 species that live in this swampland. The **Point-a-Pierre Wild Fowl Trust** (☎637 5145 or 662 4040; see p.191) is an important conservation centre for endangered species of waterfowl nestling amid an industrial wasteland, and following a successful breeding programme it now offers the opportunity to see ibis up close.

The best **book** to bring is Richard French's encyclopedic *Guide to the Birds of Trinidad and Tobago*, which describes calls as well as plumage, habitats and behaviour. For **online birding information**, visit Russell Barrow's Birds of T&T site (ⓦwww.interlog .com/~barrow) or Trinidad Birding (ⓦwww.inct.net/~billmurphy/). There are plenty of tour companies and individual guides that specialize in **birding tours** of the island (see p.53 for details). A short list of good places to go birdwatching include the **Arena Dam**, just south of Arima, and Reservoir (see p.194), **Hollis Reservoir**, **Mount St Benedict** (p.155), the Northern Range along the **Arima–Blanchisseuse Road** (p.147), the **Piarco Water Treatment Plant** near the airport, **Nariva Swamp** on the east coat (p.200) and **Oropuche Lagoon** in the southwest (p.219).

In Tobago, head for **Little Tobago** (or Bird of Paradise Island) on the windward coast (see p.311) to see seabirds in their natural environment; the **Bon Accord Lagoon** (see p.267), **Arnos Vale Estate** (p.283), **Hillsborough Dam** (p.303) and the **Grafton Caledonia Bird Sanctuary** (p.278) are also fine bird-watching sites. At the protected **Tobago Forest Reserve** (see p.299), there are plenty of well-trained guides to accompany you.

Note that you will need a permit from WASA to enter Arena dam, Hollis and Hillsborough reservoirs, and from the Wildlife Division to go to Nariva (see p.202).

## Hiking

Trinidad and Tobago are ideal for **hiking**, though you'll have to be pretty hardy if you plan to attempt long walks in the searing sun – the best plan is to start early and cover plenty of distance before the midday heat sets in, or choose a hike that goes through forest; most of the best trips do. You don't have to be supremely fit to go hiking if you stick to easy trails, nor do you need any special equipment.

## Things to bring on a hike

### Shoes
A pair of stout shoes with good grip suffice if you don't have hiking boots – trainers are inadvisable as they have less hold and don't allow feet to breathe. Clip your toenails short before a long or steep walk to prevent rubbing, and always wear socks to protect against blisters and ticks – it's a good idea to tuck your trousers into socks if walking through land grazed by animals, which will give you a barrier against mites.

### Clothes
Wear cotton trousers or leggings to protect against nettles, razor grass and insects, with a long-sleeved shirt over a vest in case you need to cool off; a hat is good protection against sun and rain and you should carry a light waterproof raincoat in rainy season. Bring a swimsuit if a dip might be on the agenda; a spare of clothes is always a good idea in case you get caught in a rain shower.

### Food
Bring a sandwich lunch as well as concentrated high-energy food such as chocolate, dried fruit or nuts; a bag of cut sugar cane is great for maintaining energy and quenching thirst. A good-quality water bottle is a necessity and you'll appreciate the worth of one that keeps your liquids cool.

### Sundries
Other useful items to bring include: map, insect repellent, sunscreen, a good torch and spare batteries, toilet paper, rope, matches and plasters.

In **Trinidad** there is excellent hiking to be had in the forests of the Northern Range especially around Paria and Brasso Seco (see p.148); the Chaguaramas hills (see p.120); and, of the numerous waterfall hikes, Guanapo Gorge (see p.162) is particularly spectacular; other areas offer less public land and are poorly geared up for walkers. The best hiking in **Tobago** is to be had in the rainforest reserve, but here a guide is recommended (see p.299).

**Don't hike alone**. In addition to increased incidents of tourist attacks on remote trails, there is no one to provide assistance or raise the alarm if you run into problems; experienced local hikers never set out with less than two people. There are plenty of **tour companies** that provide private hiking trips (see p.53), but another, less expensive option is to join one of the excellent local groups on their regular jaunts into rural areas; best of these is **Hike Seekers** (see p.53). Hikes take place most weekends: you assemble at 7am at an allotted meeting point, pay your TT$20–30 and set off. You must provide your own transport, food and water, though the group can usually get you

there if you call ahead. Call for details of upcoming walks. Over a hundred years old, the **Trinidad and Tobago Field Naturalists' Club** (PO Box 642, Port of Spain ℡687 0514, Ⓦwww.wow.net/ttfnc) is another, slightly less visitor-friendly group that hike on the last Sunday of each month; trips leave from St Mary's College in Port of Spain at 6am, and most cost TT$10. Their definitive *Trail Guide* (see "Books", p.364) makes essential reading (if you can get hold of it), describing nearly fifty walks in minute detail.

Abiding by **hiking etiquette** will ensure that the trails you walk stay beautiful. Starting a bushfire is to be avoided at all costs; do not discard matches or cigarettes and make sure that cooking fires are completely extinguished. Stick to paths and trails wherever possible; carelessly placed feet destroy plants and crops and may lead to soil erosion, as well as drastically increasing your chances of getting lost. Leaving **litter** is a criminal offence; bring rubbish – including cigarette butts – home with you, and bury or burn used toilet paper. Finally, don't collect plant or wildlife specimens, and try to keep noise to a minimum so as not to disturb wildlife.

## Watersports

While **snorkelling** and **scuba diving** are extremely popular on both islands, they are both far better in **Tobago**, where the water is clearer due to being further away from sediment-heavy currents from the South American mainland. The best dive spots are centred around Speyside on the windward coast, where you can see pristine reef and a host of fish, including deep-water manta rays and the odd shark. Other top spots are offshore Charlotteville and the Sister's Rocks on the leeward side, as well as the Shallows or Flying Reef at Crown Point; Buccoo Reef remains the most popular, as the disintegrating coral sadly reveals. Everywhere, you'll see a dazzling variety of fish, from sizeable barracuda and grouper to angel, parrot, damsel and butterfly fish as well as spiny sea urchins and lobster nestled among the coral. Throughout the Guide, we have listed reputable dive operators (most of whom also rent snorkelling gear for around US$10 per day) in relevant sections (for more details on prices, see p.248).

If you prefer to stick to **swimming**, bear in mind that undertows and strong currents make many of Trinidad's (and some of Tobago's) beaches downright risky. However, most of these are marked with red flags, with yellow and red flags marking safe areas; in their absence, don't swim until you've checked with a local. Maracas is **Trinidad's most popular beach**, due to its excellent facilities and a swathe of fine yellow sand and cool, clear green water; several more stunning places to swim lie a few miles down the road at Las Cuevas and Blanchisseuse, though all are sometimes subject to rough seas and undertows. Away from the oil refineries, many parts of the south coast offer fabulous swimming as well.

Most agree, though, that T&T's best beaches are in **Tobago**, where the water is cleaner and calmer and the tourist infrastructure more developed. The epitome of a Caribbean seashore, Pigeon Point is the queen of them all, with its crystal-clear water, white sand and pretty palm-thatched gazebos, though its overt commerciality rather mars the spot. Nearby Store Bay and Mount Irvine are also lovely, but the undeveloped allure of Castara, Parlatuvier,

Englishman's Bay and Pirate's Bay on the leeward side are far more stunning.

Both islands also offer marvellous possibilities for **freshwater swimming**. Some of the most stunning waterfalls are Argyll in Tobago and Blue Basin, Paria, Maracas and La Laja in Trinidad; though these are just a few of the many beautiful cascades.

Most of the larger Tobago hotels have all you need in the way of **non-motorized watersports** – kayaks, small sailboats, windsurfing etc. In Trinidad, Chaguaramas is the main watersports area, where you can take a guided kayak tour (see p.117). Thankfully, jet-skis have yet to make an impact in T&T, and environmentalists are already pushing for a total ban. If you're serious about **windsurfing** or want to watch one of the many local competitions, contact the **Windsurfing Association of Trinidad and Tobago** (c/o Wayne Graham ☏628 8908).

During the winter, big breakers – especially around Mount Irvine in Tobago and Toco in Trinidad – make ideal conditions for **surfing**. You can rent boards in Tobago, but in Trinidad you'll probably need to bring your own; check with the **Surfing Association of Trinidad and Tobago** (☏625 6463) for details and further contacts.

T&T also boasts excellent sport **fishing**, though at around US$250 for a half day and $400 for a full day, it doesn't come cheaply. However, as many boats accommodate up to six, and rods, tackle and bait are included, it makes sense to share the cost. For your money, you're pretty much guaranteed some excitement; main catches include marlin, sailfish, tuna and dolphin. Boats for charter are listed throughout the Guide wherever available, and if you want more information about sport fishing, contact the **Trinidad and Tobago Game Fishing Association**, 91 Cascade Rd, Port of Spain (☏624 5304).

### Yachting

The islands' main **yachting** centre is Chaguaramas. A calm natural harbour outside the hurricane belt, this strip of marinas is a haven for yachties sheltering from rough weather in other parts of the Caribbean and taking advantage of the insurance benefits, namely lower premiums, such protection affords. Chaguaramas is also the base for boat trips "down de islands" – these are normally rum-soaked party cruises to the series of islands off the north west coast (see p.124).

For more information on yachting services, contact the **Trinidad and Tobago Yachting Association** at the Sailing Centre in Chaguaramas (☎634 4210), the **Yacht Services Association** at Crews Inn marina in Chaguaramas (☎634 4938, ⓦwww.ysatt.org), or the **Trinidad and Tobago Yacht Club** at Bayshore, Point Cumana (☎637 4260). You can also consult the **Boaters' Directory**, available from marinas in Chaguaramas and the tourist board's Marine Industry Section (☎623 1932).

## Tour operators in Trinidad and Tobago

Local tour companies' offerings range enormously from eco-oriented **hiking** excursions, **birdwatching** trips and **kayaking** to more conventional **driving tours** of the islands' "highlights": Caroni Swamp, markets in Chaguanas, Ajoupa pottery, the Pitch Lake, the islands off the Chaguaramas coast and Gasparee caves, the Northern Range with birdwatching at Asa Wright and the north coast beaches. There are hundreds of tour companies in T&T, and the list below represents the very best of the bunc h. Note that you'll often get a reduced rate if you book in **groups of four or more**; some operators will not set out with less than four in any case.

Additional tour operators in Tobago are detailed on p.246.

### Adventure and naturalist tours

**Avifauna Tours** Avifauna Tours c/o Roger Neckles, Ahie Village, Sierra Leone Rd, Diego Martin ☎/ⓕ633 5614 or 788 5755, ⓔavifauna@trinidad .net, ⓦragerneckles.com. Trini-English Neckles is one of the island's most respected bird photographers, and his tours – ranging from Asa Wright to Aripo Savannah – are excellent for serious ornithologists and amateur birdwatchers alike. Many Tobago options are available too. Tours coast $75–115 per person.

**Caribbean Discovery Tours** c/o Stephen Broadbridge, 9b Fondes Amandes Rd, St Ann's, Port of Spain ☎624 7281, ⓕ624 8596, ⓦwww.caribbeandiscoverytours.com. Entertaining, informative hikes and safaris aboard a rugged Land Rover, all with a birdwatching and animal-spotting slant. One of the best for Nariva, with kayaking (water levels permitting), a walk in Bush Bush and a slap up lunch at Kernaham Village, as well as Northern Range waterfalls, a central Trinidad day tour which includes Caroni swamp, and trips to Petit Tacarib including accommodation, food, hikes and boat transfers (US$75 per day). US$50–100 per person.

**Chaguaramas Development Authority** Airways Rd, Chaguaramas (mail to: PO Box 3162, Carenage) ☎634 4364 or 4349, ⓕ625 2465, ⓦwww.chagdev .com. Waterfall and walking tours around the Chaguaramas peninsula as well as trips "down de islands", including Gasparee Caves and hiking on Chacachacare from US$8 per person (see p.120).

**Hike Seekers** Pierre Felix Drive, Diego Martin ☎632 9476, ⓦwww.hikeseekers.com. Excellent for adventurous types, the programme of hikes is led by ex-soldier Lawrence "Snakeman" Pierre, whose exhaustive knowledge of bush trails ensures trips to the less accessible parts of Trinidad, as well as Paria, Rincon, Madamas and Sobo waterfalls, Guanapo Gorge, and Tamana and Cumaca caves. Bush camping is also available. Full-day hikes US$40, overnights US$50.

### Cultural tours

**Island Experiences** 11 East Hill, Cascade, Port of Spain ☎625 2410, ⓕ627 6688, ⓔgunda@wow.net. Lively and knowledgeable tailor-made eco-cultural tours that provide an excellent insight into Trinidadian life. Great for mas camps and panyards around carnival time, and evening and daytime city tours, including bars and live calypso and steel pan, throughout the year. Daytime excursions are wonderfully offbeat, combining stock stop-offs such as Asa Wright or Caroni with more unusual places such as Arima market or St James for roti. Island tours are extremely varied, ranging from Pitch Lake and San Fernando to Chaguanas bazaar and pottery. German- and English-speaking guides available for 1–4 persons. Half-day tours from US$25, full-day from $60, evening tours $25.

**Rooks Tours** 44 La Seiva Rd, Maraval ☎622 8826, ⓕ628 1525, ⓦwww.pariasprings.com. Excellent and well-informed birdwatching and eco-tours with an experienced naturalist and a team of specialized guides. Tours include birdwatching trips all over Trinidad, Northern Range waterfall hikes,

Tamana bat caves, adventurous and soft mountain bike excursions as well as horticulture tours, turtle watches and a couple of Tobago options. US$35–85.

**Trinidad and Tobago Sightseeing Tours** 12 Western Main Rd, St James ☎628 1051, ⓦwww.trintours.com. An established company offering a range of sightseeing trips, from tours of Scarborough and Port of Spain, to tours that take you on a circuit of one of the islands for US$30–75, and a selection of naturalist tours including Nariva Swamp and Mutura Bay turtle tour (US$45-85).

**Wildways** 10 Idlewild Rd, Knightsbridge, Cascade, Port of Spain ☎/℡623 7332,

ⓦwww.wildways.org. One of the best-organized tour operators, which ploughs most of its profits back into eco-educational programmes for local schools. Hikes, kayaking trips and mountain bike rides to Trinidad's Arena forest, Tamana bat caves, Marianne, Paria and Salybia waterfalls, Mount El Tucuche and the rainforest around Grande Riviere; Tobago excursions include the Buccoo ponds, Charlotteville hikes and the forest reserve. Overnight tours, trips to Guyana and customized packages are also available. Rates vary depending on the length of the tour, and reductions are given for groups of four or more.

# Sports

Trinidad and Tobago offer a wide variety of competitive sports for both spectators and participants. Sport is as much a national pastime as liming, and local people are justifiably proud of their country's sporting prowess, most especially in cricket.

## Cricket

A Caribbean obsession, **cricket** remains a national passion in T&T, and is the source of much debate. As long as you're not foolish enough to criticize Brian Lara, the "Prince of Port of Spain" and holder of the highest Test score in the world (400) – and the highest first-class total (501), mentioning cricket to any Trinbagonian is pretty much guaranteed to break the ice. If the Windies are playing, you'll hear radios tuned into the match everywhere you go.

**Big matches,** such as major internationals, take place during March and April at the Queen's Park Oval in Port of Spain and on the central Queen's Park Savannah itself, and are great fun even if you're not a cricket fan; soca blares in the intervals, plenty of cold Carib gets downed, and fans are vocal in their support or derision, blowing whistles, beating drums, shouting raucous comments and dancing to the soca that blares out between each over. Tickets for **Test matches** cost TT$40–200 for an all-inclusive pass to the "Trini Posse" stand, where flowing drinks and a party atmosphere make it a

day's lime rather than an afternoon watching a spectator sport; tickets are available from the **Queen's Park Cricket Club**, 94 Tragarete Rd, Port of Spain (☎622 2295 or 6050, ⓦwww.qpcc.com).

Other major games take place in the south at Guaracara Park, Point-a-Pierre and at Shaw Park, Scarborough in Tobago, which hosts some international and inter-island matches. Details of forthcoming play schedules are available from the club and are also heavily advertised in the media; for further information on the local game, contact the **Trinidad and Tobago Cricket Board of Control** at Isaac Junction, Couva (☎636 1577). Alternatively, check out any of the thousands of informal amateur games that take place on Port of Spain's Savannah and any spare scrap of land every weekend; most towns and villages have their own thriving team. For online information about the West Indies team, visit their homepage at ⓦwww.cricinfo.com/link_to_database/NATIONAL/WI or the West Indies Cricket Board website, ⓦwww.windiescricket.com.

## Cricket World Cup

Anyone travelling to Trinidad for the **2007 Cricket World Cup** should be aware that the West Indies Cricket Board has made controversial decisions about raising ticket prices for these games. Check details with your local cricket board because prices vary from country to country, with England being particularly hard hit. Accommodation in Port of Spain will also have higher rates at this time.

## Other team sports

**Football** (soccer) is also extremely popular, with support for the T&T national team, known as the "Soca Warriors" (@www.soca warriors.net), nothing short of fanatical. Major matches take place at the National Stadium on Wrightson Road, Port of Spain (@623 0304 or 0305); for more information, contact the Trinidad and Tobago Football Federation, 24 Dundonald St, Port of Spain (@622 4427, @www.ttff.com). Trinidad and Tobago Football Online (@http://welcome.to/ttfootball) has everything you need to know about the game in T&T.

**Basketball** is also catching on fast with the increasing influence of American culture. The 1st National Division consists of nine teams from around the republic who often use the names of North American teams

## The rules of cricket

The **rules of cricket** are so complex that the official rule book runs to twenty pages. The basics, however, are by no means as Byzantine as the game's detractors make out.

There are two teams of eleven players. A team wins by scoring more **runs** than the other team and dismissing the opposition – in other words, a team could score many runs more than the opposition, but still not win if the last two enemy **batsmen** doggedly stays "in" (hence ensuring a draw). The match is divided into innings, when one team **bats** and the other team **fields**. The number of innings varies depending on the type of competition; one-day matches have one per team, Test matches have two.

The aim of the fielding side is to limit the runs scored and get the batsman "out". Two players from the batting side are on the pitch at any one time. The bowling side has a **bowler**, a **wicketkeeper** and nine **fielders**. Two umpires, one standing behind the stumps at the bowler's end and one square on to the play, are responsible for adjudicating whether a batsman is out. Each inning is divided into overs, consisting of six deliveries, after which the wicketkeeper changes ends, the bowler is changed and the fielders move positions.

The batsmen **score runs** either by running up and down from wicket to wicket (one length = one run), or by hitting the ball over the boundary rope, scoring four runs if it crosses the boundary having touched the ground, and six runs if it flies over. The main ways a batsman can be dismissed are: by being "clean bowled", where the bowler dislodges the bails of the **wicket** (the horizontal pieces of wood resting on the stumps); by being "run out", which is when one of the fielding side dislodges the bails with the ball while the batsman is running between the wickets; or by being caught, which is when any of the fielding side catches the ball after the batsman has hit it and before it touches the ground; or "LBW" (leg before wicket), where the batsman blocks with his leg a delivery that would otherwise have hit the stumps.

These are the bare rudiments of a game whose beauty lies in the subtlety of its **skills and tactics**. The captain, for example, chooses which bowler to play and where to position his fielders to counter the strengths of the batsman, the condition of the pitch and a dozen other variables. Cricket also has a poetry in its **esoteric language**, used to describe such things as fielding positions ("silly mid-off", "cover point", etc) and the various types of bowling delivery ("googly", "yorker", etc).

such as the Raptors, or even some players, like Shaq Attack. National team games are held at the National Stadium – for more details, contact the National Basketball Association of Trinidad and Tobago, 3 Nevls Ave, St Clair (☎623 2881). Other popular sports include **hashing**, a kind of cross-country race with lots of beer and rum drinking. The *Pelican Inn* in Port of Spain is a good place to make contacts if you want to have a go at this, and it's worth visiting the website of the Port of Spain Hash Harriers (ⓦwww.geocities.com/poshashhouse).

## Other sports and activities

While it's not the greatest **golfing** destination in the Caribbean, T&T does boast some lovely courses, most of which have clubs and carts for rent as well as in-house caddies. In Trinidad, the best is probably **St Andrew's** in Moka, Maraval (☎629 2314; TT$100 per round). The only public course is the nine-hole **Chaguaramas Golf Course**, Bellerand Rd, Chaguaramas (☎634 4227 or 4364). There are two courses in Tobago: **Tobago Plantations** (☎631 0875, ⓦwww.golf tobagoplantations.com), a pristine course on the wind-blown Atlantic coast where a round of eighteen holes will set you back US$85; or the eighteen palm-dotted holes attached to the *Mount Irvine Hotel* (☎639 8871, ⓦwww.mtirvine.com), which costs US$48 a round. St Andrews and Mount Irvine also host various professional and amateur tournaments (for details see "Festival calendar", p.47-49). For more information on the local golfing scene, contact the Trinidad and Tobago Golf Association (☎625 2115, ⓦwww.trinidadandtobagogolfassociation.com).

**Cycling** is very popular; for details call the Trinidad and Tobago Cycling Federation (☎624 0384). Though Port of Spain's Savannah is no longer a venue for galloping gee-gees, **horse racing** remains a popular sport. Major meets take place at the Santa Rosa Race Track, Arima (☎646 7223 or 2450, ⓦwww.santarosapark.com). A newer addition to the local sporting scene is **drag racing**; regular, well-attended meets take place at the Wallerfield Race Track on the Arima outskirts; for more information contact Autosport Promotions (☎671 6112).

Fitness freaks will find Trinidad well-equipped with **gyms**, which tend to get packed in the run-up to Carnival, when everyone wants to look their best in their skimpy costumes. If you want to keep up your game, you'll find **tennis** courts at the *Hilton*, *Cascadia* and *Crowne Plaza* hotels in Port of Spain and the *Mount Irvine*, *Turtle Beach*, *Crown Point Beach* and *Grafton* hotels in Tobago; the latter also has air-conditioned **squash** courts, as does the *Pelican Inn* in Port of Spain and *Cascadia* hotel in St Ann's, Port of Spain.

# Shopping

Trinidad and Tobago offers a wide variety of souvenirs and products to suit every budget. You can buy everything from woven palm hats on the beach to the most expensive jewellery in Port of Spain's Frederick Street. Local artists produce fine woodcarvings, shell and bead jewellery, paintings and beaten copper pieces. T&T also has an excellent reputation for producing good music and talented writers – purchasing a few books and CDs will enable you to carry a little of the country's culture back home.

The widest variety of shops is in Port of Spain in Trinidad and Scarborough in Tobago. **Opening hours** are Monday to Friday from 8am to 5.30pm, and on Saturdays from 8am to 2pm. Malls are open longer: Monday to Saturday from 9am to 8 or 9pm. As with everything in T&T, these times are variable – opening hours depend on the shop and the mood of the individual shopkeeper.

T&T's rich **musical culture** (see p.340–348) has spawned an astonishing variety of styles – steel drum, calypso, soca, rapso, chutney, dub and parang – and produced many marvellous songs with strong lyrics and powerful rhythms. Local labels to look out for are Rituals, Mad Bull, Engine Room and Kiskedee Records, and in Tobago Genius Records. The best places to buy music are both in Port of Spain: Crosby's, at 54 Western Main Rd in St James, and Rhyner's, 54 Prince St (www.rhyners.com). However, you'll find music shops in most malls and along main streets. For those on a limited budget roadside vendors sell inexpensive pirate copies of popular reggae and soca tracks.

Local **bookshops** are usually full of US titles and schoolbooks. The chain Trinidad Book World, 102–104 High St, San Fernando (652 3830), and the Metropolitan Book Suppliers, 11–13 Frederick St, Port of Spain (623 3462), sell the widest range of books by local authors. Many Trinbagonian authors are published by British and American publishers however, so – if you want to get a taste of T&T's culture – it may be best to buy their work before you come (see p.368).

A wide selection of inexpensive **fabric** can be found in Port of Spain shops on and around Queen Street. Imported from all over the world, the cloth on offer far exceeds any choice provided by shops in New York or London. Locally designed **clothes** range from the most elegant evening-wear to beautiful batiks.

**Local crafts** such as carved calabashes, woven palm grasshoppers, shell jewellery and carved driftwood are usually sold on or near the more popular beaches and in souvenir shops. Ornate carvings are also sold in art galleries and at individual stalls that occasionally appear on country roads. You'll often see Rastafarians selling handmade leather sandals from market stalls or on the street.

T&T has some of the highest quality **coffee** and **cocoa** in the world, unavailable outside the country, where the high grades are mixed with lower grades by multinational coffee suppliers such as Nescafé and Cadburys. Local coffee, which comes in a variety of delicious flavours such as coconut and rum, can be bought in souvenir shops. You can buy the islands' rich, creamy cocoa from small shops and street vendors – ask for cocoa sticks: these are solid blocks of cocoa that have to be melted, and then mixed with milk and sugar.

It's said that the reason the island's White Oak **rum** is not well known worldwide is because the locals keep it to themselves and consume the total production. Trinidad's famous **Angostura Brewery** (see box, p.40) produces a wide range of excellent rum as well as their ever-popular bitters. These are readily available in many local shops. Starting at TT$40 for a litre of white rum, they are excellent value and make a popular souvenir.

## Prices

**Prices** are generally higher in Tobago than in Trinidad, and most purpose-made souvenirs are hiked up as a result of the tourist trade. Paintings and woodcarvings may seem expensive in comparison with other local produce, but these works of art are unique and the prices are far lower than can be found in an art gallery back home.

If you are looking for **bargains**, check out the streetside vendors and small backstreet shops. Souvenir shops, boutiques and the malls have higher prices, though they usually have a wider variety of products on offer. Bargaining is conducted to a certain extent with street and beach vendors but not in shops. Vendors may lower the price a little but do not push for too much; this is their livelihood, after all.

# Women travellers

**Like other Caribbean countries, T&T has a predominantly macho culture. Trinbago women usually go out in groups or with their partners, so be prepared to meet surprised reactions if you're a woman travelling on your own.**

As independent travellers are still a novelty in the country, women travelling solo will experience a greater degree of **harassment** than they would in Europe, the US or Australia. However, this usually consists of verbal comments and is rarely threatening. It's customary in T&T to be friendly to strangers, acknowledge people passing in the street and even make small talk with them. As a woman you will be expected to be flattered by the attention, and the comments are often very humorous – though also very direct and sometimes very lewd. It is important that you follow all the normal safety precautions, but you are more likely to find people warning you to be careful than actually to experience any trouble.

**Foreign women**, of all ethnicities, will usually get more of this attention. The idea of women visiting the Caribbean to find romance is so entrenched that solo female travellers should expect to be approached by men with this in mind. In Tobago, the situation is so common that some men will openly introduce themselves as "beach bums", and the terms "rent-a-dread" and "rastitute" are often heard. If sex is not on your agenda, say no and mean it; giggling, blushing or presenting the boyfriend-back-home excuse will be read as a come-on. If you feel that someone has a sexual interest

in you, trust your instincts; they probably do. Even women in couples will likely be approached – so don't think because your partner is on hand you'll escape the "sweet talk".

On the whole it is best to watch the Trinbago women and learn. They are confident and assertive and will respond to comments politely but firmly, often with a joke. T&T is still a **traditional society**; in towns and cities women will be smartly dressed in shirts and skirts, leaving the more revealing outfits to fetes and parties. If you want to reduce unwanted attention it is best to follow their example. Swimsuits and bikinis should be restricted to the beach or the river – many local women bathe with a T-shirt and shorts over their swimwear, and nude or topless sunbathing is definitely not acceptable on T&T's beaches – it's also illegal. Also avoid sunbathing alone on deserted beaches and walking by yourself on remote hiking trails: there have been recent incidents of attacks on women in isolated locations. If you have rented a car always park in well-lit locations at night and don't pick up hitchhikers – some rental companies will not allow this anyway. If you are returning to where you are staying late at night by taxi, insist on being dropped off right by the front door – especially in Port of Spain, where there have been incidents of attacks on women even walking a few yards back to their hotels from where a taxi has dropped them off.

**Feminism** has made few inroads here, though women make up nearly 40 percent of the workforce, and **sexism** remains an accepted part of Trini life. Women are a favourite topic for Trinbagonian men, who usually refer to them as "tings". Trini men are known for their smooth "lyrics", as chat-up lines are known locally. These are often imaginative but usually very crude. An unending source of debate in male Trinbago culture is women's bottoms. Highly popular calypsos on this subject include *Wine up to the Big Truck* by Machel Montano and the controversial Iwer George hit, *Bottom in the Road*.

### Women's organizations

There are lots of **international organizations** based in T&T with sections dedicated to women, often with both local and foreign women members. **Network** (℡628 9655) is a subsidiary of an NGO relating to women that can put you in touch with the relevant group. The **Women's Affairs Division** (℡625 7425 ext 265) is a government department that oversees NGOs focusing on women's issues activities, and includes **Domestic Violence** (℡800 7283) and **Rape Crisis**, 40 Woodford St, Port of Spain (℡622 7273 or 622 1079) or 12 San Fernando St, Port of Spain (℡657 5355).

# Travellers with disabilities

There is little infrastructure in place for those with disabilities in Trinidad and Tobago. However, a small but growing number of hotels, guesthouses and villas do have disabled facilities; these are mentioned in the text where they are available.

If you want to make local contacts, try **Disabled Peoples' International** (℡625 6658 or 627 0203) or **Disabled Woman Network** (℡627 6431) both based at 13a Wrightson Rd, Port of Spain.

### Planning a holiday

**Organized tours and holidays** are available specifically for people with disabilities – Tripscope (see below) will put you touch with specialists for trips to a certain country. If you want to be more independent in your travels, it's important to become an authority on when you must be self-reliant and when you may expect help, especially regarding transport and accommodation. It is also vital to be honest – with travel agencies, insurance companies and travel companions. Know your limitations and make sure others know them. If you do not use a wheelchair all the time but your walking capabilities are limited, remember that you are likely to need to cover greater distances while travelling

(often over rougher terrain and in hotter temperatures) than you are used to. If you use a wheelchair, have it serviced before you go and carry a repair kit.

Read the small print on your travel insurance policy carefully to make sure that people with a pre-existing medical condition are not excluded. And use your travel agent to make your journey simpler: airline or bus companies can cope better if they are expecting you, with a wheelchair provided at airports and staff primed to help. A **medical certificate** of your fitness to travel, provided by your doctor, is also extremely useful; some airlines or insurance companies may insist on it. Make sure that you have extra supplies of drugs – carried with you if you fly – and a prescription including the generic name in case of emergency. Carry spares of any clothing or equipment that might be hard to find; if there's an association representing people with your disability, contact them early in the planning process.

## Contacts for travellers with disabilities

### UK

**Tripscope** The Vassall Centre, Gill Ave, Fishponds, Bristol BS16 2QQ ⓣ08457/585641, ⓕ0117 9397736, Ⓦwww.tripscope.org.uk. A UK-registered charity which provides a national telephone information service offering free advice on international transport for those with mobility problems.

### North America

**Directions Unlimited** 123 Green Lane, Bedford Hills, NY 10507 ⓣ1-800/533 5343 or 914/241 1700. Tour operator specializing in custom tours for people with disabilities.
**Travel Information Service** ⓣ215/456 9600. Telephone-only information and referral service.

**Wheels Up!** ⓣ1-888/389-4335, Ⓦwww.wheelsup.com. Offers discounts on airfares, tours and cruises for disabled travellers. Also publishes a free monthly newsletter.

### Australia

**ACROD (Australian Council for Rehabilitation of the Disabled)** PO Box 60, Curtin ACT 2605 ⓣ02 6282 4333; 24 Cabarita Rd, Cabarita NSW 2137 ⓣ02 9743 2699, Ⓦwww.acrod.org.au. Provides lists of travel agencies and tour operators for people with disabilities.

### New Zealand

**Disabled Persons Assembly** PO Box 10, 138 The Terrace, Wellington, New Zealand ⓣ04/801 9100, Ⓦwww.dpa.org.nz. Resource centre with lists of travel agencies and tour operators for people with disabilities.

# Directory

**Addresses and directions** Street signs and house numbers can be confusing in T&T, as some roads simply have none and most houses are completely unlabelled. Consequently addresses often include "Corner of", followed by the names of two cross streets. When someone is giving directions, they will often describe the route by landmarks, and the colour and shape of the building; people often know a street but not its name, so be aware of such visual clues.

**Children** As most local people are fond of children and used to accommodating their needs, you'll find that travelling with youngsters is rarely a problem, and can often help to break the ice. Almost all local hotels are happy to accept families, and many provide baby-sitting services; alternatively, you can usually find someone reputable by asking around. Because many of the beaches in Trinidad (and some in Tobago) can be risky for swimming, it's best to keep a close eye on small children when in the sea; even locals' favourite Maracas has a strong undertow. Tobago's Store Bay, Pigeon Point and Canoe Bay are the calmest you'll find, but Macqueripe in Trinidad can be quite benign too. Check with locals; if there's a chance of risk, stick to paddling.

**Cigarettes** The most widely available international brand of cigarettes is T&T's locally made Benson and Hedges, which also come in the lights and menthol varieties. There are also several local brands – du Maurier (strong, also available in lights and menthol), Mt D'or (strong) and Broadway (similar to B&H). Other foreign brands can be found in large supermarket chains and malls. Bidis (Indian cigarettes) are also available. Known locally as hemp, they are actually made from low-grade tobacco wrapped in a eucalyptus leaf tied with cotton – no filter, plenty of tar. They can be bought from street vendors and some local shops in Trinidad's northwest corridor.

**Departure tax** On leaving the country by air or boat you must pay TT$100 in local currency after you have checked in and before you pass through security. Ensure you have the right amount as changing TT$ outside the country is difficult and uneconomical. It is possible to avoid the queues at the departure tax desk by paying the tax through a cash machine in the airport's Bureau de Change; the machine takes the amount off your card and gives you a departure tax form.

**Electricity** Currents run on 110 or 220 volts, 60 cycles. The current is often sluggish around peak times, particularly in Tobago, making everything run a little less efficiently than at home.

**Embassies and consulates** Foreign diplomatic missions and honorary consuls are all based in Trinidad, most of them in or near Port of Spain, and are listed on p.112.

**Etiquette** T&T is generally a conservative and friendly society. As a foreigner you will be treated politely and the same will be expected of you. Outside the cities, it is polite to acknowledge people passing on the street with a nod of the head (upwards), "good day" or just "alright". Before starting any conversation, whether buying something in a shop or asking for directions, the local custom is to say "good morning" or "good afternoon". Everything is slowed down in T&T; people take a little longer to interact, converse and to serve you. If you arrange to meet someone, be prepared to wait – being on time in T&T means being 30–45 minutes after the time originally arranged, and no apologies will be given. Don't get frustrated; be flexible and tolerant and you will save yourself a lot of stress.

**Gay and lesbian** Officially it is still illegal to be gay in Trinidad and Tobago but there is a creeping acceptance of the gay community and the government is under pressure to change the law. Even though the legislation is rarely enforced, there are still no openly advertised gay clubs or bars – the scene is very underground and all events are publicized by word of mouth. Gay and lesbian travellers are unlikely to suffer any direct prejudice but even so, be aware of your surroundings and always be discreet in your behaviour if you do not want to attract any negative attention. There are a few Port of Spain bars and clubs that are gay friendly, such as the *Pelican Inn*, 2–4 Coblentze Ave, *Smokey and Bunty's*, Western Main Rd, *Just Friends*, 16 Victoria Ave and *Metal House*, Wrington Rd.

**Laundry** There are plenty of laundries in T&T that do dry-cleaning; those that also do "wet" cleaning are listed in the Guide. Hotels and guesthouses usually have facilities to do washing, whether it is a laundry service or a concrete sink out back. Some people earn a living from handwashing; ask your host for the local washer.

**Photography** Print film is less expensive in T&T than in Europe, but getting it developed can cost 25 percent more. In Port of Spain many shops develop within the hour; there are no budget rates for a longer waiting time. Slide film is very expensive and difficult to get outside the capital; there are no development facilities apart from those offered by a few professional photographers. As a result of these high prices, photography is not as common as it is in Europe or the US. People are therefore less used to having their photograph taken, and you will be conspicuous if you walk the streets with a camera round your neck. Be discreet and ask for permission when taking pictures of locals.

**Religion and mores** Religious faith still holds strong in T&T, especially in Tobago, and this affects the islanders' day-to-day behavior. Though you may see overtly sexual dancing and hear lewd lyrics, the people are still morally quite conservative. Couples in T&T tend to be very undemonstrative in public, although at fetes and parties you may see highly erotic dancing between friends and lovers. If you dance this way with a stranger you may well be considered immoral. Beachwear should be restricted to the beach; nude and topless bathing is not allowed. Obscene language is actually illegal and though the law is not often enforced, it is nevertheless important to be aware of it.

**Time** Trinidad and Tobago is four hours behind Greenwich Mean Time (five during the summer months), and one hour ahead of Eastern Standard Time.

**Tipping** Most taxi drivers in Trinidad don't expect a tip, but in Tobago, where many make their living from foreign visitors, a 10 percent tip is standard if you are the only passenger. Never tip in a route taxi or a maxi. Restaurants often add a service charge into the bill; if this is the case, a tip is not necessary – if it's not included, 10–15 percent is the norm. If you're staying in a hotel, you might consider leaving some dollars for the chambermaid.

**Working** It is illegal to take paid employment while staying in T&T on a tourist visa. Some cultural exchanges can be arranged to teach languages and specific skills, but these should be worked out before you arrive.

# Guide

# Guide

# Port of Spain and the western tip

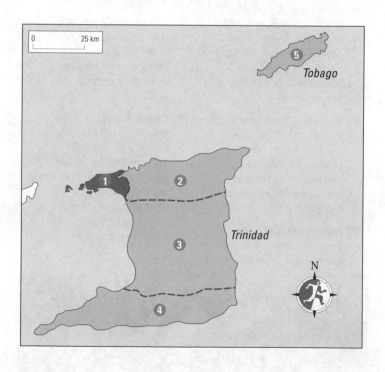

CHAPTER 1

# Highlights

✳ **Soap-box politics** Learn about the political and social concerns of Trinis at a debate in Port of Spain's Woodford Square. See p.83

✳ **Queen's Park Savannah at dusk** As the sun goes down, people gravitate to the capital's largest patch of grass. See p.86

✳ **Carnival** With panyard visits and calypso tents, huge fetes and the two-day street parade, T&T's euphoric Carnival is the best time to be in town. See p.108

✳ **Breakfast Shed** Take a seat at one of the communal tables that fill this bustling portside hangar, and indulge in some of the capital's finest Creole food. See p.104

✳ **Bar lime** Port of Spain's drinking scene is second to none, and the infa-mous *Smokey and Bunty's* is the best place to start the rum and cokes and the conversation flowing. See p.109

✳ **Paramin** Friendly people, a rich culture, beautiful countryside and some superb views are all just half an hour from the hustle and bustle of the capital. See p.102

✳ **Chaguaramas nightlife** Dance the night away under the stars at Chaguaramas' several open-air nightclubs. See p.122

✳ **Chacachacare** A one-hour boat ride from the capital and inhabited onlky by the lighthouse keepers and a diverse array of wildlife, Chacachacare offers a complete change of pace. See p.125

▲ Carnival participants

# Port of Spain and the western tip

rinidad's **western tip** – a peninsula extending towards Venezuela from the northern part of the island and dividing the Gulf of Paria and the Caribbean – encompasses both the most urbanized and some of the least developed parts of the island. **Port of Spain**, the country's capital and the commercial and cultural centre of the island, sprawls along its southern curve, between the rainforested mountains of the Northern Range and the gulf. Nearly a third of Trinidad's population lives in and around Port of Spain and for years it has enticed people from the rural areas with its employment prospects, metropolitan verve and late-night entertainment; no matter where you go in Trinidad, locals will speak of visiting the capital as "goin' to town". Port of Spain's thriving economy has also attracted many immigrants from other islands and Venezuela, making it the hub of the southern Caribbean. Although exciting in any season, the best time to be in Port of Spain is during the weeks leading up to the country's marvellous **Carnival**.

Beyond the western residential districts of Port of Spain, the landscape becomes increasingly rural. The **Chaguaramas** area, much of which is still covered by ancient rainforest, has been sensitively developed for the most part, with open-air clubs and restaurants unobtrusively incorporated into the landscape. Large areas of national parkland are etched with a network of forest trails, while the largely undeveloped beaches and sheltered coves on the north coast of the western tip offer the best opportunities for swimming.

The further west you go, the more wild and undeveloped the terrain becomes. Beyond Chaguaramas, the western tip crumbles into a series of rocky islands separated by rough, swirling channels known as the **Bocas del Dragon** – the Dragon's Mouths. Though the islands – the most accessible and developed of which is **Gaspar Grande**, the most isolated and atmospheric, **Chacachacare** – lie just a short distance offshore, they are completely free of motorized traffic. In the eighteenth century, they were a refuge for whalers, smugglers and pirates; today, they are the preserve of yachting enthusiasts, fishermen and anyone in search of tranquillity.

Port of Spain and its suburbs have a wide range of **accommodation** to suit all budgets. Whether you are visiting the city for Carnival or plan to explore

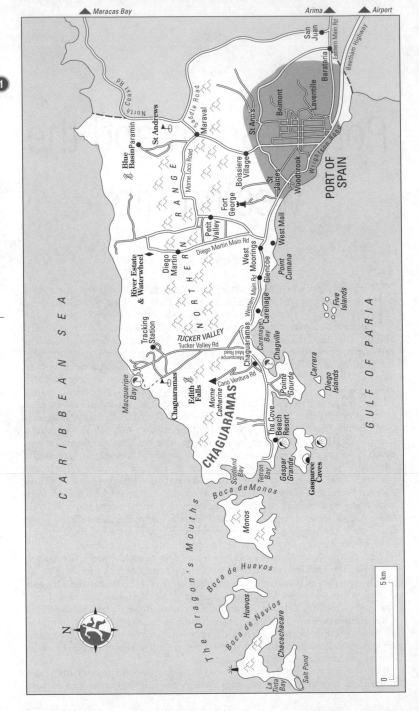

other parts of Trinidad, you will almost certainly end up staying here at some point. Indeed, it is quite feasible to base yourself in Port of Spain and visit the rest of Trinidad in day-trips from the capital, either by using the island's excellent **public transport** network or a rented **car**. Beyond the city, there are several accommodation options in the Western Tip, most of which are used by the yachties who moor at the peninsula's marinas.

# Port of Spain

**PORT OF SPAIN** occupies a crucial place in Trinidad's national psyche. It is the hub of Trinidad's booming economy, the main port of arrival for many immigrants from other Caribbean islands, and the seat of the country's government and media. The city is also the crucible of Trinidad's rich **cultural life**, with countless mas camps (see box, p.94), art galleries, panyards and theatres; it was here that Carnival was first established in Trinidad, and – in the suburb of Laventille – the steel pan was invented.

Port of Spain is a bustling city, proud of its urbanity and style. Some 51,000 inhabitants jostle for space in and around its compact centre; the latest soca tunes blare from shops, cars and pavement stalls, while locals "lime" (see "Glossary", p.370) on street corners. Yet beneath the hectic urban rhythms, you can still feel the quieter pulse of rural Trinidad. The green, crumpled folds of the Northern Range provide a constant, soothing backdrop, hand-painted advertisements co-exist with sleek new shopping malls, and street traders sell tree bark flavourings alongside disposable lighters. Despite its capital city status, Port of Spain is a small, friendly place where everyone seems to know everyone else, and at times its atmosphere can seem almost village-like.

The mish-mash of architectural styles makes for an ugly first impression, though, especially **downtown**, with its traffic-choked streets, grimy docks and frenzied commercial activity. On exploring the city, however, you'll come across many fine nineteenth-century buildings: dignified churches and state offices, the grandiose mansions of colonial planters, and quaint "gingerbread" houses, so named because of their intricate fretted woodwork. Many of these older buildings are located **uptown**, a gracious district arranged around the large open space of the **Queen's Park Savannah**, which was created by enlightened town planners in the early nineteenth century, and now gives city inhabitants some much needed breathing room.

The city's suburbs – **Woodbrook**, **Belmont**, **St Ann's**, **St James** and **Laventille**, previously old plantation estates – stretch along the flat coastal plains to the west and creep up the hills of the Northern Range. Hardly the suburban stereotype of drowsy bedroom communities, these districts pulsate with multicultural vitality: Hindu temples rub shoulders with panyards while Muslim processions and African drumming can be seen and heard on their streets. It is in the suburbs that many **mas camps** are located and where the costumes are made in the months preceding Carnival – the most exciting time to be in Port of Spain.

And during **Carnival** itself – the Monday and Tuesday before Ash Wednesday

– the city's volatile mix of style, hedonism, creativity and *joie de vivre* explodes onto the streets, and bands of fantastically arrayed revellers wind their way through the city to be judged in the grandstands on Queen's Park Savannah.

The outlying towns of **Maraval**, **Diego Martin** and **Petit Valley**, all just a few kilometres north of Port of Spain in the foothills of the Northern Range and linked to the city by frequent public transport, are essentially additional suburbs, offering a refreshing, more relaxed pace than the capital. The suburban feel peters out the further up in the hills you go, and the small, friendly village of **Paramin**, still accessible from Port of Spain by public transport, enjoys a beautiful bucolic setting, as well as being rich in cultural tradition and ethnic diversity.

## Some history

Port of Spain became Trinidad's capital almost by accident. In 1757, a series of pirate attacks on the then capital, St Joseph, left the residence of the new Spanish governor, Don Pedro de la Moneda, uninhabitable, prompting de Moneda to move the seat of government to the more convenient location of Puerto de España (a port of Spain). Though the town consisted of no more than two streets with a few hundred residents and was built on swampy, flood-prone ground, it did have the great advantage of a fine natural harbour, and was quickly made the permanent capital.

As French Catholics flooded into Trinidad in the 1780s, Port of Spain's economy boomed and the city spread. Land was reclaimed from the sea, and streets were built over the surrounding mangrove swamps and woods. The last Spanish governor, Don Maria José Chacon, greatly facilitated this expansion when, in 1787, he diverted the Rio Santa Ana (now St Ann's River) to the outskirts of the town, along the foot of Laventille Hill, alleviating the floods that had often troubled the city.

Chacon was less effective, however, when it came to defending the city against the **British**, who in 1797 invaded and took over the island. In 1808, a devastating fire led the British governor, Sir Ralph Woodford, to make a number of civic improvements, establishing the Queen's Park Savannah and developing Woodford Square. Learning from Spanish mistakes, the British also improved the city's defences by building Fort George and Fort Picton.

After **emancipation** in 1834, freed slaves left plantations to find work in the capital, squatting in the hills to the east of the city, where they established the suburbs of Laventille and Belmont. With a growing population of workers, traders and entrepreneurs, the city sprawled outwards into the old plantations of Maraval and St Ann's. Indian immigrants, brought to Trinidad under indentured labour schemes, settled in St James. In addition, settlers from China, Portugal, Venezuela and Syria all came to Trinidad to try their luck on the island and many of them settled in and around Port of Spain. Descendants of these groups, and those of the French, Spanish, African and Indian communities, ensure that Port of Spain retains its cosmopolitan mix of peoples and cultures.

As the nation's capital, Port of Spain was naturally the focus for both the **political turmoil** and the **growing prosperity** that marked the country's history during the twentieth century. From the water riots of 1903, through the independence movement of the 1950s down to the bloody 1990 coup attempt, **Woodford Square** has been an arena of political strife. The dredging of the city's **deepwater harbour** in the 1930s made Port of Spain the leading port of the southern Caribbean, while the discovery of offshore oil in the 1970s left the city with a sleek **financial district**, dominated by the imposing twin towers of the Central Bank and the futuristic Nicholas Tower. And although a slump in oil prices in the 1980s put a dent in the nation's newfound economic confidence, the last fifteen years or so has seen a wave of buoyant consumerism, with the city getting a facelift via dozens of new malls, offices and a new state-of-the-art library.

# Arrival

Port of Spain is about 20km northwest of **Piarco International Airport**, where a small **tourist information office** (daily 8am–midnight; ☎669 5196) can provide you with **maps** and **information** on the capital and the island in general. Just after you clear immigration there is a **bureau de change** (daily 24hr), while in the arrivals hall there is a First Citizen **bank** (daily 6am–10pm). You can change money at both of these places for about the same rates as in town, although they do charge a small commission (about US$1).

Official **airport taxis**, which wait outside the main entrance, will take you into the town centre for US$20 (30min, 1hr during rush hour, 6–8am and 4–6pm). Prices to all destinations, quoted in US$, are listed in the arrivals hall where the **car rental** agencies are situated. Taxi drivers will also accept local currency. Note that between 10pm and 6am fares to and from the airport increase by 50 percent.

Alternatively, take a shared **route taxi** (they pass in front of the main entrance at regular intervals during the day; less frequently at night) to Arouca Junction on the Eastern Main Road (TT$3). From there, you can catch an eastbound **red-band maxi taxi** to **City Gate**, the main transport terminus downtown (TT$4). **Route taxis** to Arouca Junction from the airport are also open to negotiation to take you direct to Port of Spain, and at TT$60–80 are a cheaper option than the official airport taxis.

A PTSC **bus** (see p.74) runs into town five times a day from the main entrance (Mon–Fri 7.15am, 7.45am, 4.10pm, 5pm & 6pm; TT$4). Departure times from City Gate in Port of Spain are 6.30am, 7am, 3.15pm, 3.45pm and 5pm.

## By sea

All ships arriving in Port of Spain dock at one part or another of **King's Wharf**: boats from **Tobago** at the **Government Shipping Service Passenger Service** opposite Twin Towers on Wrightson Road; cruise ships at the **Cruise Ship Complex**, next door on Wrightson Road. At the time of writing, boat service from **Venezuela** was suspended (you can call Global Steam Ship Company at ☎625 2547 to see if they've resumed); instead, you will have to take the boat from *Pier One* in Chaguaramas (see p.123). Private taxis tout for passengers coming off the boat from Tobago, but unless you arrive late at night, it's much cheaper to use the route and maxi taxis that run along Wrightson Road.

# Orientation and information

Port of Spain has a compact city centre based on a grid system, and most of the sights are within walking distance of each other. The **downtown** area is

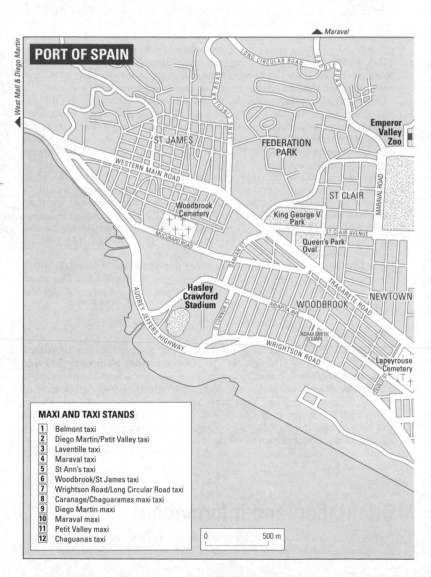

bordered by the **docks** on the Gulf of Paria and Wrightson Road. The city's most animated thoroughfare is **Brian Lara Promenade/Independence Square**, which spans the width of the city centre, running east from the financial district to the Roman Catholic cathedral. **City Gate**, the main transport terminal, and many route taxi ranks are also located in the city centre. The **uptown** area is ranged around the large green expanse of the **Queen's Park Savannah**, which becomes a focal point during Carnival.

As many of the inner suburban districts become increasingly commercialized, it is getting hard to tell where the **suburbs** begin and the city centre ends. There

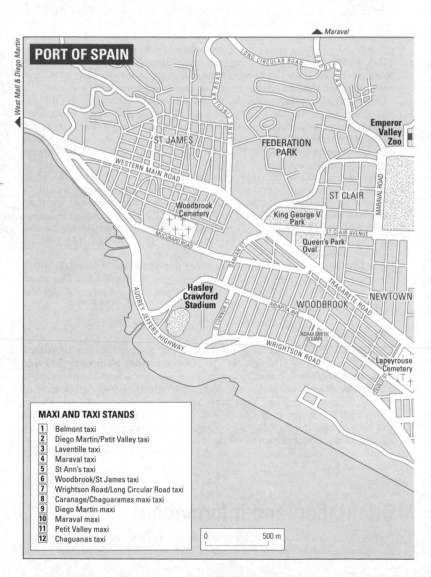

**PORT OF SPAIN**

**MAXI AND TAXI STANDS**

| | |
|---|---|
| **1** | Belmont taxi |
| **2** | Diego Martin/Petit Valley taxi |
| **3** | Laventille taxi |
| **4** | Maraval taxi |
| **5** | St Ann's taxi |
| **6** | Woodbrook/St James taxi |
| **7** | Wrightson Road/Long Circular Road taxi |
| **8** | Caranage/Chaguaramas maxi taxi |
| **9** | Diego Martin maxi |
| **10** | Maraval maxi |
| **11** | Petit Valley maxi |
| **12** | Chaguanas taxi |

0          500 m

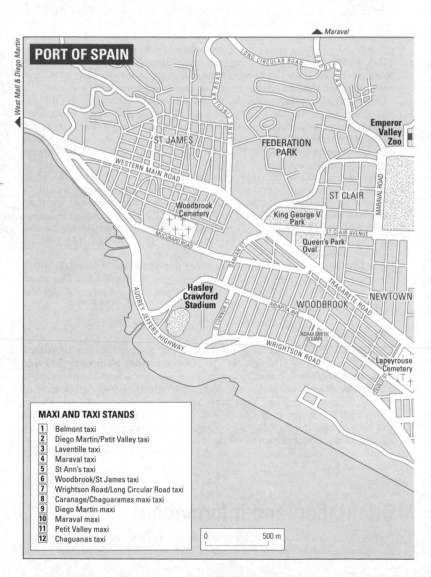

are four main roads leading out of the central downtown area. **Wrightson Road** from downtown joins the Audrey Jeffers Highway, which takes you to Diego Martin, West Mall and the west. **Tragarete Road** runs from uptown Park Street through Woodbrook before joining the Western Main Road into St James. **Saddle Road** leads from the northwest corner of the Queen's Park Savannah to Maraval and eventually Maracas Beach. From the northeast corner of the Savannah, **St Ann's Road** takes you to St Ann's and Cascade.

**Tourist information** in the form of brochures, maps, glossy magazines and approved accommodation lists is available at **TIDCO's** main office at 12–14

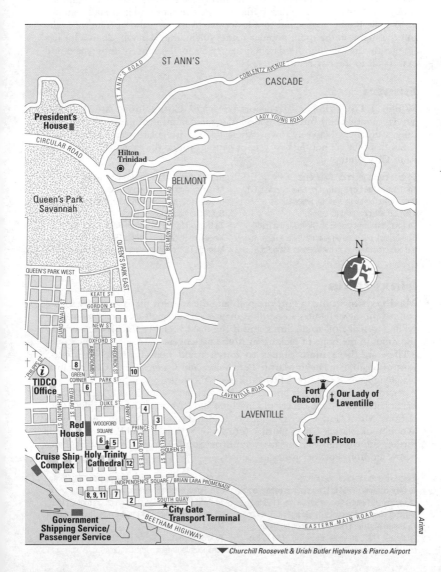

ST ANN'S ROAD
ST ANN'S
COBLENTZ AVENUE
CASCADE
LADY YOUNG ROAD
**President's House** ■
CIRCULAR ROAD
**Hilton Trinidad** ◎
BELMONT
BELMONT CIRCULAR ROAD
**Queen's Park Savannah**
QUEEN'S PARK EAST
N
QUEEN'S PARK WEST
KEATE ST
GORDON ST
NEW ST
OXFORD ST
DUNDONALD ST
ABERCROMBY ST
FREDERICK ST
PHILLIPS ST
✝
ⓘ
**8**
GREEN CORNER
PARK ST
**10**
**TIDCO Office**
**6**
RICHMOND ST
EDWARD ST
DUKE ST
**4**
HENRY ST
**3**
LAVENTILLE ROAD
**Fort Chacon** 🏰
✝ **Our Lady of Laventille**
LAVENTILLE
**Red House**
WOODFORD SQUARE
PRINCE ST
**6** ✝ **5**
CHARLOTTE ST
**1**
NELSON ST
QUEEN ST
🏰 **Fort Picton**
**Cruise Ship Complex**
**Holy Trinity Cathedral** **12**
INDEPENDENCE SQUARE / BRIAN LARA PROMENADE
**8, 9, 11** **7**
**2**
SOUTH QUAY
★ **City Gate Transport Terminal**
**Government Shipping Service/ Passenger Service**
BEETHAM HIGHWAY
EASTERN MAIN ROAD
▶ Arima
73
■

▼ Churchill Roosevelt & Uriah Butler Highways & Piarco Airport

Philipps St (Mon–Fri 8am–4.30pm; ☎623-1932). If you arrive outside of office hours, you can still get an information pack from the 24-hour security desk at the main entrance.

# City transport

There are four types of **transport** to get around Port of Spain and its environs: **buses**, **yellow-band maxi taxis**, **route taxis** and **private taxis**. There are plenty of maxis and route taxis around during the day, especially at peak hours, though note that at these times traffic jams are common and it might be quicker to walk. Route taxis – and to a lesser extent maxis – also operate throughout the night on the more popular routes (including Maraval), albeit a lot less frequently than during the day; see map, p.80 for location of most maxi and taxi stands in the city centre.

## Buses

While **PTSC** (Public Transport Service Corporation ☎623 2262, Ⓦwww.goptsc.com) **buses** provide a fast, air-conditioned means of travelling longer distances between towns, their relative irregularity and infrequency mean that they are not the best way of getting around the capital. All buses start from **City Gate**.

### Routes and fares

**To Central Port of Spain** (City Gate special): City Gate, Abercromby St, New St, Frederick St. TT$1.50, every 30min (6–9am).
**To Chaguaramas:** same as Diego Martin route (see below), but once on Audrey Jeffers Highway the bus continues on to the Western Main Rd;

passing West Mall, West Moorings, Glencoe, Carenage and Chaguaramas, ending at The Cove beach. TT$2, Mon–Fri, every 30min (5am–10pm), Sat & Sun hourly (5am–10pm).
**To Diego Martin:** Wrightson Rd, Ariapita Ave, Mucurapo Rd, Audrey Jeffers Highway, Diego Martin. TT$2, every two hours (6am–8pm).

## Maxi taxis

**Maxi taxis** operating in Port of Spain and the western tip have yellow stripes painted on them. Routes are set (see map, p.72) although some drivers may be willing to make off-route drops, and if the maxi is empty, the driver may vary the route in the hope of picking up some passengers.

There are **three main places to catch maxi taxis** for travelling around Port of Spain. For Diego Martin/Petit Valley and Carenage and Chaguaramas via Wrightson Road, the maxi rank is at the junction of South Quay and Abercromby Street. Maxis bound for Maraval (and sometimes Diego Martin) via St James start at the corner of Charlotte and Park streets, opposite the petrol station. Maxis for Carenage and Chaguaramas via Ariapita Avenue in Woodbrook, start at Green Corner (corner of St Vincent and Park streets). For further information call the maxi rank on South Quay (☎625 4053). Fares below are from Port of Spain city centre.

### Routes and fares

**To Chaguaramas** TT$4 to Chaguaramas centre, eg Chaguaramas Hotel & Convention Centre; TT$5 to anywhere beyond the centre. Route ends at The Cove.
**To Diego Martin:** TT$3; short drops on route, eg St James, TT$2; off-route drops add TT$3 to the fare. Route ends at Diego Martin waterwheel.

**To Maraval:** TT$3; off-route drops add TT$2 to the fare. Route ends at Maraval village/Paramin.
**To Petit Valley:** TT$3; short drops on route, TT$2; off-route drops add TT$3 to the fare. Route ends at Mount Coco Rd.
**To Woodbrook:** TT$2; no off-route drops. Route continues to Carenage or The Cove.

## Route taxis

The same rules apply to **route taxis** as to maxi taxis: all off-route drops depend on the driver's goodwill. Starting points for the routes are dotted around Port of Spain (see map, p.80). From around 7pm until 5am, several taxi stands relocate to Brian Lara Promenade/Independence Square.

### Routes and fares

**To Belmont:** Charlotte St, at Queen. TT$2 flat fee; off-route drops add TT$1 to the fare.

**To Diego Martin:** South Quay, at Broadway. TT$4 to the route end at Diego Martin waterwheel; short drops within Diego Martin TT$2, except from West Mall to Diego Martin, TT$3; off-route drops add TT$3 to the fare. The route goes through Four Roads and down Diego Martin Main Rd. After 6pm Diego Martin taxis can be found near the Arthur Cipriani statue on Brian Lara Promenade.

**To Laventille:** Nelson St, at Prince. TT$3 to route end at Red Hill; TT$2 to Our Lady of Laventille Shrine; off-route drops add TT$5 to the fare.

**To Maraval/Paramin:** Duke St, at Charlotte. TT$3 flat fee; off-route drops add TT$2 to the fare. Route ends at Maraval village/beginning of Paramin. Jeeps at end of route charge TT$3 up to Paramin.

**To Petit Valley:** South Quay, at Broadway. TT$4 to Petit Valley; short drops TT$2; off-route drops add TT$3 to the fare. Route ends at Mount Coco Rd at

the Capaldeo Flats. After 6pm check near the Arthur Cipriani statue on Brian Lara Promenade.

**To St Ann's:** Hart St, on the side adjacent to the Holy Trinity Anglican Cathedral. TT$3 to St Ann's hospital; TT$4 to *Cascadia Hotel*; TT$10 to the end of Ariapita Rd; off-route drops add TT$5–10 to the fare (those to the *Hilton Trinidad* are TT$10). Route ends at Bishop Ansty School.

**To St James/Tragarete Rd:** Hart St, on the side adjacent to Woodford Square. TT$3 flat fee; off-route drops add TT$5 to the fare. From around 7pm–5am St James/Tragarete Rd taxis can be found on Independence Square, at Henry St.

**To Wrightson Rd/Long Circular Rd:** Chacon St, at South Quay. TT$3 to Jean Pierre Complex, TT$4 to *Ambassador Hotel*; off-route drops add TT$3 to the fare. Route ends at *Ambassador Hotel* on Long Circular Rd. After 6pm Wrightson Rd/Long Circular Rd route starts from near the Arthur Cipriani statue on Brian Lara Promenade.

## Private taxis

Nonroute, **private taxis** tend to be cleaner and better maintained than route taxis (the two are only distinguishable by their numberplates: route taxis have an H, and private taxis have P numberplates), almost all having (functioning) air conditioning. Keep in mind, though, that while private taxis will take you direct to your destination, they are as expensive as cabs in New York or London. They are not hailed on the street, but ordered by phone or by going to their ranks, usually outside upscale hotels such as the *Hilton Trinidad* and *Kapok* or on Independence Square. Reputable firms include: **Ice House Taxi Service**, Abercromby Street, at Independence Square North (T627 6984); **Independence Square Taxi Service**, Independence Square, at Frederick Street (T625 3032); and **Kapok Taxi Service**, *Kapok Hotel* (T622 6995). The best value option, however – and the one used most by locals – is **Phone-a-Taxi** (T628-TAXI), a Maraval-based company with rates around half those of the competition.

# Accommodation

**Accommodation** in Port of Spain is plentiful and varied. Travellers on a limited budget can choose from the city's numerous small hotels and guesthouses, while more upscale hotels, including a handful of international chains, provide accommodation for business trips and package holidays. Depending on the comfort and location of your lodgings, expect to pay anything from US$20 to over US$100 for a room. Accommodation is concentrated in four areas: downtown,

## Finding a room during Carnival

The **busiest time of year** for accommodation in Port of Spain is Carnival, and if you intend to stay anywhere near the city during this time it's essential to book well in advance. Regular Carnivalgoers reserve their accommodation on Ash Wednesday for the following year, and most hotels require as much as six months' notice. Although you can sometimes still find rooms without booking that far in advance, don't expect to get your first choice when you do. A good place to look, even if you arrive in town just a few days before Carnival, are the classified sections of newspapers (see p.44), where rooms in private houses and unsold guesthouse rooms are advertised, sometimes at very reasonable rates.

**Carnival prices**, which can be over 100 percent higher than normal rates, usually apply from the Friday preceding Carnival through to Carnival Tuesday. The majority of hotels and guesthouses insist on a five- or seven-night **minimum stay** – some ask for as much as ten nights – which you'll have to pay for even if you don't stay there the whole period. Where applicable, we've listed the normal rate first, followed by the Carnival rate.

Woodbrook (including one large hotel in the neighbouring suburb of St James), Newtown–St Clair and St Ann's–Cascade; most of the rest of the city's accommodation options are in the outlying suburb of Maraval.

Staying **downtown** has its advantages, as it's obviously convenient for shops, services and sightseeing, though you may have to put up with some noise and cramped rooms. Although essentially a business and commercial district with a lighter concentration of places to stay than in other parts of the city, the downtown area does boast one big international hotel while some of the smaller places in the area offer excellent rates, especially if you are prepared to accept rooms with shared bathrooms and fans instead of air conditioning. **Woodbrook** has the lion's share of the **guesthouses**, the majority of which are moderately or inexpensively priced. Public transport to Woodbrook is good, and if you stay at the eastern end of the suburb, the city centre is only ten minutes' walk away. This area is also packed with restaurants and ideal if you're interested in mas camps, as many are based here. In addition, you will find in Woodbrook a large number of **host homes** – private houses converted to accommodate visitors, which are a good option particularly at Carnival time (see "Basics", p.32 for the differences between hotels, guesthouses and host homes). We've reviewed a few of the notable and larger ones below (many have just one room for rent); contact TIDCO for a full listing of host homes. **Newtown–St Clair**, which shares many of the advantages of Woodbrook, also has a few slightly more costly guesthouses. The **St Ann's-Cascade** area at the base of the Northern Range is greener, breezier and less urbanized than Woodbrook, Newtown–St Clair or downtown. This is an upscale neighbourhood, and consequently the accommodations tend to be among the more expensive in Port of Spain. The area's proximity to the Queen's Park Savannah makes it an excellent base during Carnival visits.

Though it lies outside the city limits to the north, **Maraval** is practically a suburb of Port of Spain; it's easily accessible and also has a good range of accommodation, the majority of which is located on Saddle Road, which runs through the centre of Maraval.

### Downtown Port of Spain

**Abercromby Inn** 101 Abercromby St ℡ 623 5259, ℻ 624 3858, ℮ aberinn@fiberline.tt. Rooms are on the small side, but clean and well equipped with cable TV, telephone and a/c; most have en-suite bathrooms but a few rooms share, and deluxe units have microwave and fridge. Communal sun deck, good central location and breakfast included.

Five percent discount for ISIC student card holders. **4**/**6**

**Copper Kettle** 66 Edward St ☎625 4381. Basic rooms, some with a/c, some with fans; all have en-suite bathrooms. Slightly run-down, but inexpensive and good value given its central location. There's also a good bar and Creole restaurant on site. **3**/**5**

**Crowne Plaza** 1017 Wrightson Rd ☎625 3366, ℱ625 4166, ℮crowneplaza@tstt.net.tt. Glitzy corporate hotel with a convenient downtown location and all mod cons: pool, three restaurants, bar, gym, business centre. All rooms have excellent views over the port and Gulf of Paria or the city, have a/c, and come equipped with hairdryer, iron and board, coffeemaker, satellite TV and phone. Breakfast is included in the rates. **9**/**9**

**Pearl's** 3–4 Victoria Square East ☎625 2158. A large old colonial mansion with a verandah overlooking picturesque Victoria Square, this is the cheapest place in Port of Spain; moreover, the rates increase only slightly for Carnival. The basic rooms have fans, sinks and 1960s furniture, and there is a communal kitchen and TV room. Friendly, helpful hosts, and perfectly situated for Carnival and downtown sightseeing. **2**/**3**

## Woodbrook and St James

**Ambassador** 99A Long Circular Rd, St James ☎628 9000, ℱ628 7411, ℴwww.ambassadortt.com. Fairly plush hotel opposite the US ambassador's residence, with a restaurant, cocktail lounge, swimming pool, ballroom and nightclub. Large, luxurious rooms with a/c, cable TV and en-suite bathrooms; ask specifically for one facing front, as those have excellent views over Port of Spain. Carnival rates include breakfast. **6**/**9**

**Ana's Place** 5 Ana St ☎627 2563, ℮anavilla@carib-link.net. Welcoming, two-room host home with some of the cheapest rates in Woodbrook. Choose from a compact en suite a/c room with cable TV, microwave and fridge or a larger apartment with a small kitchen. **3**/**6**

**Fabienne's** 15 Belle Smythe St, Woodbrook ☎622 2773. Homely atmosphere and comfortable, if rather spartan rooms featuring en-suite bathrooms and standing fans; some have a/c. There's also a small swimming pool and laundry facilities. **5**/**7**

**Johnson's** 16 Buller St, Woodbrook ☎628 7553. Friendly, helpful hosts and spotless, well-maintained rooms with fans, cable TV and a/c. Guests have use of a shared kitchen and lounge. Good value, and just ten minutes from the town centre. **4**/**6**

**La Calypso** 46 French St, Woodbrook ☎622 4077, ℱ628 6895, ℮lacalypso@tstt.net.tt. Functional but lacking atmosphere, with spartan decor and so-so service. Facilities vary from room to room – the nicer ones have a/c, cable TV, kitchenette and bathroom, while others are just a simple room with shared bathroom. There's also a jacuzzi, sundeck and use of the pool at *Alicia's* (see overleaf). **4**/**7**

**Melbourne Inn** 7 French St, Woodbrook ☎623 4006, ℴwww.geocites.com/melbournebds. Homely guesthouse with large rooms, ceiling and standing fans, and private or shared bathrooms. There's a sundeck and a large communal verandah. **3**/**6**

**Pavilion Inn** 149 Tragarete Rd, Woodbrook ☎633 8167, ℴwww.pavilioninn.com. Opposite the Queen's Park Oval and above the *Cricket Wicket* bar (see p.107), the five rooms at this bed and breakfast – each named after cricket grounds in the Caribbean – are convenient both for matches and for Carnival. All are clean and appealing, with a/c, cable TV and private bathrooms, and rates include breakfast. **5**/**7**

**Port of Spain Courtyard by Marriott** Invader's Bay, Audrey Jeffers Hwy ☎627 5555, ℱ627 6317, ℴwww.marriott.com. The newest international chain hotel to arrive in Port of Spain, the *Courtyard* opened next to the Movie Town shopping complex on Audrey Jeffers Highway in the summer of 2004. **7**/**9**

**Trinbago** 37 Ariapita Ave, Woodbrook ☎627 7114, ℱ623 9164. Inexpensive and centrally located, with a tiny pool and a balcony overlooking Ariapita Avenue – perfect for watching Carnival pass by. Rooms vary; all have a/c, while a few share very clean bathrooms. If this is full, sister property *Tourist Villa* at 7 Methuen St (☎/ℱ627 5423, ℮tourist@tstt.net.tt) offers more of the same, including a pool. **3**/**7**

**Ville de French** 5 French St, Woodbrook ☎625 4776. Thirteen large rooms in an old colonial house, most with a/c, sinks, fridge and TV, some en suite; there are a couple of self-contained units with kitchen as well. Excellent value, and breakfast is included in the Carnival rate. **3**/**7**

**Williams Villa** 69 Luis St, Woodbrook ☎628 0824, ℱ622 7782, ℴwww.williamsvilla.com. Comfortable, homely, efficient and handy for cricket matches at the Queen's Park Oval. The spacious rooms have a/c, phone, cable TV, fridge and en-suite bathroom; one has a kitchenette. The owner's late husband was a former mayor of Port of Spain. Breakfast is included. **5**/**7**

## St Ann's and Cascade

**Alicia's House** 7 Coblentz Gardens, St Ann's ☏623 2802, ⓕ623 8560, ⓦwww.aliciashouse.com. Located on a quiet road close to the Queen's Park Savannah, all the rooms at this little hotel have wicker furniture, a/c, phone and cable TV; most are en suite, but a few share bathrooms, and there's a swimming pool, sundeck and jacuzzi. Meals are available, and breakfast is included in Carnival rate. ❹/❽

**Cascadia** 67 Ariapita Rd, St Ann's ☏623 3511, ⓕ627 8046, ⓦwww.cascadiahotel.com. Well-maintained if rather sterile hotel, with excellent facilities: squash and tennis courts, gym, pool, popular nightclub, water park, restaurant and bar. Rooms are modern and bright with patio, a/c, phone, cable TV and bath. All rates include breakfast. Deposit payable to cover phone usage and the like. ❼/❾

**Chancellor** 5 St Ann's Ave, St Ann's ☏623 0883, ⓦwww.thechancellorhotel.com. Upmarket hotel tucked down a side road near the *Normandie*. The spacious, modern rooms are ranged around an attractive courtyard with a fountain and all have a/c, cable TV, phone, dataport and private bathrooms; suites are also on offer, as are fridges on request. There's a lovely pool with a waterfall, a bar and an air-conditioned restaurant serving mainly seafood. Carnival rate includes breakfast. ❼/❾

**Coblentz Inn** 44 Coblentz Ave, Cascade ☏621 0541, ⓕ624 7566, ⓦwww.coblentzinn.com. Trinidad's first – and probably only – real boutique hotel, full of quirky furnishings, most notably an Indian bridal chair in the lobby, and decorated in zesty yellows, oranges and greens. All rooms are en suite and come with a/c, cable TV, VCR, CD player, coffeemaker, fridge and microwave, and there's a shady rooftop terrace with a jacuzzi (a sauna and a massage parlour will be opening soon). The hotel restaurant is also very good (see p.105). A cozy, comfortable and trendy place to stay. Continental breakfast included. ❼/❾

**Fondes Amandes House** 9b Fondes Amandes Rd, St Ann's ☏624 7281, ⓕ624 8596, ⓦwww.caribbeandiscoverytours.com. Charming guesthouse set in the St Ann Hills with a pool and flower-filled garden that attracts local birdlife. The rooms are eclectically decorated; some have a private bathroom, and one large unit accommodates groups. Breakfast is included in all rates. ❺/❼

**Gunda's Apartments** 11 East Hill, Cascade ☏625 2410 or 756 9677, ⓕ627 6688, ⓔgunda@wow.net. Lovely, homely studio apartment overlooking the city, with spacious main room and separate kitchen and bathroom. Genial,

generous host is a great source of information on Port of Spain and Trinidad in general, and conducts enjoyable daytime and evening tours of the city. ❸/❼

**Halyconia Inn** 7 First Ave, Cascade ☏623 0008, ⓕ627 8623, ⓦwww.halyconiainn.com. Sprawling colonial mansion converted into a basic, functional, dormitory-style hostel; most rooms have bunk beds and sleep four (extremely good value if travelling in a group), and there are three agreeable doubles with a/c, phone and private bathrooms. Inn includes a large pool, kitchen facilities and a canteen dining room. Dormitory ❷; doubles ❹/❻

**Hilton Trinidad** Lady Young Rd, St Ann's ☏624 3211, ⓕ624 4485, ⓔhiltonpos@wow.net. "Upside down" hotel built down the side of a hill, with the reception at the top and the floors numbered downwards from 1 to 11. Each room has a balcony with excellent views over Port of Spain and the hotel's landscaped garden, plus all the usual *Hilton* luxuries. Facilities include tennis courts, a sauna and fitness centre, and the nicest swimming pool in town – a popular venue for pre-Carnival fetes and the perfect place to get away from the city heat. ❼/❾

**Normandie** 10 Nook Ave, St Ann's ☏624 1181, ⓦwww.normandiett.com. On a quiet cul de sac just five minutes' walk from the Queen's Park Savannah, this is one of the city's more atmospheric hotels, with a lively feel provided by the annual Carnival concerts, and by the on-site theatre, art gallery, boutiques, café and popular restaurant (see p.105). Most rooms have polished floorboards (the refurbished ones are tiled), a/c, cable TV, phone with voice mail and en-suite bathroom, and there's a lovely pool. Breakfast included in the room rate. ❼/❾

**Pelican Inn** 2–4 Coblentz Ave, Cascade ☏/ⓕ627 6271, ⓦwww.pelicaninn.co.tt. Old colonial house with verandah overlooking busy Coblentz Avenue next to a popular pub/disco; expect some nighttime noise. Functional, neat rooms with tiled floors, a/c and en-suite bathrooms. The friendly, long-serving staff and reasonable rates for this upmarket area make this a favourite with foreign visitors. Breakfast is included in Carnival rate only. ❹/❼

## Newton and St Clair

**Forty Winks** 24 Warner St, Newton ☏622 0484, ⓦwww.fortywinkstt.com. Guesthouse aimed at the business traveller who doesn't want to stay at a typical business hotel. The en suite rooms are on the smallish side, but all come with a/c, cable TV and phone. The house is nicely decorated in bright colours and has an outdoor patio and a rooftop terrace. A good breakfast is included in all rates. ❻/❽

**Kapok** 16–18 Cotton Hill, St Clair ☎622 5765, ⓕ622 9677, ⓦwww.kapokhotel.com. Elegant, stylish hotel decorated with rattan furniture and batik. All rooms are spacious with a/c, satellite TV, radio, clock, phone, dataport and en-suite bathroom; studios and suites with kitchen facilities are also available. There's a renowned restaurant (see p.105), wine and coffee bar, swimming pool, gym and sundeck on site, and breakfast is included. ⑧/⑨

**Par-May-La's Inn** 53 Picton St, Newtown ☎628 2008, ⓕ628-4707, ⓦwww.parmaylas.com. On a quiet street (though very convenient for downtown), with helpful hosts and a communal verandah where breakfast – included in the rates – is served. Very spacious a/c rooms with phone, TV and en-suite bathroom. Ten-night minimum stay during Carnival. ⑤/⑦

**Sundeck Suites** 42–44 Picton St, Newtown, ☎622 9560, ⓕ628 4707, ⓦwww.sundeck.co.tt. The self-catering version of its sister establishment, *Par-May-La's*. Offering bright, modern apartments with kitchenette, ceiling fans, a/c, en-suite bathroom and TV; half of them also have a small balcony. There's a sundeck on the roof, and facilities for the disabled. Ten-night minimum stay for Carnival. ⑥/⑦

## Maraval

**Carnetta's Inn** 99 Saddle Rd ☎628 2732, ⓕ628 7717, ⓦwww.carnettasinn.com. A great location overlooking the Maraval River with well-laid out rooms which all come with a/c, phone and cable TV, while some have kitchenette. There is a good restaurant and the owners are extremely hospitable, and a mine of local information. ⑤/⑧

**Chaconia Hotel** 106 Saddle Rd ☎628 0941, ⓕ628 7609, ⓦwww.chaconiahotel.com. Modern, expensive hotel with a Mediterranean design. The rooms, while comfortable, are not very large. All are en suite, with a/c, cable TV, phones, hairdryers and safes. The hotel has a tiny swimming pool, a restaurant and a bar-lounge which hosts Latin dancing evenings and other such events. ⑦/⑨

**Monique's Guesthouse** 114–116 Saddle Rd ☎628 3334, ⓕ622 3232, ⓦwww.moniquestrinidad.com. Long-established and friendly, with a variety of plush rooms featuring a/c, phone and cable TV – some have kitchenette and balcony, and one is fully equipped for people with disabilities. Splendid views from the rooms in the building on the hill, about 200m up the road from the main part of the guesthouse. Decent restaurant and bar. ⑥/⑧

**Villa Maria** 48A Perseverance Rd, Haleland Park ☎629 8023, ⓕ629 8641. Quiet, well-kept hotel opposite Moka Golf Course at the north end of Maraval, with a restaurant and cocktail bar overlooking the swimming pool. All rooms have a/c and en-suite bathrooms, and breakfast is included. ⑤/⑦

**Zollna House** 12 Ramlogan Terrace ☎628 3731, ⓕ628 3737. Comfortable guesthouse with one three-bedroom apartment with a/c, TV and private bathroom. Peaceful location off La Seiva Rd – a fifteen-minute walk from Saddle Rd – overlooking the Maraval Valley and ideal for groups and families. Discounts for long-term rentals. ⑤/⑦

# Downtown Port of Spain

Dating back to the 1780s, Port of Spain's **downtown** area is the city's oldest district, and it looks the part. Despite its run-down appearance, downtown is the capital's **shopping** and **finance centre**, constantly reinventing itself in a frenzy of modernization. Within the compact grid of streets surrounding broad **Brian Lara Promenade/Independence Square** and bustling **Frederick Street**, internationally known shops jostle for space with old Spanish warehouses, coffee exporters' offices, finance houses and the paraphernalia of the **docks**, while the thoroughfares are constantly jammed with traffic, pedestrians and pavement vendors.

## Brian Lara Promenade/Independence Square

Downtown Port of Spain's best known thoroughfare is a wide boulevard running the width of the city centre. **Brian Lara Promenade/Independence Square** consists of two parallel streets, divided by a paved area furnished with benches and chess tables, making it a popular after-work liming spot; stalls are

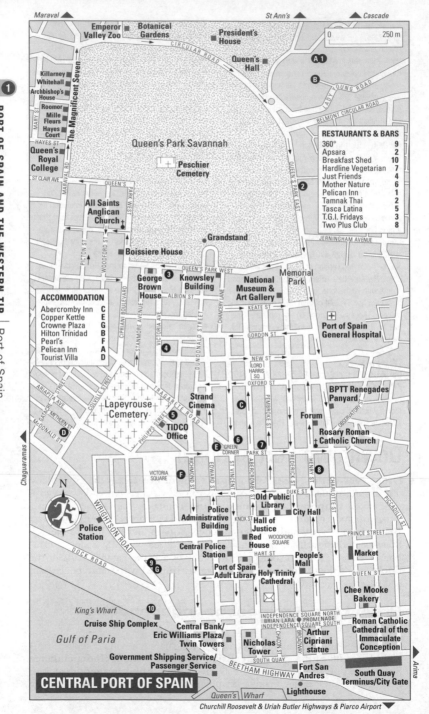

Maraval ▲    St Ann's ▲    ▲ Cascade

Emperor Valley Zoo    Botanical Gardens    President's House

CIRCULAR ROAD

Queen's Hall

Ⓐ 1

Ⓑ

LADY YOUNG ROAD

BELMONT CIRCULAR ROAD

Killarney
Whitehall
Archbishop's House
Roomor
Mille Fleurs
Hayes Court

The Magnificent Seven

MARY ST.

HAYES ST.

Queen's Royal College

ST CLAIR AVE

MARAVAL RD.

QUEEN'S PARK WEST

Queen's Park Savannah

Peschier Cemetery

QUEEN'S PARK EAST

0    250 m

**RESTAURANTS & BARS**

| 360° | 9 |
| Apsara | 2 |
| Breakfast Shed | 10 |
| Hardline Vegetarian | 7 |
| Just Friends | 4 |
| Mother Nature | 6 |
| Pelican Inn | 1 |
| Tamnak Thai | 2 |
| Tasca Latina | 5 |
| T.G.I. Fridays | 3 |
| Two Plus Club | 8 |

JERNINGHAM AVENUE

All Saints Anglican Church

PICTON ST.    WOODFORD ST.

Boissiere House

Grandstand

QUEEN'S PARK WEST

George Brown House    Ⓒ 3    Knowsley Building    National Museum & Art Gallery    Memorial Park

ALBION ST.    CHANCERY LANE

KEATE ST.

Port of Spain General Hospital

GORDON ST.

CIPRIANI BOULEVARD    STANMORE AVENUE    VICTORIA AVE.    DUNDONALD STREET

**ACCOMMODATION**

| Abercromby Inn | C |
| Copper Kettle | E |
| Crowne Plaza | G |
| Hilton Trinidad | B |
| Pearl's | F |
| Pelican Inn | A |
| Tourist Villa | D |

Ⓒ 4

NEW ST
LORD HARRIS SQ
OXFORD ST

BPTT Renegades Panyard

ARIAPITA AVE.    GATACRE ST.    METHUEN ST.    McDONALD ST.    Ⓓ

SOUVILLE STREET    TRAGARETE ROAD    ST. PHILIPS STREET

Lapeyrouse Cemetery

Ⓒ 5    TIDCO Office

Strand Cinema    Ⓒ

Ⓔ    Ⓒ 6    Ⓒ 7

GREEN CORNER    PARK ST.

Forum

Rosary Roman Catholic Church

PEMBROKE ST.    FREDERICK ST.    HENRY ST.    CHARLOTTE ST.    OBSERVATORY

Ⓒ 8

N

Police Station

WRIGHTSON ROAD

DOCK ROAD

VICTORIA SQUARE    Ⓕ

RICHMOND ST.    EDWARD ST.    ST VINCENT ST.    ABERCROMBY ST.    DUKE ST.

Police Administrative Building

KNOX ST.

Old Public Library    City Hall

Hall of Justice

Red House    WOODFORD SQUARE

Central Police Station

HART ST.

People's Mall

QUEEN ST.

PRINCE STREET

Market

PICCADILLY ST.

Port of Spain Adult Library

Holy Trinity Cathedral

Chee Mooke Bakery

Ⓒ 9 Ⓖ

King's Wharf

Ⓒ 10

Cruise Ship Complex

Gulf of Paria

Central Bank/ Eric Williams Plaza/ Twin Towers

Government Shipping Service/ Passenger Service

INDEPENDENCE SQUARE NORTH
BRIAN LARA    PROMENADE
INDEPENDENCE SQUARE SOUTH

Nicholas Tower

CHACON ST.    BROADWAY

Arthur Cipriani statue

SOUTH QUAY

BEETHAM HIGHWAY

Fort San Andres

Lighthouse

Roman Catholic Cathedral of the Immaculate Conception

▲ Arima

South Quay Terminus/City Gate

Queen's Wharf

**CENTRAL PORT OF SPAIN**

Churchill Roosevelt & Uriah Butler Highways & Piarco Airport ▼

set up against closed offices and street food vendors do a brisk trade. During the festival season, the promenade hosts **free concerts** and performances, advertised in the local press and radio. The throngs of people here have attracted a fair number of beggars, who patrol the promenade and have become very adept at latching onto foreigners.

The boulevard's cumbersome title is a result of frequent name changes in recent decades. Until independence in 1962, the thoroughfare was called Marine Square because the land it was on had been reclaimed from the sea in 1816; there's still a sign bearing this name at the centre of the promenade. Rechristened Independence Square in 1962, it was later renamed again in honour of Trinidad's most famous cricketer. Most locals still call it Independence Square, and just to make things more confusing, media and tourist publications use both names. This has resulted in an official compromise: the two parallel streets are named Independence Square north and south, while the paved area between them is known as the promenade.

### The financial district and the Arthur Cipriani statue

The western end of the promenade is dominated by the **Nicholas Tower**, a new, futuristic, 21-storey, blue and silver office block that opened in 2004, and the twin towers of the **Central Bank of Trinidad and Tobago**. These buildings are respectively the first and second highest in Trinidad. Opened in 1985, the Central Bank complex occupies the heart of Port of Spain's **financial district** and houses the Central Bank, the Prime Minister's offices and the Central Bank Auditorium.

Halfway down the promenade, at the junction with Frederick Street, is the white, near-life-sized **Arthur Cipriani statue**. A white French Creole who had served in the British West Indian Regiment during World War I, Cipriani campaigned energetically for compulsory education and self-government for the island. As president of the Trinidad Workingman's Association (later the Trinidad Labour Party) and mayor of the city in the 1920s, he was the only legislator of his day to defend workers' rights, though by the following decade his increasingly reformist stance held less appeal for many of his former supporters who had adopted a more mainstream approach. He died in 1945 and is buried in the Lapeyrouse Cemetery in Woodbrook (see p.91).

Just east of the statue, opposite the *Royal Castle* fast-food outlet, is the **UCW Drag Brothers Mall** (Mon–Sat 9am–6pm). Known locally as the "**Drag Mall**", the ten or so small shops specialize in handmade leather sandals, local arts and crafts, and Rastafarian souvenirs. If none of the sandals takes your fancy, you can have a pair made to your own design. While obviously popular with tourists, the Drag Mall does not have the feel of a tourist trap and the quality of the merchandise is generally quite good.

### Cathedral of the Immaculate Conception and Columbus Square

At the eastern end of Brian Lara Promenade, where it intersects with Nelson Street, you'll find the imposing **Roman Catholic Cathedral of the Immaculate Conception**, a legacy of Governor Woodford's post-fire reconstruction. Catholicism, the religion of the Spanish–French Creole establishment, had come to play a major role in the political and cultural life of Trinidad, and Woodford, though himself an Anglican, realized a grand building appropriate for state occasions was required. The twin-towered Gothic cathedral took sixteen years to build, and was finally completed in 1836. The ironwork frame was shipped from England, while the blue metal stone came from the local Laventille quarries; for the high altar, Florentine marble was imported from Italy. Period drawings on display in the National Museum show that when the church was completed, on newly reclaimed land, the sea lapped against its eastern wall. In 1984, the cathedral underwent extensive renovations, including the addition of sixteen new **stained-glass windows**, made to order in Ireland, which depict the many ethnic groups which have contributed to the population of Trinidad and Tobago. These windows are the highlight of an otherwise rather drab and ordinary interior. The church is open to all, and has services every evening and on Sundays. All Catholic holidays are celebrated; special masses are held at Christmas, Easter and on Ash Wednesday.

The promenade comes to an end just east of the cathedral at diminutive **Columbus Square**. Despite its brightly painted statue of the explorer, the square is very run-down, with beggars hanging out on the street corner.

## King's Wharf and the Cruise Ship Complex

The southern edge of the city is dominated by the gritty industrial area surrounding the docks. With its vast warehouses and jagged, industrialized skyline of cranes, gantries and mounds of containers, **King's Wharf**, across Wrightson Road at the eastern end of Brain Lara Promenade/Independence Square, is the hub of Trinidad's booming import–export trade. Everything from imported cars to green bananas passes through this hectic port, with most of the action taking place in the early hours when it's still relatively cool; activity gradually slows as the temperature rises.

The deep-water harbour, dredged in the 1930s, allowed Port of Spain to accommodate deep-draught ships, boosting Trinidad's economy and consolidating the city's position as the most important southern Caribbean port. The harbour is also the **arrival** and **departure point** for boats to other Caribbean islands, including cruise ships. The **Cruise Ship Complex** on Wrightson Road caters to cruise passengers during their few hours on dry land. When a ship is docked the complex comes alive in a frenetic burst of activity, with shops selling souvenirs and duty free goods, and an overpriced craft market outside. When the ship leaves, most of the shops close and the complex becomes a ghost town.

## South Quay/City Gate

Commonly referred to as **City Gate**, the grand Victorian stone building on South Quay, just to the east of the docks and one block south of Brian Lara Promenade/Independence Square, was originally Port of Spain's **train station**. The railway, established in 1876 with a line to Arima, was shut down in the 1960s and is now remembered with nostalgia as Trinidad's roads become increasingly traffic-clogged. City Gate remains Trinidad's **transportation hub**, however, now serving as the terminus for PTSC buses and maxi taxis running to all parts of the country.

Port of Spain's **lighthouse**, built in the 1880's to warn fishermen away from the rocky coastline, has since been marooned inland by reclamation. It now stands looking somewhat out of place in the middle of a traffic island on Wrightson Road next to City Gate. The heavy traffic that thunders past has turned the lighthouse into a Trinidadian version of the Leaning Tower of Pisa, skewing it 5 degrees from the vertical. Closed to the public, its only function today is to serve as an advertisement hoarding for a local paint company.

## Fort San Andres

The unassuming terracotta-painted building two blocks west of City Gate on South Quay is **Fort San Andres**, the best remaining example of a wooden Spanish fort in Trinidad. Built in 1787 – when the sea lapped against its southern stone rampart – the fort was Port of Spain's main defence when the British invaded ten years later. The National Museum runs a small **museum** at the fort (Tues–Fri 9am–5pm; free), focused solely on the **history of Port of Spain**. Drawings by Jackie Hinkson of the city's streets and buildings occupy the ground floor, while on the first floor colourful boards give potted accounts of almost every aspect of Port of Spain's history, from the Spanish rule right through to the development of banking in the capital, each description illustrated with photographs, old street maps and the odd exhibit of household items from the nineteenth century.

# Frederick Street and Woodford Square

**Frederick Street** is Port of Spain's main shopping drag, with most places of interest on the stretch between Brian Lara Promenade/Independence Square and Park Street. Here you'll find the latest imported clothes, shoes and electronics, along with street vendors selling home-made jewellery, belts, cassettes, and arts and crafts. Like much of the downtown area, Frederick Street has assumed a modern face in recent years, with many of the shops accommodated in multi-storied, air-conditioned malls complete with food courts. At the **People's Mall** on the corner of Frederick and Queen streets, small stalls and tiny shops sell clothes and shoes imported from New York, alongside hand-painted T-shirts, incense and Rasta craft.

### Woodford Square and around

A third of the way up Frederick Street, a block north of the People's Mall, you come to the pretty, tree-shaded **Woodford Square**, named after the British governor who had it built in the early nineteenth century. Its western side is dominated by the grand Edwardian facade of the **Red House**, seat of Trinidad and Tobago's parliament. On the south side stands Holy Trinity, the city's **Anglican cathedral**, while in the square itself are a picturesque colonial bandstand and an elegant, if not always functional, cast-iron fountain supported by mermaids and mermen, which dates back to 1866.

Woodford Square is best known, however, as a centre of **political activism**. As early as 1903 it was the scene of a protest meeting against the introduction of new water rates; the demonstration quickly got out of hand, and in the ensuing riots the original Red House was burned to the ground. It was in 1956, however, that the square's reputation as a political cockpit really got going with the establishment of the "**University of Woodford Square**". This was the brainchild of **Eric Williams**, historian, father of the national independence movement and first prime minister of the country, who would deliver weekly public lectures in the square on the issues of the day. In the 1970s, the square became a focal point for the Black Power movement, who renamed it the "people's parliament". It held the largest funeral ever seen in Port of Spain, that of Basil Davis, a young activist shot by the police during a Black Power protest in 1970.

Woodford Square remains a lively political forum which, along with the calypso tents, gives the people a place to speak out. On the eastern side of the square next to the public toilets a blackboard lists the topic for discussion each day. These debates typically take place at a rather unsociable 7am and anyone can join in, provided that they can get a word in edgeways; it's not a platform for the faint-hearted or soft-spoken.

## The 1990 coup

At 6.30pm on July 27, 1990, **Yasin Abu Bakr**, leader of the Islamic fundamentalist revolutionary group **Jamaat-al-Muslimeen**, announced on television that he had overthrown the government of Trinidad and Tobago. Thirty minutes earlier, members of the group had stormed the Red House and taken several government ministers hostage, including Prime Minister **Arthur Robinson**. The police headquarters around the corner on Sackville Street was firebombed and all but destroyed. **Looting** took the capital by storm, and a **state of emergency** was called, requiring all citizens to remain indoors after dark.

The Jamaat-al-Muslimeen had already had many run-ins with the authorities over a land dispute and the killing of one of its members by the police. Relying on the army to support the revolt, they also hoped to capitalize on public discontent with the government's harsh fiscal policies (satirized by the calypsonian Sparrow in his song *Capitalism Gone Mad*). Yet however little love they may have had for the government, few Trinidadians were willing to support its violent overthrow by an armed group of religious extremists. With little public support, and surrounded by loyal government troops, the rebels surrendered after a six-day siege, only after negotiating an amnesty agreement with the police which guaranteed that perpetrators of the coup would not be arrested for their activities. Nonetheless, Bakr and 113 other Jamaat members were taken into custody as soon as they surrendered, and remained in jail for two years whilst the courts debated the validity of the amnesty, which, they said, had been granted only as a means of preventing the hostages from being killed. The Jamaat members were eventually set free after a ruling by the UK Privy Council that the amnesty was invalid, but that it would be against due process to have the suspects rearrested and tried for the offences committed during the coup. The leaders remain at liberty today, and Jamaat-al-Muslimeen membership continues to rise amidst allegations of links with terrorist groups and charges of murder and drug smuggling.

Many Trinidadians found it hard to believe that such events could take place in their stable, democratic, fun-loving country. With characteristic humour, though, the crisis was soon turned into a font of amusing stories. Ask any Trinidadian about the coup and you will hear tales of wild **"curfew parties"** and imaginative explanations given to the police of the five TVs found in a neighbour's house.

### The Red House

Beneath its massive green copper cupola (which was being renovated at the time of writing), the imposing neo-Renaissance **Red House** (ⓦ www.tt parliament.org) is actually more a faded, peeling, terracotta colour. The seat of Trinidad and Tobago's parliament inherited its popular name from an earlier building on the site, which was painted bright red to celebrate Queen Victoria's diamond jubilee in 1897. The present structure, completed four years after its predecessor was burnt down in the 1903 water riots, was itself attacked in the 1990 coup (see box above), and bullet holes still scar the stonework; outside the front entrance, facing the square, an eternal flame commemorates government and security personnel who died in the coup. Members of the public can view the **parliament in session** on Fridays at 1.30pm; use the entrance on Knox Street.

### Holy Trinity Cathedral

The Anglican **Holy Trinity Cathedral** on the south side of Woodford Square was another of Governor Woodford's many initiatives to improve the public spaces of Port of Spain. The original idea was to build it in the middle of the square itself, and work was already under way when the governor bowed to popular protest and moved it to its present site. This elegant stone church, completed in 1818, was built along traditional Gothic lines, with a large clock tower. The cool, shady interior is relatively unadorned, its outstanding feature the mahogany hammer-beam roof, made in England and modelled on a medieval original in London's Westminster Hall. A life-size **effigy of Governor Woodford** lies on his tomb by the south wall; the plaques nearby commemorate various other colonial dignitaries.

## Trinidad Theatre Workshop

The immaculately restored stone building opposite the Holy Trinity Cathedral, at the southeast corner of the square, was the original home of the **Trinidad Theatre Workshop** (TTW), since moved to Rust Street in St Clair (see p.97; Ⓦ www.ttw.org.tt). Founded in 1959 by poet and playwright Derek Walcott, it established a theatrical tradition in Trinidad, made acting a recognized profession and launched the careers of many of the Caribbean's most famous actors. Errol Jones, Stanley Marshal and Albert Labeau were all influential in the development of the TTW, and among the many actors to cut their teeth here was Helen Camp, who went on to establish the internationally successful Trinidad Tent Theatre.

Although the TTW enjoyed its heyday in the 1960s and 70s, Walcott's 1992 Nobel Prize for Literature inspired a regeneration of the centre, giving rise to a new crop of talented Trinidadian actors. Many who were influenced by the TTW – including Roger Roberts, Wendell Manwarren and Cecilia Salazar – were in turn instrumental in the establishment of prestigious local theatre groups such as the Bagasse Company.

There is talk that performances could once again take place at the TTW's Woodford Square address, although currently the building is used for private functions.

## The old Public Library, Hall of Justice, City Hall and Port of Spain Adult Library

The other public buildings around Woodford Square are a mishmash of architectural styles. The oldest and most attractive is the **old Public Library** on the northeast side of the square, a large cream stone building built in 1901 and incongruously sandwiched between two brutally functional modern slabs of glass and concrete. To the right is the plain, modern-looking **Hall of Justice**; built in 1979, it houses the Supreme Court of Trinidad and Tobago. To the left is another concrete pile, the 1961 **City Hall**, home to Port of Spain's council and the mayor's office.

The new face of the city is apparent on the southeast side of Woodford Square, where the recently opened **Port of Spain Adult Library** (Mon–Fri 8.30am–6pm, Sat 8.30am–noon; ☎ 624 4466 ext 2100, Ⓦ www.nalis.gov.tt) looms over the old Trinidad Theatre Workshop building. The modern building contains a sumptuous, multi-floored library with state-of-the-art facilities and a large collection of books, newspapers and magazines. Visitors can become temporary members of the library, giving them borrowing privileges and one hour's free **Internet access** daily, on presentation of a passport and a TT$20 deposit, which is refunded when the library card is returned.

# Central Police Station

Contrary to appearances, the grey stone building with arched windows one block west of Woodford Square at the corner of Sackville and St Vincent streets is not a church, but the newly renovated version of the police station that was firebombed in the 1990 coup. Although many had wanted the site to become a museum, it was decided that the police should remain in the building, which has now become the **Central Police Station** and the headquarters of the **Criminal Investigation Department** (CID). While some maintain that the station is an eyesore that ought to be demolished, others would prefer it to remain standing as an indomitable warning to any who might think of following in the Jamaat-al-Muslimeen's footsteps.

Opposite the Central Police Station, on the other side of Sackville Street, is the **police administrative building**, which displays Trinidad and Tobago's police force emblem, consisting of a hummingbird and a police badge inside a Star of David. The hummingbird is the national symbol which replaced the crown after independence, while the star is a colonial leftover that has given rise to much confusion. Contrary to popular belief, it is not the Jewish Star of David but the symbol of Governor Picton's patron saint, St David.

## Rosary Church

At the corner of Henry and Park streets stands the **Rosary Roman Catholic Church**. Built between 1892 and 1910, this dignified Gothic Revival building is the most impressive of the city's three main churches, though its imposing towers and ornate stonework are hemmed in by buildings on all sides. You're in luck if you find it open, for the spacious interior is an oasis of peace in this hectic part of the city, and the old **stained glass**, with its finely detailed Biblical scenes, is the most beautiful in Port of Spain. Unfortunately the effect is somewhat spoilt by the fluorescent lighting, peeling paint and general dilapidation.

# Uptown Port of Spain

Ranged around the broad, grassy expanse of the **Queen's Park Savannah** and framed by the foothills of the Northern Range, Port of Spain's **uptown** area oozes prosperity. Along the wide boulevards that ring the Savannah, the palatial mansions of the colonial plantocracy compete with the residences of the republic's president and prime minister, and the glitzy modern headquarters of insurance companies. This part of town also boasts Port of Spain's main tourist attractions: a comprehensive **museum**, an above-average **zoo** and beautiful **botanical gardens**.

## Queen's Park Savannah

The **Queen's Park Savannah** is Port of Spain's largest open space, surrounded by a 3.7-kilometre circuit of perimeter roads, crisscrossed by paths and shaded by the spreading branches of old samaan trees. Originally part of the St Ann's sugarcane estate, the Savannah was bought by Governor Woodford in 1817 and developed into a city park. Subsequent attempts to build on parts of it were seen off by vigorous public protest, and the park has remained its original size.

Often deserted during the hot daylight hours, the Savannah comes to life after 4pm, with football games, joggers, couples and families taking an early evening stroll and, during the windy months of March and April, children flying kites. It is particularly busy between 4pm and 8pm, when temporary food stalls serving tasty local snacks such as bake and shark, pholouri, roti and roasted corn are set up.

The **Trinidad Turf Club** at the southern end of the park was once Trinidad's premier horse racing track. The races have now moved to Arima (see p.161), but all the Carnival competitions, including **Panorama**, **Dimanche Gras**, **Parade of the Bands** and **Champs in Concert**, are held in the track's grandstands. Many other events take place here, including musical performances by visiting international artists. Though the seats are numbingly hard, the setting is incomparably atmospheric, with performances taking place against a backdrop of the mountains and the starry Caribbean sky.

Right in the middle of the Savannah, in total contrast to the public conviviality taking place all around, is an eerie enclave of silence. From behind its high stone wall, the **Peschier Cemetery** – burial ground of the owners of the St Ann's estate – exudes an air of mystery. The graveyard is closed to the public, and all that can be seen over the wall is an ancient and towering palm tree.

## National Museum and Art Gallery

The imposing, gabled building just a block south of the Savannah at the corner of Frederick and Keate streets is an appropriately grand setting for the **National Museum and Art Gallery** (Tues–Sat 10am–6pm, Sun 2–6pm; free; ☎623 5941). Built in 1892 as part of the preparations for Queen Victoria's jubilee, it still has the legend "Royal Victoria Institute" inscribed over its door. The museum's collection is extensive, covering everything from early **Amerindian history** to the technology of the **oil industry**. Although the exhibits vary considerably in quality, the museum provides an essential overview of Trinidad and Tobago's history and culture, as well as housing an excellent collection of works by local artists, a decent natural history room and a section – albeit not as generous as you would expect – on Carnival. In addition to the exhibits and artwork related to Port of Spain in this museum, Fort San Andres in the downtown area has a museum devoted entirely to the history of the capital (see p.83).

On the ground floor, in front of the entrance, is a wall of photographs from past Carnivals which provide a glimpse of the skill of Trinidad's mas makers and designers; the selection includes Peter Minshall's seminal *Man Crab* from the 1983 presentation *The River*. In the same room, next to the photographs, there's a dusty collection of old **Carnival costumes** that, while it does scant justice to the art form, does give some idea of the detailed work involved and an impression of what mas must have been like before today's skimpy, erotic outfits took over. The room to the left holds an interesting chronology of the development of the **steel pan** as a musical instrument. The rest of the floor is taken up with racks of locally found **geological specimens**, including some enormous quartz crystals, a re-creation of a 1940s **barracks yard**, and displays on local history up to independence (look out for the yellowing photos of Port of Spain through the ages), and on local industry, from coconuts and cocoa to sugar, rum and oil.

The upper level is dominated almost entirely by a fabulous permanent exhibit of **Trinidadian art**, displayed in a brightly lit room with a magnificent wooden ceiling restored to its original glory. Rich with colour and intricate detail, **Leroy Clarke**'s huge *Queen of the Bands* and *Bittersweet Bounty* make a stunning start to the collection, while **Shastri Mahraj**'s *Check Valve* is a marvellous depiction of the madness of Carnival. Interspersed between ambitious sculptures and other installations are works by internationally known contemporary painters such as **Carlisle Chang**, **Boscoe Holder**, **Nina Squires** and **Dermot Lousion**. Many of the works draw on Trinidadian folklore, such as **Alfredo Codallo**'s rendition of local folklore characters, *Trinidad Folklore*, which includes most of the well-known suspects – from the Soucouyant (a woman who turns into a ball of fire to travel the countryside searching for human blood to drink), to Douens (faceless children who died without being christened) and La Diablesse (a beautiful woman with one cloven hoof who leads drunken men to their deaths).

The two other main rooms on the upper level, both of them air-conditioned, are filled with lithographs of the old Port of Spain and bucolic scenes of rural Trinidad by **Michel Cazabon**, as well as the various stuffed animals and trays of butterflies, beetles and spiders that make up the small but well-explained display on the island's **flora and fauna**.

## Queen's Park West

Travelling clockwise around the Savannah on **Queen's Park West** from Frederick Street, you'll come across numerous examples of gingerbread architecture by the Glaswegian architect George Brown, who mass-produced the distinctive fretted woodwork and used it extensively on all his buildings. Dating from 1904, the ornately decorated **Knowsley Building** at the corner of Chancery Lane resembles a child's fantasy doll's house; it's odd to think that it now houses the Ministry of Foreign Affairs. The black and white **George Brown House** at the corner of Victoria Avenue is somewhat plainer, though still graced by a great deal of refined fretwork. **Boissiere House** at the corner of Cipriani Boulevard is fondly called the "**Gingerbread House**" by locals, and you'd be hard pushed to find a better example of the style. It's a splendidly whimsical concoction of fretted wooden finials and bargeboards, with stained glass depicting meandering strawberry vines and a small pagoda-like roof over one room. None of these buildings is open to the public, which is a pity, since their interiors are reputed to be just as graceful and imaginative.

## The Magnificent Seven

Just off the northeast corner of the Savannah on Maraval Road stands a bizarre group of mansions affectionately known as the **Magnificent Seven**. A magical-realist parade of European architectural styles with a tropical slant, these remarkable buildings are the result of the competing egos of rival plantation owners, each of whom tried to outdo his neighbours in grandeur. All of the mansions were constructed in 1904, except for Hayes Court, which was built in 1910. Although none of the buildings is open to the public, their exteriors are easily seen from the road, most of them in dire need of repair.

Going from south to north, the first of the seven is **Queen's Royal College**, Trinidad's most prestigious school, whose former pupils include the authors VS and Shiva Naipaul and the country's first prime minister, Eric Williams. The building has a Germanic Renaissance style, with arcaded balconies and cream-and-ochre stucco offsetting the blue limestone cornerstones; the tall clock tower can be seen from all over Port of Spain.

Across Hayes Street from Queen's Royal College, **Hayes Court**, home to the Anglican bishop of Trinidad, is a grand mansion displaying a mix of French and British architectural influences.

Next door, **Mille Fleurs** is a fine example of an elaborate gingerbread house with intricate wooden fretwork. Currently in the process of being renovated for new occupants the Law Association, it was originally built for Dr Henrique Prada, a successful doctor who went on to serve as the city's most distinguished mayor, between 1914 and 1917.

The next building along is **Roomor**, a florid exercise in the French Baroque

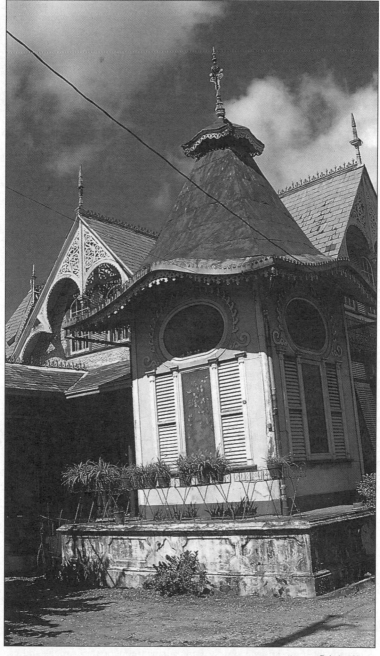

▲ Boissiere House

style which was commissioned by the estate owner Lucien Ambard. The building is composed of Italian marble and tiles from France, while its columns, galleries, towers and pinnacles are decorated with elaborate ironwork.

Crossing Flood Street you'll come to the official residence of Port of Spain's Roman Catholic archbishop, **Archbishop's House**, a weighty, neo-Romanesque pile of Irish marble and red granite, capped by a copper roof.

The next house along is **Whitehall**, a Venetian-style palazzo whose gleaming white paintwork gives it the air of a freshly iced birthday cake. Originally the home of cocoa estate owner Joseph Leon Agostini, the building has had a somewhat chequered history. It was commandeered by the US military during World War II, after which it became a cultural centre, a library and then a broadcasting unit. In 1954 it was sold to the Trinidadian government and now houses the Office of the Prime Minister.

The most outlandish structure of the seven, **Killarney**, stands at the northern end of Maraval Road just before it veers east into Circular Road. A fairy-tale castle of brick and limestone, bristling with turrets and spires, it was built for a German plantation owner named Stollmeyer (the building is actually nicknamed "Stollmeyer's Castle") by the Scottish architect Robert Giles, who modelled it on Queen Victoria's residence at Balmoral. The architectural historian John Newel Lewis perfectly captured Killarney's delicious absurdity when he wrote: "A German built a bit of an untypical Scottish castle in Trinidad and called it by an Irish name. He must have been by that time a Trinidadian, because only Trinidadians do these things." The Stollmeyer family sold the castle to the Trinidadian government in 1979, and it now houses government offices.

## Emperor Valley Zoo, Botanical Gardens and President's House

Just around the corner from the Magnificent Seven, on the northern side of the Savannah, the **Emperor Valley Zoo** (daily 9.30am–6pm; last tickets sold at 5.30pm; adults TT$4, children 3–12 years TT$2; ☎622 3530, Ⓦwww.trinizoo.com) makes a nice place to while away an hour or two. A magnet for local kids, with balloon- and novelty-sellers aplenty at the entrance, it's also worth a wander to get a close-up look at Trinidadian species that you're unlikely to see in the wild; the animals are well kept, if housed in rather compact cages. Opened in 1952, the zoo's collection of local and foreign animals – though small by international standards – is reputedly the most extensive in the Caribbean, and includes **brocket deer**, **quenk**, **otters**, a large selection of **monkeys**, aquarium fish and **snakes**, as well as **ocelots**, **spectacled caiman** and numerous **birds**, including parrots, toucans and pink "scarlet" ibis, whose carotene-supplemented diet doesn't appear to have been successful in sustaining their usual crimson plumage. (For more on Trinidad and Tobago's flora and fauna, see p.349–357.)

Next door to the zoo, and spreading east toward the President's House, are the exquisite **Botanical Gardens** (daily 6am–6pm; free; ☎622 1221), established in 1818 by Governor Woodford and the botanist David Lockhart, and home to one of the oldest collections of exotic plants and trees in the Western Hemisphere: the gardens contain an estimated seven hundred trees, around a hundred of which are indigenous to the islands. There are no official guides, but you can pick up a free map at the main gate on Circular Road. Alternatively, some knowledgeable Trinidadians frequent the gardens and can usually be persuaded to show you around for a small fee. It's a good idea to have a guide since most of the labelling has disappeared, and the tours typically come with a few anecdotes. Though guides know all the specimens' botanical names, they'll also give you the local terms: "Hat Stand", "Raw Beef" and "Napoleon's Hat" are some of the more unusual, and colourfully named, specimens. A small **cemetery** in the middle of the gardens contains the crumbling gravestones of many of the island's governors, including Solomon Hochoy. Beneath the Palmiste palms, a plaque marks another resting place, that of an Australian wallaby, a pet of the Prince of Wales which died during his visit to the island. At the weekends, the gardens are busy with school groups, parties of strollers and groups of regulars who congregate on their favourite benches for a spot of ol' talk. Otherwise, you'll often have the place more or less to yourself, except when a cruise ship is in town.

Behind the Botanical Gardens, in well-manicured gardens, stands the **President's House**. This austere, stately villa was built in 1876 as the residence of the island's British governors, and continued to fulfill this function until independence in 1962. The grounds are not open to the public, but you can get a good view of the building from inside the Botanical Gardens. The **Prime Minister's Residence** is hidden from sight behind the President's House, and is likewise closed to the public.

# The western suburbs

Crammed between the Gulf of Paria to the south and east and the uphill incline of the Northern Range, the **western suburbs** of Port of Spain are the cultural centre of the capital. For most of the year the area looks purely residential, but as **Carnival** draws near, many of the houses are converted into mas camps where the bands who organize the parades have their bases. The creative energy of **Carnival production** is concentrated in **Woodbrook**, which is likewise the culinary heartland of the capital with **restaurants** to suit all tastes lined along Ariapita Avenue. The streets and bars of cosmopolitan **St James**, meanwhile, are alive with nighttime revelry year round. The thriving commercial neighbourhood of **Newtown** also boasts several popular bars and restaurants, while the prosperous residential area of **St Clair** is the most sedate and aloof of the western suburbs.

## Woodbrook

The elegant old district of **WOODBROOK** is bounded by **Philipps Street** to the east and the **Maraval River** to the west, an area of about two kilometres traversed by two main arteries, **Tragarete Road** and **Ariapita Avenue**. The area was originally a sugar cane estate owned by the Siegert family, creators of Trinidad's famous Angostura Bitters (see p.40), and many local streets – such as Carlos, Luis and Siegert streets – bear their names. The suburb, first settled in 1911, was traditionally a middle-class residential area, and its streets are still graced by old houses with wonderful fretwork bargeboards, delicate balustrades and finials, which continue to epitomize the area despite increasing commercialization in recent decades. Woodbrook is a safe and pleasant place to stay, full of inexpensive accommodations, diverse restaurants, and close to some of the city's best nightlife.

At the eastern edge of Woodbrook, on Philipps Street, is the entrance to the **Lapeyrouse Cemetery** (daily 6am–6pm), a walled burial ground dating back to 1813. Victorian tombs adorned with Gothic spires and angels are eerily

WESTERN SUBURBS

| ACCOMMODATION | |
|---|---|
| Ambassador | A |
| Ana's Place | J |
| Fabienne's Guesthouse | D |
| Forty Winks Inn | G |
| Johnson's Guesthouse | L |
| Kapok | B |
| La Calypso Guesthouse | I |
| Melbourne Inn | N |
| Par-May-La's Inn | F |
| Pavilion Inn | C |
| Port of Spain Courtyard by Marriott | K |
| Sundeck Suites | H |
| Trinbago | M |
| Ville de French Guesthouse | O |
| Williams Villa | E |

| RESTAURANTS, BARS & CLUBS | |
|---|---|
| Chinkey's Nite-Bite | 4 |
| Club Prosperity | 1 |
| Cordials | 18 |
| Cricket Wicket | 8 |
| Home Restaurant | 6 |
| Hong Kong City Restaurant | 14 |
| Il Colosseo | 10 |
| Irie Bites | 15 |
| Jenny's on the Boulevard | 20 |
| Little Carib Theatre | 9 |
| Martin's | 19 |
| Mas Camp Pub | 26 |
| Mélange | 23 |
| Plantation House | 24 |
| Rafters | 12 |
| Shiann's | 22 |
| Singho's Restaurant | 5 |
| Smokey and Bunty's | 17 |
| Squeeze | 25 |
| Sweet Lime | 21 |
| Syps | 13 |
| T.G.I. Friday's | 3 |
| Tiki Village | 7 |
| Trotters | 16 |
| Veni Mange | 11 |
| The Verandah | 11 |

framed against the lush, tropical backdrop; long strands of ivy trail over the unkempt graves, while gravediggers, shaded by makeshift tents, dig spaces for new residents. The Siegert family is buried here, as are the Trinidadian labour leader Arthur Cipriani, the calypsonian Melody, and Charlie King, the policeman killed in the Butler Riots in the 1930s (see box, p.221). The names on the gravestones provide clues to the diverse origins – Chinese, Spanish, African, Indian and European – of Port of Spain's inhabitants, and the inscriptions reflect its varied religious affiliations: Catholics, Anglicans, Baptists and many other faiths are represented here. The cemetery's newer residents, the vagrants who sleep in the more dilapidated tombs, have been a talking point for years, often provoking press articles about the problem of homelessness.

At the western end of **Tragarete Road** – lined by a mix of shops, restaurants and offices – stands the **Queen's Park Oval** (daily 8am–4pm; ask the security guard at the gate to let you in). Originally built in 1896, this is Trinidad's premier **cricket ground**, hosting national and international matches in season (Feb–April), as well as doubling as a concert venue – the annual Soca Monarch competition is held here at Carnival time. Even if you're not a cricket fan, it's well worth making the effort to attend a Test or One-Day match here as it's a unique and hugely enjoyable experience. The game is a national obsession in Trinidad, and matches are followed with a passion, especially if local hero Brian Lara – the "Prince of Port of Spain" – is playing. The atmosphere is rowdy but good-natured, with fans draped in the national flag and music blaring from sound systems after every over and wicket. Seats in the stands typically cost TT$40–200 depending on the level of the match taking place, or you can pay TT$250–300 for an all-inclusive ticket to the Trini Posse stand (food and drink included). For box office information, call ☎628 9787.

### Carnival in Woodbrook

Woodbrook is home to numerous **mas camps**, which burst into life during Carnival season, from November to February. Now famous for its calypso nights, the **Mas Camp Pub** on the corner of French Street and Ariapita Avenue was once the workshop and headquarters of Peter Minshall's Callaloo mas camp, which subsequently relocated to Chaguaramas (see p.119).

One block away on Buller Street, the long-established **Mas Factory** run by Albert Bailey is famous for its portrayal of traditional characters and skillful wire bending in their costumes. They'll let you watch the Carnival costumes being made if you ring in advance (☎628 1178). Round the corner at 15–17 Kitchener St, **D'Midas Associates** also provide good examples of traditional Carnival design with lots of feathers, sequins and beading – all the painstaking, hand-made work which is gradually being phased out by more modern, profit-oriented bands. Again, you can see the costumes being made if you ring in advance (☎622 8233).

The **Masquerade** mas camp at 19 De Verteuil St was run by renowned designer Wayne Berkley until he suffered a stroke in 2000. Berkley was famous for his use of strong colours, his professional construction and some of the best "bikini mas" designs around, traits continued by Masquerade's current designers, Chris Santos and Gregory Medina.

Elsewhere in Woodbrook are situated some of the most popular bands of the modern era, churning out the revealing, pseudo-erotic costumes preferred by the majority of today's masqueraders. **Legends**, whose camp is at 88 Roberts St, won Band of the Year for five years in a row before the **Trini Revellers**, based at 35 Gallus St, ended the run in 2004 with their portrayal of Arabian Nights.

**Mas camps** – the headquarters of the Carnival bands – are established throughout Port of Spain in old gingerbread family homes or converted shops. In the few months prior to Carnival, furniture is stored away and the largest room turns into a workshop full of feathers, sequins and sewing machines. Some of the long-established camps have now become year-round mas factories. The camps provide a focus for the whole Trinidadian art community; many a famous Trinidadian artist, actor, dancer or writer can be found at a mas camp during Carnival season.

In recent years, costumes have increasingly catered to the desire to wear as little as possible in the tropical heat, though Peter Minshall and a few others still make more elaborate, artistic and traditional creations. Mas camps are open to all, and it is often possible to watch costumes being made if you give advance notice. Opening hours are variable; the closer it gets to Carnival, the longer the opening hours (usually from 9am until at least 10pm), while in the few days preceding Carnival some camps stay open 24 hours.

Each band will choose to portray a certain theme during Carnival. The band is then divided into different **sections**, each with its own costume (linked to the general theme) and marching position when the band assembles for the Parade of the Bands on Carnival Monday and Tuesday. If you want to participate in the Parade of the Bands or **"play mas"**, you must first register to join a mas band. Occasionally this can be done online at the websites listed below; otherwise, go directly to the mas camp and try your luck. All-inclusive registration packages, including costume, a place in a particular section of the band, security, and food and drink during the Monday and Tuesday parades can cost over TT$2000. It is also possible to buy a costume without registering with a band; prices start at around TT$800 – book early for the best choice, since designs sell out quickly.

The list below represents a selection of the best-known mas camps and their chief designers in Port of Spain: for a full list of bands, contact the National Carnival Bands Association, Queen's Park Savannah (☎627 1422, ⓦwww.carnaval.com).

**Barbarossa**
26 Taylor St, Woodbrook ☎628
6008, ⓦwww.barbarossaintl.com
(Richard Afong)
**Callaloo Company**
Building C, Western Main Road,
Chaguaramas ☎634 4491,
ⓦwww.callaloo.co.tt (Peter Minshall)
**D'Midas Associates**
15–17 Kitchener St, Woodbrook
☎622 8233 (Stephen Derek)
**Harts Ltd**
5 Alcazar St, St Clair ☎622 8038,
ⓦwww.hartscarnival.com
(Thais & Gerald Hart)
**Legends**
88 Roberts St, Woodbrook☎622

7466, ⓦwww.legendscarnival.com
(Mike Antoine and Ian McKenzie)
**Mas Factory**
15 Buller St, Woodbrook
☎628 1178 (Albert Bailey)
**Masquerade**
19 De Verteuil St, Woodbrook ☎623
2161, ⓦwww.masquerade.co.tt
(Earl Patterson)
**Poison**
75 Morne Coco Rd, Petit Valley
☎632 3989, ⓦwww.poison.co.tt
(Michael Headley)
**Trini Revellers**
35 Gallus St, Woodbrook ☎625
1881, ⓦwww.revellers.com
(Geraldo Vieira Jr)

# St James

It was in **ST JAMES**, northwest of Woodbrook, that the British first landed in 1797. Legend has it that they fortified themselves with the rum punch that they found here, which provided the courage they needed to capture Port of Spain. Once the Peru sugar cane estate, the area was settled by **Indian** indentured labourers after emancipation. The names they gave to their streets –

Calcutta, Delhi and Madras – bear witness to their homesickness.

Today, St James is one of the capital's most cosmopolitan districts, with residents from all ethnic groups. The streets are lined with modern houses possessing Indianesque capitals on concrete columns and colourful clusters of puja flags in the gardens; the upper storeys often remain unfinished, an empty frame of reinforced concrete stilts waiting for the next generation to provide the cash to build upwards. This is a bustling place, especially at night when it becomes the prime liming spot in Port of Spain. Music blasts from cars, bars and clubs; and locals dressed in clubbing gear lime alongside old men in jeans and T-shirts.

The approach to St James from Woodbrook at the start of the Western Main Road is dominated by the imposing **Roxy Building**. It was built as a cinema, but its ritzy classical-moderne colonnade now houses a branch of *Pizza Hut*. On the other side of the road is a statue in tribute to the grandmaster of calypso, the late **Lord Kitchener**. The entrance to St James itself is marked by the bridge over the Maraval River, on which an ornate green and pink oriental-style iron **archway** was built in 1997 to draw tourists and heighten local pride.

**Western Main Road**, which runs through the centre of St James, is a broad thoroughfare lined with shops, bars and takeaways. Street vendors sell vegetables, incense and crochet work on corners during the day, while at night there is a food stall every couple of metres. Halfway down the road, **St James Market** fills the air with the smell of fresh fish and meat in the early mornings. There are some old gingerbread houses, mostly turned over to commercial use – look out for the lottery outlet with the eye-catching red, gold and green surrounding wall. Towards the western end of the road you'll see the **Haji Gokool Meah Mosque**, one of the oldest in Trinidad and unfortunately not open to the public. Built in 1927, this tiny white-and-green minareted building is typical of Muslim places of worship found throughout the island. Western Main Road is most notable, however, as the scene of the annual Muslim **Hosay** processions, which take place over four days in either April, May or June (see box, overleaf). Despite the Carnival-esque twist given to Hosay in T&T, the festival is essentially a fairly solemn event, and supposed to be non-alcoholic. This has not stopped the bars of St James, however, from making a mint on Hosay night – many locals watch the proceedings with a beer or rum in hand – much to the consternation of devout Muslims.

Off Mucurapo Road at 2b Ethel St is the spectacular **Paschimkaashi Hindu Mandir**. A gleaming white modern interpretation of traditional Hindu religious architecture, the temple has tall round towers and latticed windows that allow one to view the ornate statues of Hindu gods inside. These murtis (religious images worshipped by Hindus), brought from India, represent the ten major incarnations of Lord Vishnu; at the back of the temple is a shrine to the goddess Kali. The best time to visit the temple is Sunday morning. Call the manager, Mrs Shakti Capildeo (☎622 4949), to make an appointment to be shown around.

## Fort George

To see one of the most spectacular views of Port of Spain, consider taking a taxi up to **Fort George** (daily 10am–6pm; free), a popular weekend family picnic spot, just ten minutes' drive north from the Western Main Road. Taxis leave sporadically from the corner of Western Main Road and Bourne's Road (around TT$10), or you can walk there in about an hour; after a steep climb on St James Terrace, the incline becomes gentler and it's a relaxing stroll to the top. Built in 1804, the fort defended the island against the French Caribbean fleet during the Napoleonic Wars; you can see some of the original cannons

## Hosay

The Islamic festival of **Hosay**, commemorating the martyrdom of Mohammed's grandsons Hussein and Hassan during the *jihad* (Holy War) in Persia, has been celebrated in Trinidad ever since the first Indian Muslims arrived in 1845. The festival's exposure to the island's other cultures has turned it into something resembling Carnival, with lewd dancing and loud music, but in recent years local Shi'a Muslims have taken great pains to restore the occasion's solemnity.

Hosay is celebrated in Curepe, Tunapuna, Couva and Cedros, but the best place to see it is undoubtedly in the Port of Spain suburb of St James. Trinis of all religions come here to view the festivities, which are held over four days in either April, May or June. All of the night parades start at 11pm and continue into the early hours of the morning.

In the weeks leading up to Hosay, it is possible to watch craftsmen in St James building **tadjahs**, the ornate tombs made from bamboo and coloured paper that are carried in procession; the houses where they work have large flags planted in their yards. There are only five families who build the structures each year, four based in St James and one in Cocorite. Families have to be approved by a local committee, and strict rules apply – they must be the direct descendants of Indian immigrants with an ancestral tradition of *tadjah* building. The task involves great financial, physical and spiritual sacrifice; the materials can cost up to TT$30,000, and the builders have to fast during daylight hours and refrain from alcohol and sexual activity for the duration. Understandably, perhaps, not many of the younger generation find the prospect appealing, and as the years pass fewer and fewer *tadjahs* are being built.

- The first procession is **flag night**, when hundreds of devotees walk through the streets with multicoloured flags representing the beginning of the battle of Kerbala, in which the brothers lost their lives.

- On the **second night**, two small *tadjahs* are carried slowly through the streets to the throbbing beat of *tassa* drums; the shredded paper fires at the side of the road are there to warm up the drums, which tightens the skins and produces a better sound.

- The **third night** is the most spectacular. Large *tadjahs* more than two metres high are paraded through the streets, while dancers carry two large sickle moons representing the two brothers. At midnight there is the ritual "kissing of the moons", as the dancers symbolically reenact a brotherly embrace.

- On the **fourth** day, after the moons have been paraded through the streets, the exquisite *tadjahs* are traditionally thrown into the sea, a sacrifice to ensure that prayers for recovery from sickness and adversity will be answered. These days, however, most *tadjahs* are disposed of in more environmentally friendly ways. The celebrations usually finish at around 7pm.

and cannonballs used in the fighting, and a replica of the dungeon. Stone defensive walls, surviving to a height of one to two metres, surround the wooden signal station designed by the exiled West African Ashanti prince, Kofi Nti. Fort George housed the largest contingent of British troops in the Caribbean throughout the nineteenth century. At some point these soldiers mutinied, although the details, suppressed at the time, are still buried in the depths of British military records.

## Newtown and St Clair

The area between Tragarete Road and the Queens Park Savannah consists of two smaller neighbourhoods which lack the strong sense of identity present in Woodbrook and St James. **NEWTOWN**, bordered by Queen's Park West and

Maraval Road, has plenty of shops and restaurants, but little in the way of sights. If you're passing the **Sagicor Building**, next to the US Embassy at 16 Queen Park West, pop into the lobby and take a look at Peter Minshall's 15-metre **mural** made of thousands of sequins tagged to plastic netting, colourfully depicting the flowers and hummingbirds of Trinidad.

West of Maraval Road, **ST CLAIR** is an upmarket enclave of lavish houses protected by high walls, ferocious dogs and sophisticated security systems. It is also home to the long-established **Harts mas camp** at 5 Alcazar St, run by the same family since 1959. Famous for their designs of abstract colours and revealing, erotic costumes, the Harts are at the forefront of the development of "bikini mas". One block south, at 17 Rust Sreet, is the new headquarters of the venerable **Trinidad Theatre Workshop** (see p.85), where acting workshops are held (the entrance is actually at 2 Gray St). For information on other performances, call ☎622 2217 or 628 0356, or check their website at ⓦwww.ttw.org.tt.

# The eastern suburbs

Port of Spain's **eastern suburbs**, which nestle on the lower slopes of the **Northern Range**, are also its oldest. In **Belmont**, some original wooden houses survive from the days of the area's first settlers, while the ramshackle wooden houses of **Laventille** – the city's poorest and most crime-ridden area – seem to tumble over one another down Laventille Hill. The birthplace of the steel pan, Laventille still has some important panyards in its winding lanes, making it an essential stop for the pan enthusiast. Also in the hills, north of the Queen's Park Savannah and downtown Port of Spain, **St Ann's** is a far cry from Laventille: an upscale neighbourhood which, at its northern end, is more rural than urban.

## Belmont

**BELMONT**, a maze of narrow lanes flanking the eastern side of the Queen's Park Savannah, is one of the most densely populated areas of Port of Spain. The city's first suburb, it was settled in the first half of the nineteenth century by Africans who had escaped slavery on other Caribbean islands. After emancipation, they were joined by freed slaves from Trinidad and a number of peoples from West Africa. In 1868, the tribal chieftain of the **Rada community** – a religious group from the French protectorate of Dahomey – bought land in the area to establish a settlement. Representatives from the Mandingo, Ibo, Yoruba and Krumen tribes also came to live here, and Belmont became an established African settlement. The community was well organized and close-knit, ensuring the survival of African traditions such as the Orisha religion, whose feasts and festivities are still practised in the area (see "Contexts", p.336).

## Laventille

Between the steep and twisting streets and alleys of **LAVENTILLE**, which overlooks downtown Port of Spain on its eastern side, tumbledown houses made from salvaged boards and galvanized roofing perch on the hillside in defiance of gravity. The place fairly hums with life as people bustle about their business, washing at standpipes in the road and exchanging gossip on street corners. The suburb was established in the 1840s when freed slaves squatted in the

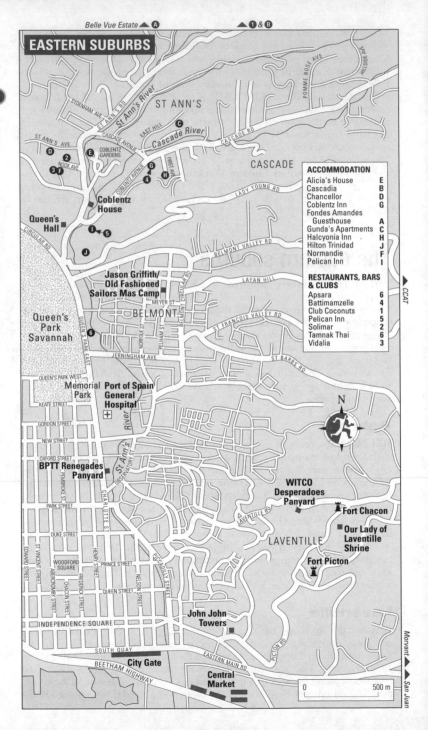

Belle Vue Estate ▲ Ⓐ        ▲Ⓞ & Ⓑ

# EASTERN SUBURBS

**ACCOMMODATION**

| | |
|---|---|
| Alicia's House | E |
| Cascadia | B |
| Chancellor | D |
| Coblentz Inn | G |
| Fondes Amandes Guesthouse | A |
| Gunda's Apartments | C |
| Halcyonia Inn | H |
| Hilton Trinidad | J |
| Normandie | F |
| Pelican Inn | I |

**RESTAURANTS, BARS & CLUBS**

| | |
|---|---|
| Apsara | 6 |
| Battimamzelle | 4 |
| Club Coconuts | 1 |
| Pelican Inn | 5 |
| Solimar | 2 |
| Tamnak Thai | 6 |
| Vidalia | 3 |

SYDENHAM AVE

ST ANN'S RD

ST ANN'S

East Hill

Cascade River

CASCADE RD

POMME ROSE AVE

HILLSIDE AVE

ST ANN'S AVE

CASCADE AVENUE

FIRST AVE

CASCADE

COBLENTZ GARDENS

NOOK AVE

Coblentz House

LADY YOUNG RD

Queen's Hall

CIRCULAR RD

BELMONT VALLEY RD

LAYAN HILL

Jason Griffith/
Old Fashioned
Sailors Mas Camp

BELMONT

ST FRANCOIS VALLEY RD

Queen's
Park
Savannah

QUEEN'S PARK EAST

MEYER ST

PELHAM ST

NORFOLK ST

BELMONT CIRCULAR RD

ST BARBS RD

JERNINGHAM AVE

QUEEN'S PARK WEST

Memorial
Park

KEATE STREET

Port of Spain
General
Hospital
✚

▲ CCAT

N

GORDON STREET

NEW STREET

OXFORD STREET

BPTT Renegades
Panyard

PEMBROKE ST

PARK STREET

OBSERVATORY ST

CHARLOTTE ST

St Ann's River

WITCO
Desperadoes
Panyard ♦    ♜ Fort Chacon

DUKE STREET

EDWARD STREET

WOODFORD
SQUARE

PRINCE STREET

ST VINCENT STREET

ABERCROMBY STREET

CHACON STREET

HENRY STREET

FREDERICK STREET

QUEEN STREET

NELSON STREET

PICCADILLY STREET

LAVENTILLE RD

■ Our Lady of
Laventille
Shrine

♜ Fort Picton

LAVENTILLE

INDEPENDENCE SQUARE

John John
Towers

SOUTH QUAY

City Gate

EASTERN MAIN RD

PICTON RD

BEETHAM HIGHWAY

Central
Market

Morvant ▲    ▲ San Juan

0        500 m

## Jason Griffith, mas legend

Today, Belmont is home to the retired **Jason Griffith**, one-time leader of the **Old Fashioned Sailors** mas band. The nautical costume has appeared in Carnival since the nineteenth century, when revellers would impersonate British sailors – a tradition that took on a new satirical edge with the arrival of the US Navy on the island in 1941. Griffith's band was one of the few to remain faithful to traditional themes (such as sailors or fancy Indians) and production techniques at a time when many were abandoning them in the pursuit of profit. Griffith himself, who brought out his first band in 1949, is extremely knowledgeable and passionate about Carnival and its eroded traditions. An approachable, eloquent man, Griffith is one of the best people to give you an impression of what Carnival used to be like. His house is on Pelham Street. Call in advance (℡624 3692) to make an appointment.

area, right "on the eyebrow of the enemy", as the Trinidadian novelist Earl Lovelace put it.

Despite all the reports of the crime that takes place "behind the bridge" (a reference to the bridge across the St Ann's River which links Laventille and downtown Port of Spain), Laventille has an undeniable – and extremely appealing – confidence and verve, perhaps born of the fact that it was within its winding streets that the **steel pan**, Trinidad's most famous instrument, was born. The area has spawned many a great pan player and calypsonian, and was celebrated by the Nobel laureate **Derek Walcott** in his poem *The Hills of Laventille*.

Laventille has often been dismissed as a slum, and many visitors are put off by scare stories involving bandits and street **crime**. Although crime in Laventille is indeed far more prevalent than in any other part of the city – and on the increase according to media reports – the warnings from some quarters not to go there no matter what are certainly exaggerated. Provided you take the usual precautions, walking around Laventille by day is as safe as in downtown Port of Spain. At night, though, it is probably best to err on the side of caution and take taxis. Exploring with a local resident will certainly help you to get more out of the area; Elwyn Francis (℡627 3377), a trained tour guide with the Chaguaramas Development Authority, conducts excellent walking tours of the area from around TT$50.

An exerting twenty-minute walk up Laventille Road brings you to a large youth facility which houses the **WITCO Desperadoes panyard**. Established by Rudolph Charles in the 1940s, the Desperadoes (they were known then as the Dead End Kids) are the longest-running steel band in Trinidad, with many first places at the annual Panorama tournament to their credit. Visitors are welcome to watch rehearsals during Carnival season.

Further up Laventille Road, at the junction with Picton Road, are the crumbling remains of **Fort Chacon**. The fort takes its name from the last Spanish governor of the island, who built it in 1770 to deter British attacks. His choice of location proved a poor one, however, as the fort did little to prevent the British from overrunning the island in 1797. There's little to be seen apart from a dilapidated stone wall, and the fenced-off remains, currently used as a telecommunications station, are closed to the public. Ask the police guarding the facility to let you climb onto the ruins for a great view of Port of Spain, northern and central Trinidad

Opposite the fort a short way down Picton Road, Laventille Hill is crowned by **Our Lady of Laventille Shrine**, an imposing landmark that can be seen from all over Port of Spain. Atop the 16-metre belfry of this white stone church stands a statue of the Virgin Mary, a gift from France in 1876. Pilgrims journey to the shrine from all over the country on the feast of the Assumption.

About five minutes downhill from the shrine on Picton Road is **Fort Picton**, built by the notorious British governor of the same name in the late 1790s. The circular stone building, with thick walls and small keyhole windows, was intended to protect Port of Spain from counterattack by the recently defeated Spanish. A tunnel is said to have linked the fort to King's Wharf. The construction of this bolthole – known as "**Picton's Folly**" – would suggest that the British at the time were still far from confident about their ability to retain the island.

The only other major attraction in Laventille is the **CCA7** or Caribbean Contemporary Arts 7, a cultural centre located at 7 Fernandes Industrial Centre (☎625 1889). To get there by car from Port of Spain, take Lady Young Road to the Morvant junction and turn right at the traffic lights onto the Eastern Main Road. The CCA7 is in an industrial complex (the Fernandes Warehouses) to your left. Focusing mainly on contemporary art, with resident artists, studio workshops and exhibitions of work by Trinidadian and international painters, the CCA7 has become a meeting place for the Port of Spain intelligentsia. This is especially so on Thursday evenings, when an appropriately arty film is screened at the centre (free of charge) at around 8.15pm.

In recent years, Laventille has become something of a political football, with successive governments outlining new plans to improve the area. The postmodern, yellow apartment blocks at the base of the hills at the start of Picton Road are the **John John Towers**, the result of an initiative to create much-needed housing.

## St Ann's and Cascade

From the northeast corner of the Queen's Park Savannah, St Ann's Road heads past the **Queen's Hall**, a favourite venue for pre-Carnival calypso revues, drama, dance and fashion shows, into the leafy suburb of **ST ANN'S**. Primarily a residential area that melts almost seamlessly into the equally chi-chi **CASCADE** district to the east, St Ann's offers little in the way of sightseeing, but there are a couple of attractions worth checking out. Starting at the Savannah, follow St Ann's Road for about five minutes until the road divides; take the right fork and you'll arrive at the *Cascadia* hotel, home of *Coconuts* nightclub and a popular **waterpark** with a couple of looping slides (Sat, Sun and public holidays 10am–5.30pm; TT$20). The left fork, Ariapita Road (not to be confused with Ariapita Avenue in Woodbrook), threads into the hills that divide St Ann's from Cascade and Diego Martin. At the end of the road, you'll meet the banks of the St Ann's River, where there are several popular spots from which to "take in the springs". Otherwise, turn off the main St Ann's Road onto Upper Ariapita Road and negotiate the steep incline to get to **Belle Vue Estate** (☎624 7717), a former cocoa plantation about 300 metres up in the hills. Now a private home and equestrian centre, Belle Vue has a small **museum** in the original cocoa house where pods were dried, with displays on the processing of these pods, as well as a small collection of **animals**, including peacocks, toucans, parrots, turtles and agoutis. You can hike a series of **trails** of varying length and difficulty around the estate and cool off afterwards in a lovely natural-style **pool** fed by spring water. If you want to exert your muscles even further, walk ten minutes uphill to "**The Pines**", a plateau surrounded by a forest of Caribbean pine that affords marvellous views of Port of Spain and its environs.

## Panyards

The best way to hear pan is live, in the open air – there is nothing as romantic as listening to its rich chiming harmonies drifting on the wind on a warm starry night. Throughout the year Port of Spain hosts events in which pan figures prominently, but for free entertainment you can go to the open-air **panyards** and listen while the musicians practise. If you're lucky, you may hear the band's full repertoire, including excellent renditions of jazz and classical numbers, as well as the usual calypso, or even get a quick lesson after the rehearsal. The most accessible of the better known panyards in Port of Spain are BPTT Renegades, BWIA Invaders, Neal & Massy Trinidad All Stars and Phase II; frequent Panorama champions – and the winner of the 2004 title – Exodus are based in St Augustine on the Eastern Main Road.

**Blue Diamonds**
George St, next to the market, Port of Spain
**BPTT Renegades**
138 Charlotte St, Port of Spain
Ⓦ www.renegades.co.tt
**BWIA Invaders**
Tragarete Rd, opposite the Queen's Park Oval, Woodbrook
**Courts Laventille Sound Specialists**
Eastern Quarry, Laventille
**Humming Birds Pan Groove**
13 Fort George Rd, St James
**Neal & Massy Trinidad All Stars**
46 Duke St, Port of Spain
**North Stars**
63 Bombay St, St James

**Pan Vibes**
St Francois Valley Rd, Belmont
**Pandemonium**
3 Norfolk St, Belmont
**PCS Starlift**
187C Tragarete Rd, Woodbrook
**Petrotrin Phase II Pan Grove**
13 Hamilton St, Woodbrook
**T&Tec Power Stars**
114 Western Main Rd, St James
**Tokyo**
2a Plaisance Rd, John John, Laventille
**WITCO Desperadoes**
Laventille Youth Facility, LP89 Upper Laventille Rd, Laventille

# Maraval and Paramin

Some five kilometres north of central Port of Spain, accessible via Circular Road at the northwest corner of the Queen's Park Savannah, **MARAVAL** lies at the base of the Northern Range, surrounded by lush green hills. Originally a small village on the outskirts of the capital, it is rapidly becoming an upmarket residential suburb, with a concentration of hotels and guesthouses aimed at middle- and upper-income visitors.

Maraval's main points of interest are stretched along its main thoroughfare, Saddle Road. At the start of Saddle Road, a short way up from the junction with Long Circular Road, the **Shoppes of Maraval** includes a Hi-Lo Supermarket, several fast-food restaurants and a pair of nightclubs, making it a focal point in a town with no real centre. About three kilometres further north, the cream and maroon neo-Romanesque **Maraval–Paramin Roman Catholic Church**, originally built in 1879 and enlarged in 1934, dominates the hillside on the right-hand side of Saddle Road, and is notable more for its picturesque location than a spectacular interior. Continuing north, you'll pass the expansive, well-kept **St Andrew's Golf Course** (see p.56) before the road takes a scenic route over the Northern Range, providing good views of the forested slopes of the Maraval Valley and eventually arriving – after many steep inclines and hairpin bends – at Maracas Beach on the north coast.

If you turn left at the church onto Morne Coco Road and walk for about 200 metres, you'll arrive at the place where jeeps (TT$3) leave for the charming hillside village of **PARAMIN**, the so-called "herb basket of Trinidad". The cottage industry here produces "Paramin seasoning", whose ingredients include French and Spanish thyme, peppermint and onions. The local population is of Spanish ancestry, the descendants not of colonial Spaniards but rather Venezuelans who came here in the nineteenth century to plant cocoa. This close-knit but friendly community maintains many of its Venezuelan traditions, most famously its **Parang** singers, who travel from house to house during the Christmas season, singing nativity songs in a mix of French and Spanish. The Monday before Christmas, Paramin hosts a **Parang festival** at the soccer field at the lower end of town. Meanwhile, on the afternoon of Carnival Monday at around 5pm, the town is overtaken with **blue devils** – traditional Carnival characters impersonating imps from Hell – dancing in the streets and attempting to drench onlookers with blue paint. **Harvest Sunday**, the second Sunday in November, is also celebrated with games, music and traditional feasts of wild meat.

**Our Lady of Guadalupe Church**, at the lower end of town, is built on a terrace overlooking the valley – a tremendously scenic location even if the church itself, with its green roof and plant-lined windows, looks more like a conservatory than a place of worship. Paramin also has what are probably the most easily accessible **bat caves** on the island. Located on Farmer's Road (walk 500m uphill from the junction in the village centre and turn right; the caves are on your left), these caves also have some lovely limestone formations, but nowhere near the number of bats present at Tamana (see p.195).

Caribbean Discovery Tours (☎624 7281) offers 4WD **tours** of Paramin which, along with the usual sights, include chats with local farmers to learn about farming methods.

# Diego Martin and Petit Valley

The residential districts of **DIEGO MARTIN** and **PETIT VALLEY**, both less than ten kilometres to the northwest of central Port of Spain, are built on land once owned by the River Estate cocoa plantation. Bought by the government in 1897, the area underwent massive development during the twentieth century. There are few specific sights, apart from the odd historic building and a scenic waterfall. Amid the suburban development of the Diego Martin Main Road, watch out for "Rainorama", a large modern corner house that was the home of the calypsonian Lord Kitchener who died in 2000, and was named after his 1973 calypso about that year's washed-out Carnival.

## River Estate

At the top end of Diego Martin Main Road (at the end of the Diego Martin maxi route) is the Diego Martin Estate, these days better known as **River Estate**, an enclave of lush greenery that forms a surprising contrast with the sprawling, suburban environment just a couple of minutes away. The old estate house – a wooden building of elegant simplicity – has benefited from a sensitive restoration, and the small **museum** (daily 9am–4pm; free, but donations are appreciated) inside has a rather bizarre but engaging diorama depicting a random history of the estate with the help of floor-pad triggered sound effects. In the basement, black-and-white photos and a slide show focus on cocoa production at the estate, which was owned by Cadbury's from the mid-nineteenth to the mid-twentieth century. Across the road, the large, nonfunctioning **waterwheel** dates back to 1845, when the estate produced sugar. An aqueduct once ran from the Diego Martin River to power the wheel, which in turn drove the rollers that crushed sugar cane for the production of molasses.

Opposite the museum, the estate's original **coach shed** is now used as storage space for the local panyard. Behind this are some original **barrack houses**, among the few surviving examples of the wooden shacks with galvanized roofs where the indentured plantation workers had to live. Each building consisted of four rooms, each of which was occupied by a family. The appalling conditions have been described by Trinidadian writers such as Alfred Mendes (see p.360). Few barrack houses are left thanks to government efforts to improve living conditions.

## Blue Basin Waterfall

One of the most accessible falls in Trinidad, the beautiful **Blue Basin** is also one of the smallest. Like so many others on the island, the six-metre cascade has been affected by the general reduction in water levels and no longer gushes with its full force. The setting, with rainforest on all sides, is still gorgeous, however, and blue emperor butterflies and exotic birds flutter through the undergrowth. The small circular pool at the base of the fall is good for bathing when water levels are at their highest (June–Dec), and while it gets busy at weekends and after school, you will often find it deserted on weekdays. To reach Blue Basin, keep on the main road past the water wheel, then turn right onto Blue Basin Road. Go up the steep hill till you reach a sign pointing to a track for the waterfall, and follow this on foot for five minutes. Route taxis run from the waterwheel near River Estate to the base of the waterfall for TT$2–5.

Blue Basin is considered sacred by some religious groups, and you may come across Baptists or Rastafarians conducting their rituals by the waters. Baptist flags fly from tall bamboo poles along the track, and offerings – candles, fruit and rice – are scattered by the waters' edge. The area around the waterfall is rumoured to be a favourite haunt of bandits out to relieve you of your wallet, however, and tourism officials are loathe to recommend the place to visitors. If you do fancy a dip, it's best to go early in the morning with a group, or visit with a local guide such as Lawrence "Snakeman" Pierre (☎632 9746). Downriver from the waterfall are various good bathing pools which are invariably filled with children at weekends.

# Eating

Port of Spain's **restaurant** scene has boomed in recent years, nowhere more so than along **Ariapita Avenue** in **Woodbrook**, where you can find several upscale establishments serving fancy – and often delicious – nouvelle Caribbean cuisine in beautifully lit surroundings, as well as some places that are more casual and convivial but still offer high-quality food. Dress smartly, though not necessarily formally, for the fine dining restaurants and take the precaution of reserving a table, especially on Fridays and Saturdays. The capital's other top restaurants can be found in the **hotels**, notably in **St Ann's** and **Cascade**, while there are a number of good places to eat, including two European-style bakeries, in **Maraval**. Menus of some of the more upmarket restaurants are published in the annual *Cre'Ole'*, which you can pick up free at many hotels. Chinese restaurants, both inexpensive and upscale, can be found all over the city; we have listed some of the more worthwile ones.

The **downtown** area is full of fast-food outlets, such as *Royal Castle*, *Mario's*, *Pizza Boys* and *KFC*, and canteen-style restaurants catering to office-workers on limited lunch breaks; many of them are only open during the day. The food courts in the downtown shopping malls are also good for a quick bite of something Chinese, Creole or Indian for less than TT$20. Then, of course, there is the huge range of **street food** – roti, doubles, bake and shark, aloo pies, corn soup and the like – sold in abundance along **Brian Lara Promenade/Independence Square** and in **St James**.

## Downtown and Uptown Port of Spain

**360° *Crowne Plaza*, 1017 Wrightson Rd ☎625 3366.** Revolving restaurant priced for diners on expense accounts that gives a fantastic 360° view of Port of Spain; the location is more of a draw than the unremarkable international cuisine, but the Sunday brunch (11.30am–2.30pm) is sumptuous. Tues–Sun 7–11pm.

**Apsara 13 Queen's Park East ☎623 7659.** Traditional Northern Indian dishes, from tandooris to rogan jhosh, served in very plush surroundings (shares the same building as *Tamnak Thai*, below). Lots of vegetarian choices and delicious desserts. Daily 11am–3pm & 6–11pm, closed Sun evening.

**Breakfast Shed Wrightson Rd, next to the Cruise Ship Complex.** Established in 1936 to provide workers' meals, and still churning out hearty, inexpensive fare, this large shed is filled with outlets selling excellent local food, served at long communal trestle tables; look around before you buy – some cooks are better than others. Delicious traditional breakfast of bake and shark and cocoa for around TT$15. Daily 6.30am–4pm.

**Chee Mooke Bakery 14 Independence Square North ☎623 4607.** Family-run bakery in business since 1931, known for its excellent fresh bread, puddings, cakes and pastries. Take-away only. Mon–Sat 6am–6pm.

**Hardine Vegetarian 34 Park St ☎623 9560.** Adorned with piles of fresh fruit and vegetables, this justifiably popular lunchtime eatery serves up delicious, healthy vegetarian meals – vegetable rice, steamed vegetables, soya stew, marinated dumplings – as well as fruit salads. The main reason for a visit, however, is for the cheap and refreshing blended fruit juices. Recommended. Mon–Fri 6am–6pm.

**Mother Nature Vegetarian Restaurant St Vincent St, at Park.** Standard, inexpensive vegetarian meals, salads and juices made with a variety of fruits and energy supplements. The buffet-style café is small with limited seating, although a new site at 44 Park St was being prepared at the time of writing. Mon–Fri 5am–4.30pm, Sat 8am–4pm.

**Tamnak Thai 13 Queen's Park East ☎625 0647.** Elegantly decorated in rich Thai style, this upmarket restaurant has indoor and outdoor sections, the latter ringed by a carp-filled pond and lush foliage. Cooked by a native Thai chef, the food is excellent: green curry, stir-fries and various rice dishes all feature on the menu. Good wine list and excellent service. Daily 11am–11pm, closed Sat evening.

## Woodbrook

**Irie Bites 71 Ariapita Ave ☎622 7364.** Very popular Jamaican jerk shack which does some of the tastiest and best value food in the city. Perfectly seasoned and cooked over pimento wood, the generous portions of jerk chicken, pork and fish are served with various side dishes such as plantain, fries or mixed vegetables and accompanied with a selection of excellent sauces. Home delivery available. Recommended. Mon–Thurs 11am–9pm, Fri & Sat 11am–10pm.

**Mélange 40 Ariapita Ave ☎628 8687.** Genteel, colonial-style decor and sophisticated international cuisine at one of the newest fine dining restaurants to open on Ariapita Avenue. Choose from seafood, steak, pork, lamb or chicken dishes, or go for a mix at the lunch buffet. Mon–Fri 11am–2.30pm, Tues–Sat 7–10.30pm.

**Plantation House 38 Ariapita Ave ☎628 5551.** Upmarket dining in an exquisitely maintained and elegantly decorated gingerbread house. Service is attentive and friendly, and the delicious nouvelle Creole cuisine ranges from chicken crepes, mussels and crab cakes to Cajun specialities – blackened shrimp, jambalaya – to Caribbean-style fish dishes. Mon–Fri 10.30am–2.30pm & 6.30–10.30pm, Sat 6.30–10.30pm.

**Sweet Lime Ariapita Ave, at French St ☎624 9983.** With outdoor tables positioned next to the *Mas Camp Pub*, this is a great spot for people-watching over a meal from a varied, inexpensive menu: mussels and shrimp for starters, and ribs, steaks, mouth-watering rotisserie chickens and several vegetarian options such as stuffed peppers and chow mein for main dishes. Mon–Sat 11.30am–midnight, Sun 3.30pm–midnight.

**Veni Mange 67 Ariapita Ave ☎624 4597.** Delicious, slightly pricey Caribbean cuisine with an international flavour and tasty vegetarian options served up in a stylish, bistro-type setting. It's a favourite spot for Trinidadian celebrities, with a friendly atmosphere and lively party scene on Fridays. Mon–Thurs 11.30am–3pm, Wed also 7–10pm, Fri 11.30am–11.30pm.

## St James

**Chinkey's Nite-Bite** Western Main Road, opposite *Smokey and Bunty's* (see p.109). Rasta-run food stall serving a loyal clientele with delicious veggie concoctions, fried fish, bake and shark, smoked herring and saltfish sandwiches, and fresh juices. A great pre- or post-clubbing option. Tues–Sun 7pm–late.

**Home Restaurant** 67 Western Main Rd ⓣ 628 3663. Tasty, no-frills, local Indian-style food. Roti fillings – with buss-up-shut or dhalpuri, paratha or sada skins – run the full range from bodi and melongene to all the meats, and you can also get pelau, stewed chicken, macaroni and other Creole food. Mon–Sat 6am–3pm, Sun 7am–3pm.

**Sing Ho** Level 3, Long Circular Mall ⓣ 628 2077. Large red and gold restaurant with an extensive menu of reliably excellent seafood, meat, poultry and some vegetarian dishes. One of the more expensive Chinese restaurants in town. Daily 11am–10pm.

## Newtown and St Clair

**Hong Kong City Restaurant** 86A Tragarete Rd, Newtown ⓣ 622 3949. Large portions of standard Chinese fare in an upstairs dining room which is plusher than the inexpensive prices would imply. Good dim sum on Sundays (11am–3.30pm). Takeaway available downstairs. Daily 11am–10.30pm.

**Jenny's on the Boulevard** 6 Cipriani Blvd, Newtown ⓣ 625 1807. Popular bar-restaurant in the basement of an attractive sky-blue gingerbread house serving average and slightly overpriced Chinese food, steaks and other American-style dishes. Becomes a lively nightspot on Friday and Saturday evenings. Mon–Thurs 11am–10pm, Fri & Sat 11am–11pm.

**Il Colosseo** 16 Rust St, St Clair ⓣ 628 1494. Fancy Italian restaurant serving authentic food, cooked by a genuine Italian chef. Good bread, excellent pasta, tasty seafood choices and some decent wines. Mon–Sat 11.30am–2.30pm & 6.30–10pm.

**Rafters** 6a Warner St, Newtown ⓣ 628 9258. Colonial stone building with an elegant dining room in which to enjoy the moderately expensive seafood dishes, steaks and other international cuisine. Mon–Sat 11.30am–2.30pm & 6.30–11pm.

**Shiann's** 3 Cipriani Blvd, Newtown ⓣ 625 1735. Small roti shop producing some of the best Indian food in Port of Spain. Choose from substantial

wrapped vegetable, channa, meat or shrimp rotis, or meals with rice accompanied by a selection of vegetables or meats, including duck. Mon–Fri 6.30am–4pm, Sat 10am–4pm.

**Syp's** 3A Cipriani Blvd, Newtown ⓣ 624 5500. Intimate coffee shop which also does breakfasts (eggs, bagels, muffins), and light lunches and dinners (sandwiches, burgers). A good place for cappuccinos, espressos, lattes and an afternoon lime. Mon–Wed 10am–10pm, Thurs & Fri 10am–midnight, Sat 5pm–midnight, Sun 4pm–midnight.

**Tiki Village** *Kapok Hotel*, 16–18 Cotton Hill, St Clair ⓣ 622 5765. One of the better hotel restaurants, with lovely views over the Queen's Park Savannah and a relaxing ambience provided by a bubbling spring and rattan furniture. The Chinese/Polynesian cuisine is excellent; go for the dim sum on Sundays or the weekday buffet lunches, which are better value than the à la carte choices. Mon–Fri 6.30am–10.15pm, Sat & Sun 7am–10.15pm.

**The Verandah** 10 Rust St, St Clair ⓣ 622 6287. Exclusive, classy restaurant in a coolly converted gingerbread house decorated with plants and local art, with a pretty open-air patio for evening dining, which is available only two days of the week. Fabulous "freestyle Caribbean" cooking: lots of fresh herbs, garden vegetables and attention to detail. Mon–Fri 11.30am–2pm, Thurs & Sat also 7–9.45pm.

## St Ann's and Cascade

**Battimamzelle** *Coblentz Inn*, 44 Coblentz Ave, Cascade ⓣ 621 0591. This Caribbean-flavoured gourmet spot has quickly gained a deserved reputation as one of Trinidad's top restaurants. Dishes include barbecue kingfish, oxtail pepperpot and crab gallette, served amidst decor that's in keeping with the hotel's hip-yet-cosy ambience. Mon–Sat 11.30am–2.30pm & 6.30–9.30pm, no lunch on Sat.

**Solimar** 6 Nook Ave, St Ann's ⓣ 624 6267. Reasonably expensive Creole, European, Latin American, Oriental and African dishes served in a restaurant resembling a rustic taverna. Holds food festivals celebrating everything from Scottish Burns Night to the curries of India, and has a bar with an extensive wine list. Sat 6pm–2am, Fri also noon–2pm.

**Vidalia** *Normandie*, 10 Nook Ave, St Ann's ⓣ 624 1181. Pasta, filet mignon and other international cuisine is available for lunch and dinner in an airy, plant-filled dining room decorated with works by local artists; while the cheaper *Café Trinidad*, also at the hotel, does breakfasts and sandwiches and salads for lunch in more casual surroundings. Daily 7am–11pm.

## Maraval

**Adam's Bagels** 15A Saddle Road ☎622 2435. Busy breakfast, lunch or early dinner spot, with a bakery selling fresh bread, humus and snacks at the front and tables in the air-conditioned rear section where you can order excellent bagels and tasty soups, salads, baked potatoes and rolls filled with Middle Eastern spiced chicken, all at moderate prices. Delivery available. Mon–Sat 7am–6pm.

**Bamboo Terrace** *Carnetta's Inn*, 99 Saddle Rd ☎628 2732. This intimate, softly lit dining room overlooks the Maraval River and is perfect for a romantic dinner. Local specials change daily, and the regular menu has all the Creole favourites including a good selection of soups and seafood. Daily 7–10am, noon–2pm & 7.30–10.30pm.

**China Palace II** upstairs at Ellerslie Plaza ☎622 5866. The ornate, upscale dining room (with a/c) belies a reasonably priced menu of typical Chinese food, including some lobster dishes. Take-away available downstairs. Sun–Thurs 10am–10pm, Fri & Sat 11am–11pm.

**Vie de France** 143 Long Circular Rd ☎628 2697. Bakery and café – one of four in Trinidad – where the food caters very much to international tastes: omelettes, fry-ups or strawberry and pineapple pancakes for breakfast, and sandwiches (sirloin steak alongside the tuna and cheese), pasta and burgers for lunch and dinner. Although expensive, the cakes and pastries are delicious; and the coffee isn't bad either. Mon–Thurs 7am–10pm, Fri & Sat 7am–11pm, Sun 8am–10pm.

# Drinking, nightlife and entertainment

Trinidadians do not restrict their partying to Carnival time. They seem to celebrate anything from a public holiday to the end of a workday, and Port of Spain is a fine place to enjoy a night on the town. There are a few excellent **nightclubs**, though most are outside the downtown area or in nearby Chaguaramas (see p.122), which, being just a thirty-minute drive from the capital, is considered as much a part of the Port of Spain nightlife scene as the clubs in the city proper. The western suburbs are packed with **bars** (often described as "sports bars"), where you'll find pumping music, TVs showing sports events or music videos, and sometimes a pool table, small dance floor and limited food menu. A couple of bars that are popular with the expat crowd, despite their vastly inflated drink prices, are *Trotters* on Maraval Road, at Sweet Briar Rd in St Clair (Sun–Thurs 11.30am–midnight, Fri & Sat 11.30am–2am; ☎627 8768) and *T.G.I. Fridays*, 5–5A Queen's Park West, Newtown (Sun–Thurs 11am–midnight, Fri & Sat 11am–2am; ☎624 TGIF). There are **rum shops** on practically every corner in Port of Spain, especially in the market area east of Charlotte Street. These tend to be small, basic shacks frequented by middle-aged men.

Most bars and nightclubs come alive after 10pm and are busiest from Thursday to Sunday. Precise **opening hours**, however, are hard to state. Many places are open "till", meaning that they close when the last customers leave, usually around 2–3am, though some, such as *Smokey and Bunty's* at the weekends, keep going all night. If a place advertises its opening hours as "anytime, anyday", it means that the owners have a 24-hour license and open and close when they feel like it.

A sign posted at the entrance to most bars and clubs gives the establishment's **dress code**. Although foreigners can usually get away with wearing the normally outlawed headgear (bandanas, for example), sleeveless T-shirts and even shorts, going "bareback" (barechested) will typically result in your being refused entry.

When Port of Spain is not preoccupied with the continuous live entertainment of Carnival season, the **theatre** becomes a popular diversion. From March through November theatre companies such as the **Trinidad Theatre Workshop** (TTW), the **Bagasse Company**, **Ragoo Productions** and

## Pre-carnival parties

During the couple of months preceding Carnival Trinidad is awash with **fetes**, especially in Port of Spain and its environs. Fetes are parties held in community centres, sports complexes, schools, car parks, hotels and venues designed for the purpose (such as the open-air clubs at Chaguaramas), featuring live music by the soca bands whose songs are played continuously on the radio prior to Carnival. **All-inclusive fetes** include "eats" and drinks – both soft and alcoholic – in the ticket price, which ranges from TT$150 to TT$400 depending on the quality of food and type of drinks on offer. **Cooler fetes** are cheaper (around TT$50) and only include entrance to the party. You can either bring your own drinks (in a cooler) or buy them there. Tickets for most of these fetes are sold in advance at various shops and businesses in towns around the island.

The **Brian Lara Fete**, held at the cricketer's house on Carnival Sunday, is one of the most prestigious (and expensive), although there are a bewildering number of others to choose from. Each one seems to attract a different type of crowd, which can sometimes be on the rough and raucous side. Ask for local advice before deciding which party to attend. The **Caribbean Brass Festival** in the week or so before Carnival is a full-scale concert – a great coming-together of soca acts from T&T and elsewhere in the Caribbean. Check the local press or radio for details of upcoming events.

**Raymond Choo Kong Productions** perform plays, often foreign comedies given a local twist, at the capital's several drama venues. Tickets cost from TT$20 for smaller amateur productions to TT$60 and above for the more well-known companies.

A number of **casinos** (tacitly known as "members clubs" to contend with local gambling laws) operate around town, particularly in Woodbrook, most with roulette, baccarat, black jack and stud poker on offer. If you fancy some gambling, try Ma Pau, Ariapita Avenue, at French Street (daily 11–4am; ℡627 6214) or Outer Limits, Royal Palm Plaza, 7 Saddle Rd, Maraval (daily 11–2am; ℡622 0100).

Port of Spain's **cinemas** are excellent value for money and as entertaining for the audience participation as the films. A double bill at Deluxe, 9–11 Keate St (℡623 6532) or Globe, St Vincent Street, at Park (℡623 1063) costs TT$20–30 and usually features American action movies and international blockbusters. Trinidad's first multi-screen movie complex has opened at Movie Towne on Audrey Jeffers Highway opposite the Hasley Crawford Stadium (℡627 8277), where tickets cost TT$30 per film.

*The G Spot* entertainment guide in Friday's edition of the *Trinidad Guardian* has movie listings, reviews of nightclubs and fetes, and a Carnival calendar.

## Bars

**Cordials** 72 Tragarete Rd, Newtown ℡628 8627. Dimly lit, social place frequented by a mature crowd, with good music – soca and Latin, for example – played by a DJ on Friday nights. There are a few tables on busy Tragarete Road for outside drinking. Mon–Sat 11am–late.

**Cricket Wicket** 149 Tragarete Rd, Woodbrook ℡628 2547. Opposite the Queen's Park Oval and next door to the BWIA Invaders panyard, this small, mostly open-air bar overlooks busy Tragarete Road. Packed when cricket matches are on, it's a laid-back spot for an evening drink, and snacks are available. Mon–Sat 11am–2.30am.

**Jenny's on the Boulevard** 6 Cipriani Blvd, Newtown ℡625 1807. Especially popular on Friday evenings, when the well-stocked bar and small dance floor are packed with professionals out for an after-work lime. DJ plays at the weekends. Mon–Thurs 11am–10pm, Fri & Sat 11am–11pm.

# Carnival calendar

Bear in mind that dates and schedules for Carnival change from year to year; check Ⓦ www.carnaval.com or Ⓦ www.visittnt.com for updated calendars of events. You can also pick up a free copy of TIDCO's annual *Trinidad & Tobago Carnival* brochure, which contains a comprehensive calendar of events, details of mas band presentations, addresses of Jouvert bands and a map of the Parade of the Bands route.
**Carnival dates** until 2010 are as follows: 2005 (Feb 7 & 8); 2006 (Feb 27 & 28); 2007 (Feb 19 & 20); 2008 (Feb 4 & 5); 2009 (Feb 23 & 24); 2010 (Feb 15 & 16).

## January
**Opening of Calypso Tents:** calypsonians battle it out in the "tents" – regular buildings, these days – for a place in the Calypso Monarch finals. The best known venues are: Calypso Revue, 111–117 Henry St (☎ 623 4949), Kaiso House, Strand Cinema, Tragarete Rd, at Dundonald St (☎ 627 2772) and Spektakula, Jean Pierre Complex, Audrey Jeffers Hwy. Yangatang, NUGFW Hall, Frederick St and Maljo Kaiso, Stalk Hill Theatre, Richmond St are "humorous" tents where the emphasis is on comedy.
**International Soca Monarch Competition preliminaries:** international soca stars sing for the prestigious Trinidad International Soca Monarch title. The finals are held in February/March.
**Junior Calypso Competition:** children compose and sing hard-hitting calypsos, full of satire, humour and social commentary. The finals are held in February/March.
**National Chutney Soca Monarch Competition preliminaries:** hear the best of Trinidad's popular soca music given an East Indian twist. The finals are held in February/March.
**Panorama Competition preliminaries:** steel pan bands display their skill in all types of music as they compete for the prestigious first prize. The finals are held on Carnival Saturday.
**Stickplay Competition:** an exciting and skilful traditional sport based on the stick fighting of the 1880s, an art thought to have originated in the practice of using bamboo sticks to fight fires in the cane field.
**Talk Tent:** Similar to the calypso tent, but featuring cabaret and comedy artists. Performances occur throughout the Carnival season.

## February/March
**Calypso Fiesta:** calypsonians engage in a battle of wit and satire for cash prizes – go with a Trinidadian who can explain the political references.
**Kiddies' Carnival:** the children's costumes and characters rival those of the adults. There are three **parades**: at the **Red Cross Children's Carnival** ten days before Carnival; at **St James Kiddies' Carnival** the week before Carnival; and at the **Junior**

Mon–Thurs 11am–10pm, Fri & Sat 11am–11pm.
**Martin's** 13 Cipriani Blvd, Newtown ☎ 623 7632. Friendly and intimate bar with a plant-bedecked open-air seating area out back, where you can hear the music from the adjacent PCS Starlift panyard. A good place to meet people, especially on Friday evenings. Mon–Sat 11.30am–midnight, Sun 6pm–midnight.
**Mas Camp Pub** French St, at Ariapita Ave, Woodbrook ☎ 627 4042. Newly refurbished, with pool tables and slot machines in a back room, and an a/c main area that's popular with an older, local

crowd, who come to dance to oldies on Sundays. There's usually a calypso show on Wednesday evenings, and other themed nights, from Latin to karaoke, throughout the week. Entrance varies; calypso show costs TT$50. Mon–Fri 11am–1/2am, Sat & Sun 11am–3am.
**Pelican Inn** 2–4 Coblentz Ave, St Ann's ☎ 624 7486. A Caribbean version of an English pub. Popular with local regulars and tourists, the enduring "Pello's" is quiet during the day, but comes to life at the weekend (Fridays and Sundays are particularly busy) with a mixed crowd, packed dance

**Parade of the Bands** in the Queen's Park Savannah on Carnival Saturday.

**Panorama Finals:** a day-long marathon pan competition, fuelled by adrenaline and free-flowing rum. Queen's Park Savannah's rowdy North Stand is the place to be if you want to party, while the grandstand is for those who want a more sedate view of the proceedings. Seats in the stands cost TT$100–250 and only go on sale two days before the event, so buy quickly. Those on a budget or wishing to move around should go on "the tracks", the road leading towards the stage where the bands practice. Carnival Saturday.

**Traditional/Individual Mas:** Held on the last Sunday before Carnival Monday, this daytime parade in downtown Victoria Square is the best place to see traditional carnival characters such as Blue Devils, sailors and firemen.

**Dimanche Gras:** the finals for the King and Queen of Carnival and the Calypso Monarch finals, held at the Queen's Park Savannah grandstands. After weeks of build-up in calypso tent competitions, the best calypsonians sing their hearts out for the prize of Calypso Monarch. The sheer size of the King and Queen costumes, and the skill, sequins and special effects expended, are amazing, though with each year the entrants are looking more and more like sculptures on wheels. Tickets cost TT$100–300. Carnival Sunday.

**Jouvert:** (pronounced *Joovay*, from **"Jour Ouvert"**, the break of day): marking the beginning of the festivities, Jouvert is "dirty mas": raw, earthy and energetic. Wear as little as possible (no jewellery) and expect to be covered in mud. Joining a **Jouvert band** such as Desert Rats (✆625 4877) or Sex and the City (✆620 7744) allows you to celebrate with more security. Starts at 4am on Carnival Monday and continues till dawn.

**Carnival Monday Parade of the Bands:** bands parade their costumes through the streets of Port of Spain; individual bands follow set routes, but there is no set route for the whole parade. Note that not everyone wears their costumes on this day. From noon.

**Carnival Tuesday Parade of the Bands:** the full display of all the costumes. The route is the same as Carnival Monday; the best place to view the bands is from the stands at the Queen's Park Savannah (tickets TT$75–250) or at the bleachers set up at the various judging points around the town. Starts 7am.

**Ash Wednesday:** International soca artists, calypsonians and DJs entertain a huge post-Carnival crowd on Maracas and Manzanilla beaches. The parties are getting busier each year; if you're driving, leave early or be prepared for a slow journey home; a quieter alternative is Blanchisseuse.

**Champs in Concert:** A parade of the winning bands, held in the Queen's Park Savannah grandstands the weekend after Carnival.

floor and resident DJ. Small cover charge at weekends. Mon–Sat 11am–2am, Sun 3pm–2am.

**Smokey and Bunty's** 97 Western Main Rd, at Dengue St, St James ✆623 3850. Named after the owners' nicknames, this local institution is a popular late liming spot, drawing a very mixed crowd – young, old, arty, gay and straight. The clientele spills onto the pavement (where there are tables), the music is loud and a funky atmosphere prevails. Mon–Thurs 11pm–3am, Fri–Sun 10pm–6am.

**Squeeze** Ariapita Ave, at Luis St, Woodbrook.

Appropriately named for its minute dimensions, this friendly bar draws a sociable drinking crowd and plays a lot of high-tempo changa (Venezuelan techno music). Mon–Fri 4pm–late, Sat 6pm–late.

**Tasca Latina** 16 Philipps St, Port of Spain ✆625 3497. Spanish taverna-style bar and restaurant with a dance floor and convivial atmosphere. Offers live entertainment and is popular at weekends, attracting a mature crowd. Entrance TT$20 when there's a live band. Mon–Fri 11am–2am, Sat 6pm–2am.

## Nightclubs

**The Attic** aka *Sabor Latino*, Shoppes of Maraval, Maraval. Nightclub which claims the credit for having introduced Latin dancing to Trinidad. Thursday's Latin night remains popular, there are salsa classes on Fridays (5.30–7.45pm), and visiting DJs from Venezuela play here. On Saturdays, when the music tends to be a mix of soca, reggae, dub and Latin, the compact dance floor is heaving until the early hours. Cover usually around TT$15.

**Club Coconuts** *Cascadia Hotel*, 67 Ariapita Rd, St Ann's ☎ 623 NUTS, Ⓦ www.clubcoconuts.com. Port of Spain's best known nightclub, with a large dance floor, sophisticated lighting and a young, fashionable crowd. Mainly soca music around Carnival time (the club organizes fetes), with more mainstream music at other times. There is also a sports bar with pool tables and video games and a cyber bar with Internet access. Wed–Sat 9.30pm–4.30am. Entrance fee varies.

**Club Prosperity** Upper Bournes Rd, St James. Brightly painted with African flags, this is the regular venue for Friday night Nyabinghi reggae jams and other special Rasta or reggae-oriented events. Best for those well acquainted with the scene.

**Forum** 111–117 Henry St, Port of Spain ☎ 623 4949. The large building next to the Ministry of Planning and Development which is the home of one of the great pre-Carnival calypso tents, Calypso Revue (many of the past and present grandmasters of the art form, including calypso monarchs, have performed here), as well as serving as a concert venue out of Carnival season. Events are advertised in the press. Entrance TT$30–75.

**Liquid** ground floor, Maritime Centre, Barataria ☎ 675 9958. One of the newer clubs in Trinidad, with a mission to attract a rather upmarket but party-hard clientele. Nights vary; expect some rock, pop and Latin along with the soca and reggae. The main room and dancefloor are lavishly decorated – check out the water features – and there's an excellent lights and sound system as well as a VIP area and black leather sofa-studded Champagne Lounge. Entrance fee varies.

**Two Plus Cultural and Recreation Club** 94–96 Henry St, Port of Spain. Near the junction with Park Street, this upstairs, somewhat hidden and unpretentious club occasionally has ballroom dancing at the weekends, utilizing the large dance floor. Otherwise, the music ranges from old calypsos to reggae and soca. No entrance fee except for special events.

## Theatres

**Central Bank Auditorium** Twin Towers financial complex, Independence Square South ☎ 623 0845. Entrance through Eric Williams Plaza. The most comfortable and high-tech theatre in Port of Spain features productions by well-known Trinidad theatre companies – usually comedies. Wear long sleeves to counteract the overenthusiastic a/c.

**Little Carib** White Street, at Roberts, Woodbrook ☎ 622 4644. Opened in 1948, this intimate and historic theatre concentrates on plays and shows highlighting local talent and culture.

**Queen's Hall** 1–3 St Ann's Rd, St Ann's ☎ 624 1284. Opposite the *Hilton Trinidad*, this is the largest arts venue in Trinidad, featuring drama, dance, music and fashion shows, as well as calypso concerts in Carnival season. Tickets TT$25–60.

**Under the Trees** *Normandie*, 10 Nook Ave, St Ann's ☎ 624 1181. Atmospheric evening performances under the stars in the grounds of the *Normandie* hotel, showcasing local artists doing everything from stand-up comedy to local plays.

# Shopping

Port of Spain's **main shopping area** is based around **Frederick Street** and the few outlying malls such as **West Mall**, **West Moorings**, **Ellerslie Plaza** in Maraval and **Long Circular Mall**, St James. **Imported goods** can be bought all over town, especially in the large malls, which are generally open Monday to Saturday from 9am to 6pm.

Since many Trinidadians have their clothes made to measure, there is an abundance of **textile** shops. Concentrated on Queen Street, these offer a greater variety of materials than you'd find in New York or London at very reasonable prices. **Mode Alive**, 34 Frederick St (☎ 627 5483), for example, is a good place to look for fabrics. Between 1984 and 1991, Trinidad banned the import of **clothes**, spurring the country's fashion industry to great heights and bringing forward a wave of first-rate designers. Look out for **Radical Designs**, which has shops in the Excellent City Centre Mall, Frederick Street and *Normandie* hotel, 100 Nook Ave, St Ann's, featuring elegant, funky clothes by Diane Hunt; the **Z Meiling** store, *Kapok* hotel, 16–18 Cotton Hill, St Clair, selling classic cuts and stylish underwear by Meiling, Trinidad's top designer; and **The Cloth**, *Normandie* hotel, for Robert Young's brightly coloured abstract designs on loose cotton.

Another field boasting plenty of local talent is art. There are several **galleries** around town, such as **Art Creators**, Flat 402, Aldegonda Park, 7 St Ann's Rd, St Ann's (Tues–Fri 10am–6pm, Sat 10am–3pm; ☎624 4369), exhibiting over 25 notable Trinidadian artists, including Karen Sylvester, and **Gallery 1,2,3,4**, *Normandie* hotel (daily 10am–6pm; ☎625 5502), a small four-room space featuring well-known local artists in all media forms. Others places with decent collections are the **101 Art Gallery**, 101 Tragarete Rd, Woodbrook (☎628 4081) and **On Location**, West Mall, Westmoorings (☎633 3404).

Of the several places to buy **Carnival supplies**, the best is **Samaroo's**, 11–13 Abercromby St (☎624 8431), which has all the multi-coloured clothes, beads, sequins and the like to make your own costume.

**Bookshops** in Port of Spain don't carry a huge range, concentrating mostly on school textbooks and imported cookery books. There are a few exceptions, though. Downtown, visit **Trinidad Book World**, 87 Queen St (☎623 4316), which is particularly strong on Trinidadian writers, stocking several of the titles mentioned in "Books" p.358, or **Metropolitan Book Suppliers**, upstairs at Colsort Mall, 11–13 Frederick St (☎623 3462), good for books on the country's history and culture. The biggest selection, however, belongs to **Classic Book Services**, 7 Royal Palm Plaza, Maraval (☎628 4811), where you'll find everything from novels by writers from Trinidad and Tobago and the Caribbean to tomes on history, politics, religion, culture and cookery.

**Crafts** can be found at street stalls and, at higher prices, in the malls. **Poui Designs**, 60 Ellerslie Plaza, Maraval (☎622 5597), has a wonderful selection of locally made crafts, from miniature wooden rum shops to hand-painted postcard-sized watercolours and classy ceramics from the Ajoupa pottery. For the best selection of hand-made leather sandals and Rastafarian goods, visit the shops at the **United Craft Workers Drag Brothers Mall**, just east of the Arthur Cipriani statue on Independence Square South. **African Trophies**, 39 Tragarete Rd (☎622 9476), specializes in fine African carvings, furniture, clothes and jewellery, and also functions as a cultural centre with a library and space to view videos on African culture. If you're looking for **Indian crafts** and **ornate filigree jewellery**, however, the best place to shop is in Chaguanas. Among the other miscellaneous craft shops worth a look is the **T&T Blind Welfare Association**, 118 Duke St (☎624 1613), where you'll find a large selection of wickerwork on sale; **Susan Dayal**'s beautiful hand-crafted wire decorations at the *Normandie* hotel (☎625 3197); and the **Yesteryear Antique Shop**, 63 Church St, St James (☎622 1040), specializing in mainly Caribbean antiques.

**Local music** is sold by street vendors touting the latest soca CDs, though these are poor-quality pirate copies. For retail CDs, try any of the music stores on Frederick Street, such as **Cleve's One Stop Music Shop**, at the back of a small mall at no. 58 (☎624 0827); **Crosby's**, 54 Western Main Rd, St James (☎622 SOCA), also has a good selection. If you're inspired to become a pan player or a Parang singer, head for **Music and Equipment Ltd**, 36 Duke St (☎624 5834), **The Music House**, 116 Oxford St (☎627 1914), or **Lincoln Enterprises**, 19 Gallus St, Woodbrook (☎628 7267) to buy a cuatro or a **steel pan**.

# Listings

**Airlines** American, 69 Independence Square North ☎627 7013; BWIA, 30 Edward St ☎627 2942 (also Tobago Express); Caribbean Star, 13A Pembroke St ☎623 6522 (also Dutch Caribbean Airlines); LIAT, 9–11 Edward St ☎627 6274; Air Canada, Piarco Airport ☎669 4065.

**Airport** 24hr information line ☎669 4866 69

**Banks** Numerous branches in the downtown area and the suburbs, including: Citibank, 12 Queen's Park East ☎625 1040; First Citizen, 50 St Vincent St ☎623 2576; Republic Bank, 9–17 Park St ☎623 1056; Scotiabank, 1 Frederick St ☎623 1253.

**Car rental** Convenient, Tropical Marine, Western Main Road, Chaguaramas ☎634 4017; Econo Cars, 191–193 Western Main Rd, Cocorite ☎622 8072; Kalloo's, 31 French St ☎622 9073; Signal, Chaguaramas Convention Centre, Chaguaramas ☎634 2277 or 800 2277; Singh's, 7–9 Wrightson Rd ☎623 0150; TCM, 132 Roberts St, Woodbrook ☎675 0145.

**Embassies and high commissions** British High Commission, 19 St Clair Ave, St Clair (Mon–Fri 7.30–11.30am; ☎622 2748, Ⓕ622 4555, Ⓦwww.britain-in-trinidad.org); Canadian High Commission, 3–3A Sweet Briar Rd, St Clair (Mon–Thurs 7.30am–noon & 12.30–4pm, Fri 7.30am–1pm; ☎622 6232, Ⓕ628 2619); US Embassy, 15 Queen's Park West (Mon–Fri 7.30–11am; ☎622 6371, Ⓕ628 5462).

**Hospital** Port of Spain General, 169 Charlotte St ☎623 2951–52 – you may have to wait a few hours to be seen if you turn up at casualty. Two efficient options if you're in a hurry and have good medical insurance are the private Community Hospital, Western Main Rd, Cocorite ☎622 1191 or 628 8330 and St Clair Medical Centre, 18 Elizabeth St, St Clair ☎628 1451 or 8615.

**Internet** In downtown Port of Spain, Inet Café, upstairs at Town Centre Mall, Frederick St, just north of Independence Sq (Mon–Thurs 8am–5pm, Fri 8am–6pm, Sat 8.30am–3pm, TT$10 per hr); Port of Spain Adult Library, Hart St, at Woodford Sq (Mon–Fri 8.30am–6pm, Sat 8.30am–noon; members get 1hr free Internet daily). In Newtown, Euro+, 11A Marli St (Mon–Fri 9am–7pm, Sat 1–6pm; TT$8 per hr). In Maraval, Rikmer Technologies, 36 Saddle Rd (Mon–Fri 10am–4pm; TT$10 per hr).

**Laundry** Ashleigh Phillip's Coin Laundry, 10 Western Main Rd, St James ☎628 2268 (another branch at 44 Diego Martin Main Rd, Diego Martin ☎632 9026); Simply Clean Laundromat, 99 Saddle Rd, Maraval ☎628 1060.

**Money transfers** Moneygram, at Hi-Lo stores all over town ☎627 2000; Western Union, 44–58 Edward St ☎623 6000.

**Pharmacies** Alchemist, 57 Duke St (daily 6.30am–midnight; ☎623 2718); Bhagan's, 10 Broadway, next to *KFC* (Mon–Thur 6.30am–11pm, Fri 6.30–midnight, Sat 8am–midnight, Sun 9am–10pm; ☎627 5541); Express Drugs, 102 Western Main Rd, St James (Mon–Sat 7.30am–11pm, Sun 7.30am–10pm; ☎628 1527); Kappa Drugs, Saddle Rd, at La Seiva, Maraval (Mon–Fri 7.30am–10.30pm, Sat & Sun 8am–10.30pm; ☎628 0544).

**Photography** Buy and develop film at: Film Processing Ltd, 6 Broadway, Port of Spain ☎625 3907; Fotomart, 20 Frederick Street, Port of Spain ☎623 8070; Photo World, Excellent City Shopping Mall, Frederick Street, Port of Spain ☎627 7627.

**Police** Report crimes at the Central Police Station, St Vincent St, at Hart ☎625 1261 or 2684. In emergency, dial ☎999.

**Post office** TT Post has several branches, including: 23 Chacon St (Mon–Fri 7am–5pm, Sat 9am–2pm); City Gate, South Quay (Mon–Fri 7am–6pm, Sat 8am–1pm); 177 Tragarete Rd, next to Roxy roundabout, Woodbrook (Mon–Fri 7am–5pm, Sat 8am–noon).

**Sport facilities** Hasley Crawford Stadium, Ariapita Ave, at Audrey Jeffers Hwy ☎623 0304, contains an athletics track and football field, and hosts both local and international events. The Jean Pierre Sports Complex next door has facilities for lawn tennis, netball, basketball, table tennis, gymnastics, badminton and a gym. Events are advertised in the local media.

**Swimming pool** YMCA, Benbow Rd, off Wrightson Rd (Mon–Fri noon–12.45pm & 7.15–8pm, Sat 3.45–4.30pm, Sun 3–5.15pm; ☎625 9622). TT$10 for a 45min session. You can swim at the *Hilton Trinidad* for TT$30 and the *Cascadia* hotel for TT$20.

**Tour operators** Island Experiences, 11 East Hill, Cascade ☎625 2410 or 756 9677, Ⓕ627 6688, Ⓔgunda@wow.net are best for city and panyard/mas camp tours. For excellent eco-based tours in the city and surrounds, call Caribbean Discovery Tours, 9B Fondes Amandes Rd, St Ann's ☎624 7281, Ⓕ624 8596, Ⓦwww.caribbean discoverytours.com and Paria Springs, 44 La Seiva Rd, Maraval ☎622 8826, Ⓕ628 1525, Ⓦwww.pariasprings.com.

**Travel agents** Alstons Travel, 67 Independence Square ☎625 2201, Ⓕ625 3682; Haygem, 55 Edward St ☎625 5328, Ⓕ624 4889.

# West to Chaguaramas

From Port of Spain, the Western Main Road winds its way along the coast, past the turn-off to the residential suburbs of Diego Martin and Petit Valley. The first 5km stretch of the Western Main Road from Port of Spain is characterized by high-rise apartments, the plush shopping centre at **West Mall** and exclusive suburbs such as **West Moorings** and **Glencoe**. After Glencoe, however, the landscape becomes less obviously urban and the communities smaller, with the odd rum shop and rickety wooden stall selling fruit and vegetables the only things lining the road until it reaches the most built-up part of the western tip, the down-to-earth town of **Carenage**, about 10km from Port of Spain. A few hundred metres after Carenage the Western Main Road enters the **Chaguaramas National Park**, a tranquil area of wide expanses of grassland and mountainous, largely untouched rainforest. Beyond the nondescript town of **Chaguaramas** – a cluster of former military buildings a couple of kilometres west of Carenage left over from World War II when the US Army had a huge military base on the peninsula – a plethora of **yachting** facilities drawing thousands of vessels each month line the Western Main Road for the next 4km or so until the road comes to an end at *The Cove Beach Resort*. These boats come to be serviced or to wait out the hurricane season, and provide the most popular means of visiting the rocky, forested islands in the **Bocas**, the farthest flung of which lies about a one-hour boat ride from the mainland.

There is regular **public transport** along the Western Main Road, with PTSC **buses** and **maxis** linking Port of Spain and *The Cove*, stopping at all points in between. To explore the Chaguaramas National Park, however, you will either need to **rent a car** or, for the more energetic, a **bicycle**. Maxis continue to run throughout the night between Port of Spain and the nightclubs in Chaguaramas, even if they are much fewer and farther between and fill up quickly when available. The **taxi** fare between Port of Spain and Chaguaramas with Phone-a-Taxi (☏628-TAXI) is TT\$60–70.

## West Mall, West Moorings and Glencoe

The area stretching from Diego Martin to Carenage, a swamp until it was reclaimed in the 1940s, consists of a series of largely indistinguishable and upmarket residential communities known as **WEST MALL**, **WEST MOORINGS** and **GLENCOE**. Driving along this part of the Western Main Road, you'll pass luxury houses defended by high walls and fierce-looking dogs, and postmodernist apartment blocks by Stephen Mendez (one of Trinidad's foremost architects) without necessarily realizing that you have left one community and entered the next. West Mall, just past the turn-off for Diego Martin, is identifiable by its American-style shopping mall full of expensive clothes shops, while Glencoe, a few minutes further down the Western Main Road, is the home of the **Trinidad and Tobago Yacht Club** (☏637 4260), which provides yachting facilities and offers **deep-sea fishing trips** – US\$315 for four hours, US\$400 for six hours, US\$475 for 8 hours; contact Mr Sagomes ☏637 8711 or Mr Da la Rosa ☏637 7389. Opposite the Yacht Club, a mini shopping mall houses a Hi-Lo supermarket and *Pizza Boys* and *Vie de France* food outlets.

# Carenage

The first clearly recognizable town on the Western Main Road, **CARENAGE**
sprawls far into the hills, its winding lanes flanked by modern concrete homes,
dilapidated huts and general stores covered in posters and hand-painted adverts.
There is little to see in Carenage, apart from the crumbling **St Peter's Chapel**
at the water's edge, next to the petrol station on the main road. On St Peter's
Day (the last Sunday in June), the clergy bless fleets of fishing boats here.

The town owes its name to the fact that it was here that the Spaniards
brought their ships to be careened (scraped clean of barnacles). After the
Spanish departed in 1797, Carenage sank into a century-and-a-half-long tor-
por as a sleepy fishing village, but its character changed drastically with the
arrival of the Americans in 1941. All of the peninsula's residents were forcibly
relocated to Carenage when Chaguaramas was turned into a US military base.
The town soon acquired a seedy reputation as a place where American soldiers
went to have fun and find local women, and there are still a couple of flop-
houses around. Today, Carenage has more of a maritime flavour again, with the
masts of pleasure yachts moored at the marinas visible over the rooftops.

# Chaguaramas

A few hundred metres west from Carenage, past the large white bauxite loading plant that juts into the sea, the Western Main Road enters **CHAGUARA-
MAS** (pronounced Shag-ger-*rarm*-ms). Home to red howler and capuchin
monkeys, armadillos, ocelots and anteaters, much of this land has remained virtually untouched, with shallow beaches and miles of virgin rainforest in its
mountainous interior, and is now a protected **national park**. Leisure development has, for the most part, been sensitive and unobtrusive. The strip of flatlands along the south coast is the only built-up area, and is also where you will
find **Chaguaramas town**, with its scattering of restaurants and nightclubs.
There is a string of unappealing **beaches** along the south coast, fronted by a
rather polluted sea. Better swimming can be had on the north coast at
**Macqueripe Beach**, a delightful cove that's easily accessible by road provided
that you have your own transport.

Come to Chaguaramas on a weekend and you'll see people liming on the
beaches, fighting the currents in kayaks, cycling and jogging along the quiet
roads that strike off the Western Main Road toward the north coast, and hiking in the forests; while at night, a more glamorous crowd comes in from Port
of Spain to frequent the open-air nightclubs.

### Some history

The name Chaguaramas, derived from the Amerindian word for the palms
which once lined this coast, is the only remnant of the area's indigenous population. The region's natural harbour provided the **Spanish** with a hiding place
for their ships when the **British** invaded in 1797, though when it became clear
that defeat was inevitable, the ships were scuttled. The harbour was also the reason the **US military** wanted Chaguaramas as its Caribbean base during World
War II, one of the sites they leased from the British in 1940 in return for fifty
used destroyers. At this time, the population was relocated to Carenage and the
military base which now forms Chaguaramas town was hastily constructed.

The American soldiers, initially greeted with a warm welcome, quickly

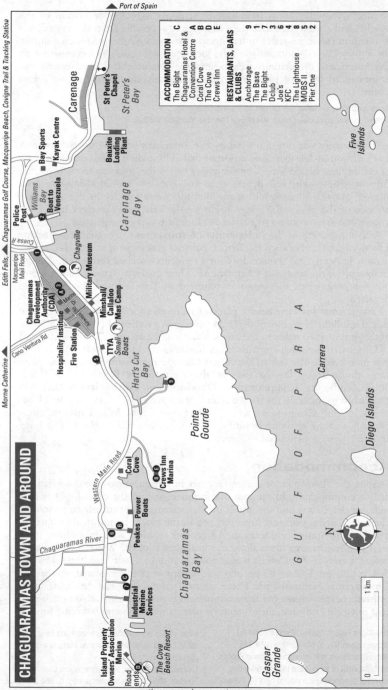

CHAGUARAMAS TOWN AND AROUND

ACCOMMODATION
The Bight                                    C
Chaguaramas Hotel &
Convention Centre                            A
Coral Cove                                   B
The Cove                                     D
Crews Inn                                    E

RESTAURANTS, BARS & CLUBS
Anchorage                                    9
The Base                                     1
The Bight                                    7
Dclub                                        3
Joe's                                        6
KFC                                          4
The Lighthouse                               8
MOBS II                                      5
Pier One                                     2

Port of Spain

Carenage

St Peter's Chapel
St Peter's Bay

Bauxite Loading Plant

Bay Sports
Kayak Centre

Williams Bay
Boat to Venezuela
Police Post

Carenage Bay

Five Islands

Edith Falls ◆  Chaguaramas Golf Course, Macqueripe Beach, Covigne Trail & Tracking Station

Macqueripe Mail Road

Chagville
Military Museum

Chaguaramas Development Authority (CDA)

Minshall/Callaloo Mas Camp

Hospitality Institute
Fire Station

TTYA Small Boats

Hart's Cut Bay

Cano Ventura Rd

Pointe Gourde

GULF OF PARIA

Carrera

Diego Islands

Morne Catherine ◆

Western Main Road

Coral Cove
Crews Inn Marina

Chaguaramas River

Peakes Power Boats

Chaguaramas Bay

Industrial Marine Services

Island Property Owners' Association Marina
Road ends

The Cove Beach Resort

Gaspar Grande

N

1 km

0

T&T Coast Guard (authorized personnel only) ◆

became unpopular. Many Trinidadians resented the US occupation of the beaches and countryside that were most easily accessible from the capital, not to mention the social effect of having so many young American men living in the region. The GIs outnumbered the local men, who could not compete with the Americans' ostentatious wealth, and the resentment this generated was immortalized by Lord Invader in his famous calypso *Working for the Yankee Dollar*:

**Rum and Coca-Cola, Go down to Point Cumana,**
**Both mother and daughter, Working for the Yankee Dollar.**

The situation was not improved by the Americans' attitude towards **race**. A 1945 edition of *Life* magazine reported that "US soldiers confused by the mix of colour lines would keep a brown paper bag at the doorway to their parties. Anyone whose skin was lighter than the bag was considered white (and allowed entry)." Some would argue that this persists today in the admission policies of the peninsula's glitzy nightclubs, where cover charges have been known to vary according to the skin colour of prospective patrons.

With the growth of the **independence movement**, Chaguaramas became a focus of conflict between the British colonial government and the local population. In April 1960 thousands of local residents marched through the rain to campaign for the return of Chaguaramas. Their goal was achieved the following February, when the area was returned to Trinidad and the Americans departed.

Chaguaramas has long been a place of recreation for Trinidadians, and with this in mind the government declared the region a **national park** in 1961, also granting protected status to the area's wildlife and rainforest. The built-up part of Chaguaramas, which contains many buildings abandoned by the Americans, was promoted as the seat of the future Caribbean parliament, but these plans were thwarted by the collapse of the West Indian Federation in 1962. Subsequently, the **Chaguaramas Development Authority** (CDA) was established to maintain the nature reserve and encourage leisure-oriented businesses. In 1999, Chaguaramas served as the venue for the **Miss Universe** competition, and the resulting beautification saw an upgrade in the CDA's hotel and cavernous conference facilities.

## Accommodation

Despite the abundance of leisure facilities in Chaguaramas, there is relatively little accommodation in the area; most visitors stay in the capital, just twenty minutes' drive away, and the hotels in Chaguaramas cater mainly to a yachting clientele. During Carnival, however, not all the places bump up their rates so it may merit some consideration. All accommodation is located either in or west of Chaguaramas town along the final stretch of the Western Main Road before it ends at *The Cove*. It is also possible to rent a tent from the CDA (see box, p.120) for TT$40–80 per day and **camp** at two designated sites in the Chaguaramas National Park. There are no facilities, save the drinkable water from the nearby stream, but the environment is awe-inspiring as you pitch your tent in virgin rainforest, surrounded by parrots, monkeys and bubbling brooks.

**The Bight** Peakes Marina, Western Main Rd, Chaguaramas Bay ☏634 4839, ℱ634 4387, ℮pys@cablenett.net. Ten smart rooms in Peakes boatyard west of town, used mainly by visiting yachties. Overlooking the marina right by the sea's edge, rooms are tastefully furnished and have a/c, cable TV and en-suite bathrooms. There is a coin-operated laundry. ❺–❻

**Chaguaramas Hotel and Convention Centre** Western Main Rd, Chaguaramas town ☏634 2379,

ⓕ634 2377, ⓦwww.chagdev.com/Pages/CHACC .htm. Refurbished to house the 1999 Miss Universe Pageant entrants, this is a somewhat soulless but functional place where the modern, tiled rooms all have cable TV, phone and a/c. There's a restaurant and bar on site, and a pool and gym are planned for 2005. **❹**

**Coral Cove** Western Main Rd, Chaguaramas Bay ⓣ634 2040, ⓕ634 2248, ⓦwww.coralcove marina.com. Newish, rather uninspired but efficient and friendly hotel. Rooms are on the expensive side but clean and modern, with a/c, cable TV, phone and kitchenette. **❻**

**The Cove Beach Reort** Western Main Rd, Chaguaramas Bay ⓣ634 4319, ⓕ634 4278. Spacious, peaceful and well-maintained self-cater-ing apartments sleeping two to four. Most have TV and fridge, and daily maid service is provided. Use of *The Cove's* beach and swimming pool, which the public must pay to use, is free for guests, and meals are available. **❺**

**Crews Inn** Point Gourde, Chaguaramas Bay ⓣ634 4384, ⓕ634 4175, ⓦwww.crewsinn.com. Overlooking the busy marina and patronized mostly by a well-to-do yachtie crowd, this is the smartest and most expensive place to stay in Chaguaramas. The tiled, sparkling rooms have all mod cons, kitchenette and balconies overlooking the sea, and there's a good restaurant, bar, gym and a lovely pool. Carnival rate includes breakfast. **❽–❾**

# Williams Bay

Just before arriving at Chaguaramas town, the Western Main Road trundles along the south coast parallel to the sea, its twists and turns revealing lovely vistas out to the Bocas and back to Port of Spain, before descending towards **Williams Bay**, where there is a narrow beach lapped by brownish waves tinted with petrol rainbows from the boats moored at *Pier One* nightclub on the western side of the bay.

Williams Bay gets busy at weekends with local bathers, who bring coolers packed with food and drink and make a day of it, but as with the rest of the south coast of the peninsula, swimming isn't recommended. Better to rent a **kayak** from the Kayak Centre (daily 6am–6pm; ⓣ633 7871), in a signposted building in the concrete lot on the eastern side of the bay. Paddling about in the waters off Chaguaramas costs TT$25 for a single kayak and TT$35 for a double; both rates are per hour and rise by TT$5 at weekends. Another option for the energetic is to rent a **mountain bike** from Bay Sports next door (Sat & Sun 6am–6pm; ⓣ687 0566 or 681 8887). A straight rental costs TT$20 per hour, but you're better off paying an additional TT$10 for a **guided ride** along the paved roads in the interior of the national park – one of the nicest (as long as it's not too hot) and least intrusive ways to see Chaguaramas's wildlife and natural beauty. Tours should be booked a day in advance, though turning up on spec is usually fine at the weekend.

### Ferry to Venezuela

Willams Bay is where the **ferry to Venezuela** departs from. There is one sailing per week, on Wednesdays. The boat leaves *Pier One* at 9am, arriving in the Venezuelan town of Guiria at 12.30pm. The return leg of the trip departs Guiria at 3pm on the same day, reaching *Pier One* at 6.30pm. Fares are as follows: one-way US$48.30, return US$96.60, same day return US$72.45. Departure tax for Trinidad is TT$75 and for Venezuela US$23. Those travelling between Trinidad and Venezuela by this means will need a Yellow Fever Vaccination Certificate.

## Chaguaramas town

Beyond Williams Bay, the Western Main Road straightens out to become the main drag of **Chaguaramas town**, flanked on either side by the rather ugly structures that were constructed in three months in 1940 by the US military and local labour, and turned over to civilian use in 1961. Nowadays most of the aircraft hangars, warehouses and official buildings have been converted for use by businesses or government departments, and the **Chaguaramas Hotel and Convention Centre** with its curving, incongruously grand flagpole-lined driveway looks out of place amidst its no-nonsense neighbours.

Several minor roads strike off north from the Western Main Road here toward a gently inclining parallel road that's simply known as "the back road", home to training camps for firemen and soldiers with the Trinidad Defence Force. Penned in by the high hills that spread back from the coast, the heat can get oppressive here, but it's worth braving the sun to check out the surprisingly interesting **military museum** and, in Carnival season, Peter Minshall's **Callaloo mas camp**. Also, if you plan on exploring the fantastic rainforest of the Chaguaramas interior, you would also do well to visit the offices of the **Chaguaramas Development Authority** (see box, p.120), from where you can book tours and arrange access to more remote parts of the peninsula.

## Chaguaramas Military History and Aerospace Museum

Located on the Western Main Road at the western edge of town, just a couple of hundred metres from the Chaguaramas Hotel and Convention Centre next to the Coast Guard's training ground and heliport, the **Chaguaramas Military History and Aerospace Museum** (daily 9am–5pm; TT$20; T634 4391, Ⓔcm-ham@carib-link.net) is hard to miss – there's a large sign out front and a collection of military hardware on the forecourt, including a monumental 88-ton, US Army LARC (lighter amphibious resupply cargo) vessel, a rusting tank, a plane and the gutted remains of a helicopter. Inside the main building, wedged between somewhat smaller pieces of military equipment, the exhibits chronicle the military history of Trinidad and Tobago from 1498 to the present. Although the presentation can be somewhat haphazard, it's an absorbing, and occasionally touching, array, worth a glimpse if only because it so sharply counteracts the usual beaches-and-palms image of the Caribbean.

Among the first exhibits are a recreation of a World War II trench and a German machine-gun bunker, complete with flashing lights simulating explosions and battle sounds. These are followed by a series of photos and explanatory panels highlighting the extensive (and often overlooked) role of local soldiers in international warfare. Paintings and text deal with famous pirates, the history of the Trinidadian police, and local battles, with detailed drawings of the Battle of Scarborough Bay in Tobago and the British takeover of Trinidad. Newspaper photographs from the 1990 coup provide a glimpse of the turmoil in Trinidad during the six-day siege. The collection ends at a small shop that sells military prints, pamphlets and a good selection of greeting cards.

## Callaloo mas camp

The **Callaloo mas camp** (Mon–Fri 9am–5pm, Sat 10am–2pm; ☎634 4491, Ⓦwww.callaloo.co.tt), opposite the old heliport in a large warehouse-type building surrounded by a wire fence, is the workshop of Trinidad's most famous mas band, led by designer **Peter Minshall** (see box opposite). Known for innovative techniques, high quality and immensely detailed mas presentations, Minshall and his crew use everything from leaves to bottle tops to lengths of fibreglass to manufacture the amazing costumes that have often won them the title of **Band of the Year**. While most mas camps are based in Port of Spain, Callaloo was leased this building as a reward for its contribution to Trinidad Carnival. Open year-round, the camp is busiest in the run-up to Carnival,

## Peter Minshall and the Callaloo Company

**Peter Minshall**, who shared the Emmy for costume design for the 2002 Winter Olympics opening ceremony, is the most controversial and admired of T&T's Carnival designers, his unique combination of traditional Carnival characters and innovative techniques presented with a strong sense of theatre.

Born in Guyana and raised in Trinidad, Minshall studied theatre design at the Central School of Art and Design in London. Indeed, he designed his first Carnival band for London's **Notting Hill Carnival** in 1975, returning to Trinidad soon afterwards to bring out **Paradise Lost**, the first of his many nationally acclaimed bands. Minshall's **Callaloo Company**, formed in 1991, includes many of Trinidad's top actors, dancers and artists, and functions as a production company, mas factory and performance group. This close-knit and loyal crew takes its name from Trinidad's national dish, whose various ingredients reflect the country's ethnic mix; "all ah we is one" is the company's philosophy.

Unlike many Carnival costumes, which are thrown away on Ash Wednesday, Minshall's creations decorate houses throughout Trinidad. While most contemporary mas presentations tend to concentrate on escapist, fantasy themes with minimal costumes, Minshall's lavish and detailed works deal with spiritual and political issues – the environment, the interconnectedness of humanity, the transience of life. Many of his pieces are more like kinetic sculptures than costumes in the traditional sense, where puppets have moving limbs and butterflies fluttering wings. In emphasizing the aspect of Carnival that allows people to escape their own identity by playing a role, Minshall is continuing the tradition of Carnival as theatre for all: "In most countries", he has often remarked, "people pay to see others perform. However in Trinidad, people pay *to* perform".

Sadly, however, Minshall's dissatisfaction with the bikinis and good-time carelessness that make "pretty mas", alongside the general lack of regard for the creative traditions of Carnival, have seen him take a step back from mas in Trinidad in recent years. Though he continues to make work overseas, it remains to be seen if his fabulous designs will cross the Savannah stage again.

when the crew work 24 hours a day in a whirl of fabric, sequins and natural materials. The camp also makes costumes and puppets for international events such as the **Olympic Games** and **World Cup** ceremonies, and **Jean Michel Jarre** concerts; workers here even make and restore furniture. Visitors are welcome, though bear in mind that during Carnival season production is at its most hectic; look around as quickly and quietly as possible, to avoid disrupting production.

### Chagville Beach and Small Boats

The unremarkable strip of pebbles and sand which stretches along Carenage Bay for about half the length of Chaguaramas town, is called **Chagville Beach**. It's fringed by grass and almond trees and separated from the Western Main Road by a car park and a garish *KFC* outlet. Although swimming is not recommended during the wet season due to downstream pollution, the water still gets packed with bathers at weekends and public holidays. Facilities are limited: basically toilets and showers, a car park, a bar and a handful of kiosks selling snack foods, basic hot meals and cold drinks.

A calmer – though not necessarily any cleaner – spot for bathing can be found by walking fifteen minutes west along the Western Main Road, where, just beyond Chaguaramas town adjacent to the Trinidad and Tobago Yachting Association (TTYA), you'll find a small beach known locally as **Small Boats**. There are no facilities here; and to buy drinks at the TTYA's bar, you must first sign in (officially with a member).

## Chaguaramas Development Authority (CDA)

Behind the *Chaguaramas Hotel and Convention Centre* on Airways Road is the orange-painted facade of the **Chaguaramas Development Authority (CDA)** (Mon–Fri 8am–4pm; ☎634 4227 or 4312, ℻634 4311, ⓦwww.chagdev.com), which was set up to promote and maintain this pristine countryside region. They offer excellent and educational **tours**, led by experienced and knowledgeable guides, into the **Chaguaramas National Park**, most of which pass through the lush vegetation, rivers and cultivated forest of the **Tucker Valley**, the first citrus plantation on the island. Perhaps the best hike is to **Covigne River**, a fairly strenuous 3km, one-hour hike along a river bed, which includes a beautiful section of twisting gorge and a rope-aided climb up a waterfall to an emerald bathing pool surrounded by rainforest. On the way back, you can pick your own nutmeg at an abandoned plantation and bathe in a spring. The CDA also provides guides for the **Edith Falls** trail and trips to the **Bocas**. Much of the CDA's work is with local school groups, and if you're lucky, you'll be able to join one of these hikes at a fraction of the normal rate – it's well worth calling ahead to check the schedule of tours. Otherwise, regular rates are between US$8 and $25, which cover transport from the CDA office to the start of the hike and back. You should bring water and snacks with you on all trips as there's nowhere to buy them and, unlike many tour companies, the CDA do not provide refreshments.

# Tucker Valley

The area immediately north of Chaguaramas town is called the **Tucker Valley**, accessible via Tucker Valley Road, which strikes into the interior toward the north coast from the Western Main Road; the junction (look for the Macqueripe Mail Road) is just west of the police post at the eastern edge of Chaguaramas town. You will need your own transport to travel up Macqueripe – a truly beautiful drive, with pastures and fields dotted with enormous, bromeliad-smothered samaan trees to each side, gently rising to meet forested peaks.

After a couple of minutes' drive, you'll pass the unmarked right-hand turn-off to the Covigne trail (see box, above) and, a few minutes' further, a haphazard group of gravestones and the dilapidated St Chad's church to your right. This is pretty much all that's left of **Mount St Pleasant** village, a thriving settlement that was home to workers during the colonial era, when this fertile valley was planted with citrus, cocoa and coffee as part of the Tucker Estate. Among the plain gravestones you can pick out the rather grand tomb of Amelia Tripp, daughter of the estate's former English owner, William Sanger Tucker.

### Edith Falls and Chaguaramas Golf Course

Back on Tucker Valley Road, you'll soon pass the well-signposted left turn to **Edith Falls**. This will take you onto Bellerazand Road, from where the beginning of the trail to the falls – on the left of the road just before the practice range of the Chaguaramas Golf Course – is clearly marked. It's an easy 30-minute (1.5km) walk through the rainforest, which is rich in **exotic flora and fauna**: fluffy stands of enormous bamboo, halyconia flowers, fishtail palms, rubber trees seeping black sap, red howler monkeys, yellowtails and bluejays, and large blue emperor butterflies. At the end of the trail, you must scramble up a few boulders to reach the waterfall itself. Water seeps through the steep craggy rockface, sending showers tumbling 180 metres into the shallow pool below (not deep enough for swimming). Bear in mind, though, that the falls slow to a trickle in dry season (Nov–June). They are rarely overcrowded and if you visit during the week, you are likely to be alone.

Beyond the falls trail, Bellerazand Road cuts straight through the nine-hole **Chaguaramas Golf Course** (US$10 per round; ☎634 4227), located at the base of the falls and built on a former tonka bean plantation by American servicemen during World War II. From the golf course, you can follow a 2.5km-long **hiking trail** up through the forest to Macqueripe Beach, with gorgeous views of the north coast at several points. To find it, you'll need to enlist the services of a CDA tour guide (guided walks from Macqueripe Beach to the golf course cost US$8).

### Macqueripe Beach and the Tracking Station

Tucker Valley Road ends at the small, picturesque cove of **Macqueripe Beach** (daily 7am–6pm), on Trinidad's north coast. Entry to Maqueripe is free, but you'll be charged TT$10 to drive down to the car park overlooking the beach, from where some fairly steep steps lead down to the water. A curve of coarse brown sand sheltered beneath a steep, wooded hillside, it's an idyllic spot with stunning sunsets and a distant view of Venezuela's Paria Peninsula, marred only by a concrete platform built when the beach was the favoured swimming spot of US servicemen. The sea on this side of the peninsula is unpolluted and good for swimming (if a little chilly), and though the beach can get crowded at weekends, you'll often find it deserted. Keep in mind that strong currents make it unwise to swim out too far. Although Macqueripe was a fashionable resort in the 1930s and 1940s, the haunt of movie stars such as Errol Flynn, none of the facilities remain. There is a changing room (TT$1) in the car park, but that's it; you should bring your own food and drink.

Almost opposite the security station where you pay to use the Maqueripe car park, a signposted right turn leads to the **Bamboo Cathedral**, a rather whimsical but nevertheless apt name for the tunnel of bamboo that encloses a section of the tarmac, the thick foliage allowing shafts of green-tinged sunlight to filter through. It was a pretty enough spot to inspire renowned Trinidadian artist and national hero **Michel Cazabon**, who included the Cathedral in the many paintings he did of the Tucker Valley in the nineteenth century. Once through the bamboo, the road snakes upward toward the rusting bulk of the **tracking station** at the top of the ridge. This huge dish was erected by the US military in the 1950s to track nuclear missiles; however, its main claim to fame is less sinister. The dish's technology soon became redundant, and the radar scanner was converted into a radio transmitter in 1960; on August 12 of the same year it was used to transmit the first radio signal to be bounced off a **satellite** – the signal was received at Floyd Air Force Base in New York. The station was used to develop the technique until 1972, when it was abandoned. The tracking station stands on a nine-acre plateau which affords gorgeous **views** of Tucker Valley, the north coast and of Venezuela. On the way down, keep an eye (or an ear) out for the wide variety of **birds** and troops of **howler monkeys** that inhabit the area.

## Morne Catherine

Opposite the military museum, Cano Ventura Road snakes northwards into the hills, arriving after a steep and beautiful climb along a road overhung with trees and bamboo at the **Morne Catherine**, the highest peak in the Chaguaramas National Park. The way is barred by a gate, so you'll need to contact the CDA if you want to drive up; walkers and cyclists have free access. A fork off to the right leads to a radar dish, but there's nothing much to see there; instead, stop anywhere along the road to appreciate the abundant birdlife, from toucans to oropendolas and hummingbirds, which will interest casual observers and more serious birders alike.

## The marinas: Crews Inn, Coral Cove, Power Boats, Peakes and Industrial Marine Services

Once the Western Main Road has cleared Chaguaramas town, it passes several **marinas** before coming to an abrupt end at The Cove. These marinas have been developed in recent years to look after the rapidly growing number of yachts which dock in Trinidad to avoid the hurricane season in the rest of the Caribbean. Even if you're not a yachtie, you'll find the marinas useful for their extensive facilities. Moving from east to west, upscale **Crews Inn** accommodates the **immigration office**, an attractive restaurant, a Hi-Lo supermarket, a bank (Mon–Fri 9am–4pm) and a series of smart shops selling everything from marine equipment to books. **Coral Cove Marina** also has several maritime-oriented shops, a newsagent which sells Chris Doyle and Jeff Fisher's indispensable *Cruising Guide of Trinidad and Tobago* and a **post office** (Mon–Fri 7.30am–5pm, Sat 9am–1pm). There is a supermarket and fast-food outlet at **Power Boats** (℡634 4303), while a little further down the road **Peakes** (℡634 4420) has a well-stocked boat shop and an **Internet café** (TT$18 per hr). **Industrial Marine Services** (℡625 2105) provides technical and maintenance support for yachties and their craft.

The chunky *Boater's Directory of Trinidad & Tobago* is a free guide containing information on marinas, tide tables and other subjects of nautical interest, in addition to more general tourist titbits. *The Bocas*, meanwhile, is a free monthly magazine written by and for the yachting community.

## The Cove

**The Cove Beach Resort** (daily 7am–6pm), at the end of the Western Main Road, is a narrow beach of imported yellow sand with the most developed and well-maintained facilities along this stretch of coast. The sea is calm and regular pollution checks have cleared the water for swimming. A lifeguard is on duty during the day, and facilities include changing cubicles, showers, toilets and a swimming pool. It costs TT$10 to use the beach and TT$20 for the beach and swimming pool. There is also a bar serving refreshments and light meals (Sun–Thurs 8am–11pm, Fri & Sat 8–2am), as well as a hotel (see p.117) should you wish to base yourself here and use the beach, pool and facilities without paying the daily fee.

The land due west of The Cove belongs to the Trinidad and Tobago Coast Guard and is closed to the public.

## Eating, drinking and nightlife

What Chaguaramas lacks in decent **restaurants** – virtually all of the places to eat are found at the marinas along the Western Main Road west of Chaguaramas town – it makes up for in atmospheric and trendy open-air **nightclubs**, some operating every weekend, others hosting pre-Carnival fetes, concerts and privately organized parties. Getting to these clubs from Port of Spain after dark is possible by maxi, although departures are a lot less frequent than during the day. Taxi fares from the capital to Chaguaramas start at around TT$30 with Phone-a-Taxi.

**Anchorage** Hart's Cut ☎634 4334. Formerly an upscale restaurant with one of the most romantic views in Trinidad, but now operating as an open-air venue in a dreamy location right on the water for fetes and the like. Entrance fee varies.

**The Base** Western Main Rd, at Macqueripe Mail Rd ☎634 4004. Huge hangar of a place hosting live shows, fetes and one-off parties, most of which attract a young, well-to-do crowd. The club has, however, been the subject of press allegations that it operates a racist door policy. Car park parties here tend to be looser affairs. Entrance fee varies.

**The Bight** Peakes Marina, Western Main Rd ☎634 4839. This neon-bedecked a/c bar, with its two pool tables, huge TV for showing sports fixtures, plus breezy verandah restaurant overlooking the marina, is a popular yachtie hangout. The international menu is hugely varied, from good local and continental breakfasts, to salads, sandwiches and burgers for lunch, and seafood, steaks and chops for dinner. Mon–Fri 7am–11pm, Sat & Sun 8am–11pm.

**Dclub** next to *Chaguaramas Hotel and Convention Centre* ☎634 1656. The Trinidad and Tobago Defence Force recreational facility, with its tinted windows, khaki-clad patrons and large room reverberating with soca, is a more down-to-earth place to have a drink than the trendy clubs elsewhere in Chaguaramas.

**Joe's** Coral Cove Marina, Western Main Rd ☎634 2332. Simple Italian café chain serving unremarkable but reliable salads, steak sandwiches, burgers, hoagies, pasta and pizza. Takeaway is available, and it's a useful stopgap if you need to eat in a hurry. Mon–Sat 11am–10pm

**The Lighthouse** Crews Inn Marina, Point Gourde Rd ☎634 4384. Attractive open-air restaurant and bar overlooking the marina, underneath a red-and-white striped lighthouse. Aimed mainly at a yachting clientele, it serves tasty international food with Creole specialities and good desserts. Daily 7am–11pm.

**MOBS II** Welcome Bay, Western Main Rd ☎634 2255, ⓦwww.mobs2.com. Expansive open-air venue for fetes and concerts only. The location overlooking Small Boats beach is especially picturesque at night, and the amphitheatre terrace design ensures good views of the stage. Entrance fee varies.

**Pier One** Western Main Rd, Chagville ☎634 4472. Pretty open-air nightclub overlooking the sea and attracting a yuppyish crowd. Best for Thursday's steaming Latin night (dance classes available), with a variety of other styles of music, including live acts, at the weekends. Also a popular venue for fetes. Entrance fee varies.

# The Bocas

When you hear Trinidadians refer to the **BOCAS**, they talk of "down de islands" in tones of wistful longing. These rocky islets are separated from the mainland, and from one another, by the **Bocas del Dragon** (**Dragon's Mouths**), a series of channels connecting the Gulf of Paria with the Caribbean. The name is appropriate, for the coastlines here are jagged and rocky, and the sea hides treacherous currents and undertows that can make even the short journey to the nearest island, **Gaspar Grande**, a rough ride. Dolphins frequent the waters hereabout, so keep your eyes peeled; if you're lucky, you may even see a leatherback turtle or a pilot whale.

The islands had a thriving **whaling industry** in the eighteenth century, with whaling stations on Gaspar Grande, **Monos** and **Chacachacare**. Today the Bocas are sparsely inhabited, their interiors covered with dense forest, and lacking any roads. Scattered around the coasts are a few holiday homes, accessible only by boat. For Trinis the islands have always been a popular weekend getaway from the mainland, when yachts drop anchor in the bays for an afternoon of eating, drinking and swimming. However, few people explore the islands themselves and, apart from the *Bayview* resort on Gaspar Grande, there are no hotels, guesthouses, restaurants or bars. Chances are that you'll be alone with the birdsong and the sound of the sea. The atmosphere is so still that it can verge on the uncanny, especially on deserted Chacachacare, with its abandoned leper colony and tales of ghosts.

## Getting to the islands

The **Island Property Owners' Association** marina on the Western Main Road just before The Cove is the base for boats, known locally as **pirogues**, that make regular trips to the islands. Prices are for up to six people, so it's cheapest to go in a group or else share a boat with mainlanders who commute to and from their jobs at holiday homes on the islands. One-way fares are TT$50 to Gaspar Grande, TT$60 to Monos and TT$400 to Chacachacare; for more information, call ☏681 8167.

If you want to **tour the Bocas** for the day, you can also rent a boat (and driver) for about TT$600. Alternatively, both the CDA and Caribbean Discovery Tours (☏624 7281) run a variety of day-trips to the Gasparee Caves, Chacachacare and other islands.

# Gaspar Grande

Just fifteen minutes by boat from the mainland, **GASPAR GRANDE** (also known as **Gasparee** and **Fantasy Island**) is the most accessible of the islands. The eerie **Gasparee Caves** at Point Baleine – "Whale Point", named for its former role as a whaling station – were once used by pirates to hide their booty; these days, the only thing that glitters are the walls and the huge, green-tinged stalactites and stalagmites. It's also an excellent place to observe the **fruit bats** which inhabit the caves and the many local species of bird which congregate outside them. If you want to **visit**, you'll first need to contact the CDA; turn up unannounced, and you're likely to find the entrance locked up. CDA tours, including the boat from the mainland, cost US$20; alternatively, you can arrange your own vessel and pay the TT$20 fee, though you'll still need to let the CDA know when you'll be visiting.

Of the eight caves on the island, the largest is also the one that's open to the public; to get there, follow the signposted concrete path from the jetty through the forest; look out for unusual tan-coloured trees, whose rather politically incorrect nickname, "naked Indian", derives from the colour of their peeling bark. If you've prearranged your trip, you'll meet your **CDA tour guide** by the white-and-mustard-painted wooden house just before the mouth of the cave. If you are visiting independently, proceed directly to the cave. The cave itself is an impressive, cathedral-like cavern some 35 metres deep, a mysterious and weirdly beautiful place, silent but for the chirping fruit bats and dripping water. Reflected sunlight causes calcium crystals in the rocks to sparkle, and a deep, clear, marvellously turquoise tidal pool, the **Blue Grotto**, reflects the extravagant colours and strange shapes of the stalactites and stalagmites; swimming is officially prohibited, but you may be able to take a dip if touring with a small group. Past the pool, there's a short path to the back of the cave, where you can gaze up at roosting bats and pick out the rock formations that have been given apt nicknames such as "the Lovers", "Buddha" and the "Virgin Mary".

On your way to Gaspar Grande, the small rocky island to the east is **Carrera**, Trinidad's equivalent of Alcatraz. Its only building is the prison, established in 1876, where convicts still do hard labour. It's said that a few individuals have braved the strong currents and shark-infested waters to swim to the mainland, but officially, there's never been a successful escape.

# Scotland Bay, Monos and Huevos

Though actually part of the mainland, **Scotland Bay** is always considered as being "down de islands", since it can only be reached by boat. This idyllic small cove right at the end of the peninsula is blessed with soft sand and calm waters that are good for snorkelling. Yachts are often moored in its shelter, although the beach has no facilities. Spreading back from the shore is some gorgeous primary rainforest inhabited by multiple exotic creatures, including red howler monkeys. It was from nearby **Staubles Bay** that the government shelled the Northern Range during the Black Power uprising in the 1970s.

Scotland Bay looks out across the swirling waters of the Boca de Monos to the island of **Monos**, uninhabited except for a few holiday homes belonging to rich Trinidadians. Monos's densely wooded interior once supported a large colony of red howler monkeys – the island's name is Spanish for apes – but these are now confined to the mainland. Beyond the sheer western ramparts of Monos and another fierce *boca* lies the privately owned and seldom-visited island of **Huevos**.

# Chacachacare

Utterly peaceful **Chacachacare** (*shak*-a-chak-ar-ee) is the largest island of the Bocas and, at an hour's boat ride from the mainland, also the farthest-flung. It has none of the well-to-do holiday homes found on the other islands, and the mountainous interior is covered in dense forest. There is just one useable road, leading from the jetty to the lighthouse; the others, which once serviced the **abandoned leper colony**, have long been overgrown, and only tracks remain.

The island's name may derive from *chac-chac*, the Amerindian word for cotton, which grows profusely on the island, or might also have something to do with the chattering of the monkeys once found here. According to discovered remains that dated from around 100–400 AD, it was once inhabited by Amerindians. Under Spanish rule it became a cotton plantation, and subsequently a whaling station was established. It developed into a popular health and holiday resort with Trinis from the mainland until, to their consternation, a leper colony was established in 1887. The Dominican nuns ran the colony like a prison, and conditions provoked strikes among the patients to gain such rights as male-female fraternization. The last 30 patients left in 1984, and all that remains are the decaying wooden houses, the infirmary (with bottle and papers still on the shelves), the nuns' quarters and the chapel, all visible on the right as you approach the island from the mainland. You're free to explore the structures, but as they're all derelict, you should watch your step. Also on this stretch are a string of lovely **beaches**, with pale sand and shallow, calm, crystal-clear water; these see some traffic at weekends, but are often deserted during the week.

Chacachacare is now uninhabited except for its wildlife (look out for unusually large iguanas) and the two men who work the small, white **lighthouse**, built in 1885. On the southwest of the island is **La Tinta Bay**; the name, meaning "ink" in Spanish, alludes to the black sand of its beaches. Once a favourite place for smugglers, today this coarse-grained beach is deserted save for the refuse washed up by the tide, and the odd iguana and scavenging hawk. Nearby is the **Salt Pond**, a marsh-fringed sulphurous lake that provides the perfect habitat for unusual trees such as the campecho, known locally as the bread and cheese tree on account of its textured fruit with a cheesy taste. The odd manchineel tree also grows on the island's beaches. Its beautiful yellow flowers hide the fact that it produces a sinister fruit, used by the Amerindians to make poisoned arrows. Avoid contact with any part of this tree: its sap causes painful blisters (see p.26). The CDA offers guided walks to the lighthouse or the salt pond for US$25 including transport.

# The North

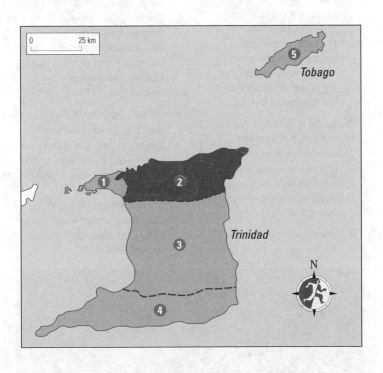

CHAPTER 2 # Highlights

✳ **Maracas meal** Having a cold Carib, and a fresh shark and bake, is the perfect restorative after a day spent riding the waves and displaying your best beachwear on Trinidad's most popular beach. See p.134

✳ **Asa Wright Nature Centre** Overlooking a valley deep in the Northern Range rainforest, the verandah of this bird-watcher's paradise attracts an incredible variety of technicolour tropical species. See p.148

✳ **Turtle watch** Watching a giant leatherback turtle complete the laborious process of laying her eggs on the beach is a truly magical experience. See p.166

✳ **Northern range hikes** From a wet and wild hike up Blanchisseuse's Marianne River to a kamikaze trek through Guanapo Gorge, Trinidad's lush mountain range offers endless possibilities for adventure. See p.143 & p.162

✳ **Mount St Benedict Monastery** With a stunning view over the central plains, St Benedict's offers a soothing, secluded respite from the maelstrom of the Eastern Main Road below. See p.156

✳ **Grande Riviere** This village makes for a perfect retreat, featuring a stunning beach where rainforest tumbles down onto golden sand, a clutch of great places to stay and endless possibilities for waterfall swims. See p.171

▲ Maracas Beach

# The North

T he north of Trinidad is an eighty-odd kilometre stretch dominated by the rainforested mountains of the Northern Range, which form a rugged spine through the region's centre and boast the island's highest peaks, El Cerro del Aripo and El Tucuche. North of the range, the coast is lined with Trinidad's most stunning beaches; at the weekends the enduringly popular Maracas Bay and Las Cuevas play host to what is seemingly the entire population of Port of Spain. Beyond Las Cuevas lies the glorious seashore of Blanchisseuse, where the North Coast Road dissolves into kilometres of undeveloped coastline. The Arima–Blanchisseuse Road then swings south through the forest, providing an opportunity to see most of the island's prolific bird life at the Asa Wright Nature Centre.

Scattered around the uninhabited, jungle-smothered hills are some of Trinidad's most **densely populated** areas outside of Port of Spain and home to the majority of the island's **African** population. Though you'll see the odd temple, mosque and prayer flag, Indian culture is far less visible here than in the south; Creole cooking reigns supreme and the soundtrack that blares from shops, bars and maxis is **soca** and Jamaican **dancehall** rather than chutney (see p.344).

To the south of the mountains, in the area called the **East–West Corridor**, a string of busy communities crowd along the traffic-choked **Eastern Main Road** (EMR) and the faster flowing **Churchill Roosevelt Highway** which runs parallel to it; both start at Port of Spain and end abruptly just east of Arima, replaced by the winding minor roads that span the weatherbeaten northeast coast. The EMR is the route to a host of interior attractions; there are **waterfalls** and **river swimming** at **Maracas Valley**, **Caura** and the **Hollis Reservoir**. The **Heights of Guanapo Road** boasts two of the island's most spectacular cascades, **La Laja** and **Sombasson**, as well as the challenging **Guanapo Gorge**. Many of the towns along the EMR are equally absorbing, particularly **St Joseph**, the island's first Spanish capital, with its historic church and barracks. The largest town in the region, **Arima**, is great for window shopping and for the town's **Carib** parade in late August at the **Feast of Santa Rosa**.

Past Arima, the road continues to the **northeast tip**. This wild and rugged peninsula, jutting some 20km into the Atlantic Ocean, is Trinidad's best-kept secret. Despite the area's outstanding beauty and its overwhelmingly friendly populace, relatively few make the effort to venture so far off the beaten track. It's a shame, really, as along the **Toco coast** on its northern side and **Matura beach** to the east, **leatherback turtles** clamber up the wave-battered sandy beaches to lay their eggs between March and September.

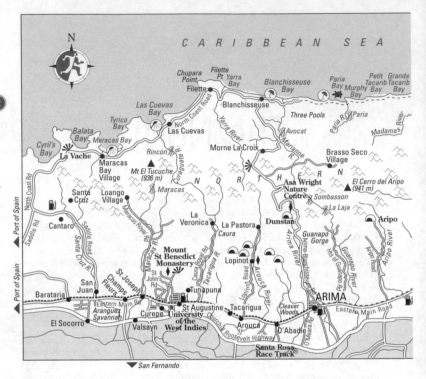

Though parts of the north are well served by **public transport** – buses, taxis and maxis serve every village and town along the East–West Corridor – a **car** is useful to visit the more remote north coast, where you're likely to encounter long waits if you rely on the intermittent public transport; it's about a three-hour drive from Port of Spain to the far end of the Northeast Tip. Surprisingly, there is not a huge amount of **accommodation** in the region; though there are lovely guesthouses at Blanchisseuse and Grande Riviere and a couple of luxury options along the east coast, it's often easier to simply explore from Port of Spain as you can see all the sights during day trips. The exception to this is the remote Northeast tip, at least three hour's driving from town; you'll need a few days and nights here anyway to fully appreciate it.

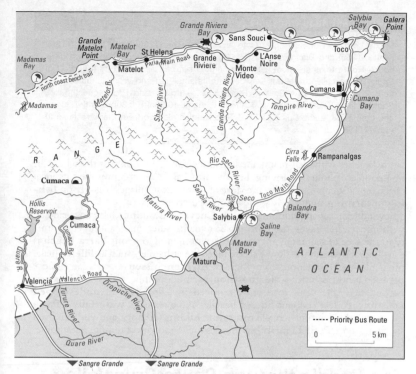

# The Saddle and the North Coast Road

Driving the **Saddle Road** (usually called "the Saddle") makes for one of the region's most scenic journeys, as you climb the western flank of the range dividing Maraval valley from Port of Spain, squeezing through a narrow mountain pass to where it forks, and descend east into lush **Santa Cruz** valley. However, most visitors drive straight past the Saddle turn-off and continue upwards, navigating the coastal fringes of the Northern Range along the **North Coast Road**. Smooth and spectacularly enhanced by the glittering Caribbean coastline and cliffs smothered with tangled jungle, the North Coast Road becomes quite crowded at the weekends when the multitudes descend from nearby Port of Spain heading for **Maracas Bay** and some of the finest **beaches** on the island. Even though it's Trinidad's major concession to sun, sand and sea, Maracas is definitely not a "tourist beach", and like the other seashores in the region, it has more local than foreign devotees soaking up the sun. Nonetheless, the Maracas does represent the island's most **tourist-oriented** region, a ravishing coastline sprinkled with rest stops selling crafts and cold drinks, designated "scenic areas" to stop and admire the view, and miles of

## North Coast Road transport

**Maxis** from Port of Spain City Gate run to Maracas (TT$8), Las Cuevas (TT$9), Filette (TT$9) and Blanchisseuse (TT$15) fairly frequently, especially during peak hours. **Route taxis** are more limited in number but can be picked up from Port of Spain. The excellent rural bus service, with its small red-and-yellow shuttles, runs from Port of Spain City Gate to Blanchisseuse (to Almond Brook guesthouse). Shuttles leave Blanchisseuse at 5.30am, 6.30am, 10.30am, 3.30pm and 7.30pm, and cost TT$8; a short drop is TT$2. The shuttles also go from Blanchisseuse to Arima (TT$8).

sandy beaches with well-maintained facilities. You can whisk past the whole lot in a couple of hours of driving, but the area hasn't yet compromised its local character or succumbed to leisure development; most villages still rely on **fishing** or **farming**, and hotels are few and far between.

Beyond Maracas and shimmering **Las Cuevas**, a beautiful sandy cove riddled with underwater **caves**, the north coast remains quiet, maintaining equanimity in the face of seemingly inevitable development. Gorgeous **Yarra beach** is usually deserted and the slow-paced village life at hamlets such as **Filette** make for a pleasant distraction from the sea. At **Blanchisseuse**, you can choose between a host of small-scale **guesthouses** and a number of rugged beaches; beyond here, the coast road ends, replaced by kilometres of **undeveloped coastline**. Perfect coconut-littered beaches and a series of **waterfalls** – Paria is particularly beautiful – make this prime **hiking** territory, and you can even stay in the area; **Petit Tacarib Bay** houses the island's most remote guesthouse.

# The Saddle through Santa Cruz Valley

Not long after gliding by the last of Maraval's grand residences and St Andrew's Golf Course, the roadside buildings gradually give way to abundant rainforest, and after a succession of hairpin bends, a **junction** is marked by two four-metre high stone pillars. To the left is the **North Coast Road** (see opposite); to the right, **Saddle Road** squeezes through a narrow gorge of solid rock (if driving, beep your horn and approach with caution) before meandering downhill through pastoral **Santa Cruz valley**, a half-hour scenic jaunt through cattle pastures and farmland south towards the EMR and the urban bedlam of San Juan (see p.151).

Following the Saddle through the Valley, neat cocoa groves, crumbling **tapia** houses and dilapidated gingerbread mansions are punctuated by towering samaan trees and impressive clumps of bamboo, mango, sapodilla and banana; unfortunately a thriving nearby **quarrying** concern has gouged messy yellow scars into the hillsides. Cricket legend **Brian Lara** spent his childhood in **Cantaro Village**, about 3 km along the road, the valley's largest community. The place has a friendly, suburban feel, its main focus the lively main street, lined with small restaurants and roti shops, shops, and rum bars, which swings off from Saddle Road. Past the village, the Saddle cuts through the countryside for several beautiful kilometres before the roadside houses of the San Juan suburbs block the views.

A serene Port of Spain satellite cut off from the city and the coast by mountains rather than distance, **San Juan** is the starting point for a hilly but popular **hike** to Maracas Bay along the **La Sagesse trail** – less often attempted are treks to Las Cuevas or the Maracas–St Joseph valley, for which experienced guides are essential to prevent you from getting lost. As the La Sagesse–Maracas Bay route is so heavily travelled, it's pretty easy to follow on your own; however, reports of robberies make it sensible to travel with a group, and preferably with a local guide; see "Basics" p.51 for a list of options. It's a pleasant eight-kilometre, two- to three-hour up-and-down hill walk through secondary forest with good views of the northern coastline on the descent; to get to the start, turn off the Saddle at Gasparillo Road (marked by a signpost for a quarry) and carry straight on, passing the quarry on the right. The hike begins where the houses end; ask for directions to the first stretch of path.

# The North Coast Road to Maracas

Taking the **left turn** at the Saddle-North Coast Road pillars sets you off on one of Trinidad's most dramatic drives, teetering along 300-metre cliffs and tunnelling past precipices of teeming rainforest with the occasional view of faraway peaks swinging into sight. Bois cano trees drop claw-like leaves onto the tarmac and mineral springs pour down into roadside gullies; the water is chilled, delicious and safe to drink, and in places has even been channelled through bamboo pipes at which people stop to fill bottles. Despite its spiralling course, this is also one of the smoothest roads on the island, built by US Army engineers in 1944 as a recompense for the American occupation of the Chaguaramas peninsula (see p.114), which deprived Port of Spain residents of sea bathing at Macqueripe and other western bays. This route to Maracas Bay was offered as the alternative and it's still sometimes called the "American Road".

Looking back, the first of many panoramas stretches over the Maraval valley and across the hills to the tiny spice and parang centre of Paramin (see p.102) and down into the outskirts of Port of Spain, with the sea just visible over Hasley Crawford Stadium and the compacted buildings of Woodbrook and Mucurapo. Cliffs and jungle close in beyond here (though you get a few glimpses of Santa Cruz to the right), but a few kilometres further on, the vegetation dissolves to reveal a marvellous coastal prospect, the ocean far below dotted with rocky islets. The largest of these is **Saut D'eau island**, a 100,000-square-metre breeding colony for brown pelicans and home to the chestnut-collared swift and the rufous-necked wood rail.

## Down to Cyril's Bay

Getting down to the sea isn't easy from this stretch of the road, though; the cliffs are steep and most bays are only reachable by boat. However, if you are prepared to undertake a stiff 20-minute walk, the reward is a secluded dip at the pebble beach of glorious Cyril's Bay, just before the La Vache lookout point. To make the descent, look for a cream-painted board house past which is a road sign saying "slow, sharp bend"; beyond this and a couple more hairpin bends is the overgrown mouth of the path, next to a grassy lay-by where you can park. The agreeably strenuous walk weaves down through balata-dominated evergreen forest humming with bird and animal life. As the path nears the sea, you pass a stone house; if at home, owner Frank welcomes visitors to his menagerie of ducks, geese, dogs and squirrels. You must also pass through his land to get to a three-metre **waterfall** which he has harnessed and dammed – as it's his drinking water, swimming is definitely discouraged. He also guides trips to nearby islands and caves aboard his pirogue; one nearby cavern supports

A small stretch of apparently ordinary tarmac between La Vache and Maracas Bay
has a unique claim to fame; according to local folklore, this is the **"magnetic road"**,
where vehicles roll up the incline in defiance of gravity. Though it cannot be ration-
ally explained, it's easily experienced. Stop just before the North Coast Road begins
its descent to Maracas Bay. As the cliffs to the right recede, revealing the Northern
Range, the road ahead appears to have a definite upward incline. On stopping your
vehicle, putting the gears in neutral and releasing the handbrake, you'd assume that
the car would obey the rules of gravity and roll backwards; however, you move in
what you would imagine to be completely the wrong direction. Although the more
level-headed conclude that this apparent marvel is nothing more than an optical illu-
sion, more romantic locals insist that the contrary movement is the work of God,
obeah (see p.338) or a bizarre magnetic field.

a colony of **oilbirds** (see p.356). Swimming in the bay is pretty safe – the
murkiness of the water is the result of sediment from the River Orinoco rather
than pollution, and there are a couple of offshore rocks that you can dive from.

## La Vache Scenic Area

Past Cyril's Bay, the North Coast Road continues its stomach-lurching cir-
cumnavigation of the cliffs. The route is punctuated by fruit stalls, as well as
refreshment huts, one of the best of which is the brightly painted *Hot Bamboo
Hut*, a friendly roadside stop for soft drinks and coconut candies, though it's
usually only open on weekends; cool breezes and sea views add to its allure.
Tourist trinkets and coconut shell or crystal jewellery are on sale, as are chess
pieces fashioned from shark bones. The air cools noticeably as you climb to **La
Vache Scenic Area**, a viewpoint overlooking the sea from the highest point
on the North Coast Road; the coastal views are marvellous. At weekends, vendors sell fruits and cold drinks to the hordes on their way to Maracas beach,
and likely-looking targets are sometimes serenaded by a resident **busker**, who
improvises calypsos and will expect a few dollars if he makes you laugh.

Below the viewpoint, a precipitous tarmac road leads about 300m down the
cliff to a former cocoa estate house on a secluded bluff. It's a lovely spot, with
magnificent views of Balata Bay to the right and Cyril's to the left, occasional
glimpses of Venezuela, and a **beach** so seldom used it might as well be private.
The house (until recently a hotel) is also the point from which to explore
**Balata Bay**, a pretty beach of coarse sand with two small rivers running into
the ocean; take the concrete path that leads off to the right just before the estate
house, and ask permission from the caretaker who lives on the estate surrounding the bay. There's also a bench trail, or wide footpath, which runs west-
ward back along the coast to Cyril's Bay.

# Maracas Bay

The smell of burning brake linings fills the air as the North Coast Road
plunges toward **MARACAS BAY**, three-quarters of an hour's drive from Port
of Spain. The most popular stretch of shore on the island, this is much more
than a beach – it's an institution. Thousands make the traditional Sunday pilgrimage from Port of Spain to show off their newest swimwear, frolic in the
water and promenade around *the* place to swim, sunbathe, network – and be

seen by everyone else to be doing it in style. Deck chairs, umbrellas, coolers packed with beer or rum and hampers of cooked food are de rigueur, while boogie boards flash through the surf, muscle-men play beach tennis and local lads put on the occasional acrobatics display – if they can find space between the beach accoutrements. The numerous picnic tables covered by coconut leaf-thatched gazebos are ideal lunching spots, but you'll need to get there early on a weekend to find a good one. Maracas Bay is also the island's main Ash Wednesday chill-out site, where revellers come to relax after the mayhem of Carnival, and sound systems keep the prostrated bodies twitching to the beat.

A concrete pillar with silver lettering and silver waves stands in the center of a roundabout, heralding your arrival. The left-hand road leads down to the village while the North Coast Road carries on to the east where you'll find a large car park on the right-hand side for beach goers. Unusually for a Caribbean beach, Maracas is wholeheartedly dedicated to locals rather than tourists, and you'll find yourself sharing the sand with everyone from Port of Spain's fashionable elite to extended families enjoying a day in the sun and spreading out into the grassy area behind the beach for games of football and cricket. On weekdays, however, Maracas Bay is a much quieter place – the sand is almost empty, numerous food outlets are closed, the extensive facilities built by the tourist board look a bit out of place and you might wonder what all the fuss is about.

That said, it remains a beautiful beach. Its long, generous curve of fine off-white sand bordered by groves of skinny-stemmed palm trees is a fantastic place to explore and soak up the sun. Wherever you **swim out to sea** at Maracas Bay, you'll get a sublime view of the beach and its backdrop; cloud-tipped peaks rise up in a majestic swell of deep green, while the forested bluffs funnel breezes on even the hottest of days. Licked into a fury by passing currents and the wind tunnel effect of the surrounding headlands, the waves often reach a metre high and make for an exhilarating swim; the water is usually clear and emerald green. It's never a good idea to go out too far, however, as the tides and undercurrents are often dangerously strong; stick to the areas between red and yellow flags. **Lifeguards** stand by (daily 10am–6pm), whistling furiously at anyone who goes too far out. In addition, the wind, when especially strong, can kick up the sand and blast it against your skin and into your eyes.

If you tire of sun, sand and shark and bake, you can have a go at the energetic two-hour trek across the mountains to St Josephs' valley (see p.153). Ask in the village for start of the trail.

### Practicalities

Built by the tourist board in the mid-1990s, Maracas' **facilities** have transformed the beach and somewhat obscured its beauty; concrete huts interspersed with palm-thatched shade covers are scattered all over the main stretch of sand. The huge car park (TT$10 per entry; you'll get a ticket if you park elsewhere at weekends) has a block of showers, changing rooms and toilets (daily 10am–6pm; TT$1).

**Transport** from Port of Spain to Maracas is erratic. Maxis cost TT$8 but are unreliable on the weekends; most locals travel by private car, and it's not uncommon for people to hitch a ride home with friends they've made during the day; otherwise the roundabout is where to wait for public transport away from the beach. The petrol station at the eastern end of the bay is now closed and derelict, so, if you're driving from Port of Spain make sure you have enough petrol to get back before you set off.

**Accommodation** in the Maracas Bay area is limited. The main option is the imaginatively named *Maracas Bay Hotel* (T669 1914, Wwww.maracasbay.com; ⑥): once a symbol of the grand and modern plans for the beach as a whole, this bland and somewhat run-down hotel at the west end of the bay has rooms with en-suite bathrooms, a/c, and sea facing balconies, but they are also tatty, plain and do not justify the high price. At the western edge of the beach right in the middle of the village's fishing cooperative – where fish is bought and sold – is *Bab's Guesthouse* (T669 4064; ⑤), a bright blue building with a charming elderly owner who rents out a large apartment downstairs consisting of two bedrooms, a lounge, kitchen and bathroom. Sparsely furnished, dark and a bit shabby, it's in a great location nonetheless. You may also be able to rent a room elsewhere in the village if you ask around.

Five minutes' drive east of Maracas Bay between Tyrico and Las Cuevas beaches is the delightful *Oropendola Cottage* (T669 1772; ⑤). Perched above Diamier Bay, this spacious, rustic, wooden two-storey house has two bedrooms, fans, a lounge, a well-equipped kitchen and a lovely sundeck with views of neighbouring Maracas Bay. Set in tropical gardens with mango trees and antherium lilies, and a bath outside serving as a makeshift pond, the cottage is fantastic value for the space and setting – though you'll want a car if don't want to feel cut off. There's also a small bar on the property decorated with oropendola's nests which gets busy on Sundays. Alternatively, the nearby hotel at Las Cuevas (p.137) is a good accommodation option.

When it comes to **eating**, shark and bake is the obvious choice; you'll find it for around TT$12 from multiple takeaway outlets. If you don't fancy shark, some shacks serve kingfish instead, or you can easily find aloo and fish pies or roti and veggie bake. As the long queues and filled tables hint, *Richard's* and *Natalie's*, both in the car park, are two of the top choices. Most places close down at around 6pm, although *Richard's* stays open later and serves a hearty flying fish and fries for TT$10 into the night.

The only real option for a sit-down evening meal is the *Bandanya* restaurant at the *Maracas Bay Hotel* (see above). More pleasant than the rest of the hotel, the food is moderately priced, and the extensive menu includes fish creole (TT$69), chicken and chips (TT$55) and a few vegetarian options.

If you just want an evening drink there is a small bar at the hotel, while on the beach, alcohol is sold by most of the shark and bake vendors. At the eastern end of the bay is *Uncle Sam's* bar and grocery store (closed Mon), with its brightly coloured outside seating, and a sound system pumping reggae and soca over the sand. The only other option is the *Bay View* bar on the headland west of the bay just before Morro Point.

## Maracas Bay Village

To the west of the bay, a river divides the bathing area from **Maracas Bay Village**, a fishing hamlet whose catch is in demand throughout the north; super-fresh carite, cavalli, shark and "small fry" are sold here once the boats return in the afternoon. Here you'll find a couple of snack parlour-cum-rum bars, a small grocery store, post office, a loose arrangement of houses, lots of beached pirogues and drying nets and a very pretty cream-and-blue church set back from the road next door to the *Maracas Bay Hotel*. The village is also home to a profusion of scavenging dogs and fewer bathers; most stick to the main beach to avoid the odd fishy entrail. It is possible to join local fishermen aboard their pirogues for a day or night for a couple of hundred dollars, but make sure you've got your sea legs before setting out.

## The North's best beaches

Blanchisseuse p.142
Grande Riviere p.171
Las Cuevas p.137

Maracas p.134
Paria p.146
Toco p.169

**②**

**THE NORTH** | Las Cuevas Bay and around

## Tyrico Bay and Diamier Bay

Hidden from Maracas Bay by a steep headland, **TYRICO BAY** is about one kilometre east. The entrance can be found on the left hand side of the North Coast Road, two hairpin bends after Maracas Bay and marked by a black and white pole. Popular with the Indian community who flock here for weekend picnics, family beach cricket tournaments and camp-outs, the bay is roughly half the size of Maracas with slightly less in the way of wave action, making it a better choice if you are travelling with children. There's also a small lagoon on the west side of the beach for very safe paddling. Luxuriant, fine yellow sand and a gentle shelf add to the feeling of calm, and as there are no food and drink vendors, Tyrico is quieter and more unspoiled than its neighbour. The only buildings are the lifeguard towers (guards are on duty daily 10am–6pm) and portable toilets, and you can drive right down to the sand.

Even quieter is the isolated beach at **DIAMIER BAY**, a few minutes' drive, or half an hour's walk, east from Maracas Bay, just past Tyrico Bay. Just a few metres after the turnoff from the North Coast Road, the lane divides and drops steeply down to the bay on the right (don't drive down, though, as there's no room to turn around at the bottom). The small, pebbly beach has a sheltered bit of sand on its far side, overlooked by the houses perched high on the hill above; the sea in front of you is calm and practically windless. Bring your own food and drink as there are no facilities.

# Las Cuevas Bay and around

After an inland curve that provides impressive views of the jagged double apex of Mount El Tucuche, Trinidad's second highest mountain (see p.154), the North Coast Road turns back to the sea at **Las Cuevas Bay**, the north coast's longest and second most popular strip of sand after Maracas, with a fishing village spreading uphill to the east of the beach. A ten-minute drive from Maracas Bay and still an easy day trip from Port of Spain, Las Cuevas is less of a fashion parade at the weekends than Maracas, and during the week it's often deserted, although the fishing community is still very active. So far, the locals have managed to resist large-scale development on this wide, clean and unadorned swathe of whitish sand, fringed by coconut palms and inviting green sea. It is surrounded by headlands which enclose the bay in a tight horseshoe and provide protection from the wind and a relatively gentle surf. Keep in mind, though, that the legendary **sandfly** population, a particular problem in the late afternoon or after rain, can make for unpleasant sunbathing – take repellent and try to cover up as the day wears on. Named by the Spanish after the caves that riddle the rocks to the west end of the bay as well as the seabed, Las Cuevas offers better swimming than Maracas and is a great place for beachcombing, especially along the seldom-visited western reaches, littered with shells and stones.

△ Football on the beach at Las Cuenas

## Practicalities

For getting to Las Cuevas by **public transport**, maxis and route taxis are the easiest and best option. Maxis cost TT$9 from Port of Spain, while route taxis are a couple of TT$ extra. Since buses are set up for commuters to Port of Spain, they tend not to be as good an option for a shorter trip to the beach.

Though there's no development on the beach itself, there is a large car park above the bay (free), as well as changing rooms, showers, toilets and a first aid room (10am–6pm; TT$1). Lifeguards patrol and put out yellow and red flags to mark safe bathing spots (daily 10am–6pm). If you're **hungry**, head to the western edge of the car park and try *McLean's* bar, a favourite with local fishermen, serving budget-priced Creole breakfasts and lunches alongside beer and rum; in addition to the ubiquitous roti, wild meat including manicou, iguana or agouti is on offer if you ask in advance. There are usually vendors on the beach selling coconuts, as well. The *Las Cuevas Rec Club*, to the right on the North Coast Road before the bay, is a low-key **drinking** spot; they also sell pholouri and aloo pies.

*Las Cuevas Beach Lodge* (☎669 6945, ⓦwww.lascuevasbeachlodge.com; ❻), an appealing, brand-new hotel precariously balanced on a ridge above the beach, is the only **place to stay** in Las Cuevas, and an excellent base from which to explore the whole stretch of coastline. All of the lodge's comfortable rooms have tiled floors, en-suite bathrooms, a/c and great views of either the beach or the hills behind. The attractive wooden terrace bar and *Bougainvillea* restaurant, decorated with fairy lights and fishing nets and overlooking the peninsula, serves a good range of dishes, from fish curry (TT$65) to reef and beef ($230). If you want to **camp** in the area, you're pretty much limited to the beach itself.

## One Thousand Steps Beach

On the eastern outskirts of Las Cuevas, you'll find the secluded **One Thousand Steps Beach**, so-called because of the seemingly endless concrete steps which wind down the cliffs to the sand. Easily missed, ideal for a secluded swim and popular with local fishermen, this curve of soft, greyish sand is backed by almond trees – one growing horizontally over the sand – and a few **manchineels**, which should be treated with caution (see p.26). At the eastern end, the sea has pounded a lookout hole through the rocks, and you can climb over boulders at the western corner to another deserted bay. Though the water is often glassily smooth, you should be careful when swimming here, keeping to a depth you can stand in – the tides can be strong even on apparently calm days, and there's no one to help if you encounter problems.

To find the beach, turn down Mitchell's Trace, a dirt track opposite the larger Rincon Trace, which strikes inland from the North Coast Road a kilometre or so east of Las Cuevas. The latter is also the route to spectacular **Rincon Waterfall** and pools, a two-and-a-half-hour uphill walk through the bush. You'll need a guide to find this and nearby **Angel Falls**, though the latter is often dry or filled in by small landslides. Laurence Pierre, a guide at Hikeseekers (see p.162), knows the area intimately. East of Las Cuevas is **Fort Abercromby**; a small, aged French fort whose wooden structure has deteriorated. There's now little to see apart from the cannons marking the headland, but the small beach is good for snorkelling.

## Filette and Yarra

As you take the North Coast Road past Chupura Point, with its new and expanding cluster of private homes, beach houses and holiday villas, it narrows and becomes increasingly potholed before entering the fishing village of **FILETTE**, about 5km from Las Cuevas, an improbably pretty cluster of neat houses and blooming front gardens straddled over two hillocks. A parlour in the centre of town (opposite a phonecard booth) sells groceries and snacks, while a rum bar on the western outskirts is good for watching the world go by with a "beastly" cold beer or for gossiping with the fishermen about the rumoured **contraband** landing spots on this part of coast.

Beyond the village, after a long, straight stretch of road, traffic is forced to slow down to cross a rickety plank bridge over one of the **Yarra River's** many strands. There are four smaller plank bridges to cross before the road passes through a teak plantation (teak is slowly replacing coffee and coco crops and may offer the area a renewable resource), after which you enter **YARRA**, a rather deserted hamlet made up of grand beach houses. Look out for a grassy turn-off towards the sea, the only one not leading to a house; this goes to **Yarra Beach**, another perfect, deserted seashore. Wide and sweeping, with white sand fine enough to remain on your limbs long after a shower, Yarra has two main bays which shift in size and shape according to the season. Offshore is a rock painted with the legend "Yaradise Bay", and, as you're likely to have the whole place to yourself, it's not difficult to imagine that you really are in Eden. Another Yarra River tributary runs down to the sea, and is sometimes deep enough so that one can white-water body surf right into the ocean, where the water is pleasantly active and clear. As always on this coast, take care while swimming and be sensible if you feel strong tides. About 30m past the entrance to the beach, look out for another offshore rock on which the word "**hollyweed**" has been painted in foot-high letters – an allusion to the bales of marijuana which are said to be imported and exported from these beaches.

# Blanchisseuse

The five-minute drive along the narrow, jungle-lined stretch of the North Coast Road from Yarra passes by a number of new houses, mainly holiday homes for wealthy Trinidadians, before bringing you back to the coast and into **BLANCHISSEUSE** (pronounced "blaan-she-shers"), which is the last village before the road trails off into the bush. With a population of around three thousand, Blanchisseuse isn't exactly a hamlet, and the clutch of ever-growing flashy holiday homes on the western outskirts – some garish, some tasteful – are testament to its popularity as a retreat. Even so it's still pretty quiet; the atmosphere is relaxed and supremely friendly, and there are as many local holidaymakers as there are foreign. During the weekends the beaches bustle with activity and an increasing number of visitors, including many day-trippers from Port of Spain, which is an easy drive away. Tourists divide their time between visiting the succession of marvellous sandy **beaches**, and hiring a local guide and hiking through the rainforest for river swimming in the unpolluted waters of nearby **Three Pools**, or sights further afield on the Arima–Blanchisseuse Road (see p.147).

**Maxis and taxis** to Blanchisseuse are somewhat sparse, with only a small, though increasing, number continuing east from Las Cuevas. Taxis for Blanchisseuse (TT$16) from Port of Spain leave from the corner of George and Prince streets. Maxis (TT$15) leave from City Gate as does the rural **bus service**, clustered around peak hours. Buses from Blanchisseuse to Arima and Port of Spain run early in the morning and late in the afternoon for commuters (TT$8 to Port of Spain). The maxis are marked with yellow bands and have "North Coast" written on them (TT$20); there are also three pale blue mini buses which ply the route, but are not properly licensed (TT$15).

## Accommodation

While Blanchisseuse has the greatest number of **rooms** along this part of the coast, it's still wise to book ahead if visiting on weekends or national holidays when Trinidadians come down for a bit of rest and relaxation. All the guest-houses are small scale; tucked away at the very end of the road, *Laguna Mar* is the largest with twelve rooms, but the rest of the guesthouses strung along the North Coast Road, primarily in the more lively upper village, are all good options. If you've got a tent – or even just a piece of tarpaulin, the local material of choice – you can **camp** on the beach at the *Marianne Beach Resort* for TT$30 per tent; this includes the use of toilets, showers and rather lax security protection.

**Almond Brook** North Coast Rd ⊕ 669 5456, ⓦ www.lagunamar.com. By far the most atmospheric place in the upper village, its wood-panelled rooms decorated with shells and plants; all have mosquito nets, private bathroom and queen-size bed; one has a full kitchen, the others fridges. Breakfast is included in the rates, and the extremely genial owner also rents a two-bedroom beach house in its own garden with a verandah and full amenities. **⑤**

**Laguna Mar** ⊕ 669 2963 or 628 3731, ⓕ 628 3737, ⓦ www.lagunamar.com. The most established hotel in Blanchisseuse, *Laguna Mar* takes pride of place at the end of the north coast road with its own access to Marianne Beach. The rooms are on the inland side of the road, housed in blocks of six with a lovely communal balcony; each has two double beds, fans and private bathroom. Free boogie boards are available for guests and the German/Trinidadian owners are well-known local figures and great hosts. They also have a 3-bedroom villa to rent. **⑤**

**Northern Sea View Villa** North Coast Rd and Wilson Trace ⊕ 669 3995, ⓔ elope@tstt.net.tt. The least expensive option in town, these two basic apartments offer little in the way of luxury, but the location opposite Marianne Beach is great and the owners are extremely friendly. Both apartments have two bedrooms, as well as a fan, kitchen, verandah and living room. Excellent if in a group or on a budget. **④**

**North Star View** North Coast Rd ⊕ 637 7619 or 4619. Owned by the same family as *Northern Sea View*, this spacious yellow villa, on the hill before the road descends to Marianne Beach, has clean, basic rooms with a shared bathroom or a self-contained studio apartment with wooden floors, double bed, kitchenette with microwave and a constant sea breeze from the balcony. **❼**

**Second Spring on the Sea** LP191, Paria Main Rd ⊕ 669 3909, ⓕ 638 7393, ⓦ www.geocities.com/secondspringtnt. Small bed and breakfast which have friendly owners and is close to the beach. The nicely decorated rooms have fan, mosquito nets and kitchenette. There is also a cottage for rent. **⑤**

**Surf's Country Inn** North Coast Rd ⊕ 669 2475, ⓕ 669 3016. Precipitously placed above the surfers' beach, this attractive hotel has three double rooms and one suite which are great value, attractive and fully mosquito-screened, with terra-cotta floor tiles, fridge, fan, nice bathroom and verandah or terrace. The on-site restaurant is excellent (see p.144); rates include breakfast. **❸–❹**

**Vista Del Mar** North Coast Rd ⊕ 662 7534, ⓕ 663 1454. A coolly attractive blue and white building overlooking the surfer's beach; two self-contained apartments with rattan furnishings, a/c, full kitchen, living room and a verandah with great sea views, while bedrooms and bathrooms are suitably luxurious. There's a sundeck, hammock-dotted gazebo and barbecue pit on the lawn below – meals available on request. **⑤**

Another accommodation option is the wonderfully secluded **forest lodge** at Petit Tacaribe, a half-hour boat journey or four-hour walk east along the Bench Trail from Blanchisseuse. Stephen Broadbridge of Caribbean Discovery Tours (see p.146), can organize all transport and accommodation and help with an itinerary.

## The village

**Lower Blanchisseuse** to the west is the older portion of the village, an attractive assortment of weather-beaten board houses and crumbling tapias wreathed by rambling bougainvillea and neat croton hedges. Steep cliffs plunge down to the ocean, while breaks in the palms or almond trees reveal the white-tipped waves of the intensely blue sea below. The small village atmosphere is reinforced by a couple of rum bars, a fishermen's co-operative building, a post office (Mon–Sat 8am–4pm) and a boxy, single-spired Catholic **church** overlooking the sea, complete with three bells housed in an outdoor tower. In this dozing place, young men watch as a vehicle passes by, octogenarians while away the hours in front of the bars and chickens pick for scraps in the middle of the tarmac.

**Upper Blanchisseuse** begins after the Paria Main Road descends the hill and loops inland to meet the Arima–Blanchisseuse Road (see p.147). This is the main residential section of Blanchisseuse, dominated by the attractive arched windows and blue porticoes of the Georgian-style **police station**. General stores and pastel-painted homes cluster by the roadside, while residential streets trail uphill into the bush. Behind the police station is the community centre and a playing field which sees some serious football in the late afternoon. A small roadside restaurant, *Wayside Hut,* has a nice gazebo to sit in and watch the world go by. Further up opposite *Almond Brook* guesthouse is Bob's Artistic Creations, which sells beautifully carved walking sticks, masks, mirror frames and wall hangings made from calabashes and poui, cedar and mahogany.

Past the shop, buildings start to thin out, apart from the odd luxury beach house, and another downhill stretch brings the North Coast Road to sea level, running parallel to Marianne beach, the town's largest (see opposite). The last building is the *Cocos Hut* restaurant (see p.144); beyond here, the road runs parallel to the Marianne River lagoon, a popular swimming spot, to the **Orange Suspension Bridge** which straddles the water and is a popular place to dive from. Over the bridge, the road carries on for a short way past a development of new houses on the left hand side. It then becomes little more than a rutted dirt track which you can drive on for another kilometre or two (not recommended in the rainy season), but otherwise, the only means of progressing east to Paria and beyond is on foot (see p.145).

## Blanchisseuse beaches

Like most beaches on this section of coastline, those of **Blanchisseuse** are ruggedly beautiful. However, while it's unlikely that you'll be swept away during your first dip, they do have a reputation for rough and **treacherous waters**, particularly between November and February when mighty breakers crash onto the sand and the surfers come into their element. Whatever the time of year, it's wise to ask local advice before taking the plunge, and to keep at a depth you can stand in.

The first of Blanchisseuse's **three main beaches** can be reached via a walkway opposite *Surf's Country Inn*. Popular with crowds of sun-bronzed surfers, the beach has been locally renamed in their honour as **surfer's beach**; its true name – **L'Anse Martin** – is seldom used, though it is marked as such on the sign. The seashore here is wide and open with an almost imperceptible shelf that makes for excellent waves. Craggy rocks border each end and the forest drips down from the cliffs onto the sand. It's also popular for a spot of late afternoon **fishing**, with anglers casting lines from the water's edge.

The second main beach is accessible by an easy path next to the fishermen's co-operative in the lower village. This fishermen's beach is a better place to lime and admire the view rather than swim, since the measly pebble shore is littered with dead boats and straddled by a half-built wooden jetty; the concrete foundations of the unbuilt portion are gradually being eroded by the surf. Just 50m further down the road, though, down some steps marked by a broken sign atop a green pole, is a marvellous bathing beach, with around 200m of soft grey sand and a completely secluded feeling. Headlands provide protection and gentle waves, while almonds and sea grapes tangle down the cliffs. Watch out for a few offshore rocks while swimming.

**Marianne** is the longest and most popular beach in Blanchisseuse, stretching around 2km from the busiest portion of the upper village, where concrete steps lead down to the sand, right to the *Cocos Hut* restaurant (see p.144) and the river lagoon at the end of the North Coast Road. It's a completely breathtaking seashore, wide and straight with yellow sand battered by crashing waves and awe-inspiring views of the uninhabited coast beyond – the perfect place to watch the moon rising over the headlands from the east. At the eastern end is a huge, vegetation-smothered boulder; past this, the clear Marianne river water is partially dammed by the ever shifting sands into a **lagoon** – an inviting place to swim, particularly if the sea looks rough. Watch out however for the mosquitos which gather around the water towards the end of the day. Locals tend to congregate at the lagoon for an after-work bathe or cricket match, and fishermen paddle rough canoes in search of freshwater salmon.

The owners of the *Laguna Mar* resort (see p.141) have cut a path through the swampland which divides the eastern portion of the beach from the road, and put in a couple of benches. There are showers and toilets at a sandy car park grandly named the *Marianne Beach Resort* (TT$5), 100m or so west of the *Laguna Mar* entrance. You can pitch a tent here for TT$30 and park your car for TT$10. There is also a small **café** here which sells soft drinks and snacks – you'll have to get there early on a weekend to find a seat at one of the handful of tables outside.

## Marianne River and Three Pools

Spanned by the **Orange Suspension Bridge** – graceful and still solid despite its hundred-plus years – the **Marianne River** is the source of much local recreation, as well as the village's name: dating from French Creole times, "Blanchisseuse" refers to the laundresses who once washed clothing in the river. Regular buses of **bird-watchers** park up at a lay-by to the side of the bridge to see the green woodpeckers, yellow orioles and silvered antbirds that congregate here.

The Marianne itself is a typical Northern Range watercourse, originating at Brasso Seco (see p.148) and tumbling downhill, carving deep swimming pools and waterfalls along the way. You can take a watery trek south along the riverbed to **Three Pools**, an hour or so from the mouth of the Marianne. Most people hire a guide in the village to lead the way and draw attention to the abundant plant, bird and animal life, but it's a fairly straightforward route that you can follow independently if you wish. Following the riverbed is the fastest way to get there, the journey being a combination of splashing through calf- (and sometimes waist-) deep water and swimming (sticking to the banks takes a lot longer), so don't carry anything that can't get wet. To reach the pools by yourself, take the path into the woods to the right of the road just before the bridge (the "No Entry" sign is universally ignored); you meet the water after five minutes. Overhung by vines, ferns and huge buttress-rooted trees, it's a gorgeous and easy wade, bar the odd overhanging bank. Though the water deepens to form several enticing swimming pools along the way, the stunning Three Pools easily surpass any of the other swimming spots.

The first of the three, around 12m across, is the least impressive, though it does have a **water-slide** of sorts, formed by the current coursing through a narrow channel in the rock. Passing over the smooth, grey rock which forms the first pool, you'll find the second one, with huge boulders rising out of water so deep you'll find it difficult to touch the bottom. A second gushing channel creates a **natural jacuzzi**. The third pool is the most impressive, despite being the smallest. Overhung by tall cliffs, the water here has carved the rock into bizarre folds and small caves you can swim into and climb up to see the waterfall above.

To go beyond this point to the spectacular and isolated **Avocat Falls**, you'll need a guide; almost everyone in the village knows the way, or you can go with jovial Eric Blackman, owner of *Northern Sea View Villa* (see p.141). He leads a two-hour trip to Three Pools that includes kayaking, hiking and swimming (TT$80 per person), an all-day tour of the Avocat Falls (TT$50) and a four-hour walk to Paria (TT$50). Eric also rents kayaks on the beach by the river mouth ($TT20 for 30min), and for TT$10 he'll take an instant photograph of you on the beach.

## Eating and drinking

Blanchisseuse has a good but limited selection of low-key **restaurants**, most of which offer a choice of meat, fish or vegetarian dishes. You should, however, give advance notice (at breakfast time) for dinner as many kitchens cook to order or close early. Prices are moderate – expect to pay around TT$100 for dinner.

Grandest are the **hotel restaurants**, such as *Cocos Hut* (☎628 3731), a converted cocoa drying house across the road from *Laguna Mar*. Owned by the charming Fred Zollna, the restaurant is decorated with an appealing mix of memorabilia from his home country of Germany and his travels while a US marine and afterwards in the Caribbean. This intimate eatery with indoor and outdoor seating is great for a sit-down meal at any time of the day. Moderately priced dinners consist of tasty, local-style fish, chicken, beef or pork, though vegetarians are catered for – ask in advance as there are no printed menus and all dishes are cooked to order. The bar is especially nice for an evening drink, its end-of-the-road location and regular clientele providing a sense of cosy isolation.

Another option for semi-upmarket dining is the lovely open-air restaurant at *Surf's Country Inn* (☎669 2554), beautifully located on a boardwalk overlooking the sea and shaded by silk cotton boughs. The primarily seafood-based menu is inexpensive and innovative; they also do breakfast and lunch. In the upper village, try *Gilbert's*, a shack perched on the cliff by a bend in the road with a couple of tables overlooking the sea. Their breakfasts of bake and scrambled egg, bacon or cheese sandwiches, and lunches or dinners of stew or jerk chicken, peas, vegetables and potatoes with onions are all tasty and relatively cheap. Just before *Surf's Country Inn*, *Wayside*, a small takeaway, serves inexpensive sweetbread, guara and other snacks.

Blanchisseuse tends to quiet down early, but as the locals still need to lime and unwind at the end of a day's work, the **rum shops** are fairly lively after dark, particularly on a weekend. In the lower village, *Casbah* is a classic Trinidadian drinking hole with a pool table, dim lights, a verandah for catching the breeze and "no bareback, spitting on the floor or obscene language" notices painted on to the walls. The *Butterfly Rec Club*, behind the playing field in the upper village, is more or less the same, bedecked with coloured fairy lights.

# East of Blanchisseuse: the north coast bench trail

Beyond Blanchisseuse, the North Coast Road gives way to the only remaining piece of **undeveloped coastline** in Trinidad. The next piece of tarmac is some 30km to the east in Matelot (see p.174); in between, you'll find some of Trinidad's most impressive **hiking** along a **bench trail** (the local name for the old donkey tracks cut in the late nineteenth century for transporting goods and produce between the villages and servicing the then-thriving cocoa estates). Well-trodden, the trail dips and climbs through the remnants of abandoned estates and secondary forest, with the sea swinging spectacularly in and out of view.

There are periodic government proposals to construct a **road** along this stretch of the coast, but environmental groups and landowners (most of the coast is in private hands) have so far successfully lobbied against the idea. While most agree that it's only a matter of time before tarmac is laid through the forest, the area remains a sanctuary for bird and animal life, and many of the beaches are prime laying spots for the **leatherback turtle** (see p.354).

Though few attempt it, you can hike the bench trail all the way from Blanchisseuse to Matelot, but only the fittest could hope to complete the journey in a day. Most make the trip in two stages, camping in the bush along the way. Though the trail is easy to follow, it is not a good idea to walk in this area alone; it's remote enough to make getting help difficult if you run into trouble, and reports of drug smuggler landings at deserted bays suggest that you may feel safer if accompanied by a guide (and his/her cutlass). If you prefer a solitary hike, do so during the week; Saturdays, Sundays and public holidays are prime times for local hiking groups or individual ramblers to take to the bush.

## Blanchisseuse to Paria Bay

The most often-attempted hike from Blanchisseuse is the moderately challenging round-trip trek to **Paria Bay** and its inland **waterfall**, which you can do in a couple of hours at a good pace, though most stop to admire the scenery and make a day of it. Past the Orange Suspension Bridge (see p.142), the track passes beach houses for the first couple of kilometres; an uphill fork makes an attractive if unnecessary detour, bringing you back to the main trail after a few minutes. Logging vehicles have widened the bench trail in some parts, and as a result it can get muddy in the rainy season, but little can detract from the marvellous forest around: look out for massive bachac nests and a splendid specimen of the weird **cannonball tree**, with its heavily perfumed, rotund pink flowers and dangling, twisted branches which sprout five-centimetre-wide brown "cannonballs" from the base of the trunk to the main boughs. There is a constant accompaniment of birdsong, though the soothing calls are often shattered by the raucous shriek of passing parrots.

### Alternative routes to Paria

There are a variety of **ways to get to Paria** other than the trek detailed above. You can hike to Paria Bay and waterfall from Brasso Seco (see p.148), but you'll need a guide. Caribbean Discovery Tours ($US75; ☎624 7281, ⦿www.caribbean discoverytours.com) organize tours, or contact Carl Fitz-James Jnr (☎667 5968), who lives in Brasso Seco. Alternatively, local fishermen are often willing to take you by boat. Ask at your hotel or around town.

## Petit Tacaribe

*Petit Tacaribe* is undoubtedly the **most unusual resort in Trinidad**, a magical and completely secluded place, drenched in natural beauty and comprised of three cedar-framed bamboo cabanas and a cooking shed overlooking the bay (c/o Stephen Broadbrisge 9b Fondes Amendes Rd, St Ann's, Port of Spain; ☎624 7281, Ⓦwww.caribbeandiscoverytours.com; Ⓖ). Rates cover all meals (though you should bring any extras – beer, rum, chocolate, etc) and transport, including boats and excursions into the forest. Most people get there via boat from Blanchisseuse (organized by the *Tacaribe* owners), which costs TT$200 each way and takes about half an hour; six people and their baggage can cram in, but you can always hike if you're feeling hardy. Leatherbacks lay eggs on the sand during the March–June season, and as the surrounding bush is well-stocked with agouti, armadillo, manicou and quenk, you may get wild meat for dinner. Days are spent lazing on the beach or in the hammocks, hiking to Madamas, hunting in the bush or bird-watching, and if you like the natural life, this is a chance in a million.

Depending upon your pace, you'll reach Paria Bay about two to three hours after leaving Blanchisseuse. The **beach** is an idyllic 1km of fine, coconut-littered golden sand with a true *Treasure Island*-style background jungle and groves of palms. Other than a fisherman's shelter, it's completely undisturbed, with craggy grey rocks out to sea and a river at the eastern end; the high headland above is **Paria Point**. A cliff at the western corner has been eroded at the base to form an arch. Swimming is safe and the waves are usually moderate. If you want to press on to the **waterfall**, walk two-thirds of the way up the beach and head inland at the track. The path, through anthurium lilies and forest, meets the Paria River, which brings you to the waterfall in about fifteen minutes. At the waterfall, crystal clear and freezing cold spring water crashes down the 5-metre cascade into a deep swimming pool around 10m across. While you should always start your hike with a full bottle of water, you can drink from the safe and pure streams along the way.

## Paria Bay to Matelot

Past Paria Bay, the bench trail is less well-travelled and a little more overgrown. After ten minutes' walk, you come to another attractive beach, **Murphy Bay**. You can carry on up the coast from here to **Petit** and **Grande Tacarib bays**; the walk to Petit Tacarib will take around an hour and a half. Both have marvellous sandy beaches and are separated by half an hour's walk and the inexplicably named **Trou Bouilli-Riz Point**; from here, it's a six-hour walk back to civilization at Matelot.

Another hour and a half east from Grande Tacarib along the bench trail through jungle will bring you to **Madamas Bay**, a curve of deserted off-white sand which rivals Paria in beauty. Half an hour inland from the beach is another gorgeous cataract, **Madamas waterfall**, though you'll need a guide to find it. However, if you want to see the area without straining your muscles, you can arrange to **stay** at the forest lodge at **Petit Tacaribe** (see box above), but as preparing for guests is time-consuming, the resort only takes groups of four or more, preferably for stays longer than four days.

# The Arima–Blanchisseuse Road

Inland from Blanchisseuse, the **Arima–Blanchisseuse Road** cuts south through the middle of the steamy Northern Range forest, climbing high into misty, breeze-cooled peaks and descending to the **Asa Wright Nature Centre**, one of the Caribbean's finest birdwatching sites. The sharply winding, potholed and generally ill-kept road is not for the faint of heart, but the payoff is tremendous. Small villages like **Morne La Croix** and **Brasso Seco** seem contentedly stuck in a time warp, and make excellent starting points for exploring the **waterfalls** that course through the mountains. Light filtering through the overhanging canopies of mahogany, teak, poui, cedar and immortelle colours the tunnel-like road green, and every available surface is smothered in plant life: mosses, ferns and lichens cover rocks and tree trunks already laden with massive wild pine bromeliads, and vines and monkey's ladder lianas trail down to the tarmac. Just as dense as the vegetation is the sound of the manic calls of crested oropendolas and bearded bellbirds echoing across the peaks.

Wet and humid, the first portion of road from Blanchisseuse to Asa Wright is carpeted with composting leaves. A succession of hairpin bends sets a slow pace as the road begins a gentle climb up from the coast, each quarter mile marked by a roadside post, remnants of English control of the island. Just before the twenty-and-a-quarter mile marker, look out for a neat grove of pommerac trees to the left; here, a track leads past a few modest dwellings and provision grounds to the **Avocat Falls**. After a ten-minute walk, you reach a river (a tributary of the Marianne); turn left and walk along the banks or the shallow riverbed for twenty minutes until you reach a watery junction. Wade across the river and grab hold of one of the roots that wreathe the steep bank. Haul yourself up, and straight in front of you is a pretty 12-metre cascade with a deep pool below; there are even some vines for swinging on. Local guides are available to help you explore the area – contact the Paria Springs Eco-community (see p.148).

## Morne La Croix

South of Avocat Falls, the Arima–Blanchisseuse Road climbs a steep hill before entering the tiny hamlet of **MORNE LA CROIX**, a picturesque village about 7km from Blanchisseuse where most of the inhabitants still speak French Creole as well as Trini English. Development comes slow in the middle of the Northern Range; when the government planned to install electricity poles in 1996, there was much debate over whether the villagers wanted a current at all. Apart from a small general store there is nowhere to buy food and drink in Morne La Croix. Just beyond the town, look for a hedge of purple-flowered vervain, a favourite haunt of yellow-breasted ruby-topaz **hummingbirds** and the red-crested tufted coquette. There are some impressive views of the mountains below here, too, and you're more or less guaranteed to see **bird life** wherever you stop; the spectacular metre-long, teardrop-shaped nests of the crested oropendola are commonplace. As the road climbs ever higher, you pass a lookout point adjacent to a dirt road called Andrew's Trace. A break in the forest and an elevation of just over 600m provides chilly breezes and sweeping views across the valleys, with the sea just visible if the mists haven't set in; above you can often see hawks coasting on the thermal updraughts as they scan the bush for food.

# Brasso Seco

The only sizeable village between Morne La Croix and Arima is **BRASSO SECO**. Named after the term for a dry branch in reference to the fact that the surrounding area has never been cultivated and remains virgin rainforest, the community is tucked away at the end of a signposted turn-off from the Arima-Blanchisseuse Road, about 3km beyond Morne La Croix. A ten-minute drive east past converted cocoa houses and still-occupied tapia houses brings you into the village's main street, where there's a rum shop-parlour, a church, a school and an overwhelmingly languorous atmosphere. Kids play cricket in the middle of the road, young men lime outside the rec club and everyone has time to greet each other with an exchange or a wave.

There are some lovely walks in the area; naturalist Courtenay Rooks of the Paria Springs Eco-community (☎622 8826, ⓦwww.pariasprings.com) guides **nature hikes** and **birdwatching trips** from their base, a ten-minute drive from the centre of the village. These include a difficult hike up Morne Bleu to see virgin rainforest and blue-capped tanagers, a birdwatching tour along the Paria/Arima/Blanchisseuse Road, and a leisurely stroll to the Madamas Waterfalls whilst butterfly- and birdwatching – he also does the latter on mountain bikes for US$50. Rates vary from US$35 for a half-day tour to up to US$85 for some full day trips. Individual itineraries can be created to suit visitors' requirements and mountain bikes can be rented for US$10 per day. For more details on his island-wide tours, see p.162.

There are a number of **host homes** in the Brasso Seco area, all of which offer a fabulously tranquil setting in which to while away a few days and cost US$25 per person per night, plus US$5 for breakfast, and US$10 for lunch or for dinner – you're best off taking the meal options, as there's nowhere to buy food hereabouts (contact Paria Springs Eco-community for booking and details, see above). Airport transfers can be arranged for US$25. As most of the host homes have been converted from private houses, facilities vary enormously. *Peña Blanca*, an old cocoa house high in the hills with wonderful views over the valleys and an outside porch for barbecues, is one of the most attractive. The four bedrooms all have double beds, and there are two bathrooms, a kitchen and living room. Tucked into the hillside, *Paria Heights Mountain View* is an equally good choice, with basic but serviceable bedrooms featuring mosquito nets, and a shared kitchen, bathroom and living room.

# Asa Wright Nature Centre and around

A birdwatcher's paradise situated inside the 800,000 square-metre Spring Hill estate, the **Asa Wright Nature Centre** (PO Box 4710, Arima, Trinidad; ☎667 4655 or in the US 1-800/426 7781, ⓔasawright@tstt.net.tt, ⓦwww.asawright

.org; ❻–❼) was originally a coffee, citrus and cocoa plantation. In 1947 it was bought by Dr Newcome Wright and his Icelandic wife, Asa. Both were keen amateur naturalists and bird-watchers, so when the New York Zoological Society set up the Simla Tropical Research Station on neighbouring land in 1949, the couple began to accommodate visiting researchers. After her husband died, Mrs Wright sold the land on condition it remained a **conservation area**; a nonprofit-making trust was set up in 1967, which established a nature centre to accommodate naturalists and birdwatchers, a first in the Caribbean. Simla closed in 1970, but donated its land and the research station to the centre – botanists and ornithologists still study here.

Today, Asa Wright is Trinidad's most popular **birdwatching retreat**. This nonprofit organization revolves around its nearly century-old **great house**, a maze of polished mahogany floors, stately heirlooms and antique furniture with a **verandah** overlooking the spectacular Arima valley. At 360m above sea level, the views of the rainforest are incredible, and since Mrs Wright began feeding them in the 1950s, the verandah has attracted a huge variety of **birds**; you can see up to forty species per day. If you're not staying at the centre itself but still wish to do some birdwatching, it's a good idea to get there before 10am to avoid the rush. Face-level feeders on the great house's verandah attract dazzlingly colorful, thumb-sized hummingbirds, and trays of fruit below are gorged upon by green- and red-legged honeycreepers, blue-grey tanagers and white-bearded or golden-headed manakins. There are also a large number of the ever-present and precocious bananaquits, not to mention a host of more sporadic visitors. Matte lizards and agoutis clear up the scraps, and the surrounding trees glitter with the brightly coloured feathers of nesting and roosting birds: rufous-tailed jacamars, toucans, mot-mots, woodpeckers, trogons, yellow orioles and the yellow-tailed crested oropendola, which nests in a bois cano tree to the left of the verandah. The multitude of birds that flock about the Asa Wright's great house attracts daily crowds of birdwatchers, the low murmur of voices broken by the excited squeals of an unusual sighting, or by the whirr and click of paparazzi-standard zoom lenses.

A network of well-marked **trails** of various lengths threads through the grounds, which you can only explore in a group tour. The best option for day visitors is to join one of the expertly conducted introductory **guided tours** which take about an hour and a half (daily 10.30am & 1.30pm; included in entrance fee). On the tours and at all times while in the centre visitors are requested not to touch the flowers or pick fruit. Residents of more than three nights get a tour of **Dunston Cave**, which houses the world's most accessible colony of **oilbirds**.

### Practicalities

The centre is open to the public (daily 9am–5pm; US$10); the entrance fee includes an hour-and-a-half tour and access to the verandah and its library. You can have an excellent buffet lunch for TT$50 (Mon–Sat, TT$25 more on Sun); sandwiches and drinks are available on the verandah if you don't want a cooked meal. There is also a small shop selling locally made crafts, field guides, local coffee and bird feeders. Resident guests tend to be middle-aged American bird fanatics toting state-of-the-art binoculars or camera equipment, and checklists of a day's sightings are enthusiastically compiled over sunset rum punches.

**Accommodation** is situated in a luxurious 24-room lodge. All rooms have large screened verandahs, en-suite bathroom and two double beds; rates include three meals a day and afternoon tea, and access to a natural grotto on a free-running rainforest stream which acts as a swimming pool for residents. Informed field trips accompanied by experienced guides to Trinidad's other premier birdwatching sites including the Caroni Swamp (see p.183) are also on offer to resident guests. These can be designed to meet individual requirements and cost between US$35 and US$55 per person.

For those who want an even closer brush with nature, the *Alta Vista Rainforest Resort* (☎629 8030, ⓕ629 3262, ⓦwww.come.to/alta-vista; ❷), a couple of bends up from Asa Wright, offers the total natural rainforest experience at bargain prices. Six rudimentary log cabins, sleeping up to three people with bed and curtained-off shower, toilet and sink are surrounded by lush rainforest, gardens and a verandah for bird-watching. Steps descending under christophene plants lead to a freshwater pool fed by a mountain spring. Electricity is provided from solar power and meals (TT$15–40) use home grown herbs, vegetables and fruit. If you're the only guests, you can use the communal kitchen, otherwise a cook is brought onto site. Day visitors pay TT$150 entrance fee to use the picnic facilities and walk one of the variety of trails.

You may also consider staying in Blanchisseuse (see p.140) – it's a good, less expensive option for those who want to visit Asa Wright, and many of the hotels and guesthouses will even arrange transport to here from Blanchisseuse.

## South to Arima

Heading **towards Arima** the road dips downhill, rounding spectacular corners and passing hillsides cleared for christophene cultivation, the vines, (commonly used in Chinese cooking are supported by a rough trellis network), and former cocoa and coffee estates left to grow wild as the younger generations leave the land. Here the road is cool, shady and beautiful, and decorated with numerous prayer flags fluttering along the way. As you near Arima (see p.159), the jungle thins out and a few sporadic buildings – including a bar – appear at the roadside. A number of quarries are located on the stretch of road between Verdant Vale and Arima, hence the scars on the hillside and large the trucks heading towards Arima on the road. Also look out for the tiny do-it-yourself Hindu temples to the left of the road just before the right turn to Arima's Calvary Hill; locals refer to the area as "**temple village**".

# The East–West Corridor

Running along the southern flank of the Northern Range, the **East–West Corridor** is the main route between Trinidad's east and west coasts. It is traversed by the **Eastern Main Road** (EMR), a driver's nightmare for the unfamiliar, ruled as it is by capricious local driving practices. If they're not avoiding the rush by taking the **Priority Bus Route** – a fast-track commuter thoroughfare built where the now-obsolete **train tracks** were once in service – the maxis and route taxis that shuttle between each community seem to delight in stopping abruptly with a careless abandon that's terrifying if you're behind the wheel, but extremely convenient if you're relying on **public transport**.

Hot and dusty as the EMR is, the grinding pace of traffic at least allows you to absorb the commercial chaos: lined with shops, stalls, restaurants, bars and offices, the EMR buzzes with life – shoppers dodging delivery trucks throng the pavements and vendors fill the air with the sweet aromas of street food. The mercantile aspect doesn't let up until you've passed **Arima**, the corridor's largest town and home to what's left of Trinidad's **Carib** community. In between Arima and the eastern suburbs of Port of Spain some interesting towns are slung along the road; bustling **San Juan**, with its frenetic crossroads, and the old Spanish **capital** of **St Joseph**, where elegant colonial edifices sit incongruously with a more recent rash of concrete, are both worth exploring for their historical connections and varied architecture, but most of the communities are so close together, it's hard to tell where one district tails off and another begins.

Although it can be a nightmare to drive, the EMR is nevertheless the most convenient route from Port of Spain to a number of engaging attractions. Inland of St Joseph, the **Maracas Valley waterfall** crashes magnificently down 90m of sheer rock to a decent bathing pool; the area is a holy spot for followers of the Hindu, Orisa and Spiritual Baptist faiths. At 240m above sea level, the **Mount St Benedict Monastery** dominates the hillside above **Tunapuna**, providing a panoramic view of the Caroni plains and a restive spot for **afternoon tea**. East of Tunapuna are access roads leading north to **Caura** and **Lopinot**, which have plenty of possibilities for **picnicking**, **hiking** and **river swimming**; the latter also has a network of **caves** to explore.

Beyond Arima, the buildings on either side of the road let up and are replaced by an almost-impenetrable wall of rainforest, pierced by a few country lanes leading to some marvellous natural attractions. **La Laja** and **Sombasson waterfalls** are two of the most impressive on the island, while **Guanapo Gorge**, a deep water channel overhung by towering grey rock, is completely breathtaking. At **Aripo**, you can hike through undisturbed forest to the island's largest cave network and see a colony of squawking **oilbirds**; the forests are also richly populated by the full quota of Trinidad's **mammals**, and hunters make regular forays after agouti, armadillo, wild pig and manicou; if you're really lucky, you might catch sight of an ocelot on the flanks of **El Cerro del Aripo**, the island's highest mountain. Inland of the hub-town of **Valencia** – where the EMR turns south, and the Valencia road begins – the **Hollis Reservoir** lies like a sea in the middle of the forest, a host of birdlife twittering in the trees.

The EMR is paralleled by the snaking **Churchill Roosevelt Highway**, which doubles up as an impromptu market place; fruit and vegetable stalls, and trucks marked "fresh Maracas fish", line the hard shoulder while itinerant vendors hawking everything from Portugal oranges and Congo peppers to steering wheel covers and toys lie in wait at the traffic lights, and road signs tacked to the bridges – locally called "walkovers" – exhort you to "relax and enjoy the drive". The highway comes to an abrupt **end** after Arima, replaced by a smaller dual carriageway which takes you on to the Eastern Main Road and Valencia.

# San Juan

The westernmost of a succession of communities that sprawl along the length of the Eastern Main Road, brash, commercial **SAN JUAN** (pronounced sahwah) avoids being a Port of Spain satellite by the skin of its teeth. The town's focal point is the "**croisee**" (pronounced *kwaysay*), a bustling junction marked by the Scotiabank clock tower, which was named when French Creole was the main local vernacular – "croisee" translates as "crossroads". It's a scene of agreeable, organized pandemonium; doubles vendors, fruit and vegetable stalls and racks of sportswear line the streets while gangs of limers compete for the pavement with perusing buyers, and fleets of taxis honk endlessly. The croisee is equally lively after dark, when the flambeaux of oyster salesmen throw up whiffs of pitch oil and "power punch" milkshake vendors provide party-goers with sustenance.

South of the croisee, between the EMR and the highway, is **El Socorro** district, a community dominated by the **Aranguez Savannah**, a main venue for the annual **Phagwa** celebrations in March (see p.47). If you're **hungry**, forgo the host of eateries on the EMR and head for San Juan's Back Chain Street, adjacent to the Savannah, where *Ali's* serves up particularly delicious roti.

# St Joseph

Past the vast West Indian Tobacco Company and Carib beer factories at **Champs Fleurs** on the outskirts of San Juan, a major junction of the EMR leads to the Uriah Butler Highway, the route to the "deep south" (see p.205); left of the highway is the smart Eric Williams Medical Science Complex at Mount Hope, Trinidad's best-equipped **hospital**. After the junction, the EMR's commercial trappings temporarily thin out; once you pass the Water and Sewerage Authority (WASA) offices, a venue for one of the larger **carnival fetes**, you're in **ST JOSEPH**, Trinidad's oldest European town and first official **capital**, as well as one of the better places along the EMR to get a flavour of the East–West Corridor. Because of the town's historical pedigree, the streets of St Joseph are lined with genteel colonial French and Spanish architecture jostling with newer concrete structures and market stalls.

### Some history

In 1592, acting on behalf of Spanish Governor Don Antonio de Berrio y Oruna, Lieutenant Domingo de Vera founded a town on the site of an Amerindian settlement. Christening it **San José de Oruna**, de Vera built a church, a prison-cum-police barracks, Governor's residence and a *cabildo* (town hall). In 1595, **Sir Walter Raleigh** attacked San José, burning down the church and the barracks in an attempt to seize control of the island; by 1606 both were rebuilt, only to be destroyed by the **Dutch** in 1637 and ransacked by **Caribs** in 1640. In 1687, Capuchin missionaries arrived from Spain, settling in a monastery adjacent to the church, and San José struggled along for the next eighty years. Neglected by Spain, which dismissed Trinidad as little more than a convenient stop-off during journeys to South America, the 500-odd residents scratched a living through small-scale farming.

During the eighteenth century, San José began to prosper as a **plantation town**, but in 1766 was hit by a devastating **earthquake**. The hard-luck town never really recovered from this blow, and eighteen years later Don José Maria Chacon, the last Spanish governor, relocated the capital to Port of Spain. San José's troubles weren't over yet, however; in 1837, a detachment of the West Indian Regiment stationed at the police station **mutinied**. The soldiers, led by a Yoruba ex-slave known as Daaga, were protesting against the apprenticeship system that kept freed Africans in a state of semi-slavery for four to six years after so-called emancipation. They set fire to the barracks, seized ammunition and fought for several days before being overwhelmed. In the aftermath, forty

Africans lay dead; Daaga and two of his comrades were **executed** by a firing squad in front of the police station. Things are much quieter here these days, the town having grown into a bustling commercial centre, with residential districts expanding to the north into what has become Maracas–St Joseph Valley.

## The Town

Old meets new as you cross the bridge into town; on the right is the imposing and elaborate **Mohammed Al Jinnah Memorial Mosque**, resplendent with a crescent- and star-topped main dome flanked by two minarets; there's not much to see inside, but if you want to take a look, check at the caretaker's house, left of the Muslim school behind the mosque. Directly opposite is the old **police station** and **barracks**, the graceful curves and porticoes smothered by a coating of blue paint.

From the police station, **Abercromby Street** strikes uphill into the mountains. A couple of hundred metres up is **St Joseph's Catholic Church**, which has undergone many changes since it was first consecrated in 1593. Its three previous incarnations were sacked along with the rest of the town, and today's Gothic-style stone and red-brick structure dates back to 1815. Impressed by the religious devotion of the townspeople who clubbed together to fund the first stages of construction, British Governor Sir Ralph Woodford, though a Protestant himself, donated £2000 towards construction and even laid the foundation stone. Inside, beautiful **stained-glass** windows depict the Holy Family, St John and St Andrew; the ornate Italian marble **high altar** was imported from Dublin in 1912. The graveyard behind contains headstones with inscriptions in French, English and Spanish; the oldest tombstone in the island, a weathered slab known as the **tombstone of the pirate**, is marked with a skull and crossbones and the date 1682, but no one knows the identity of the buccaneer interred beneath. Further up Abercromby Street and framed by elegantly fretworked colonial houses, **George Earl Park** was the old Spanish town square, used for evening promenades, military parades and as a burial ground; the single remaining stone, dated 1802, commemorates one Mr Thomas.

## Accommodation

**Accommodation** in St Joseph itself is limited, but there are two good options nearby. Tucked away on the upper reaches of Upper Quarry Drive in Champs Fleurs (follow the signs), the excellent-value *Mountain View Guesthouse* (☎645 0700; ❹, ❺ at Carnival time) has apartments with sitting room, full kitchen, TV and a/c; they can accommodate four people. Route taxis, which run all day from the junction of Quarry Drive and the EMR, can take you there for about TT$3. Slightly further away at 108 Valley View Drive in the Maracas–St Joseph Valley (see below), *La Belle Maison* (☎/☎663 4413, ⓦwww.la-belle maison-tt.com; ❹), is a beautifully designed private home with a verandah that's good for birdwatching. Owner Merle Lynch is a mine of local information, and *La Belle* is an excellent, friendly base for exploring the area. The three rooms have lovely valley views and private or shared bathrooms; breakfast is included and tours of the island are available.

## The Maracas–St Joseph Valley and around

Turning inland opposite the mosque, Abercromby Street becomes **Maracas Royal Road** less than a kilometre from the EMR, crossing the grand First River Bridge and winding north into the lush **Maracas–St Joseph Valley**, overlooked all the way by the peaks of **El Tucuche**, the island's second highest mountain. **Maracas** itself is a tiny place, all but swallowed by the suburbs of St Joseph; once you've passed its postal agency and steepled church of St Michael, the houses thin out, separated by clumps of fluffy bamboo and neat provision grounds. Some 10km north of the EMR, the Maracas Royal Road ends at **Loango Village**, where there's a bar and a parlour. The bumpy tarmac of San Pedro Road, which makes a T-junction with the end of the Maracas Royal Road, provides easy access to the **bathing pools** along this section of the Maracas River, the deepest usually being filled with swimmers from the village. The riverbed is scattered with the sparkling bronze sedimentary rocks which fed rumours of local **gold** deposits in the early twentieth century. Route taxis run from Curepe junction to Maracas Valley between 7am and 6pm; the fare is around TT$4; you'll pay more if you go off-route along Waterfall Road.

From the pools you can **hike** over the mountains to Maracas Bay (see p.134), a stiff two-hour trek along an old fisherman's trail that's been more or less unused since the construction of the North Coast Road. Another possibility – if you've got stamina and don't mind heights – is to climb the 936-metre **El Tucuche** (variously pronounced *tuh-cutchee* or *too-koosh*). It's an 8-hour round trip, and some of the trail is bordered by a terrifying 300-metre cliff, but you'll be rewarded by spectacular epiphyte-laden **montane** forest as well as high-altitude, mist-drenched **elfin** forest. If you're lucky, you'll see **red howler monkeys** and the **golden tree frog**, Trinidad's only endemic animal, which lives in the waterlogged leaves of wild pine bromeliads. If you want to tackle Tucuche, a **guide** is essential – see p.53 for a list of options.

### Maracas Waterfall

Most people head to the valley in order to get to **Maracas Waterfall**, which is one of Trinidad's highest; to get there, turn right from the Maracas Royal Road onto the signposted Waterfall Road; the turn is about 8km from the EMR. At the end of the road you'll find a secure car park where you can also locate a guide (participants of the National Service Programme in conjunction with the agriculture ministry; ☎622 4521), a good idea, considering the reports of robberies in the area. After twenty minutes of uphill walking along a wide rocky track lined by groves of tall balata trees, a path strikes off to the right. This leads to the **first cascade**, three tiers of mini-waterfalls with two swimmable, ice-cold **pools**; the main waterfall is another twenty minutes' walk. Signs warning "no candles" posted on tree trunks are puzzling until you near the falls; here you'll see clusters of black and red candles or pools of wax on the rocks, left by followers of the Hindu, Spiritual Baptist and Orisha religions, who regard the waterfall as a sacred place, marking it with tall coloured flags among the trees. Rumours that some of the rituals performed here are not altogether wholesome give the place a somewhat eerie feel, but little can detract from the awesome beauty of the waterfall. Falling some 90m down a sheer rock face, the water splashes on to a rocky basin, the sunlight shimmering rainbow prisms through the droplets of spray. Water levels are low during the dry season, but you can almost always take a shower.

# Curepe and around

Loosely arranged around the Eastern Main Road, **CUREPE** is another of the EMR's busy transport hubs. The Priority Bus Route runs parallel to the road here, and maxis and taxis trickle off to park up outside the bus terminus – a converted train station – and hawk for trade. Cars heading for the Southern

Main Road or Churchill Roosevelt Highway create a constant traffic jam, and there's little to stimulate the imagination, though it's a convenient base for exploring sights in the surrounding area, such as **Mount St Benedict** and **Caura Valley**.

Just past the junction, the Priority Bus Route mounts an attractive cut-stone flyover under which a road takes you to the **University of the West Indies St Augustine Campus**. Usually referred to by its acronym, UWI (yoo-wee) also has branches in Jamaica and Barbados. The spacious campus was formerly a sugar plantation, and the great house now serves as the principal's home. The students are a cosmopolitan Caribbean mix, and the campus is the annual venue for Trinidad's priciest **all-inclusive Carnival fete**, a massive party which usually boasts every single soca performer of note.

### Practicalities

Curepe is an ideal place to start your exploration of the Northern Range: route taxis and maxis use this as a hub with spokes to Port of Spain, west along the EMR and inland along all the major roads – though if you're heading to more remote destinations, such as Lopinot, you may have a long wait. Most inland taxis leave from the EMR and the appropriate junction; ask locals where to catch one.

Of the few **accommodation** options available, *The Caribbean Lodge*, 32 St Augustine Circular Rd (☏645 2937, ℻645 2358; ❷), is by far the best choice, a supremely friendly, attractive place adjacent to UWI campus. Rooms are not fancy, catering mainly for visiting students, but they are functional and very clean with shared or private shower; some have a/c and kitchenette. There's an area for washing clothes and meals are available. Those who don't mind a few restrictions can try the rather overpriced *Hosanna Hotel*, Santa Margarita Circular Road, St Augustine (☏662 5449, ℻662 5451, ⓦwww.hosanna hotel.com; ❺); signs warning "no smoking, no unmarried couples, no arms and ammunition, no alcohol" are pasted up in reception. Rooms are quite nice, with a/c and TV, and there's a restaurant and intermittently-filled pool. Connected to the CONCACAF "football centre of excellence" – a modern complex used for development of Caribbean football players and coaches with a 6000-seat stadium, practice fields, swimming pool and, most dramatically, a giant football at its entrance – *Le Sportel Inn* (Macoya Road, Tunapuna ☏663 3905, ⓦwww.concacafcentre.co.tt; ❹) is a new and very simple, but comfortable option. The box-like rooms have two double beds, a/c and not much else, though breakfast is reasonable at US$3.50 per person.

For **food** and **drink**, you'll find the usual selection of local restaurants and darkened rum shops along the EMR; there are late night roti and doubles vendors at Curepe junction, while *KFC* and *Pizza Hut* share a building on the highway. If you're in the mood to **party** on the EMR, between St Augustine and Tunapuna you'll find the excellent Sunday School outdoor dance party (10pm–4am; TT$10) run by the Twelve Tribes Rastafarian sect; look for the red, gold and green Rasta flags draped over the entrance on the side of the road. The Kay Donna drive-in **cinema** is on the corner of Churchill Roosevelt Highway and the Southern Main Road, just turn right at Curepe junction.

## Mount St Benedict

Just east of Curepe's centre, where the EMR intersects St John's Road, sits the **Exodus panyard**, its pans stacked neatly in the practice space. Winners of the 2001 and 2004 **National Panorama** title, awarded to the nation's best pan band during Carnival, and led by long-time arranger Pelham Goddard, Exodus can sometimes be seen practising at night.

Crucifix-lined St John's Road climbs uphill through the village of St John to the **Mount St Benedict Monastery**, which is a place of pilgrimage to this day. Taxis for Mount St Benedict leave from the corner of St John's road and the EMR – just wait by the Scotia Bank; an unreliable bus service also plies this route every half an hour from 6am to 6pm (TT$4), or you can join the evening power walkers who hike up the hill to keep fit. At 243m above sea level, the monastery commands spectacular views south across the Caroni plains to the Trinity Hills and Mount Tamana.

An eye-catching network of white-walled, red-roofed buildings dominating the hillside, the monastery was established in 1912 by Benedictine monks fleeing religious persecution in Brazil. The first of its kind in the Caribbean, the monastery initially consisted of nothing more than a mud-walled, thatch-roofed *ajoupa* at the peak of Mount Tabor, which was eventually abandoned in favour of this more accessible site. Additional buildings were added over the years, including in 1918 a gorgeous burnt orange central tapia house, now slowly crumbling. With a boxy steeple tower forming the tallest portion of the complex, the imposing **church** was consecrated as an **abbey** in 1947. In keeping with their motto *ora et labora* (prayers and work), the 25-odd resident monks are a vibrant, active community, maintaining an apiary and producing delicious yoghurt and honey for commercial sale, as well as coffee and vegetables for domestic use. Mount St Benedict houses the Caribbean's main regional training college for priests, the **St John Vianney and the Uganda Martyrs Seminary**, which is also UWI's theology faculty. The nearby **St Bede's Vocational School** is run by the monks, who teach local youngsters practical skills such as machining, welding, plumbing and carpentry.

## Pax Guest House

Constructed in 1916 to fulfill the Benedictine tradition of welcoming travellers, **Pax Guest House** (T/F 662 4084, W www.paxguesthouse.com; ❻), adjacent to the monastery, is the oldest guesthouse in Trinidad and remains the most popular place for local Trinidadians to come and celebrate a special occasion. *Pax* is also a traditional spot for **afternoon tea** (daily 3–6pm; moderate), a feast of homemade breads, cakes and pastries taken at the tea garden or a terrace facing the hills. A favourite haunt of American soldiers based in Trinidad during World War II, today the guesthouse caters for birders, nature lovers and anyone in need of tranquillity – you can even hand-feed the hummingbirds from the terrace. In keeping with their monastic history, the rooms –

---

### Birdwatching at Pax

*Pax*'s manager Gerard Ramsawak organizes **birdwatching tours** through the two square kilometres of surrounding land, which are home to a huge array of birds; the elevation means that raptors – hawks, vultures, kites and falcons – are particularly common, as are woodpeckers, parrots and hummingbirds. Five **trails**, ranging from half an hour to two hours' walking weave through jungle and secondary forest of Caribbean pine; a beautifully illustrated trail guide is available from the guesthouse. For a panoramic view of Trinidad that surpasses even the vistas at the monastery, take the Alben Ride trail and climb the **fire tower**, built to give warning of blazes in the cane fields below; the views are awe-inspiring, particularly at dusk when the sun disappears behind faraway Port of Spain and the town's lights twinkle in the distance. While you can explore these trails alone, recent reports of mugging along them suggest it is much wiser to hire a guide to come with you. Recommended local ornithologist Kenny Caulderon is the main tour guide at *Pax*.

which lead from an impeccably clean, dormitory-like corridor – are simple and fitted with solid furniture, some of which was made by the monks.

**Rates** include breakfast and an excellent three-course dinner of Caribbean fare; after a complimentary glass of rum punch, the dinner gong echoes through the corridors at 7:30pm and dinner is served on a large, candlelit terrace facing the rainforests of the Northern Range. Non-guests can eat for US$10, but only if space is available and they ring ahead.

Past *Pax Guest House* the road twists around a few more hairpin bends before coming to an abrupt halt at St Benet's Hall. This building houses an art gallery as well as *Chez Glorie* restaurant (℡645 1905, @ opmount@trinidad.net), whose south-facing dining terrace commands amazing views over the Caroni plains and is a perfect spot for watching sunsets.

## Caura Valley

Curepe merges imperceptibly into **Tunapuna**, yet another nondescript collection of shopfronts and residential roads which uses the EMR as its main street – of the many food shops here, *Loveys* is particularly good for roti. Just to the east, the Caura Royal Road turns north to the **Caura Valley** – one of the most popular **picnic spots** in the East–West Corridor. Carved by the serpentine Tacarigua River, the valley was nearly turned into a reservoir in the 1940s: the inhabitants were even relocated to Lopinot (see below), but the proposed **dam** was thwarted by the sandy soil and never built.

About 6km up the Caura Royal Road from the EMR is a right turn that will take you to a popular **swimming spot**. Picnic tables line the bamboo-fringed riverbanks, and at the weekends, cooking fires smoulder and the water is crowded with families enjoying a dip – be aware, though, that there are rumors of pesticide pollution from runoff here and the shallow water often looks murky in the dry season. You can see a graffiti-smothered abandoned building here, the last vestige of the abandoned dam project. From this point there are several walkable dirt tracks of varying lengths into the **Tacarigua Forest Reserve**, an attractive patchwork of abandoned plantations and lower montane woodlands. Hikes range from ten-minute jaunts to whole-day treks to the peak of El Tucuche (see p.154).

Past the picnic spots, high walls of bamboo form an intermittent tunnel over the road, opening up occasionally to reveal the small-scale farmlands and homes of **La Veronica** hamlet. As the Royal Road emerges onto the riverbanks again, the water deepens a little and picnicking is more secluded. The road is eventually terminated by a tributary of the Tacarigua. The drive back to the EMR affords some spectacular views of the central plains that are easily missed on the way up.

# Lopinot

Uninspiring and easily missed if you're not scanning a map, **Arouca** is really notable only as the point where you turn off the EMR in order to get on Lopinot Road, which shoots north through gorgeous, undulating countryside of richly fruited vales and hillsides of jungle and Caribbean pine. The junction of the EMR and Lopinot Road is marked by the Arouca Industrial Estate where the crowds of customers confirms the quality of the Indian takeaway dishes sold at a number of food stalls here. Eight kilometres from the EMR, **LOPINOT** is a pretty hamlet clustered around a sports field and the neat flower beds of the **Lopinot complex**, a former cocoa estate that has been transformed into a beautiful, secluded picnic spot (daily 6am–6pm; free). Lopinot's annual harvest – a festival of parang fuelled by excesses of food and drink – usually takes place on May 17, though a shift to July has been known. The route **taxi** fare from Arouca to Lopinot is TT\$3; cars are fairly frequent (Mon–Sat 5am–6pm), but the service is reduced on Sundays.

The valley was first settled by one Charles Josef, **Compte de Lopinot**, a planter who fled Haiti following Toussaint L'Ouverture's 1791 revolution. After a spell in Jamaica, he arrived in 1800 with his wife and 100 "faithful" (so the on-site board assures us) slaves. It's not difficult to see why he chose to settle in this absurdly abundant alluvial valley surrounded by high, protective mountains. Lopinot's cocoa thrived, allowing him to build a tapia estate house, a prison and slave quarters and to amass a small fortune before his death in 1819. The Compte is buried alongside his wife by the Arouca River, which runs through the valley, and local legend has it that on stormy full moon nights his ghost rides through the estate on a white horse.

The modest **great house** has been carefully restored, with a glassed-over section showing the original mud walls behind the newly rendered exterior. Meticulously maintained, the surrounding gardens are linked to the road by a quaint wooden bridge, its roof smothered with ferns and wild pine bromeliads, while picnic tables are shaded by several enormous samaan trees with branches laden down by epiphytic plants. On the grounds are a restored cocoa drying house, a dirt oven and a cave. The estate makes a good spot for watching birds such as the white-shouldered tanager, the bare-eyed thrush and the violaceous euphonia. Inside the great house, a small **museum** (6am–6pm, free) is dedicated to the culture of local residents. The community, of Spanish, African and Amerindian descent, was relocated here when the Caura dam was proposed (see p.157); it has spawned some of Trinidad's finest parang players, inspiring villagers to call Lopinot the "**home of parang**". The village is one of the few places where, each Christmas, a band of roving players still serenades each household. Site caretaker Martin Gomez is a parang master who delights in treating visitors to a song, accompanying himself on the cuatro. The museum displays photographs of local parang elders, as well as a couple of dusty Amerindian artefacts and the dried-out husks of large grasshoppers and tarantulas, presumably on show to scare the tourists.

The boxy, cut-stone **La Veronique RC church**, by the roadside on the other side of the playing field, was originally built in Caura in 1897, but was taken piece by piece from the neighbouring valley during the Caura evacuation and reassembled here. Past the church and the primary school, lichen-smothered cocoa trees line the road, and a downhill turn-off leads to the **La Pastora** chapel and shrine, one of many on the island to share the title. This dedication to the Virgin of Shepherds stems from Capuchin monks who established several missions on the island during the late seventeenth century, instilling devotion to La Pastora in their Amerindian converts. Carved in the 1940s, the plain white shrine inside the chapel depicts the Virgin Mary, and is said to have been chipped directly from the mountain.

After passing several small, friendly villages, the road eventually forks; taking a left down San Francisco Road brings you to a series of deep, swimmable **pools** on the river. There is good **hiking** in the surrounding mountains; Martin Gomez (see above) can arrange a guide who'll take you to nearby bat-filled **caves** – Mr Gomez actually discovered one of them himself, and it bears his name.

Should you find a need to stay overnight, you might try *Sadila House*, on Waterpipe Road, which is close to the Five Rivers junction at Arouca on the

EMR (☎ 640 3659, ⓦ www.sadila.com; ❺); ring first for directions as it can be difficult to find. Rooms are clean and comfortable with a/c, en-suite bathroom and a shared communal area with TV. Breakfast is included in the rates.

# Arima and around

East of Lopinot, the EMR takes on a distinctly more rural aspect, with the shops and offices interspersed with the odd cattle pasture or overgrown empty lot. At the diminutive village of **D'Abadie**, the EMR wreathes through the pines and cocorite palms of **Cleaver Woods**. On Cleaver Trace, there's a gravel car park and the entrance to an **Amerindian museum** (daily 7am–6pm; free). Though the museum, housed in a thatch-roof ajoupa hut, is a bit neglected, the displays are interesting, including pottery, hunting traps, bows and arrows and equipment used to process cassava, which was farmed by Amerindians and formed a major part of their diet. The surrounding forest has a few short **trails** and picnic tables, and on the southern side of the road there's a small spring popular with local Rastas.

Named "Naparima" by the Amerindians who were the first to settle here, **ARIMA** is situated smack in the middle of the East–West Corridor, about six and a half kilometres from the Lopinot turnoff. The largest town in the area, it's also one of the easiest places to get lost if you're driving, as the EMR departs from its normally ruler-straight path and gets swiftly swallowed up in an endless-seeming urban clamour of shops, banks and wandering pedestrians. Far away from the tourist centres and especially busy on Saturdays, workaday Arima's attraction is primarily the facilities it offers and lower prices for commodities such as clothes, shoes and music.

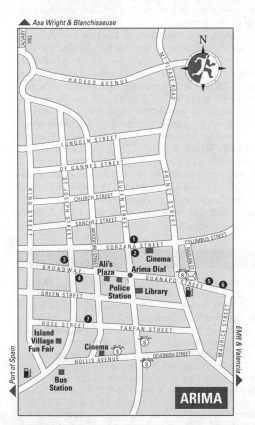

▲ Asa Wright & Blanchisseuse

**ARIMA**

---

**RESTAURANTS, BARS & CLUBS**

| | | | |
|---|---|---|---|
| Cantonese Kitchen | 5 | Fifth Element | 1 |
| Casa Caribe | 3 | Friendship Restaurant | 2 |
| Chee's Chinese Creole | 4 | Home Restaurant | 6 |
| Cool Top | 7 | | |

The town has a far deeper history than its commercial facade would suggest, however, as it is home to what's left of Trinidad's **Carib** community, most of whom live around the crucifix-strewn **Calvary Hill**, a precipitous thoroughfare that overlooks the town and connects to the Arima–Blanchisseuse Road. You can still see remnants of Indian features in these distant relatives of the Carinepogoto tribe who once inhabited the Northern Range, but links are becoming ever-more tenuous as intermarriage slowly erodes the physical aspect of the **Karina nation**, as they like to be known – Carib is regarded as a European corruption of their correct title. However, Carib culture still has a stronghold here, and **the Santa Rosa Carib Community Association** was formed in 1974 to look after the interests of the dwindling tribe. Their headquarters on Paul Mitchell Street, behind the cemetery, sells good quality traditional Amerindian craft such as woven baskets or carved calabashes, as well as giving information about local Carib culture. The only remaining **ajoupa** – the traditional Carib thatched building – on Calvary Hill sits in the front yard of Christo Adonis, a local Carib shaman and vociferous defender of his people; if you can catch him at home, he's a mine of information on Amerindian medicine and all things pertaining to the Karinas.

Exploring Arima is best done on foot as everything is close by and the one-way street system is confusing for drivers; there's a free car park behind the blue bus terminus on Hollis Avenue. Walking is also a good way to see the odd old house – especially as you wander away from the central cluster of streets – soak up the hustle and bustle of town life and be entertained by the latest soca/reggae blaring out from numerous loud speakers and music stalls around the centre of the town. Arima's main landmark and traffic roundabout, the **Arima Dial**, features a four-faced timepiece, originally presented to the townspeople in 1898 by their mayor, John Wallen, and recently restored after being knocked down by a truck in 2000. On **Hollis Road**, the line of local street vendors stops at a small park where the statue of venerated calypsonian **Lord Kitchener** will hold your attention briefly before you're drawn to the fabulous open-air **market** nearby; it's liveliest on Fridays. The adjacent Arima Velodrome is the setting for many a wild Carnival fete. Weekend evenings are especially busy, with locals tending to lime by the savannah wall and engaging in a little "ol' talk". On St Joseph's St, at the west end of town, a children's fun park known

## The Feast of Santa Rosa

During the last weekend of August, Arima's Carib community celebrates the **Feast of Santa Rosa de Lima**, making the town the only place in Trinidad where the first canonized Roman Catholic Saint of the "New World" is honoured. Following a morning of church services, a Carib King and Queen are crowned, and a white gowned statue of Santa Rosa is paraded through the streets, the procession bedecked with white, yellow, pink and red roses. An all-day party ensues; rum flows, and traditional Amerindian foods such as pastelles and cassava bread are eaten. The origins of the festival are somewhat murky, but in true fairytale style, Carib elders relate that three hunters chanced upon a young girl lying in the woods, and brought her back to Calvary Hill. She disappeared three times, only to be returned to the community. A local priest told the Caribs that this was no normal child, but the spirit of Santa Rosa and that they should make an image of her while she was still with them, for if she vanished again, her physical body would never more be seen. They made the statue, and the girl duly disappeared, leaving only a crown of roses at the spot where she had first been discovered. Ever since, Santa Rosa has been the patron saint of the Carib community.

as the **Island Village Fun Fair** (daily, no set hours; TT$20) has a ferris wheel, merry-go-rounds and some more adult-oriented fairground rides, while the **Santa Rosa Race Track** (⚎646 2360 or 2450, ⊛www.santarosapark.com), off the highway, holds regular **horse racing** meets. Highlights of the racing calendar include the Midsummer Classic, run on the first Saturday in July, and the Derby Stakes, run in August or September. Leaving town along the Eastern Main Road, you pass **Nutones panyard** on the right.

### Practicalities

Because it is the region's main transport hub, Arima has three **petrol stations** and a number of banks – the RBTT bank on the corner of Devonish and Queen streets has an ATM. The **library** (Mon–Fri 8.30am–6pm, Sat 8.30am–noon) can be found directly opposite the music stalls on Queen Street and has free **Internet** access, allowed in half an hour slots. There is also an Internet café (TT$5 per half-hour;   ⚎667 7168), upstairs in Ali's Plaza on Broadway, and another at the shop Eastech, Queen and Farfan sts (Mon–Sat 9am–7.30pm; ⚎667 4556; TT$9 per hour).

**Taxis** to Sangre Grande (TT$4) and Valencia (TT$2) leave from the Dial, and taxis to Port of Spain (TT$5) can be caught on Broadway. Alternatively, catch the ECS **bus** to the capital outside the courthouse on Hollis Avenue (TT$4). **Maxis** for Port of Spain leave from the northern end of St Joseph Street (TT$4), while maxis for Sangre Grande (TT$3), Manzanilla (TT$3), Toco (TT$7), Mayaro (TT$7) and Grande Riviere (TT$15) leave from the corner of Raglan Street and Broadway.

There are few **places to stay** in and around Arima. On the town's southern outskirts there is the *Hotel California*, at the Havana Social Club on Nelson Street (⚎667 2209; ❸) – catch a route taxi from the Malabar taxi stand on Queen Street just past the RBTT bank. A well-maintained yellow-and-brown building, the hotel's carpeted walls, dark rooms and music are perfect for its primary clientele: lovers with nowhere else to go. The rooms are clean and cheerful, and there's a friendly bar downstairs. *MK's Haven*, Lot 70 Swift Drive, Phase 3, Malabar (⚎643 4681; ❸), is a comfortable nearby host home.

Arima is full of fast **food** and low-key eating places, the best of which are: *Home Restaurant*, Guanapo St (⚎667 5020), a very popular eating place selling top quality local fare such as rotis (from TT$9) and salt fish (TT$5.50); the *Cantonese Kitchen*, almost next door, which prepares an excellent range of Chinese and Cantonese dishes at around TT$14; *Friendship Restaurant & Take Away*, Queen St (⚎667 7567), with its distinctive Far Eastern décor and tasty curry special (TT$13); and *Chee's Chinese Creole & Indian*, Broadway (⚎667 3405) where a superb fish, calalloo and rice costs TT$15.

Street food in Arima is tasty and great value. Coconut water can be bought from vendors on Hollis Avenue, doubles and roti are always available by Arima's excellent outdoor fruit and vegetable market and an excellent stall outside the *Friendship Restaurant & Take Away* serves mouthwatering Asian dishes. At night refreshing punches can be bought from the stalls on Queen Street, and further up delicious doubles are cooked while you wait by roadside vendors.

There's no shortage of **entertainment** in the town, with plenty of rum shops, upmarket bars and pool halls, two cinemas and a nightclub, all of which are well patronized by the locals. It's rare that you'll see a foreigner hanging out in a rum shop or catching a movie in Arima, making it a good town to come to if you're tired of the glitz of the more upmarket tourist-orientated places in Port of Spain. The two **cinemas** – Kabsco, on Sorozano Street (⚎667 4003; screenings 4.30pm and 8.30pm), and Windsor, on Hollis Avenue (⚎667 3274;

screenings 3pm and 8.15pm) – both show double bills of the usual Hollywood action fare (TT$10–15). The relatively new *Fifth Element* **nightclub**, on the corner of Queen and Sozano streets, has a student night on Thursdays, after-work limes on Fridays, and dub/dancehall/hip-hop on Saturdays that attracts a young and trendy crowd. *Casa Caribe*, St Joseph Street, is a sports **bar** with pool tables and a nice open-air section, and serves tasty inexpensive food such as hot dogs and rotis. *Cool Top*, at the corner of Woodford and Farfan streets, is a great bar with indoor and outdoor seating and pool tables on the rooftop; its good views also make it an ideal spot to cool off with a beer during the heat of the day.

## Heights of Guanapo Road

On the eastern outskirts of Arima, the EMR switches abruptly from commercial thoroughfare to rural road, either side dominated by farmlands and cattle pastures rather than shopfronts and honking traffic. Just after the Arima Bypass meets the EMR, a turn-off at the WASA Guanapo Waterworks sign brings you to the **Heights of Guanapo Road** which runs along the Guanapo River for 3km before petering out into a country lane, churned up by logging vehicles, muddy and best accessed with a four wheel drive vehicle. North is the Heights of Guanapo, a hikers paradise which, while beautiful and peaceful, is not a place to explore without the help of a knowledgeable **guide**. Though you can drive further uphill to **La Laja Heights**, which gives lovely views over the Guanapo Valley, it's a good idea to park in the large clearing below where logging workers have built a hut, and then walk, as from here onwards the road becomes treacherous with potholes. The main attractions of the area are the breathtaking **Guanapo Gorge**, and the **La Laja** and **Sombasson waterfalls**. With effort, you can see both the falls and the gorge in a day, but you'll need to be pretty fit.

### Guanapo Gorge

A little nearer to the EMR than the waterfalls, the **Guanapo Gorge** is a narrow channel whose vine-wreathed walls of smooth grey rock rise 15m to 30m above the water. Dark and cool even on a hot sunny day, the gorge runs for some 400m; exploring it – wading and swimming all the way – can be quite hard work. Though you can start the trek from the southern (downstream) end, a far more exciting option is to begin upstream, where a large boulder blocking the river has created a small waterfall. From here, you can enter the gorge by simply jumping from the boulder into a deep pool and swimming for a few yards before your feet meet the riverbed. Water levels vary according to the time of year, but you shouldn't have to swim further than 25m; this is quite simply one of Trinidad's most thrilling journeys due to the sense of danger it provokes. The tiny **Tumbason River** threads through rocks to meet the Guanapo at the southern end of the gorge; if you walk up the riverbed for about 45min, you'll come to a small **waterfall** with a deep **pool**.

### The La Laja and Sombasson waterfalls

The **La Laja** and **Sombasson waterfalls** are hidden deep in the folds of the Northern Range. Getting to them necessitates a long and difficult hike, passing through abandoned cocoa plantations and forests of bois cano, sandbuck, nutmeg, balata and silk cotton. The trail dips and climbs constantly, but frequent use by hunters, who come here for the rich stocks of wild meat, have kept the majority of the trails fairly free of bush, though you may need to blaze a trail in the last stages of the walk, marking your path by slashing the undergrowth or leaving other easily recognizable marks. The first of the falls, **La Laja** is the smaller at about 20m high, with a couple of good pools below; the water is kept icy cold by the overhanging cliffs and dense foliage. Above La Laja, you're in virgin forest, and the trek to **Sombasson Falls** is harder, but the three-tiered fifty-metre cascade with deep pools is worth the effort.

## Aripo Road

East of Guanapo, more lonely fields line the EMR for a couple of kilometres before it meets the nondescript-looking **Aripo Road**, which runs north into the mountains following a valley cut by the Aripo River. The road follows a pretty, meandering uphill route deep into the bush for about 14km. From its end, you can hike up to Trinidad's largest system of caverns, **Aripo Caves**, which support one of the island's few **oilbird colonies**, or follow a different route to climb Trinidad's highest mountain, **El Cerro del Aripo**. Note that if you're going to the caves, you will need to have a **guide** with you, not just to keep you from getting lost on the confusing trail but to take care of the special permissions required to enter the area, as it is a scientific reserve.

### Aripo Caves

Even though they're weather-beaten and battered, you can still make out the forestry department signs along Aripo Road which point the way to the **Aripo Caves**; follow them past **Aripo**, the last village, where you should be able to hire a guide. After a cocoa grove – which sports fruits that turn purple when ripe rather than the usual orange – there's a sign for the caves by a grassy clearing where you can park. The fairly taxing two- to three-hour trek, with plenty of hills and gullies to navigate, is best undertaken in the dry season (Jan–March), when the three rivers that cross the path usually slow to a trickle; if it's been raining, you'll have to wade them. In the rainy season, you'll also have to get wet to enter the caves, as a river courses straight into the mouth; take care, as the going can be slippery.

The forest is thick, but if you squint through the leaves you can get the occasional view of the Central Plains below. On nearing the main entrance of the caves, you'll start to hear the unearthly rasping shriek of the **oilbirds** inside (for more on oilbirds, see p.356). The **mouth** is large and dramatic, with a musty mist rising constantly from the depths. Water drips from the limestone roof, and every surface is covered with fruit stones dropped by oilbirds returning from night-time feeding forays as well as a thin film of guano. With a good torch, you can navigate the rocks and go fairly deep inside, but doing so increases the oilbirds' cries to an ear-splitting pitch; it's not difficult to imagine why the Amerindians named them "Guacharo", meaning "the one who wails and mourns". If you want to go any further into the caves, you'll need rope, a compass and some caving experience.

**El Cerro del Aripo**

At 941m, the peak of **El Cerro del Aripo** is covered with prehistoric-looking elfin forest; short, scrubby and smothered with lichen, mosses and epiphytic growth. It's a tough full-day hike from the top of the Aripo Road, but as the temperature at the peak is some ten degrees lower than in the lowlands, overheating is one thing you don't have to worry about. As the Aripo Road is rough and periodically potholed, you'll need a car with high clearance if you're driving; in the wet season, a four-wheel drive is a good idea. It's a pretty route, tracing the valley and passing through some quiet rural communities; artist **Leroy Clarke** has a home up here. If you're in the mood for a **river swim**, look out for a metal arch with the inscription "Jai Guru Data" soldered from iron rods; take the steps down the hill to a deep **pool**.

# The northeast tip

Stretching from **Matura** on the east coast round to **Matelot** on the north coast, the wild and rugged coastline of Trinidad's **northeast tip** feels far more remote than anywhere else in the region; it takes a minimum of three hours to drive from Port of Spain to Matelot, where the paved road ends. Cut off from most of the island by a break in the North Coast Road and by the dense rainforests of the Northern Range, the region seems suspended in a time warp; people and houses are few and far between and an air of hypnotic quiet pervades. The villages strung along the coast are close-knit and spirited communities, with proud residents clipping verges and planting flowers in voluntary beautification projects and making their own entertainment at the **rum shops**, country parties and fishermen's fetes. Locals here run the only community radio station on the island – Radio Toco 106.7FM – which is great for giving you a taste of local life and music. **Farming** and **fishing** are the mainstays of the economy: tiny roadside stalls offer fresh fruit and vegetables at knock-down prices and you'll lose count of the signs advertising shark oil, salt fish and sea moss for sale.

The narrow "Matura Road" (also called the Toco Main Road) loops northeast from Sangre Grande to Matura Point, where it swings north through neat farmlands and stark, untamed bush, with unreachable rocky coves enticing you to scramble down the cliffs. Warnings against frequent landslides and collapsing tarmac are clearly signposted and long-standing potholes thoughtfully circled with white paint. At wind-whipped **Matura**, **leatherback turtles** lumber up the sand to lay eggs, while the eastern headlands provide plenty of sheltered spots for a dip in the foaming Atlantic. At weekends, sublime stretches of yellow sand such as **Saline** and **Balandra bays** become popular retreats for seclusion-seekers, as does the reef-fringed seashore adjacent to **Galera Point**, where a lighthouse guides ships through the treacherous waters between Trinidad and Tobago. Inland, **Rio Seco Waterfall** is one of the island's best, and you'll usually have it all to yourself. The largest town in the area, **Toco**, is relatively tiny, but has lent its name to the surrounding region, with its awe-inspiring, untamed coastline of weather-beaten cliffs and crashing sea. Along

## Transport to Toco and beyond

Sangre Grande, in Central Trinidad, is the region's main transport hub; all **public transport to Toco** starts here. The rural bus service has seven buses a day during the week (3.30am, 5.30am, 7.30am, 9.30am, 1.30pm, 3.30pm, 5.30pm) and four on weekends (5.30, 8.00, 13.00, 16.00) costing TT$9 to Matelot. Maxis leave regularly from Sangre Grande for Cumana (TT$6), Toco (TT$8) and Grande Riviere (TT$9), and they also run to Matelot (TT$20) twice a day, in the early morning and evening (TT$20); route taxis run with the same frequency to Cumana (TT$7), Toco (TT$8), Grande Riviere (TT$10) and Matelot (TT$20). A cheaper and quicker option for Matelot is to take the rural bus from Sangre Grande to Grande Riviere, then take a taxi to Matelot from there (TT$4). The larger hotels may be able to arrange transport from wherever you might be.

the north coast, **surfers** ride the breakers at **Sans Souci**, and the **rivers** and **waterfalls** inland from **Grande Riviere** and Matelot make jungle hiking a rewarding adventure.

Most people visit the Northeast Tip in a day as there are not a lot of **accommodation** options, though more are springing up each year. The fabulous *Mt Plaisir Estate Hotel* on the beach at Grande Riviere is one of Trinidad's best, however, and there are plenty of **beach houses** advertised for rent in the classified pages of the national newspapers. To explore the Northeast Tip easily you'll need your own car, though there is a rural **bus** service – concentrated at peak periods – and the occasional **maxi** and **taxi**. If you're **driving** from Port of Spain, it's quicker to avoid the car-choked EMR and take the Churchill Roosevelt Highway; turn left at the end of the highway and then right onto the quiet portion of the EMR to Valencia, from where the Valencia Road swings north to the Toco coast.

Stakeholders Against Destruction (SAD ☎670 1452, ⓦwww.toco.inter connection.org) provide services and information for the area, including community-based eco-tours, and help with finding accommodation and features of local interest.

# Valencia and Matura

The small town of **VALENCIA** sits about eight kilometres down the EMR from Arima, its bustling centre hosting a few shops, including a mini market, a petrol station (the last one before you get to Cumana) and the odd bar (including the lively *D'Ponderosa*), not to mention plenty of coconut vendors to quench your thirst. The **Hollis Reservoir** – a serene spot good for bird-watching if you go early in the morning – is on the eastern side of town; take the Quare Road turn-off from the Valencia Road – watch out for the "North West Water Project" sign. You'll need a permit from the Water and Sewage Association (WASA) to enter – call ☎662 2301. Further east is the well-posted North Oropuche River recreational facility – a rather grand name for picnic tables by the river; this pretty spot is a popular place for families on weekends taking a river swim and having a barbecue. Though there's a sign, the sharp left-hand **turn** for the **Toco Main Road** is easy to miss – watch out for the large Radio Toco sign; if you don't take this turn you'll be heading straight south to Sangre Grande (see p.198).

Starting at the east edge of town, the straight and smooth **Valencia Road** swings through mile upon mile of open country; other than the odd home or

## Nature Seekers Incorporated and Matura's leatherback turtles

If you want to see the leatherback turtles on Matura's beach, a permit (TT$5) and guide (US$10) can be organized and purchased through **Nature Seekers Incorporated** (☎668 7337, ✉natseek@tstt.net.tt) on the main road next door to *Joe's Lounge Bar*. Established in 1990, Nature Seekers is run by a team of twenty full-time dedicated volunteers who patrol the beach and offer a guide service aimed at educating locals and visitors on the importance of conserving this endangered species. Many of the guides come from the local community, whose indiscriminate hunting of the turtles was once the main cause of concern. Now, instead of poaching, they earn a living as guides and by patrolling the beach day and night. As well as accompanying visitors onto the sand, the guides move nests from areas where they are at risk from erosion or flooding, an activity which saves over 500 turtles every year. If you can visit during the nesting season, Nature Seekers can arrange for you to watch the amazing nesting process; you can also get more involved in the conservation process as a volunteer. The institution runs a lovely new guesthouse, costing TT$200 per night for bed and breakfast.

### How to help the turtles
1. Avoid buying souvenirs made from turtle shells and eating turtle meat.
2. When on the beach walk close to the water to prevent compacting the sand and soil above nests.
3. Don't discard plastic bags on the beach – turtles mistake them for jellyfish and try to eat them.
4. Adopt a turtle. As a way to raise funds Nature Seekers run a turtle adoption scheme. For US$35 visitors are given the opportunity to become a "Parent" for one of the hundreds of marine turtles which nest on Matura Beach. After choosing its name, you will receive a certificate of adoption and regular updates when your turtle hits the beach.

For details on how to behave if you come across a nesting turtle see p.354.

small provision field, signs of human habitation are few and far between and it's rare to pass another car. 19km east along the road from Valencia, the one-street town of **MATURA** consists of little more than a police station, a school, a health centre, a couple of grocery stores and a few modest houses slung along the tarmac. Other than stopping for a drink at one of the rum shops, the only reason to spend any time in the area is the **beach**, a windswept, four-kilometre stretch of fine yellow sand strewn with coconut husks, chip-chip shells, driftwood and the odd bit of flotsam and jetsam washed up by the fearsome waves. Though local people often take a dip, it's not a place for the uninitiated to swim, as the currents are extremely powerful. There are two entrances to the beach, both marked by Forestry Division signs. The first is in the centre of Matura; follow a challenging tarmac and gravel road to the right. The other end of the shore, reached from the far side of town down a dirt track, is known as **Rincon Beach**, which is well signposted. The whole beach is a protected area and a permit and guide are required at all times to enter (see box above). These restrictions are due to the presence of Matura's real attraction: the **leatherback turtles** which haul themselves on to the sand to lay eggs. Known locally as "Caldon", an adult turtle nests between five and seven times a season (March 1–Aug 31), usually at night, although sometimes in the late afternoon.

# Salybia and the Rio Seco Waterfall

Past Matura, the Toco Road meets the east coast for the first time. The view is often obscured by a thick cover of bush, though you do get some stunning views of small, wave-battered coves. On the other side of the road the bush conceals recent quarries that scar the landscape for a short stretch after Matura. The next community along this road, about 4km north, is the tiny village of **SALYBIA**, basically just a government school, *Friday's Grocery & Rest* bar and the Silver Gates Recreational Club.

By far the biggest reason to come here is the *Salybia Nature Resort and Spa* (T668 5959, Wwwwsalybiaresort.com; ❻), one of the most luxurious spots for miles around. In addition to panoramic views over Salybia Bay and on to Matura Beach, there's a fantastic oceanfront pool complete with waterfall, hidden caves and swim-up bar, and a splendid spa offering hydrotherapy, aromatherapy, massage and energy healing treatments. Standard rooms come with all sorts of amenities and the more expensive ones have the added extra of a sea-facing jacuzzi bath. The on-site restaurant is one of the best places to eat in the area and surprisingly moderately priced: main course options vary from shrimp in pepper sauce (TT$165) to stuffed aubergine (TT$100). The hotel also organizes guided hikes to the Rio Seco Waterfall (see below).

The small rugged beach in front of the hotel is not safe for swimming nor good for sunbathing. Although there are plans to build an artificial reef and create a white sand beach for hotel guests, currently the best option is the nearby **Saline Beach**. After a short downhill stretch past the resort, a large concrete bridge crosses the Rio Seco. Just before you reach the bridge you'll see a small hut selling tasty roasted corn and other snacks. A turn-off to the right leads down to the sands, which are a popular chill-out spot during the weekend when families come to bathe and picnic. For less crowded swimming, a small lagoon at the point where the river meets the sea is ideal for children; a lifeguard patrols the beach from 10.30am–3.30pm at weekends.

Opposite the car park is the clearly signposted trail to the **RIO SECO WATERFALL**, the route to one of the area's more spectacular **waterfalls** (known locally as **Salybia Waterfall**), beautifully placed in the **Matura Forest Reserve**. You can drive up for about ten to fifteen minutes if there's been no recent rain, but if the ground is wet, it's best to leave your car at the beach car park and tackle the rocky, uneven road on foot. It's a pleasant walk up a gentle incline enclosed by thick forest. Look out for a tall royal palm just before the pink house.

Past the house, the road has been churned into a muddy, rutted track by the wheels of forestry department vehicles. After 10 minutes, you should pass a wooden house on a hill to the left; carry straight on, skirting a small field of dasheen and sweetcorn and passing signs warning "Take only pictures, leave only footprints" and "Stay on the trail". After ten minutes' walk through the forest, the trail splits; you can follow the left-hand side to the river and an attractive, fairly deep swimming pool, while the right-hand, uphill track leads to the falls. A mossy picnic table and chairs carved out of felled trees and some rather incongruously placed signs punctuate the path; for no discernible reason, one of them declares the place a "nature habitat". You cross a river tributary and climb another hillock before descending to the falls – it's possible to follow the river all the way up to the main waterfall, passing some small cascades.

The trail's last stretch, bordered by rickety rails, is steep, but you get a good prospect of the waterfall below. The trunk of a huge silk cotton tree forms a bridge over the riverbed rocks and into a blue-green pool, 7m deep and 12m wide – a great place to bathe. The waterfall itself tumbles some 8m down the rocks, with plenty of handholds for an easy climb up and a dive from the top. Emerald light filters through the surrounding canopy, while a break in the cover above the water provides some direct sunlight. From the road, the walk should take about an hour, and the falls make a great picnic spot.

# North to Toco: Balandra, Rampanalgas and Cumana

After cutting inland across some wild and undeveloped bush, the Toco Road rejoins the coast at **BALANDRA**, a pretty fishing village with a popular beach but minimal facilities and no accommodation. The main entrance to the **beach** is at the western end, and is marked by a small sign; you should be able to find a space in the car park unless you visit at a weekend, when cars line the path to the road.

Backed by the fishing village and fringed by palm trees and Indian almonds, the beach is wide and inviting, with clean yellow sand and moderate waves. Most of the weekend crowds swim by the sheltered walled area past the car park, though swimming is safe along the whole length of the beach. A small shack by the car park sells soft drinks, pies and pholouri, and a rudimentary shower is located behind the fishing depot.

The next settlement along the coast, the sizeable village of **RAMPANAL-GAS** clings to the landward side of the road. It's a friendly sort of place – the local hot-spot is the unmissable *Arthur's Grocery* on the outskirts of town, which boasts a lively bar with a pool table, a grocery that sells cakes, sandwiches and crab and dumplins, and a postal agency. From a backroad which strikes off the Toco Road just past the sign announcing the village, a trail leads inland to the **Cirra Falls**. The trail crosses a stream and winds uphill, passing a rather grand wooden house on the right; after a ten-minute walk you'll come to a river, where crazy paving put in by the villagers leads to the cascade. The water-fall is small but attractive, with a deep, greenery-wreathed pool and a tree stump which forms a diving board for local kids. You can climb up the bank to the top of the falls, where there's another, smaller cascade.

Three kilometres past Rampanalgas the Toco Road goes uphill to the wild and beautiful **Guayamara Point**, a jut in the headland whose wooden bench-es are perfect for a picnic or simply to admire the fantastic views stretching far south to Matura Beach, Manzanilla Bay and the Trinity Hills.

The next village along the Toco Road, **CUMANA**, about another 4km north, was once the focal point for missionary work in the area. Today the town is still home to a number of churches as well as the last **petrol .station** (Mon–Sat 8.30am–6pm, Sun 8.30am–noon) on this road before Toco. There are also several noisy but friendly **bars** in the town, the most popular of which is *Oscar's* bar and roti shop on the corner of Archibald Street. *Rose's*, on the western outskirts, is another excellent option for food, selling all kinds of snacks including roti and salt fish and bake.

## Accommodation in Rampanalgas and Cumana

The two sleepy villages of Rampanalgas and Cumana are slowly changing as more **accommodation options** spring up in the area. *Jasmine's Ocean Resort*, 1 Simmons Drive, Rampanalgas (℡670 4567 or 625 8385, from the US

877/202 5567, from Europe 888/509 9852, ⓦwww.jasmines.net; ⑤), which is more established than others in the area, sits at the top of a steep, tree-lined and very potholed road. Although magnificent chandeliers still adorn the lobby, this once-plush hotel has seen better days. Its main attractions are a large pool, bar and sundeck with superb sea views overlooking Balandra Bay, and a reasonably priced restaurant that serves locally made wine. The somewhat plain rooms have satellite TV, a/c, phone and en-suite bathroom; the tiny balconies for the more expensive "standard" rooms do not justify the rates. There are nature trails on the hotel grounds and a beautiful rugged cove is a five-minute walk away through a small gate opposite the hotel driveway which is locked at night. Another attractive cove with wooden benches can be found just past *Jasmine's* after the road has gone downhill and over a small wooden bridge.

In Cumana, a right turn just before the Jehovah's Witness Hall leads to the fabulous French-style villa *Hotel Esterel* (ⓣ/ⓕ662 4084 or 670 4767, ⓦwww.hotelesterel.com; ⑧), sister hotel of *Pax Guesthouse* in Mount St Benedict (see p.156). In addition to a luxury rooftop penthouse, this spa resort has nine individually designed rooms furnished with French antiques and all come with a/c, mini-bars, TV, phones, hairdryers, Internet access, whirlpool baths and private balconies. This unique hotel's grounds are equally unusual. Intricate secret gardens complete with covered gazebos, meditation areas and birds and butterflies galore can be explored to the front, while at the back a series of ornate terraces lead down to the sea, a swimming pool, sauna and small poolside bar. Spa treatments, the fabulous French Creole *Restaurant Beaulieu sur Mer*, birdwatching trips and a nearby beach complete the resort's offerings – well worth a day's visit even if you don't stay overnight.

A more budget-conscious option in Cumana is the *Agro-Tourism Centre* (ⓣ670 0068 or 670 3694, ⓔrooks@pariasprings.com; ④), which has eight simple, comfortable rooms with shared bathrooms, as well as dormitory accommodation for twenty; rates include breakfast. To find it, turn off the main road just before the petrol station onto Anglis/Harris Road; continue through the village for about 1.5km, and turn right at the football ground – the *Centre* is on the left.

# Toco and Galera Point

North of Cumana, the quality of the road deteriorates until it reaches the largest community along this stretch of coast: **TOCO**, an attractive, quiet fishing village which retains a distinctly antiquated air. This proud, close-knit community has one of the largest concentrations of Baptists in the Caribbean, which helped inspire one of its sons, the great Trinidadian writer Earl Lovelace, to write *The Wine of Astonishment*, a novel about Baptist persecution under colonial rule (see "Books," p.358). Most of the buildings are dilapidated gingerbreads made of weather-beaten wood. Though most residents make their money from fishing or farming, many have recently begun to sell off family land to prospective developers, tempted by the high real-estate prices that would be brought about by the oft-mooted suggestions to build a **ferry terminal** here, forming a second sea bridge to Tobago, which is a mere 20km away and easily visible on clear days. The plan would entail oil bunkering facilities, docks for cruise ships and trawler traffic, but local protest has shelved it for now.

As you enter the town, **Galera Road** strikes off to the right; this is where Radio Toco is based – tune in at 106.7FM – a local landmark and an integral part of island life. Behind the station is *Wad-P's Kitchen,* a good place to stop for a local lunch. The road continues past the Toco Composite School, site of the **Toco Folk Museum** (open during school hours 8am–3.30pm, or ring to make appointment ☎670 8261; TT$3 adults, TT$2 children). Started as a school project, this small museum houses Amerindian artifacts, local shells, snakeskins, butterflies and insects, and household items, including a gramophone and some rare 78rpm calypso records, which can be played if requested. The curators, mainly school teachers, are an excellent source of local history. The road continues to a good **beach**. A gorgeous double horseshoe of yellow sand scattered with white fragments of finger coral, the beach is busy on weekends, when it's a popular spot for a cook-out, and fried fish, soft drinks and local sweets are sold from a thatch-roofed stall. Surfers skim along beyond the reef, but the water close to the shore is translucent and pretty calm.

### Practicalities

Most of the **route taxis** from Sangre Grande turn around at Toco; if you're heading further west, you may have to wait here for quite a while, or hitch a lift. Unless you want to spend time in the town or see Galera Point, it's a good idea to try and find a ride to Matelot or Grande Riviere.

There are some basic **places to stay** in Toco, mostly catering for local surfers – ask in the village. For more upscale accommodation, try the *Blue Haven Resort* (c/o Marlene Clark ☎670 1563; ❼), a blue-and-white wooden apartment above *Annifar's Snack Bar.* The spacious three-bedroom unit sleeps up to six people and has a fully equipped kitchen, bathroom, TV, wooden floors and a verandah decorated with a colourful mural. The snack bar downstairs serves good local **food** at bargain prices, if you can't be bothered cooking. If you are staying for a few days, watch out for Toco's fortnightly Under the Sapodilla Tree Lime, a long-standing local party with music and rum to spare.

## Galera Point

Past Toco's beach, Galera road meanders to **Galera Point**, Trinidad's extreme eastern tip and site of the Galera **lighthouse**. A stocky tower built in 1897, the lighthouse flashes its red beacon over a notoriously treacherous stretch of sea known to fishermen as the "graveyard". If the keeper is in a good mood, he'll let you climb all eighty-three rickety steps to the top for a fantastic view over inland coconut estates, down the coast to Matelot. Below the lighthouse is a windblown, rocky bluff – known as Fishing Rock – pounded by crashing waves that send up mists of salty spray; several currents swirl in the shallows, a blowhole under the rock gives off occasional moans, and the point where the royal blue Caribbean Sea meets the murky, pastel-blue Atlantic Ocean is easily visible far out to sea. It's a strange, wild spot, filled with an uneasy energy; the lighthouse keeper maintains that the point is haunted, relating tales of car doors slamming when there is no car, and ghostly wails in the still of the night. It's likely that these tales spring from an incident that occurred during a 1699 **rebellion** at a Spanish encomienda in San Rafael in which Amerindians killed three Capuchin monks. Incensed, Spanish forces pursued the culprits to Galera, where they leapt off the cliffs to their deaths rather than be killed by their slave-masters.

## The Toco Foundation

During the 1980s, the traditional agricultural and fishing economy of the Toco region fell into decline. Local residents reacted by forming the **Toco Foundation** (Ⓦ www.opus.co.tt/toco/), which works to create sustainable solutions to poverty in the region through various community-based initiatives, including tourism. Two such successes have been the extremely influential Radio Toco and the *Eastern Voice* newspaper. As well as local music and events information, Radio Toco broadcasts public service and health information. *Eastern Voice* is a monthly paper (TT$1) that carries local and national news, event information and, perhaps most importantly for the traveller, advertising for local services.

# Sans Souci and around

Past Toco, the road Toco Main Road becomes **Paria Main Road** as it turns west onto the north coast, running perilously close to the cliffs and making for a beautiful, if heart-stopping, drive. Shattering all illusions of what a Caribbean seashore should look like, huge waves crash onto the wild and rugged coast, and jagged rocks poke out of a surging ocean in which only the suicidal would swim. There are several relatively safe beaches, however, around the next village, **SANS SOUCI**, all boasting waves large enough to make this the island's **surfing** capital and a regular venue for competitions. One of the biggest annual events, staged in late October or early November, is the International Adventure Festival, with mountain biking, surfing and hashing competitions (for info: ℡ 622 8826, Ⓦ www.pariasprings.com).

From San Souci's beaches you can see Tobago on a clear day and its lights on a clear night. The largest beach is known simply as **Big Bay**; here the waves are a little smaller and there are two places to eat on the road, both serving excellent food. *The Beach Break Café* serves up sandwiches and cold drinks, while the adjacent *Beach Break Rest & Bar* serves inexpensive Creole dishes and is the centre of the village's nightlife.

There are a few places **to stay**: Kathleen Manswell (℡ 670 1345; ❸) rents out a simple but roomy apartment with two bedrooms sleeping up to four, with furnished kitchen, lounge and verandah, two minutes from the beach. A little further away from the sand, but right on the river, on the western side of the village, Carmen Joe (℡ 670 1867; ❷) is the caretaker for a basic wood and brick cottage with three bedrooms sleeping up to nine people – a real bargain. Past the bay, Paria Main Road winds inland through impossibly lush rainforest which lets up only at the tiny **Monte Video** village, notable mostly for the cold beers on sale at the lone bar. Further west is the tiny village of **L'Anse Noire**, home to *Violet's Holiday Resort* (℡ 637 3973; ❷), a spacious two-bedroom house with 1960s wooden furniture and a dark kitchen, just ten minutes' walk from the beach. Beach house rentals are advertised by weather-worn signs on placards and houses along this stretch of road if you're looking for other options.

# Grande Riviere

One of the most appealing villages on this stretch of the north coast, **GRANDE RIVIERE** is where the rainforests of Trinidad's Northern Range tumble haphazardly onto deserted beaches lapped by impossibly blue waters. Nicknamed "beyond's God's back", Grande Riviere is the only community on this coastline which has any kind of tourist infrastructure. The beautiful *Mount Plaisir Estate* hotel (see p.173), right on the beach, has spurred a host of local residents to open up **guesthouses**, but the remote location has kept development low-key, and the town remains one of the most unspoilt, idyllic places you'll find anywhere on the island. Interaction between visitors and local people has none of the money-oriented duplicity of other resorts, and local people tend to be incredibly welcoming, often throwing parties for guests who are leaving.

Named after the wide, fast-flowing river which originates deep in the Northern Range and runs down to the sea at the eastern end of town, Grande Riviere also boasts a superlative **beach**, a wide, gentle curve of coarse yellow sand with a few unobtrusive buildings blending seamlessly into otherwise unbroken jungle. Tall forested headlands border the sand to the east, where you can take a freshwater bath in the river, while a good kilometre away, the western end is sealed from the rest of the coast by rocky outcrops. Strong waves provide passable surfing or an invigorating swim, and give **leatherback turtles** the extra push they need to haul themselves up the sand at laying time; Oxbill and Olive Ridley turtles also nest on these sands. As in Matura, the beach is a protected area between March 1 and August 31, and you need a permit to enter between dusk and dawn during this part of the year, which can be purchased from *Mount Plaisir Estate*.

The liveliest part of the beach centres around *Mount Plaisir Estate*, where the **bar** is a favourite liming spot and a lovely stall on the beach sells fine calabash art and locally made jewellery. Most people who stay in town divide their time between the beach and the interior, where there are hosts of **waterfalls** and **river walks** as well as excellent **bird-watching** – the rare **piping guan**, a kind of wild turkey that has died out in more developed areas, is quite common here. Other activities include horse riding – ask at the hotel – snorkelling and boat trips. Most guides in the village work through either the hotel or the **Grande Riviere Nature Tours Guide Association** (T670 8381), housed in a small hut between *Mount Plaisir Estate* and the *Le Grande Almandier* hotel (see opposite); if this is closed ask in the village for Michael James. You can be taken by pirogue to Paria beach and hike to Paria Waterfall (TT$700), or go fishing (TT$150 for 1hr 30min) or sail to Tobago (TT$900). Guides are also available for hikes on nature trails in both Grand Riviere and Matelot (TT$50), or you can rent kayaks for TT$20 an hour. Another guide is Cyril James (see *Le Grande Almandier* below) who organizes a night's **camping** in the bush, which includes building a treehouse at the end of a day's hike. Local character Jakatan, the originator of the "**Earth People**", a loose family group who lived the natural life deep in the bush according to their own set of customs, also takes groups to "Jakatan Falls", a waterfall that he "discovered" and which has been locally named in his honour. Jakatan makes an excellent source of information on local folklore and is working on a campsite in the hills. Most of his tours cost around TT$100 per person. The hotels can also help to organize other tours, such as **snorkelling** trips to nearby Langosta Cove, **boat trips** to remote beaches as well as day trips to Asa Wright, Blanchisseuse and Port of Spain.

A good way to explore both village and beach is to take a loop walk; start in the village and walk east from Guy's Rec Club, turn left at the faded sign welcoming you to Grande Riviere, then another left at the fork; a shady, flat track leads past the Grande Riviere Fishing centre to the beach and is a good place to spot birds and butterflies. Walk back to the village along the beach to complete the loop.

The rural **bus** service runs seven buses a day during the week from Sangre Grande to Grande Riviere (3.30am, 5.30am, 7.30am, 9.30am, 1.30pm, 3.30pm, 5.30pm) and four on weekends (5.30am, 8am, 1pm, 4pm) costing TT$8. Maxis also leave for Grande Riviere from Sangre Grande (TT$9) as do route taxis (TT$10); see also p.198.

## Practicalities

One of the finest **places to stay** on the island is right on the beach at the eco-friendly and easygoing *Mount Plaisir Estate* (T670 8381, F670 0057, Wwww.mtplaisir.com; ④). The en-suite rooms here are fitted with solid, locally made furniture, while beautiful paintings hang on the walls and surfaces are decorated with driftwood oddities. Most rooms sleep four people, some six; try and get one with a stable door overlooking the beach. The hotel also boasts the fantastic *Ylang Ylang* **restaurant** (daily 8am–9pm); the menu, printed on handmade paper made in local schools, could easily hold its own in the swankiest of Port of Spain's eateries: local creole cuisine, as well as Indian and Italian dishes are complemented by an extensive wine list and imaginative vegetarian options. Breakfast and lunch are available, and three-course dinners cost TT$100–165. The hotel is also famous for its "botanical garden in the forest" where they grow some 50 different types of fruit to produce the juice and jams served in the restaurant. The hotel will also take you to the airport (US$85).

Across the track which leads to the beach is *Le Grande Almandier* (T670 1013, Wwww.legrandealmandier.com; ⑥), owned by Cyril James. The pleasant rooms of this attractive and friendly hotel, situated off a large sea-facing sun deck, can sleep four, have a fan and en-suite bathroom, and rates include breakfast and free use of the hotel canoes. The lovely beachfront bar and restaurant downstairs is a popular place for an evening drink. The restaurant serves contemporary Creole-French cuisine (10am–11pm; dinner TT$70–100) and is an excellent spot for lunch – burgers and sandwiches from TT$30–50.

Turn left at the *Mount Plaisir* turn-off to find *McEachnie's Haven*, Bristol and Thomas sts (T670 1014 or 642 0477, Wwww.mchaventt.com; ⑤). This yellow guesthouse perched on the hillside provides clean, homely rooms sleeping up to four, with fans, mosquito nets and en-suite bathroom. *Haven* is run by a multitalented family: the owner, Ingrid, cooks delicious, inexpensive meals, such as chicken in coconut and ginger sauce; her husband, Eric, is "Roots" of the local band Roots and Branches, which started the careers of many famous local musicians; and their children are all tour guides.

In the village, you can stay at the dingy but economical apartment above *Guy's Rec Club* (T670 0048; ②); there are three bedrooms, a living room and a kitchen. The bar downstairs is a lively liming spot, with music (turned down if guests request it) and a pool table. Opposite the community centre and playing field, Miss Freda (no phone; ②) has several simple double rooms above her home; bathroom and kitchen are shared. Mr Roseman (no phone – ask for him in the village or at *Mount Plaisir*) has a pink, two-bedroom house on a hill overlooking town with two bedrooms, a kitchen, outside shower and toilet, and a verandah with a gorgeous view; the rent is TT$200 per week.

There are also numerous small guesthouses and host homes in the village; look out for signs in the village or ask around – good options include *The Fatherless Rest* (②–③) opposite the school playground and *Bumpings Guesthouse* (②–③) to the right as you enter the village.

You'll have to make your own **entertainment** in Grande Riviere; apart from the strains of Roots and Branches, the local band, whose nightly sessions echo over the village from the rehearsal hall on top of a hill above *Guy's*, things are quiet in the evening. *Jamesy's Stone Wall Bar* on the main road is a friendly spot, though, as is the *First and Last Bar*. You can buy **snacks** and **food** from Guy's Grocery and there is a post office in the village.

# Matelot and around

Of the many plank-lined bridges that pepper the recently restored Paria Main Road past Grande Riviere, the one crossing **Shark River** is the largest. The river is a popular swimming spot, with a couple of deep **pools** just before the water meets the sea and plenty more upstream; during holiday weekends, campers pitch tents along its banks. Walking upriver makes a great excursion, though you have to clamber over some mighty rocks to reach the best pools, and you'll need a guide – contact the local *Pawi Culture & Eco Club* (T670 1816) to negotiate several tributaries and the occasional swing off into the bush.

Beyond the river and past the tiny village of **St Helena**, a ten-minute scenic coastal drive takes you to the fishing hamlet of **MATELOT**, the last settlement on the Paria Main Road. The village square is flanked by a plain Catholic church and a couple of rum shops; from here, a track leads down to the fishermen's beach. Houses, some of them quite grand, meander up the hillsides. The best recreation round here is swimming in the **Matelot River**; follow the main road to the left and bear right. There's a wooden bridge, and the water runs crystal clear down to the sandy **beach**. A sparse thatched hut provides an outdoor cooking space. The adjacent football field sees plenty of action at dusk; in one corner a large TIDCO sign points the way to the Madamas River Nature Walk, the start of the bench trail to Blanchisseuse. A Glasgow University research project has inspired locals to form the *Pawi Culture & Eco Club*, a group of fourteen licensed **tour guides** who can take you into the forest interior, to the Paria and Matelot waterfalls and the undeveloped beaches between Matelot and Blanchisseuse; like their counterparts in Matura, they are part of the monitoring and protection programme for leatherback turtles. **Entertainment** is focused around the *Sea Breeze Recreational Club* (T670 1724; ❷) on Pyke Street, the main bar in the village. The owners – Janet and Raymond Joseph – also rent out two rustic wooden **cottages** in the village for bargain prices (❷–❸). One overlooks the river and the other has a sea view, and both come with equipped kitchen, fan and bathroom. Other rooms are available in the village – ask at *Sea Breeze* for more information. There are **no restaurants** here, but if you don't want to cook, Mr James, who runs the grocery shop opposite the church, prepares excellent local **meals** for reasonable prices. Rural buses leave Grande Riviere for Matelot three time a day during the week at 6am, 1pm and 6pm (TT$2); maxis run infrequently throughout the day from Sangre Grande (TT$20 or TT$3 from Grande Riviere) as do taxis (TT$20 or TT$4 from Grande Riviere).

Past here, the road ends; there's nothing but a bench trail along the wild and undeveloped coast to Blanchisseuse, 19km to the west (see p.140). Local fishermen can usually be persuaded to take you along the undeveloped coast from Matelot, Paria, Madamas or Blanchisseuse; a round trip will take about four hours depending upon conditions, route and number of people travelling (around TT$700 per boat for the whole stretch). Ask at the fishing depot in Matelot. The forest inland of Matelot is riddled with hunters' trails, including a half-day trek to the 3-metre **Matelot Waterfall**, with its wide, deep pool. Logging over the past year has churned up the path and taken some of the magic out of the walk – especially around Madamas Bay, which is especially muddy after rain. Following recent incidents of assaults on tourists along this path the services of a guide are essential; contact *Pawi Sport Culture & Eco Club* (T670 1816, or ask around in the village).

# Central Trinidad

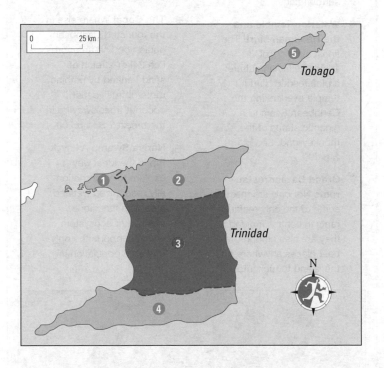

CHAPTER 3 # Highlights

✳ **Bat- and bird-watching**
Witness the awesome
en-masse exodus of
over one million bats
from the Tamana caves
(p.195) or the roosting of
thousands of scarlet ibis
at the Caroni Swamp
(p.183), both occurring
at dusk in magnificent
surroundings.

✳ **Waterloo Temple and
the Hanuman Murti** The
finest symbols of
Trinidad's Indian culture:
a picturesque Hindu
temple overlooking the
Caribbean Sea and a
gigantic statue of the
monkey-god. **See p.188
& p.190**

✳ **Grand Bazaar restaurants** Not only are these
some of the only restaurants in central Trinidad,
they are also among the
best places anywhere on
the island to tuck into

Indian, Italian and
Chinese food. **See p.182**

✳ **Pointe-a-Pierre
Wildfowl Trust** Gawk at
scarlet ibis, muscovy
duck and the like in the
middle of an oil refinery:
a striking juxtaposition of
two very different sides
of Trini life. **See p.191**

✳ **The Cocal** Where else in
the touristed Caribbean
could you find an unbro-
ken 24km-stretch of
sand flanked by nothing
more obtrusive than
coconut trees swaying in
the breeze? **See p.200**

✳ **Nariva Swamp** A kayak
trip is the ideal way to
explore this internation-
ally recognized wetland
area with its unique
freshwater ecosystem
which supports the only
manatee population in
Trinidad. **See p.200**

▲ Prayer flags

# Central Trinidad

A compact area of roughly 350 square kilometres, **central Trinidad** encompasses an astonishing variety of landscapes. The **west coast** is for the most part gritty and industrialized, punctuated by brash commercial towns such as **Chaguanas**. But even in this relatively more urbanized region you can still find natural oases like the **Caroni Swamp**, home of the scarlet ibis, and, further south, the **Pointe-a-Pierre Wildfowl Trust**, whose pristine pools are nestled incongruously on the grounds of a huge oil refinery. Inland, the flatlands of the agricultural **Caroni Plains** – dotted with somnolent villages and the country's only airport at **Piarco** – rise gently to the wooded **Montserrat Hills** in the south. Also in the inland area you'll find the awesome **Tamana bat caves** as well as the country's two largest dams and reservoirs, **Caroni Arena** in the Caroni Plains and **Navet** in the Montserrat Hills. The only town of any size in the more rural **east coast** region is the busy market centre of **Sangre Grande**, south of which lies the stunning **Manzanilla Beach**, with its seemingly endless avenues of palms, and the starkly beautiful **Nariva Swamp**.

Central Trinidad's population is mostly descended from Indian indentured labourers who came here in the 1840s to replace freed slaves. This heritage is visible in the Hindu shrines that adorn practically every other yard as well as **Indian festivals** such as Diwali and Phagwa which are celebrated much more vigorously in places like Chaguanas than elsewhere on the island. Indeed, when you visit the outstanding **Waterloo Temple** and **Hanuman Murti**, both just southwest of Chaguanas, you could be forgiven for thinking you were in India rather than the southern Caribbean.

Much of this part of the island remains deeply traditional or, as Trinis put it, "countrified". Some people here still subsist by growing breadfruit, ground provisions and dasheen bush, though things are slowly modernizing. These days instead of the traditional mud *tapia* houses built by the indentured Indians, you are more likely to see concrete homes built on stilts as a protection against frequent floods. Mechanical harvesters now reap the fields in place of labourers with machetes, and most produce is taken to the market or factory in trucks instead of a buffalo cart.

On the Caroni Plains, wide, flat expanses of **sugar cane and coconut estates** stretch as far as the eye can see, while in the heart of the island around the Montserrat Hills, huge reserves of awe-inspiring **rainforest** shelter countless species of flora and fauna. **Wildlife**, including scarlet ibis, manatees, red howler monkeys and caimans, can easily be seen by visiting the swamps, reserves and reservoirs, and with many of the island's 430 avian species nesting in the protected areas, the region is excellent for **birdwatching**.

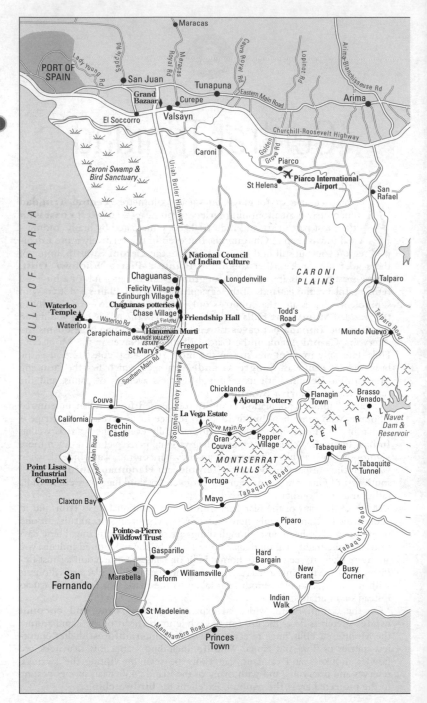

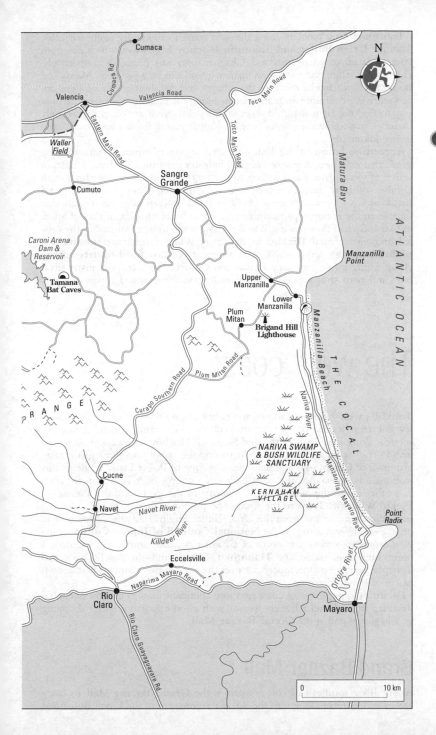

**Transport** is no problem along the west coast; its towns are easily accessible from the **Uriah Butler and Solomon Hochoy highways**, which run from Port of Spain to Chaguanas and Chaguanas to San Fernando, respectively. However, reaching the rural areas further inland can be a problem. **Maxis** and **taxis** take long, circular routes to the villages, and the absence of road signs can make driving confusing. In many places, asking for directions is often the only way to find the right road, although country directions are often frustratingly vague – "just round the corner" could mean anything from a hundred metres to five kilometres.

**Accommodation** in this little-touristed region is minimal, with the few hotels that exist geared more toward oil industry personnel (or Trini couples in search of some privacy and willing to pay by the hour). There are also a small number of **host homes** which can be contacted through the Bed and Breakfast Co-Operative Society (☎/🖷 663 4413). Keep in mind, though, that since even the remotest parts of this region can be reached from Port of Spain in two and a half hours or less, it makes more sense to base yourself in the capital and visit central Trinidad in day trips. While formal **restaurants** and **nightlife** are also very limited, there are plenty of **fast-food outlets** serving cheap, filling meals, especially Indian and Chinese food, and the many small **bars** and **rum shops** are good for friendly conversation and a night out.

# The west coast

Trinidad's **west coast** is a sometimes rather uneasy mix of nature and industry. Oil refineries and cement factories rub shoulders with workers' dormitory suburbs along the Uriah Butler and Solomon Hochoy highways, which connect Port of Spain and San Fernando, passing the rapidly developing commercial town of **Chaguanas** and the industrial zone of **Point Lisas**. Yet despite its inauspicious appearance, the coast harbours a couple of rich habitats for birds and other fauna: the huge **Caroni Swamp** in the north and the **Pointe-a-Pierre Wildfowl Trust** to the south. The predominance of Indian culture is immediately noticeable from the Uriah Butler Highway, as the 12-metre statue of Swami Vivekananda at the **National Council of Indian Culture** complex looms into view just north of Chaguanas; while south of Chaguanas a more impressive statue, the **Hanuman Murti**, and the lovely **Waterloo Temple**, perched picturesquely out over the sea, are the country's best known places of Hindu devotion.

**Facilities** along the west coast are more abundant than in the rest of central Trinidad (though still relatively sparse), with good opportunities for shopping in Chaguanas and at the **Grand Bazaar Mall**.

## Grand Bazaar Mall

About 10km southeast of Port of Spain is the **Grand Bazaar Mall**, its fancy arches and turrets poking into the sky at the junction of the Uriah Butler and

Churchill Roosevelt highways. The Mall is a major landmark on the route between Port of Spain and Chaguanas, and maxis and route taxis will stop there on request. Although it has a wide array of **shops** (mostly Mon–Sat 10am–5pm) selling everything from books to swimwear to Carib beer merchandise, it also holds the best **restaurants** in central Trinidad. *Imperial Garden* (Mon–Thurs 11am–10pm, Fri & Sat 11am–11pm; ☎662 6971) is a swish place offering a good selection of Chinese dishes, complemented by a variety of mouth-watering and occasionally spicy sauces, as well as ribs. Directly opposite is *Botticelli's* (Mon–Fri 11am–11pm, Sat 3–11pm; ☎645 8733), ostentatiously decorated with Roman columns and a fountain outside, and serving a generous selection of delicious Italian dishes, some given a Creole twist by the use of local fish and vegetables. The pick of the bunch, however, is *Rasam* (Mon–Sat 11am–11pm; ☎645 0994), where the magnificently furnished dining room is redolent of the prawn coconut curry, several types of *dosa* and the other excellent southern Indian specialities served here. All of these places are on the expensive side (main courses at *Botticelli's* and *Rasam* are TT$100 and up) and reservations are recommended.

# Caroni Swamp and Bird Sanctuary

A few kilometres further south on the Uriah Butler Highway from the Grand Bazaar Mall is one of Trinidad's most heavily promoted environmental attractions, the **Caroni Swamp and Bird Sanctuary**. This is the island's only roosting place for the national bird: the elegant, long-billed and spectacularly red **scarlet ibis**. These sixty square kilometres of tidal lagoons, marshland and mangrove forest bordering the Gulf of Paria between the mouths of the Caroni and Madame Espagnole rivers are home to 157 species of birds, including white flamingos, egrets and blue herons, while caimans, snakes, opossums, racoons and silky anteaters can be observed in the water and the surrounding mangroves. Caroni Swamp was designated a protected wildlife area in 1953, but poaching still occurs, and the reserve also suffers the effects of industrial waste pollution. Nonetheless, it remains a quiet, mysteriously beautiful place, and well worth a visit. The mangrove trees themselves have an otherworldly appearance: some have twisted aerial roots growing downwards into the water, while others have roots that grow upwards, emerging from the murky depths like stalagmites.

To visit the swamp you must take a **boat tour**, usually in a 15-seat wooden pirogue. The boatmen know the swamp and its wildlife well, and will point out birds, plants and animals of interest as they lead you through a maze of tunnel-like channels to the mangrove islands where the scarlet ibis roost at dusk. Once the boat engines shudder to a halt, a spectacular scene unfolds: as the birds flock in, an area of green mangrove gradually turns a vibrant red. It is not possible to get close to the birds' roosting spot without disturbing them, so bring binoculars or a powerful zoom lens, or you'll see little more than red specks against the dark green foliage.

The ibis's intense red plumage owes its pigment to carotene, derived from the bird's main prey – shrimp, worms and the tree-climbing fiddler crabs which inhabit the swamp in their millions; carotene substitutes don't do the trick, and in captivity the birds turn a faded pink. During the day the scarlet ibis fly to Venezuela to feed – about an 18km trip – returning at dusk to roost in the upper branches of mangrove islands in the midst of large lagoons. In April and May, breeding pairs construct flat, open nests in the mangroves from twigs and their own droppings. Once laid, the eggs incubate for just under a month before all-black hatchlings emerge – it's another few months before their diet replaces the dark feathers with brilliant crimson.

**Driving** to the swamp from Port of Spain, you'll need to leave at 3pm to catch the 4pm tour, as rush-hour traffic can be terrible. The exit off the Uriah Butler Highway is well signposted. **Maxis** and **route taxis** run from Port of Spain to Chaguanas; ask them to drop you at the Caroni Swamp exit, from where it's a five-minute walk. Aside from an incongruously large car park, facilities at the swamp are limited to toilets, while drinks are sold from coolers in the boats. Make sure to bring plenty of insect repellent during the rainy season (June–Dec), when mosquitoes go on the offensive.

**Tours** of the Caroni Swamp (TT\$60/US\$10) leave daily at 4pm from the assembly point in the car park and last two and half hours; advance booking is advisable. Contact Nanan (℡645 1305) or James (℡662 7356) for more information and to make bookings.

# Chaguanas

The Uriah Butler Highway ends and the Solomon Hochoy Highway begins roughly halfway down the west coast at the sprawling settlement of **CHAGUANAS**, one of Trinidad's oldest and (fourth) largest towns. A major **shopping centre** with a couple of glitzy malls alongside its rambling old market, Chaguanas is also one of Trinidad's great centres of **Indian culture**: just outside town is the **National Council of Indian Culture**, an important venue for Hindu festivals, while the elegant **Lion House** on the main thoroughfare is the birthplace of the acclaimed Indo-Trinidadian novelist V.S. Naipaul.

The town, which derives its name from an Amerindian tribe, the Chaguanes, who once lived in the region, was pretty much a one-horse town until Indian indentured labourers came in the 1840s to work on nearby sugar and cocoa estates. By the 1880s Chaguanas had become the most important **market town** in central Trinidad, connected to Port of Spain by rail lines and steamer ships. As the sugar industry declined in the early twentieth century, many Indians moved into professions such as journalism and the law, creating the middle-class intelligentsia from which **V.S. Naipaul** emerged and that would serve as the milieu for some of his early novels. Though the trains and steamer are long gone, the construction of the Uriah Butler and Solomon Hochoy highways in the late 1940s ensured that at least the town remained easily accessible. The 1970s **oil boom** gave Chaguanas a new lease on life; conveniently located near the oil-rich south, it has since developed into a shopping centre for those who prefer not to travel all the way into Port of Spain, and its swanky suburbs such as Lange Park are testament to the area's growing prosperity.

## Arrival and information

Chaguanas's **post office** is located at 11 St Yves St (Mon–Fri 7am–5pm, Sat 8am–2pm) and there are several **banks** in the town centre. Javinco Limited in the Centre Pointe Mall offers cheap **Internet access** (Mon–Sat 9am–6pm; TT\$5 per hr).

There is no **accommodation** to speak of in Chaguanas, though the town is easily reached in about 30 minutes from the capital. **Maxis** from City Gate, Port of Spain, take you to the maxi stand next to the Mid Centre Mall in Chaguanas for TT\$4. **Route taxis** from Broadway, Port of Spain, will also drop you opposite the Mid Centre Mall for TT$6. **PTSC buses** leave City Gate for Chaguanas every 30 minutes and cost TT$4; the stop in Chaguanas is next to *KFC* at the entrance to the Uriah Butler Highway. Maxis and route taxis to the rest of the west coast can be taken from the transportation stands at the Mid Centre Mall.

## The Town

Ranged around the junction of Chaguanas Main Road and the old Southern Main Road, the centre of town is a busy amalgam of new shops, hand-painted signs and street-side clothes stalls. It is dominated by two large malls: the **Mid Centre Mall** and **Centre Pointe Mall** (also known as Ramsarran Plaza), both great places to find bargains in shoes and clothes imported direct from New York and India.

The big, old-fashioned **market area**, which lines the southern edge of Chaguanas Main Road and the narrow alleys behind it, offers a complete – and far more absorbing – contrast to the town's malls: the pavements are chock-a-block with countless wooden stalls selling dirt-cheap clothes, ornaments and fashion accessories; whatever you're after, you're more or less guaranteed to get it cheaper here than in Port of Spain. Be prepared to haggle, though – it's expected. The stalls start to thin out as you approach the **fruit and vegetable market**, an industrial-style hangar bedecked with bright red wrought-iron arches; inside, old women sit behind stalls groaning under the weight of plantain, dasheen, chillies, ground provisions and artfully arranged piles of fruit. Chaguanas' busiest trading days, and the best times to visit even if you're not shopping, are Friday and Saturday.

### Lion House

The imposing **Lion House** (Ⓦwww.lionhouse.com), a stocky, arch-fronted edifice a few hundred metres further down Chaguanas Main Road from the market, was the birthplace and childhood home of Trinidad's most famous writer, V.S. Naipaul. This fine, glaringly white-painted example of North Indian architecture takes its name from the lions that adorn the stout columns supporting its grand arcade. Built in 1926 by the Pundit Capildeo, it became the residence of the Naipaul family when the writer's father Seepersad married Capildeo's daughter Droapatie. In his 1961 novel *A House for Mr Biswas*, Naipaul describes his experience of growing up in this house, surrounded by his mother's wealthy, religious and domineering family. Still a private residence, the Lion House is not open to the public, although the impressive exterior can easily be viewed from the road.

## National Council of Indian Culture

The large complex of the **National Council of Indian Culture** (☎671 6242), also known as the **Diwali Nagar** site, on the Uriah Butler Highway near the Endeavour overpass, about 2km north of Chaguanas, is dominated by a 12-metre statue of **Swami Vivekananda**, a nineteenth-century thinker from Calcutta held in high regard in Trinidad for his insistence that Indians should find freedom through education, technology and physical fitness.

Built as a venue for traditional Indian festivals, the complex consists of little more than the statue, a large fenced-off area, a portakabin office and a concrete structure where stalls can be set up. But during the numerous festivals that punctuate the Indian year – all of which are attended by many of the country's top dignitaries – the place is utterly transformed. The highlight of the year is

## Phagwa

A lighthearted, joyous celebration of the new year and the arrival of spring, the Hindu Holi festival – known in Trinidad as **Phagwa** (pronounced "pag-wah") – is held around the first full moon in March to mark the end of the Hindu calendar's twelfth month (Phaglun). Upbeat and Carnivalesque – to the horror of more traditional Hindus, who consider this attitude *adharamic* (anti-religious) – Phagwa celebrations are massive outdoor parties that represent a symbolic triumph of light over darkness and happiness over suffering. In Indian religious mythology, the festival commemorates the death of Holika, the sister of an evil king, Hiranyakashyapu, who repeatedly tried to murder his son Prahalad because of the latter's insistence on worshipping Vishnu as the only God. Immune to flames, Holika carried Prahalad into a fire, but the gods ensured that she burned to death; her brother was later slain by Vishnu. Holika's conflagration is re-enacted the night before the main festivities, when sins amassed in the previous year are ceremonially consumed by the flames of large bonfires.

The main festivities revolve around traditions such as the singing of devotional folk songs called **chowtals**, composed specifically for Phagwa to tell the story of the festival and accompanied by goatskin *dholak* drums and brass cymbals called *ghanj*. Local businesses sponsor *chowtal* competitions in the weeks preceding Phagwa, and the winners perform on the day itself. The principal focus of the festival, though, is an intense fuschia-pink dye known as **abir**, which is strewn about as powder or mixed with water and squirted from a plastic bottle renamed a *pichakaaree*; participants wear white to make the most of the ensuing glorious mess. Accompanying the *abir* squirting are **pichakaaree songs** – topical ditties sung in a mix of English and Hindi which relate current issues and religious concepts – while classical Indian dancers display their movements and chutney soca fuels the more risqué dancing. Games add to the fun; adults participate in **makhan chor**, where teams form a human pyramid in order to grab a suspended flag; and children compete in roti-eating contests in which skins are strung through the middle and tied in a line to be eaten with no hands allowed.

Chaguanas hosts one of the largest celebrations in Trinidad, the **Kendra Phagwa Festival**, in an open space off Longdenville Old Road. There are other gatherings at Aranguez Savannah in San Juan and at Couva, but none are widely publicized – to find the exact date, you'll have to scan the community events listings in the newspapers, or call TIDCO (☎623 1932).

**Diwali** (the festival of lights), nine days and nights of celebration at the end of October. All aspects of Indian culture in Trinidad are represented during Diwali: the complex is decorated with paintings and statues of Hindu gods; every type of music, from Indian classical to chutney (the Indian version of soca), is played; and there are performances of Indian folk theatre and modern dramas. The dozens of stalls provide a fascinating mix of culture and commerce: those selling burglar alarms and furniture do a roaring trade alongside those surrounded by people trying to find their Diwali souvenir trinket.

Christian and Muslim Indians also have their own festivities at the site for Christmas and Eid-ul-Fitr, respectively, while **Indian Arrival Day** (May 30) re-enacts the docking of the *Fatel Rozack*, which carried the first 225 Indian immigrants to Trinidad in 1845. Displays in the fenced-off area of the complex reveal the way of life and working conditions of the indentured labourers.

## Eating and entertainment

Chaguanas has no shortage of **fast-food outlets**: along with *KFC*, *Blimpies* and the like on Chaguanas Main Road, there is a plethora of roti and doubles stalls and Chinese food vendors all over town, and *Vita Force* in the Centre Pointe Mall (Mon–Sat 9am–6pm) is good for freshly blended fruit juices or a veggie sandwich. For something slightly more upmarket – or at least somewhere to sit down for your meal – there are also a few actual **restaurants**. On the cheaper end of the scale there's *Eagles*, 44 Eleanor St (Mon–Thurs 10am–9pm, Fri & Sat 10am–10pm; ℡665 6825), a dark eatery serving inexpensive but decent Chinese food, while over the road at the corner of Eleanor and Marc streets the canteen-style *Brilliant Bargain Food Paradise* (Mon–Sat 7am–7pm; ℡672 4945) offers a wide selection of economical Chinese, Creole and Indian dishes in a garishly decorated dining room. The more upscale *Kam-Po*, a haunt of the Indian elite located opposite the Centre Pointe Mall at 55 Ramsaran St (Mon–Thurs 10.30am–10pm, Fri & Sat 10.30am–11pm; ℡665 4558), has a vast and varied menu ranging from steaks to classic Chinese dishes – service is excellent and the dining room is air-conditioned.

The only real entertainment in Chaguanas comes in the form of the **cinema**; you can take in a Bollywood film at the Jubilee, 13 Chaguanas Main Rd (℡665 5812) or new US releases at the Globe on Market Street (℡665 1463).

# Felicity Village and the Chaguanas potteries

In the couple of kilometres south of Chaguanas, the buildings lining the Southern Main Road (known as the Felicity Main Road between Chaguanas and Felicity Village) thin out, and the tarmac is bordered to the left by acre upon acre of undulating sugar cane. To the right, backstreets lead into **FELICITY VILLAGE**, an Indian community where you'll see a mini-temple outside most homes. Come **Diwali**, Felicity residents are particularly lavish with their decorations; thousands of *deyas* (pottery lamps produced for the festival) and strings of fairy lights give off an incredible glow in the evening. Indeed, this is one of the best places on the island to take in the celebrations, with *tassa* drummers, Indian dancers and loads of delicious food to sample. Since traffic slows to a standstill around here during Diwali, it's best to park closer to Chaguanas and walk to Felicity (about 15 minutes).

Past Felicity, the Southern Main Road winds through a string of indistinguishable Indian communities which are most attractive at night when neon shop signs flash a rainbow of garish colours over the traffic. As you pass through the otherwise unremarkable Edinburgh Village, look out for the ornate, white-painted **Edinburgh Temple** on the right, its walls, arches and turrets richly embellished with plaster reliefs and with a colourful shrine to Kali outside.

A few hundred metres further down the Southern Main Road a number of stalls lining the road are known collectively as the Chaguanas Potteries, the oldest and most famous of which is Benny's Pottery Works (daily 8am–6pm; ℡665 4267), at the back of Radika's Pottery Shop. The thousands of *deyas*, windchimes, wall plaques, pots and ornaments on sale in Radika's are all produced in Benny's workshop using traditional Indian methods passed down from the present owner Radika Benny's grandfather, who learnt his craft in India. It's a fascinating process to watch. The clay, dug from the nearby Carlsen

Field (site of a World War II US airbase), is soaked and kneaded by foot to remove stones and lumps. It is then hand-rolled or shaped on a wheel before being fired in the large open kiln that dominates the centre of the workshop. Fuelled by wood, the kiln has no temperature gauge – the process relies entirely on the potter's experience and judgement. There is something for every budget in the shop, and if you don't see what you want, Sylvan or Andy Benny (Radika's sons) will make it for you.

## Friendship Hall

A little further down the Southern Main Road on the eastern side, halfway between the sign for Chase Village and the turn-off to Waterloo Village, is the grandiose **Friendship Hall** (also known locally as MacLeod House or the House of One Hundred Windows). With its elaborate balconies, steep gables, corner turret and fanciful roofscape clad in rusting galvanized iron, it's a fine, if rather dilapidated, example of the estate houses that were common throughout Trinidad in the mid-nineteenth century. It was built in 1864 by a Scotsman, Hugh MacLeod, whose fascination with Indian imagery led him to create most of the ornate exterior plasterwork by hand. On his deathbed, MacLeod bequeathed the house to his estate agent, whose family still live there today. Though the house isn't open to the public, the owners will usually let you poke around the splendid exterior if you ask.

# Carapichaima and Waterloo Village

About a kilometre south of Chase Village, another small Indian community with little in the way of specific sights, the Orange Field Road cuts west off the Southern Main Road through the Orange Valley Estate to join the signposted Waterloo Road down to the sea. This is prime **sugar territory**: fields of cane stretch out on either side, and graceful royal palms tower over the road as they have done since the early plantation days, when the land was owned by the Tate and Lyle sugar company.

At the junction of Orange Field and Waterloo roads stands the quiet village of **CARAPICHAIMA**, a cluster of neat bungalows built in the 1920s for sugar estate managers and occupied today almost entirely by Indo-Trinidadians. The village's ethnic makeup meant it was as logical a place as any to build the majestic **Hanuman Murti**, a statue depicting the Hindu monkey-god Hanuman and, at 26 metres, the largest Hanuman Murti outside of India. Consecrated in June, 2003, the statue was a gift from Ganapati Sachchidananda, the Swami (spiritual teacher) of Mysore in southern India. The statue's workmanship rivals anything to be found in Asia, its beautifully detailed and colourful relief work the product of twenty craftsmen, well versed in twelfth-century Dravidian temple architecture, sent over from Mysore by the Swami. They also renovated the bright pink **temple** (Mon–Fri 6am–noon & 5–8pm, Sat & Sun 6am–noon & 4–8pm) attached to the **Sri Dattatreya Ashram**, which is surrounded by some superb bas reliefs of Hindu deities and is located about one hundred metres from the Hanuman Murti. To arrange guided tours, contact the President of the Temple, Ramesh Persad Maharaj (☎689 6581).

To reach Carapichaima by **public transport**, take a route taxi from the Mid Centre Mall in Chaguanas to St Mary's Junction (look for the *KFC*) on the Southern Main Road just beyond the Orange Field Road turn-off (TT\$2.50), where you pick up another taxi to the junction of Orange Field and Waterloo roads.

△ Hanuman Murti

From Carapichaima, route taxis continue west down Waterloo Road, passing through another sleepy, predominantly Indo-Trinidadian village called **WATERLOO**, where Hindu prayer flags flutter in the gardens next to trees with blue plastic bottles hanging from their branches – an old Trinidadian superstition to ward off maljo, or bad luck – arriving after five kilometres at the sea. During this drive look out for an old and pretty former railway station on the right, a remnant of the days when Waterloo was a stop on the Port of Spain–San Fernando train line.

## Waterloo Temple

West from the village by about a half-kilometre, opposite an old Anglican cemetery which includes a plot reserved for Muslim burials, the gleaming white, onion-domed **Waterloo Temple** stands on a pier, surrounded, at high tide, by fishing boats bobbing in the waters of the Gulf of Paria, or by extensive mudflats at low tide. With the temple, the flatlands, the funeral pyres at the water's edge and the flags (*jhandes*) – representing prayers and offerings – flapping in the breeze, visitors could be forgiven for thinking they were standing on the shore of the River Ganges.

The octagonal temple – used by the local Hindu community for weddings and *puja* ceremonies, in which fruit and flowers are offered to the gods – covers an area of over 100 square metres, with coloured glass windows that enable you to see the brightly painted stone and marble gods inside. Anyone can enter the temple (Tues, Wed, Sat & Sun 8am–3pm; though note that these times depend very much on when the caretaker arrives), provided they remove their shoes first. The pier (gate open daily 6am–6pm) – planted with hibiscus and bougainvillea – allows visitors to walk to the temple and get good views of the rich array of **birdlife**, including terns, gulls, whimbrels and skimmers, which feeds in the mudflats around Waterloo throughout the year.

In the middle of the car park before the temple is a life-size statue of **Sewdass Sadhu**, an Indian labourer to whose zeal and persistence the temple owes its existence. Sadhu built the original temple on the shore in 1947, but since the land was officially the property of the state sugar monopoly Caroni, the government bulldozed the structure five years later, and sent him to jail for fourteen days. Sadhu then decided to rebuild his temple in the sea, where no permission was required. A lonely, determined figure, he struggled single-handedly for the next 25 years, using a bicycle to carry the foundation rocks out into the water and placing barrels full of concrete on the sea floor at low tide. It was a Sisyphean task, though, as no sooner had he constructed one part of the building than the sea would erode his previous work, ensuring that the shrine was never completely finished. Help finally came in 1995, when the 150th anniversary of the arrival of Indians in Trinidad inspired the government to declare the temple an Unemployment Relief Project (URP). With labourers paid by the state to rebuild the structure, the temple was swiftly completed.

# Inland to Ajoupa Pottery

Back on the Southern Main Road, a few kilometres south of Chase Village, a signposted left-hand turn-off at St Mary's Junction takes you into the relatively bustling little village of Freeport. From here, another signposted minor road heads for **Chicklands**, a rural community that's home to the **Ajoupa Pottery**, 326 Chickland Rd (tours by appointment Mon–Fri 8am–4pm; ☏673 0605,

ⓕ673 0604, Ⓦwww.ajoupapottery.com), producers of the distinctive, classy ceramics you'll see on sale in most of T&T's gift shops, decorated with beautiful, deep-coloured glazes and featuring all manner of local animal life – the lizards-on-a-plate series are worth looking out for, but they sell fast. This family-owned business produces all their ceramics – plus furniture and their increasingly popular mosaics – at this site, in an open-sided and overstuffed workshop. Tours are very informal, with a quick explanation of ceramic production from sourcing and blending clay to the exquisite glazing that Ajoupa is known for, and usually finish with a visit to the main house, a beautifully restored wooden former estate home. Inside the house is a small shop where you can buy the pottery and other Ajoupa products – and pay far less than you would in Port of Spain.

# Couva and around

Of the smoggy, industrial towns that line the west coast below Chaguanas, the liveliest is **COUVA** – but that doesn't mean it's much of a destination. Although the town's main drag (the Southern Main Road) is lined by beautiful, deteriorating old gingerbread houses – which include the **Holy Faith Convent**, a fine old colonial plantation house at the northern end of the drag – many of them are unfortunately being torn down in favour of cheap, concrete structures.

A short way down the Southern Main Road at 8 Edgar St, *Bal Tar Zzzar* (Mon–Sat 11am–10pm; ⓣ636 1294) is Couva's best **restaurant**, serving standard, inexpensive Chinese food plus a daily Creole special such as baked chicken or wild game in a dark, chandelier-lit dining room. For **Internet access**, try High-Speed Internet Café on the main road opposite Scotiabank (Mon–Sat 6.30am–6pm; TT$10 per hr). To get to Couva (from where you can catch public transport to La Vega Estate – see p.196), take a **route taxi** from the Mid Centre Mall in Chaguanas or a **maxi** from High Street in San Fernando.

## Point Lisas Industrial Complex

Just south of Couva on the Southern Main Road is **California**, a drab residential suburb of the massive **Point Lisas Industrial Complex**, whose belching chimneys are already visible from the Southern Main Road. The complex was built as a flagship for the Trinidadian economy during the oil boom years of the 1970s, and no expense was spared in creating the factories, which produce liquefied natural gas, steel and fertilizers – the complex has the unfortunate distinction of being the largest exporter of fertilizer in the world. Industrial as it is, Point Lisas still has its wildlife. Every year between December and June, thousands of **blue crabs** make the hazardous journey from the swampland beside the complex across the main road to lay their eggs in the sea. During these months, the noise you're most likely to hear as you drive past Point Lisas is the crunch of crabs under car wheels.

# Pointe-a-Pierre Wildfowl Trust

Past **Claxton Bay**, an industrial suburb cloaked in dust from the nearby cement factory about halfway between California and San Fernando, you come upon a stunning oasis of nature, located (oddly enough) on the extensive grounds of the Petrotrin Oil Refinery at Pointe-a-Pierre. The only nature reserve in the Caribbean maintained by the oil industry, the **Pointe-a-Pierre Wildfowl Trust** (Mon–Fri 8am–5pm, Sat & Sun 10am–4pm; TT$8; ☎658 4200 ext 2512, ⓦwww.trinwetlands.org) came into being in 1966, when a hunter who worked at the refinery realized that wildfowl stocks were diminishing, and set aside an area within the complex to breed the birds. In time it became an established reserve, supported (though not financially) by the refinery.

The Wildfowl Trust consists of 250,000 square metres of attractively land-scaped grounds around two lakes filled with waterlilies and lotus flowers and bordered by wooden walkways. Many **rare bird species** can be found here, including the wild Muscovy duck, the red-billed whistling duck and the white-cheeked pintail. Notwithstanding the fact that some of the rarer birds, including scarlet ibis, are caged to allow breeding programmes to continue, the reserve doesn't feel at all like a zoo. Indeed, the ibis breeding programme has been something of a landmark project, particularly as the released birds have chosen to stay on the site, allowing you the only chance you'll get in Trinidad to see wild ibis up close. (For details on visiting Caroni Swamp, home of the scarlet ibis, see p.183). The well-maintained **learning centre** at the entrance has good photographic displays of the flora and fauna found on the reserve, a collection of shells and insect specimens, and a small collection of Amerindian artefacts, with a very informative account of the culture and belief systems of Trinidad's original inhabitants. The Trust's guides are vastly knowledgeable not only about the bird life, but also the **medicinal qualities** of the indigenous plants: a chemical in the white periwinkle, for example, is used to fight leukemia, while certain mango leaves reduce nervous tension.

## Practicalities

To **drive** to the Trust from Port of Spain or San Fernando, leave the Solomon Hochoy Highway at the Gasparillo exit and follow the signs to the Petrotrin Oil Refinery. On **public transport**, the Chaguanas–San Fernando maxi route passes in front of the Petrotrin Oil Refinery. Of the refinery's several entrances, the one closest to the reserve is located between oil drums 84 and 85, on the left-hand side of the Southern Main Road if coming from the north. Once inside, turn left on Regent Road and walk for about twenty minutes to get to the Trust entrance. The best time to visit is before 11am or after 3pm, as the animals hide in the shade during the hottest part of the day.

There are a couple of **hotels** around Pointe-a-Pierre which, like the modest selection in nearby San Fernando (see p.205), cater mainly to oil workers and businessmen. A five-minute drive north of the Wildfowl Trust on the Southern Main Road (take the turn-off under the red railway bridge) will take you to the quiet, good-value *Mikanne*, 15 Railway Ave, Plaisance Village, Pointe -a-Pierre (☎/ⓕ659 2584, ⓔmikanne@tstt.net.tt; ❺), which has TV, a/c and en-suite bathrooms in all rooms, a small swimming pool, sun lounge and an inexpensive restaurant. Unless you're with what Trinis call your "outside" man or woman, avoid *Reflections* guesthouse, just opposite the turning for *Mikanne*, where rooms are rented strictly by the hour. A little back north along the Southern Main Road in Claxton Bay, *Cara Suites* (☎659 2272, ⓕ659 2202, ⓔcarasuitespap@carahotels.com; ❽), is an expensive business hotel where rooms have all mod-cons and often even a private balcony affording good views of the Gulf of Paria. There is also an attractive swimming pool and com-plimentary Internet access for guests.

# The Caroni Plains

The **Caroni Plains**, just one or two hours from Port of Spain, are an ideal place to enjoy Trinidad's countryside and escape from the city. Most of the island's sugar cane is produced here, and apart from **Piarco International Airport** and its immediate environs, the area is deeply rural. The plains are bounded to the south by the Montserrat Hills and to the east by the **Caroni Arena Dam and Reservoir**, where a wide variety of birdlife and other flora and fauna can be found, while at the nearby **Mount Tamana**, over a million bats darken the sky every nightfall.

Although most settlements in this part of the country are just one or two hours from Port of Spain, **public transport** is slow and occasionally non-existent. Perhaps more than anywhere else on the island, **renting a car** is the best way to explore the Caroni Plains. The only **accommodation** is located around the airport; **food** can be bought at the numerous fast-food outlets at the airport or at roadside snack parlours; and what **entertainment** there is revolves around village rum shops.

## Piarco International Airport and around

The "town" of Piarco, 24km southeast of Port of Spain, actually consists of very little except for the island's sole airport and a few small houses, the homes of airport workers. Built in 1931, **Piarco International Airport** (ⓦwww .piarcoairport.com) is the base of British West Indian Airlines (BWIA). Fondly referred to as "Bee wee" by locals, BWIA was set up during World War II to provide a transport route which avoided the German submarines prowling the Caribbean. More recently, Piarco was given a multi-million-dollar facelift in the form of a brand new terminal, all glass roofs and state-of-the-art technology, making arrivals and departures a far more hassle-free affair. There is also a food court, currency exchange booth, taxi rank and car rental desks adjacent to the arrivals area. For details of **public transport** to and from the airport, see p.71.

Although best known for the airport, the **Piarco area** is actually an overwhelmingly rural landscape of winding country roads and small villages. **St Helena**, a somnolent village 1km south of the airport, consists of little more than a cluster of houses, but is slowly expanding as a result of airport trade. On the outskirts by the airport you'll pass a few traditional, whitewashed *tapia* houses, built of mud on a bamboo frame, though most of these have now given way to concrete buildings.

There are three **hotels** within five minutes of the terminal building. On Golden Grove Road, the approach road to the airport, the *Bel Air International Airport Hotel* (Ⓣ/ⓕ669 4771, ⓦwww.belairairporthotel.com; ⓞ) is an expensive 1940s hotel. All rooms have a/c, phone and en-suite bathroom, and there's a swimming pool and a restaurant/bar with live entertainment on Saturdays. (The owners of the *Bel Air* are building a new hotel north of the airport terminal that should be finished in 2005.) Slightly closer to the airport at 8–10 Golden Grove Rd, the *Piarco International Hotel* (Ⓣ669 3030, ⓕ669 1739; ⓞ) is pricier and newer than the *Bel Air*, with a pool, restaurant, three bars and comfortable rooms with all the amenities. The area's sole budget option is the *Airport View Guesthouse*, opposite the gas station on the main crossroads of the small village of St Helena (**℡/℻**669 4186; **❹**), a basic, rather dark but spacious and functional place, where all rooms have a/c, TV and private bathroom; there's a 10 percent discount for stays longer than a week, except during Carnival. All of these hotels have **complimentary shuttles** to and from the airport.

# The northern plains

**San Rafael**, 9km east of St Helena through a flat landscape of cane fields and citrus groves, is scarcely larger – a church, a school and a few old board houses. Its peaceful aspect hides a violent past, however. In 1699, the local Amerindians rebelled against Spanish missionaries who tried to forcibly convert them to Christianity and use them as slave labour in the construction of churches. The Amerindians killed the priests, dumping their bodies into the foundations of those same churches they were being forced to build, and then ambushed the Spanish governor, José de León y Echales, and his party, killing them all. In retaliation, the Spanish massacred the region's entire Amerindian population. Ironically, today a statue of St Raphael, the healer of all wounds, presides over the village's main junction in front of the modern-day church.

**Waller Field**, which sits another 10km or so from San Rafael in the northeastern corner of the Caroni Plains, recalls more recent conflicts. When it was occupied by the Americans during World War II, this was the largest and busiest airbase in the region, but the hangars, barrack blocks and control rooms are long gone; what's left of the airstrip is used for weekly drag racing. The rest of the plains are dotted with small villages. **Cumuto**, about 5km south of Waller Field, is typical of this area: a quiet place with the odd bar and shop, it has declined since its heyday in the early twentieth-century when it was the centre of the region's large-scale cocoa cultivation. In the 1940s, the community was reinvigorated by its proximity to the US base at Waller Field, but like Carenage (see p.114), its reputation suffered as the village became a playground for lonely young soldiers, and rumours of wild parties and immoral behaviour ran rife. Not all Trinidadians regard the US occupation as entirely negative, however; it is said that the money earned from the Americans during these years funded new housing developments in the region during the 1970s.

# The Caroni Arena Dam and Reservoir

From San Rafael, Talparo Road runs south through serene rainforest where you'll rarely meet another car. As you pass the tiny settlement of Brazil and continue on towards Talparo, the first low foothills of the Central Range appear, hidden beneath luxuriant vegetation: bamboo thickets jostle with papaya, mango, banana, cashew and breadfruit trees. The blooms of the golden poui dominate the woodlands in April, while from December to March the magnificent immortelle trees blaze a fiery red. In the seventeenth century, the forests sheltered Amerindians fleeing Spanish persecution – many of the Amerindian artefacts in the National Museum in Port of Spain (see p.87) were found here.

The **Caroni Arena Dam and Reservoir** (daily 8am–6pm) lies a kilometre or so due east of Talparo Road on Caroni Arena Road – the dam is 9km southwest of Cumuto and 3.5km southeast of San Rafael. The turn-off on Talparo Road for the dam is well signposted by the Water and Sewerage Authority of Trinidad and Tobago (WASA), but Caroni Arena Road itself is bumpy and, in local parlance, "mash up" – meaning that after heavy rains it is often impassable, so check with WASA before starting out. Completed in 1981, the dam is the largest in T&T, reaching 40.85m at its highest crest elevation, while the reservoir provides a water storage area of over 680 hectares. It's a favourite weekend spot for families, with picnic tables, swings and climbing frames, but swimming is not allowed in the reservoir.

The **wildlife** is astounding: parrots, hawks and white egrets fly around the dam; blue emperor butterflies flutter among the bamboo and settle on the reeds by the water's edge; caimans lurk in the swamps bordering the reservoir, while red howler and capuchin monkeys, toucans and tree porcupines inhabit the surrounding forest.

Visiting the Caroni Arena Dam and Reservoir requires time and effort, which is worth it provided that you come during the week when there are no crowds and the wildlife is undisturbed. In the absence of any **public transport** to the area, you must either book a **taxi** for the day from Arima or Port of Spain (around TT$150), **rent a car** or take a **tour** with Paria Springs (☎622 8826), which concentrates on birding at the dam itself and in the forests around it. Before setting off, make sure that you have purchased a **permit** (TT$10). To do this, you must go in person to the WASA headquarters on Farm Road in St Joseph (Mon–Thurs 8am–4.15pm, Fri 8am–4pm), where you may be asked to present a letter, written by yourself, explaining the reasons for your visit.

# Mount Tamana's bat caves

Just east of the Caroni Arena Dam and Reservoir, the distinctive, flat-topped **Mount Tamana**, highest in the Central Range at 308 metres, and visible from as far as the Northern Range, was created thousands of years ago when geological shifts pushed what was a coral reef out of the sea. Over the centuries, underground water flows eroded Tamana's porous limestone core, creating a series of lengthy **cave systems** which provide the perfect home for the huge colonies of **bats** that inhabit the caverns today. The gentle thirty-minute walk up Tamana's slopes is pleasant enough, threading through shady groves of lichen-covered cocoa trees and under giant silk cotton trees and moras, with the occasional eye-popping view over the Caroni Plains. However, the real draw here is the bats, which make a spectacular exit en masse at **dusk** to feed. It's best to arrive around 4pm, in order to have enough time to walk up and enter the first of the caves, peek at the ceiling – almost every inch is covered with roosting bats – and exit before the sun goes down. As dusk approaches, the first stragglers make their way out, and as the darkness thickens, the trickle becomes an ever-increasing stream as about a million and a half bats shoot past like furry, flapping balls, their sonars clicking away as they avoid flying into you.

Though it's bang in the centre of Trinidad, Tamana is easiest to reach from Sangre Grande in the northeast of the region, (see p.198) via the Cunapo Road. From there, it's a precarious journey along winding, heavily potholed and landslide-wrecked minor roads, but as the route isn't signposted, and there's no easy way to find the path to the caves unless you know it, it's difficult to visit Tamana independently. Your best bet is to go with a tour (see p.53).

# The Montserrat Hills

The most picturesque part of the Central Range is its western part, known as the **Montserrat Hills**, a countryside characterized by rolling hills that begins just a kilometre or two east of the Solomon Hochoy Highway and which shelters huge, run-down cocoa estates and enfolds the grandeur of the **Navet Dam and Reservoir**. More of Trinidad's sleepiest villages dot the scenic hills, accessed via winding roads with rickety wooden bridges. The nineteenth-century English novelist Charles Kingsley, who visited the region in 1870, described "the panorama from the top of Montserrat" as "the most vast and most lovely which I have ever seen". Most of the villages have little specific to recommend them apart from the odd picturesque colonial house and a great deal of rural charm. In the early twentieth century, many of these villages bustled with activity thanks to the highly productive cocoa estates that surrounded them. However, as the estates declined the settlements returned to their former somnolence. The landscaped gardens and exotic plants and flowers of **La Vega Estate** is a good place to experience the wonderful nature and some of the only facilities for visitors in this part of the country.

The closest **accommodation** and **restaurants** are in San Fernando or Port of Spain, and if you're intending to visit this area in a day-trip from either of these two cities, you can get to the La Vega Estate by **public transport** (which leaves from the town of Couva), but not the Navet Dam and Reservoir.

## La Vega Estate

An experimental commercial nursery dedicated to cultivating exotic plants, with a few recreational activities for visitors as well, the **La Vega Estate** (daily 9am–5pm; free if you've come to shop, TT$12 to picnic and walk the signposted nature trail; ☎679 9522) lies about 7km west of Flanagin Town on the Couva Main Road, just west of Gran Couva. The on-site nursery has the largest variety of ornamental plants in Trinidad, including fifty different species of **bougainvillea**, spiky-fruiting rambutan trees from Malaysia, and caryota plants, bedecked with distinctive mop-like tendrils. The whole estate covers about a square kilometre, of which nearly a quarter consists of exquisitely **landscaped gardens** open to public recreation. Guided tours (TT$25) and nature trails highlight the work of the estate and the variety of flora, as well as providing an opportunity to spot local wildlife such as **manicou**, **agouti** and **wild deer**. There are large ponds for **fishing** (TT$20) and **paddleboating** (TT$40 for 30min; public holidays only), picnic tables in sheltered bamboo groves, bromeliad and Japanese gardens, a meditation space and a childrens' play area.

Infrequent **route taxis** set out for La Vega Estate from next to the *KFC* at the eastern end of Couva (TT$5). To get there by **car**, take the Gran Couva exit from the Solomon Hochoy Highway and follow the road past Gran Couva for about twenty minutes.

# Tortuga

**TORTUGA**, which sprawls up the slope of the Montserrat Hills just fifteen minutes from the Solomon Hochoy Highway and about 4km south of La Vega, is a collection of old board houses interspersed with the odd rum shop. The primary reason to come here is to see the Catholic **Church of Our Lady of Montserrat**, a grand, green-painted wooden gingerbread house at the top of the village which was built in 1872 with a big gable and a graceful arcade. Inside are many old plaster statues, carved wooden Stations of the Cross and, to the left of the altar, a shrine containing a **Black Virgin**. The small statue, half a metre high and swathed in an oversized white dress, was brought to the island by the early Capuchin missionaries.

From the church, you get an excellent **view** north over the rolling plains of central Trinidad, with the distinctive, half-flattened San Fernando Hill in the distance to the south.

## Navet Dam and Reservoir

A couple of kilometres south of Tortuga, you come to the intersection of the Tabaquite Road, which runs eastwards along the southern slopes of the Montserrat Hills. The road is bordered by sugar cane, cocoa and coffee estates, while the undulating slopes are clad in seemingly endless tropical rainforest. Past the tiny village of Tabaquite, you come to an abandoned **railway tunnel**. A few kilometres further on, the road edges up a valley towards the towering **Navet Dam and Reservoir** (daily 8am–6pm). Completed in 1966, this dam is the second largest in T&T after Caroni Arena (see p.194), while the **reservoir** behind it stretches out in several directions, forming an intricate pattern of inlets and coves, some as much as 6km in length. With only the minuscule hamlet of Brasso Venado nearby, it's an isolated place, excellent for quiet picnics and birdwatching – many species of wildfowl frequent the reservoir in the early mornings and late afternoons.

The public facilities are not as good as those at the Caroni Arena Dam and Reservoir, however: just one picnic table and some toilets. Nor is there any **public transport**. As with visits to Caroni Arena, you must first buy a **permit** (TT$10) at the WASA headquarters on Farm Road in St Joseph (Mon–Thurs 8am–4.15pm, Fri 8am–4pm).

# The east coast

South of **Sangre Grande**, the largest town on this side of the island and a transportation hub of considerable commercial vigour, central Trinidad's **east coast** is dominated by the **Cocal**, 24km of unbroken sand, lined by grove upon grove of swaying coconut palms, that begins at **Manzanilla** and stretches south to Mayaro. The lure of the seashore and a slow but steady increase in tourism has ensured a few places to stay around Manzanilla Village, but otherwise the area has few facilities for visitors. The Manzanilla–Mayaro Road runs the length of the beach, fringed inland by the pristine rainforest and mangrove-smothered wetlands of **Nariva Swamp**, a primary breeding ground and habitat for all manner of rare and exotic animals and birds.

The east coast is also the source of most of the **coconuts** sold in Trinidad. The area's coconut estates add to the breathtaking environment, with their deserted beaches and waving palms reminiscent of Hollywood film backdrops and high-class fashion magazines. So far, despite the slight increase in tourism, the estate owners have declined to sell the property to hotel developers, and the beach and protected swamp still retain their idyllic seclusion.

# Sangre Grande

A thriving market town slung along the Eastern Main Road, **SANGRE GRANDE** ("big blood", after a long-forgotten battle) – pronounced "sandy grandy" but usually just called "grandy" – is the largest town in the east, a bustling transportation hub and the only place in the region where you can get to a bank or ATM. Residents of surrounding villages crowd the pavements every Friday to deposit their wage cheques, shop at the **market** stalls, take a fast-food fix at the conglomeration of neon-flashing takeaway chains along the main street and drink the night away at the rum shops.

Most people pass through Sangre Grande to change taxis and maxis, and aside from the shopping, there's no real reason to spend much time here unless you need to stock up on food, fill your petrol tank or exchange money. Most **route taxis** and **maxis**, as well as **PTSC buses** to Arima and Port of Spain, leave from the square behind *Royal Castle* in the middle of the main drag; ask around to find the correct queue. Maxi fares are TT$7 to Port of Spain and TT$4 to Arima; route taxis cost TT$9 to Mayaro and TT$5 to Manzanilla Beach (Manzanilla Beach taxis leave from just past the police station next to the Republic Bank on the eastern side of town). *Royal Castle*, *KFC* and other fast-food outlets are the most obvious **places to eat**, while the market is a good place to buy picnic provisions, including fresh fruit. There are several **banks** and **petrol stations** (one of which is open until midnight) along the Eastern Main Road, while cheap **Internet access** is available at NJ's, up the stairs directly behind *Royal Castle* (Mon–Fri 9am–5pm, Sat 2–3pm; TT$5 per hr).

# Manzanilla and around

South of Sangre Grande, the Eastern Main Road cuts a picturesque and winding 8km route toward the Atlantic coast; underground waterflows regularly cause substantial subsidence below the tarmac, so if you're driving, take things slowly, as dangerous spots can be poorly signposted. A quiet and attractive village strewn with gingerbread houses at the end of the Eastern Main Road, **MANZANILLA** can effectively be divided into Upper and Lower sections, though note that these are not official names and locals make no distinction between the Manzanilla on the Eastern Main Road (**Upper Manzanilla**) and the coastal part of the village (**Lower Manzanilla**).

The section of **beach** next to Lower Manzanilla is the most popular part of the whole four-kilometre stretch that makes up Manzanilla Beach, and the only place where there are any facilities; **to get there**, follow the Eastern Main Road through Upper Manzanilla and turn left opposite Plum Mitan Road. After passing a handful of small groceries and rum shops, you'll find yourself on the seashore, at the beginning of the Manzanilla–Mayaro Road. (South of here, the beach runs the whole length of the east coast, with only the odd decrepit building interrupting palm groves that line the wide, expansive stretch of fine, brownish-grey sand.) Windswept and exposed, Manzanilla Beach is usually deserted during the week, but becomes a popular swimming spot at the weekends. The water is often quite bracing, and you should take care while swimming as the undercurrents can be dangerous. The beach has experienced something of a renaissance in recent years; there are now lifeguards and TIDCO has put in changing and showering facilities at the northern end (daily 10am–6pm; TT$1), as well as a car park that rivals Maracas (see p.135) in capacity. Indeed, Manzanilla is fast overtaking Maracas as Trinidad's most popular Ash Wednesday chill-out spot (in addition to being a venue for massive Easter beach parties), with more space for the crowds of revellers to sunbathe or dance to the sound systems that are set up in the northern section. If you're planning to visit Manzanilla for the Ash Wednesday or Easter beach parties, try to set off early – it's not unknown for the traffic jams to start as far away as Valencia.

### Practicalities

If you want to **stay** near Manzanilla Beach, there are a few options. *Calypso Inn* is very close to the sand (℡691 5939 or 671 7369; ❻), at the end of a dirt track at the extreme northern corner of the beach. Beautifully located on a stretch of the coast protected by the headland separating Manzanilla from Matura Beach (see p.166), the hotel has smart double rooms with a/c, TV and balconies overlooking the sea. There's a bar and **restaurant** with outdoor and indoor eating and drinking areas, while hammocks slung between the seashore palm trees and a swimming pool in landscaped gardens make for nice spots to relax. A less expensive option, but also just metres from the sand, is *Amelia's Guesthouse* (℡668 5308; ❹), on the same dirt track that leads to the *Calypso Inn*. The three functional rooms sleep up to four people and come with private bathroom, microwave, fridge and a choice of a/c or fan. On the Eastern Main Road as it winds down to Manzanilla Beach, roughly two hundred metres from the sand, is *Hotel Carries on the Bay* (℡668 5711, ℻691 0146; ❺). Relatively new and still with a rather unlived-in feel, the breezy, modern rooms, all with tiled floors, a/c, satellite TV and private bathroom, are pleasant enough. There is also a restaurant providing a cheaper, more Creole-based alternative to the one at the *Calypso Inn*. Walk fifteen minutes up the Eastern Main Road from the beach to get to *Dougies* (℡668 1504; ❷), a large block of rooms adjacent to a rum bar and grocery, and by far the cheapest accommodation available in Manzanilla. Basic rooms have fan and private bathroom, but self-contained two-bedroom apartments sleeping up to four people are also on offer (❸); the place is friendly and the rum shop is a lively liming spot after dark.

### Brigand Hill Lighthouse

Built in 1958, the stubby white **Brigand Hill Lighthouse** (daily 8am–5pm; free), about 5km south of Upper Manzanilla, is one of only three in Trinidad. Although it's not possible to enter the lighthouse itself, you can climb the twenty-odd iron stairs that run up the outside for a magnificent view stretching from Toco in the north to Galeota Point in the south, taking in the Caroni Plains and the flatlands of Nariva Swamp. Red howler monkeys inhabit the trees around the lighthouse, and if you're lucky, you'll see a troop passing by.

To **get to** the lighthouse from Manzanilla, take the Plum Mitan Road off the Eastern Main Road after Upper Manzanilla, and turn off at the signpost. It's a steep climb; a hard twenty-minute walk or a five-minute drive. **Route taxis** departing from just past the police station next to the Republic Bank on the eastern side of Sangre Grande will drop you at the lighthouse junction on Plum Mitan Road (TT$5). A word with the security guard will gain you entry at the gate. Note, however, that to visit Brigand Hill Lighthouse in a large group or with young children, you need to write for permission to the Ministry of Works Maritime Services, Second Floor, Ansa House, Queen Street, at Henry, Port of Spain (☎625 3858).

# The Cocal

The large coconut estates that line the Manzanilla–Mayaro Road (as the continuation of the Eastern Main Road is named south of Manzanilla) are known collectively as the **Cocal** and it's an awe-inspiring drive: 24km of graceful, leaning coconut trees dancing in the wind, with unspoilt, wave-pounded beach to one side and preserved rainforest and the wetlands of Nariva Swamp (see below) to the other. If you're lucky, you may see an experienced coconut-picker climbing up and down a tree in the flash of an eye. The docile, long-horned animals grazing amongst the coconuts at the edge of the road are **buffalypso**, kept for their meat and milk. The result of selective breeding of water buffalo, they are highly profitable; a farmer can raise four of them for the same cost as one cow, and each will command a higher price at market than a cow. There are no **hotels** or **restaurants** anywhere along the road between Manzanilla and Mayaro, but you will come across a few roadside stalls selling the shellfish known as chip-chip, freshly caught crabs, black conch, fish and, in season, watermelon.

Nearing Mayaro (see p.232), the Cocal runs past a small grove of huge coconut palms, their nuts processed at a plant recognizable by the huge mounds of husks that surround it. After miles of bendy, leaning palms, these tall upright specimens stand out in firm resolution against the sea breeze that whips in constantly from the Atlantic. Between 5.30pm and 6pm every night the air around here is raucous with the calls of the **red–chested macaws** that come to roost in the trees (binocular-toting birdwatchers usually mark the spot), while the surrounding swampland is a popular spot for southern lapwing and the rare red-breasted tanager. The ponds in this area are full of **cascadura**, a small brown freshwater fish, properly known as an armoured catfish, with a tough skeletal covering. They can be spotted by circles appearing on the pond surface, and are caught on a line or by using nets. It's said that if you eat their chewy brown, tuna-like meat (invariably served curried), you'll return to end your days in Trinidad, but it's a messy business as you have to pick and suck the flesh from beneath the armour.

# Nariva Swamp

One of Trinidad's most significant wildlife areas, the internationally recognized wetland of **Nariva Swamp** covers 15 square kilometres behind the coconut estates along the coast south of Manzanilla. The area is made up of agricultural land (rice and melons are the main crops), as well as reed-fringed marshes, and

## Coconuts

Grown on estates throughout eastern Trinidad and the southwest peninsula, **coconuts** are in constant demand on account of their sheer versatility. Depending on when they are harvested, they can be a source of drink, food, flavouring, oil, soap or animal feed, while their fibrous husk makes an alternative to peat for potting plants. Green nuts are full of sweet **water**, a popular drink sold fresh from the fruit from many an old Bedford van around the country. As the nut matures, much of the liquid is replaced by an edible white **jelly**. A few weeks later, the jelly solidifies into firm white flesh, which can be grated, dried and roasted in cooking. Later still, a **bread-like substance** grows in the centre of the fruit; if caught at the right time, it makes a tasty snack. Soon afterwards it develops into a sprout, from which a new tree will grow. Depending on the type, a tree will take five to ten years to mature and live for many years after that, producing nuts all year round.

eerie mangroves between the Mayaro–Manzanilla Road and the swamp itself. Also, deep in the southwestern corner of the swamp is **Bush Bush Island**, which is actually a peninsula standing around three metres higher than the surrounding land, bordered by palmiste and moriche palms and covered in hardwood forest and silk cotton trees.

Nariva is hard to explore in any real depth independently, but if you're just passing by, it's worth taking a stroll along one of the paved roads that swing in from the Manzanilla–Mayaro Road about two-thirds of the way down from Manzanilla, connecting the residential **Kernaham Village** with the coast. Just on the edge of the swamp and reachable via the signposted Kernaham Trace, the village is little more than a widely dispersed collection of picturesque board houses, mostly on stilts, that are home to a friendly, overwhelmingly Indian community of small-scale rice farmers and fishermen. It's a beautiful scene, with the flatlands opening up huge expanses of open sky. Nariva Swamp is a unique freshwater ecosystem that harbours large concentrations of rare **wildlife**, with some 58 species of mammals, 37 species of reptiles, and 171 species of birds. The swamp also harbours 92 species of mosquito, so remember to bring your insect repellent.

The 1996 **Ramsar Convention** – to which Trinidad and Tobago is a signatory – designated the swamp a "Wetland of International Importance," placing a legal obligation on the government to ensure the area is protected and maintained. In an area of low employment, however, it is not always easy to reconcile human economic needs with the demands of conservation. Many people turn to hunting as a means of subsistence, and large-scale illegal rice farming has destroyed some of the habitat. The government eventually expelled the big rice farmers after pressure from environmentalists, but small-scale cultivation continues. In addition, **bush fires**, often deliberately set by farmers to clear land, have ravaged almost half the territory, and as a result, access is often prohibited during the dry season.

Nariva is the only place in Trinidad where you can see the cute but threatened **manatee** or sea cow, a peculiar elephantine mammal that once fuelled rumours of mermaids lurking in the brackish depths. These shy, bizarre creatures can grow up to three metres in length, weigh over 900 kilograms, and live in freshwater ponds, where they feed on water hyacinth, moss and waterlilies. They are currently in danger of extinction: in the 1970s hundreds inhabited the swampland, but their numbers are now down to below one hundred as a result of increased human activity in the area, notably boating. The swamp is also an excellent place to view **caimans**, **freshwater turtles**, **red howler**

**monkeys** (whose rather alarming, otherworldly roars reverberate around the forest), white-fronted **capuchin monkeys** (which have been known to shower human intruders with a hail of twigs), three-toed and silky **anteaters**, **opposums**, **porcupines** and a wide variety of birds including **savannah hawks**, **dicksissels**, **orange-winged parrots** and the **yellow-capped Amazon parrot**. Its most alarming inhabitants, however, must be the **anacondas**, reputedly washed here from South America on the current of the Orinoco River. These terrifyingly large, dangerous, greenish-brown, black-spotted snakes grow up to nine metres long; they're the heaviest reptiles in the world, and the largest in the Americas.

If you want **to visit** the sanctuary, you must first obtain a free permit from the **Wildlife Division** of the **Forestry Department** on Farm Road in St Joseph (Mon–Fri 8am–4pm; ☎662 5114); the division will advise you about which guides to contact. Caribbean Discovery Tours (☎624 7281) offer a marvellous Nariva trip, with a walk through Bush Bush, kayaking if water levels permit and an excellent Indian lunch cooked by residents of Kernaham Village and served in a private home. If you're a serious ornithologist, opt for the excellent birding tours offered by Paria Springs (☎622 8826).

# San Fernando and the south

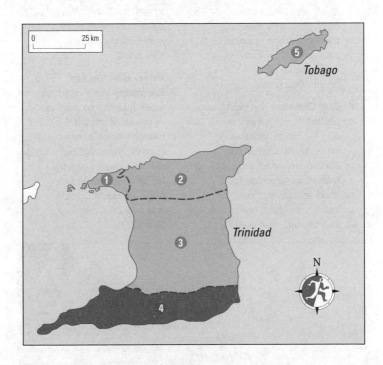

# CHAPTER 4

# Highlights

✳ **The Pitch Lake** Take a tour to understand the nuances of this fantastic geological wonder, the largest of its kind in the world. **See p.222**

✳ **Southwest peninsula drives** The beauty of rural Trinidad is best experienced along its quiet, undulating roads, often lined with teak plantations and coconut estates, and typically ending at an idyllic beach. **See p.218**

✳ **Gulf City Mall** The best place to meet people in San Fernando, especially on Friday and Saturday afternoons, when the mall's cosmopolitan food court and several bars and dance clubs are jam-packed. **See p.217**

✳ **Moruga** Isolated, but still accessible, this quiet and deeply religious fishing village has a unique atmosphere all its own. **See p.230**

✳ **Mayaro Bay** The country's longest stretch of sand is a much quieter and more relaxing place to kick back for a few days than the island's north coast beaches. **See p.232**

✳ **Trinity Hills Wildlife Sanctuary** You'll need to make an effort to get the most out of this off-the-beaten track nature reserve, but could be rewarded with sightings of Trinidad's rarest animals, including ocelots and capuchin monkeys. **See p.235**

▲ Mayaro Bay

# San Fernando and
# the south

Geographically, Trinidad's **south** presents a mirror image of the north: a long littoral extending beyond the main body of the island, with the low ridge of the forested Southern Range as its spine. In the Gulf of Paria, where the southwest peninsula crooks a finger towards Venezuela, Trinidad's second city, precipitous **San Fernando**, sits at the base of its oddly shaped landmark hill.

That's as far as the comparison with the north goes, however; even though San Fernando is a serious, booming business town, beyond its city limits this region is the most sparsely populated in Trinidad. Although many inhabitants still earn a living from agriculture – mainly sugar and rice – and fishing, the economy here is really based around **oil**. Ironically, this is what has left the region so unspoiled; with its well-paid jobs, oil money means that the local population do not have to pander to the tourist dollar – a refreshing experience for Caribbean holidaymakers. In addition, the petroleum business leases from the government large expanses of forest, which remain largely undeveloped apart from a few discreet oil pumps. Most of southern Trinidad is covered with untouched and barely-accessible rainforest – an environmentalist's dream. In the deep **southeast**, the protected rainforest of the **Trinity Hills Wildlife Reserve** shelters countless species of birds and exotic mammals such as the ocelot, while the **Oropuche Lagoon** southwest of San Fernando is a wildlife-rich mangrove swamp seldom visited by tourists.

Development is never far away, though, and in the built-up areas the architecture, like elsewhere in Trinidad, is changing rapidly. Brand new suburban malls are springing up around San Fernando as well as industrial towns like **Point Fortin** on the peninsula's north coast. Even though the inland towns of **Siparia** and **Fyzabad** still have a few old colonial gingerbread buildings interspersed among modern concrete structures, they hold little appeal.

Without the clear seas and the more developed beaches of the north to tempt them, tourists rarely venture this far south – those that do tend to make a bee-line for the **Pitch Lake**, the only potted attraction in these parts: a vast, volcanic pool conveniently located just thirty minutes west of San Fernando. Few make it as far as the **southwest peninsula**'s picturesque areas of **Cedros** and **Erin**, or the remote and eerie fishing village of **Moruga** on the south coast, even though the drives to these destinations are among the most scenic in

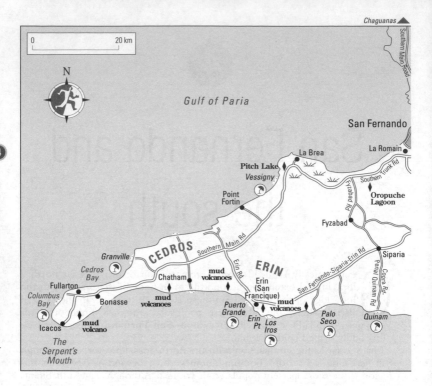

Trinidad. **Mayaro**, a gorgeous swathe of sand on the southeast coast, has long been a popular holiday resort with Trinidadians, but remains almost entirely undiscovered by foreign visitors. On the whole, **beaches** in the south are best visited during the dry season (December to May) when the sea and sand are clear. Note that from June to November beaches at Vessigny, Point Fortin and Guayaguayare are polluted by brackish water and litter swept downstream.

The lack of tourism is a mixed blessing, meaning there are no crowds but also few facilities for visitors in the region. The largest concentration of **accommodation** is along Mayaro Bay, which is fine if you intend to spend your whole time by the beach, but not all that practical for visiting other parts of the south. The ideal base is San Fernando, even if the modest selection of hotels there is underwhelming. Check with TIDCO (☎623 1932) for a list of host homes in the area, though don't bank on there being a huge choice. All of the towns and villages in the south, along with many of the beaches, are accessible by **public transport**. Again, San Fernando is the best place to start your journey; taxis and maxis go direct from there to the major towns, as well as some of the more far-flung destinations such as Erin and Cedros.

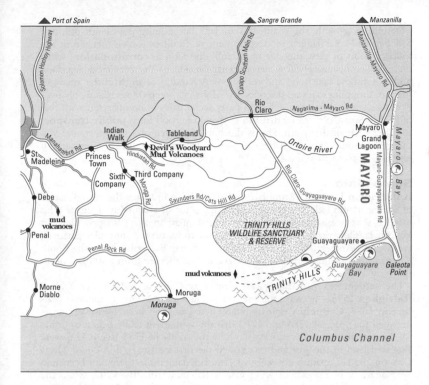

# San Fernando

Nestled against the base of the bizarrely shaped **San Fernando Hill**, the city of **SAN FERNANDO** enjoys the most striking location of any in Trinidad. Considered the industrial capital of Trinidad and Tobago (Port of Spain being the financial capital), it has a surprisingly old-fashioned charm. The city's steep streets and sea views are reminiscent of a miniature, low-key San Francisco and make San Fernando a more aesthetic city than Port of Spain, while a warren of old winding lanes still retain some enchanting gingerbread buildings that have survived the city's rapid industrial development of recent years.

San Fernando – usually referred to as **"Sando"** by Trinis – has always maintained an independent spirit. The city has scant regard for its arch rival Port of Spain, which in turn has a habit of belittling San Fernando. This said, all of the capital's soca stars, Calypsonians and steel bands make regular visits to San Fernando during Carnival season. San Fernando is scarcely promoted as a tourist destination; an oil city first and foremost, it gets many business visitors but few sightseers, meaning that tourists are basically left to get on with their own business. This can make San Fernando seem more sterile than it actually is. Essentially a friendly place, getting to know Sando's people is easy enough provided that you make the effort – and often the first move.

Despite its growth, the result of Trinidad's burgeoning petroleum industry, San Fernando has lagged in development of facilities for visitors. From the tourist's point of view the city is woefully short on **accommodation**, while there are comparatively few **restaurants** outside of the inevitable fast food outlets, Chinese takeaways and roti shops. A handful of **nightclubs**, many of them in shopping malls on the outskirts of the city, keep things reasonably lively at weekends, although the Sando party scene pales in comparison with that of Port of Spain. One thing that San Fernando is good for is **public transport** to other parts of the south. This is the hub of the region's transport, and you can get a maxi or taxi from here to just about anywhere on the peninsula, as well as points north and east.

## Some history

**Amerindian legends**, dating back to 8000 BC, emphasize the sacred nature of San Fernando Hill. It was the final resting place of Haburi the Hero and his mother, who were fleeing from the Frog Woman in the Orinoco Delta in Venezuela. They reached Trinidad safely, only to be turned into "Anaparima", the original Amerindian name for the hill. Amerindian tribes from the South American mainland made annual pilgrimages to the site from 6500 BC up to the early 1900s.

The settlement's first European contact was the arrival of **Sir Walter Raleigh** in 1595 – he was unimpressed and sailed on. Nearly a hundred years later in 1687, **Capuchin priests** established a mission here. However, it was between the years of 1784 and 1792 that the settlement really began to flourish. French plantation owners attracted by the *cedula* of 1783 (see p.322) were allocated land in the area and established the first estates. In 1784, José Maria Chacon, the last Spanish governor of Trinidad, named the town San Fernando de Naparima in honour of King Carlos III's new son. By 1797, when the British captured the island, San Fernando had more than a thousand inhabitants, twenty sugar mills and eight rum distilleries. Surrounded by fertile agricultural land, the town continued to grow, and by 1811 the population had trebled. In 1846, Sando was officially recognized as a town.

By around the mid-nineteenth century, San Fernando had become the **hub of the south**, a busy trading centre for the region's successful planters, with a regular coastal steamer to Port of Spain – the overland route took three days of rough riding through forests and swamps. The arrival of the **railway** in 1882 led to another population increase, and by the late 1880s San Fernando had been thoroughly modernized. Suburbs grew as the plantations disappeared – the result of falling sugar prices in the 1920s – and the town became dominated by the expanding **oil industry**. The municipality grew with little planning or design through the twentieth century until it was finally designated a city in 1988.

San Fernando continued to expand through the early 1990s, bringing the northern city limits up to the oil refinery at Pointe-a-Pierre and increasing its population by around 10,000 (it's a little under 60,000 today). This relative boom has created a need for new housing and a general improvement of the city's infrastructure, challenges which still face this bustling city determined to outgrow its second-city status.

# Arrival, information and getting around

Public transport **from Port of Spain** will drop you in one of three places, all in the centre of San Fernando. **PTSC buses** (ECS: Mon–Fri every 15min 4.45am–7.30pm, Sat every 30min 6am–6.30pm, TT$6; Transit: Mon–Fri hourly 4am–9pm, Sat 5am–9pm, TT$4) arrive at their terminal at the bottom of Queen Street, by the fish market; **maxis** (TT$6) arrive behind the Chancery Lane Market; and **route taxis** (TT$12) finish in Library Corner, at the top of High Street. A large car park between the Chancery Lane Market and the San Fernando General Hospital serves as the city's **main transport stand**, from where you can catch maxis and taxis to most destinations in the south of the country (for details of transport **out of San Fernando**, see box below).

There is no TIDCO office in San Fernando and little documented **information** on the city outside of what appears in the tourist publications. A useful **website** for background information and discussion of local issues is ⓦ www.whatsouthsay.com.

Given the sprawling layout of San Fernando and its numerous hills, it makes sense to use public transport to **get around** the city. Only **route taxis** ply the city's streets, operating around the clock and charging a flat fare of TT$3 for most journeys, with an added dollar or two for off-route drops. Be aware, however, that finding out which taxis go where is an exercise in frustration. Almost all routes originate – or at least pass through – **Library Corner**, but be sure to ask the driver where he is going before boarding any taxi. A good place to wait for a taxi in Library Corner is next to the *KFC*, where you can catch "**Round the road**" taxis, which follow a loop around the city centre, circling San Fernando Hill, as well as taxis to the town's main shopping malls, **Cross Crossing** and **Gulf City**. To get to **St Joseph Village**, take a Gasparillo taxi from High Street (TT$5). Two local **private taxi** firms are Mattadeen's Taxicab Service (☎658 4973) and St Anthony's Taxicab Co-Operative (☎648 3941). If you want to **rent a car**, contact Convenient, Southern Main Road, Claxton Bay (☎634 4017).

---

## Moving on from San Fernando

The **main transport stand** for rides to the rest of the south is adjacent to the San Fernando General Hospital on Chancery Lane. **Maxis** go from here to La Brea (TT$5), Vessigny (TT$5), Penal (TT$4), Siparia (TT$6), Fyzabad (TT$4) and Point Fortin (TT$6). For Palo Seco, you will have to take a maxi to Siparia and then change. **Route taxis** from this stand run to La Brea (TT$7), Vessigny (TT$7), Erin (TT$10), Siparia (TT$7), Palo Seco (TT$10) and Point Fortin (TT$10).

Other destinations have their stands located around the city centre. Maxis for **Pointe-a-Pierre** (TT$2), **Couva** (TT$4) and **Chaguanas** (TT$4) depart from St James Street between Penitence and Mon Chagrin streets, while those for **Princes Town** (TT$3) go from Coffee Street. Route taxis to **Penal** (TT$5) leave from High Street and those to **Fyzabad** (TT$6) and **Princes Town** (TT$4) depart from the corner of Mucurapo and Lord streets. To go to **Granville** and **Icacos**, you have to change at Point Fortin. To reach **Mayaro**, you need to go via Princes Town and Rio Claro, or Sangre Grande in the northeast.

For information about **PTSC bus** services, ring ☎652 3705 (ticket office: Mon–Fri 4.45am–8pm, Sat 6am–7pm, Sun 6am–6.30pm). All buses to Port of Spain run from the main bus terminal at the bottom of Queen Street (see above), Chaguanas (same times as Port of Spain bus; ECS: TT$4; Transit: TT$2.50), Point Fortin (Transit: Mon–Fri 3am–7.30pm, hourly, Sat & Sun 6am, 9am, noon, 3.30pm & 6.30pm, TT$3) and La Brea (Point Fortin bus; TT$3).

Marabella, Point-a-Pierre & Port of Spain ◄

**RESTAURANTS & BARS**

| | |
|---|---|
| Atherly's by the Park | 13 |
| Belle Bagai | 8 |
| Canton Palace | 15 |
| Club Celebs | 18 |
| Gallery Pub | 18 |
| Hi RPM | 18 |
| Jenny's Wok & Steakhouse | 17 |
| KFC | 5 |
| Kolumbo | 9 |
| Nam Fong Lotus | 6 |
| The Pagoda | 10 |
| Petroleum Club | 14 |
| Platinum | 16 |
| Puff 'n Stuff | 3 |
| Richie's Paradise | 12 |
| Shashell's | 2 |
| Soong's Great Wall | 4 |
| Swiss Grill | 11 |
| Tree House | 1 |
| Willie's Ice Cream | 7 |

VISTABELLA

ST JOSEPH VILLAGE

GULF OF PARIA

San Fernando Hill (200 m)

King's Wharf

PTSC Bus Terminal

Fish Market

Maxis for Port of Spain

Chancery Lane Market

Main Maxi & Taxi Stand

City Hall

Church of Our Lady of Perpetual Help RC

Carnegie Free Library

Police Station

San Fernando General Hospital

Paradise Cemetery

Naparima Bowl

Carib House

Skiffle Bunch Panyard

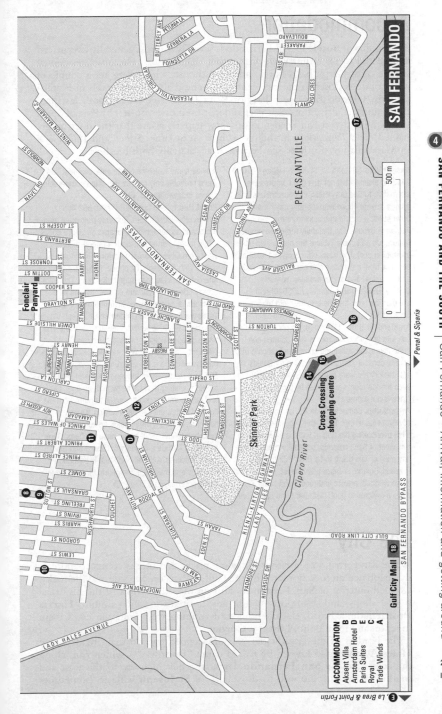

4

SAN FERNANDO

▶ Penal & Siparia

▲ La Brea & Point Fortin

◀ ▲ ❸ Penal & Siparia

**ACCOMMODATION**
Aksent Villa          B
Amsterdam Hotel    D
Paria Suites         E
Royal               C
Trade Winds         A

Fonclair Panyard ■

Skinner Park

Cipero River

Cross Crossing shopping centre

Gulf City Mall ⑱

PLEASANTVILLE

0                    500 m

# Accommodation

The choice of **hotels** in San Fernando is severely limited, generally overpriced and geared to oil industry workers rather than visitors. The quiet residential suburb of St Joseph has a hotel and a guesthouse, while there are a couple of other options closer to the city centre. You could also stay at hotels in Pointe-a-Pierre/Claxton Bay (see p.191) or Point Fortin (see p.223), both less than thirty minutes' drive from San Fernando, or even base yourself in Port of Spain (see p.69) and visit San Fernando on a day trip. Be aware that the disarmingly named *Hotel Tokyo*, right in the city centre on St James Street, and *Villa Capri* in Marabella just north of San Fernando, are actually both brothels.

**Aksent Villa** 58 North St, St Joseph Village ☎683 2413, ⓔaksent@tstt.net.tt. A good, impressive alternative to Sando's hotels, this guesthouse is in a large private house with a pretty garden on a quiet street a couple of blocks from the San Fernando Bypass. The tastefully furnished rooms feature a/c and cable TV, and the house also has a swimming pool. The hosts offer a myriad additional services from cell phone and car rental to laundry, and breakfast and dinner are also available. Weekly (US$290) and monthly (US$690) rentals are possible, and there is a three-night minimum booking. ❺

**Amsterdam Hotel** 11 Todd St; no phone. Small, box-like but functional rooms with painted concrete floors, fan, toilet and shower, all ranging off a central corridor plastered with rules for guests. A satisfactory and safe place for tourists to stay; even though rooms are rented by the hour, this place is not a brothel. ❹

**Paria Suites** Southern Trunk Rd, La Romaine ☎697 1442, ⓕ697 1445. This renovated hotel on a hill overlooking the Gulf of Paria is a few kilometres west of San Fernando, but easily reached on any maxi or taxi going to La Brea, Point Fortin, Fyzabad, Siparia, or other points west. Rooms come with a/c, private bathrooms and cable TV, while a swimming pool, restaurant and sports bar

provide some welcome onsite entertainment, but you'd probably only choose this if the comparable places in town are full. ❻

**Royal Hotel** 46–54 Royal Rd ☎/ⓕ652 4881, ⓦwww.royalhoteltt.com. Recently renovated after a fire, and as conveniently located as you're going to get in San Fernando, about a fifteen-minute walk from Library Corner. Comfortable, bright rooms with a/c, cable TV, phone, fridge, jacks for Internet access and en-suite bathrooms. There's a breezy open-air restaurant on site, as well as a pleasant, reasonably large swimming pool. ❻

**Tradewinds Hotel** 38 London St, St Joseph Village ☎/ⓕ652 9463, ⓦwww.tradewindshotel.net. The best equipped hotel in the south, occupying a pleasant – albeit not a very central – location on a breezy hill in the quiet suburb of St Joseph Village. The best rooms are in the renovated and ultra-modern building next to the swimming pool, bar and restaurant, though the noise at night from the bar and restaurant can be annoying. All rooms have a/c, cable TV, fridge, minibar, kettle and en-suite bathrooms, while some have kitchens. Other amenities include a large gym, jacuzzi and free Internet access. A buffet breakfast is included in the rates and there is a complimentary shuttle to the airport daily at 5.30am. ❻

# The City

While San Fernando is a rather sprawling place, its centre is compact and easily negotiated on foot, bordered by the Gulf of Paria on one side and the rocky, wooded outcrop of **San Fernando Hill** on the other. Most of the historical sights, shops and transport stands are located on and around **Harris Promenade**, a broad, elegant boulevard running west from the city's main junction and focal point, **Library Corner**.

The borders of the city's wider area are defined by two main roads: **Lady Hales Avenue** (also known by its old name, "Broadway"), which runs along the coast, and the **San Fernando Bypass**, a belt highway to the west and south. Further out, the well-to-do suburb of **St Joseph Village** (sometimes referred to simply as "The Village") sprawls up the slopes of San Fernando Hill, while more recent developments such as **Pleasantville** and the large **shopping malls** are located on the outskirts, on or not very far from the bypass.

## San Fernando Hill

At 200 metres high, **San Fernando Hill** overshadows the town centre. For many years the hill was quarried to provide gravel for the building of the city's streets, giving it its strange profile – half the hill is flattened with steep protruding points, while the other half maintains its natural outline. In 1980 it was declared a national park, providing a pleasant recreation area with picnic tables, planted flowers, a children's playground, fountain, public toilets and several lookouts from which to enjoy the panoramic views. The clearly signposted road to the summit (daily 9am–6pm) lies next to *Soong's Great Wall* restaurant (see p.216) on the hill's northeast corner. Though you can drive a car to the top, it's only a twenty-minute walk. Once at the summit, you are rewarded with a good view of San Fernando, the Gulf of Paria and the flaming Petrotrin chimneys, or, to the other side, the undulating sugar cane flats and agricultural plains of the interior.

Just past *Soong's Great Wall*, several other streets wind up the hill into the upscale residential suburb of **St Joseph Village**, the location of some of San Fernando's most sumptuous houses, the majority of which enjoy fine views over the city. The main reason tourists venture up to St Joseph Village, however, is to enjoy a meal and some live entertainment at the popular *Tree House* restaurant (see p.216) at the *Tradewinds Hotel*.

## Harris Promenade and around

**Harris Promenade** is the centre of San Fernando's civic life and the location of many of its official buildings. Named after the British governor of Trinidad from 1846 to 1854, the promenade stretches from the long 1950s-style facade of **San Fernando General Hospital** to Library Corner in the east, and consists of two relatively short, parallel streets with a paved centre lined with benches and tables, the odd statue and an ornate Victorian bandstand. Like Port of Spain's Brian Lara Promenade (see p.79), it has been beautified to provide a pleasant hang-out for the city's residents, but is more picturesque than its equivalent in the capital, lined with attractive colonial buildings and virtually devoid of the beggars and hustlers that patrol Brian Lara Promenade.

On the south side of the promenade towards its western end stands an old-fashioned, round-arched yellow stone building reminiscent of an English parish church or country mansion – this is actually the city's **police station**. Across the road, the grand Neoclassical **City Hall** was built in 1930 and dominates the western end of the promenade – though it faces stiff competition from the Catholic **Church of Our Lady of Perpetual Help** just one block to the east, a huge white modern building with a tall clock tower that can be seen from most places in the city. Although impressive from the outside, its interior is unusually stark for a Catholic place of worship.

At the centre of the promenade is the **Mahatma Gandhi Statue**, brought to Trinidad from India in 1952. On Gandhi's birthday (October 2), the day of his death (January 30) and Diwali (see p.49), the local Gandhi Seva Sang Organization holds a commemorative service on the promenade below the statue. The Afro-Caribbean population's aspirations are similarly acknowledged at the eastern end of the promenade by a brightly painted statue of Jamaican black rights activist **Marcus Garvey**, typical of Trinidad's more modern monuments which use plenty of colours to make them as life-like as possible.

At this point the promenade's two roads converge in front of the **Carnegie Free Library** (Mon–Fri 8.30am–6pm, Sat 8.30am–noon; ℡652 3228), a large, ornate terracotta building built in 1919 and financed – like many others the world over – by the Scottish philanthropist Andrew Carnegie. Behind the library, on the promenade, an old **steam locomotive** recalls the last run from Port of Spain to San Fernando in 1968. People packed the carriages, hanging out of the windows to be part of this historic occasion, which was subsequently immortalized by the late Lord Kitchener's famous calypso *Last Train to San Fernando*. Engine 11, which stands on the promenade today, is not the actual machine that pulled the final train, but one of the last to be used by the sugar estates. The chaotic junction of seven roads just east of the library is known as **Library Corner**, at the centre of which stands a modern four-faced clock. This spot is a popular rendezvous – "meet meh library corner" is a common refrain among the city's residents.

Walking west down **High Street** from Library Corner brings you into the busiest part of town. This is San Fernando's main shopping street, lined with clothes stores and shops selling household goods, while street vendors hawk everything from plastic trinkets to leopardskin underwear on the pavement. At its western end, as High Street doglegs into Queen Street, the sea comes into view. This area, ironically known as **Happy Corner**, is the most run-down in the city, but a few colonial buildings, including *Hotel Happy Corner* (a flophouse) with its pretty balcony overlooking the junction of Queen and King streets, provide some architectural interest, while the patrons of the local rum shops add a touch of raffish zest. It's an interesting spot that allows you to experience another, more laid-back side of San Fernando, away from the glut of shops and malls that otherwise tend to characterize the city. Happy Corner gives on to **King's Wharf**, a scruffy tarmac dock lined with dilapidated wood and galvanized iron huts fronting a small harbour where fishing boats bob up and down on the swell. In the **fish market**, a plain whitewashed building just south of the wharf that has changed little since it was built in 1924, the fishermen gut, clean and sell their catch – snapper, kingfish and shark, alongside the occasional deep-sea monster.

## Carib Street and "The Coffee"

Along the southern verge of San Fernando Hill runs **Carib Street**, fringed by ramshackle old colonial houses. Though less picturesque than its wooden neighbours, the stuccoed **Carib House** – the cream-and-red eighteenth-century Spanish colonial building on the corner of Upper Hillside Street and Carib Street – is the oldest building in San Fernando. Despite its age, there is no plaque or sign indicating its history or date of construction, although there have been rumours recently that it has been slated for renovation, perhaps to open in the future as some sort of museum.

**Coffee Street**, which turns south off Carib Street at about the hill's midpoint, takes its name from the coffee plantations that once thrived here. "The Coffee" – as the street is familiarly known – was the original home of many of the south's **steel bands**, including the highly acclaimed **Fonclaire**, led by inimitable panman Ken Professor Philmore. The Fonclaire panyard is now located on Dottin Street, one block south of Coffee Street. A brightly painted statue of a pan player at the junction of Coffee and Cipero streets celebrates the area's musical heritage. A little further down Coffee Street opposite the Southern Food Basket supermarket is the panyard of the **Skiffle Bunch**, a regular participant in the Panorama Finals at Carnival time and a particularly good performer at the World Steel Band Festival in October (see p.49). One of the walls on the narrow decaying building on the panyard's left-hand side is decorated with frescoes known as the **Dancing Walls**, painted in 1994 by local artist Glen Steel. The animated figures – executed in spiky black outline – capture the energy and excitement of the steel band as they trace its development from the tamboo bamboo of the 1940s (see p.345) to the present day. Interwoven with the pan players are traditional Carnival characters such as Jab Molassis and the sailors (see p.330). The Coffee is particularly lively during the run-up to Carnival, when practice sessions ring out into the street; it's an excellent time to be in the area.

## South San Fernando

Lady Hales Avenue skirts the coast on the western edge of San Fernando before veering east and cutting through the southern part of the city (where it runs parallel with the Rienzi-Kirton Highway). This is not the most attractive of Sando's neighbourhoods, but is nevertheless the location of San Fernando's two major shopping malls (see p.217) and one other useful facility. Just before intersecting with the San Fernando Bypass, Lady Hales Avenue passes **Skinner Park**, an outdoor sports and concert venue where many of San Fernando's pre-Carnival concerts, Calypso tents and fetes are held. On the other side of the San Fernando Bypass (where Lady Hales Avenue becomes Cipero Road), the unremarkable suburb of **Pleasantville** is an example of San Fernando's recent residential development.

# Eating

Grabbing a quick fix of roti, chow mein or fried chicken is hardly a problem in San Fernando, where numerous **fast-food outlets** line the streets. There's an especially high concentration of informal places for weekday lunches or early dinners along High Street, while the large food court at the Gulf City Mall (see p.217) is heaving on Saturdays and offers a variety of food for most tastes. Finding a more formal **restaurant** suitable for a leisurely meal is less straightforward, with your choices basically restricted to one or two upmarket Chinese places, the hotel restaurants and a handful of other eateries dotted around town.

**Atherly's by the Park** 104 Gooding Village, near Cross Crossing Shopping Centre ℡652 7373. Roadside diner close to Skinner Park with an a/c main room and a couple of tables outside, serving inexpensive, reliable Creole and Indian dishes, principally at lunchtime. The menu changes daily and there is a buffet on Wednesdays. In the evenings, although snacks such as fried chicken wings and sandwiches are available, the place becomes more bar than eatery (see p.217). Daily 10am–2am.

**Belle Bagai** 20 Gransaul St. Nice place for lunch or for dinner and drinks, with a simple menu of snacks – wontons, fish and chips, burgers – as well as more substantial steaks or fish dishes. Good service and relaxed atmosphere in a pretty old colonial house with a cool verandah on one of Sando's quieter streets. Mon–Thurs 3pm–late, Fri & Sat 1pm–late.

**Canton Palace Restaurant** Cross Crossing Shopping Centre ℡652 5993. Moderately priced Chinese restaurant with pleasant decor and a/c, recommended for its crab and pepper shrimp and tasty appetizers such as Har Gau (shrimp), Siu Mei (pork) and Chinese dumplings. Mon–Sat 11am–10pm.

**Jenny's Wok & Steakhouse** 175 Cipero Rd, Victoria Village ℡652 1807. Located some distance from the town centre in a warehouse-dominated industrial area, but a popular after-work liming spot all the same, with its large, three-sided American-style bar and decent, though somewhat pricey, Chinese food, steaks and seafood. Delivery available. Mon–Thurs 11am–10pm, Fri & Sat 11am–11pm.

**Kolumbo Restaurant** 34 Sutton St ☎653 7684. International cuisine such as gourmet burgers, patés and steaks. Occupying a restored colonial building, this stylish restaurant set on two levels is very romantic at night. Tues–Sat 4pm–midnight.

**Nam Fong Lotus Restaurant** 91–93 Cipero St ☎652 3356. Serves huge Chinese lunches and dinners – the signature dish is Char Sue Kai Fan (chicken, pork and rice) – at inexpensive prices. A relaxing, comfy and more refined atmosphere than the usual plastic tables, and better value than the other upmarket Chinese restaurants in town. Recommended. Mon–Sat 10am–10pm.

**The Pagoda** 59 Independence Ave ☎657 6375. Cosy restaurant serving usual, affordable Chinese fare; the steamed fish dressed with garlic and ginger, however, is outstanding. Mon–Thurs 10.30am–10pm, Fri & Sat 10.30am–10.30pm.

**Petroleum Club** Top Floor, Cross Crossing Shopping Centre ☎652 4069. Intimate restaurant decorated in cosy Mediterranean style, offering creative international cuisine from kebabs to steaks and seafood platters, all of which comes at a price. Mon–Fri 11.30am–10pm.

**Puff 'n Stuff** 40 Circular Rd ☎657 5920. Bakery owned by the same people as the *Tradewinds Hotel*, selling excellent fresh cakes, pastries, sandwiches, moist brownies, fluffy tuna puffs and rum fruitcake. Take away only. Mon–Sat 6am–9pm, Sun 6am–8pm.

**Royal Hotel Restaurant** 46–54 Royal Rd ☎652 4881. Comfortable hotel restaurant serving international breakfasts with Creole touches such as

saltfish buljol, sandwiches at lunch, and steak or fish dinners, served either under an open-air pavilion or in an a/c dining room. Daily 6am–10.30pm.

**Soong's Great Wall** 97 Circular Rd ☎657 5050. High-quality and slightly higher-priced Chinese food – as well as international cuisine such as steak dinners – served in an ornate pagoda-shaped building; some outdoor seating. Buffets every Wed evening. Mon–Thurs & Sun 11am–10pm, Fri & Sat 11am–10.30pm.

**Swiss Grill** Prince Albert St, at Rushworth ☎657 9295. Swiss-run restaurant with a not very Swiss-like menu including steaks and pasta dishes, but known for its succulent mahi-mahi steaks and other delicious grilled fish. The warm colours of the teak-walled dining room give the place a relaxing ambience. Mon–Sat 11am–11pm, Sun 4pm–11pm.

**Tree House** 38 London St ☎653 8733. Lively place at the *Tradewinds Hotel* – a popular haunt for locals and expats alike. Built round the trunk of a large cedar tree, the plant-bedecked balcony affords good views over the city. The menu is varied, featuring crab backs and shrimp bruschetta, seafood and steaks, and Mexican and Cajun dishes, although the portions are disappointingly small for the high prices. Reservations recommended for dinner. Sun–Thurs 5am–10pm, Fri & Sat 5am–2am.

**Willie's Ice Cream** 43 Coffee St ☎673 0537. One of the largest and most elaborate branches of this national ice cream chain, full of tubs of exotically flavoured ice cream such as soursop, sapodilla and barbadine, as well as a complete children's playground with swings and slides in the back of the shop.

# Nightlife and entertainment

Although you won't be coming here for its nightlife and entertainment, San Fernando still has enough on offer to while away an evening or two. The city's numerous **rum shops** are the ideal place to meet the locals and partake in some inane, drunken conversation, while **bar/restaurants** are your best bet for an evening lime and some **live music**; their busiest evening tends to be Friday. For a dance in more energetic company head for the **nightclubs**, several of which are located in the shopping malls. Predictably, Friday and Saturday evenings are the busiest times for nightclubs, when the music tends to be a mix of soca, hip-hop, dub and reggae. The bars and clubs of Gulf City Mall are also very lively on Saturday afternoons; *HiRPM* and *Club Celebs* organize popular gatherings intended for, but not restricted to, teenagers and young adults. In the **build-up to Carnival**, Skinner Park (☎657 7168; entrance tickets vary), on Rienzi-Kirton Highway at the southern edge of the city, is Sando's main venue for fetes, pan and soca competitions, calypso tents and other pre-Carnival events. At other times, this venue is used to host local football and baseball games. The **Naparima Bowl**, 19 Paradise Pasture (T657 8770), is another venue for big calypso and steel band events, as well as being a comfy theatre and outdoor amphitheatre hosting plays, which regularly come here after showing in Port of Spain. Ticket prices vary depending upon what's on.

San Fernando has three **cinemas**, each catering to distinctly different tastes: Hobosco II, 21–23 Mucurapo St (T652 4543), shows kung-fu films; Metro, 41–43 Harris Promenade (T652 4107), specializes in Bollywood, while National Cinema, Keate St, at Gomez (T652 2343) screens double bills of Hollywood fare.

**Atherly's by the Park** 104 Gooding Village, near Cross Crossings Shopping Centre T652 7373. Popular, friendly restaurant/bar that's good for a drink, especially at night or if you're waiting to attend an event at Skinner Park over the road. Sit in the softly lit a/c indoor section or at the tables outside, the ambience of which is spoilt a little by the rather noisy street. DJ plays a nice selection of calypso, reggae and old hits Tues–Sun, and there is a happy hour on Friday evenings. Daily 10am–2am.

**Belle Bagai** 20 Gransaul St. Elegant bar/restaurant in a wooden gingerbread house, all creaky floorboards and polished mahogany. The open-air verandah on a quiet street is perfect for a low-key lime or a game of pool. Mon–Thurs 3pm–late, Fri & Sat 1pm–late.

**Club Celebs** Top Level, Gulf City Mall T652 7641. A modern club playing a wide variety of music to a crowd that tends to be in its teens or twenties, especially on Saturday afternoons. Soca, hip-hop and the like predominate on Saturdays and Wednesdays, while your best chance of hearing some techno is on Fridays. Cover charge varies. Wed, Fri & Sat 10–4am.

**Gallery Pub** Top Level, Gulf City Mall T688 9329. Straightforward pub offering the usual selection of beers and spirits, plus a few cocktails. Especially busy on Fridays and Saturdays, both at night and in the afternoons as shoppers in the mall stop off for a quick lime. Attracts a more mature crowd than the clubs here at Gulf City Mall. Mon–Sat 11am–midnight, Sun 2–10pm.

**HiRPM** Top Level, Gulf City Mall T652 3760.

Longstanding club that takes the credit for introducing rock music to San Fernando. Wednesday's rock nights remain very popular, while at weekends it's the typical hip-hop, dub and soca. Techno-lovers are catered to on Tuesdays. Cover charge usually around TT$20. Daily noon–4am.

**Platinum** in the old Southland Mall, opposite Cross Crossing Shopping Centre. Sando's newest and most popular club. On two floors with a large dance floor and free drinks included some nights in the cover charge, which varies. Wed–Sun 6pm–4am.

**Richie's Paradise** Cipero St T653 0711. Bar-cum-club with a big dance floor that attracts a mature crowd and lots of couples; music ranges from back-in-times (retro) to dance. Moderate cover charge – usually around TT$20. Wed–Sun 6pm–late.

**Shashell's** 137a Lambie St, at Pointe-a-Pierre Rd, Vistabella T652 5836. Fridays at this nightclub in Vistabella – a suburb west of St Joseph Village – see a younger crowd for the soca and reggae, while Saturday's calypso and soca draws more mature revellers. Moderate cover charge. Fri & Sat 5pm–late.

**Tree House** 38 London St T653 8733. The restaurant's friendly, intimate cocktail bar is good for a drink and a lime, as well as being a popular meeting place for expats. Handmade cigars are on sale, there's a good selection of wines, and live music in the form of a pianist or steel band is laid on Mon–Thurs & Sun. The tempo of the music is higher and the place much busier on Fri & Sat. Sun–Thurs 5am–10pm, Fri & Sat 5am–2am.

# Shopping

The best place for shopping is **Gulf City Mall** (Mon–Thurs 10am–8pm, Fri & Sat 11am–9pm, Sun 2–8pm), at the southern edge of the city on the San Fernando Bypass (the mall is officially located in La Romain). This is Trinidad's most enjoyable mall, a bustling place crammed with diverse shops on two levels – as good for meeting people in one of its many bars and clubs as it is for finding the latest imported fashions. Another shopping complex with far fewer outlets and none of the conviviality of Gulf City is the **Cross Crossing**

**Shopping Centre** opposite Skinner Park on Lady Hales Avenue. For more local goods, the **Chancery Lane Market** at the western end of High Street features a number of stalls selling local arts and crafts made by Rastafarians, who make up a significant proportion of San Fernando's residents. Sandals, hats, jewellery, belts and straw goods can be found here for very reasonable prices.

## Listings

**Banks** First Citizens, High St, at Penitence ☎652 2757; Republic, 92–94 Cipero St ☎652 3736; Scotiabank Cipero St, at Rushworth ☎657 7109. All have ATMs.

**Hospital** San Fernando General, Independence Ave ☎652 3581.

**Internet** You can get 30min free Internet access a day at Carnegie Free Library (Mon–Fri 8.30am–6pm, Sat 8.30am–noon). Otherwise, try Browwwser's Cyber Café, Coffee St, near Library Corner (Mon–Sat 7am–7pm; TT$10 per hr) and TT

**Surf Cyber Café**, Top Level, Gulf City Mall (Mon–Sat 8am–8.30pm, Sun 2–8.30pm; TT$12 per hr).

**Laundry** Chee's, Gulf City Mall ☎657 5505 (dry cleaning); Ng Pack Laundry, 4 Mucurapo St ☎652 3276 (steam laundry).

**Pharmacy** Shiva's Pharmacy, 42 Royal Rd ☎652 4604. Daily 8am–8pm.

**Police** The main police station is at the western end of Harris Promenade ☎652 3206.

**Post office** Carlton Centre, St James St. Mon–Fri 7am–5pm, Sat 8am–2pm.

# The southwest peninsula

Trinidad's **southwest peninsula**, known locally as the "deep south", offers a mix of gritty oil towns and marvellous drives through sleepy backwaters, forested hills, and teak and coconut plantations, all of it lined by beaches of soft brown sand backed by red-earth cliffs and lapped by calm seas. The pace of life is very slow here, so take time to enjoy the relaxed atmosphere and incomparable countryside.

Despite its proximity to industrial San Fernando, the hard-to-get-to mangrove swampland of the **Oropuche Lagoon** is a wildlife haven, teeming with birds and seldom-visited. Indeed, it's rare for tourists to explore this area beyond the well-publicized **Pitch Lake** at **La Brea**, an interesting and worthwhile excursion; though you should also consider travelling on south to the areas of **Erin** and **Cedros** at the tip of the peninsula for a glimpse of some of Trinidad's prettiest countryside. Down here, small fishing hamlets line the coast, while the beaches are like an escapist's fantasy of small sheltered coves, usually deserted apart from the odd fisherman or truant child. Taking the Southern Main Road down to **Icacos Point**, the extreme southwest tip and the closest point to the Venezuelan mainland, is one of the most spectacular drives in Trinidad, lined with coconut plantations where herds of buffalypso graze.

The larger towns on the peninsula, such as **Point Fortin** and the **Siparia-Fyzabad conurbation**, revolve around the oil industry and are almost entirely given over to industry and commerce, in stark contrast to the laid-back villages further along the peninsula. These towns are also the main **transportation hubs** in the southwest outside of San Fernando, and the time it takes to change maxis or taxis will normally be enough to take in the limited amount that they have to offer.

There is limited **accommodation** in Point Fortin, as well as one or two guesthouses by the beach in Cedros and Erin, but that's about it.

# Oropuche Lagoon

The **Oropuche Lagoon** – 56 square kilometres of tidal mangrove swamp alongside the Southern Trunk Road (as the Southern Main Road is called between San Fernando and La Brea) 6km south of San Fernando – features on the itineraries of very few tour companies. That's just how the government plans to keep it – a sanctuary for fish and endangered wildfowl bred in the Pointe-a-Pierre Wildfowl Trust (see p.191).

Oropuche's rather inaccessible location amid swampy marshland discourages hunters as well as visitors, and as a result it teems with animals and birdlife. It is an excellent place to view **butterflies**, as well as **birds** such as egrets, black-bellied whistling duck, American bittern, ringed kingfish and a variety of herons. The swamp is home to several types of fish including tarpon and catfish, and the area is known for its shrimping grounds. Though it is less disturbed than the Caroni Swamp (see p.183), the lagoon is under threat from pollution due to oil leaks from pumping jacks – there are more than 1600 scattered around the south, including several in the vicinity of the lagoon, and damaging oilspills occur fairly frequently.

Paria Springs (☎622 8826) include the Oropuche Lagoon on its excellent West Coast Wetlands and Icacos birding **tours**. Otherwise, if you have your own transport, there is nothing to stop you visiting the lagoon independently, although a guide is recommended if you want to do some serious wildlife spotting. The Oropuche Lagoon is accessible via a turn-off on the Southern Trunk Road just before the intersection with Fyzabad Road.

# The Siparia-Fyzabad conurbation

Some 10 to 13km south of San Fernando is the **Siparia-Fyzabad conurbation**, powerhouse of the country's oil industry and surrounded by the rolling pastures and endless sugar cane fields of the **Philippines Estate**. The government has designated the magnificent untouched forest on either side of the San Fernando–Siparia–Erin Road as the **Palmiste National Park**. The small agricultural town of **Penal**, which produces a large proportion of the country's rice, holds little of interest for the visitor, but it marks the beginning of the built-up area; from here it is easy to drive into the lively old Spanish town of **Siparia** without noticing where one starts and the other ends. The urban area sprawls a few kilometres north of Siparia, also encompassing **Fyzabad**, a gritty place that played a crucial role in the development of Trinidadian trade unionism and the struggle for civil rights. The hectic towns of the conurbation are excellent places to buy **Indian** sweets, pies and snacks that are sold on roadside stalls in the little wooden glass cases known locally as "safes".

Away from the urban hustle and bustle is **Quinam Beach**, the most popular beach on Trinidad's south coast, located a few kilometres south of Siparia where the calm seas attract both swimmers and Baptists, who believe that the waters in these parts have mystical qualities.

## The Festival of La Divina Pastora

Held on the second Sunday after Easter in Siparia, the **Festival of La Divina Pastora** – The Divine Shepherdess – was brought to Trinidad from Andalucia by way of Venezuela in the eighteenth century. Decked out in new clothes, the locals make offerings to the **Black Virgin** statue, carried in procession through the streets, and celebrate with general feasting and merrymaking. Some believe that the wooden statue was in fact the prow of the ship in which the priests travelled from the mainland, and taken from a shipwreck on Quinam Beach by passing Warwarrhoons Indians. Others claim it was brought to Siparia from Venezuela by a Spanish priest whose life it had saved. Whatever its origins, many miracles have been attributed to the statue, even by non-Catholics. Local Baptists attribute mystical powers to the Black Virgin, and in the 1890s, Hindu indentured labourers saw in the statue's dark features the goddess Kali, the destroyer of sorrow. Renaming the statue Soparee Kay Mai, the Hindus started their own form of worship – if Kali answered their prayers, Hindu women would offer the statue locks from their children's first haircut. The Catholic Church attempted to discourage this devotion in the 1920s, but the cult had already grown too strong, and to this day, Hindu devotees are well represented at the festival.

## Siparia

The action in **SIPARIA** is focused on the main street, lined with a smattering of attractive **colonial houses** which are juxtaposed with more modern constructions and rickety market stalls. A busy place full of shoppers and market vendors, there are few specific sights in Siparia, unless you are interested in the variety of vegetables, ground provisions and fruit on offer.

The town was originally settled in 1758 by Spanish Capuchin priests who established a mission to convert the Amerindians in the area. The legacy of Catholicism is still very much in evidence in the feast day of **La Divina Pastora** (see box, above) held in Siparia three weeks after Easter. During the festival, the **Black Virgin**, a small statue of the Virgin Mary normally housed in the church at the top of the hill (follow the road that branches off the Southern Trunk Road opposite the Republic Bank), is carried through the streets to the beat of tassa drums and showered with offerings of gold bracelets, flowers, olive oil and money. The festival is one big street party, with the whole town coming out to celebrate in their best clothes.

## Fyzabad

Just as bustling as Siparia, 5km to the south on Fyzabad Road, **FYZABAD** occupies a unique place in the history of **trade unionism** and the struggle for equal rights in Trinidad. Established in the nineteenth century by Canadian Presbyterian missionaries, Fyzabad took its name from the district in Uttar Pradesh, India, where most of its settlers originated. After oil was discovered in the area in 1917, however, the character of this hitherto nondescript village changed dramatically. Fyzabad quickly developed into a busy industrial town, the centre of the emergent labour movement, while the original Indo-Trinidadian Presbyterian community were soon outnumbered by migrants who came from Grenada and St Vincent to work on the oilfields, and whose descendants still make up the majority of the town's population.

The compact commercial centre, a blend of dilapidated colonial buildings and modern concrete structures, clusters around Charlie King Junction. The

Oil Workers' Trade Union Hall (OWTU) and the painted statue of the workers' leader **Uriah Butler** (see box below) in his black suit and bowler hat, dominate the junction, ironically named after **Charlie King**, the policeman killed when he tried to arrest Butler for political agitation. The junction is also the focus of the annual **Labour Day** (June 19) celebrations organized by the OWTU. The streets are blocked, a stage is erected and a street party, with a political message, ensues – union leaders make fiery speeches, a wreath is laid on Butler's grave and DJs entertain the crowd.

## Uriah Butler

**Tubal Uriah "Buzz" Butler** – Trinidad's foremost trade union activist – was a Grenadian who came to work in Trinidad's oilfields in 1921. After an industrial accident in 1929 left Butler unfit for oil work, he joined the Moravian Baptist church and became a preacher, developing the rousing oratorical skills that characterized his political career. Disillusioned with Cipriani's Trinidad Labour Party (see p.325) after it failed to support an oilworkers' strike in 1935, he established the **British Empire Workers** (BEW) to further the "heroic struggle for British justice for British Blacks in a British colony".

The BEW campaigned for better pay and working conditions in the oilfields, where many of the managers were white South Africans who had instituted an apartheid-type regime. Among the workers' many grievances were low wages, long working hours and the frequency of industrial accidents, for which there was no compensation. Workers were liable to be dismissed on the spot and, once sacked, a blackballing system made it impossible for them to find work elsewhere.

In June 1937 strikers started a **sit-in** at the **Forest Reserve oilfield**. The police broke up the protest, and in response the strikers set fire to two wells in the Apex oilfield. When the police arrived at Fyzabad to arrest Butler on a charge of agitation, they found him addressing a large crowd. As they attempted to serve the warrant, a riot broke out. One plainclothes officer, the deeply unpopular **Charlie King**, fled into a nearby shop, found himself trapped, and jumped from an upstairs window, breaking his leg; the furious crowd burned him alive, and when his colleagues tried to retrieve his body, a British police officer was shot dead. A 1938 calypso caught the popular mood: "Everybody's rejoicing, How they burned Charlie King, Everybody was glad, Nobody was sad, When they beat him and they burned him, In Fyzabad."

**Strikes** spread like wildfire, and became increasingly violent, with a mounting death toll on both sides. Butler, in hiding after the riot, was soon discovered and sentenced to two years in prison. But the strikes won important concessions: public workers were granted an eight-hour day and a higher minimum wage. The government recognized the trade unions, though the police continued to harass trade union officials. On his release in 1939, Butler was given a hero's welcome, but during his imprisonment the BEW had changed, adopting a more mainstream position, and he was soon expelled. In September 1939 Butler was once again incarcerated for sedition, and remained behind bars till the end of World War II.

Butler continued to be politically active after his release in 1945, campaigning in the national elections; but though his party won the largest block of seats in 1950, he was outflanked by the rise of Eric Williams's nationalist politics (see p.326), and his star faded. In remembrance of his role in defending workers' rights, the Princess Margaret Highway linking north and south Trinidad was renamed in his honour in the 1960s. In 1971 the government awarded him the Trinity Cross – the highest honour in the land, and June 19, the day of the riots, was declared a public holiday.

## Quinam Beach

A well-signposted, if rather bumpy, 7.5km-drive south from Siparia down the Coora Road/Penal Quinam Road, through teak plantations and forest inhabited by deer, takes you to **Quinam Beach** on the south coast of the peninsula. The sands here are fine and brown, though at high tide they disappear beneath the waves; the waters are calm and good for swimming; and Baptist flags flap in the breeze on the seashore – followers of the faith believe the sea here has mystical qualities.

This is the most popular beach on the south coast – on weekends the small car park on the seafront is packed with Trinis coming to take a swim. The **Quinam Bay Interpretive Centre** (daily 9am–6pm), just by the beach, displays pictures of the local flora and fauna, and also provides sheltered picnic facilities, firewood cooking stoves and a special praying area for Hindus, Muslims and Spiritual Baptists. You'll need to bring your own food and drink unless you want to buy aloo pies, snow cones or soft drinks from the beach vendors who ply their trade mainly on weekends. There is no **transport** to the beach, but you can persuade a Siparia taxi driver to take you there for an agreed fare (around TT$10–20). To return, you might be able to catch a lift with a Trini at the weekend. However, during weekdays when the beach is much quieter, you had better make an arrangement with the taxi driver to either wait for you or pick you up at an appointed time.

# La Brea and around

Eighteen kilometres south of San Fernando on the Southern Trunk Road, a turn-off winds through rainforest and teak plantations to **LA BREA**. The village's name, Spanish for pitch, announces its main claim to fame: the nearby **Pitch Lake**. There's little else to see – the most memorable feature of the village itself is its excruciatingly bumpy roads, a car suspension's nightmare, caused by the underground volcanic eruptions that replenish the lake. La Brea's residents put up with it, finding compensation in the free pitch that bubbles up all over the place, used as rather unattractive paving for driveways and as an unconventional garden weedkiller.

## Pitch Lake

Some of the world's finest quality asphalt comes from **Pitch Lake** (daily 9am–5pm; for more info, call ☏623 6022), well-signposted 1.5km south of La Brea on the Southern Main Road. Trinis claim it as the eighth wonder of the world, although from a distance it bears a remarkable resemblance to a car park or the wrinkly hide of an elephant. However, closer inspection with a knowledgeable guide reveals this site's intriguing complexities.

Five to six million years ago, asphaltic oil flowed into a huge mud volcano here, developing over time into the pitch that is now extracted from the lake, refined into asphalt and used to pave roads the world over – including the one in front of London's Buckingham Palace. The depth of the lake is estimated at 55m and the level of pitch rises naturally after each excavation – calculations suggest that there is enough pitch in the lake to last four or five centuries. Covering more than 40,000 square metres, the lake probably represents the largest deposit of its kind in the world, of which there are few to begin with; others exist in Los Angeles, Norway and Lake Maracaibo, Venezuela, which is actually connected to La Brea by veins that run under the sea.

Bird of Paradise flowers grow around the lake's edge, in stark contrast to the unsightly factory that excavates 180 tonnes of pitch daily. If you visit between 7am and 11am or noon to 4pm, you'll see the workers loading pitch onto trolleys and dragging their load across the surface to the factory. The **"mother of the lake"** – soft parts that are not firm enough to walk on and virtually impossible to remove if caught on clothing – occupies some 25 percent of the lake's total surface area. This gooey, tar-like substance feeds the pitch, but is in itself useless for making asphalt. If it rains after the pitch has been excavated and before the lake has had time to rise to its original level, pools of sulphuric water are created. These become popular spots for locals to take an evening dip, mostly to capitalize on the reputed healing qualities of the waters, said to be good for mosquito bites, rashes and various skin conditions.

According to local **legend**, a Carib tribe who killed and ate the sacred hummingbird to celebrate a tribal victory angered the Great Spirit of the Amerindians. The spirit punished them by trapping them forever under the Pitch Lake – a story reinforced by the many Amerindian artefacts yielded up by the lake over the years, and now displayed on shelves in local homes as well as in glass cases at the National Museum in Port of Spain. **Sir Walter Raleigh** discovered the pitch lake in 1595, used the pitch to caulk his ships, and reported on its quality to Queen Elizabeth I. The lake was not commercially exploited until the 1860s, however, when it was developed by the British, who continued to control the excavation of pitch until 1978.

Although free to enter, it is well worth **visiting** Pitch Lake with a guide (TT\$30, expect to leave a tip), who will explain the lake's history and its various geological features, as well as help you to avoid walking on the treacherously soft "mother of the lake" patches. Indeed, it is not advisable to strike out onto the lake alone, since soft patches are difficult for the uninitiated to recognize. Authorized guides wait at the main entrance and are identifiable by their badges and green shirts. Wear shoes with low heels. The fee for the guide also includes access to a small **museum** of dubious interest, being full mainly of photographs of pitch being excavated and the places around the world where Trinidadian asphalt has been used to line the streets.

## Vessigny Beach

Three kilometres south of Pitch Lake along Guapo Bay, **Vessigny Beach** (facilities open daily 10am–6pm; small fee charged) is a delightful little cove of brown sand lapped by calm seas. This is the only developed seaside on the south coast: a popular spot with Trinis at the weekends, and a favored destination for evening excursions that often turn into high-spirited beach parties. There are no lifeguards on duty, so be careful when swimming. Its well-maintained facilities include a snack bar (open weekends and during school holidays), changing rooms and picnic tables. Trinidadians sometimes **camp** on the grass by the beach – this is not an official campsite, and there is no charge if you wish to do the same.

## Point Fortin

Five kilometres down the Southern Main Road from Vessigny beach, through forest, bamboo groves and small villages, is the oil town of **POINT FORTIN**. Evidence of the industry is everywhere: large storage tanks pop up in the suburbs, and the rhythmic motion of an oil pump will often catch the corner of your eye from a side street. Shell, which once owned the refinery and tank farm, built extensive facilities for its expatriate management; scattered around town are tennis courts, a golf course and an old country club, while the suburbs are full of large houses with satellite dishes and barking dogs. On some roads the old **workers' houses** can be seen – rough concrete boxes that are a far cry from the luxurious mansions of the managers.

There is little to see in Point Fortin unless you have a personal interest in the oil industry. The place only comes to life after 4pm, when the workers come out to lime in the **bars** and hang around the main junction. The best time to visit is for the annual Borough Day in May, a mini-Carnival event; contact TIDCO (☎623 1932) for exact dates. Locals swim at **Clifford Hill Beach**, by the oil storage tanks. To get there, follow Point Fortin Main Road past the police station on your left and the oil tanks on your right – about a twenty-minute walk from the town centre.

Unlike most towns in the south, Point Fortin does have **accommodation** geared to the foreign visitor. *Cinnamon House*, 118 Cinnamon Drive, Clifton Hill – just past Clifford Beach behind Clifton Court tennis courts (☎648 2349, ℉648 1419; ❺), is an attractively decorated small hotel with a/c and cable TV in all rooms, most of which are en suite; the comfortable **restaurant** serves good Creole/international food. The other, pricier option is the fifteen-room *South Western Court*, 16 Cap-de-Ville Main Rd – obliquely opposite the market (☎648 4734 or 0075, ⓦwww.innsouth.tripod.com; ❻), a guesthouse aimed very much at business visitors, with large dining and conference facilities and bright a/c rooms, some with balconies and all with phones and satellite TV.

# Cedros and Erin

The areas of **Cedros** and **Erin**, occupying the tip of the southwest peninsula, are some of the most picturesque and untouched in Trinidad. The **environment** here is simply stunning, as the teak plantations that line the Southern Main Road to the northeast are replaced by miles of palm and coconut trees. There are some appealing **beaches** here, too: lovely sheltered coves lapped by a calm sea and – unimaginably in the tourist-saturated Caribbean – you'll often find them practically deserted. At the furthest point of the southwest peninsula, **Icacos Point** looks out across the swirling waters of the **Serpent's Mouth** to the South American mainland just 11km away.

The atmosphere in this part of Trinidad is irresistibly low key – and this tranquillity, along with the scenery, is the main reason for making the three- to four-hour drive from Port of Spain. Most residents earn their living by fishing, and village life usually centres on the bar and the football field, where lively games take place in the cool light of dusk. Charming **board houses** line the road, their occupants watching the occasional passer-by from their verandahs, while small groceries sell traditional snacks such as fruit preserved with salt, lime, pepper and herbs. Visitor facilities are very limited in this part of the country, although Los Iros cove in Erin and Icacos Point in Cedros each boast a **guesthouse**.

## Cedros

The extreme tip of the southwest peninsula is called **Cedros**, taking its name from the **giant cedar trees** that lined the bays in the early 1700s, though sadly none of these have survived. It was first settled by Spaniards, whose influence lingered longer in this isolated region than in the rest of the island; despite an influx of Indian indentured labourers, Spanish was still widely spoken until the 1880s, almost a century after the British had captured Trinidad. A little over a hundred years ago, during the nineteenth-century heyday of the sugar estates, Cedros was a bustling place with a population twice as large as it is today. Famed for its rum, this small district once boasted no less than seven distilleries, though now that these have shut down, there's little going on today.

Every bay in Cedros seems to have a picture-postcard **beach**, usually a small sheltered cove with soft brown sand and calm waters. The idyllic settings more than compensate for the total lack of facilities. The beach at **Granville** is so far off the beaten track – 5.5km from the Southern Main Road through the well-kept village of the same name, about halfway between Point Fortin and Icacos Point – that it's often completely deserted. Its fine sands are a very light brown and the waters are calm, though underwater currents that drag sand from the bottom give the water a somewhat murky aspect. Unless you fancy walking to the sea from the Southern Main Road (not much fun in the heat of the day), you'll have to negotiate a fare with a taxi driver from Point Fortin.

Though Cedros is actually the name of the whole area south and west of Granville, many people from outside the district use it to refer specifically to **Bonasse**, a charming village on **Cedros Bay**, a 10km beach used mainly by local fishermen. Two kilometres from neighbouring **Fullarton** is the lovely 3km beach on **Columbus Bay**. This stretch of sand is very quiet during the week and large enough to avoid bumping into people at the only slightly-more-crowded weekends. The view has changed little from the one that greeted Columbus when he visited these sands after his landing at Moruga in 1498 (see box, p.230).

### Icacos Point

From Columbus Bay the road winds on southwest through a huge, spectacular coconut plantation, down to the sleepy little village of **Icacos** (*Ih-car-cus*). A little further on the road comes to an end at **Icacos Point**, the southwesternmost point in Trinidad; to get there, turn right when you arrive at the village and walk for about twenty minutes along a track bordered by coconut trees. There's nothing much to see at this faraway spot apart from the crumbling sea wall, the pelicans, the buffalypso herds, the surrounding coconut trees of the Constance Estate – once the largest in Trinidad – and the vague outline of the Venezuelan coast. The dividing channel is called the **Serpent's Mouth** – an apt description, for the bay forms the shape of an open mouth, while the three rocks jutting out at sea at the northern end resemble the serpent's fangs. The serpent fails to scare the **drug smugglers** who use these beaches to bring in cocaine from Colombia via Venezuela. Rumours abound that the area is awash with drug money now that the Caroni Swamp – the smugglers' previous entry point of choice – is well patrolled by the T&T coastguard and this stretch relatively unguarded.

Nine kilometres across the sea to the west, you can see the craggy silhouette of **Soldado Rock**. This small, 60-metre-high island marks the division between Venezuela and Trinidad's territorial waters – its name means "the soldier". The only major seabird breeding site in Trinidad, it has been a wildlife sanctuary since 1934, and is home to frigate birds, grey-breasted martins and brown pelicans, and the nesting site of sooty and noddy terns. During nesting season – March to July – these birds lay over 5000 eggs on the rocky protrusion. Its varied and dramatic rock formations are of great interest to geologists, and even amateurs can spot the many fossil beds. Those interested in visiting

the island should negotiate with one of the fishermen from Icacos. It is difficult to land on the rock, however, and you must be careful not to sail into
Venezuelan waters unless you fancy a night in a South American jail.

To get to Icacos you must first go to Point Fortin (see p.223), where taxis
leave from School Road near the town's main junction for Icacos (TT$10).
The only **accommodation** is the *Icacos Beach House*, Icacos Beach Rd,
halfway between the village and Icacos Point – ask for Michelle's house (T690
3350; ❸), where you can rent a comfortable en suite room with kitchen and
fan or a three-bedroom apartment with a balcony affording views of the sea.
Paria Springs (T622 8826) conduct excellent birding **tours** around Icacos
Point, either at dawn (3.30am departure from Port of Spain) or at dusk. More
rarely, they also run tours to Soldado Rock.

## Erin

The part of the southwest peninsula that lies east of Cedros and south of La
Brea is known as **Erin**, an area blessed with many pretty villages and little–visited beaches. The **village of Erin** (**San Francique** on many maps) is one of
the most picturesque, with old board houses set in flowering gardens and
colourful fishing boats bobbing on the seashore. Little changes here – the population is roughly the same size as it was a hundred years ago, when it had the
reputation of producing some of the finest cocoa in the world. These days this
is Trinidad's most important **fishing village**, with the biggest catches in the
country. During Erin's fishing season (June to December), the village is frenet-
ically busy with fishermen landing their catch, and buyers and sellers haggling
on the shore. From January to May the community returns to a more peaceful existence, as the fishermen depart for Moruga where the catch is greater.

**Erin's beach**, known as **Puerto Grande**, is the centre of its fishing activities. Fishermen painstakingly mend their nets with huge needles, weigh fish on
large old-fashioned scales and discuss prices in discreet tones. A busy working
beach, with a fishy scent to the air, this is not really the place to take a swim.
However, it is the best place in the region to buy fresh fish; you can watch your
purchase being pulled out of the water and you will pay half the price advertised in the supermarkets of Port of Spain. There are a few snack parlours and
bars on the waterfront which cater to the fishermen. You can catch **taxis** from
Erin village to San Fernando (TT$10), Siparia (TT$6) and Point Fortin
(TT$6); they all leave from in front of the yellow church in the village centre.

If you want a more private bathing spot, try the pretty cove of **Los Iros**, 2km
east of Puerto Grande. **Taxis** from the Los Iros turn-off cost TT$3, or it's a
thirty-minute walk to the beach from the San Fernando–Siparia–Erin Road.
The water is calm and clean, and though the sandy beach is popular at weekends, you'll find it deserted during the week apart from the odd fishing boat.
There is a small snack parlour and a bar nearby, but if you are planning to spend
the whole day, follow the Trini example and bring your own food; at weekends
it is common to see whole families with pots, containers and coolers, as they
bring their large Sunday lunch down to the beach.

Los Iros cove boasts the only **accommodation** in Erin. The *Beach Boys Guest
House* (T649 8569 or 657 9826 in San Fernando; TT$250 per night
Mon–Thurs, TT$450 per weekend including Fri; phone ahead to confirm prices
and make sure that someone is there to let you in) consists of four basic but functional self-catering apartments 15m from the beach. Each has two bedrooms
with double beds, a lounge with TV and fans, and a kitchenette. Book early, especially for the holiday weekends, and remember to bring your own food.

## Trinidad's fishing industry

Over the last 25 years the **fishing** industry in Trinidad has developed from local self-sufficiency to an organized business, becoming an excellent earner of foreign exchange. The industry's potential persuaded the government in 1977 to provide incentives to encourage people to become fishermen. The policy was highly successful: the industry now employs 8000 people, and in 2001 Trinidad exported US\$4.4 million worth of fish, mostly red snapper, carite and kingfish.

This success story has brought its problems, however. T&T's fishing grounds are becoming seriously depleted, and disputes regularly arise when Trinidadians are caught in Venezuelan waters. Declining fish stocks are variously blamed on increasing pollution and the large foreign trawlers that haunt T&T's waters, though some point the finger at the use of "ghost" nets – transparent plastic netting banned in many other countries – by their own countrymen. The fishermen argue that they are obliged to use ghost nets to ensure a decent catch during the day, since increasing crime has prevented them from fishing at night, when most fish feed and hence larger catches can be hauled.

Eight kilometres east of Erin village is another marvellous **beach** at Palo Seco Bay. Turn onto **Beach Road** by the YKC & Son supermarket at Palo Seco village. This takes you past the Petrotrin beach club, where it is best to park, as beyond it the road degenerates into a steep dirt track. This leads to a 4km beach scattered with driftwood and lapped by the typical calm seas of the region. It is a fifteen-minute walk from the San Fernando–Siparia–Erin Road, the route of the maxis from Siparia or taxis from San Fernando.

# The southern central region

The **southern central region** is one of the most impenetrable in Trinidad. The only transport artery, made up of the Manahambre and Naparima-Mayaro roads, runs from the west to the east coast, through rolling plains of sugar cane, linking the region's two main towns, **Princes Town** and **Rio Claro**. The road is dotted with Hindu temples, Muslim mosques, Christian churches and agricultural villages, with little to interest the visitor beyond the well-publicized **Devil's Woodyard** – with its over-hyped mud volcanoes – and a predilection for bizarre place names.

**South of the main road**, much of the landscape is swathed in wild forest punctuated by the occasional oil well. There are very few passable roads in this region, signs are almost nonexistent and trying to follow a map is a lesson in frustration – what is marked as a road may turn out to be no more than a dirt track. If you need directions, it's best to ask how to get from A to B – few locals know the official names of the roads. This said, you are well advised to stick to the main roads and not venture onto the dirt tracks – many are dead ends, or lead to no more than an oil pump. Moruga Road is the only decent road that penetrates this wilderness, running down to the small fishing village of

**Moruga** on the south coast – a strange, isolated place, undisturbed by visitors and steeped in ancestral African faiths that give the place an eerie and mystical atmosphere.

**Maxis** and **taxis** are frequent along the Naparima–Mayaro Road from Princes Town to Rio Claro (TT$6). To go to **Devil's Woodyard** — roughly halfway between the two towns – take a maxi from San Fernando to Princes Town (TT$3), change here and get a taxi from the main stand direct to Devil's Woodyard (TT$6). You can also get a maxi or taxi to **Moruga** from Princes Town for TT$6. The maxi stand in Princes Town is in the Nipdec Car Park on the main drag just east of the market; the taxi stand is on the main drag next to the market.

**Accommodation** is extremely limited in this area, but the two nearest concentrations of hotels – in San Fernando (see p.212) and Mayaro (see p.232) – are easily accessible. **Restaurants** in the American or European sense are nonexistent, but there are many Chinese fast-food parlours and the usual roadside stalls selling snacks, homemade pies and preserved fruit.

# Princes Town and around

The unremarkable **PRINCES TOWN**, 7km east of San Fernando where the Manahambre and Naparima–Mayaro roads meet, resembles a permanent traffic jam. En route you pass the blackened chimneys of the **St Madeleine Sugar Factory**, a rather incongruous sight in the midst of rolling fields and lines of palm trees – during harvest season, the smell of burnt sugar fills the air along with ominous billows of smoke. Princes Town itself is developing faster than its infrastructure can cope with. New buildings are springing up in every imaginable style, competing with traditional places of worship such as the grand mosque with its copper dome and steel-plated minarets on the east side of the town centre. The town's most curious feature, however, is the **Tyre Warehouse**, a large, pink tyre shop on Manahambre Road just before it meets the Naparima–Mayaro Road, covered in wonderfully colourful murals and reliefs of Hindu gods and the Statue of Liberty. Around the corner on the left stands the austere Anglican **St Stephen's Church** – its two poui trees were planted by Prince Albert and Prince George in 1880. It was this visit by the future kings Edward VII and George V that led to the village, previously known as Mission, being renamed in their honour. The English novelist Charles Kingsley visited the town in 1870, and is commemorated in a street name.

The tiny villages of **First**, **Third**, **Fourth** and **Fifth Company** surrounding Princes Town are a legacy of the **black American soldiers** of the War of 1812. These former slaves had fought on the British side in return for promises of land, and after the British defeat they were allocated lots in Trinidad. There is no village called Second Company – this unit was lost at sea on the voyage to Trinidad. The soldiers settled here in 1816, bringing with them the Baptist faith that still has a strong influence on village life. They cleared the land and established successful plantations in uncharted jungle, earning themselves the reputation of pioneers. They complained bitterly to the then-governor, Ralph Woodford, about the condition of the land they had been granted, but without success; he wanted to open up the interior, and also to keep the radical black soldiers isolated from potentially rebellious slaves elsewhere on the island.

The small village of **Indian Walk**, 5km east of Princes Town, is of little interest except for its unusual name, which recalls the many Amerindian traders who once travelled this route selling parrots, food and ornaments. Seven kilometres to the east, the small village of **Tableland** has what is claimed to be the second oldest Hindu temple in the Western Hemisphere (the oldest is in Martinique). The small temple was built on the northern side of the road in 1904 by Pundit Mahant Moose Bhagat Dass, an indentured labourer who had migrated from Bharat Desh in India. The story goes that he had removed some stones from a stream and placed them near his house. That night in a dream, the spirit Shiva Bhagwan asked him to build a temple, as Shiva's previous home in the stones had been disrupted by Pundit Mahant's action. To this day the stones remain in the temple, housed in the shrine of Shiva.

# Devil's Woodyard

**Devil's Woodyard** is marked on all the tourist maps, but despite the intriguing name, the sight is disappointing: the famous **mud volcano** being merely a series of metre-high hillocks oozing gunge (for more details, see box below). The name for the Devil's Woodyard came about in 1852 when a large eruption shook the surrounding houses, scattering the planks like matchsticks. The route to it runs down Hindustan Road, 4.5km past Indian Walk; it's a pretty but bumpy drive through rolling pastures, and teak and citrus plantations. Take a **taxi** from the top of Hindustan Road (TT$3) or from Princes Town direct to Devil's Woodyard (TT$6).

Local Amerindians believed the mud volcanoes were passages between this world and the one below, and that the explosions were the Devil coming out to shake the earth. The present reality is less dramatic – little more than a few small mounds of earth with grey mud bubbling lazily to the surface. If you are curious to see a mud volcano, though, this is the most accessible, and has the best facilities, including a children's playground, picnic tables, and (though the latter are often locked). Bear in mind that like all natural phenomena, the volcanoes' levels of activity can vary; most of the time the eruptions splutter harmlessly, though in some years the eruptions have been violent enough to shower the nearby picnic tables with mud.

## Mud volcanoes

The many **mud volcanoes** scattered around southern Trinidad are promoted as environmental curiosities by TIDCO, which highlights them on its maps. The majority are largely inaccessible – unless you like taking hikes through dense forest – and in most cases it's not worth the effort. The volcanoes are small mounds mostly less than a metre high that seep and bubble grey sulphuric mud, which is believed to be good for skin conditions.

The volcanoes can appear anywhere: in the middle of the bush, in people's back gardens and by the road. They are usually ignored, though those who live near them do so at their peril, for they have a tendency to explode every few years. The most recent and damaging explosion was in Piparo in central Trinidad in 1997, where a road was completely destroyed; the villagers had to endure repeated tremors and the pungent smell of sulphuric gas, while the mud-filled gutters provided an excellent breeding ground for mosquitoes.

# Moruga

**MORUGA** is a pretty, isolated village on the central south coast, 21km from Princes Town, by a sheltered cove lined with soft brown sand. The place seems to have changed little since it was settled by black American soldiers of the War of 1812 (see p.228): the bright, contrasting colours of the old board houses have weathered to pastel shades; colourful wooden fishing boats lie on the seashore; and fishermen while away their spare hours liming outside the two shops on the main road.

The Catholic church on the seafront dominates both the physical surroundings and the life of the villagers. This is a place of strong – but heterodox – beliefs; villagers may avow allegiance to Catholicism, to the Baptist faith, or to obeah (see p.338), but many actually believe in aspects of all three. As a result of this (and, likely, the area's isolation), a palpably religious, well-nigh superstitious, atmosphere pervades the village. Locals speak of **obeah spells**, and stories abound of **Papa Neiza**, an African herbal doctor, immortalized by the calypsonian Sparrow in his song *Melda*, who could allegedly exorcise devils – and instil them in people as well.

The village's main event is its **Columbus Festival**, held on August 1 each year. Situated near the spot where Columbus briefly landed in 1498 (see box below), Moruga is the only place left in Trinidad which observes **Discovery Day** (celebrated during the Columbus Festival), a holiday replaced elsewhere by Emancipation Day, also on August 1, which commemorates the abolition of slavery (see p.48). The organizers hold the controversial view that without Columbus, the majority of Trinidadians would not have the benefit of living on the island, or of the Catholic faith. Besides, the yearly festival brings in much-needed money and provides the locals with a good party and street bazaar. The festivities take place on the beach, where three boats are decorated as fifteenth-century galleons and locals play the part of Columbus and the Amerindians who greet the explorer peacefully and exchange gifts – hardly an accurate account, but it makes an entertaining spectacle.

## Columbus in Trinidad

**Christopher Columbus** had nearly run out of drinking water when, on July 31, 1498, he sighted the three peaks of the Trinity Hills (see p.235), which are said to have inspired him to name the island Trinidad. He landed near present-day **Moruga**, where he gathered fresh water from the river. His crew reported seeing fishing implements that had clearly been abandoned in haste, and realized that they had arrived in a region that was already well populated. In fact, there were some 35,000 **Amerindians** (from the Arawak, Shebaio, Nepoio, Carinepagoto and Yao peoples) then living on the island which they called "Ieri", the land of the hummingbird.

Columbus sailed west and encountered the island's residents the next day while he was anchored off Icacos Point. Twenty-four Amerindians armed with bows and arrows set off in a large canoe to investigate the foreign ship. Upon sighting them Columbus ordered a drum to be played and the sailors to dance, believing the indigenous population would be entertained by this spectacle. However, the Amerindians mistook it for a war dance and rained arrows on the Spaniards; as the latter returned fire, the Amerindians fled. That night, Columbus had little sleep as strong currents tossed the ship. Huge waves crashed against the boat, rocking it so violently that the anchor broke. A bewildered and fearful Columbus named the passage the Serpent's Mouth, and quickly sailed away.

Catholicism also inspires the two other celebrations in Moruga. On **St Peter's Day** (the last Sunday in June) the fishermen's boats are blessed, and there is also a street festival on the Sunday after **Easter**.

# Rio Claro

Located on the Naparima–Mayaro Road some 24km east of Princes Town, **RIO CLARO** is the administrative hub for the central and southeastern region. This makes it a busy place compared with its surroundings – but that's not saying much in this somnolent corner of the island. The town enjoyed a period of prosperity between 1914 and 1965, when it was connected to Trinidad's major cities by the railway. Rio Claro has been in a long decline ever since the railway shut down, as young people abandoned agricultural work here for more profitable jobs in the oilfields and the bigger cities.

As you enter Rio Claro from the west, you'll pass between a grand wedding-cake-pink and ice-blue **Catholic church** and a resplendent white **Hindu temple** with a stepped dome and gold and blue trimmings. After this majestic entrance you come upon the main junction and town centre, with its lively stalls and **maxi stand**, from where you can get maxis to Princes Town (TT$5) and Mayaro (TT$4). A large mosque commands the main road going out of town to the east, amid a cluster of businesses and banks. The town's Spanish heritage emerges towards Christmas, as Rio Claro's famous **parang** singers (see p.340) come out to entertain the clientele of the local bars and clubs. **Internet** access is available at Red Rock Internet Café (Mon–Fri 9am–7pm; TT$10 per hour) on Cunapo Road at the town's main junction.

# The southeast

Trinidad's **southeast** is bounded on its Atlantic coast by **Mayaro Bay**, the longest beach in the country, an astonishing 22.5km of palm-fringed sand running from Point Radix in the north down to **Galeota Point**, a small peninsula that marks the country's southeasternmost extremity. Just inland from Mayaro Bay, the low Southern Range rises to the **Trinity Hills**; swathed in dense rainforest, they are part of a rugged, unspoilt and seldom-visited **wildlife reserve**. Despite the presence of the oil industry in and around Galeota Point and the nearby town of **Guayaguayare**, the southeast has a holiday atmosphere, and many Trinidadians take their vacations here. This said, the place is nevertheless uncrowded and perfect for getting away from it all, soaking up the sun and, as the Trinis say, "just chilling".

**Accommodation** in the form of self-catering apartments, beach houses and larger-scale resorts has proliferated on Mayaro Bay to such an extent that there are more choices in this area than in the rest of south Trinidad, including San Fernando. You can get to the region on **public transport** from Port of Spain (via Sangre Grande) and San Fernando (via Princes Town and Rio Claro).

# Mayaro Bay

**Mayaro Bay's** greatest attraction is its beach, a gentle, coconut tree-lined curve of clean, soft brown sand. The only settlement of any size is the holiday village of **Mayaro**, towards the northern end of the beach, a couple of kilometres from the bay's northern limit at Point Radix. All of the facilities for tourists are south of Mayaro village, where you will also see, with increasing frequency, the large luxurious houses built by the oil companies for their managers and workers. Men sell fresh fish by the roadside, and small boys will tempt you with strings of crabs and conch; sadly, these delicacies are rarely served in restaurants. Despite its stunning setting and wonderful beach, Mayaro still remains practically undiscovered by foreign visitors; enjoy the peace and quiet while you can.

## Some history

Originally inhabited by the Amerindians, the bay was settled by French royalist planters fleeing the wars and rebellions that ravaged the West Indies in the 1790s. The place boomed in the nineteenth century on the strength of its cotton and coconut estates. With the opening of a train service in 1914, it began to flourish as a seaside resort, but after the railways were closed down in 1965, Mayaro village went into economic decline. Mayaro Bay's fortunes revived during the oil boom of the late 1970s, when it once again became a popular holiday resort with Trinidadians, and hotels and beach houses lined the coast. After the boom went bust in the mid-1980s, many of these facilities fell into disrepair, and the largest hotel was taken over by an oil company as a retreat for its workers. Nowadays, the steady stream of mainly local visitors has prompted the opening of more tourist accommodations.

## Arrival

If you're **driving** to Mayaro from Port of Spain, the quickest route is via the Churchill Roosevelt Highway to Valencia, through Sangre Grande and down the east coast via Manzanilla (see p.198), in total about a two-hour drive. This is also the quickest way if you are going by **public transport** – take a maxi to Sangre Grande (TT$7) and then a taxi down to Mayaro (TT$9). If you're coming from San Fernando and the west coast, drive east along the Manahambre and Naparima–Mayaro roads. Maxis go from San Fernando to Princes Town (TT$3); change here for a maxi to Rio Claro (TT$5), where you can get another one to Mayaro (TT$4).

## Accommodation

All of the **accommodation** on Mayaro Bay is south of Mayaro village and mostly within walking distance of the village itself. Either walk along the Mayaro–Guayaguayare Road, where signs indicate the turn-offs for each establishment, or along the beach. Since a good deal of the accommodation is in private houses, you should phone ahead to make sure that you are expected. The places below are listed according to their proximity to Mayaro village.

**Westside House** Beaumont Rd ☎ 652 8276. A 3-bedroom house sleeping up to twelve people, just 50m from the beach. It's clean but basic, with no a/c or fans, and you'll have to bring your own dishes and linen. ❼ for the weekend (may·be able to negotiate cheaper rate during the week)

**Precious Poolside Resort** Beaumont Rd, the green building behind *Westside House* ☎ 630 7642. Brand new hotel with en suite a/c rooms ranged around a good-sized swimming pool. Meals

△ Handpainted shop-sign, Princes Town

are available to guests, but must be ordered in advance. ⑤

**New Sun Haven Beach Resort** Gill St, diagonally opposite *Westside House* ☎646 2625. The main reason for staying here as opposed to the similarly equipped *Westside House* is that the two 3-bedroom apartments with fans are situated on the beach itself. ⑥

**Amar's Beach Resort** well signposted on a dirt track off the Mayaro–Guayaguayare Rd ☎662 2494. This clean, fully furnished house by the beach has three bedrooms that can sleep up to ten people, but you'll have to bring your own linen. Good for groups, since you must rent the whole house. ⑦

**RASH Beachfront Resort** Church Rd, Radix Village ☎630 7274, ⑤656 0193, ⑩www.resort-trinidad.com. A collection of brightly painted 1- to 4-bedroom self-contained apartments with a/c, full kitchens, TV, balcony and ocean views; you'll need to bring blankets and towels, though linens are provided. There's a covered, hammock-slung gazebo for barbecues and chilling out, and recliners for relaxing on the beach. ④

**Radix Beach Resort** Church Rd, Radix Village ☎630 6676. Some of the rooms are a little dark, but all come with a/c, private bathrooms and TV. There is also a swimming pool and a pay phone on the premises, both useful if you are staying at the other resorts on Church Road. ⑤

**Queen's Beach Hotel & Holiday Resort** Church Rd, Radix Village ☎630 5532, ⑤630 5607. One of the largest beachside properties, a full-blown but friendly place with a personal touch. The large rooms have a/c, TV, fridge and en-suite bathrooms, plus there's a restaurant and a lively bar with a pool table. ⑤

**Azee's Guest House** 3 1/2 mile marker Mayaro–Guayaguayare Rd ☎630 4619, ⑤630 9140. A small, friendly hotel just two minutes' walk from the beach. All rooms have a/c, cable TV, telephone, fridge and en-suite bathrooms, and there's a homely bar and an open-air restaurant serving grilled foods to guests and non-guests alike. ⑤

**Harry's Guest House (aka The Seagull)** 3 3/4 mile marker Mayaro–Guayaguayare Rd ☎659 2539, ⑩www.harrys4u.com. Family-orientated place with various facilities including volleyball and basketball courts, football and cricket pitches, and a fishing pond. Studio, 2-, 3- and 4-bedroom apartments all come with a/c and private bathrooms, while a kitchen is available for communal use. ④

**B's Host Home** 485 Mayaro–Guayaguayare Rd, third house after the fenced Amoco complex, 4.5 miles from Mayaro village ☎630 8510. Run by Beulah Parriag, a pillar of the local community and an informative and friendly host. The comfortable rooms have a/c and cable TV and an excellent breakfast is included. Recommended. ⑤

## Mayaro village and Plaisance Beach

**MAYARO** – 16.5km east of Rio Claro and 24km south of Manzanilla – has grown out of two old French villages, Pierreville and Plaisance, and is still marked as such on some maps. **Pierreville**, on the Mayaro–Guayaguayare Road, is the business end of town, a small nexus of shops and local businesses. A side road cuts east to the village's seaside quarter, **Plaisance**, a lovely place with a thoroughly relaxing atmosphere. The **beach** here is one of the most popular bathing spots on Mayaro Bay, along with **Queen's Beach** a couple of kilometres further south, though it only gets crowded at the weekends. Note that there are no changing rooms, toilets or other facilities on this or any other beach along the bay, but there is a lifeguard on duty from 10am to 6pm. The Queen's Beach resorts all have restaurants and there is a swimming pool at the *Radix Beach Resort* (enquire at the hotel if there is any charge to use the pool; at quiet times you might be able to use the facilities for free). The sea in this area has **strong currents**, so it is important to exercise caution.

## Eating and drinking

There are not many places to eat in Mayaro – Trini holidaymakers tend to barbecue their own food on the beach. There is a *KFC* in the village centre, as well as a few other **fast-food outlets**, mostly selling roti, and snack parlours, both in the centre and down by Plaisance Beach. For more formal dining, the **restaurant** at *Azee's Guest House* (see above) serves delicious, inexpensive

Creole food, while the larger air-conditioned restaurant at *Queen's Beach* does a good Sunday brunch (noon–2pm; TT$50) when the hotel is reasonably full, in addition to lovely breakfasts, and lunches and dinners: fish broth, salads, chicken and fish. There are also a few lively **rum shops** on the road leading down to Plaisance Beach if you feel like a drink and a lime.

# Galeota Point and Guayaguayare

**Galeota Point**, the southeasternmost tip of Trinidad, is strictly the domain of American oil companies. The area is dotted with oil storage tanks, and many oil wells can be seen offshore. The point itself is owned by Amoco, who do not permit public access to the end of the peninsula.

Two kilometres past Galeota Point on the south coast is the small town of **GUAYAGUAYARE**. The sea has been eroding the coast here for centuries, but the growing population seems unconcerned; the inhabitants build their houses away from the seafront, and a sea wall has been erected. The brown sandy **beach** is 4km long, with good calm seas for swimming.

Although not much to look at today, Guayaguayare actually changed the fortunes of Trinidad, for it was here that oil was first discovered on the island in 1819, and the village blossomed in the early twentieth century when the petroleum industry really got going. Unless you are here in connection with the oil business, however, it's a quiet and uneventful place. Local residents still remember the big day a few years ago when a smuggler's ship, chased by the T&T coastguard, abandoned its cargo of cocaine. Large quantities of the drug were washed up on Guayaguayare beach, giving some of the locals an opportunity to make a quick killing before the authorities arrived.

The *Sea Wall Beach Resort* (☏ 630 6369; ❸, negotiable during quiet periods) on Guayaguayare Main Road west of the village has three cheap and very basic rooms overlooking the sea. This place also operates as a lively **bar and nightspot**, serving inexpensive **meals** of freshly caught fish. Three times a year – at Easter, August and November – they hold large **parties**, attracting heaving maxis full of people from all over the country. The owners also run the Eastern Divers Company (☏ 630 8572), whose internationally qualified (PADI) instructors can teach you to **scuba dive**; there are no spectacular reefs around here, but they do offer unusual trips under oil rigs, and will teach you **spear fishing** out on the open seas.

**Public transport** to Guayaguayare leaves from the centre of Mayaro village. The maxi fare is TT$3, while a route taxi will cost TT$5.

# Trinity Hills Wildlife Sanctuary

The **Trinity Hills Wildlife Sanctuary and Reserve** encompasses 65 square kilometres of evergreen forest in the southeastern corner of Trinidad, running alongside the Rio Claro–Guayaguayare Road down to the sea. Situated in the highest part of the Southern Range, it includes the famous Trinity Hills and Mount Derrick, at 314 metres the tallest peak in the south. The hills form a watershed that's vital to the nation's water supply, ensuring that the area was declared a reserve as early as 1900; it received wildlife sanctuary status in 1934.

The many **rivers**, **streams** and **waterfalls** in the reserve are excellent for bathing. The lush forests of carat, redwood, cooperhoop and bois pois trees shelter wild animals such as lappe, agouti, quenk, tatoo and red howler monkeys, and you may even see such rare creatures like ocelots, capuchin monkeys, buck deer, armadillos and opossums. The wide variety of birds includes the mountain quail dove, while deep in the hills there are mysterious caves harbouring many species of bats. A 45-minute hike from the road is a **mud volcano** and lake known as **Lagoon Bouffe**, at 100 metres wide one of Trinidad's largest.

**Information** on the reserve is hard to find due to its remoteness and the paucity of visitors. Caribbean Discovery Tours (☎624 7281) have been running **tours** to Trinity Hills for many years. They cost US$80 and include breakfast, snacks and lunch. It is possible to visit independently (the turn-off is on the Rio Claro–Guayaguayare Road, about halfway between Rio Claro and the south coast), though you'll need to get a free permit from Petrotrin, who have a pipeline running through the reserve (call ☎649 5539 after 4pm Mon–Sat; on Sundays and public holidays call ☎649 5500 or 5501). There are, it's alleged, marijuana fields in the hills, so it is wise to go with a local to avoid stumbling into dangerous areas.

# Tobago

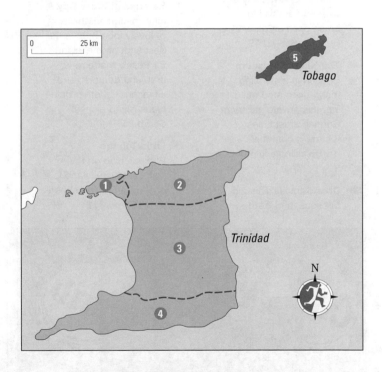

CHAPTER 5 # Highlights

✳ **Englishman's Bay**
Framed by lush rainforest, the pristine white sands of this beautiful and isolated beach represent the Caribbean at its most unspoilt.
See p.298

✳ **Sunday School** Dance your cares away any weekend at this big, brash open air party in Buccoo. See p.277

✳ **The Kimme Museum**
Housed in a stunning mural-decorated building, this private gallery of German artist Luise Kimme is crammed with her beguiling sculptures.
See p.277

✳ **Charlotteville** This picturesque, end-of-the-road fishing village provides a taste of the real Tobago. See p.313

✳ **Tobago's rainforest** The oldest protected rainforest in the Western Hemisphere is also a sublime location for a hike. See p.299

✳ **Eateries at Store Bay** A local institution, this row of lovely food huts is the best spot on the island for freshly made rotis, crab and dumplin' and all manner of other delicious island dishes.
See p.256

✳ **Little Tobago**
Birdwatching on this lush sanctuary island is a once-in-a-lifetime experience. See p.311

▲ Tobago rum shop

# 5

# Tobago

An elongated oval just 41 by 14 kilometres, **TOBAGO** features an astonishing richness within her craggy coastal fringes. Abounding with natural allure – deserted palm-lined beaches, pristine coral reefs and a wealth of lush rainforest – the island is a tropical idyll still mostly unfettered by all-inclusive resorts but nonetheless suitably geared toward visitors. **Tourism** has taken root here with breathtaking speed – 68,000 people visited the island in 2003 and 100,000 are expected in 2004 – and the subsequent reliance upon foreign money has inevitably had some negative effects, eating away at the very attributes which make the island so special. Resort developments are springing up along hitherto undisturbed seashores, and in the tourist strongholds, the traditional values held high in the otherwise deeply religious, close-knit communities are being replaced by a hustler mentality.

Still, Tobago is hardly the typically jaded resort island. Instead, it's a place where locals and tourists co-exist in an easy equilibrium, with everyone frequenting the same beaches, bars and nightclubs. Moreover, celebrations such as the Easter **goat races** are attended by more Tobagonians than tourists, and local culture is honoured at the annual **Heritage Festival** each August. The uniquely friendly Tobagonian mentality can especially be seen at **Harvest Festivals**, where entire villages open their doors to passing revellers. Tobagonians take their culture – and their heritage – very seriously, though, and it's difficult to penetrate very far beneath the surface of this clannish, almost insular small-island community. This close sense of community also means that Tobago is very **safe** – especially outside the Crown Point area – and if you use your common sense you should be fine.

Physically, Tobago is breathtakingly beautiful; heavy industry is confined to Trinidad, so the beaches here are clean and the landscape left largely to its own devices. The flat coral and limestone plateau of **the southwest tip** is the island's most heavily developed region, comprising commercialized beaches such as **Pigeon Point** and **Store Bay**, as well as quieter stretches of sand along the area's smart hotel coast, where glass-bottom boats head for **Buccoo Reef**, palms sway over the **Mount Irvine** golf course, and **Plymouth** hotels run night excursions to watch giant **turtles** laying eggs on the beach. Strong currents in this area provide some excellent **surfing** possibilities, with the rough seas between November and February (the height of the tourist season) producing massive breakers at bays like Mount Irvine.

But Tobago isn't just sun, sand, surf, and the tourist dollar. The commercial clamour of the southwest tip is kept in check by the capital, **Scarborough**, a lively, picturesque port town tumbling down a lighthouse-topped hillside. Pummelled by the dark-green, wave-whipped Atlantic, the island's rugged

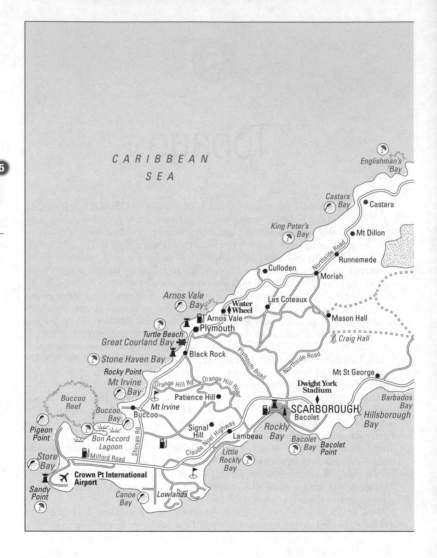

windward (south) coast is lined with appealing fishing villages; **Speyside** and
**Charlotteville** in the remote eastern reaches have **coral reefs** as ornate as
you'll find anywhere in the Caribbean and **scuba diving** is a burgeoning
industry. Tobago is an excellent and inexpensive place to learn to dive, and
there's plenty of challenging drift diving for the more experienced, while the
many reefs within swimming distance of the beaches make for fantastic
**snorkelling**. Coral sands and glassy Caribbean waters along the **leeward**
(north) **coast** provide some of Tobago's finest beaches; some, like
**Englishman's Bay**, are regularly deserted, while at **Castara**, **Parlatuvier** and
**Bloody Bay**, you'll share the sand with local fishermen.

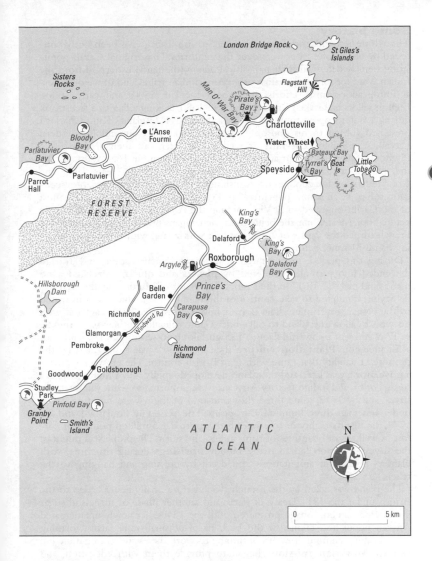

The landscape of the eastern interior rises steeply into the hillocks and rolling bluffs which make up the central **Main Ridge**. These mountains shelter the **Forest Reserve** – the oldest protected rainforest in the western hemisphere – an absurdly abundant tangle of mist-shrouded greenery dripping down to fabulous coastlines, often with neither building nor road to interrupt the flow. Ornithologists and naturalists flock in for the **bird** and **animal** life that flourishes here; David Attenborough filmed parts of his celebrated *Trials of Life* series at **Little Tobago**, a solitary seabird sanctuary off the coast of Speyside. For more casual visitors, the squawking, chirruping forest offers plenty of opportunities for birdwatching or a splash in the icy **waterfalls**.

## Some history

Though treated with indifference by the Spanish, Tobago has been hotly contested by other colonial powers over the centuries. The original **Carib** population fiercely defended their paradisical *Tavaco* (the name is derived from the Indian word for tobacco) against other Amerindian tribes, and drove off several European colonists' efforts throughout the late 1500s and early 1600s. English sailors had staked Britain's claim in 1580, tacking a flag to a tree trunk during a water stop en route to Brazil, and in 1641, England's King Charles I presented Tobago to his godson James, the Duke of Courland (in modern Latvia). A group of **Latvians** arrived a year later, but their settlement at Plymouth suffered constant attacks from the Caribs, and in 1658 was taken by the Dutch, who called it "Nieuw Vlissingen". Twenty years later, the Courlanders left for good, but, astonishingly, a group of their Latvian descendants still make an annual pilgrimage to Plymouth. In the following years, most of the Caribs migrated to St Vincent, and the Amerindian population slowly petered out. Meanwhile, the belligerent shenanigans of the Dutch, English and French turned the coasts of Tobago into a **war zone**, with the island changing hands 31 times before 1814.

During this period, forts sprang up at every vantage point, and Tobago descended into turmoil, plundered by **pirates** and officially declared a no man's land in 1702. In 1748 the French Governor of Martinique, the Marquis de Saylus, attempted to take control of the island, an act which was disowned by the French government. The British, however, worried by this act and with no wish to allow the island to fall under Gallic rule, flexed their naval muscle in 1762 and sent a powerful fleet to Tobago, taking possession of the island with swift precision. **Plantation culture** then began in earnest, sustained by the promise of stability that came with firm British control. The crown appointed a **governor** a year later, and the island developed rapidly into a highly efficient sugar, cotton and indigo factory. Africans were imported to work the estates as slaves, and by 1772, some three thousand-odd of them were sweating it out under less than three hundred Europeans. The economy flourished and, by 1777, the island's eighty or so estates had exported 1.5 million pounds of cotton, as well as vast quantities of rum, indigo and sugar. The numerical might of the slave population led to many bloody **uprisings** during this time, with planters doling out amputations and death by burning and hanging to the rebels.

The island was taken by the French twice before finally being ceded to the British under the 1814 Treaty of Paris, and another phase of successful sugar production ensued. Tobago prospered until the 1840s, her newly emancipated African population taking to the bush to plant small-scale farms, forming coastal fishing communities or continuing to work the estates as free men and women. **Moravian missions** began to provide them with education, and many converted to Christianity; the faith has since been incorporated with African belief systems to form the Spiritual Baptist sect (see p.336). When Britain removed its protective tariffs on sugar sales, however, Tobago's unmechanized industry was unable to compete with other, more efficient producers. A severe hurricane in 1847, along with the collapse of the West India Bank (which underwrote the plantations), marked the beginning of the end of the sugar trade in Tobago.

In the aftermath of the **Belmanna Riots** (see p.307), Tobago's Legislative Council relinquished its tenuous rule, and the island became a Crown Colony in 1879. Having reaped all it could from the island and its sugar industry, England had little further need for troublesome, ailing Tobago. In 1899, Tobago was made a ward of Trinidad, effectively becoming the bigger island's poor relation with little control over her own destiny. With the **collapse of the sugar industry**, the islanders fell back upon other crops, planting the acres of limes, coconuts and cocoa that still stand today. Boosted by the arrival of **free Africans** in the mid-1800s, the black population clubbed together to farm the land, tending their food crops in the efficient **"Len-Hand" system** of shared labour that is still celebrated in the annual round of Harvest Festivals. By the early 1900s the island was exporting fruit and vegetables to Trinidad, and in 1927, the island was granted a single seat on the legislative council.

In 1963, **Hurricane Flora** (see p.300) ravaged Tobago, razing whole villages and laying waste to most of the island's crops. In the restructuring programme that followed, attempts were made to diversify the economy and the first tentative steps were taken towards developing a tourist industry. By 1980, the island had her sovereignty partially restored when the **Tobago House Of Assembly** (THA) was reconvened, but it had authority only over the island's more mundane affairs while the main decisions were still made in Trinidad. Although Tobago has a stronger profile now in the republic's affairs, the island is still looked down on by the bigger Trinidad, much to the resentment of the local populace. As the sharp increase in the number of visitors reflects, Tobago's economy now revolves around tourism. That said, apart from the commercialized Crown Point area, the island has resisted the most ruinous aspects of the industry it depends on, and a majority of residents remain proud of the place they rightly consider to be paradise.

# Arrival and information

Most people arrive in Tobago via **Crown Point International Airport**, an airy, open-plan complex that is small enough to feel overwhelmed by the arrival of a single jet. Upstairs in the airport terminal is a **bureau de change**; opposite the terminal is a Republic Bank branch (Mon–Thurs 8am–3pm, Fri 8am–1pm & 3–5pm) with an ATM, useful for **currency exchange**; there is a free standing ATM just past the terminal building on the right hand side. Opposite the terminal is a row of shops, among them a small newsagent where Local and Companion **phonecards** (TT$20, $30, $60, $100 + VAT) can be purchased; and two **restaurants** – the fast-food chain *Royal Castle* and the cheerful and busy *Tri-Star Restaurant*. Note that all visitors to Tobago must pay a departure tax, in local currency (TT$100), at the smoked-glass window at the front of the airport complex (daily 6am–10pm).

For **information**, head to the tourist board office, the last shop on the left of the row (daily 6am–10pm; ☎639 0509). The staff here can advise on accommodation, transport and activities. The B&B Association is also based out of this office. If you're heading anywhere further than Plymouth or Scarborough (eg Charlotteville or Speyside), it makes sense to arrange accommodation through the tourist board as chartering a taxi is quite expensive and many hotels throw in free airport pick-ups as an incentive. The tourist board also has copies of the free, tourist-oriented *Tobago Today* listings newspaper as well as the latest version of the more detailed *Discover Tobago* booklet. An attractive, detailed map of the island can be bought here for TT$17.75, but the free visitor maps contain just as much information on the island's road system.

Some visitors also come to Tobago via the **ferry** from Port of Spain which docks at Scarborough (see "Basics," p.32).

# Getting around

Tobago's **public transport** system is improving all the time, as is the width and the quality of the island's roads. Although the blue and grey buses and blue and white **maxi taxis** are not that frequent to more remote corners of the island or at the weekends, the extensive **route taxi** network is convenient for short hops in the western portion of the island; travelling between Crown Point, Buccoo, Mount Irvine or Plymouth simply involves standing on the right side of the road for your destination, sticking out your hand and asking the taxi driver where they're heading. In Tobago, vehicles that appear to be route taxis but don't have the usual "H" taxi registration plate also stop to pick up passengers – they are easily recognizable with their multiple passengers and driver clutching a wad of dollars. Be warned, although locals and tourists alike use these cars, only those with the "H" registration are insured to pick up passengers.

For all forms of public transport make sure you have plenty of small denomination notes – drivers often don't have much change. If you're heading further afield, say to Castara, Charlotteville or Speyside, you'll need to travel into Scarborough, where route taxis and buses depart to the rest of the island; see p.285 for details. If your time is limited, **renting a car** is essential to see the island independently and avoid the hassles and long waits that are sometimes experienced with route and maxi taxis or buses.

## Taxis

From the airport, you can walk to most of the hotels in Crown Point, but if you're travelling further, for example to Scarborough, Mount Irvine, Plymouth, Charlotteville or Speyside, check the taxi price list on the wall of the arrivals lounge. The rates are used by all the **licensed taxi drivers** who meet each flight – they're high, but not wildly so. If you're on a budget, you can cross the street and haggle with the sometimes-cheaper unlicensed drivers. It is possible to hire a taxi, for all or part of a day to help you explore Tobago – many of the local tour guides also offer this service (see p.246) – just let them know your requirements. This can often work out cheaper than hiring a car and you'll probably get a commentary on the island along the way. For reputable operators to call (including a woman driver), see "Listings", p.254.

---

### Driving times

Although the roads around Scarborough can be busy during peak times, these approximate driving times remain constant: around the island:
Crown Point to Scarborough – 15min
Scarborough to Roxborough – 45min
Roxborough to Speyside – 25min
Speyside to Charlotteville – 5min
Scarborough to Plymouth – 15min
Plymouth to Bloody Bay – 1hr
Scarborough to Castara – 40min
Bloody Bay to Roxborough – 45min
The speed limit is 30mph/50kph throughout the island.

## Bus fares

Scarborough to:
Belle Garden: TT$5
Castara: TT$5
Charlotteville: TT$8
Crown Point TT$2
Delaford: TT$6
Glamorgan: TT$4

Mason Hall: TT$2
Mount St George: TT$3
Parlatuvier: TT$6
Pembroke: TT$4
Roxborough: TT$5
Speyside: TT$8

## Buses

Tobago's **public bus system**, the Public Transport Service Company (PTSC), makes public transport on the island a convenient and inexpensive option. An hourly shuttle service operates between Crown Point (there's a stop just outside the airport complex) and the island's main **depot** on Greenside Street in Scarborough; buses leave at half past the hour from Crown Point and on the hour from Scarborough from 5am to 8pm.

From Scarborough, buses run **along the windward coast** to Mount St George, Studley Park, Glamorgan, Argyll Falls, Roxborough, Delaford, King's Bay, Speyside and Charlotteville (Mon–Fri 4.30am, 5am, 9am, 11am, 2.30pm, 4pm and 5.30pm; Sat 6am, 9.30am, 1pm and 5pm; Sun 9am, 12.30pm, 2pm and 5.30pm). The **leeward coast** route extends from Scarborough to L'Anse Fourmi via Moriah, Castara, Englishman's Bay, Parlatuvier and Bloody Bay (Mon–Fri, 4.30am, 8.30am, 10.30am, 12.30pm, 1.45pm, 5pm and 6pm; Sat, 6am, 9.30am, 1pm and 5pm; Sun 8.30am, 12noon, 2pm and 5.30pm). Buses run north from Scarborough to Mount Thomas via Les Coteaux and Golden Lane (Mon–Fri 5.30am, 6.30am, 3pm, 4pm and 6pm); they also go from Scarborough to Plymouth via Mount Irvine and Black Rock (Mon–Fri, 5am, 6.30am, 7.15am, 8am and then hourly on the hour until 8pm). All tickets must be **pre-purchased** as drivers will not accept cash; they are available from the shops opposite the airport complex or from bars and mini-marts throughout the island. For information on bus times and where to buy tickets locally call ☎639 2293.

## Car and bike rental

Most of the international **car rental** firms – as well as the local operators with two or three vehicles to rent – are clustered around the airport. You can generally expect to pay about US$45 per day for either a car or a jeep. If you are hiring a car in Tobago, it is best to use a **licensed rental company**. Local operators tend to be cheaper than their international counterparts, but the smaller the company, the less likely you are to be offered 24-hour assistance and adequate coverage in case of an accident; the most reliable among them is Sherman's, based in Lambeau (☎639 2292, ⓦ www.shermansrental.com). Friendliest amongst the internationals is the local franchise of Thrifty (☎639 8507, ⓦ www.thrifty.com), which has efficient service and a wide selection of vehicles. Most companies ask for some kind of **deposit**, usually a credit card imprint; a notable exception is Auto Rentals (☎639 0644, ⓔ mail@autorentals.co.tt), which has one of the largest fleets in Tobago.

It is essential to hire a vehicle with an "R" (for rental) registration. Some less reputable companies try to rent both cars and jeeps with a "P" (for private) registration – this is illegal, and if a company tries to hire you one, insist on an "R"

The sharp rise in the number of visitors to Tobago has led to an increase in the number of **tour companies and guides** operating on the island. As the options range from the highly qualified and experienced to the downright charlatan, it is worth spending time considering the options before parting with your cash. Several established tour companies offer rather sterile itineraries of Tobago's main sights, ranging from snorkelling on the Buccoo Reef and a barbecue at No Man's Land to trips to Scarborough, Fort George, Little Tobago, the Forest Reserve, Plymouth and the mystery tombstone. These tours are great if you want a zero-hassle overview of the island, but they can also feel completely distanced from what flashes by through the window. **Full-day tours** almost always include lunch and cost US$55–75 per person; groups must be of four or more. Most people book through reps who visit the main hotels or trawl the beaches, but you can sign up individually as well. Recommended companies include: Frankie's Tours (T639 4527, Wwww.frankietourstobago.com), who run a varied selection of fishing, hiking and sightseeing tours; Classic Tours (T639 9891, F639 9892, Wwww.classictoursltd.com), with an office at Crown Point Airport; and Sun Fun Tours (T639 7461, F639 7561, Wwww.sunfuntour.com).

### Hiking and wildlife tours

The tourist board holds a list of well-established, trained guides offering **hiking and wildlife tours** – all of which display an identification badge issued by the Department of Tourism. Part-time Store Bay lifeguard and certified tour guide Harris McDonald (T639 0513, Wwww.harris-jungle-tours.com) runs half-day rainforest and birdwatching walks (US$45), including breakfast, and full-day excursions including a rainforest walk, snorkelling at Angel Reef (US$95), glass bottom boat tours to Little Tobago (US$60) and night trips to the rainforest and turtle watching in season. Renowned naturalist David Rooks (T/F639 4276, Wwww.rooks-tobago.com) leads informed, professional and popular tours to **Little Tobago** (Thurs, 8–9hr; US$65) and the Forest Reserve (Sat, 7hr; US$45). Trained by David Rooks, Ali Baba (T639 1096, Wwww.alibaba-tours.com) is an excellent tour operator working from Castara. In addition to the standard island trips (Little Tobago and such) he organizes romantic sunset cruises and lagoon parties (US$65), full day snorkelling, fun fishing and beach barbeques (US$80), and island sightseeing tours – which can be arranged to suit whatever you want to see (half day US$55, full day including lunch US$70). Darren Henry of Nature Lovers (T639 4559, Wwww.angelfire.com/at2/naturelovers) is a trained forester and licensed tour guide who takes trips into the **forest reserve** (1hr 30min–2hr; US$25) and to Little Tobago (2 hr; TT$150), a short tour of the Botanical Gardens (45mins; TT$50) and a hike to Mason Hall Waterfall (2hr 30min; TT$80). Margaret Hinkson's thoughtful Educatours (T639 7422, magintob@hotmail.com) organizes excursions with local guides, custom designed to suit your interests. Prices start from US$65 for a guided trek through the rainforest and on to Argyll Waterfall (6hr), including lunch. Pioneer Journeys (T660 4327, Epturpin@tstt.net.tt) puts together more rugged jaunts, including a hike along the **Louis D'Or River** to see crayfish, crab and wetland birds; prices start from US$30–40 for transport to the hike area. Mark Puddy (T639 4931) leads fabulous offbeat hiking trips to deserted beaches (6hr; US$40) or seldom-visited waterfalls (4hr; US$25); rates include transport to and from your hotel as well as drinks and snacks. Some hotels have a guide based with them, such as the highly experienced Mr B (T796 7830) who operates out of *Inn on the Bay* (see p.270) and offers a rainforest tour (US$60), Golden Island Tour (US$120) and Trinidad Tour US$164. More information on Forest Reserve tour guides can be found on p.301.

### Jeep, dirt bike and mountain bike safaris

**Jeep and dirt bike safaris** booked through *Coconut Inn* (T639 8493, F639 0512) take you to less accessible parts of Tobago, following ancient trails through deserted plantations, stopping at beaches and waterfalls; you can ride pillion on request. All-day bike

TOBAGO | Getting around

5

and jeep tours cost US$65; both include food and drink. One of Tobago's female taxi drivers, Liz Lezama (☎639 2309 or 758 1748) offers an extensive island tour, including lunch, with plenty of stops at small rum shops (US$60). **Mountain bike tours** can be organized with Eamon Healy-Singh at Slow Leak Tobago Mountain Tours (☎635 0641, ⓦwww.tobagomountainbike.com), a certified game warden. Ranging from beginners to expert, the selection of tours start at US$35 for 2 hours' easy riding to US$50 for 4 hours of extreme downhill cycling – helmets, gloves, snacks and water are provided with every tour. Alternatively, Trinidad-based *Wild Ways* (☎623 7332, ⓦwww .wildways.org) organize Tobago cycling tours, either with a guide or self guided.

## Boat tours, activities and cruises

One of the most popular ways to explore the brine is a pleasure boat **cruise**. Several operators work the waters – their prices for a full-day trip vary little (usually around US$35 per person for a 2hr sunset trip and US$75 for a 6–8hr cruise) and usually include lunch, snorkelling at Bon Accord Lagoon, Englishman's Bay or other similarly deserted coves, and an open bar; private charters or sunset and moonlight dinner trips are also on the roster of most operators. The atmosphere varies from racy booze cruises to sedate sightseeing. Best of the bunch is *Natural Mystic* (☎639 7245, ⓕ639 7888, ⓔmystic@tstt.net.tt), a trimaran that unfurls its sails when the wind allows, cruising to deserted beaches for fantastic snorkelling and a sumptuous freshly cooked barbecue lunch and as much drink as you can handle. Kalina Cats (☎639 6306, ⓦwww.trinidad.net/kalina) organize a range of fun day cruises, sunset sails and private island charters (all inclusive day trip US$75) on their luxury 50ft sailing catamaran. Exhilarating trips on **hobie cats** – mini-catamarans built for speed and balanced by the bodies of the passengers – are available from Cool Runnings at Mount Irvine Bay (☎639 6363, ⓕ639 4755, ⓦwww.outdoor-tobago.com; 1hr with or without instructor US$50); they also offer all-day trips aboard the hobies. Chartering a **sport fishing** boat is exciting but expensive; rich pickings of marlin, sailfish, tuna and dolphin are caught year round. A speedy boat accommodating up to six and equipped with rods, tackle and bait will cost in excess of US$275 per half day, US$400 for a full day; try Dillon's Deep Sea Charters (☎639 8763, ⓔdillons@tstt.net.tt), or local character Captain Frothy's boat *Hardplay* (☎639 7108, ⓔhardplay@tstt.net.tt). **Glass-bottom boat** tours of Buccoo Reef (US$20) leave from Store Bay, Pigeon Point and Buccoo. Tobago Sea Kayak Experience (☎660 5514, ⓦwww.seakayaktobago.com) run a programme of full and half day **sea kayaking** trips for both the novice and experienced paddler including beginner 3-hour trips around Man O' War Bay (US$35) and 6-hour adventure sea kayaking complete with a visit to the rainforest and time for snorkeling (US$55).

## Aerial tours

If you want to do a little **aerial sightseeing**, you could consider chartering a small plane or helicopter from Hummingbird Helicopter Services in Crown Point (☎639 7159 or 622 7159, ⓦwww.hummingbirdhelicopters.com), who offer 20- (US$300) and 40-minute (US$500) tours of the island for a minimum of four people. Romantics can opt for the sunset soiree tour (US$300 per couple) which includes a bottle of wine with the flight.

## Horseback riding tours

Those who prefer a slower, more earth-bound tour can go **horseback riding** with Essentially Tobago (☎639 9379, ⓔtobago@pobox.com, ⓦwww.essentially tobago.com); a 2-hour tour costs US$50. Other options are Friendship Riding Stables (☎660 8563) who offer horse trekking – including beach rides – and tuition; and Looking Out Stables (☎682 2408, ⓦwww.action-tobago.com) whose twice daily riding times start at 8am and 3pm.

Tobago is one of the best **scuba diving** spots in the southeastern Caribbean, yet it has relatively few divers visiting its pristine coral reefs, volcanic formations and marine wrecks. The island is internationally recognized for its exciting, though difficult, drift dives, caused by the Guyana current, which results from the confluence of the Caribbean Sea and the Atlantic Ocean. The aquamarine seas around Tobago are home to 300 species of South Atlantic coral and a variety of spectacular multicoloured fish, including the neon orange-and-blue parrot fish, the black-and-yellow-striped sergeant majors and every species of angel fish, not to mention such larger species such as whales, stingrays, sharks, dolphins, turtles and squid. While it's even possible to see rare species such as toadfish and shortnose batfish, the island is best known for the enormous number of manta rays that are frequently encountered on diving trips. Adding a touch of history to underwater encounters are the sunken pirate ships, Spanish galleons and dozens of World War II troop and supply carriers that litter the sea floor. Speyside (see p.309) is known as "the Disneyland of diving", offering a variety of spectacular sites surrounding the offshore islands: Goat Island is popular for drift dives, St Giles for its rocky pinnacles and underwater canyon and Little Tobago, where 70 percent of dives encounter manta rays. Popular dives in this area include London Bridge, Bookends, Angel Reef, The Cathedral and Kelliston Drain – the site of the single largest brain coral in the Caribbean, and possibly the largest in the world. For more advanced divers, Sisters Rocks – with the sea shelf falling to 667 metres – is especially popular for larger species of fish including hammerhead sharks.

Tobago's **diving industry** was only established in the 1980s but since then scuba diving operations have multiplied with many hotels, beaches and guesthouses sporting their own centres. Prices vary slightly between operators; in general one to three dives cost US$30–35 each, one-day resort courses US$55–65, five-day PADI open water certification courses from US$375–425, advanced open water from US$225 and skin diving around US$35.

When deciding who to dive with it's worth contacting the Association of Tobago Dive Operators for advice (℡660 5445, Ⓦwww.tobagoscubadiving.com) who can provide a list of certified scuba diving operators. **Safety** comes first. Always check for the prominent display of a dive affiliation, such as NAUI, PADI, SSI or BSAC. A good operator will always ask you to fill in paperwork and present a diving certification card. The rental equipment should be well rinsed; if you see sand or salt crystals this may indicate careless equipment care. Inspect all equipment thoroughly, check hoses for wear, see that mouthpieces are secure and ensure they give you a

registration vehicle. It is also important to check that there is a certificate of insurance in the vehicle and that you carry your driving licence with you at all times when driving. Tobago police make regular checks on the roads and if you are stopped in one of their road blocks you will be required to produce both of these documents immediately.

If you're driving into Pigeon Point, avoid parking under a coconut-laden palm – a single nut can cause a lot of damage if it lands on your vehicle. In general, be careful on the roads after a rain shower, when innocent looking puddles often hide large potholes. Also remember that it's not illegal to **drink and drive** in Tobago and many people do, so be appropriately cautious.

**Scooters** are available from some beach outlets and cost approximately US$20–25 a day. **Motorbikes** are catching on fast and there are several places offering dirt bikes for about US$30 per day. Some places offer discounts for extended rental (take a bike for six days and you get a seventh free), and most depth gauge and air-pressure gauge. Listen for air leaks when you gear up and smell the air, which should be odourless. If you smell oil or anything else, search for a different operator. If anything does go wrong, Tobago has a recompression chamber in Roxborough (☎660 4000).

### Reliable scuba operators

**Adventure Eco-Divers Ltd** Stone Haven Bay ☎639 8729, Ⓦwww.adventure ecodivers.com. Standard dive packages and equipment rental.

**Dive Tobago** Pigeon Point ☎639 0202 or 2150, Ⓔcohel@tstt.net.tt. A tried and tested operator on the island whose catchphrase is "go down with a local".

**Man Friday** near Man O' War Bay beach in Charlotteville ☎660 4676, Ⓦwww .manfridaydiving.com. Resort and certification courses, single dives and packages, and snorkelling equipment for rent.

**Manta Dive Centre** based on Pigeon Point Road and opposite the *Crown Point Beach* hotel ☎639 9969 or 9209, Ⓦmantadive.com. General operators with more than 13 years experience in Tobago,

**Proscuba** based at *Rovanel's* resort on Store Bay Local Rd and *Surfside* on Milford Rd ☎639 7424 or 682 9673, Ⓦwww.diveguide.com/proscuba. Offering "scuba phones" for easy communication underwater, as well as Dutch-, German- and French-speaking dive masters.

**R & Sea Diving Company** based at Spence's Terrace on Milford Road and Pigeon Point ☎639 8120, Ⓔrsdivers@tstt.net.tt.

**Sal's & Stina Scuba** *Conrado's* on Pigeon Point ☎639 1142, Ⓔsalstinascuba @tstt.met.tt. Special accommodation rates for divers who stay at the hotel.

**Scuba Adventure Safari** Pigeon Point Rd ☎660 7333 or 7767, Ⓦwww.dive tobago.com. A new dive operator offering state of the art equipment.

**SubLime** Arnos Vale Bay ☎639 9386, Ⓔsublime@tstt.net.tt; or *Tropikist Beach Hotel* in Crown Point ☎639 9642 or 8512.

**Tobago Dive Experience** *Turtle Beach Hotel* in Black Rock and *Manta Lodge* in Speyside ☎639 7034, Ⓦwww.tobagodiveexperience.com.

**Undersea Tobago** *Coco Reef* at Crown Point ☎639 7759, Ⓦwww.underseatobago .com.

**Wild Turtle Dive Safari** Pigeon Point ☎639 7936, Ⓦwww.wildturtledive.com. Offers a variety of day and night dives at locations all around the island.

**World of Watersports** *Tobago Hilton* ☎660 7234, Ⓦwww.worldofwatersports.com. Has staff speaking English, German, Afrikaans and Dutch.

also offer accompanied tours along off-road trails. Check your bike and helmet before you ride away, as some are less than perfect. As with renting a car or bike, it's imperative that you take note of every bump and scratch as well as checking the tyres (especially the spare and the jack), headlamps and indicators. If the vehicle is damaged, let the company know immediately, and on no account let anyone unauthorized drive the car; as Tobago is so tiny, someone is bound to catch you at it, and you are liable for any damage. For details of reputable operators, see "Listings", p.253.

**Bicycles** are a good way of seeing the island, although it is worth noting that some local drivers go very fast, many do not signal and the coast roads are often nothing but blind corners. The best time to cycle is early evening when both the temperature and the number of cars on the road have dropped. Or, for a safer cycling experience, book a cycle tour with one of the local operators. For details of reputable operators, see "Listings", p.253 and box on pp.246.

# Accommodation

There is no shortage of good quality **accommodation** options in Tobago. From luxury resorts to cosy inns and guesthouses, to a rich array of private villas, you should have little trouble finding somewhere to fit both your taste and your budget – although it is advisable to book ahead during the busy times of Carnival and Easter. A recent rise in the demand for accommodation has led to an increase in the number of small guesthouses in Tobago. These are often great value for money and very friendly places to stay. It is not compulsory for any guesthouse to be registered with the tourist board and many perfectly good ones are not; however, if they are it means that they have been inspected and approved.

The sheer number of **hotels** and **guesthouses** crammed into Crown Point makes choosing accommodation there mind-boggling, and the tourist-friendly location keeps prices relatively high; you pay less for the same standard of room in more remote areas, and there are few bed and breakfasts or host homes here. Tobago's most **upmarket** hotels are clustered along the beaches between Buccoo and Plymouth, and the exclusive **villas** (see box, below) around the Mount Irvine golf course offer some of the plushest private accommodation you'll find, but you don't necessarily have to be well-heeled to stay here. There are plenty of middle bracket hotels and guesthouses along this stretch, and the area makes one of the most appealing bases on the island; you're close to the action of Crown Point without being stuck right in it, transport is easy (taxis run along Shirvan Road from early morning to late at night), and the beaches are marvellous. Also close to the main tourist areas, Lambeau and Little Rockly Bay are home to a growing number of hotels, guesthouses and villas at a range of prices, while nearby Scarborough is the place to find both first-class romantic hotels and numerous inexpensive host homes. Away from the densely populated southwest, you can find an abundance of cheaper accommodation options and some of the most stunningly located luxury hotels Tobago has to offer.

Those wanting to **camp** should head for Canoe Bay (see p.268), where you pitch a tent for US$15 per night; security, lighting and bathrooms are included.

## Villas

Though **villas** are conventionally seen as luxury accommodation, they can work out to be quite cost effective if you're travelling in a large group. Most of the newer villas are aimed at the wealthier traveller, ranging from packed, estate-type complexes – the majority are set around the Mount Irvine golf course – to the secluded villa of one's dreams. Reviews of individual villas are included in accommodation listings for each area, but there are useful go-betweens: Villas of Tobago Ltd (⊕639 9600, ⓦwww.villasoftobago.com), a well established and professional agency with an excellent range of properties for all budgets; the Tobago Villas Agency on Shirvan Road (PO Box 301, Scarborough ⊕/ⓕ639 8737), representing properties throughout the island, whose villas rent from US$110 per day; Essentially Tobago (⊕639 9379, ⓔtobago@pobox.com, ⓦwww.essentiallytobago.com) are agents for five large, plush villas (starting at US$395 per night) overlooking Mount Irvine golf course – they also organize tours and watersports.

For further villa listings – including the exclusive *Being Villa* (US$1200 a night) – visit the See Tobago website (ⓦwww.seetobago.com), a fount of accommodation information. Take note that you might have trouble finding reasonably priced villas from outside the island as they're unlikely to be advertised by foreign travel agents.

## Tobago street food

Trinidad-style **street food** has yet to make an impact in Tobago – even in Scarborough, it's impossible to find a good corn soup – but one notable exception is *Block 22*, a hulk of concrete at the Canaan end of Milford Road that makes the best fried chicken in Tobago; spicy batter and rum shop ambience keep the cars double parked until 1–2am on the weekends. Also in this section of Milford Road, the popular morning stopoff *Golden Girls Bakery* makes excellent buljol or smoked mackerel and hops as well as sandwiches, pastries and a cracking carrot juice and peanut punch. You'll inevitably be drawn in by the local staples – "roti, conch and all kind ah ting" – served up by the stalls at Store Bay (see box, p.256), while a few hundred yards up Airport Road, try *Triple B Burger Grill* for fish, beef or chicken burgers and fried potato wedges – usually open until 11pm. You'll find food stalls springing up wherever there is nightlife – the *Golden Star* restaurant and bar is a favourite place for them to pitch – where you can get chicken, souse, boiled corn and fish tea.

# Eating

While the highlights of **Tobagonian food** – crab and dumplin' or pacro water – are sublime, there isn't much variety, particularly in the southwest tip where it can be difficult to escape the expensive and bland tourist-oriented offerings; pasta or steak often take pride of place over *coocoo* or conch. It's not impossible to find good Tobagonian cooking, though, and even some of the smartest restaurants allow their callaloo to remain unadulterated by cream or a blender. If you're here in the slow season (April 15–Dec 15), bear in mind that many kitchens close at around 9pm. In the reviews included in this chapter, we've included phone numbers only for restaurants where you might need to book a table. Check whether menu prices include tax (up to 15 percent) and service charge (usually 10 percent). If a service charge is included, you don't have to leave a tip.

# Entertainment and nightlife

Tobagonians tend to display less of the frantic party enthusiasm that characterizes Trini "feting", and much of the local nightlife revolves around the **bar** scene, a mix of rum shops and more tourist-oriented dives. Tobago isn't inundated with heaving dancefloors, and even the comparatively bright lights of Crown Point offer limited options after dark, but you can still find excitement most nights of the week. Consult roadside posters or ask around to find out about the current and ever-changing hotspots; Monday and Tuesday are often quiet as everyone recovers from the excesses of the weekend.

Other than the weekly bacchanal of **Sunday School** at Buccoo (see box, p.277), Friday (pay day for locals) is the biggest party night, when the Lowlands echo with bass notes. Aside from a flirtation with soca during Carnival time, Tobagonian music policy is R&B, hip hop and, primarily, dancehall reggae – Sean Paul and Sizzla are guaranteed floor-fillers.

Larger hotels provide nightly **entertainment** for guests and nonguests alike, usually avoiding the rather tacky limbo and fire-eating ilk of other Caribbean islands. Occasional **stageshows** are held at Shaw Park football ground or *Golden Star*; you'll see promotional billboards all around the island – this is also the method of choice for advertising the marvellous round of summer fishermen's **fetes**.

Your only other entertainment options are the **casinos**: the *Crystal Palace* in Scarborough (see p.293); the popular *Kaiso Club* casino in Canaan; and Tobago's newest, the *Royalton Casino* (daily 7pm–3am), next door to *Crown Point Hotel*, which has both a dress code and cocktail bar. Note, though, that when it comes to gambling, most locals opt for a round of easy-to-learn "all fours" played at home, in the street and at some bars

# Shopping

There is an abundance of locally made arts, crafts and unusual souvenirs to be found on Tobago, even in the remotest of areas, making **shopping** an engaging diversion here. Although an increasing number of outlets selling pottery, clothes, leather goods, calabash art and jewelry are springing up all over the island, make sure to also investigate the plethora of road- and beach-side stalls. These are often run by local craftspeople and artists who sell good quality hand made goods at reasonable prices.

The widest variety of crafts – carved calabashes, Rasta hats and such – are sold at the huts adjacent to Store Bay beach, but you'll get better deals at the vendors' mall in Scarborough and the stalls that line Milford and Wilson Road around the market square area. Also in town, Tobago Treasures on Carrington Street sell a nice line in colourful fish carvings. On the Arnos Vale Road, inland of Plymouth, keep a sharp eye out for a small, brightly painted shop selling drums and beautifully tailored African-style clothing. The Doux Doux shop on Milford Road, adjacent to Viewport Supermarket, stocks good handmade sandals, clothing and knick-knacks, whilst Shore Things on Old Milford Road in Lambeau sells high-quality crafts, jewelry and local paintings, and serves lovely light lunches on its sea facing terrace. Drum lovers should head straight for the Culture Barn (Mon–Sat 8am–7pm ☎639 9022) at Fort Bennett, Black Rock, where Malcolm Melville crafts beautiful, innovative drums from mango, mahogany, cedar and breadfruit woods; he also sells drums at booth nine at Store Bay beach. The Art Gallery (✉artgal@tstt.net.tt), just off the Claude Noel Highway opposite the *Tobago Hilton* entrance has an ever-changing collection of Tobagonian art, including gorgeous watercolours of gingerbread homes and local life, oils, prints and crafts. Sculptures and gifts imported from a dozen West African countries are on sale just up the road at the African Art Gallery and Gift Shop.

Funky and distinctive **clothing**, for both men and women, can be bought from Radical Designs on the corner of Main and Bacolet streets in Scarborough; their trademark T-shirts are far more chic than your average souvenir specimen and they also sell lovely linen clothes at reasonable prices. Known for its wide range of batiks, arts, crafts, jewelry and beachwear is the Cotton House on Bacolet Street. Batiki Point situated next to *La Tartaruga* restaurant in Buccoo – unmissable with its beautiful murals adorning the outside walls – stocks a fantastic range of batik wall-hangings, wraps, T-shirts and clothes (this shop opens on a Sunday evening to catch trade from the Sunday School revellers see p.277). Also in Crown Point, Things Natural on the corner of Pigeon Point and Milford Road has a good selection of clothes, leather craft, accessories and gifts, and D'Pottery and Batik House above Penny Savers supermarket stocks a varied range of Caribbean handicrafts, clothes, bags, jewelry and wall hangings. For more unusual souvenirs head for Planet Ceramics on Milford Road, the island's only working pottery. Their range of colourful, distinctive ceramics can also be found in a number of other shops on the island.

**Duty-free goods** are sold at Stetchers in the airport departure lounge and a duty free store opposite the airport terminal – avoid the local jams and honey on sale here, though, as these are best bought from supermarkets. Zoom Caribbean on Pigeon Point beach carry quality T-shirts and Carib memorabilia, and calypso, soca and reggae records, tapes or CDs are available from One World Music Shop on Airport Road, opposite *Dillon's* restaurant.

In order to protect local endangered animals, avoid buying products made from turtle shell, black coral, conch or bird feathers.

# Listings

**Car and bike rental** The most reliable companies for cars and jeeps are Sherman's (☎639 2292), Rattan's (☎639 8271) and Thrifty (☎639 8507). For motorbikes and bicycles try Baird's, who are another good bet for cars (☎639 2528). Bicycles are also available from Glorious Rides at Pigeon Point junction (☎639 7124), Fun Rides (☎639 8889) on Shirvan Road and Marco Polo Tourism (☎639 7420) based at the car park at Mount Irvine beach complex – expect to pay about TT$60 per day. Scooters can be hired from R & Sea Diver's Company on Pigeon Point Road, who charge US$20 a day, with discounts for long-term hires. Fun Bikes on Milford Road, Bon Accord (9am–4pm; ☎631 0352) rent motorbikes for TT$150 per day – with a TT$300 deposit.

**Courier service** As the postal service in Tobago can be anything but speedy, you might want to try the local branch of DHL in Lowlands (☎639 9244) if you need to send something abroad in a hurry.

**Dentist** Dr. D. Serrette, 109 Sherwood Park, Carnbee ☎631 0902

**Emergency numbers** Fire and ambulance ☎990, police ☎999, Coast Guard ☎ 639 1461, hospital ☎ 639 2551, emergency health service ☎660 7955

**Internet access** There's been an explosion of Internet facilities in Tobago in recent years, focused mainly round Crown Point and Scarborough. Usually you'll pay between TT$20–30 an hour with 30-minute options also available and economy rates for longer periods. In Crown Point: *Cybercafe*, next to Sun Fun Tours by the airport; *House of Pancakes*, Milford Rd, Bon Accord; and the *Clothes Wash Café* on Airport Rd. In Scarborough: *J Putertech*, 20 Burnett St, opposite James Park; *CIRC* in the Elias Building, Wilson St; *CITI*, Bernard St, *Cybercafe*, Bacolet St; and in Speyside at *NKY Internet Café*, 46 Tophill St. Alternatively there is free use of the Internet at the

library (see below), bookable in half hour slots.

**Laundry** Machine washes are available at White and Bright on Milford Road (Mon–Sat 8am–5pm ☎639 0921), which charges TT$30 if you load the wash yourself, or TT$35 for a wash and dry service, detergent is TT$3; and at the Clothes Wash Café (Mon–Sat 9am–5pm) on Airport Road, Crown Point, next to *Coco Reef* hotel.

**Library** Tobago's public library is temporarily housed at the end of Happy Haven Road in Signal Hill – opposite a Red Cross Building and two minutes' drive from the Claude Noel Highway (Mon–Fri 8.30am–5pm, Sat 8.30am–12.30pm). The building at its main location in Scarborough was damaged in an earthquake tremor and once repairs have been carried out, the library will return there. Visitors can register to borrow books and are charged TT$10 for each. Alternatively, books can be rented from *New Horizons*, Orange Hill Rd, Spring Garden, Scarborough (☎678 2401). Membership is TT$40 and books are then rented out at TT$5 for three days or TT$7 per week. *Shore Things* in Lambeau (see p.269) also has a selection of used books for exchange.

**Medical** Complete with an Accident and Emergency department, Tobago's only hospital is just below the fort complex in Scarborough (☎639 2551 or 2552). For an ambulance, call ☎990. If you need a doctor, try any of the physicians practising at the Triangle Building, Crooks River, Scarborough (☎639 1115) or Dr Melville (☎639 1722, 639 7586 or 678 8369). The best gynaecologist, according to local opinion, is Dr Francis Jacobs in Scarborough (☎639 5727).

**Money** Apart from the bureau de change at the airport and hotels, all money-changing must be made at the banks; there's one branch of Republic Bank at Crown Point airport and an RBTT bank on Airport Road, both have ATMs. All other banks are in Scarborough (see p.285); and all are subject to the same opening hours (Mon–Thurs 8am–2pm, Fri 8am–noon & 3–5pm). 24hr ATMs are located at Crown Point airport, the corner of Milford Rd and Pigeon Point Rd, the ferry terminal and adjacent to the Scarborough banks; all provide cash advances on credit cards. Wire transfers can be collected at any of the banks.

**Newspapers** Published on Fridays, *The Tobago News* (ⓦ www.thetobagonews.com) is the island's main newspaper and the place to find out about local news, sports and entertainment.

**Petrol stations** In Crown Point, the Canaan garage on Milford Road is the only port of call (Mon–Sat 7.30am–1pm & 3–9pm, Sun 8am–2pm); you can also try the Carnbee petrol station (Mon–Sat 6am–9pm, closed Sun) – take the first right from Shirvan Road or the turn-off from the highway marked for Auchenskeoch. Roxborough petrol station is open Mon–Thurs & Sun 7am–9pm, Fri 7am–5pm, Sat 6pm–9pm, Plymouth's Mon–Sat 6.30am–9pm, Sun 5.30am–9pm, Charlotteville's Mon–Sat 6am–8pm, Sun 6am–11am & 8.15pm–8.30pm. Scarborough petrol station on Milford Road is open Mon–Sat 6am–9pm, Sun 6am–1.30pm; and the Taxi Co-Operative garage on Wilson Road stays open until midnight daily. None of these petrol stations is self-service and at the time of writing it cost approximately TT$120 to fill an average-size tank. As a last resort, seek out one of the local fishermen who often keep a spare container or two.

**Pharmacies** Late-opening pharmacies in Scarborough include Scarborough Drugs, opposite *KFC* on the corner of Carrington Street and Wilson Road (Mon–Sat 8am–7.30pm, Sun and public holidays 8.30am–noon; ☎ 639 4161), and Tobago Pharmacy on Carrington Street (☎ 639 3784, Mon–Thurs 8am–7pm, Fri 8am–8pm, Sat 8am–2pm). In Crown Point try Dove Drugs (Mon–Sat 8am–7pm, Sundays and public holidays 9am–noon; ☎ 639 2976) in the Real Value Plaza, located on Buccoo Bay Road, which runs from Claude Noel Highway to Shirvan Road, signposted for Auchenskeoch.

**Photography** Fotomart have a shop on Burnett Street in Scarborough for film and developing (one-hour service available) as well as two easy-access booths (☎ 639 4010, Mon–Fri 8am–6pm, Sat 8am–2pm), located at Mount Irvine beach complex and Store Bay. Their Crown Point branch on Airport Rd (☎ 639 0489) is open daily 8am–6pm.

**Police** There are five police stations in Tobago; Scarborough (☎ 639 2512 or 4737), Old Grange (☎ 639 8888), Moriah (☎ 639 0029 or 0100), Roxborough (☎ 660 4333) and Charlotteville

(☎ 660 4388). The island-wide emergency police line is ☎ 639 1200; alternatively, dial ☎ 999 for police ☎ 990 for fire and ambulance.

**Post** The main post office is located in the ferry terminal building in Scarborough (Mon–Fri 7.30am–6pm, Sat 9am–1pm). There are sub-post offices in most towns and villages (Mon–Fri 8am–4.15pm) and nearly all hotels can send letters and postcards for you.

**Radio** Tobago's Radio Tambrin – 92.1FM – (☎ 639 3437, ⓔ tambrin@tstt.net.tt) is an excellent way of keeping informed on local issues and music.

**Supermarkets** The best supermarket is Penny Savers on Milford Road at the Canaan end; it's competitively priced, well stocked and has lots of imported foods (Mon–Sat 8am–8pm, Sun 8am–1pm). In Crown Point, try the small but convenient Francis mini-mart just before Fort Milford in Crown Point (Mon–Sat 8am–6pm), or the View Port Supermarket (Mon–Thurs 8am–8pm, Fri & Sat 8am–9pm, Sun 8am–8pm), opposite the Tobago Taxi Co-Op in the Canaan section of Milford Road. The well-stocked All in 1 Tobago Supermarket at the corner of Glen and Darrell Spring roads is open late (daily 7am–11pm) – turn left from the highway just past the Scarborough turn-off. Morshead Delicatessen, on Buccoo Road (turn off Shirvan Road) sell imported cold meats and cheeses.

**Taxis** You can hail a car on almost all of Tobago's roads – make sure that you settle the price before getting in. Most large hotels have registered drivers, but they can be expensive. If you want to call a cab, try Tobago Owner Drivers' Association (☎ 639 2692) or Tobago Taxi Co-Operative (☎ 639 2659). Both have set rates which are pretty reasonable; drivers work until midnight or thereabouts. For a 24hr taxi service contact James Wise (☎ 660 8294) and if you'd prefer a woman taxi driver, contact Liz Lezama (☎ 639 2309).

**Telephones** There are pay phones all around the island, most using the pre-paid TT$20 phonecards available from small stores and pharmacies – these can only be used for local calls. However, making a call in the remote eastern end of the island is difficult; the only call-boxes in Speyside and Charlotteville are often out of order, so you'll have to resort to a hotel, which usually means a hefty mark-up on local and international calls. You can always make international calls from the ferry terminal booths or buy a pre-paid companion card (TT$30, 60, 100 + 15 percent VAT) from local shops and the main Post Office in Scarborough, which allows you to phone abroad from a private phone. The local phone company (TSTT) in the Caroline Building, Wilson Rd, Scarborough (Mon–Fri 8am–4pm) offers inexpensive international calls and a send-and-receive fax service. *Comserve Ltd. Overseas Calling Centre* (Mon–Fri 7am–10.30pm, Sat & Sun 10am–10pm; ☎635 1150) on Castries St in Scarborough arranges calls to the USA, UK and Canada for TT$1 per minute from private booths and an overseas fax service for TT$5 plus call charges. Be careful when calling abroad from any phone: if the number rings for more than 10 seconds, even if the call is not answered, you will be charged for the international connection.

**Therapies and treatments** A wide range of alternative therapies and treatments, including ayurvedic massage, reflexology and shiatsu costing approximately US$50 per hour, are available at *Kariwak Village* hotel in Crown Point (see p.260), which also has a programme of early morning yoga and Tai Chi classes – some of which are free to guests. *Sea Spray Spa* in Lambeau ☎639 3533 offers a range of massage, aromatherapy, reflexol-

ogy and hydrotherapy treatments from US$45 and the *Exhale Acuppressure Touch Therapy Studio* (☎639 7422) at *Shore Things* café in Lambeau provides acupressure, meridian oil massage and Jin Shin energy rebalancing treatments from TT$150.

**Weddings** Since 1996 it has been possible for couples to marry in Trinidad and Tobago as soon as three days after their arrival. Many hotels offer sumptuous honeymoon suites, and *Tobago Weddings* (☎639 1400, ☎639 3253, ☒http://tobagoweddings.com) will make all of the necessary arrangements. You will need passports, airline tickets, and if either you or your soon-to-be spouse is divorced or widowed, also the decree absolute or death certificate, along with proof of name change if it differs on the document. Under 18s must also have a documented consent form from parent or legal guardian.

# The southwest tip

Sometimes referred to as "the Lowlands", Tobago's flat, low-lying **southwest tip** is the island's most heavily developed, accessible and populated region, home to the vast majority of its hotels, restaurants and nightclubs, as well as its most popular beaches. This area is centred around a crowded five-kilometre stretch of **Milford Road** from the airport and Store Bay beach – a tiny area known as **Crown Point** – east through **Bon Accord**, **Canaan** and **Mount Pleasant**, and up **Shirvan Road** which runs north along the coast through **Buccoo**, **Mount Irvine** and **Plymouth**. The highly commercialized concrete-and-neon hodgepodge around Milford Road, as well as the less frenetic beaches and smart hotels that shoot off Shirvan Road, mean that the southwest tip should hardly be considered the "real Tobago". But the region's animation and industriousness more than make up for its occasional lack of aesthetic charm and, whether you like it or not, the concentration of facilities and activities means that you could well have to spend some time here.

Tobago's most popular **beaches** are within shouting distance of the airport – **Store Bay** is just a couple of minutes on foot, and **Pigeon Point** is only ten minutes further. The terrain between the two is jam-packed with all the familiar tourist trappings – craft stalls, restaurants and bars advertising happy hours, and endless resort hotels – and many people never make it any further into the island. East of the beaches, Milford Road continues in the same vein, cutting through Tobago's tourist heartland to quieter stretches of sand; you'll find peace and tranquility at **Canoe Bay**, and past here, the vacation ethic slackens a little; the **Lambeau** and **Signal Hill** communities are the almost exclusive preserve of locals. Set atop the foothills of the island's modest mountains, both villages provide beautiful views of the unravelling flatlands to the west, with **Little Rockly Bay** a rugged cove below.

Another rash of tourism development lies along Shirvan Road, which cuts north from Milford to run along the coast. **Buccoo** harbours two main attractions: an abundant **reef**, trawled by fleets of glass-bottom boats carrying snorkellers out to the coral and the Nylon Pool, a metre-deep bathing spot on a sandbar in the middle of the bay, as well as **Sunday School**, Tobago's biggest, brashest open-air party. Dominated by a palm-studded eighteen-hole **golf course**, **Mount Irvine** heralds the start of a series of glorious **beaches**, while historic **Plymouth**, with its cluster of **forts** and **mystery tombstone**, is also heavily visited. Further north, potted attractions like the **Arnos Vale water wheel** complex and the Kimme **art exhibition**, as well as plenty of restaurants and the fabulous prospect of watching a **turtle** lay eggs metres from your hotel room, draw enthusiastic crowds of locals and tourists alike.

# Crown Point and around

If you arrive by plane, your first introduction to Tobago will be **CROWN POINT**, just minutes walk from the airport tarmac. This is the hub of Tobago's **commercial tourist industry**, full of bright lights, lively bars, up-beat restaurants, fashionable shops, tourist trappings and the odd hustler. It is also via Crown Point that you gain access to two of Tobago's most popular beaches, Store Bay and Pigeon Point. However, Crown Point is also a million miles away, culturally, from the rest of Tobago; a visitor who never goes beyond this admittedly enjoyable area will leave with a very distorted picture of this laid-back and peaceful island.

## Accommodation

Space is at a premium in the Crown Point area and many **accommodation** establishments are built back to back with little individuality and scant regard for aesthetics; rooms are kept dark to keep them cool. Forget about peace and quiet: discos blare soca into the night air and road traffic is pretty constant, scaring away bird and animal life and making the place feel like the Costa Del Sol rather than an unspoilt Caribbean paradise. However, there are definite advantages to staying in the area; you'll be within walking distance of the busiest

---

### Store Bay dining

An essential part of any visit to Tobago is a plate of **crab and dumplin'**, **macaroni pie with callaloo**, or **curry goat and vegetable rice** from one of the row of attractive, cream brick takeaways facing Store Bay beach. All are open daily from around 8.30am to 8.30pm, but the flow of custom usually dictates. This strip of eateries (from right to left there's *Miss Jean's*, *Miss Trim*, *Miss Joycie's*, *Alma's*, *Silvia's* and *Miss Esmie*) are the best places for a tasty, local-style meal; in fact, you'll probably find yourself heading to Store Bay come lunchtime even if you aren't planning to grace the beach. The rewards of eating here are simple; it's inexpensive, convenient and almost always tasty, and the covered sea-facing gazebo with seating and tables is an attractive place to sit, eat and watch the world go by. The fare varies little from stall to stall: bake with fish or eggs, buljol and smoked herring for breakfast and goat, beef, chicken or vegetable roti, stewed beef or chicken, conch or crab and dumplin', pelau, vegetable rice, stewed lentils, macaroni pie, callaloo and ground provisions. They also offer a range of soft drinks and punches including peanut, sea moss and carrot.

beaches, restaurants and bars, and among the uniform, you'll find some of Tobago's most appealing hotels. The proximity of the airport (jet noise isn't a problem due to the infrequency of flights) also means that you can often walk straight from the tarmac to your room, though many hotels offer **free transport** from the airport or Scarborough sea port.

A number of low-priced **guesthouses** can be found along John Gorman Trace – a left turn by *Toucan Inn* – don't be put off by the gravel track, this location is quiet, close to the action and offers some of the cheapest options in this high-priced area. There are also guesthouse options along the busy Airport Road.

**Arthurs by the Sea** Airport Rd, Crown Point ℡639 0196, ℻639 4122, ⓦwww.trinidad.net/arthurs. Small, simple and dark rooms, each with a balcony overlooking the pool; all have a/c, en-suite bathroom, cable TV and fridge. Overpriced despite the nice sundeck and pool area. ❼

**Belleviste** Sandy Point, Crown Point ℡/℻639 9351, ⓦwww.trinidad.net/belleviste. Directly opposite the airport runway. An unattractive block-like exterior masking spacious, well-designed apartments. All have wooden fittings, a/c, cable TV and full kitchen. Outside is a garden with barbecue pits, pool, children's play equipment, gazebo overlooking the sea and a path to the beach. ❻

**Classic Resort** Sandy Point, Crown Point ℡639 0742. Tiny place with small, basic rooms that have seen better days, and shared bathroom and kitchen facilities. Good for Tobagonian ambience. ❸

**Coco Reef** Airport Rd, Crown Point ℡639 8571, in US and Canada 800/221 1294, ℻639 8574, ⓦwww.cocoreef.com. Peach-painted enclave of contrived luxury with perimeter walls beside an artifical white sand beach. Two restaurants, two bars, health spa, gym, pool, watersports and rooms with every associated frippery offer opulence at the expense of atmosphere, due mainly to package tour bookings and overworked staff. Restaurant food is good but overpriced. ❾

**Conrado** Milford Extension Rd, Pigeon Point ℡639 0145, ℻639 0755, ⓔconrado@tstt.net.tt. The closest you can stay to the much-vaunted Pigeon Point; modestly proportioned garden- or sea-view rooms with a/c, cable TV, phone and balcony. Busy, but with its own stretch of beach, as well as a restaurant and bar. ❻

**Coral Inn Guesthouse** John Gorman Trace, Crown Point ℡/℻639 0967, ⓔcoralinntobago@yahoo.com. Small, friendly guesthouse five minutes' walk from the airport on a quiet road. All of the self-contained apartments have cable TV, kitchenette and a/c, and there is a swimming pool on the grounds. ❹

**Crooks Apartments** Store Bay Local Rd, Crown Point ℡/℻639 8492, ⓔcrooksapts@hotmail.com. Friendly hosts run these large, clean studio rooms that include kitchenette, en-suite bathroom, a/c and cable TV. Some rooms sleep up to six. Guests can use the pool at the adjacent *Store Bay Resort* (see p.260). ❹

**Crown Point Beach** Store Bay Rd, Crown Point ℡639 8781, ℻639 8731, ⓦwww.crown pointbeachhotel.com. The largest hotel at the westerly side of Store Bay beach with currently unsightly concrete-block rooms – due for renovation in 2004 – softened by sprawling cabana-filled gardens overlooking the sea; cabanas are the better option. Both have kitchen, a/c, phone, cable TV and small patio, and there's a pool, restaurant and tennis courts on site. Usually busy with a Trinidadian/European crowd. ❻

**Golden Thistle** Store Bay Local Rd, Crown Point ℡/℻639 8521, ⓦwww.caribbean -connexion.com/hotels/thistle.htm. Tucked away behind Store Bay Local Rd, and good for groups wanting relative seclusion with middle-bracket luxury, rooms have a/c, TV, phone, kitchenette and patio; there's also a pool, bar and infrequently functioning restaurant on site. Discount available for four nights or more. ❻

**The Hummingbird** 128 Store Bay Local Rd, Crown Point ℡/℻635 0241, ⓦwww.thehumming birdonline.com. Centrally located, yet quiet, this friendly, family-run hotel has a pool, restaurant and bar and eight spotless, ensuite rooms named after tropical flowers – six have a/c and the other two fans. ❹–❺

**Jeffrey's Guesthouse** Airport Rd, Crown Point ℡639 0617, ⓔhsorace@hotmail.com. Close to Store Bay and Pigeon Point, these very sparse rooms with a/c and en-suite bathroom share a communal kitchen and lounge. Clean and inexpensive with amiable Tobagonian hosts. Discounts are available for stays longer than a week. ❸

**Jetway** Crown Point ℡/℻639 8504. Directly opposite the airport, this is a good place to get your bearings. Clean and functional rooms with a/c and kitchenette; friendly atmosphere but expect some airport noise. ❺

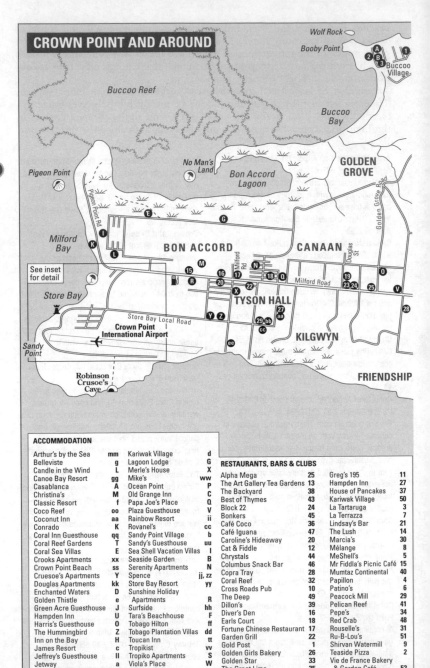

CROWN POINT AND AROUND

Wolf Rock

Booby Point

Buccoo Village

Buccoo Reef

Buccoo Bay

GOLDEN GROVE

Pigeon Point

No Man's Land

Bon Accord Lagoon

Golden Grove Road

Milford Bay

BON ACCORD

CANAAN

Douglas St

See inset for detail

Store Bay

Milford Road

TYSON HALL

Store Bay Local Road

Crown Point International Airport

KILGWYN

Sandy Point

Robinson Crusoe's Cave

FRIENDSHIP

## ACCOMMODATION

| | | | |
|---|---|---|---|
| Arthur's by the Sea | mm | Kariwak Village | d |
| Belleviste | g | Lagoon Lodge | G |
| Candle in the Wind | L | Merle's House | X |
| Canoe Bay Resort | gg | Mike's | ww |
| Casablanca | A | Ocean Point | P |
| Christina's | M | Old Grange Inn | C |
| Classic Resort | f | Papa Joe's Place | Q |
| Coco Reef | oo | Plaza Guesthouse | V |
| Coconut Inn | aa | Rainbow Resort | ii |
| Conrado | K | Rovanel's | cc |
| Coral Inn Guesthouse | qq | Sandy Point Village | b |
| Coral Reef Gardens | T | Sandy's Guesthouse | uu |
| Coral Sea Villas | E | Sea Shell Vacation Villas | I |
| Crooks Apartments | xx | Seaside Garden | B |
| Crown Point Beach | ss | Serenity Apartments | N |
| Cruesoe's Apartments | Y | Spence | jj, zz |
| Douglas Apartments | kk | Store Bay Resort | yy |
| Enchanted Waters | D | Sunshine Holiday | |
| Golden Thistle | e | Apartments | R |
| Green Acre Guesthouse | J | Surfside | hh |
| Hampden Inn | U | Tara's Beachhouse | F |
| Harris's Guesthouse | O | Tobago Hilton | ff |
| The Hummingbird | Z | Tobago Plantation Villas | dd |
| Inn on the Bay | H | Toucan Inn | tt |
| James Resort | c | Tropikist | vv |
| Jeffrey's Guesthouse | ll | Tropiko Apartments | S |
| Jetway | a | Viola's Place | W |
| Jimmy's Holiday Resort | nn | VIP | ee |
| Johnston Apartments | rr | Woods Castle | pp |
| Jordine's House | bb | | |

## RESTAURANTS, BARS & CLUBS

| | | | |
|---|---|---|---|
| Alpha Mega | 25 | Greg's 195 | 11 |
| The Art Gallery Tea Gardens | 13 | Hampden Inn | 27 |
| The Backyard | 38 | House of Pancakes | 37 |
| Best of Thymes | 43 | Kariwak Village | 50 |
| Block 22 | 24 | La Tartaruga | 3 |
| Bonkers | 45 | La Terrazza | 7 |
| Café Coco | 36 | Lindsay's Bar | 21 |
| Café Iguana | 47 | The Lush | 14 |
| Caroline's Hideaway | 20 | Marcia's | 30 |
| Cat & Fiddle | 12 | Mélange | 8 |
| Chrystals | 44 | MeShell's | 5 |
| Columbus Snack Bar | 46 | Mr Fiddla's Picnic Café | 15 |
| Copra Tray | 28 | Mumtaz Continental | 40 |
| Coral Reef | 32 | Papillon | 4 |
| Cross Roads Pub | 10 | Patino's | 6 |
| The Deep | 49 | Peacock Mill | 29 |
| Dillon's | 39 | Pelican Reef | 41 |
| Diver's Den | 16 | Pepe's | 34 |
| Earls Court | 18 | Red Crab | 48 |
| Fortune Chinese Restaurant | 17 | Rouselle's | 31 |
| Garden Grill | 22 | Ru-B-Lou's | 51 |
| Gold Post | 1 | Shirvan Watermill | 9 |
| Golden Girls Bakery | 26 | Teaside Pizza | 2 |
| Golden Star | 33 | Vie de France Bakery | |
| The Great Lime | 35 | & Garden Café | 52 |
| Green Shop | 23 | Waving Gallery | 42 |

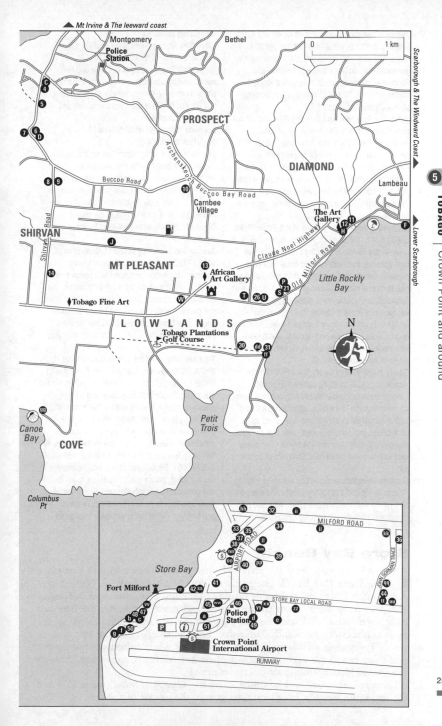

▲ Mt Irvine & The leeward coast

Montgomery          Bethel

**Police Station**

PROSPECT

DIAMOND

Lambeau

Buccoo Road

Carnbee Village

**The Art Gallery**

SHIRVAN

MT PLEASANT

**African Art Gallery**

Little Rockly Bay

**♦Tobago Fine Art**

L O W L A N D S

**Tobago Plantations Golf Course**

Petit Trois

Canoe Bay

COVE

Columbus Pt

Scarborough & The Windward Coast ▲

Lower Scarborough ▲

N

MILFORD ROAD

Store Bay

**Fort Milford**

**Police Station**

**Crown Point International Airport**

RUNWAY

JOHN GORMAN TRACE

STORE BAY LOCAL ROAD

**Jimmy's Holiday Resort** Airport Rd ℡639 8292 or 8929, ℻639 3100, ✉jimmys@tstt.net.tt. 1-, 2- and 3-bedroom self-contained apartments right on the road between Store Bay and Pigeon Point. Functional, clean and drab, with sitting room, kitchenette, a/c, TV and phone, and a swimming pool and mini-mart on site. ❺

**Johnston Apartments** Store Bay Rd, Crown Point ℡639 8915, ℻631 5112, ⊛www.johnston -apts.com. Set right above Store Bay and sharing the pool and restaurant of its larger neighbour, *Crown Point Beach*, these studios and 1- and 3- bedroom apartments are huge (some sleep eight) with fully equipped kitchen, living room, a/c, cable TV and phone, and instant access to the sand and sea. ❻

**Kariwak Village** Store Bay Local Rd, Crown Point ℡639 8442, ℻639 8441, ⊛www.kariwak.co.tt. A jewel in the middle of bustling Crown Point: the lush gardens, thatched-roof cabanas, excellent personal service and peaceful atmosphere give a real feeling of retreat. Cabanas are split in two and furnished using local wood crafted on the premis- es; each has a/c and phone. There's also the option of larger and more luxurious garden rooms, and facilities include a pool, jacuzzi, and a fabu- lous restaurant/bar (see p.264), though there is intermittent airport noise. ❽

**Sandy Point Village** Sandy Point ℡639 8534, reservations 639 8533, ⊛www.sandypt.net. Large, clean studio apartments with fully equipped kitchen, en-suite bathrooms, satellite TV, a/c and phone, furnished in wicker and teak. Good value for facilities that include a mini-gym, two jacuzzis, two pools, a dive shop and car rental. The restau- rant has stunning views over Sandy Point beach. ❺

**Sandy's Guesthouse** Store Bay Local Rd, next to *Toucan Inn* ℡639 9221. Very simple and inexpen- sive rooms with en-suite bathroom, fans and a communal kitchen, overseen by good-natured Tobagonian hosts. ❸

**Store Bay Resort** Store Bay Local Rd, Crown Point ℡639 8810, ℻639 7507, ✉sbaymair@cablenett.net.tt. Clean and well- maintained apartments with kitchen, living room, a/c and cable TV. Genial owners, there's a pool, and it's just five minutes from the airport and beaches, to boot. ❺

**Surfside** Milford Rd ℡/℻639 0614, ✉surfside@tstt.net.tt, ⊛www.surfsidetobago.com. Set on the road to Pigeon Point beach, with wall murals and truly Trinbagonian decor in roomy units with kitch- enette, a/c, fan, cable TV, and patio area and pool. Vibrant, popular with Trinidadian holidaymakers and well located on the road to the beach. Discounts are available May–Nov for stays over a month. ❹

**Toucan Inn** Store Bay Local Rd, Crown Point ℡639 7173, ℻639 8933, ⊛www.toucan- inn.com. This welcoming hotel is a haven of tran- quility in the middle of Crown Point's bustle. The unusual, octagonal cabana rooms are set in attrac- tive gardens around a pool; all have a/c and fit- tings made from local teak and pine. *Bonkers* – the on site restaurant – is a local institution (see p.264). ❻

**Tropikist** Store Bay Rd, Crown Point ℡639 8512, ℻639 9605, ⊛www.tropikist.com. Popular with British tour groups and a real holidaymaker kind of a place with volleyball nets, pool and a large grassy tanning area overlooking the beach. White tiles, a/c, phone, radio, fridge and glass patio doors give rooms a handsome degree of luxury, and there's a restaurant, bar and car rental on site. ❼

**VIP** Store Bay Local Rd, Crown Point ℡639 9096, ℻639 0581. Slightly out-of-the-way apartment block offering peace and competitive rates for the self-contained units; studios and 1- and 2-bed- room apartments have full kitchen, TV, phone, a/c and balcony. Car rental is available on site. ❸

## Store Bay Beach

A two-minute walk from the airport brings you to Crown Point's best place to swim, **Store Bay beach** (lifeguards on duty 10am–6pm; free). Named after early Dutch settler Jan Stoer, this is some of the most popular sand in Tobago, and deservedly so; it's close to the airport and main hotels, has the best and most inexpensive food available and is a great place to buy crafts. It's one of the liveliest places on the island: Trinidadian holidaymakers consume vast quanti- ties of curry crab and dumplin' (see box, p.256) while fishermen pull in the odd seine net to the accompaniment of clicking cameras, soca thuds through the air and glass-bottom boat operators prowl.

Though fairly small and hemmed in by the *Coco Reef* hotel (see p.257) and the rocks, the beach is excellent: tides govern the extent of the fine, off-white sand, and lifeguards patrol the areas flagged off for safe bathing. With a gentle shelf and crystal-clear, mirror-calm water, Store Bay is a good choice if you're travelling with children, but be careful with them as the beach occasionally sees some big breakers. Store Bay is the finishing point for the annual Great Race power-boat contest each August (see "Festival calendar", p.48) as well as a venue for open-air parties around Easter weekend, and the bars opposite are a popular liming spot, particularly during and after sunset.

Opposite the beach is a car park, pristine shower/changing facilities (daily 10am–6pm; TT$1 per entry) with lockers for rent (TT$10 per day) as well as a couple of bars blasting reggae and soca, an ice-cream kiosk and the row of shacks housing the irresistible cookshops from which most people purchase their lunch (see box, p.256). If you don't fancy local staples, try the café at the Tobago Taxi Co-Op for generous portions of chicken or fish with fries, sandwiches and hot dogs. The **craft shops** (8am–8pm) are excellent for souvenirs.

# Fort Milford, Sandy Point and around

The road that shoots off toward the airport behind the Store Bay craft stalls is the main route from the beach to hotel-filled Sandy Point and the **Fort Milford** stockade. The fort was preceded by a Latvian settlement and a Dutch redoubt named Belleviste. The landscaped ruins of gun-slitted coral stone which visitors see today were built by the British in 1777, and briefly appropriated by the French during their 1781–93 occupation of Tobago. Surrounded by bench-studded lawns that make a quiet chill-out spot for Tobagonians and tourists seeking some peace and shade after the intensity of Crown Point, and a favourite haven for artists, the fort gives a panoramic perspective over Store Bay beach and Milford Bay right up to Pigeon Point.

South of the fort, the road swings left, skirting hotels and restaurants before meeting the fences of the airport runway. A right turn at this junction takes you onto what's known as NP Road, so called because there's a National Petroleum garage at its far reaches. As it circles the runway, the road passes the pretty and often deserted **Sandy Point beach**. Obscured by trees and shrubs, the beach is easy to miss; take the first dirt road into the bush (just opposite the end of the tarmac) and you'll emerge onto a picturesque strip of fine white sand and translucent sea bordered by sea grapes and palms. Swimming is safe if you stick to the left of the beach; currents get strong around the headland to the right which divides this stretch of sand from the more popular beach at Store Bay. At the point where the road meets the beach there's a secluded covered bench – a perfect spot to enjoy panoramic views of the ocean and an unrivaled vantage point from which to watch planes landing at the airport.

## Robinson Crusoe's Cave

After passing Sandy Point Beach, the NP Road doubles back on itself to lead along the south edge of the runway from the other side. At a point that's roughly parallel to the airport terminal, a hand painted-sign announcing "**Crusoe's Drive and the Cave**" marks a right-hand turn off the NP Road. A five-minute drive through cow pasture interspersed with the odd rambling home takes you to a clearing; ask for Mrs Crooks at the last house; her family own the land which leads to the cave, and she'll collect the entry fee (TT$3) and direct you down. The concrete steps and rocky pathway constructed for easy access are treacherous and do little for aesthetics, the cave itself is small, incredibly unimpressive, with craggy limestone walls stained green by mineral drips and only about 5m deep. The Crusoe connection came about via the

## Robinson Crusoe's isle

"The Life and Strange Surprising Adventures of Robinson Crusoe of York, Mariner; Who lived eight and twenty Years all alone, on an uninhabited Island on the coast of America, near the mouth of the Great River of Oroonoque; Having been Cast on Shore by shipwreck, wherein all the Men perished but himself." Thus reads the introductory blurb to the first edition of Daniel Defoe's *Robinson Crusoe*, dated April 25, 1719 and the oft-cited rationale behind the claim that Tobago was the setting for Defoe's epic. In the book, the fabled island was situated, like Tobago, off the coast of (South) America near the mouth of the Orinoco River.

In the late seventeenth century, the then-sovereign Duke of Courland commissioned an Englishman, John Poyntz, to develop the island. Poyntz wrote a pamphlet praising Tobago's beauty and natural riches as well as giving a physical description of the island. Believers argue that Defoe got hold of the document and used it as the basis for his novel.

However, this clashes with the accepted notion that Defoe based the book on the experience of Alexander Selkirk, a crew member on the ship of English explorer and pirate William Dampier. During a voyage in the Pacific Ocean, Selkirk quarrelled with another crew member and, rather than continue in his company, volunteered to be put ashore at the tiny island of Juan Fernandez, off the coast of Chile. He spent four years alone there before Dampier rescued him. After Selkirk's return to England in 1711, his story became well known through various pamphlets, on which Defoe's novel was almost certainly based.

fertile imagination of the late Mr Crooks; having read Defoe's novel, he sided with the local rumour that Tobago was Crusoe's isle and concluded that this was as legitimate a base as any other on the island for the fabled castaway. Whatever the reality, it's an uninspiring spot and best avoided – the coastline is tatty and strewn with car tyres.

## Pigeon Point

Running north from the airport past the entrance to Store Bay, Airport Road becomes Milford Road as it swings to the right some 50 metres from the complex. Here, a left-hand turn (marked by the neon constellation of the *Golden Star* bar and restaurant, see p.265 and p.268) leads to **Pigeon Point Road** (also known as Milford Extension Road), taking you to the spot where the Atlantic Ocean meets the Caribbean Sea. The shoreline here – unlike the majority of Tobago's rugged beaches – is definitively Caribbean: powdery white sand with turquoise sea on one side and the ubiquitous swaying palms on the other – an attractive remnant of the time when the area was part of a coconut plantation. This is the entrance to **Pigeon Point**, what some see as the island's best **beach**, though you have to pay for it – it's private land and an entrance fee is charged (daily 8am–7pm; TT$18 per visit or TT$300 for a year pass).

The beach itself is a strip of glaring sand backed by almond and palm trees, shady picnic spots, shower blocks, volleyball courts and a flotilla of yachts moored around Tobago's most photographed pier, with a weathered wooden boardwalk with a thatch-roofed hut at the end. White sand on the sea floor gives the water that impossibly bright blue tint which typifies a postcard-style Caribbean beach, while the gentle shelf and tame currents make swimming benign. There's ample space here to stake out your niche without feeling cramped, and if in the mood for a wander, you can take a long walk east around the headland to another, less pretty, marshy stretch of sand that borders the **Bon**

**Accord Lagoon** (see p.267) – if you're visiting during the rainy season, note that mosquitoes from here have a field day at Pigeon Point, making insect repellent essential. A series of shops selling beachwear, clothes and upmarket souvenirs nestle into the landscaped area around the busy central **bar** – a popular liming spot at sundown, when steel pans play away the last rays; cameras click, rum punch is downed and camcorders capture the best **sunset** view on the island.

Picturesque as it appears, the beach is a source of **controversy** among locals. It was the first beach to charge an entry fee, and regularly increases rents for beach vendors. There is meant to be free access to all beaches in Tobago, so the entry fee is actually for the use of the facilities and road; as such it is possible to avoid paying by simply walking along the beach at low tide into Pigeon Point. Be warned, however, that the area is patrolled by security guards who are looking out for the small, plastic bracelets that visitors are given to wear once they've paid to get in – not wearing one could draw unwanted attention. Many locals now refuse to go to Pigeon Point, especially after a fisherman was fatally shot when he tried to enter without paying. This history, and the increased tourist-driven development, have diminished the beach's appeal and natural beauty.

Pigeon Point is also one of the few places on Tobago to suffer from **development and commercialization**, a fact that quickly becomes evident even before one gets there: the entrance roadway is lined with watersports outlets and crafts stalls. Fast-food chains have ousted the local cafés, though it's sometimes possible to buy roti and the odd local dish from the food outlets on the beach for around TT$20–30. The groynes constructed to curtail beach erosion have reduced the water circulation, and this – along with general pollution and poor management – has allowed algae to flourish on the sea floor, making local people question the sagacity of swimming in what on a bad day resembles a rather milky soup. Though water quality is monitored by local environmental groups, and the chance of getting sick is pretty scant, try to shower off as soon as you leave the water and avoid immersing your head; there's little to see in any case.

## Watersports in southwest Tobago

The southwest is the best place to indulge in watersports, with a large variety of outlets and operators. Buzzing **jet-skis** have not yet become a regular feature amid the surf (though you can rent them from R & Sea Divers Den on Pigeon Point, US$25 for 20min), and nonmotorized watersports are freely available at the main Crown Point beaches and from the all-purpose outlet Essentially Tobago (Ⓣ639 9379, Ⓔtobago@pobox.com, Ⓦwww.essentiallytobago.com) at Mount Irvine beach complex (see p.277). You can rent **snorkelling** gear from itinerant vendors or scuba concessions for US$5–15 per day, while **kayaking** costs about US$10 an hour at Pigeon Point. Wild Turtle (Ⓣ639 7936, Ⓦwww.wildturtledive.com) at Pigeon Point rents out kayaks (TT$30 for 30min, TT$60 for 1hr). World of Watersports (Ⓣ660 7234, Ⓕ660 8326, Ⓦwww.worldofwatersports.com) is based at the *Tobago Hilton* and offers **water-skiing** and **inflatable bananas** (TT$80 for 15 min) as well as **jet skiing** (TT$200 for 20min) and **windsurfing** (TT$200 for 1hr). Water-skiing, windsurfing and sailing lessons are also available (TT$320 for 1hr). The most popular local **surfing** site is Mount Irvine beach – early morning often sees twenty to thirty surfers riding the waves. A well-kept secret, local surfers are trying to keep it that way, making it difficult to find places that rent equipment; keen surfers should bring their own. Note that the water here is shallow and directly over coral reef, so surf fins can be badly damaged and no protective footwear is allowed (this is done to protect the reef from overeager surfers jumping in and damaging the coral).

# Eating, drinking and nightlife

To satisfy the sheer number of visitors who stay in Crown Point, there are **eating** options for all tastes and budgets, mostly well within walking distance of the main hotels and guesthouses. In high season, beach barbecues at Pigeon Point or Store Bay are advertised by vendors distributing fliers. Flambeaux and a steel band provide atmosphere; US$35-plus covers drinks and all the freshly cooked seafood you can eat.

## Eating

**The Backyard** Airport Rd, Crown Point. Cosy café serving excellent, well-filled sandwiches on toasted French bread, as well as salads. The owners also provide takeaway and picnic lunches. A small shop on site sells beautiful local batiks. Affordable and easygoing. Mon–Fri noon–6pm.

**Bonkers** *Toucan Inn*, Store Bay Local Rd, Crown Point ☎ 639 7173. This excellent and popular restaurant serves tasty Tobagonian food at moderate prices under a shady pavilion or at poolside tables. Breakfast is local and European-style, while lunch usually includes sandwiches and soup. Dinner is from 7pm and highlights include voodoo shrimp, lambaabaa curry and taboo tenderloin – all served with fresh vegetables and salad. There's a good and varied wine list and a regular "limetable" of live music.

**Café Coco** Pigeon Point Rd, Crown Point ☎ 639 0996. One of Tobago's newest restaurants, serving a mix of local and international dishes – highlights include beef stew cubano, and a range of salads and pizzas – in swish surroundings.

**Café Iguana** Store Bay Local Rd and Airport Rd by the police station ☎ 631 8205. This lively bar and restaurant serves great and decently-priced Caribbean cuisine and range of cocktails. Live jazz and salsa on Friday and Saturdays. Daily from 6pm.

**Chrystals** Store Bay Local Rd and Airport Rd. Low-key, inexpensive bar/café serving fruit juices, bake and shark, flying fish and take away roti and sandwiches. The sheltered tables outside make a good spot for street gazing.

**Columbus Snack Bar** Store Bay Rd, Crown Point. Popular drinking spot opposite the airport that also dishes out great, cheap Tobagonian staples: flying fish, buljol or smoked mackerel breakfasts; roti, fried chicken and rice or stew pork for lunch and dinner. The Friday night barbecue is popular, offering a good lime as you eat.

**Copra Tray** Store Bay Local Rd. International menu, good for a light lunch – shrimp wonton, chicken wings, beef or fish salad, burgers and filled croissants – or a pre-drinking dinner of meatloaf, vegetable quiche, lasagne, calamari or pizza, in a pleasant garden setting back from the road.

**Dillon's** Airport Rd ☎ 639 8765. Busy seafood restaurant midway between the turn-offs for Pigeon Point and Store Bay beaches, with an a/c dining room and outdoor tables. They prepare sumptuous, moderately-priced, carefully prepared Creole dinners of fish, lobster and shrimp. Live music most nights. Mon–Sat from 6pm.

**The Great Lime** Milford and Pigeon Point rds, Crown Point. Claiming to have the biggest menu in Trinidad and Tobago this mural decorated restaurant serves a range of not-too-expensive local and international dishes in a shaded, but close to the main road spot. There's also a bar and pool table.

**Kariwak Village** Store Bay Local Rd, Crown Point ☎ 639 8442. Fresh herbs and spices, inventive slants on local staples and genuine love in the kitchen make this restaurant, attached to the hotel of the same name (see p.260),one of best and most expensive places to eat in Crown Point. Breakfast and dinner menus are set – usually with a meat, fish or vegetarian option – and everything is supremely fresh, succulently cooked and completely delicious. Accompanied by live music, the Saturday night buffet is particularly good. Great service and vegan food available.

**Marcia's** Store Bay Local Rd, Crown Point ☎ 639 0359. The genial owners make this one of the most welcoming small restaurants in the area. Open for dinner from 6.30pm (call the day before to order lunch) and offering great, affordable local food: red snapper Creole, lobster in coconut garlic sauce, stewed or curried conch and Sunday-style stewed chicken with macaroni pie and callaloo, all served with rice and ground provisions. Gorgeous cassava pudding for dessert.

**Mumtaz Continental Restaurant** Airport Rd, Crown Point, opposite *Jimmy's Holiday Resort*. Serves excellent budget Indo-Trinidadian food including rotis, Korma and samosas, with steak, lobster and shrimp dishes available for tamer tastes. Simple surroundings with Indian kitsch decoration. Open for breakfast, lunch and dinner Mon–Sat; dinner only on Sunday.

**Pelican Reef** Airport Rd, Crown Point ☎ 631 8080. Tobago's newest liming spot has galley style surroundings complete with fishing nets and pirates, serving a range of moderately expensive steaks and seafood. The wine list is extensive and the desserts excellent. Open from 5pm Tues–Sun.

**Pepe's** Store Bay Rd, off Pigeon Point Rd ☏639 7304. Varied and expensive menu served in the lively, open sided and attractive restaurant. Usually full of foreign visitors gorging on sesame chicken wings or stuffed crab-back appetizers and a huge range of chicken preparations, including red wine and mushroom sauce and curry and coconut. The pepper shrimp is excellent, and soup, salad and rum punch are included with every evening meal.

**Red Crab** Sandy Point Rd, Crown Point ☏631 8318. Adjacent to the *Tropikist* hotel (see p.260), this new, brightly coloured Chinese restaurant has an extensive and excellent menu of medium-priced Chinese fare.

**Ru-B-Lou's** Sandy Point, opposite James Resort ☏639 8046. This extremely genial place offers hearty, inexpensive and flavoursome American-style breakfasts, and English fry-ups on request. Their simple dinner menu (served daily from 6pm until the last customer leaves) features fresh and tasty meat and fish dishes prepared in both local and international styles. It's a small venue so come early or call ahead.

**Steak & Lobster Grill** *Sandy Point Village*, Sandy Point ☏639 8533. Stunning setting overlooking Sandy Point beach, accompanied by the sound of the sea. A combination of mediocre local and international food at high prices, though weekly buffet (Tuesday) is good value for money. Nightly entertainment of local dancers and musicians livens up the atmosphere.

**Vie de France Bakery and Garden Café** Crown Point. This is hardly a garden café, but the pretty green and yellow terrace is filled with lots of plants. A good and affordable lunch option, serving a range of pasta, sandwiches and salads and a varied selection of teas and coffees.

**Waving Gallery** Store Bay beach facilities. Upstairs dining spot offering no-frills food – fish sandwiches, hamburgers, hot dogs and salads and an extremely inexpensive buffet on Friday night. The best and least expensive grilled shrimp in Tobago. Barbecue on Sundays.

### Drinking and nightlife

**The Deep** *Sandy Point Village* hotel, Crown Point. Air-conditioned subterranean disco popular with upwardly mobile locals and tourist crowds – good for a hassle-free dance. Moderate cover charge; women usually get in for free. Open Fri & Sat.

**Golden Star Restaurant and Bar** Pigeon Point Rd, Crown Point ☏639 0873. One of Tobago's busiest nightspots with an outdoor stage that remains popular with a young crowd of tourists, locals and especially those on the lookout for company. The entertainment varies every evening; karaoke, "Latin" night (Thurs), and the marvellous "Scouting for Talent" show, an annual competition for Tobagonians with stars in their eyes. TT$20 plus cover charge.

# Bon Accord, Milford Road and Canaan

Bisecting Tobago's low-lying southwest tip, ruler-straight **Milford Road** is the area's artery, a busy main road connecting Crown Point to the Bon Accord, Tyson Hall, Canaan and Friendship communities. Trucks, cars and route taxis fly past the limers who congregate on every corner – even the supermarket forecourt becomes a choice drinking spot on a Friday evening – and the whole stretch is the busiest you'll find away from Scarborough. One community melts seamlessly into another (boundaries seem to be a law unto themselves which only local residents can grasp), but as this is probably the most well-travelled thoroughfare on the island, the strip rapidly becomes familiar. Taxis travelling along Milford Road are usually plying the Scarborough–Crown Point route, but some turn off at Shirvan Road to Buccoo, Mount Irvine, Black Rock and Plymouth.

## Accommodation

Away from Crown Point things get much quieter very quickly as you enter a more residential area. A range of high quality, peaceful and sometimes inexpensive **accommodation** options can be found in these friendly communities along Milford Road, which are still within easy striking distance of the popular beaches. The places listed below are included on the map on p.258–259.

**Candles in the Wind** Lot 145, Bon Accord Estate ☎631 5335, ⓦwww.candlesinthewind.8k.com. This very friendly hotel, just a minute from the airport, contains eight en-suite rooms with cable TV and a/c. There are two fully equipped shared kitchens and laundry facilities on site. ❺

**Canoe Bay** Canoe Bay Beach Resort, Cove Estate ☎631 0367, ⓦwww.holidayintobago/canoebay.html. Set in 44 acres of beautiful landscaped gardens, Canoe Bay is one of Tobago's newest and most secluded resorts. Each self-contained apartment contains a bedroom, a/c, TV, balcony, furnished kitchen and bathroom. A quiet and clean beach with changing facilities and a bar and café is on your doorstep. ❺

**Christina's** Roberts St, Bon Accord ☎/☏639 7834. Good value and German-owned guesthouse set in a peaceful backstreet behind Milford Road, ten minutes' walk from Pigeon Point beach. Huge rooms have a/c, radio, TV, fridge, phone and en-suite bathroom. On-site restaurant serves German cuisine, and breakfast is included in the rates. ❻

**Coconut Inn** Store Bay Local Rd, Bon Accord ☎639 8493, ☏639 0512, ⓦwww.coconut-inn.com. Distinctly Teutonic ambience – clean lines, spotless rooms, well-mown lawns and no-hassle atmosphere – nestled behind the *Copra Tray* bar (see p.264). Apartments have kitchenette, a/c and verandah, and there's a pool onsite. The seriously spacious "budget" rooms are set in another block; all have fans and shared access to showers, kitchen and TV lounge. Standard ❻ budget ❹

**Coral Sea Villas** Bon Accord Estate, Bon Accord ☎639 9600, ⓦwww.coralseavillastobago.com. A series of pretty and distinctively pink Mediterranean styled villas, each sleeping a maximum of eight people and set in landscaped gardens with a pool, jacuzzi and barbecue. ❽

**Cruesoe's Apartments** Store Bay Local Rd, Bon Accord ☎639 7789, ☏631 0155, ☏janmarc@tstt.net.tt. Spacious self-contained apartments, tastefully decorated in blue and orange with a/c, cable TV, fully furnished kitchen and pool. Excellent value. ❺

**Douglas Apartments** John Gorman Trace, Milford Rd ☎/☏639 7723, ☏dougapp@tstt.net.tt. Sparkling clean, spacious and varied apartments with a family atmosphere at the Bon Accord end of Milford Road, with one and two bedrooms – each with a couple of double beds for large groups – as well as a lounge, full kitchen, patio, a/c, and TV. Car rental is available on site. ❺

**Harris's Guesthouse** Golden Grove Rd, Canaan ☎639 0513, ⓦwww.harris-jungle-tours.com.

Home of one of Tobago's best tour guides, Harris McDonald, this fabulous guesthouse, situated on a quiet road, has two spotless, double rooms with private patios and one family room – all are en-suite, and have fans. There is a shared TV area and a free rainforest tour is included for stays of seven nights or more. Freshly cooked, local breakfast is included in the rates and dinner is available for an extra TT$60. ❹

**House of Pancakes** Milford Rd and John Gorman Trace, Bon Accord ☎639 9866, ☏kittycat@tstt.net.tt, ⓦgeocities.com/original-houseofpancakes_tt. Three rooms at the back of this popular Milford Road restaurant, all very home-style with varied decor and double, single or bunk beds, TV, a/c or fan, and shared or private bathroom. There is also a suite with a kitchenette. Clean and comfy but a bit cramped. ❹

**Merle's House** 7 Kilgwyn Bay Rd, Bon Accord ☎639 7630, ☏imarcell@tstt.net.tt or imarcelle@hotmail.com. This guesthouse is basic but good value, featuring homely rooms all with a/c, kitchenette, en-suite bathroom and porch. ❸

**Mike's** Store Bay Rd, Crown Point ☎639 8050. Excellent value and two minutes from the airport, this busy place has small but clean and inviting 1-, 2- and 3-bedroom apartments with a/c, cable TV and kitchenette. There's a mini-mart on site. ❹

**Papa Joes Place** George and Guy sts, Canaan ☎/☏631 7272, ⓦwww.papajoesplace.com. Ten colourful, luxury apartments, each with a/c, kitchenette and cable TV in a village style setting close to Pigeon Point. ❻

**Plaza Guesthouse** Milford Rd, Canaan ☎639 9269. Very basic rooms in a friendly Tobagonian-run guesthouse right on the road. You pay for what you get; a bed, fan and en-suite bathroom, all somewhat down at heel. ❷

**Rainbow Resort** Milford Rd ☎639 8271, ☏639 9940, ☏Ratt@tstt.net.tt. An unimaginative concrete exterior contains clean, functional white-tiled rooms with kitchenette, en-suite bathroom, cable TV, a/c and radio. Some rooms are adapted for disabled guests. Car rental is available, and there's a pool on site. Pigeon Point beach is a 5min walk. ❹

**Rovanel's** Store Bay Local Rd, Bon Accord ☎639 9666, ☏639 7908, ☏rovanels@tstt.net.tt. Palatial splendour set in landscaped gardens, with a pool, restaurant and bar, as well as a mini-zoo of sorts featuring a monkey, deer and some rabbits in tiny cages. Rooms have phone, TV, a/c, hairdryer and patio; some have kitchenette. ❺

**Sea Shell Vacation Villas** Bon Accord Estate, Bon Accord ☎639 9600, ⓦwww.seashellsvillas.com. Each of these fifteen colourful villas clustered close to Pigeon Point and

Store Bay beaches sleeps six, is set in its own landscaped private gardens with swimming pool and has a lovely first floor covered deck area – perfect for alfresco dining. ❽

**Serenity Apartments** 14 Centre St, Canaan ⌕ 639 0753, ✉ serenapt@tstt.net.tt. All the rooms in this well-established guesthouse on a quiet side street have a self-contained kitchen, TV and a/c. ❹

**Spence** Store Bay Local Rd, also a branch on Milford Rd ⌕/⌕ 639 8082, ✉ myorkeol@hotmail.com. Simple, faded rooms,

but inexpensive and close to the airport with a pool and restaurant. Eclectic design: some rooms are split level, some have bunk beds, others are doubles; and all have a/c, TV and kitchenette. Popular with a German clientele. ❹

**Sunshine Holiday Apartments** Milford Rd, Bon Accord ⌕ 639 7482, ⌕ 639 7495, ✉ sunapt@tstt.net.tt. A ten-minute walk from Pigeon Point beach, these good-value rooms all have high ceilings, kitchenette, en-suite bathroom and porch, and phone, a/c and cable TV. A pool is also available. ❹

# Bon Accord

Following the right-hand curve of Airport Road/Milford Road takes you east into the **BON ACCORD** district, though it's an area as loosely demarcated as any of the mini-villages skirting this central thoroughfare. North of the road is **Bon Accord Lagoon**, a sweeping oval of mangrove swamp and reef-sheltered, shallow water which forms one of the most important fish nurseries on the island. Though the marine life has been adversely affected by run-off from a nearby sewage treatment plant, the lagoon remains a sanctuary for conch, snails, shrimp, oysters, crab, urchins and sponges – if you can see them amongst the thick sea grass.

As most of the land skirting the swamp is **privately owned** – Britain's Princess Margaret stayed at one of the beach houses during a 1950s sojourn – access is problematic. You can get pretty close by turning down Golden Grove road from Milford (though the road becomes extremely bumpy after the small bridge, and is impossible without four-wheel drive in the wet season) and taking the first dirt track you come to – passing the crumbling remains of a windmill and cocoa drying house, once part of the Bon Accord sugar estate. Adolphus James (⌕ 639 2231) is an excellent guide for birdwatching around the lagoon; better still is to see it on a Buccoo Reef boat tour (see p.275) that includes a barbecue at a deserted sandy spit on the lagoon's north side known as **No Man's Land**, an idyllic place to swim. You'll have to move fast to catch the area in its current unspoilt state, though, as the Golden Grove estate encompassing this land is starting to build villas here.

# Canaan

Tyre shops, dusty rum bars and the obligatory coconut palms prevail as Milford Road continues eastward about 4km from the airport into **CANAAN**, an unremarkable district dominated by a row of shops in front of sprawling Milford Court, the southwest's largest housing scheme. The entire area was once carved up into individual sugar plantations; some – like Friendship Estate – have not yet shed their colonial names, while Canaan (and Bon Accord) received their unusual titles from Moravian missionaries who arrived in Tobago in 1789 to convert the populace. You can still pick out the odd bit of period architecture, such as the old windmills housing the *Peacock Mill* restaurant (see p.281). These days, though, this stretch of Milford Road, with its peppering of rum bars, is a nice place to stop off for a **drink** and a spot of "ol' talk", the inconsequential rum-fuelled banter which goes hand-in-hand with the liquor. Due to the presence of a roti stall and an outlet of the renowned *Block 22* fried chicken chain (see box, p.251), it also stays comfortably busy during the evenings.

## Canoe Bay

Just after the turn-off for Buccoo (see p.273), a right-hand gravel track sign-posted for **Canoe Bay Resort** leads south to a pretty and quiet **beach** (daily 9am–5pm; TT$12, includes use of showers and bathroom) that was once the site of a large Amerindian settlement; the English named it Canoe Bay after the Indian pirogue fleets moored here. Today, the 56 acres around the bay are beautifully landscaped and an appealingly peaceful place to spend the day (or even overnight; see p.266 for accommodation). The main area boasts lawns, thatched gazebos, picnic tables and a supremely private beach of clean yellow sand and calm waters – the view stretches right down to Crown Point and there's some good snorkelling to be had. The facilities are good and there's a small bar serving drinks, food and ice cream all day. This is an excellent place to come if you're travelling with children – the sheltered water makes for safe swimming and the large grassy areas are perfect for ball games.

## Eating and drinking

**Alpha Mega** Milford Rd, Canaan. Local-run, inexpensive café serving up fish and chips, roti, bake and shark and fruit juices. Mon–Sat 7am–10.30pm.

**Caroline's Hideaway** Douglas St, Canaan. This small and basic but friendly and locally run restaurant serves up a range of cheap local dishes – such as split peas and rice.

**Diver's Den** 7 Roberts St, Bon Accord ☎639 0287, ⊛ www.diversdentobago.com. This recently refurbished bar and grill is Tobago's newest late-night lime – karaoke night on Tuesdays is particularly popular.

**Fortune Chinese Restaurant** Milford Rd ☎639 8818. A new, plush Chinese restaurant with an excellent range of well-priced dishes, as well as a good vegetarian selection, to eat in or take away.

**Golden Star** Milford and Pigeon Point rds ☎639 0873. Chiefly recommendable for its easy-access location. Food is mediocre – the fish, chicken, steaks, lobster and club sandwiches hold no surprises (or nasty shocks), but it's open late, prices are decent and service is cheerful.

**Green Shop** Canaan, Milford Rd, opposite Milford Court. Popular rum shop, good for a game of dominoes or a quiet lime.

**House of Pancakes** Milford Rd, Bon Accord. Good breakfasts of cinnamon- and nutmeg-laced pancakes with fresh bananas and walnuts; omelettes, bacon and eggs are also on offer. Dinner is Cajun-style: blackened fish or shrimp, shrimp jambalaya or seafood and okra gumbo. The roadside setting is noisy but central, and the shady terrace good for watching the world go by. Closed for dinner Sun & Mon.

**Kaiso Club** George St and Milford Rd, Canaan ☎631 1000. One of Tobago's popular casinos offering stud poker, blackjack, roulette and a few slot machines. There's also a bar and free hotel pickups can be arranged. Mon–Sun noon–3am.

**Lindsay's Bar** Milford Rd, Bon Accord. Another Milford rum bar patronized mainly by locals, inexpensive and good for catching up with local gossip.

**Mr Fiddla's Picnic Café** Milford Rd. Claiming to be a place where "friends meet flavours" this inexpensive, funky little yellow outdoor café is open for breakfast and lunch to eat in or take away. The homemade ice cream is particularly good.

# Lowlands, Lambeau and Little Rockly Bay

About 1km east of Canaan on Milford Road, the tarmac widens as you approach Claude Noel Highway, named after the local boxer who was a world lightweight champion in the early 1980s, and built several years later as a swifter route into Scarborough than the narrow Milford Road, which swings off right from the highway after the *Tobago Hilton* turn-off. The area trapped between Milford Road and the Atlantic – known as the **Lowlands** – was once a swampy peninsula, but is now home to Tobago's largest development project:

**Tobago Plantations**. The development includes villas, condominiums, a shopping centre and a 9- and 18-hole golf course (US$85 for 18 holes, ☎631 0875, ⓦwww.golftobagoplantations.com), all centered around the *Tobago Hilton*, a sprawling complex of plantation-style buildings overhanging the ocean.

The hotel itself has twenty acres of ocean front, but the best beach in the Lowlands, **Petit Trou**, is actually to the east of the hotel, where the Milford Road turns left onto **Old Milford Road** – on the way, keep your eyes peeled for Tobago's only mosque. Petit Trou is used extensively by locals and also patrolled by security guards from *Tobago Plantations*, but is most notable for its multitude of kiteboarders, whose colourful sails soar above the water they skim along (kiteboarding lessons can be organized with Cool Runnings ☎639 6363, ⓦwww.outdoor-tobago.com). Swimming is not recommended here as the undercurrents are strong and there are no lifeguards, but the beach makes a slow descent into the ocean, so wading is pleasant.

## Lambeau and Little Rockly Bay

Heading east from the Lowlands up the Claude Noel Highway, just past the Old Milford Road turning, you'll drive past a forest-like plantation of coconut palms to the left. From here, the road begins to climb; once you've passed the Auchenskeoch Road (a convenient shortcut to Buccoo and Mount Irvine), you come to a set of traffic lights marking a crossroads. A left turn here will take you to Signal Hill (see below), while a right leads to the hilly residential community of **LAMBEAU**, a tight-knit and completely untouristed village – if you visit on a Sunday morning stop by the sea-facing church and listen to the singing.

Lambeau is best used as the approach to **Little Rockly Bay**, which occupies a wide swath of coast just north of Petit Trou and was once used as a site for horse racing before the construction of Shirvan racetrack. Just opposite the *Cat & Fiddle* pub in Lambeau (see p.271) is a reef-protected beach on the bay known locally as "warm pool", whose shallow waters and constant cooling breeze make it a popular spot for local picnickers and bathers. The beach is decorated by a small monument dedicated to calypso champions Lord Kitchener and Calypso Rose. Lifeguards are on duty here Mon–Fri 10am and 6pm and are based in a small concrete building at the Petit Trou end of the sand – look out for their red and yellow flags which mark where it's safe to swim. Unlike most beaches, the area is often busy in the evenings, especially Fridays, when the *Cat & Fiddle* and the neighbouring *Greg's 195* bar (see p.271) become popular meeting places.

Beyond Lambeau, as Little Rockly Bay becomes **Rockly Bay**, the coast gets rougher and the shoreline is strewn with local litter, such as bottles and car tyres, and the flotsam and jetsam of yachts and the shipping industry. The ruggedness of the coastline, undercurrents in the surrounding sea and proximity to Scarborough, which ensures the murky broth floating on the water is seasoned by sewage, makes swimming here pointless and dangerous.

## Along the highway

Heading east on the highway, a left-hand turn at the crossroads leading to Lambeau will take you up the steep route to **Signal Hill**, a great vantage point to take in the panoramic **view** of the Lowlands and Crown Point beyond the forest-like coconut plantations. Throughout Tobago's chequered history, Signal Hill has been used as a lookout point, notably by signalmen communicating out to sea and to nearby forts. Today, the area is temporary home to Tobago's **library** (see Listings p.253), as well as a base for the Trinidad and Tobago, Regiment; listen out for strains of their marching band at practice.

The next right-hand turn-off from the highway, about 1.5km further, is the route to **Shaw Park football ground**, a sprawling facility which doubles as a concert venue, hosting many pre-carnival and Heritage Festival events. Sport is the main focus of the place, though, with football taking precedence. Advertised on the radio and in *Tobago News*, the games are great fun to attend, and as most take place in the cool of the night, the floodlights are the best way to tell if a match is on. Next door to Shaw Park is a cricket ground where minor international and local matches are held – both grounds have great views of low hills on one side and the ocean on the other. The hill overlooking both stadiums is the home of a striking yellow pipe sculpture known as **"the matchstick man"**: a cryptic monument designed as part of Tobago's millennium celebrations and standing as an ironic reminder of what happened – the island spent more than TT$40 million on the sculpture and a large concert, only to have a dismally low turnout.

Another kilometre down the highway is the next set of traffic lights, where a left hand turn brings you to quiescent **Orange Hill Road**, a rambling route to Mount Irvine on the leeward coast (see p.273). Past the attractive Spring Garden Moravian church, the road splits: left takes you into **PATIENCE HILL**, an attractively quiet rural community that makes a pleasant drive and is a great way to get completely lost along the winding country roads; if you can find it, there's a fantastic view of the Lowlands from the top of what locals call "Patience Hill Back Bottom Road". The right fork will bring you into sparsely populated but pretty **ORANGE HILL** itself, its bougainvillea hedges and overgrown empty lots sliding loosely into the town of Bethel and down to the leeward coast.

## Accommodation

The area stretching from the Lowlands east to Lambeau contains a variety of accommodation – all cheaper than their Crown Point counterparts, but conveniently close to both there and Scarborough. The places listed below are included on the map on pp.258–259.

**Coral Reef Gardens** All Fields Crown Trace off Old Milford Rd, Little Rockly Bay ☎639 2536, ℱ639 0770, ✉janicejo@tstt.net.tt. Clean, simple and somewhat cramped rooms with 1960s furniture; some have a/c, others have fan only. Studio apartments have kitchenette and TV. Special rates for groups of ten or more, and meals are available on request. There's also a small pool. **❸**

**Green Acre Guesthouse** Daniel Trace, Carnbee Village ☎639 8287. Slightly north of the Lowlands area, this recently renovated Tobagonian-run guesthouse has basic rooms with en-suite bathroom and ceiling fan. Some apartments have kitchenettes, but meals are available on request. **❹**

**Hampden Inn** Old Milford Rd, Lowlands ☎/ℱ639 9866, ⓦwww.seetobago.com/tobago/resorts/ hampden. Efficient, friendly and German-run (popular with German clientele as well) but stuck in the backwoods. Large rooms are scattered around a

landscaped garden, all with a/c, cable TV, a huge bathroom and patio with hammocks. There's a good restaurant on site. **❻**

**Inn on the Bay** Old Milford Rd, Lambeau ☎639 4347, reservations 639 7173, ⓦwww.innbay.de. *Toucan Inn*'s sister hotel set in tropical gardens and across the road from a small beach. The staff at this vanilla-painted hotel are supremely friendly and the rooms are spacious with mahogany furniture and teak floors; all have phone, a/c, en-suite bathroom, balcony and sea view, and TV on request. There's also a small, deep pool, attractive sundeck and an on site restaurant serving a good range of dishes – often with live local entertainment – and a bar that's open all day. Standard **❻** Brand-new villa sleeping four **❼**

**Ocean Point** Old Milford Rd, Hampden Lowlands ☎/ℱ639 0973, ⓦwww.oceanpoint.com. Self-contained, spotless and semi-plush studios and suites on quiet Old Milford Road, with a/c, cable TV, full kitchen and wood fittings. All rooms have a sea view, and there's a small pool and sundeck, as well as a restaurant on site. **❻**

**Tara's Beachhouse** Old Milford Rd, Little Rockly Bay, Lambeau ☎ 639 1556, ⓦ www.tarasbeach house.com. Unusual red-brick building with spacious but simple and clean apartments, sun decks and a small pool, perched on the hillside overlooking Little Rockly Bay. All with kitchenette, TV, small bathroom and innovative chairs made from car seats. **❺**

**Tobago Hilton** Lowlands ☎ 660 8500, ⓕ 660 8503, ⓦ www.hilton.com. Subject to gusty sea winds, this sprawling mock colonial pistachio-coloured hotel has all the mod cons expected of this chain. All rooms have sea-facing balconies, minibars, phones with data ports and cable TV. The more expensive suites feature a jacuzzi on the balcony. Facilities include a small gym, sauna, tennis courts, swimming pool, children's activity centre, and watersports (nonmotorised are free). Excellent local art adorns the walls, but the rooms do not justify the high rates. **❾**

**Tobago Plantations Villas** Lowlands ☎ 639 8000 or 1025, ⓕ 637 1025, ⓦ www.tobagoplantations.com. Situated in the Lowlands near the *Tobago Hilton*. Choose from 2- and 3-bedroom condominiums or luxurious 3- and 4-bedroom villas with their own pool. The complex borders a golf course, but the nearby beach is one of the dirtiest and most windswept on the island. **❾**

**Tropiko Apartments** 26 Old Milford Rd, Lowlands ☎ 660 8724, ⓔ stay@tropiko.com, ⓦ www.tropikotobago.com. Two spotless and tastefully decorated apartments, each with large kitchen, lounge and dining area, and two white and pine bedrooms. Some bedrooms have TV and a/c. Guests can use the pool at nearby *Ocean Point* hotel, and the *Tobago Plantations* golf course is five minutes away. Excellent value. **❺**

**Viola's Place** Birchwood Triangle, Lowlands ☎ 639 9441, ⓕ 624 8765, ⓦ www.violasplace.com. Just off the Claude Noel Highway opposite the *Tobago Hilton* entrance, these spacious, comfy apartments – for two to eight people – come with fully equipped kitchen, bathroom, a/c, phone and cable TV. Meals are available on request, and there's also a pool. Excellent for what you pay, with a friendly atmosphere and popular with Germans, though there is some noise from the nearby highway. Five minutes from the *Tobago Plantations* golf course. **❺**

# Eating and drinking

**The Art Gallery Tea Gardens** Hibiscus Drive, Lowlands ☎ 639 0457. Set in the delightful gardens of the *Art Gallery* this intimate and expensive venue serves local teas accompanied by poetry readings, steel drum music and discussions on art. Thurs & Sun 5pm–9pm.

**Cat & Fiddle** Old Milford Rd, Lambeau ☎ 639 4347. An excellent and extremely popular Friday night option, adjacent to the *Inn on the Bay* in Little Rockly Bay, where live music, a barbeque and late night DJ are the perfect way to kick start the weekend for many locals and tourists alike.

**Coral Reef** *Tobago Hilton*, Lowlands ☎ 660 8500. Pricey restaurant overlooking Little Rockly Bay specializing in seafood and international fare. Mon–Sun 6.30pm–11pm.

**Cross Roads Pub** Buccoo Rd, Carnbee. Expansive bar which comes to life each Saturday night for a "Back in Time" dance where an older set groove to 1960s, 70s and 80s music.

**Garden Grill** *Ocean Point Hotel* ☎ 639 7312. Informal restaurant serving reasonably priced chicken, steak and fish dishes. Creole buffet on Monday, East Indian buffet on Wednesday and bar-

becue on Thursday. Mon–Sun 7am–11pm.

**Greg's 195** Old Milford Rd, Little Rockly Bay. Adjacent to the *Cat & Fiddle*, this local liming spot, an open-air wooden board bar, is good for its intimate and friendly atmosphere and sea views.

**Hampden Inn** Old Milford Rd, Lowlands. Good in-hotel restaurant serving medium-priced European fare; American or continental breakfast, sandwiches, salads, burgers and soups for lunch, and pizza, spaghetti, curried or stewed fish, chicken and shrimp for dinner, accompanied by an African drumming show each Sunday.

**Rouselle's** *Tobago Plantations*, Lowlands ☎ 639 9582. Swish, international-style restaurant overlooking the *Tobago Plantations* golf course, specializing in seafood. Tues–Sat 11.30am–11pm, reservations required.

**Shore Things** Old Milford Rd, Lambeau ☎ 635 1072. A delightful, well-priced café in a brightly painted old house with verandah overlooking the sea. Serves delicious light lunches, pizzas, pastelles, quiches and salads, plus fresh pastries and fruit juices. High-quality regional crafts and furniture also on sale. Mon–Sat 10am–6pm.

△ Argyll Waterfall

# North to Buccoo

A kilometre or so before Milford Road widens into Claude Noel Highway, **Shirvan Road** strikes off to the left. Bristling with signs tacked up by enterprising restaurateurs and hoteliers, this is the route to Buccoo Bay and its famous **reef** (see p.275) as well as several wide yellow-sand **beaches** and the neat coastal town of Plymouth. The first stretch is bordered to the left by a plantation of towering coconut palms and to the right by thick hedges masking what was once Shirvan Park **horse racing track**. A fire in 1985 put a permanent stop to horse racing in Tobago, and the site then had a brief incarnation as popular nightspot *Starting Gate* before turning into *The Lush*, the place to "large it".

Studded with swanky restaurants, fruit stalls and simple board shacks, Shirvan Road continues north, passing turn-offs to quietly residential Mount Pleasant and Carnbee Village – the latter has a supermarket and petrol station. There's another cluster of tourist-oriented signposts at the next crossroads, known as **Buccoo Junction**. Here, route taxis running between Scarborough and the north coast pick up and drop off passengers, so you'll often see beckoning hands if you're driving. The right turn at the crossroads is Auchenskeoch (pronounced or-kins-styor)/Buccoo Bay Road – take any left from here and you'll climb into the midst of one of Tobago's smartest residential areas, Mount Irvine, with its towering satellite dishes, a lavish golf course, fantastic views of Buccoo Reef/Pigeon Point, and opulent villas sporting swimming pools.

A little further up the road and you're at the outskirts of tiny **BETHEL**, a precipitously situated and completely charming rural village once home to infamously eccentric German artist Luise Kimme (see p.277); there are several wonderful views of the Lowlands and the Buccoo coast from the village. From Bethel, Orange Hill Road eventually meets Claude Noel Highway a couple kilometres west of Scarborough.

# Buccoo and Mount Irvine

The left turn at Buccoo Junction takes you past a small supermarket and into the small settlement of **BUCCOO**, haphazardly built around the calm and beautiful bay that shares its name. Fishing remains a major industry here – the day's catch is sold by the beach facilities when the boats return in the late afternoon – but ever since the nearby reef became a premier attraction, this close-knit community has become more dependent on tourism. Shopfronts are daubed with "Welcome to Buccoo", and the green space in front of the bay is the venue for the annual **goat races**, a highlight in Tobago's tourist calendar – the scoreboard is left up year-round as testament to the bitterly fought contests which take place each Easter (see box, p.276). Buccoo gets a weekly energy injection when the masses descend for the **Sunday School** debauchery (see box, p.277) and the village is completely taken over. The rest of the week sees a quieter scene, with the community (and its posse of skinny dogs) tidying up the revellers' rubbish and enjoying their peace and quiet while they can; families chat over garden walls and small boys take pleasure in diving off the fishing pier, despite the scummy waves that lap against the coarse grey sand.

Don't become too relaxed, though, as Buccoo has the **highest crime rate** in Tobago and although it's little more than petty theft this is not a place to let guard down – especially if you're visiting Sunday School. Also, the unfortunate combination of a muddy sea bed and the bay being used as a urinal on Sundays have made Buccoo a terrible place to swim, though the palm-lined western fringe of the bay is more appealing, with cleaner water and plenty of shells and coral fragments to collect. There are run-down government-built beach facilities, but hardly anyone uses them these days. This is, for the most part, a place to come for events like Sunday School or the races, and then promptly depart.

## Accommodation

Tobago's most **upmarket** hotels are clustered along the beaches between Buccoo and Plymouth, and the exclusive **villas** around the Mount Irvine golf course are some of the plushest private lodgings around, but not all the accommodation is just for the well heeled. There are plenty of middle-bracket hotels and guesthouses, and the area makes one of the most appealing bases on the island; you're close to the action of Crown Point without being stuck right in it, transport is easy (taxis run along Shirvan Road from early morning to late at night), and the beaches are mostly marvellous. The places listed below, around Buccoo and Shirvan Road, are included on the map on p.258–259.

### Buccoo and Shirvan Road

**Casablanca** Battery St, Buccoo ⓣ/ⓕ 639 0081, ⓔ peiser@tstt.net.tt. Spotless rooms with fan, sink and cable TV, kitchenette and en-suite bathroom. For those on a limited budget, there's a dormitory with bunk beds and shared kitchen. All rooms have wheelchair access. Standard ❸ dormitory ❷
**Enchanted Waters** Shirvan Rd ⓣ /ⓕ 639 9481, ⓦ www.kpresorts.com. Adjacent to *Patino's* restaurant (see p.281), this hotel's luxurious rooms are a bargain; all have a/c, cable TV, phone, radio, hairdryer, en-suite bathroom and an open-air, but covered kitchenette on the balcony. The beautiful honeymoon suites include a four-poster bed and jacuzzi. Landscaped grounds feature a pool and a 75ft-wide waterfall, and the location is convenient for Mount Irvine beach and route taxis. ❻
**Hillcrest** Buccoo Rd, c/o Max Baden-Semper in UK ⓣ 020/8741 9264 or 563 0423, ⓔ cimbs@yahoo .com. Set on a hilltop off Shirvan Road near *Morshead's* deli, the verandah of this sumptuous five-bedroom villa commands a panoramic view of Buccoo Reef and the Atlantic coast all the way to Scarborough. A living room, dining room, full kitchen, gorgeous infinity pool and spacious grounds complete the perfection. Rates cover ten people and include staff. ❾
**Old Grange Inn** Buccoo Junction ⓣ/ⓕ 639 9395, ⓦ www.trinidad.net/grangeinn/index.html. Get a look at your room before paying as there are two options: appealing rooms with wooden floors, a/c, phone and fridge; or else rather gloomy self-contained units with kitchenette, phone, a/c, TV and small patio. The inn features a large pool and a good restaurant, and the golf course is close by. ❺

**Seaside Garden** Buccoo Bay ⓣ/ⓕ 639 0682. ⓔ theseasidegarden@tstt.net.tt. Clean rooms with mosquito nets, ceiling fans and en-suite bathrooms, all within staggering distance of the Sunday School venue. ❸

### Mount Irvine

**Blue Horizon** Jacamar Drive, Mount Irvine ⓣ 639 0433, ⓕ 639 0432; in US ⓣ 305/592 1434, ⓕ 305/592 4935, ⓦ www.blue-horizonresort.com. Commanding great views over the golf course and the sea from a hilly setting (you'll need a car), these spacious, shady rooms have a/c, cable TV and phone, living room, patio and full kitchen; some can sleep up to six. The atmosphere is friendly, and the service laid-back but efficient. There's also a pool. Free airport pickup. ❻
**The Fourteenth Green** Mount Irvine ⓣ 639 9600, ⓦ www.tobagovilla.co.uk. Specially equipped for wheelchair users and those with walking difficulties, this fully-equipped 3-bedroom villa comes complete with its own pool, guest cottage and maid service. ❾
**Golf View Apartments** Buccoo Junction, Mount Irvine ⓣ 639 9551, ⓕ 639 0979, ⓦ site.yahoo.com/golfview-apts/. Excellent prices for these clean and spacious, self-contained apartments with a/c, TV, phone and optional kitchenette. There's a restaurant and bar on site, and a large pool in a pretty garden out front. It's a bit close to the road, however. ❺
**Mount Irvine Hotel and Golf Club** Mount Irvine ⓣ 639 8871, ⓕ 639 8800 ⓦ www.mtirvine.com. Built around a coral stone sugar mill and other plantation remnants, this grand old lady of Tobago hotels maintains a sophisticated elegance.

❺

Amenities include tennis courts, sauna, huge pool, three restaurants, five bars plus a private stretch of beach and an 18-hole golf course (guests get a 15 percent discount on green fees). Rooms are luxurious with a/c, phone, satellite TV and patio; self-contained 2-bedroom bungalows are available as well. **❾**
**Rolita** Jacamar Drive, Mount Irvine ☎ /⒡ 639 7970. Extremely friendly and accommodating

atmosphere with great views down to Pigeon Point. The good-value rooms are plain, clean and breezy with fan and double bed. There's also a pool and meals are available on request. **❸**
**Villas on the Green** Jacamar Drive, Mount Irvine ☎/⒡ 639 9748, ⓦ www.golftobago.com. Each villa has 3 bedrooms, 3 bathrooms, a small pool and a jacuzzi, and every imaginable amenity. There's also a large communal pool. **❾**

# Buccoo Reef and Nylon Pool

Covering around twelve square kilometres of Caribbean sea bed between Pigeon Point and Buccoo Bay, **Buccoo Reef** is the largest and most heavily visited reef in Tobago. Home to forty-odd species of hard and soft coral, the reef has taken around ten thousand years to grow into today's magnificent labyrinth. The predominant corals are hard stag and elkhorn, though you'll see waving purple sea fans and peach-coloured fire coral, all of which make good feeding for the brilliantly coloured trigger, butterfly, surgeon and parrot fish which thrive here. To the south of the reef is **Nylon Pool**, a gleaming coralline sandbar forming an appealing metre-deep swimming pool smack in the middle of the sea. It's said to have been named by Princess Margaret during her stay in the 1950s; she supposedly remarked that the water was as clear as her nylon stockings – nylon had just been invented.

Sadly, however, human interference is taking a devastating toll. Carelessly placed anchors and thoughtless removal of coral souvenirs – not to mention the inevitable pollution – mean that many parts bear more resemblance to a coral graveyard than a living reef. Large sections have died off completely, leaving white skeletons in their wake, while overfishing has reduced the fish and crustacean populations, and poorly-aimed spear guns have ripped chunks from the coral. The situation became so bad that Buccoo was declared a protected national park in 1973, but with scant resources to enforce the law, the legal status meant little and the damage continued practically unabated. Today, glass-bottom boat operators are more conscientious, anchoring only on parts of the dead reef and warning visitors that touching or removing reef matter and shells is illegal, but they still hand out plastic shoes, making it possible for a single footstep to damage or kill hundreds of years' growth. You can do your bit by standing on the sea bed only and refusing to buy any coral trinkets.

If you want to see the reef, you'll have no difficulty in finding a **glass-bottom boat** to take you; they leave from Store Bay, Pigeon Point and Buccoo – though if you choose the former, snorkelling time may be reduced as it's a longer journey to the reef. Basic tours include a trip across the unscathed deep-water coral garden as well as snorkelling and a dip in Nylon Pool; a two- to three-hour trip costs around US$20–25. Some operators make a day of it by including a beach barbecue at No Man's Land for around US$40. Some of the most reliable operators are Buccoo-based Johnson and Sons (☎ 639 8519); Mr Power, who makes daily trips on his boat *POWER1* from Pigeon Point; or Hew's (☎ 639 9058) – you can also just ask around on the beaches. These operators time their trips with the low tide, when **snorkelling** is at its best, while others will go any time you want.

## Goat and crab races

Easter weekend is to Tobago what Carnival is to Trinidad: an unofficial national holiday when the hotels are filled to the brim and the island erupts with festivities. A succession of huge open-air parties and well-attended harvest feasts culminate on Easter Tuesday at the **Buccoo goat races**, a tradition since 1925. Though attempting to race one of the world's most intractable and belligerent animals may seem a little ridiculous to the uninitiated, these tournaments are taken very seriously by aficionados, who study the form (and character) of the sleekly groomed animals and place bets on their favourites. Raised separately from the run-of-the-mill roadside grazer and given fanciful names like Dance Hall King, Nobody Wants Me, Nasty Man or Ben Johnson, racing goats usually don't end up in the pot, but instead undergo a rigorous training routine and return to the tracks year after year. Prize specimens live out their days as stud goats to breed more potential champions.

The preliminary round at the Mount Pleasant Family Fun Day on Easter Monday gives everyone a chance to see which goat is running best, and by Tuesday, Buccoo – still reeling from the two largest Sunday Schools of the year – is transformed; the track is clipped and fenced in, the scoreboard resplendent with a new coat of paint and the starting gates in place. Food vendors and craft stalls line the streets and a carnival atmosphere builds as fast as the crowds, who are kept entertained by dancing and drumming in between stakes. Smartly attired in white shorts and coloured vests, the jockeys limber up by the side of the tracks; a necessary exercise, as their ability to keep up with their goat (and keep hold of it) has more influence on their success or failure than the capabilities of the goat itself; animals are raced at the end of a rope, and guided or encouraged with the help of a long stick. Sponsored by local businesses and given grand titles like White Oak Classic or Penta Paints Stake A, the actual races are a joy to watch once the jockeys manage to manoeuvre their malignant charges into starting position. With wild-eyed stares, the goats tear haphazardly down the track, often taking a diagonal course that trips up other goats and runners alike, to the delight of the spectators. The best of the bunch battle for supremacy in the final "Champ of Champs" race, while "Champion Jockey", "Champion Trainer" and "Most Outstanding Goat" prizes are also presented.

The equally improbable **crab races** are taken a little less seriously. Plucked from the ocean a couple of weeks before, the crustaceans are encouraged to run both by tugs on a piece of string and by temporary withdrawal of food; choice morsels placed at the end of the wooden alleys which keep the crabs on course are the incentive for the sideways dash to the finishing line. Once all the races are over on Tuesday, the final all-night party swings into action, and the dancing continues until dawn.

## Mount Irvine

The swaying palms and shaven greens of Tobago's first **golf course** herald the outskirts of **MOUNT IRVINE**, the next coastal village north from Buccoo. Straddled across Shirvan Road, the course was opened in 1968 as the main attraction of *Mount Irvine* hotel (see p.274), which still owns and maintains the greens. This professional standard, 72-par, 18-hole course with several onerous water holes and some wicked undulations, offers a challenging game and plays host to the Tobago Pro-Am tournament every January. Green fees are US$30 for nine holes, US$48 for eighteen – there's also a weekly rate of US$264 and hotel guests get a 15 percent discount.

Past the golf course, the hitherto hidden Caribbean sea coast swings spectacularly back into view; yachts bob on the waves and craggy volcanic rock formations bordering Buccoo Point make an arresting backdrop to the west.

There's a lovely section of beach known as Mount Irvine Wall behind a low concrete bulwark just past the golf course; it's very popular with locals who often sit chatting in the emerald-green water.

Around the next bend is **Mount Irvine Bay Beach**, a busy slip of fine yellow sand with just enough room for beach tennis and volleyball, surrounded by cutesy covered gazebos and the ubiquitous palms and sea grape trees. The slightly run-down facilities (daylight hours; TT$1) are adequate, and there's a bar/restaurant doling out mountains of fried shark and bake. During the summer months, the water here is calm enough to make exploration of the ornate offshore **reef** a joy. However, Mount Irvine is most exciting to visit between December and March, when it becomes one of the island's best **surfing** beaches, with huge breakers crashing against the sand. Boards can be rented from Mt. Irvine Watersports (☎639 9379) right next to the beach complex; they also rent out windsurfing and snorkelling equipment as well as Sailfish boats (for more information on surfing, see "Basics", p.52). Though it lacks atmosphere, the semi-private section of beach maintained here by the *Mount Irvine* hotel is a little superior to the public area; nonguests are still welcome to swim, and you can use the showers if you're drinking from the bar.

## Kimme museum

Nestled in the hills behind the beach along Orange Hill Road – take the right turn just past the Mount Irvine golf course then follow the signposts – is the **Kimme Museum** (open Sun only, 10am–2pm, appointments taken for other days; TT$20; ☎639 0257, ⓦwww.luisekimme.com), the private gallery of German sculptor Luise Kimme, who settled in Tobago in 1979. Her eerily beguiling wood sculptures are on display in the *Tobago Hilton* (see p.271) and the *Kariwak Village* hotel (see p.264), and her bronze head of local politician A.P.T. James graces James Park in Scarborough. Works are also dotted around

---

### Sunday School

A Tobago institution, **Sunday School** is most definitely not for the pious. A massive beach party that the whole island seems to attend, Sunday School is the highlight of the week's nightlife, completely taking over Buccoo village with swarms of people, food stalls and cars squeezed sardine-style into available spaces. The action begins at around 8pm, when the Buccooneers Steel Orchestra plays pan for a couple of hours. The crowd begins to thicken around 10–11pm, when the sound system at the covered beach facilities starts up, competing for the highest decibels with the music pumping out of *Hendrix Bar* across the road ($5 cover). Music policy at the beach is inevitably Jamaican dancehall with the most popular soca tunes thrown in alongside hip-hop and R&B, while you'll hear oldies (disco, Michael Jackson), soca, calypso and a little reggae at *Hendrix*. Either dancefloor is invariably jumping, as experienced winers (see "Glossary," p.371) display their skills, foreigners let loose or take a wining lesson, and the gigolos (and tourists) scout for a partner – Sunday School is well known as a kind of **pick-up joint**, so it's the ideal place to watch the intricate mating dance of thrill-seeking foreigners and those hard-working beach bums. Sunday School is not just for the young – locals and tourists of all ages come here to chill out and many tour guides offer Sunday School trips for visitors for about US$17. Even if you want to experience Sunday School on you own, to avoid car parking hassles it's a good idea to book a taxi to collect you at a prearranged time. Though Buccoo is busy every Sunday night, the largest Sunday School of the year takes place each Easter Monday, when several more sound systems add to the cacophony and parked cars back up all the way to Mount Irvine.

the surrounds of her quirky, mural-decorated fretworked home, the "Fairyhaus" – known locally as "the castle". The collection is stunning; three-metre-high figures carved from whole trunks of oak depict the subtlest nuances of Tobagonian dancing, and her interpretations of local folklore characters Mama L'Eau, La Diablesse and the Soucouyant are powerful. Meeting Luise Kimme – ever the eccentric artist – is an experience in itself; she's always on hand to provide further insight into her work. You can buy copies of her evocative Tobago diary, *Chachalaca* (see "Books", p.362), as well as photograph booklets of her pieces for TT$100.

# ⑤ Grafton Beach and Black Rock

Past Mount Irvine, Shirvan Road's name changes to Grafton Road. Its narrower forefather, Old Stone Haven Road, ran closer to the sea, and though pot-holed and semi-private looking, you can still drive or walk along it to access an excellent **beach** – usually referred to as **Grafton Beach** after the resort hotel which dominates the sand from above. Just past the turning for the nearby bird sanctuary (see below), a left-hand turn will bring you down to the beach. A glorious, wide swathe with coarse sand and year-round crashing waves that attracts turtles to lay eggs (see p.354), the beach (or **Stone Haven**, as it's officially called) makes for marvellous swimming. The hotel's proximity makes this a rather commercial beach in some ways, though; washing lines strung between the almond trees display pretty batik sarongs and you'll be periodically approached by roving craft vendors.

Adjacent to the entrance to *Stonehaven Villas* on the main road (see p.280) is a sun-bleached sign marking the entrance to the **Grafton Caledonia Bird Sanctuary** (daylight hours; free). Now somewhat run-down, the sanctuary was

---

### The Tobago hustle

Though **tourist harassment** in Tobago is far less of a problem than in many other destinations where the industry is a major earner, aggressive and unsettling attitudes are becoming increasingly common among a small number of people who seem bent on stressing you out, either through sexual harassment at the bars and clubs or over-insistent hustling of overpriced crafts on the more touristy beaches. It can be irritating and frustrating, but it's important not to lose perspective. Many tourists do come to the island with a holiday romance in mind, so you can't blame locals for trying it on just because it's not on your personal agenda; most hustlers are simply struggling to make ends meet. Be aware that HIV infection is high on the island, though, the result of hedonistic holidaymakers, so if you do have sex, make sure you use protection, otherwise you could be returning home with an unwanted souvenir. Tobagonians on the whole are hugely generous hosts, warming to visitors with genuine respect and taking pride in showing you their island. That said, it's hardly surprising that constantly having to pander to others' needs – especially those of comparatively wealthy tourists with little knowledge of conservative Tobagonian culture – can get frustrating and occasionally boil over into heavy-handed hustling or downright rudeness.

If you do feel harassed, maintain your sense of humour, say no if someone's selling something you don't want, and remember that local women are not expected to dance with anyone but their lovers or friends, so you needn't feel pressured to accept an invitation. Should you be unlucky enough to need to, report an incident to the police at the nearest police station (see p.254).

founded by the late owner of the surrounding estate, Eleanor Alefounder, who began feeding hungry local birds following the devastation wreaked by Hurricane Flora in 1963 (see p.300). Today, 4pm is feeding time for the flocks of mot-mot, cocorico, bananaquit and practically every other feathered specimen found on the island, many of which will peck right out of your hand. There are extensive trails through the property which make for excellent, easy and scenic **hiking**.

## Black Rock

Continuing northeast, Grafton Road narrows as it enters **BLACK ROCK**, a busy, friendly village with a couple of nice rum shops. On the western outskirts of town is a signpost for **Fort Bennet**, a still-intact stockade built by English mercenary Lieutenant Robert Bennet in 1680. During the plantation era, the fort was expanded by British troops, who built a red-brick oven to heat up the metal used to make cannonballs and placed two cannons here to defend the bay against US warships during the American War of Independence. A gazebo has been added, and the view over Mount Irvine Bay and the Pigeon Point headland is spectacular, particularly at sunset. Close by is the Culture Barn (☎639 9022), a small shop run by Malcolm Melville, renowned internationally for his unique and innovative hand-crafted drums.

## Turtle Beach

Beyond a grating stretch of potholes marking the end of Black Rock, the road swings around a blind bend before entering a straight stretch. Trees mask the lovely **Turtle Beach**, a picturesque kilometre of coarse yellow sand flecked with the occasional swathe of volcanic grey; there are several dirt tracks from which to enter the bay from the road. The water shelves steeply from the beach and the waves are large, making for exhilarating swimming, while a river at the western end can sometimes be nice for a freshwater dip, but it's often dammed up and stagnant in the dry season. Jealously guarding pole position in the centre of the bay (only guests are allowed to use the purpose-built sun shelters), the two-storey *Turtle Beach* hotel (see p.280) dominates the sand, and the constant presence of well-heeled guests has generated an ideal captive market for itinerant vendors. Like Grafton next door, the sand here is patrolled by craft and aloe-purveyors who offer their high-priced wares with varying degrees of insistence, and the strip in front of the hotel is one of the few places in Tobago where you might feel hustled (see box opposite). If you do, head for a spot further away from the hotel; however, the centre of the beach is the only place where you can buy drinks and snacks. A Team (☎639 0531), a tour operator, puts on a **beach barbecue** every Wednesday and Friday – for TT$200 you can have grilled fish, chicken, rice and salads, and rum punch whilst being entertained by limbo dancers and calypso music.

Though the beach is officially called **Great Courland Bay**, it acquired its colloquial title on account of the **turtles** that still lay eggs here in the dark of night (see box, p.354). The main laying season runs between March and August, and six weeks after the eggs are laid, hatchlings make a dash for the sea; both equally moving sights. All of the hotels along this stretch organize a turtle watch during the laying and hatching seasons, but if you're not staying in the area, contact Nick Hardwicke at *Seahorse Inn* (☎639 0686) for turtle watching expeditions, or Save Our Sea Turtles Tobago (☎639 9669), a charity run by local forest rangers, for information and free tours.

# Accommodation

**Coral Sunset House** Black Rock ☎639 9600, ⓦwww.tobagohouserentals.com. This fabulous villa was lovingly designed, built and decorated by an American surfer. With spectacular views and a unique combination of luxury and quirky, this villa sleeps up to six and is a gem. ❾

**Grafton** Black Rock ☎639 0191, ⓕ639 0030, ⓦwww.grafton-resort.com. Now an all-inclusive hotel – most guests arrive on package tours – this resort hotel dominates Stone Haven Bay. Comprehensive amenities include pool, tennis and squash courts, games room, two restaurants and a beach bar, nightly entertainment, watersports and a scuba centre. Rooms are tastefully decorated with balcony, a/c, fan, safes, TV and phone, but don't justify the high walk-in rates. ❼

**Indigo** Pleasant Prospect ☎/ⓕ639 9635, ⓦwww.indigo-tobago.com. Nestled above the bar and restaurant of the same name, Caribbean colours and batiks decorate these basic but pleasant rooms which have a/c, mosquito nets, fridge, tea/coffee-making facilities and en-suite bathroom. Each has a balcony, some overlooking the beautiful Stone Haven Bay. A family room with TV is also available, and breakfast is included in the rates. ❻

**Jema's** Turtle Beach ☎639 7724, ⓦwww.jema -guesthouse.de. Tucked behind Turtle Beach, this three-bedroom, Tobagonian/German-run outfit is beautifully decorated with rattan furniture and a nice verandah. Rooms are simple with mosquito nets and fans; the kitchen and bathroom are shared, and breakfast is available on request. ❹

**Le Grand Courlan** Stone Haven Bay Rd, Black Rock ☎639 9667, in US 800/468 3750, ⓕ639 9292, ⓦwww.legrandcourlan-resort.com. Favoured by airline crew and package tour operators, this all-inclusive, swish pink-and-blue resort features an extensive spa, gym overlooking the sea and all the mod cons of a luxury hotel. There's a large sundeck area and pleasing decor, but no atmosphere. Rates include one spa treatment a day. ❾

**Over Seas Cottage** Fort Bennett, Black Rock ☎639 7995 or 0819. These three Tobagonian-run apartments are basic with kitchen, lounge, bedroom with fan, bathroom and small verandah/sundeck. Steps lead down from the apartments to Stone Haven Bay. ❺

**Plantation Beach Villas** Stone Haven Bay Rd, Black Rock ☎639 9377, ⓕ639 0455, ⓦwww.plantationbeachvillas.com. Gorgeous colonial-style 3-bedroom villas with gingerbread fretwork, wraparound verandahs overlooking the sea, beautiful fittings (four-poster beds, rocking chairs) and all mod cons, as well as washing machine and dryer, dishwasher, well-equipped kitchen and spacious living room. Bar and pool are on site and the sea is a minute away. ❾

**Sanctuary Villa Resort** Grafton Estate ☎639 9556, ⓕ639 0019, ⓦwww.sanctuaryvillas.com. Attractive and well designed, these 25 two-, three- and four-bedroom villas have all mod cons, TV, a/c, phone, verandah, full kitchen, beautifully decorated living room and private pool. Opposite Grafton Beach and there's plenty of peace and quiet. ❽

**Seahorse Inn** Stone Haven Bay Rd, Black Rock. ☎639 0686, ⓕ639 0057, ⓔseahorse@trinidad.net.tt, ⓦwww.seahorseinn.com. Small and right on a turle nesting beach, these four comfortable rooms have appealing quirks like arched windows and teak floors and a patio with great sea views, a/c, ceiling fan, en-suite bathroom and cable TV. There's a good restaurant on site (rates include huge breakfast) and evening entertainment during the high season. ❼

**Stonehaven Villas** Grafton Estate, Black Rock ☎639 0102 or 9887, ⓔstonehav@tstt.net.tt, ⓦwww.stonehavenvillas.com. Fourteen huge colonial villas fitted with mahogany, marble and granite and every conceivable luxury: four poster beds, a maid's room for those travelling with servants, personal pool and stunning views over Stone Haven Bay. The complex includes a club house with bar and open-air restaurant and a conference centre. ❾

**Two Seasons** Pleasant Prospect, Shirvan Rd ☎639 7713. Bargain accommodation set back from the road between Mount Irvine and Stone Haven beaches. Rooms are plain with wood floors, fan, mosquito net and a bed, but the atmosphere is friendly and this is an excellent budget choice. Meals are available from the restaurant downstairs, and there's also a communal kitchen, lounge and bathroom. Guests must like animals as there are cats and dogs on the premises. ❷

**Turtle Beach** Turtle Beach/Stone Haven Bay. ☎639 2851, ⓕ639 1495; in UK ☎020/8741 5333, ⓕ741 9030; in US ☎800/255 5859, ⓕ305/471 9547, ⓦwww.rexcaribbean.com. A member of the *Rex* chain, this 1970s-style concrete edifice is right on the beach and is predominantly all-inclusive. Popular with tour groups, the rooms with sea view are suitably well equipped with a/c, phone, king-size or twin bed and balcony. Amenities include tennis courts, pool and watersports, and there's also a restaurant on site. The first child under 12 stays free; additional children are charged the adult rate. Pleasant accommodation, but does not justify the expensive walk-in rate. ❾

# Eating and drinking

Most of the **restaurants** along Shirvan/Grafton Road tend to be touristy and pricey, but you can get inexpensive local lunches from hole-in-the-wall eateries in Black Rock. All of the restaurants listed below are good for a **drink**, but the most scenic place to sink a few beers is the beautifully located *Ocean Edge* rum shop perched on a cliff top overlooking Stone Haven Bay; a great place to while away the sunset hours.

**Black Rock Cafe** Grafton Rd, Black Rock ☎639 7625. Popular open-air restaurant on the town's outskirts serving medium-priced soups, salads and fabulous fish dishes for lunch, and daily dinner specials of steak, chicken and fish.

**Blue House** Shirvan Rd ☎639 8242. Open in the high season from Dec to April, this pleasant restaurant set on the road serves reasonably priced meals inspired by Italian, German, American and local cuisine. Things liven up at the weekend with Latin dance and barbecue on Saturday and steel band and barbecue on Sunday.

**The Emerald** Pleasant Prospect ☎639 8272. Just off the road between Mount Irvine and Stone Haven bays, *The Emerald* has a breezy upstairs setting, good for somewhat pricey seafood, tender lobster, steaks and great Creole-style shrimp. For those with smaller appetites there is a kids' menu.

**Indigo** Pleasant Prospect ☎639 9635. Friendly restaurant/bar with changing daily menu specializing in seafood and clever combinations of spices and fresh herbs all in the medium-price range. Food served 7pm–11pm. Bar frequented by both locals and tourists for a lively lime, open 5pm till late.

**La Tartaruga** Buccoo Bay ☎639 0940. Tobago's best Italian restaurant with an open-air patio near the sea, owned and run by a mercurial Italian émigré. The select menu features top class cuisine, including a selection of authentic regional Italian specialities such as Sicilian caponata, bassioico bruschetta and fresh tuna carpaccio. Homemade pasta with rock lobster, fish and shrimp is the house specialty. Make sure you leave room for the to-die-for desserts, including Drambuie crème caramel and homemade Italian ice cream. Extensive wine list and somewhat high prices. Closed Sun.

**La Terrazza** Shirvan Rd ☎639 8242. Open for lunch and dinner, this is another first-class Italian restaurant serving a range of authentic and moderately pricey Italian cuisine in a relaxed atmosphere. Extensive wine list and cigar club.

**Le Beau Rivage** Mount Irvine Golf Course ☎639 8871 ext 327. An exclusive, tastefully decorated restaurant that features an international menu specializing in seafood, such as lobster and shrimp, and vintage wine at equally exclusive prices.

Dinner from 7pm. Closed Tues.

**Mélange** Shirvan Rd ☎631 0121. Popular Creole restaurant housed in a pretty yellow colonial-style building. The affordable menu features grilled lobster, goat's cheese and duck salsa, steaks and fresh pasta. Live entertainment most nights.

**MeShell's** Shirvan Rd ☎631 0353. Peach-painted restaurant serving expensive international cuisine with a Caribbean twist. Good for seafood, especially shrimp and lobster.

**Papillon** *Old Grange Inn*, Buccoo ☎639 0275. Classy, pricey dining on a leafy patio or in an a/c room. Huge menu adds pastelles, conch in coconut milk, lamb kebabs, and shark in rum and lime to the usual fish and chicken selections. Deeply satisfying pone with ice cream for dessert.

**Patino's** Shirvan Rd ☎639 9481. Friendly Trinidadian/Canadian hosts serve Polynesian-style food which works extremely well in a congenial setting. A waterfall wall with changing coloured lighting and garden patio provide romantic atmosphere to meals featuring seafood, ginger beef with Chinese mushrooms, hot and sour shrimp and lobster Polynesian. This upmarket restaurant has a different theme every night ranging from Thai to seafood – supremely fresh and tasty.

**Peacock Mill** Shirvan Rd, Friendship Estate ☎639 0503. Decorated in a multitude of greens this old windmill serves tasty light meals such as sandwiches and baked potatoes at good prices. Open Mon–Sun 3pm–11pm.

**Seahorse Inn** Stone Haven Bay Rd ☎639 0686. Imaginative and expensive menu based around international staples; sandwiches, fish, shrimp and a good tuna pasta salad for lunch, and more sophisticated offerings for dinner: stuffed peppers, chef's paté, lobster bisque or fish chowder to start and excellent seafood, steaks, pork chops and chicken for the main course. The chocolate gâteau is delicious. Happy hour between 5.30pm and 6.30pm and nightly entertainment.

**Shirvan Watermill** Shirvan Rd ☎639 0000. Upmarket restaurant with tables beautifully set under the cut stone roof of an abandoned water mill. The "international" fare (steak, lobster and so on) is beautifully cooked and the prices match the decor; cocktails are served at 5pm, dinner from 6pm.

**Teaside Pizza** Battery St, Buccoo Point ☎639 8437. Unpretentious, appealing and tucked away behind Buccoo Bay; the pizza is good and reasonably priced with seven standard toppings. Wholewheat bases are available, as are natural juices – fig (banana) is recommended. Toasted sandwiches and home-made cookies are good, too; they'll deliver to hotels and guesthouses in Crown Point.

**Two Seasons** Pleasant Prospect ☎639 7713. Next door to *The Emerald*, the tasty, freshly made pizza comes with a white or whole wheat base and plenty of toppings. Brown rice and vegetables

is a good option for non-meateaters. Local food and breakfasts are also served at bargain prices.
**Under the Mango Tree** Black Rock ☎639 8964. Lovely yellow-and-green roadside café serving inexpensive sandwiches, pizza, salads and hot entrees including coconut crusted chicken in peanut sauce, all freshly made and served inside or under the shady mango tree. Delicious fruit juices and amusing signs, "Beware – falling mango", toilets marked "mango" and "womango" complete the atmosphere. Sat–Thurs 1–9.30pm for lunch and dinner.

# Plymouth

Over a kilometre past Turtle Beach, Grafton Road meets a junction: going straight will put you on the Plymouth Road to Scarborough, while to the left, a narrow bridge over the Courland River brings you to the outskirts of **PLY-MOUTH**. Tobago's first European community, Plymouth was settled by a group of roving Latvians, usually referred to as Courlanders, then by the Dutch and finally by the British (see p.242). Today, it's an attractive little town, with neat board houses and an over-abundance of rum shops lining the grid-patterned streets. Life in Plymouth centres around the large grocery on the main street, opposite the *S&B Tasty Roti* parlour (Mon–Sat 11am–2pm). Reggae blasts out from cars and shops, bringing the street to life, while the local youth lime outside. If you're driving up the coast, it's wise to fill your tank at Plymouth's **petrol station**, as it's the only one for miles (Mon–Sat 6.30am–9pm, Sun 5.30am–9pm)

## Accommodation

**Adventure Eco Villas** Arnos Vale Rd, Plymouth ☎639 2839, 🅕639 4597 or 4157, 🆆www .adventure-ecovillas.com. Two wooden wendy house-type villas overlooking the Adventure Farm and Nature Reserve (see p.283), with kitchen, a/c, satellite TV, iron, hairdryer and double bed, plus sofa bed – a cot is available on request. ❾
**Arnos Vale** Arnos Vale Estate ☎639 2881, 🅕639 4629, 🆆www.arnosvalehotel.com. One of Tobago's grandest hotels and set on 400 hillside acres of beautiful bird- and flower-filled private land. Close to a gorgeous protected cove of brown sand and reef-filled sea, which is great for snorkelling. The rooms are chintzy with rattan furniture, phone, TV, a/c and balcony. There's a swimming pool onsite and bird feeders in the restaurant attract the local birds. Buffet breakfast (included) and lunches are good; and from 4pm to 6pm tea is served and the birds are fed on the restaurant terrace. Dinner here is a romantic option, but pricey. ❾
**Cocrico Inn** North & Commissioner sts, Plymouth ☎639 2961, 🅕639 6565,

🆆www.coricotobago.com. Comfortable, family-run and very friendly with a restaurant, pool and quiet location in residential backstreets. Eclectic accommodation ranges from clean, simple rooms with fan to larger units with a/c, fridge, TV and kitchen. They also rent basic or luxurious self-contained one-, two- and three-bedroom houses in Plymouth and a plush villa on Great Courland Bay. ❻
**Footprints** Culloden Bay Rd, via Golden Lane ☎660 0118, 🅕660 0027, in the US ☎868/660 0118, 🆆www.footprintseco-resort.com. Overlooking Culloden Bay, down a long, windy, potholed road, this remote, 62-acre self-styled "eco resort" has its own nature trails, saltwater and freshwater pools, excellent snorkelling just steps from the rooms and plenty of peace and quiet. Accommodation ranges from standard suites to self-contained villas with jacuzzi and pool, and a "lovers' retreat". There's an excellent restaurant, boutique, library, and a mini-museum displaying local artefacts. ❼
**Seekei's Ville** North Street ☎639 1352. Friendly and comfortable family-run apartments with

kitchen, fan and cable TV. Popular with Trini holidaymakers. ❸

**Top O' Tobago** Arnos Vale Estate ☎639 3166, in UK 01225/859 530, ℱ859916, ⓦwww.topo tobago.com. Perched above Arnos Vale Bay with pretty gardens, a distant sea view and plenty of bird life. The comfortably opulent main 2-bedroom house sleeps up to seven and has a large sitting room, two bathrooms, fully equipped kitchen, patio, cable TV, stereo, and washer and dryer. Smaller cabanas are stylish with kitchenette and all have use of the pool. Cabana and house can be rented separately or as a package. Remote enough to merit a car but excellent value. Cabana ❻ cabana/house ❾

## The Town

Turning left from the main road at the phone box will take you to Plymouth's main attractions; the so-called **mystery tombstone** and **Fort James**. Well signposted and sitting alone on a concrete platform close to the sea, the eighteenth-century tombstone is an enigmatic, if rather depressing, reminder of Tobago's history of slavery. The double grave of a child and her 23-year-old mother, Betty Stiven, the "mystery" is the inscription on the stone slab: "What was remarkable of her; she was a mother without knowing it, and a wife without letting her husband know it, except by her kind indulgences to him". Betty is said to have been the African slave (and lover) of Alex Stiven, a wealthy Dutch planter, and the general hypothesis has two strands. In the first theory, she gave birth to Stiven's child and he took charge of it, raising it as his but not acknowledging Betty as the mother, giving her "freedom" to carry on as his lover and making her a "mother without knowing it". The other theory proposes that the affair between Alex and Betty was illicit and scandalous but passionate, carried out in secret to save the face of a white man. When she died giving birth to his child, he was so overcome with grief that he left this cryptic message as a commemoration of their love.

Opposite the tombstone, a road leads down toward the sea; turn right and you'll see the stark concrete blocks of the **Great Courland Bay Monument**, testament to the "bold, enterprising and industrious" Latvians who colonized the area and lent their name to the bay. Carrying straight on past the tombstone brings you to Fort James, the oldest stockade in Tobago. The solid, roofed coral stone structure and four cannons that remain today are a British legacy, added in 1811, and there's an excellent view of Turtle Beach from the mown lawns behind.

The Plymouth main road leads back onto the Arnos Vale Road, where, on the eastern outskirts of town, a small weather-beaten sign on the left-hand side directs you to the **Adventure Farm and Nature Reserve** (Mon–Sat 7am–5pm; US$5, guided tours US$8; ☎639 2839). There's little adventure to be had on this twelve-acre site, though there is plenty of nature with motmots, green herons and chachalaca and other birds that regularly appear to feed in the late afternoon to the sound of an antique ship's bell. There's also a butterfly garden, an organic farm where you can pick your own fruit and toy-like cottages in which to stay (see opposite).

## Arnos Vale and north

From the centre of Plymouth, a well-signposted but narrow road meanders through the greenery toward **Arnos Vale**, one of the few sugar estates to keep its land, parts of which have been opened up to the public while a resort hotel straddles the beachfront section of the property. The main point of access is at the old estate **water wheel** (daily 9am–10.30pm; adults TT$12, children TT$6; ☎639 2881) where new buildings constructed from natural materials housing a modest **museum** – displaying a small selection of Amerindian pottery and colonial artefacts found on the estate – and gift shop are connected by wooden walkways that allow visitors to view the atmospheric remains of the large wheel, pump, fermenting house and steam train that once transported sugar around the plantation. It's a pretty spot, and lavish, with flowering plants and lush foliage, and the only place on the island where Tobago's plantation history can truly be grasped. There's a classy, romantic and expensive Caribbean **restaurant** here; highlights of their eclectic and delicious menu are toasted lobster, mignon with brandy and peppercorn sauce, and duck in Grand Marnier sauce. Arnos Vale is also a great place for a relaxing drink at the **bar** – where freshly squeezed juice from fruit grown on the estate is served.

Past Arnos Vale, the resurfaced road passes the tiny but attractive villages of **Golden Lane** and **Les Coteaux**; the latter is known as a centre for obeah, and rumours of witchery and potions abound – the community hosts spooky story sessions during the Heritage Festival celebrations. Road improvements have linked Arnos Vale with the rest of the leeward coast, but you can also get to Moriah and Castara from Scarborough via the Northside Road (see p.294).

# Scarborough

Tobago's raucous, hot and dusty capital, precipitous **SCARBOROUGH** (population 18,000), is an immensely appealing place. Poking through the treetops, the houses and roads of this town spill higgledy-piggledy down the hillside while the Atlantic provides a magnificent backdrop for the silhouettes of the **lighthouse** and **Fort King George**, perched at the top of the hill. The island's administrative centre and its main **port**, Scarborough is a flourishing town, brimming with a brisk vibrancy. Devoid of any touristic pretensions, the town still throbs with activity; street corners swarm with liming locals, clothes stalls are perused by the shoppers, while the **market**, with its artistically arranged displays of intensely coloured fruit and vegetables, and constant sales banter of the stallholders, is irresistible. Away from the bustle of the main town, the shady suburb of **Bacolet** is home to some of Tobago's most upmarket hotels and the beautiful, secluded Bacolet Bay beach – playground of many a rich and famous visitor to Tobago.

Though the largest town on the island, Scarborough is still pretty tiny; the docking of the **ferry** from Trinidad is spectacle enough to draw crowds of onlookers – prospective passengers scurry by clutching parcels, while cars and lorries inch along as they wait to board. Although the commercial clamour, traffic and steep climbs can make Scarborough a bit of an ordeal, the cool breezes and views from the port offer respite. Friday afternoons the town throbs with life as people celebrate the end of the week, while Saturday afternoon is a much quieter time to visit. On Sundays Scarborough is practically deserted as most locals head out to Sunday School (see p.277).

### Some history

The **Dutch** were the first Europeans to settle what became one of Tobago's most hotly contested pieces of land. They navigated the treacherous harbour rocks in 1654, and constructed a fort and a few buildings, naming it

**Lampsinsburgh**. Around the same time, a group of Courlanders (Latvians) were building up their stronghold on the opposite coast at Plymouth (see p.282). In 1658, the Dutch captured Plymouth – an act that led to the destruction of their own settlement when, in 1666, an British fleet came to the aid of the Latvians and blew Lampsinsburgh to smithereens.

The British officially won the island in 1672, but didn't maintain a presence, allowing the Dutch to return and build Lampsinsburgh into a more substantial settlement, with houses, a single street and a church, as well as warehouses and wharves at the harbour and a new fort. However, during the French assault of 1677, the newly improved fortifications proved to be the undoing of the Dutch; a French cannonball hit the fort's ammunition dump, and the resulting fireball destroyed the structure and killed all 250 occupants. Though still commemorated in the current name Dutch Fort Road, there's nothing left today of that original settlement.

The British bestowed the name **Scarborough** upon the town when they regained control of Tobago in 1762, establishing the House of Assembly and constructing Fort King George. The **French** returned to take control, after a bloody and prolonged fight, in 1781. Scarborough was renamed Port Louis, while Fort King George – with finishing touches added by French soldiers – became **Fort Castries**. The town ricocheted between the British and French until Tobago was finally ceded to the British in 1814. Though Scarborough was a thriving commercial centre during the plantation era, it was the first place to suffer when the sugar industry collapsed in the 1870s; the House of Assembly was disbanded, and not reconvened until 1980.

# Arrival, getting around and information

Most people enter Scarborough by **road** along the Wilson Road turn-off from Claude Noel Highway and follow the one-way system toward the wharves bordering Carrington Street – home of the central terminal for **ferries** to and from Trinidad (for departures and prices, see "Basics", p.32) – the other primary means of arrival into the town. Free parking is available at the wharf lot on the corner of Carrington and Castries streets, in the NIB Mall car park off Gardenside Street (strictly speaking for shoppers only) and the lot behind the *KFC*.

There are two **taxi** stands on Carrington Street, a one-minute walk from the ferry terminal, while the **bus depot** is located five minutes away on Greenside Street behind the NIB Mall. Buses to all corners of the island run daily between 4.30am and 8pm; for details see p.286; remember to purchase your tickets before boarding. As Scarborough is so small, there are no bus services within the town, but that's no problem as you can easily see all the sights by foot.

For **information**, head to the offices of the Tobago House of Assembly, Division of Tourism, 197 Doretta's Court, Mt. Marie (8am–4pm; ☎639 2125 or 4636, Ⓕ639 3566, Ⓦwww.visittobago.gov.tt) or the TIDCO (Tourism and Industrial Development Company) office in Unit 26, ADC Mall, 8–10 Sangester's Hill (8am–4pm; ☎639 4333, Ⓕ639 4514, Ⓦwww.visittnt.com).

For **currency exchange**, there's the Republic and Scotiabank on Carrington Street opposite the wharf, Royal and Republic banks on Main Street and First National Bank on Lower Milford Road; of all of them Royal is the most efficient. All are subject to local opening hours (see "Basics", p.18) and all have ATMs; there is also an ATM at the ferry terminal. There are two late-opening **petrol stations** on Milford Road (see "Listings", p.254).

Scarborough is the departure point for **route taxis** serving the whole of the island, though finding where to catch your ride can be confusing. For Crown Point (TT$5–6), Mount Irvine (TT$5), Buccoo (TT$4), Carnbee (TT$3), Bethel (TT$4), Plymouth (TT$4) Black Rock (TT$4) and Lambeau (TT$2) go to the "west end" taxi rank directly outside the ferry terminal. For Carnbee and Mount Pleasant (TT$4), go to the phone booth opposite *KFC* on Carrington Street. Taxis running the Northside Road to Castara (TT$6) and Parlatuvier (TT$10) leave from Carrington Street opposite the port, while cars going to L'Anse Fourmi (TT$12) leave from the NIB Mall car park on Gardenside Street. Taxis to Speyside and Charlotteville leave from Republic Bank, Main Street. (TT$11–13). Sometimes route taxis will only go as far as Roxborough where you will need to catch another one to complete your journey. Alternatively, **maxis** to Charlotteville leave a few times a day from outside the James Park on Burnett Street (TT$10). With all of these taxi stands it can be confusing to know exactly where to wait – but if you're not sure just ask around as there are always plenty of people who will help.

# Accommodation

Though Scarborough and the Bacolet suburbs were popular in the 1960s and 1970s during the early years of Tobagonian tourism, the Lowlands are now the most tourist-developed areas. Some excellent options remain, though, particularly in suburban Bacolet. Prices are lower, and access to public transport is good. Staying in a host home or bed and breakfast (see "Basics", p.34) can be great if you're on a budget or fancy a little more intimacy with local lifestyles than a hotel can provide. The tourist board recommends a number of **host homes** in their standard accommodation listings booklet (available from offices worldwide) – most rent at around US$35–55 per person, but you can often get a room for less than this, particularly if you're visiting in the off-season.

**Ade's Domicil** 19 Old Lighthouse Rd, Bacolet Point ☎ 639 4306, ☏ 639 3779, ⓦ www .adesdomicil.de. This lovely spacious white plantation-style house is a few minutes' away from the beach. All rooms have en-suite bathroom, a/c or ceiling fan, cable TV, fully equipped kitchen and a sea view. Good value. ❺

**Bacolet Bay Apartments** Bacolet St ☎/☏ 639 2955, ⓔ cross@Cariblink.net. Past its heyday but very friendly, great value and just a step away from Bacolet beach. Studios have kitchen, TV, a/c and a patio, suites are much larger with a living room; all rooms are clean and serviceable. There's also a pool and a laundry service is available at TT$28 per load. ❸

**Blue Haven** Bacolet Bay ☎ 660 7400, ☏ 660 7900, ⓦ www.bluehavenhotel.com. The best luxury accommodation on the island and recently renovated, this historic hotel – a continually popular hideaway for celebrities and honeymooners – was originally an outpost of Fort King George and retains its stunning panoramic views of the bay it once protected. The stylish rooms have four-poster

or sleigh beds, a/c, TV, minibar, phone and modern artwork, spacious bathrooms and a balcony overlooking stunning Bacolet Bay. There's a swimming pool with ornamental waterfall, mini-gym, spa and tennis court, and an excellent restaurant on site as well as a small bar on the adjacent palm fringed Bacolet beach. Close to restaurants, with Scarborough a ten-minute walk away. ❾

**Della Mira** 36 Bacolet St ☎ 639 2531, ☏ 639 4018 or 5226. Set in a pretty colonial-style house overlooking the sea with a pool, bar and restaurant on site. The basic rooms with bathroom and a/c are somewhat down at heel, but the rates are reasonable and there is a shared kitchen and TV area. Monthly lets are available. ❹

**Federal Villa** 1–3 Crooks River ☎/☏ 639 3926, ⓔ maredwards@hotmail.com. All the rooms in a private house in the Scarborough suburbs are basic with fan and shared bathroom, and have a pleasant atmosphere. ❷

**Half Moon Blue Hotel** 73 Bacolet St ☎ 639 3551, ☏ 639 6124, ⓦ www.halfmoonblue.com. The rooms of this hotel are comfortable, decorated in

# SCARBOROUGH

▲ *Plymouth & the leeward coast*

▲ *Mason Hall, Moriah & the leeward coast*   ▲ *windward coast*

*Fort King George, Lighthouse & Tobago Museum* ▶

*Bacolet Hotels & the winward coast* ▶

**RESTAURANTS & BARS**

| | |
|---|---|
| Bar Code | 7 |
| Blue Crab | 9 |
| Ciao Café | 5 |
| Club Renes & Royal Castle | 1 |
| Crystal Palace Casino | 8 |
| KFC | 2 |
| King's Well Inn | 3 |
| La Patisserie | 6 |
| MJ's | 10 |
| Roti & Pizza Boys | 4 |

**ACCOMMODATION**

| | |
|---|---|
| Federal Villa | B |
| Hope Guesthouse | C |
| Jacob's Guesthouse | A |
| Mill's Guesthouse | E |
| Sandy's Guesthouse | D |

an unusual mixture of traditional and modern styles, and come with fridge, TV, phone, fans, and great views of Bacolet Bay from private balconies. Unfortunately the kitchen area is rather shabby and the high rates are not justified; the open-plan penthouse suite is fabulous, if you've got the money. There's also a spacious garden, an overflow pool and a restaurant on site; rates include continental breakfast. Airport transfers on request. ⑧

**Hope Cottage** Calder Hall Rd ℡639 2179, Ⓔhopecottage100@hotmail.com, Ⓦwww .surfmaster.btInternet.co.uk. Set in a 100-year-old colonial building just before the hospital, this is one of Tobago's oldest guesthouses and remains a great bargain, though admittedly it has seen better days. Rooms are plain, some have private bathroom and kitchenette, and there's also a 3-bedroom cottage with shared kitchen on the grounds. ②

**Horizons Tobago** 89 Bacolet Point ℡0121 709 1648, Ⓦwww.horizonstobago.com. Cream-and-brown concrete building in a lush setting housing 5 apartments, 1- and 2-bedroom, furnished with rattan and decorated with local artwork; all have a/c, phones, cable TV, kitchens and mosquito nets. There's a swimming pool, a shared utility area for washing clothes, and maid service is also provided. ⑥

**Jacob's Guesthouse** Crooks River ℡639 2271. The small dark rooms are clean and simple; all have fans and washbasin, some have en-suite shower and toilet, and a few sleep four. Two minutes from Scarborough's centre. ②

**Mill's Guesthouse** Young St ℡639 2193, Ⓕ660 7812, Ⓔcristalj@hotmail.com. The rooms of this pretty, blue guesthouse set high on a hillside, are pleasant and well maintained – some have a/c and TV. Breakfast is an extra US$5 and dinner US$15. ③

**Mt Pelier Cottage** Montpelier ℡639 4931, Ⓔpuddy@tstt.net.tt. Unique and utterly fabulous home away from home in the hosts' self-built wooden house perched on Scarborough's hillside. These airy rooms (double, twin or single) have lattice windows, creative hand-carved decor and shared bathroom. Meals are served on a balcony – frequented by mot-mots, blue jays and bananaquits – overlooking the forest. Rates include excellent home-cooked breakfast, huge evening meals and the owner as personal guide and driver. ⑤

**Noon's Holiday Cottage** 97 Bacolet Pt ℡639 5567, Ⓔpat_denoon@hotmail.com. Spacious 2-bedroom apartment with fully furnished kitchen, lounge and fan on the ground floor of the owner's home. Located in a quiet residential road five minutes' walk from Bacolet Bay, the apartment has a back garden to relax in and is good value for the space. ③

**Sandy's** Robinson St ℡639 2737, Ⓕ660 7748, Ⓦwww.tobagobluecrab.com. Run by Auntie Alison, the hospitable owner of the *Blue Crab* restaurant (see p.293), this wonderful guesthouse has four pretty and spotless rooms with a/c and private bathroom. Breakfast included. ⑤

**Seaview Guesthouse** Bacolet St ℡639 5613, Ⓕ639 6243, Ⓔverleen@tstt.net.tt. Overlooking the sea just a two-minute walk from the centre of town, this guesthouse offers superb value and a warm atmosphere. The basic but sparklingly clean apartments have full kitchen, fan, hot water and beautiful views; all share a communal patio. Meals and laundry facilities are available on request. ④

# Lower Scarborough

Entering Scarborough along car-choked Wilson Road, a left on Darrel Springs and then a right down Gardenside Street will take you past the bus station and the back of **NIB Mall** to the right, and the **Botanical Gardens** to the left. The largest shopping centre in Scarborough, NIB Mall houses Christian bookshops, fast-food outlets and pharmacies.

On the same block as the mall is a car park that doubles as a venue for Carnival celebrations and sound system dances, as well as the food **market**. Main trading days at the market are Friday and Saturday, but throughout the week, vendors loudly hawk every tropical fruit and vegetable imaginable. The indoor meat section is an odoriferous melange of goat, beef, lamb, mutton and chicken, while fish on ice gleam at the back of the market, where stallholders attract customers by blowing on a **conch shell**. Trading reaches a peak on Friday, when the heavily scented fruits and earth-encrusted ground provisions are piled up alongside leather sandals, incense, mounds of soap powder, clothing and dry goods, and all the while carts selling snow cones, doubles and boiled corn do a roaring trade. It's a friendly and absorbing scene, great for bargains and interaction with Tobagonians away from the resorts. If you're after souvenirs, check out the **vendors mall**, a ramshackle collection of tarpaulin-covered stalls just south of the NIB Mall, where you'll find knitted Rasta hats, sandals, wood carvings and carved calabashes. Stalls also line the busy Wilson Road, while heading towards Kings Well, the small indoor **Crooks River Mall** situated next door to *Roti Boy* has a selection of clothes shops.

Another, quieter way, to enter the town is along the wide Milford Road, which leads back west to the Lowlands and here runs adjacent to the **waterfront** – a nice place to hang out and escape the crowds and noise of Scarborough. Though some older buildings remain in Scarborough's steep heights, most of the waterfront is being overtaken with new development. Souped up in 1990 by the addition of a deep-water cruise ship pier, the harbour is being revived as attractive stalls are being built on Milford's **promenade** to replace the glut of temporary ones currently lining the road. This half-kilometre-long stretch of road, although quiet compared to the rest of the town, has some good bars and cafés. At the western end of the promenade you'll find a small mall containing Tringo Tours – whose offices have bargain **Internet** access at TT$10 per hour – a bookstall and stationers, doctors and the *East Ocean* restaurant (see p.293).

## The Botanical Gardens

Opposite the bus station on Gardenside Street is the back entrance to the **Botanical Gardens** (daily, daylight hours; free), a soothing oasis after the heat-retaining concrete and constant traffic fumes of downtown; it can also be accessed from a signposted layby on the Claude Noel Highway. Covering eighteen acres of former sugar estate, once part of the Dal Fair and Rockly Vale plantations, the land was originally requisitioned by the British in the late nineteenth century with the intention of creating a public botanical garden. Today, the broad sweeps of lawn interspersed with planted beds and shade trees could indeed pass for an English park, were it not for the garish crimson of towering African tulips, flamboyant trees and the yellow and pink cascades of the poui trees, all bearing labels for easy identification. Near the botanical station is an **orchid house** displaying most of T&T's indigenous orchids as well as a few imported species. The gardens are overall an enchanting place, often deserted save for the odd office worker taking lunch under a shade tree. At its highest point there is a covered gazebo which affords a nice view over town and the sea. There are no guided tours as such, but the gardeners are usually on site to answer questions. Alternatively trained forester and licensed tour guide Darren Henry (℡639 4559) does a 45-minute tour of the gardens for TT$50.

# Upper Scarborough

As Milford Road leads into Carrington Street, the promenade turns into the waterfront wharf, with the brand-new **ferry terminal** its central focus. As well as the ferry ticket office, the complex also contains a few shops and Scarborough's main **post office** (Mon–Fri 7.30am–6pm, Sat 9am–1pm) which is the best place to post mail, being far quicker than the small regional postal agencies.

Proceeding east from the wharf along Carrington Street, you soon reach a junction known as **King's Well**, originally the site of the town's main water-course, but now home to a bar of the same name and a new Italian café. A sharp left from King's Well takes you out of town along Northside Road and the edge of the botanical gardens, while the sharp right is Castries Street, which takes you to Main Street. Between the two, steeply inclining **Burnett Street** is one of Scarborough's best places for knick-knack **shopping**, its tarmac decorated with white-painted palm trees and hibiscus flowers by a local shopkeeper.

As Burnett reaches a plateau, you enter **James Park**, once the town's main marketplace but now simply a small walled square decorated with Luise Kimme's bronze of A.P.T. James, a former Minister of Tobago Affairs. The park is bordered to the north by the imposing old **courthouse**, which has housed the administrative offices of the Tobago House of Assembly since the judiciary were shifted to their current Bacolet Street base in the late 1980s. Built between 1816 and 1825, the cut-stone structure was supposedly considered one of the finest examples of Georgian architecture in the Caribbean on completion. Subsequent alterations have, unfortunately, smothered the original brickwork with white paint and removed the pillars, leaving it a shadow of its former glory. A small monument outside, dating from the reign of King Edward VII, bears the inscription "One flag, one king, one empire". Across the park from Burnett Street, **Jerningham Street** houses a paved mini-park with benches, a fountain and a relief map of Tobago which gives you a good idea of the island's topography.

## Main Street and around

Carrying straight on past James Park along Burnett Street brings you directly onto the bustling shop-and-office-lined **Main Street**. One hundred yards or so uphill are traffic lights marking the right turn on to **Bacolet Street**, the route to the fire station, the main police station (and only jail) as well as **Gun Bridge**. This short bridge, just a minute's walk from the turning, marks the transition into Bacolet and has stone walls embellished with four cannons, two at either end, taken from Fort George – a commemoration of the town's historical discord. The small **juice bar** just before Gun Bridge is a must – it serves fantastic freshly squeezed fruit juices and punch (TT$8–12) and delicious rotis. A few yards past the bridge is **St Andrew's Anglican Church**, originally built in 1819 but razed by Hurricane Flora in 1963 and reconstructed a year later. The fire station is across Bacolet, while the police station is behind the church on Jerningham. Further south down Bacolet Street, the buildings thin out as you enter the quiet and attractive Bacolet suburbs (see p.292).

Back on Main Street, a weathered sign pointing to Cuyler Street on your left leads you to the eclectic **Scarborough Heritage Parlour** (Mon–Fri 9am–5pm; free), containing displays of furniture from the old plantation houses, slave shackles, coins and antique uniforms – all allowing a glimpse of Tobago's social history. Before carrying on up the hill take a quick detour to **Radio Tambrin**, Tobago's radio station (see p.254), which keeps Tobagonians up to date on the island's current affairs and whose building – just around the corner from the Heritage Parlour on Piggot Street – is situated close to an ancient tamarind tree which was once the slave market for male slaves.

# Fort King George

Follow Fort Street off Main as it twists its way up a steep hill past the imposing Methodist Church and some attractive but dishevelled colonial architecture; this is the way to one of the most prominent sights in town, **Fort King George**. If the precipitous walk looks too much and you decide to **drive**, you can almost always find a parking space in the lot adjacent to the museum and main fort. Refreshments are available at a kiosk opposite the hospital, but as it's often closed, you should probably bring your own, particularly if you're walking up.

Near the top of the hill, a vine-wreathed red brick building to the right is all that remains of an old **prison**, once part of the fort complex above; time and the elements have opened its tiny, dingy cells to shafts of sunlight. Just past the old prison, around the next bend, is **Tobago County Hospital** and the start of the recently renovated Fort King George complex. The first building on the left is the dome-shaped cover of an old **well**, built in 1926 to service the hospital. Opposite is the red brick **Officers' Mess**, now home to a local craft centre (Mon–Fri 9am–1pm).

A grassy path next to the Officers' Mess leads below the main fort to a landscaped **park**, lush with poui trees and colourful planted beds. Benches are perfectly placed here for soaking up marvellous views back of Scarborough and the Orange Hill district. In the shade of a massive, buttressed silk cotton tree is the decrepit **powder magazine**, its inner walls blackened by fires. The main fortification above the magazine is the largest in Tobago, built by the British and initially composed of some thirty buildings but reduced to around ten by an 1847 hurricane. The fort was occupied by French troops between 1781 and 1793, who built the solid stone perimeter walls. Inspired by the French Revolution, the soldiers **mutinied** in 1790, imprisoning their officers and razing the town below.

Today, this peaceful spot 140m above sea level is favoured for its constant sea breezes and spectacular views of Bacolet Bay, Minister Point and the rugged interior to the west, and Rockly Bay and the north coast of Trinidad to the east. By night it's a suitably deserted destination for a bit of in-car canoodling. Despite the profusion of cannons still pointing out to sea, the place's tranquil atmosphere makes it hard to imagine its military history. Behind the old officers' mess is the **lighthouse**, a squat structure transferred from Galera Point in Trinidad in 1958; the Fresnel lens beams fifty kilometres out to sea and sweeps spectacularly over the Scarborough suburbs.

## Tobago Museum

The rest of the fort's buildings are ranged around the tidy lawns of Barrack Square. The buildings house the Culture Division of the Tobago House of Assembly, as well as the must-see **Tobago Museum** (Mon–Fri 9am–4.30pm, closed public holidays; adults TT$5, children TT$1; ☎639 3970). Acquired by the Tobago Trust, this small but fascinating collection of idiosyncratically labelled artefacts includes Amerindian plates, cooking wares, tools and talismans (one shaped like a penis, presumably for fertility) dating back to 2500 BC as well as pre-Columbian nostril bowls, used to inhale the intoxicating tobacco water favoured by the Indians. One unnerving exhibit is part of the skeleton of a young Indian unearthed during construction work at Mount Irvine beach in the 1970s; teeth, skull and ribcage are all clearly visible. Satirical colonial prints depicting the exploits of "Johnny Newcome in the West Indies" are well worth a look, as are the shells, fish fossils and military paraphernalia. Upstairs, there's a gallery of ancient maps, imported African drums, sculptures and some fascinating logs of the colonial era, including notes on the sale of plantation slaves.

# Bacolet

As Bacolet Street eases out of town south along the coast past Sandy Hall and Fairfield Complex – the main administrative base of the Tobago House of Assembly as well as the Tobago Hall of Justice court and the island's main cemetery – the roadside homes become noticeably upmarket. Though **Bacolet** suffered a lull when its eponymous street was replaced by Claude Noel Highway as the main route to the windward coast – Bacolet Street is also known as Old Windward Road – this is still a suburb of choice for Tobago's elite; the grand structures built along Bacolet Point stand as testament to their owners' wealth.

The area enjoyed a heady prestige during the late 1960s and early 70s, when the area boasted a couple of luxury hotels, the *Bacolet* and *Blue Haven*, and even the **Beatles** frolicked on Bacolet Bay beach. The *Blue Haven* (which is still in business and recently somewhat restored to its former glory, see p.286) was once part of Tobago's battlements: a cannon still resides on the hotel's grounds, its base is surrounded by stone walls dating back to 1770 and the bay itself was the site of many sea battles. The hotels tried to cordon off the sand in the 1960s but Dr Eric Williams – the premier who once declared that he had no intention of ruling "a nation of waiters and bellhops" – intervened to keep the beaches public.

The best reason to linger here has long been the charm of crescent-shaped **Bacolet Bay Beach**, brought to the silver screen during the filming of Walt Disney's *Swiss Family Robinson*. It's a lovely spot, the white sand lapped by the vigorous green Atlantic and shaded by palms and Indian almond trees, and it remains a popular beach for local football matches. The coral reef which protects it and Scarborough ensures good swimming despite its location on the Atlantic side of the island – but be aware of the occasional dangerous undercurrents and rough seas in winter when it becomes popular with surfers. From the road concrete steps lead down the cliff side to the sand, where a thatched beach bar serves up ice-cold drinks for thirsty sun worshippers.

South of the beach, the houses thin out as Bacolet Street swings left to meet with the highway and the traffic on its way along the windward coast (see p.301).

# Eating, drinking and nightlife

Scarborough's **dining scene** offers everything from excellent low-cost meals to the most exclusive eatery. Cafés for working men and women have food on a par with the priciest restaurants, though the latter have a wider range of international options. The town's most popular **roti** outlet is at the coastal end of Dutch Fort Road in the small plaza, but many locals still opt for the foreign allure of *KFC* on Wilson and Carrington streets or stick with what they know best at *Royal Castle* on Wilson Road – the spicy fried chicken, fish or veggie burgers and fries are available till 1am Thursday to Saturday. Another fast-food favourite is the *Pizza and Roti Boys* chain – although their prices are low you pay for what you get. For drinks there are plenty of **bars** along Carrington Street well worth checking out; *King's Well Inn* at the junction with Crook's River has the best terrace from which to watch the world go by.

When it comes to **nightlife**, Scarborough is not most visitors' first choice. Those that do venture into the capital at night will find a number of lively bars and the *Crystal Palace* casino (Tues–Sun 7pm–3am), on the corner of Milford and Mount Marie roads, which offers blackjack, roulette and poker tables. There's also sometimes a sound system jam in Market Square on Friday and Saturday – late-night fun with plenty of reggae and best experienced in the company of locals.

**Aroma Salt & Pepper** Crooks River Mall. This bustling café on the mall's second floor serves basic local dishes at low prices and has great views overlooking busy King's Well below.

**Bar Code** Milford Rd ☎635 2633. Scarborough's liveliest bar, complete with big screen and free hotel pickup service.

**Blue Crab** Robinson and Main sts ☎639 2737, ⓦ www.bluecrab.com. This busy, friendly restaurant has both indoor seating and a lovely shady terrace with sea views – even though located on the edge of Main Street, it feels a million miles away from the bustle. The decently priced excellent Creole food is popular with an office crowd; highlights are the green fig salad, crab curry and the unsweetened, freshly squeezed juices. Lunch Mon–Fri 11am–3pm, dinner by reservation only.

**Ciao Café** King's Well ☎639 3001. This fantastic, popular Italian café and bar with outside terrace serves authentic cappuccino, over twenty different flavours of delicious homemade ice-cream, fine Italian wine, good beer and colourful cocktails.

**Club Renes** Wilson Street, above the *Royal Castle*. This bar is busiest every Friday and Saturday when reggae and soca is spun for a mixed but predominantly local crowd. 10.30pm–4am; small cover charge.

**East Ocean** Milford Rd ☎639 4535. The best Chinese restaurant in Tobago, overlooking the sea and offering a menu of cheap, familiar dishes. Order takeaway or eat in the a/c dining room; they also deliver large orders.

**Glendale's Local Cuisine** Glen Rd, just outside town on the north side of the highway. Huge servings of well-priced local staples, pilau, chicken and goat lure a steady stream of cars from the highway. Particularly good for lunches.

**La Belle Creole** 73 Bacolet St, ☎639 3551. This somewhat expensive restaurant of the *Half Moon Blue Hotel* (see p.286) sits on a high terrace with views out over Bacolet Bay. Open for breakfast, lunch and dinner, the evening menu offers both a la carte and set menu options and a good variety of rum cocktails.

**La Petite Patisserie** Cuyler St ☎660 7971. Cheap, delicious and authentic French pastries, bread and coffee. Freshly made cakes are available from 11am – a must is their to-die-for rum-soaked chocolate cake. Mon–Fri 7am–4pm, Sat 7am–1pm.

**MJ's** of Bacolet and Main sts. Good for a fast, affordable snack, serving vegetable pies, pastries, pizza and cakes all day – there's also Internet access upstairs.

**Mr D's** NIB Mall. Caters for vegetarians, with a daily changing menu including roti and buss-up-shut. Cheap.

**Rouselle's** Old Windward Rd, Bacolet ☎639 4738. Stylish restaurant with hardwood decor, a breezy verandah setting and relaxed sophistication reminiscent of a Port of Spain hangout. Food is chic and tasty nouvelle cuisine, with correspondingly small portions and moderately high prices. Dishes to try include lobster in lemon, white wine and garlic sauce, Creole-style fish or chicken, and charcoal-flamed pork chops with garlic and mustard; reservations are recommended for dinner. Tues–Sat 3–11pm.

**Salsa Kitchen** 8 Pump Mill Rd ☎639 1522. This fabulous and pricey restaurant has a great atmosphere and enticing menu of pizza, pasta, tapas and grilled food, along with fresh fruit juices and locally grown coffee. At weekends it livens up with nightly entertainment of Latin music and dancing. Tues–Sun 6–11pm.

**Shutters on the Bay** *Blue Haven Hotel*, Bacolet Bay ☎660 7400. On a par with any exclusive eatery in New York or London, with prices to match. A sophisticated setting with an international menu that changes daily and always includes a fresh fish, meat and vegetarian option.

# The leeward coast and Tobago Forest Reserve

Beyond Plymouth, the dramatic and sparsely populated **leeward coast** feels more wonderfully remote than any other part of the island; here, the local claim that Tobago is not just paradise, but the capital of paradise, begins to ring true. Tourist development has been minimal, with the ravishing beaches at **Castara**, **Englishman's Bay**, **Parlatuvier** and **Bloody Bay** much the same as they were decades ago. Locals still make a living off the land and sea: clusters of bobbing pirogues in every bay and seine nets drying in the sun hint at the importance of **fishing** to this area, and you'll often see machete-wielding fellows trudging the route to small-scale plantations or meandering along with a pack of hunting dogs.

Inland of Castara and Bloody Bay, the area is dominated by the steep and lush terrain of the stunning, protected **Tobago Forest Reserve**, traversed by the Roxborough-Parlatuvier Road, which connects the leeward and windward coasts. Although even the most confirmed city-dweller shoud have no trouble finding the managed trails cutting through the thick and impenetrable-looking rainforest, any in-depth exploration of its ancient interior requires an experienced guide.

Although you might assume the most direct way to the leeward coast would be the coast road from Plymouth, this is actually the slowest route, due to its twists and turns; your best bet is to take the Northside Road up from Scarborough.

**Buses**, **maxis** and **route taxis** serve the leeward coast from Scarborough (see p.286 for more details), although it is ultimately far more convenient to explore this coast and the forest preserve by **hiring a car**.

## The Northside Road

Less than a kilometre east of Scarborough on the Claude Noel Highway, the well-signposted **Northside Road** strikes right across the middle of Tobago and connects the windward with the leeward coast. Barely 50 metres down Northside Road, the right-hand turn by the bridge takes you up a narrow, near-perpendicular road to **French Fort**, the site of a Gallic garrison in the 1780s. It's now home to several towering radio transmitters and satellite pylons and the only hint of its history is a plaque nestled in the trees. The journey up to the fort is definitely worthwhile, though, for its panoramic **views** of Scarborough, Fort King George, Rockly Bay and Lowlands, the northern coast around Plymouth and Arnos Vale, and the southeast as far as Granby Point. Past the fort turn-off, the Northside Road swings past the armed guards and clipped hedges flanking the **President's House** (closed to the public), and continues its snaking climb uphill, passing through the quiet villages of **Concordia** and **Cinnamon Hill**.

Not much further along the road lies the larger and close-knit residential community of **MASON HALL**, situated about halfway between the coasts.

The village features a massive football pitch, clusters of snug gingerbread homes, a general store, roti shop and a few good drinking spots such as *Mason Hall Recreational Club* and *Pub Unique*, which often have live music on weekends. A marvellous **waterfall** is hidden on the village's outskirts. To find it, look for the roadside WASA sign for the Craig Hall water intake. Half an hour's walk from the road along the Sandy River will bring you to **Mason Hall Falls**, one of the island's tallest at about 50 metres. Taking the Craig Hall route leads you to the top of the main cascade, where there's another, smaller waterfall with a pool deep enough to jump into without touching the bottom. Darren Henry, a trained forester and licensed tour guide, leads hikes to Mason Hall Falls (2hr 30min, TT$80; ☎639 4559, ✉darren@tobagobirding.com).

If you fancy **staying** in the area, *Oasis Apartments* (☎660 7218; ➋) has a simple, somewhat shabby three-bedroom apartment with bathroom and kitchen; you can also rent on a monthly basis, though you'll need a car here if you're not to feel cut off.

## Moriah and around

Continuing north, the road begins its winding ascent of the lumpy, egg-carton-like undulations that surround **MORIAH**, a roadside village teetering at the top of a particularly steep precipice which plummets straight into a valley from the road. The views from here are superlative, with terraces on the surrounding hills supporting crops of pigeon peas and ground provisions, and Baptist prayer flags fluttering in the breeze. At the heart of Moriah are a few wonderfully decorated buildings including *D'Pan Man's* restaurant and bar and its neighbour *Randy's Night Light Saloon*, whose brightly coloured murals bring a sense of vibrancy to this small community. There are a couple of other **rum shops** well worth a visit, if only for their eccentric names and interesting decor; the *Hardest Hard Rec Club*, on the road before you enter town, has a shady outdoor section, further down the hill is *Green Corner*, a lively spot on the weekends when the DJ plays the latest tunes and local youths turn the nearby road into an impromptu disco.

On the outskirts of Moriah the *Immortelle* **hotel** (☎660 0895; ➒) has sixteen two-storey wooden cabanas spread over a hundred acres in the Woodland Hills forest behind the village. The air-conditioned cabanas are spacious with beautiful wood and stone fittings and offer prime views across the forest reserve; some have a pool and jacuzzi. Facilities include a restaurant, squash courts, health spa with gym, two bars, small boutiques and a library. Worth it if you can afford it, though you'll need a car to negotiate the windy roads down to the beach.

A potholed downhill turn-off to the left as you leave Moriah leads to **King Peter's Bay**, a seldom-visited but beautiful yellow-sand beach named after a Carib cacique. If you strike west from the beach into the bush over the next bluff you'll find an even more beautiful strip, with a good reef to boot. Past the King Peter's Bay turnoff, Northside Road heads for the coast, providing breathtaking views as you pass through the tiny communities of **Des Vignes** and **Runnemede**. Look out for a truly monumental **silk cotton** tree at the roadside; its buttressed roots are said to be haunted by jumbies (ghosts). For one of the best vistas around, turn right at the fork just after Runnemede to **Mount Dillon**, where benches are set up to admire the unravelling coastline and, on a clear day, the island of Grenada. There's also a small take-away snack shop and a colourful souvenir stall.

## Cuffie River Nature Retreat

If you're looking for a peaceful hideaway, they don't come much better than *Cuffie River Nature Retreat* in Runnemede (☎660 0505, ℱ660 0606, ℗www .cuffie-river.com; ❻). Nestled into the forest on the site of an old sugar plantation, all the large, airy and comfortable bedrooms come with en-suite bathroom, a/c, radio and balcony. There is also a fantastic honeymoon suite with panoramic views of the rainforest. Guests can make use of a swimming pool, play table tennis or relax in the lovely shared lounge areas – complete with board games and books. Its forest-facing restaurant is also open to non-residents (call ahead for reservations) and serves delicious meals, freshly prepared with local ingredients – breakfast is included in the rates, lunch is US$15 and a three-course dinner US$20. *Cuffie* also organizes a wide selection of tours and hikes of the surrounding forest, as well as island wide trips for both residents and non residents.

# Castara

As the Northside Road makes its final steep descent into **CASTARA** it passes a small layby – a perfect place to stop and admire the postcard-perfect view of the bay and village, all framed by the lush green tips of the rainforest. Castara is an attractive, easygoing fishing village that's slowly developing a nonchalant tourist-friendliness; low-key **guesthouses** are scattered on a hillside, while visitors dribble in to swim at the marvellous **beach** or splash in the nearby **waterfall**. Although the number of guesthouses is growing, Castara seems unlikely to be eaten up by resort hotels and beach bars anytime soon. Fishing remains the main earner around here, and the beach is one of the best places to participate in the pulling of a **seine net**, still in constant use by the supremely friendly posse of Rasta fishermen. The village abandons its languid air each August, when the beach is packed with revellers attending the **Castara Fishermen's Fete**, one of Tobago's biggest; the drinking, dancing, eating and swimming start at about midday and continue until well after dark.

## Accommodation

Castara is the only village along this section of coast where you'll find a choice of **places to stay**, though almost all of the guesthouses are small and located on a bluff overlooking the eastern portion of the beach. The town is becoming increasingly popular, so it's wise to reserve a room before turning up in high season. If you're stuck, finding someone to put you up in their home shouldn't be a problem.

**Blue Mango** Second Bay Rd ☎639 2060, ℗www.blue-mango.com. More upmarket than the competition, these simply furnished, stylish 1- and 2-bedroom self-contained cottages have great bay views, cool breezes, well-equipped kitchens, mosquito nets and plenty of privacy; the owners also manage two cottages at nearby Little Bay and an old wooden house perched on a hill 5 minutes' walk from the beach. The "Sea Steps" cottage is the best – a tropical dream house, with indoor and outdoor shower, sundeck overhanging your own private cove, from where you can watch dolphins and lilies growing over the entire cottage. There's also an excellent restaurant on site. ❻
**McKnight's Golden Palace** Castara Village ☎639

4664. Overlooking Castara on the eastern side of the village, these spacious, airy and basic studio apartments have kitchenette, fan and balcony, as well as great views of the forest. ❸
**Naturalist** Castara Village ☎639 5901, ℱ660 7166, ℗www.seetobago.com/tobago/resorts /natural/. Right on the beach, the small, aging rooms are well equipped and clean; all have radio, TV, private bathroom and a kitchenette; some have a/c. The extremely genial staff will cook for you on request – you can eat on their porch overlooking the beach. The name refers to nature-lovers rather than potential strippers; "no nudity" was added to the roadside advertisements after guests got the wrong idea. ❹

**Paradise Point Villa** Castara Village. no phone, ⓦwww.paradisepointvilla.com. This luxury 2-bedroom villa commanding panoramic views of Castara Bay has both a terrace and a balcony; private trails lead to a waterfall with a pool. ❾

**Sandcastles** Northside Rd ☎635 0933, ⓦww.holidaytobago.com. Opposite *Sundeck* (see below) this sand-coloured building resembling a fairytale castle houses two apartments: a family-sized one downstairs, and two rooms sharing a kitchen and lounge upstairs. Basic decor, large bathrooms and great views out to sea; the family apartment has a/c. There are also plans to build 12 villas within the next three years. ❾ for one upstairs room per week.

**Sea Level** Second Bay Rd ☎660 7311, ⓕ660 7549, ⓔirie_Horizon@hotmail.com, ⓦwww

.tobago.de. Just up the hill from the *Naturalist*, this guesthouse is the largest in the village and excellent value. All rooms have a balcony, spacious bathroom, mosquito nets and fan. They plan to open a bar and restaurant in 2005. ❹

**Sundeck Apartments** Northside Rd ☎639 1410, ⓦwww.sundeckapartments.com. This yellow-and-green building, the first hotel you'll pass on entering Castara, has compact studio apartments with kitchen, mosquito nets, huge bathrooms, TV and VCRs (two complimentary videos included); most rooms have fans, one has a/c. Ask for apartments facing the sea, which have great views. Meals provided on request. Steep hike to a private beach or 15min walk to Castara beach. There's also a lovely communal sundeck and garden complete with hammocks. Minimart on site. ❹

## The village and beaches

Straddling the Northside Road, the main body of the village consists of a post office and a few weather-beaten rum shops interspersed with simple board homes. Souvenir hunters should head for *Zingah's* on Depot Road and check out their wide selection of local arts and crafts including hats, wraps, jewellery and calabash art. A bridge at the eastern edge of town crosses the **Castara River**; a ten-minute walk southeast along the riverbed brings you to a small **waterfall** with a fairly deep swimming pool below. Crossing the playing field behind the bridge cuts the walking time, and the pool is popular among local lads cooling off after a game of football; these frenetic, foul-filled tournaments take place in the late afternoon, and often attract a small crowd of spectators.

The main focus of the town, though, is its **beach**, a generous swathe of coarse, shell- and pebble-strewn sand divided by the fast-flowing Castara River. If there hasn't been rain, the water is a joy – crystal clear and relatively calm due to the protection of the surrounding forested headlands – but during the rainy season it turns a murky brown. Flotillas of seagull-infested pirogues bob out to sea, and there's always activity around the Fishermen's Co-Op building, where the day's catch is weighed, scaled and sold; impromptu gutting usually draws a posse of mangy pot-hounds that clear up the entrails with gusto. Unfortunately for visitors, changing facilities (daylight hours; TT$1) are directly opposite the Fishermen's Co-Op.

There is another small beach close to Castara, perfect for those seeking total peace. As you drive out of the village past *Blue Mango* look out for a sharp left hand turn onto a track which, after approximately 25 metres, leads to a quiet stretch of sand. There are no facilities here except for a small café.

Of the enterprising locals who take visitors on **tours**, one of the more reliable operators is David Williams, also known as "King David" (☎660 7906, ⓦwww.kingdavidtobago.com), who offers snorkelling and fishing trips, sunset cruises and barbecues from his sun-roofed boat, providing all equipment (US$50) – if he's not around ask in the village for colleague Michael Scotland. Duck's Tours (☎660 7785) also offer fishing and snorkelling tours and organize beach barbecues. One of Tobago's most unique experiences is the Boboshanti (☎660 0005, ⓦwww.reageer.nu/boboshanti), a wooden stall on the beach where you'll find Rudi, who offers relaxing herbal steam baths (from TT$250), massages, teas and purgatives (from TT$300) and more rigorous tours of the area (US$50), taking in waterfalls and prime spots for birdwatching. The stall, usually run by his wife, is open every day except Saturday, and sells locally made batik, tie-dye and jewellery.

### Eating and drinking

There are limited places to **eat** in Castara; among them, the inexpensive *L&H Sunset*, set on a lofty patio next to the Fishermen's Co-Op, is most popular with locals. Their classic Tobagonian cooking, usually revolving around fish, is excellent; the traditional Sunday dinner of chicken, callaloo and macaroni pie is a gastronomic triumph, as is the cow heel soup. Right on the beach, *Cascreole* (☎639 5291) is a great, spacious bar and restaurant decorated with beautiful sea-themed murals and equipped with a pool table, table tennis, table football and comfy sofas. The tasty and inexpensive menu consists mainly of fish, lamb and shrimp dishes. The bar also makes a good all-day **drinking** spot, staying open as long as there are customers and often featuring live music. Intermittently open, but still worth seeking out, is *The Boathouse* (☎660 7354) a colourful, cosy, sea-shell-decorated restaurant on the edge of the beach whose daily changing menu always includes chicken and fish. Blended fruit drinks (and a rudimentary selection of fresh vegetables) are available from a stall on the hilly eastern edge of the village, and *Vera's*, a stall on the left hand side of the Northside Road as it winds out of this end of Castara, serves hot and tasty rotis. Slightly more expensive, but with friendly service and excellent food, including delicious coconut and ginger marinades, *The Clay Kitchen* at *Blue Mango* cottages is a popular hang-out for locals and tourists alike; their verandah makes for a fine setting. *Wallace's* bar on the hill by *Sea Level* (see p.297) is another congenial hangout for those who want to lime with the locals to the sound of "back-in-times" music.

## Englishman's Bay to Bloody Bay

East of Castara, houses, shops and most of the traffic melt away, and the Northside Road is flanked by enormous tufts of whispering, creaking bamboo, broken occasionally to reveal marvellous, unbelievably green, jungle-clad hilly prospects. The next worthy beach, about 1.5km along the Northside Road, is **Englishman's Bay**, hidden from the road by a thick cover of bush; look out for the blue and white sign marking a left hand turn and the gravel track which leads to the beach's small car park. Utterly ravishing and virtually undeveloped, the bay offers a perfect crescent of pure white sand, deep blue water, offshore reef and nothing else – from the sea, the forested hillside appears completely untouched, as the bush drips right down to the sand. The bay remains delightfully remote, the quintessential "deserted beach" destination of many a pleasure boat cruise. Hot meals including roti, chicken, fish and lobster are on offer, as well as ice cream, soft drinks and bamboo crafts at the fabulous *Eula's Café by the Sea* (☎639 6408), which also serves dinner by reservation, from a shack on the edge of the beach. Next door, a selection of rough-hewn stalls sell a larger range of arts, crafts and colourful wraps. There are no lifeguards here, but beach chairs can be rented from one of the stalls.

The coast road climbs upward and inland beyond Englishman's Bay, passing through the diminutive community of **Parrot Hall** after about 3 km before descending to reveal one of the most arresting views on the island: **Parlatuvier Bay** is another crescent of pearly sand flanked by an absurdly pretty hillside scattered with palms, terraced provision grounds and the odd house. The pier in the middle of the bay is testament to the village's dedication to fishing, as

are the gulls which roost on the rocks at either side of the bay, patiently await-
ing the return of the boats. **Swimming** here is a vigorous experience as waves
are usually quite strong and the water deepens sharply from the sand, be careful as there is no lifeguard on duty here.

Built around the bay, the village of **PARLATUVIER** consists of a few houses, a school and a number of shops; one sells tourist souvenirs, *Philip's Book
Centre* next to the beach sells books, stationery and phonecards, while the
other, presided over by local character Duran Chance, sells everything from
floor wax to bread and rum. Above the shop, the excellent-value *Parlatuvier
Tourist Resort* (☎639 5629; ❸) has breezy apartments with fan or a/c, bathroom, kitchen and balcony overlooking the gorgeous beach. Inexpensive and
delicious **meals** are available from *Gloria and Anthony Joseph's Riverside
Restaurant* (☎639 4935) on the Northside Road, where you get lavish portions
of local-style fresh fish, lobster or shrimp with ground provisions for about
TT$40 for lunch and TT$50–100 for dinner. Below the restaurant are a couple of dark, basic rooms to rent with fan and kitchenette (❸).

The last accessible beach on the coast – turn off the road at the large mango
tree lookout roughly 2km beyond Parlatuvier – is **Bloody Bay**, named for a
battle between English soldiers and African slaves in 1771 that was fierce
enough to turn the sea crimson with blood; Dead Bay River, which runs across
the sand and into the sea, is named for the same event. The beach itself is fine
brown sand, strewn with pebbles and driftwood and frequented by no one
except the odd fisherman. From here, directly opposite the bay and clearly visible five kilometres out to sea, the **Sisters Rocks** form an attractive cluster of
tiny, verdant islands.

Beyond Bloody Bay, the smooth tarmac continues to the lofty village of
**L'Anse Fourmi**, which is remote enough to make just the sight of a tourist a
talking point. The *Living Fountain* and *Punnet* **bars** are two good places to
refresh yourself before turning around, for past here only the bravest of drivers
and hardiest of 4WD vehicles or dirt bikes can manage the track east to
Charlotteville (see p.313). At the time of writing, however, the road was being
paved, with an estimated completion date of spring 2005.

# Tobago Forest Reserve

Swinging inland from the Northside Road at Bloody Bay, the
Roxborough–Parlatuvier Road is the route to the **Tobago Forest Reserve**
and the central mountain range. Construction of the road began in 1958 –
prior to which the two sides of the island were only linked by small trails.
However, Hurricane Flora (see box, p.300) ravaged it mercilessly five years
later, and the road was not repaired until the mid-1990s. Now it's a beautifully quiet half-hour drive through the rainforest; the tarmac is in good shape and
traffic is rare.

The reserve itself acquired its status as the oldest protected rainforest in the
western hemisphere during the plantation era, when British scientist Stephen
Hales began researching the relationship between rainfall and trees and com-
municated his findings to Soame Jenyns, a British MP responsible for the
development of Tobago. At the time, the island was abundant with flourishing
plantations concentrated in low-lying areas. Gradually, though, the planters
began encroaching on the more precipitous forest areas, felling trees for fuel or
clearing land to make way for yet more sugar cane. It took Jenyns ten years to

convince Tobago's planters that if they continued to cut down the forest, the island would soon be incapable of supporting the smallest of shrubs, let alone a massive sugar plantation. Ultimately, he was successful, and on April 13, 1776, 14,000 acres of central Tobago were designated a protected Crown Reserve.

The main point of access into the rainforest is the **Gilpin Trace**, marked by a huge slab of rock by the road in front of **Bloody Bay Lookout**, essentially just a wooden hut with benches and toilets nearby. This is a great lookout spot over the Caribbean, with views stretching all the way out to the Sisters Rocks. The 5km trail which strikes straight into the forest from here is well marked and maintained – though often very muddy – taking you through some spectacular forest dotted with huge bachac ant nests, where lianas and vines block out most of the light. The trail comes out of the forest just after the reserve boundary, towards the windward side, approximately 3km north of Roxborough – remember that it is a steep uphill walk along the road back to the start of the trail if you've parked there.

Tempting as it may be to walk this trail alone, it's advisable to hire a **guide**: you'll understand a lot more about forest dynamics, and you won't get lost. If you do decide to walk alone, remember that the sun sets quickly on the island and in addition to a rapid drop in temperature and the increased possibility of getting lost, there are also the recent incidents of tourist mugging in the rainforest to worry about. Guides are often hanging around at Gilpin Trace offering their services to tourists, but be suspicious of anyone who tries to inveigle you into a rain forest tour – not all of these guides are reputable (for recommendations, see box, opposite).

If you are looking for **refreshments** in the area there are two options before entering the rainforest. Look out for the *Inner Forest*, a restaurant and bar which also organises nature walks in the forest, and the *Rainforest Roti Shop*, along the Parlatuvier-Roxborough Road before you get to Gilpin Trace. In addition, there is sometimes a self-service fruit stall on the side of the road just before the forest boundary. For last minute souvenirs pause at *Parrot Man's Bird's Nest* colourful stall (see box, opposite). On the other side of the rainforest as the Parlatuvier-Roxborough road enters Roxborough you'll find the *Riverside Fruits & Fruit Juice Bar*, which serves excellent juices made fresh while you wait and has a bamboo terrace with superb rainforest views.

## Hurricane Flora

On September 30, 1963, **Hurricane Flora** swept over Tobago and completely devastated the island. Most of the banana, coconut and cocoa plantations were wiped out, and large tracts of the forest reserve laid to waste, with 30-metre-high trees toppling like matchsticks. The catastrophic Flora killed 30 people, injured hundreds and razed to the ground 60 percent of the island's fragile board houses. Moriah, Concordia, Argyll and Richmond were completely demolished, roads were impassable and there was no mains water or electricity outside Scarborough for more than six weeks.

A relief fund helped to repair the worst of the damage, and the United Nations provided foodstuffs that fed the population for nearly a year, while other Caribbean islands donated items as various as fevergrass (a bush remedy for colds and fevers) and roasted breadfruits. Though there are few signs of the damage left today, other than some toppled trunks in the forest reserve, the hurricane had a profound influence on Tobago's future; a tentative agricultural economy was abandoned, and the island began to devote its energy to tourism. Tobagonians still remember Flora with a shudder, but thankfully her force has not since been repeated.

Training programmes have greatly increased the number of **knowledgeable guides** in the area, most of whom are from local villages such as Parlatuvier and Roxborough. All of them are also far cheaper than the hotel-arranged guides.

The highly experienced Harris McDonald (☎639 0513, ⊛www.harris-jungle -tours.com) is recommended, as is David Rooks (☎639 4276, ⊛www.rooks tobago.com). At the *Parrot Man's Bird's Nest Café* on the Main Ridge road after the Bloody Bay junction you'll find the "Parrot Man" – Curtis James (☎660 7893) – who does a two-hour tour for TT$200 and a three-hour tour, with food and drink, for TT$500. His brother Dexter James (☎660 7852 or 639 6936) – in the second house after the Northside Road/Parlatuvier–Roxborough Road junction – is cheaper; his three-hour tour is TT$220 and 1hr 30min tour TT$120.

Alternatively try one of the guides belonging to the Nature Explorers group who offer a standard package of a 3hr trip for TT$200 and a 1hr 30min trip for TT$100: Junior Thomas (☎660 7847), Shurland James (☎660 7883 or 639 6936), Fitzroy Quamina (☎660 7836) and Darlington Chance (☎660 7828 or 7823). The only woman of the bunch, Shurland also does a 5hr hike to Charlotteville from L'Anse Fourmi (TT$450), and Fitzroy Quamina takes full moon nature hikes as well as an easy hike to Palm Tree Falls in Bloody Bay (TT$100). Another excellent woman guide is Alison Bascombe (☎660 6208) who runs rainforest, waterfall and birdwatching tours as well as fishing trips, and the colourful Mr B (☎639 4347), based out of the Inn on the Bay (see p.270), who specializes in rainforest tours.

# The windward coast

Rugged and continually breathtaking, Tobago's southern shoreline is usually referred to as the **windward coast**. It's spanned by the Windward Road, which is narrow and peppered with blind corners and potholes, sticking close to the sea, and providing fantastic views of choppy Atlantic waters and tiny spray-shrouded islands. The parade of languid coastal villages is a complete contrast to the more developed southwest; groups of limers congregate outside rum bars, ladies in curlers chat on the pavement and football games on salt-seasoned grassy pitches are the height of an afternoon's activity.

Though rip tides and strong undercurrents make some of the most attractive-looking **beaches** unsafe for swimming, there are still plenty of sheltered bays to take a dip in the cool Atlantic. Some – such as **King's Bay** – have showers and changing rooms, but more often, you'll share the sand only with fishermen. Tour buses make regular rounds, stopping off at stock attractions like **Argyll Waterfall** and period plantation home **Richmond Great House**, but most of the windward traffic is headed for the tiny village of **Speyside** and its smattering of guesthouses and small hotels. Nature is the main attraction along this coast; Speyside's **reefs** rank among Tobago's best, while the **Little Tobago** island bird sanctuary has long been a magnet for ornithologists and amateur birdwatchers alike. Fifteen minutes' drive from Speyside and directly opposite on the Caribbean coast, picturesque **Charlotteville**, with its attractive hillside houses and perfect twin beaches, is the last point of call on the windward route – the tarmac ends here, replaced by a treacherous and often impassable stretch of coastal track which divides the town from the rest of the leeward coast.

There's also plenty to see away from the firmly beaten track. You can **hike** to many of the infrequently visited waterfalls scattered throughout the hilly southern interior, passing the crumbling remains of water wheels and sugar boilers along the way, while the wetlands and rivers surrounding the central **Hillsborough Dam** are great for bird and reptile watching.

# Mount St George to Granby Point

The first stretch of highway ends abruptly a couple of kilometres east of Scarborough (see p.284), just after the Dwight Yorke football stadium – named after the national soccer hero who won a European Champions League medal with Manchester United in 1999. The last fast and straight section of road then sweeps past the glorious **Hillsborough Bay** about 2km later, where although the long stretch of windswept sand looks inviting, stick to paddling – the riptides are dangerous. Past the beach and over a narrow bridge, the road swings round a sharp corner and into tiny **MOUNT ST GEORGE**, on the eastern side of this large bay, its roadside houses with attractive flowered gardens. There's no discernible sign that this was once **Georgetown**, the island's first British **capital**, named in honour of King George III. The British began to develop Georgetown after they captured the island in 1762, building houses and a base (now destroyed) for the House of Assembly, which held its inaugural meeting here in April 1768. British occupation was short-lived, however; by 1769, they shifted the capital to Scarborough. There's still one tenuous connection to sovereignty in the town, though; set at the top of a breezy hillock overlooking the village below is the official residence of the prime minister, a seldom-used, whitewashed structure that's closed to the public. A little further into the interior is Mount St George Youth Camp, where budding bad boys are forcibly sent to learn a trade.

If you're in the mood to linger, stop on the roadside at the genial *Little Sparrow's Rest* or the easygoing *Hibiscus Bar*, right for inexpensive and tasty lunchtime roti and a cool beer. You can also **stay** at *Vicky's Guesthouse* (☎660 2089, Ⓔⓔeverace@tstt.net.tt; ❸), an expansive building west of the village that's often used for local weddings. The basic but clean rooms are of varying quality, but meals are available, and all rooms have a/c, bathroom and kitchen.

Past the main body of Mount St George, the road is littered with the small white stones that fall from trucks travelling from the Studley Park Quarry, a busy commercial enterprise that's steadily eating into the surrounding hillsides. Approximately 3km past Mount St George, a fanfare of brightly painted wooden walls and blooming flowers just before the next village, of **STUDLEY PARK**, announces the *First Historical Café*, which makes an interesting stop even if you don't need refreshment (see also below). The pet project of charming retiree Kenneth Washington, the colourful café is a shrine to the history of the island, with every inch of wall space covered with handwritten accounts of Tobago's turbulent past and local anecdotes. Be warned, however, the owner charges TT$5 to read the information on the walls and considering that you can't help but do so, all visitors are expected to pay this fee. Aside from soaking up the written word, this is a comfortable place to sit and watch pelicans taking rich pickings from the shoals of small fish inhabiting the bay; seine nets are sometimes pulled in at the small **beach** below, which you can reach from the bar.

Less than half a kilometre past the café, a right-hand turn onto a short gravel track leads to the sea at **Granby Point**. The track ends at a car park where you will find a small children's **playground** as well as a bar/restaurant. A flight of concrete steps leads off the car park and through some rather fly-infested bush to **Fort Granby**, originally built on Granby Point by the British to protect Georgetown and briefly occupied by the French between 1781 and 1787. Nothing remains of the original fortification; the cannons are long gone, replaced by pretty gazebos, mown lawns and picnic tables. The views of the sea and nearby **Smith's Island** are fantastic, and there is excellent swimming to be had on either of the **beaches** which flank the point. Barbados Bay to the left is the more populated; the fisherman's shacks on the sand make it a good spot to hang out, while the more deserted **Pinfold Bay** on the other side is a better bet if you fancy sunbathing; neither has any facilities, however, and both are only accessible from Granby Point.

Your best **food** options in the area are to be found on the Windward Road. The unmissable *Punnies Midway Bar*, a large yellow building not far from the turning, is a good place for a drink, quick snacks and a lime with the locals; while a little further along is the well-signposted *Eco Spot* (☎660 2470), also known as "the bar on the rocks", a great restaurant and bar whose views over Granby Point make up for its higher-than-average prices. The budget-priced *First Historical Café* (see above), is a good, if often painfully slow, choice; they serve breakfast from 9am, and inexpensive salads, burgers and sandwiches for lunch.

# Inland to Hillsborough Dam

To get to the birdwatchers' paradise of **Hillsborough Dam**, head inland from Mount St George or Studley Park to the often muddy and rutted Castara Road – it's a 45-minute drive from the coast that requires a 4WD vehicle. (Take note that the road doesn't actually go to Castara, tailing off into an often impassable dirt track miles from the coast.) To enter Hillsborough Dam – a man-made reservoir built to hold half of Tobago's drinking water – you are officially required to obtain a pass from the local water authority WASA, but hardly anyone bothers, clearing entrance with the security personnel on the gates instead. Though the reservoir's concrete banks are pretty unattractive, they're overhung by the thick forest which provides an ideal habitat for the herons and other waterfowl which frequent the area. A more arresting sight than the birdlife are the cayman which heave themselves onto the banks to bask in the sun; obviously, this is not a great place to swim. There are good possibilities for **river hikes** along the gentle streams which feed the reservoir, though it's best to go with a local guide (see p.246.) as you can easily lose your way.

If you push on north beyond Hillsborough, the road eventually swings west, passing small-scale farms and homes to Mason Hall (see p.294), from where you can head north for the leeward coast, or west for Scarborough and Lowlands.

# Goodwood to Pembroke

As the Windward Road swings into the tiny village of **GOODWOOD**, with its appealing gingerbread houses and neat playing field, you'll start to see the views for which the windward coast is famous – starting with a spectacular panorama of the unravelling coast and distant **Richmond Island**. On entering the village proper a large sign on the left-hand side directs you to **Genesis Nature Park & Art Gallery** (Mon–Sat 9am–6pm; US$5; ☎660 4668) where a variety of animals, including capuchin monkeys, a boa constrictor, cocoricos – the national bird of Tobago – and wild hogs (in small cages) are housed on the landscaped grounds. The entrance fee includes a complimentary drink and a tour of the grounds and the not-as-interesting art gallery, which exhibits sculptures and paintings by the owner. There's a track leading from the centre of Goodwood down to the **beach**; the palm trees and greyish sand are nothing to shout about, but it's nevertheless a pleasant place for a swim, and popular with locals.

A few kilometres up the road in **GOLDSBOROUGH**, a small village with a pretty cricket pitch by the sea, is the signposted left turn to **Rainbow Falls**, a series of privately managed cascades along the Goldsborough River, worth seeing, if you have the time. If you need a **place to stay**, *Rainbow Nature Resort* (☎/☎660 4755 or 6715, ✉rainbownatureresort@tstt.net.tt, ⊛www .smallhotelstobago.com/rainbow_nature_resort.htm; ❺) offers spacious rooms with en-suite bathroom and fan; some have TV. The quiet hotel overlooks the Tobago Forest Reserve and is just a twenty-minute walk from the falls. Rates include breakfast, and there's a restaurant and bar on site.

## Pembroke

As the houses of Goodwood recede, the road climbs into yet another Lilliputian-sized village, **PEMBROKE**, a serene fishing community spreading down to the sea from the road. It's a friendly place with a smattering of rum bars and a pretty clapboard Anglican church set on cliffs overlooking the Atlantic. As the road dips down again, there's a right-hand turn to the **beach**, which is mostly dedicated to fishing, but nice enough for a swim. Pembroke is the venue for the annual **Salaka Feast** celebrations, now an important part of the July/August Heritage Festival. A kind of African thanksgiving to ancestors, the feast commemorates the community's founding by the first slaves brought to the area, and honours obeah spirits through dancing, singing, storytelling, drumming and offerings of fruit and other foods, followed by plenty of eating and drinking.

Pembroke is a lovely place to absorb unadorned Tobagonian life, and if you want to **stay**, three self-contained apartments are available to rent at the *Paradise Villa* (☎660 4933; ❺), a real bargain that's signposted and set just off the road. None of the apartments is the height of luxury but all are scrupulously clean with two small bedrooms, a bathroom, fans and a kitchen; the airy upstairs unit comes with TV and phone; rate includes a huge breakfast. Even cheaper is the friendly *White Castle Hotel and Resort* (☎/☎660 5287; ❸), just two minutes from Pembroke's small beach; rooms are simple with fan, en-suite bathroom and kitchenette, and breakfast is included. A good place for a drink and reasonably priced seafood meals is the affordable *Kountree Forest Cocktail Lounge* (☎660 5380) on the eastern side of Pembroke. This quirky corner building perched on the rockface just beside the road was built by the owners themselves from bamboo-like Roseau wood, coconut shell and coral stone; it makes a lovely place to while away the hours with fruit bats for company and a great view over the sea. You'll have to park down the road from the restaurant, or on the almost vertical incline of parking space, as the restaurant is located on a dangerous bend.

# Richmond Great House and Argyll Waterfall

A narrow bridge not far up the Windward Road marks your entry to **Glamorgan**, a little bigger than neighbouring Pembroke and beautifully located atop its own hillock. Just out of town, the road widens, dipping down and up again through a small valley, the perfect spot to overtake any slow-moving vehicles in front of you.

On the other side of the valley is the signposted left turn for **Richmond Great House** (T/F 660 4467; ❻), a hotel, restaurant and essential point of call for almost all of the tour buses that travel the Windward Road. Built of solid brick and whitewashed board in the eighteenth century, it was the great house of the old Richmond sugar estate, and offers fantastic views over the jungle-smothered interior hills. It's now owned by Professor Hollis Lynch, a Tobagonian who used to lecture at Colombia University, and his extensive collection of African art and textiles is on display; tours (daily 10am–4pm; TT$15) are available. You can also visit for lunch, but you'll need to call ahead for dinner; prices run high. The colonial-style bedrooms are gorgeous and cool with varnished wood floors and a private bathroom, and there's a pool and tennis courts on site. Rates include breakfast.

Beyond Richmond, the Windward Road passes the Richmond water works on the right. The small budget café on the left, *Caribbean Splendour* (Mon–Sat 7am–7pm), serves delicious roti, buss-up-shut and inexpensive local dishes and fruit juices. The road then returns to the coast at the tiny village of **Belle Garden**. Another few kilometres further along Carapuse Bay will take you to the village of Argyll, just beyond which a cache of guides is always waiting at the entrance road to **Argyll Waterfall** (daily 7.30am–5pm), waving frantically for you to stop. To access the falls, turn off the road and follow a muddy but easily passable cocoa tree-lined path to a grassy parking lot where you'll see the clapboard booth of the Co-Op offices. Here, you can buy soft drinks and snacks, pay the entrance fee (TT$30 for adults, TT$10 children) and hire a guide (TT$30); doing so is recommended, as they point out birds and flowers and show the way to the less accessible cascades – a tip is expected. Unofficial guides will charge anything up to TT$80. The official guides, who carry IDs and wear khaki uniforms, work for the Roxborough Visitor Service Co-Operative Society (T 660 4154)

The falls themselves are a pleasant fifteen-minute walk away, and you can hear the water long before you reach it. Argyll is the island's highest waterfall, tumbling 54 metres out of the greenery into a deep pool. Even though it is also one of Tobago's most accessible falls, to see the best parts you'll have to exert yourself a little and climb up the right-hand side along steep and sometimes bushy paths. There are three main cascades; the second is particularly strong – increased flow during the rainy season creates a constant fine mist that soon soaks you to the skin. The second tier is great for a dip in a natural jacuzzi, as there are plenty of rocky seats on which to perch and get a pounding shoulder massage. If you're feeling energetic, you can climb up even further to the deepest swimming pool – and the smallest section of waterfall – where you can dive or swing in Tarzan-style on a vine. If the climb doesn't appeal, you can drive right up to the highest swimming spot.

△ Turtle Beach

# Roxborough

The **ROXBOROUGH** environs are **cocoa** country; just before you enter town on the main road, half a kilometre past the Argyll Falls turn off, a left fork cuts straight through the old Roxborough Estate, one of Tobago's largest plantations – home of the only working cocoa house remaining from the colonial era in the Caribbean. Sadly, cocoa is a declining industry these days, as local youth turn away from agriculture in favour of the easy money to be made in tourism. The cocoa estate road swings back to the Windward Road at the outskirts of town, adjacent to the expansive fire station and community centre, and the inland **Roxborough-Parlatuvier Road**, the route north through the forest reserve and to the Caribbean coast.

Roxborough is the largest town along this section of the coast. Its main drag runs parallel to the sea, although – unlike almost everywhere else on the windward parade – there are also a few residential streets stretching inland. Despite the profusion of small shops, including a small minimart and *KiTambi's* who sells inexpensive clothes and batik, a large stadium and even a petrol station, it's a peaceful and friendly place, though that hasn't always been the case. In the hard times that followed emancipation, Roxborough was the scene of the infamous and bloody **Belmanna Riots** (see box, below). Apart from filling up your gas tank, there's no real reason to stay here; the **beach** is nothing special and beyond a few low-key rum bars there's little to do.

If you want to linger, you should be able to find someone who's willing to put you up. Ask for *Carter's* **guesthouse** on Roberts Street. Good **places to eat** are thin on the ground; try the *Pelican View Atlantic Beach* restaurant on the main road for budget chicken sit-down meals, *Mus Be Molly* for pies and fish and chips or *Beat the Heat* for ice cream. Delicious blended fruit drinks are sold from a roadside kiosk at the town end of the cocoa estate road. As you leave the town, you can get a good overview of some local blooms and fruit trees at Louis D'Or Nursery, just outside Delaford (open daily, daylight hours, free).

## The Belmanna uprising

Disgusted with the low pay and abysmal working conditions which dogged the ailing sugar industry after emancipation, African plantation workers from the Roxborough Estate **revolted** in 1876, burning down the estate manager's home and rioting in the streets with such vigour that one of their comrades was killed by police. Enraged, the workers surrounded the police station and demanded that the chief officer, Colonel Belmanna – whom they held responsible for the death – should come out and confront them. Unwisely, he did; the mob descended, gouging out his eyes, mutilating his body and beating him to death. As the ranks of the workers swelled with sympathizers from surrounding villages, the unrest continued. Hopelessly outnumbered, the police could do little but retreat and call for external assistance; it came a week later in the form of a British warship, which transported hundreds of the dissenters to Scarborough, where they were slammed into jail and put on trial, most receiving a life sentence or banishment from the island.

The riot left self-governed Tobago in turmoil. Feeling they had completely lost control of the island and its predominantly black population, and fearing total chaos, the Legislative Council swiftly washed their hands of the whole affair and handed the running of Tobago back to the British. On January 1, 1877, Tobago became a Crown Colony, but the Belmanna repercussions were not to be quelled so easily. Continual unrest that followed throughout the island contributed to the final collapse of the sugar industry and the overall economic decline which led to the official coupling of Trinidad and Tobago in 1879.

# King's Bay

Turning inland past Roxborough, the Windward Road swings through the hilltop village of **Delaford**, making one almighty bend at the outskirts to reveal a breathtaking view of the spiky coconut plantation surrounding the beautiful, deep blue **King's Bay** below. In the midst of a cool green arbour of cocoa trees at the bottom of the next hill is the spacious parking lot for **King's Bay Waterfall** (daily, no set hours; free). The most heavily manicured of any on the island, the waterfall was presented as a gift to the nation in 1987 by Delaford philanthropists James and Dorothy Rosenwald. It's a five-minute walk to the falls along a neat pathway well cropped by cattle. Sadly, the actual cascade is a disappointment; damming has drastically reduced the flow of King's Bay River, reducing the waterfall to a shadow of its former glory. The worn rocks are the only sign that a torrent once crashed down on them, but nowadays you're unlikely to see more than a trickle, even at the height of the rainy season. The once-deep pool at the base is murky and stagnant, and the only fun to be had is climbing the thirty metres to the top.

A far more satisfying time is to be had at **King's Bay beach** (daylight hours; free), one of the few beaches along the windward coast to provide changing facilities (TT$1 to enter) – turn off at the large sign for *Pedro Point Rest & Bar*, just past the waterfall. With gentle waters, reefs and fine dark sand, King's Bay is one of the best beaches in the area, but apart from a handful of bathers, it's mostly favoured by fishermen, and is a great place to watch – and participate in – the pulling in of a seine net. The profusion of Carib Indian artefacts found here (on display at the Tobago Museum – see p.291) indicate that King's Bay was once the site of a large settlement; some suggest that the bay is named after Carib cacique (chief) King Peter, though it's more likely that that honour goes to King Peter's Bay on the north coast (see p.295).

## Practicalities

For **accommodation** in the King's Bay area, there are a couple of basic places nearby. Just before the King's Bay cocoa plantation, 2km past Roxborough, a road branches off to the sea, identifiable by the signs promoting a variety of guesthouses. This road leads down to Delaford Beach – a smaller beach frequented by locals and fishermen. Follow the rocky road for a couple of minutes until you reach a junction opposite a bar; turn left to reach *Ocean View Cottage* (☎660 4220; ❸), where the clean but basic small rooms have fan and en-suite bathroom, and are steps away from the sea. The owner of *Ocean View* also has rooms for the hard-pressed traveller at the *Sea Gardens Guest House* (signposted on the main road as *Restrite*; ❸). Set on a rather raggle-taggle section of the otherwise beautiful Delaford Beach, the two rooms are small, dark and a bit downat-heel, but the waves lap on your doorstep. Both have patio space, two tiny bedrooms, shower and rudimentary kitchenette. *Crab Inn* (☎660 4285; ❷) on the other side of the bay at King's Bay Beach, also has basic rooms for rent; ask for Mr James Edwards. If you don't want to feel isolated staying here, you'll need your own car – the nearest shops and **restaurants** are in Speyside or Delaford. At Delaford, try *King's Bay Café* ("we specialise in freshness"), beautifully situated with a sweeping view of the bay from the back verandah, where hot meals, snacks, pastries, espresso and cappuccino are served at budget prices. A little further down the road behind *Liz Café & Bar* is the *Riverside Guesthouse* (☎660 4383; ❸), just five minutes' walk from King's Bay Beach, with two rooms – clean and basic with a fan and en-suite bathroom – available to rent.

# Speyside

The coast swings out of view as the road turns inland beyond King's Bay and through lush hills and green valleys broken only by the odd roti shack. Constant hairpin bends and a steep incline make the going pretty treacherous, so if you're driving, don't let your surroundings become too much of a distraction. However, it's hard not to get sidetracked by the amazing view which opens up as you round the last corner before the descent into **SPEYSIDE**. From the bench-dotted **lookout** point, marked by a colourful souvenir stall, you get a marvellous panorama of the town, the turquoise waters of **Tyrrel's Bay** and the stunning sight of **Little Tobago** and **Goat Island**. There's good forest hiking to be had along Murchiston Trace, a tiny road that strikes off to the right from the Windward Road just before the Speyside lookout; ask in the village for a local guide.

## Accommodation

With plenty of demand for **rooms** with marvellous views and the sea as background music, you'll need to book well in advance if visiting during the high season. If you turn up with nowhere to stay, head for the small orange and blue tourist **information shop** just before the right hand turn to the beach facilities. They will be able to advise you on accommodation options in both Speyside and the whole of Tobago. If you get stuck without a roof over your

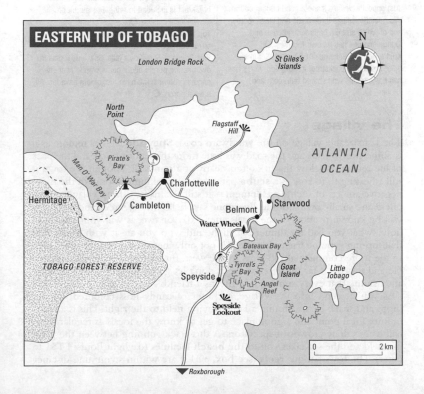

head, just ask around in the village; there are a number of non-registered guesthouses and if you get stuck for accommodation someone will probably be willing to put you up in their home.

**Blue Waters Inn** Bateaux Bay ⊤660 4341 or 4077 or 2583, ⓕ660 5195, ⓦwww.blue watersinn.com. Speyside's largest and grandest hotel, set around the semi-private and totally stunning Bateaux Bay, is separated from the village by a steep walk. All rooms are spacious, with rattan furniture, batik decor, a/c, porch and a sea view; choose from a standard unit or 1- and 2-bedroom self-catering rooms and bungalows. There's a restaurant, bar, dive shop and tennis court as well as 200,000 square metres of lush tropical grounds with two nature trails. Use of kayaks, and sun-tanning beds are all free. Popular with divers – this is a PADI International Gold Palm Resort and Training Facility. ❽

**Country Haven Guesthouse** Main Rd, Speyside ⊤660 5901, ⓦwww.caribinfo.com/countryhaven. Three cramped rooms in a family-run guesthouse perched on Speyside's hillside; all have fan, mosquito net and en-suite bathroom, some have kitchenette. ❸

**Davis Atlantic View** Main Rd ⊤/ⓕ660 4231. Just opposite *Jemma's* and a good budget option, this guesthouse has three basic and clean rooms, two of which have a bathroom, kitchen and lounge and one has its own facilities. ❺

**Kurt's** Housing Scheme ⊤660 4232. Set in a quiet residential backstreet in Speyside, *Kurt's* has two basic rooms with shared bathroom and kitchen. ❹

**Manta Lodge** Main Rd ⊤660 5268, ⓕ660 5030, in US ⊤800/544 7631, ⓦwww.mantalodge.com. Colonial-style luxury catering for scuba enthusiasts. Standard rooms are small but stylish with ceiling fan and balcony; "superior" rooms provide more space and a/c, while the quirky attics have the lot plus a private sundeck on the roof. There's a good restaurant (breakfast included in the rates), pool and dive shop on site, and you can access the nature trails which network the grounds. ❼

**Speyside Inn** Main Rd ⊤/ⓕ660 4852, ⓦwww.caribinfo.com/speysideinn/. Simple and beautifully styled with priceless bay views, and accommodation options that vary from a circular tower to octagonal corner rooms; all have bathroom, balcony and fan. There's an excellent restaurant on site (rates include breakfast) and good swimming is just a step away. ❼

**Suncrest** Main Rd ⊤660 6027. Perfect bay views, lively and popular with a young crowd. Three of the four rooms overlook the sea; all have a/c and bathroom. The bar below can mean late-night noise; breakfast is included in rates. Restaurant on site serves local cuisine. ❹

**Top Ranking Hill View Guesthouse** Main Rd ⊤/ⓕ660 4904, ⓦwww.caribinfo.com/toprank. Pink house in Speyside's hills. Spacious rooms in overbearing purple decor come with kitchenette and bathroom; some have a/c, others have fan. All have a porch. ❹

# The village

The last sizeable village on the windward coast, **Speyside** feels as remote as it is; some twelve years ago the road was little more than a dirt track, and the pace of life remains so slow that it's often nearly at a standstill. Though the town is still adjusting to its role as a **scuba** paradise – and taking on some of the more negative aspects of such development – it still retains its fishing village atmosphere and small-town attitude. Everyone says hello on the street, and your face will be known to most of the locals after a day or two, as will your choice of hotel, what you had for dinner last night and who you ate it with. You'll find that forging genuine friendships here is not only inevitable but a lot easier than in the more commercialized areas to the west. Interaction between local people and tourists is far more relaxed, but don't let go of all your common sense and assume that every smiling face means a friend.

As you descend into the village, a cluster of candy-floss coloured grocery shops and snack bars surround a large playing field to the right. This is a community focal point and a good place to get to know the locals as regular football games draw crowds of spectators. A dirt track running between the playing field and the sea takes you to the **beach** facilities (daylight hours; TT$1 to enter). The bay's famous **reefs** (see box, p.312) are within swimming distance from here and it's also a good place to organize a **fishing** trip aboard a local pirogue; the fishermen will also be happy to take you to Little Tobago for in excess of TT$75, though if you're interested in birdwatching, it's probably better to go in more expert company (see p.312).

Carrying on along the main road brings you into the main village, a short parade of small shops and a couple of bars. Past the next corner is what could loosely be termed the tourist strip, though expect concrete and neon. In Speyside, tourism means **diving**, so the strip consists of several dive shops, some hotels and a couple of restaurants, including the famous *Jemma's* – built into a tree overlooking the sea. *Jemma's* also sells local flavoured coffee and food products, while other tourist trinkets can be purchased from the two craft stalls opposite, which both carry the usual bamboo, calabash and coconut craft items.

Just past *Manta Lodge* hotel, the road forks; left takes you across the island's interior and on to Charlotteville (see p.313), while the right turn is the route to the astonishingly blue waters and rich reefs of **Bateaux Bay**, site of the luxurious *Blue Waters Inn*; north of this point the coast is almost completely uninhabited. The road to picturesque **Belmont** and **Starwood** bays is often impassable; if so, ask a local fisherman to take you aboard a pirogue. Both bays offer great snorkelling and diving.

## Little Tobago and Goat Island

Of the two misshapen islets sitting five kilometres or so out in Tyrrel's Bay, **Goat Island** is the closer. You'll see one white house nestled in its centre, built as the Tobagonian holiday home of Caribbean devotee Ian Fleming, author of the James Bond novels. The house and the island are privately owned and closed to the public. However, birdwatchers and hikers flock to the larger island, **Little Tobago**, a kilometre further out to sea. The most easterly point of the T&T republic, the two-square kilometre outcrop has been known as "Bird of Paradise Island" since the beginning of the twentieth century, when it was bought by keen ornithologist Sir William Ingram. In 1909 he transported 24 **greater birds of paradise** (*Paradisaea apoda*) from Aru island in New Guinea. Over the years, however, the birds were slowly extinguished by hurricanes and hunters. When Sir William died in 1924, his heirs gave Little Tobago back to the government on condition that it receive protected status. It has remained a bird sanctuary ever since, uninhabited except for one of the Caribbean's largest seabird colonies, which includes impressive flocks of frigate birds, boobies, terns and the spectacular red-billed tropic bird. You'll also hear the crows and clucks of feral cocks and chickens brought here by the now-departed resident caretaker, who was unable to round up his private flock before leaving the island.

Several trails cut during the island's brief spell as a cotton plantation mean there are good possibilities for **hiking**, though as Little Tobago is only 1.5km long at its widest point, these are hardly marathon treks. Make sure you have enough drinking water with you, however, as no refreshments are available. All the boats dock at a small beach facing the mainland, from where you get beautiful views of the town and Pigeon Hill above, one of Tobago's highest points. Here, there's a wooden shelter with toilets, benches, tables and a long list of dos and don'ts for visitors: no smoking, squatting or fires and so on. Concrete steps lead up the hillside, passing the ramshackle caretaker's house, long-deserted but still displaying framed posters of Little Tobago's most common bird species. Well-signposted trails lead off from here through the dry and scrubby

Speyside's main attractions are the amazingly rich coral **reefs** which network Tyrrel's Bay. Generally pristine with little sign of bleaching or human damage, the reefs flourish on a rich diet of nutrients flowing in from Venezuela's mighty Orinoco River along the Guyana Current, ensuring a huge variety of marine life and some dazzling hues among the coral. Speyside also boasts one of the world's largest **brain corals**, an awesome four metres high and six metres across. Apart from the regular shoals of small fish – butterfly, grunt, angel, parrot and damselfish – the currents also attract a number of deep-water dwellers, including **nurse sharks**, **dolphins** and, most notably, **manta rays**. These regular visitors are usually around seven metres long, and are so accustomed to the divers' touch that it's now common practice to hitch a ride by grabbing on to the body just beside the horns – known as taking a "Tobago Taxi", though this is not recommended. Local operators claim that as the mantas make the first approach, they actually enjoy contact with humans, particularly a scratch on the back.

The **most popular Speyside dive sites** include Japanese Gardens, Angel Reef, Bookends and Blackjack hole, and most dives are of the drift variety. Operators to trust are Tobago Dive Experience at *Manta Lodge* (T660 5268, Wwww.tobago diveexperience.com); the first operator to set up in the area, Aquamarine Dive at *Blue Waters Inn* (T660 4341, Wwww.aquamarinedive.com) who are also the most expensive; Tobagonian-owned Tobago Dive Masters next to *Jemma's* (T639 4697); and *Redman M Dive* (T660 6117, Eredmanm_dive@yahoo.com) next door to *Redman's* restaurant. For sample prices see box, p.248. All of these operators rent **snorkel** equipment for around US$10 per day, and *Aquamarine* offer snorkelling tuition for a rather inflated US$55 per person.

**Glass-bottom boats** are a good way to see the reefs if you don't want to get wet, though you can always jump overboard for a spot of snorkelling as well. Frank's (T660 5438), based at *Blue Waters Inn*, offers a basic tour with snorkelling at Angel Reef (US$15), drift snorkelling at Little Tobago (US$17), as well as a boat tour around St Giles Island (US$35). Top Ranking Glass Bottom Boat (T660 4904), also at the inn, offers reef and snorkelling and a trip to Little Tobago (US$17), reef tour and snorkel (US$14) and reef tour alone (US$12). Fear Not (T660 4654), based at *Jemma's*, also do inexpensive Angel Reef tours (1hr 30min; US$14).

landscape; head for the cliffside nesting grounds of the red-billed tropic bird, where a lookout point provides sweeping views and an opportunity to see birds up close. To get the most from the guide, hire an experienced guide, such as David Rooks (T639 4276, Wwww.rooks-tobago.com), the man who persuaded David Attenborough that Little Tobago was sufficiently unique to be included in his famous BBC *Trials of Life* documentary. For other firms, see the box on Speyside watersports, above.

# Eating and drinking

Speyside isn't exactly a metropolis even during the high season, but in the low season, you'll find the town pretty much deserted as some of the cafés and dive operators close up shop. It is always advisable to make dinner reservations for Speyside **restaurants** as they are busy during the high season and sometimes won't cook unless guests are assured during the low season.

**Birdwatcher's Rest and Bar** Main Rd. Unmissable red, gold and green café with indoor and outdoor eating areas. Friendly staff serve all the usual staples of chicken, fish and Creole dish-

es as well as a range of sandwiches and hot dogs. Good food at good prices.
**Fish Pot** *Blue Waters Inn* T660 4341. Designed with American package tourists in mind, the menu

is somewhat bland resulting in average-tasting, expensive seafood. The setting is pleasant though, decorated with fishermen's accessories and windows overlooking Bateaux Bay.

**Green Moray** *Manta Lodge* ☎ 660 5268. Well-executed seafood cooked for international tastes. The menu includes lobster, shrimp, kingfish and shark in an exclusive setting. The restaurant is open for breakfast, lunch and dinner and the bar is open all day.

**Jemma's Treehouse** Main Rd ☎ 660 4066. Popular with every island tour bus, this place perches crazily in the boughs of a tree with a fantastic sea view and serves decently priced tasty Creole-style food. Breakfast (Sun–Thurs 9am–9pm, Fri 9am–4pm) is eggs, bacon or local fish dishes; lunch (available until 4pm) includes breadfruit or eggplant casserole, tannia fritters, fried plantain and salad; and dinner – fish, lobster and shrimp – is excellent, as are the puddings.

**Marlene's** Main Rd. On the right hand side as you enter Speyside, this white shack serves great roti.

**Paradise Cuisine & Beer Garden** Main Rd, opposite *Suncrest* bar in the main village. Simple, inexpensive café/bar good for quick snacks, pies, rotis, alcohol and light refreshments.

**Redman's** Main Rd. This basic restaurant in the attractive blue building next door to *Jemma's* has a lovely sea facing terrace. Open for breakfast, lunch and dinner and serves a range of local dishes at low prices.

**Speyside Inn** Main Rd ☎ 660 4852. This inn's onsite restaurant features lots of imaginatively cooked local ingredients: chicken with mango and banana and excellent coconut shrimp, as well as a mean chocolate cake and key lime pie; moderately expensive.

**Suncrest** Main Rd ☎ 660 6027. Popular with locals, this lively bar, decorated with a fish and diving mural, blasts soca music all day long. Dark interior, at night it becomes the local hotspot. No food.

# Charlotteville

From Speyside, the Windward Road strikes inland on its way from the Atlantic to the Caribbean coast, climbing steeply upward through jungle-like mountain foliage before plummeting down to the opposite shoreline. Tobago's most easterly portion of tarmac marks the last sign of "civilization"; northeast of here, the countryside is completely undeveloped, with no electricity or piped water for the hardy handful of small-scale farmers, bush hunters and fishermen. Just before the descent to the Caribbean, there's a stunning perspective of Charlotteville and the sea from **Flagstaff Hill**; to get there, take the signposted right turn from the main road – though be aware it's quite bumpy and may require 4WD in the rainy season. At the crest of the hill, the road opens up to reveal a battered coastguard's hut and tall navigational beacon, a swathe of grass with a covered gazebo and a fantastic view of Man O' War Bay, Booby Island, Cambleton Battery and, much further out, Sisters Rocks. This excellent vantage point was once used by British and French soldiers, who used mirrors to warn their colleagues stationed at Cambleton Battery below of an approaching ship.

As the Windward Road begins its seaward plunge, the absurdly pretty fishing town of **CHARLOTTEVILLE** swings into view; houses tumble willy-nilly down a hillside met by calm Caribbean waters, while frigate birds swoop overhead and hissing cicadas keep up a constant refrain. Snugly situated under the protective cover of two-kilometre-wide **Man O' War Bay**, Charlotteville is one of Tobago's foremost fishing communities – more than 60 percent of the island's total catch is brought in by local fishermen. Bordered on each side by steep forested hills, the town has an isolated feel, as though time were suspended and commercial concerns put aside. Though the tourist dollar is steadily encroaching upon this self-contained, tight-knit community, the atmosphere is still so friendly that it's hard not to relax. Indeed, Charlotteville is known as a place where visitors come for one night only and stay for months.

Despite its small–town atmosphere and "end of the road" feel, Charlotteville, with its 5000 residents, is actually one of Tobago's biggest communities and one of its oldest, first settled by Caribs and then by the Dutch in 1633 – for many years the bay was known as Jan De Moor Bay after an early Frisian occupant. During the plantation era, the area was divided into two successful estates, Pirate's Bay and Charlotteville; sugar shipments made regular departures from the bay, and the town prospered. In 1865, both estates were purchased by the Turpin family, who still own much of the surrounding land.

## Accommodation

Between December and April it's wise to book ahead for **accommodation**, as guesthouses fill up quickly in what is fast becoming Tobago's most popular retreat. To cope with demand, many local residents rent out rooms during high season, so if you find yourself without accommodation, ask around for possibilities, or call any of the numbers listed in the box, opposite.

**Banana Boat** 6 Mac's Lane ☎660 6176, ⓦwww.banana-boat-tobago.com. This quirky, brand-new hotel is a great budget option. Set on the edge of the beach, it has eight basic and unusual rooms all with ensuite, fans or a/c and banana related décor, as well as one king size, sea-facing room with mini fridge. Free airport transfers are included for stays of seven nights or more. A bar and restaurant can be found on site and vehicle hire, nature and forest tours, boat trips and diving can all be arranged with the fluent German-, French- and English-speaking owner. ❸

**Belle Aire Cottage** Belle Aire St ☎/ⓕ660 5984. One hundred metres up the road from the Pirate's Bay track, these basic, white-painted rooms have fan, en-suite bathroom and fridge. All have porches and shared kitchen and dining room. ❹

**Charlotte Villa** North Side Rd, Cambleton ☎660 5919, ⓦwww.travel-tobago.net/cvilla.htm. A small, simply decorated place, just two minutes from Man O' War Bay, with one apartment with two bedrooms (with double beds) and one bedroom (with twin beds), fans, kitchen and en-suite bathroom. ❹

**Cholson Chalets** Man O' War Bay ☎/ⓕ639 8553. Completely charming green and white houses overlooking the beach at the Pirate's Bay end of town. The deliciously antiquated feel of the six simple rooms makes the basic romantic: muslin curtains and wooden floors, fans, private bathroom, optional maid service and a few kitchenettes; the upstairs flat is most appealing. Advance booking is recommended. ❺

**Green Corner Villa** Pirate's Bay Track, ☎660 5991. This basic but friendly guesthouse next door to *Gails* has small rooms, one ensuite, and all with shared kitchen. ❹

**Man-O-War Bay Cottages** Man O' War Bay ☎660 4327, ⓕ660 4328, ⓔpturpin@tstt.net.tt,

ⓦwww.man-o-warbaycottages.com. Situated right on the bay in pretty landscaped gardens, the cottages are different shapes and sizes, with one to four bedrooms. All have fan, bathroom, hot water and kitchen, simple but attractive decor, books on the shelves, driftwood ornaments and an overwhelming feeling of peace. There's also a small commissary on site. Hiking tours are available and the maid/cook service is optional and costs extra. ❻

**Mitchell Alleyne** Belle Aire St ☎660 4423. Pleasant rooms, simply decorated, with fan, shared toilet, shower and kitchen. Five metres from Pirate's Bay track and convenient to the best beach in the area, making this option a bargain. ❷

**Moore's Guesthouse** Belle Aire St ☎660 4749. Located on the hillside overlooking the bay, meaning you'll need strong legs to get there, *Moore's* has large, basic rooms and shared kitchen, lounge with plastic-covered sofa and simple bathroom. ❹

**Ocean View** 11 Mission Rd ☎660 4891. These small cosy rooms perched on Charlotteville's hillside and overlooking the serene Man O' War Bay each have fan, en-suite bathroom and small kitchen, done in typical Tobagonian decor. ❹

**Pirate Bay Eco Home** Pirates Bay ☎631 0266. At the top of a steep path, with no access for vehicles, 20 minutes from the village, this inexpensive option has 4 2-bedroom apartments, which are spacious, rustic, clean and set amongst fruit gardens. ❹

**Top River Apartments** 32–34 Spring St ☎660 6011, ⓕ660 6011, ⓦwww.topriver.com. This lovely new accommodation, away from Charlotteville's main seafront area, offers well maintained self contained apartments with ceiling fans, and a large communal sun deck complete with hammocks and views of the bay; the downstairs cappuccino bar is a pleasant place to hang out. Hiking, deep-sea fishing, rainforest tours, diving and snorkelling can all

## Additional Charlotteville accommodation numbers

Almondoz: ☎639 2631
Cambleton House: ☎660 2217
Mrs Budd: ☎660 5607

Mrs McKenna: ☎660 4446
Mr James: ☎660 5605
Sharon's: ☎660 5036

be arranged for guests. **❺**
**Uncle Man's Castle**, c/o Sherryl, 29 Belle Aire St
☎660 6073. Two basic rooms in the friendly

host's home overlooking Charlotteville harbour.
Furnished with ceiling fan and shared kitchen and
bathroom. **❹**

# The village

If you're seeking peace, quiet and great beaches, it's hard not to become utterly besotted with Charlotteville. The "town centre" with its hole-in-the-wall shops, petrol station (Mon–Sat 6am–8pm and Sun 6am–11am & 8.15pm–8.30pm), post office, and sprinkling of restaurants sticks close to the sand; the streets that stretch uphill form the residential section. There's little to actually do here but enjoy the sea, whether you arrange a **fishing** trip aboard the many pirogues which moor up in the bay, or just while away the hours on the fine brown sand of **Man O' War Bay beach** – site of Tobago's most popular fisherman's fete, held to celebrate St Peter's Day. The bay is clean, calm and inviting, with good snorkelling and changing/shower facilities (daylight hours; TT$1) as well as a lively beach bar and restaurant. Just past the main swimming area is the busy Charlotteville **Fishermen's Co-Operative** building, with its blackboard displaying the day's catch alongside messages to its members. Benches along the sea wall, the fishing pier and a covered pavilion are popular liming spots, great for fishermen to dry their nets and anyone soaking up the village scene. Maurice Alleyne sells his beautifully handcrafted calabashes from a small stall called *Jah One* behind the pavilion.

Beyond the square, the coastal street turns inland, but a dirt track continues along the shoreline to the town's – and Tobago's – most attractive beach, **Pirate's Bay**. At the bottom of a long concrete stairway, you're rewarded with a stunning horseshoe of calm emerald green water and fine yellow sand, with a backdrop of trees, ferns and foliage. A tumbledown fisherman's hut and a smart pair of pit toilets are the only buildings in sight, and there's even a freshwater rinse, courtesy of a stream trickling down from the hills. The bay's translucent waters offer fantastic **snorkelling**, especially on the left-hand side. The seventeenth-century buccaneers after whom the bay was named may have gone, but the bay still has its freebooters, a large colony of **frigate birds**, which feed by snatching recently caught fish from the beaks of smaller seabirds. These, and other birds such as terns and pelicans can be found at St Giles Island a few kilometres to the north, but strong currents make it difficult for small boats – and thus birdwatchers – to get there.

In terms of practicalities, **Internet** access is available at *De Maximum*, a small shack opposite *Green Corner Villa*, which also organizes mobile phone rental, and *Pioneer Net Café* (from 9am Sun–Fri) next door to the *Banana Boat*. **Buses** from Charlottesville to Scarborough, serving the whole windward coast, depart at 8am, 10am, 11am, 2pm, 4pm, 7pm and 8pm (TT$8). This timetable is very flexible, however, so be prepared to wait around and if you have to get back to Scarborough it is advisable not to rely on catching the 8pm bus which is infamous for not turning up at all. In addition, Charlotteville's isolation is not just one of its attractions, but also a huge drawback in an **emergency**, as it can take quite a while for an ambulance to reach the town – if you're really stuck the *Banana Boat* staff are first-aid trained.

## Cambleton Battery

Reached via a steep and potholed lane striking off from the main road on the western outskirts of town, **Cambleton Battery** (no set hours; free) was built by the British in 1777, who placed two cannons here to defend against attack from marauding American warships; the sweeping views of Charlotteville, Booby Island and Pirate's Bay explain why they chose this site. It's now a popular cooling-off spot for locals, who lime away under the shade of the gazebo. Past the battery, the track continues upward, but if you're driving, it's wise to go no further than the sign that warns "treacherous road – proceed at your own risk". If you have a dirt bike or 4WD vehicle, you can proceed as far as the next bay, **Hermitage**, without too much trouble, but bear in mind that almost all of the island's rental companies will hold you fully responsible for any damage incurred along this stretch, and though it's attractively deserted with a shingle beach and plenty of washed up flotsam, the bay isn't really worth the trouble; rip tides also make swimming precarious. If you do decide to attempt the full stretch, it will take about an hour to cover the three kilometres to **L'Anse Fourmi**, where the tarmac begins again and will take you eventually to Bloody Bay (see p.299). At the time of writing, this stretch of road was being improved and was due to be completed in spring 2005 at the earliest; until then it is not advisable to attempt to drive on this road.

## Eating and drinking

Though many of the available accommodations are self-catering, Charlotteville offers limited **food shopping**. Basic needs are covered by two minimarts – one of which is a decent size – and shops and fruit stalls along Man O'War Bay and Main Street; you can buy fresh fish daily from the Fishermen's Co-Operative. **Restaurant** pickings have improved in recent years, though opening times can be erratic. *Gails*, by the Pirate's Bay track, serves excellent, inexpensive local food for breakfast and dinner, while budget-priced *Eastman's* by the town square has a catch of the day with chips, burgers and sandwiches, served up on a verandah overlooking the fishing pier. Small parlours on the beach front – such as *Lyda's*, a striking blue shack next to *Cholston Apartments* – sell roti and the popular fish or chicken and chips; and good coffee, fresh milkshakes and ice cream are served at *Top River Pear's* (Mon–Sat 8.30am–6.30pm) cappuccino bar on Spring Street.

On the other side of town, *G's* (8.30am–9pm) serves a good selection of local dishes and has a nice little bamboo shelter for those who want to eat whilst

## Watersports in Charlotteville

If you want to visit the excellent **scuba diving** sights in the area, the only reputable local operator is Man Friday (☎660 4676, ✉mfdiving@tstt.net.tt; ⊛www.man fridaydiving.com) near Man O' War Bay beach. They offer resort and certification courses, single dives and packages, and rent out single and double **kayaks** (US$30/45 per day) and **snorkelling equipment** (US$8 per day). Locally run Workshop Sea Tours (☎683 4069, wkshoptours@excite.com) offer fishing trips for US$25 per hour as well as offshore island tours and bird and dolphin watching expeditions. Tobago Sea Kayak Experience (☎771 4247, ⊛www.seakayaktobago.com) also provide kayaking tours and instruction – full day US$50 and half day US$35.

watching the waves and listening to the latest dancehall. Across the way, local institution *Sharon and Pheeb's* (9am–late) is known for some of the best food in Tobago, serving fantastic breakfast, lunch or dinner. Michelle Jack (☎660 5206 or 4419) on Parrots Bay Road also serves local dinners from her home from TT$50 per person. Fries, fish or chicken meals, drinks and good company are on offer at the beach bar, which also puts on a lively sound-system party on Friday and Saturday nights. A new addition, on this side of town, is the bar and restaurant at the *Banana Boat* (see p.314). Complete with a large cage of parrots, this friendly establishment features fantastic murals and is open for reasonably-priced lunches – crab claws a speciality – and fabulous dinners. A daily happy hour (5–6pm) is the time to enjoy an inexpensive sundowner cocktail on the terrace and watch the sun set and the stars come out. This is also the best place to be on a Friday night in Charlotteville – some travel from around the island – to celebrate the end of the week by propping up the boat shaped bar and enjoying one of the extensive range of cocktails.

# Contexts

# Contexts

# A brief history of Trinidad

rinidad was the first inhabited island of the Caribbean, having been settled by Amerindians from South America as early as 5000 BC. The early
settlers were Arawaks – peaceful farmers and fishers – though after 1000
AD they were joined by more warlike Carib tribes. The Amerindians
called the island "Ieri", the land of the hummingbird.

## The Amerindians and the Spanish

When **Christopher Columbus** "discovered" the island in 1498, the population numbered around 35,000, most of whom lived in the coastal areas. There
was a structured society, with organized villages and chiefs, and a self-sufficient
economy that exploited the abundant natural resources and extensive trade
with the South American mainland. Sighting the three peaks of the Trinity
Hills, Columbus is said to have renamed the island **Trinidad**, landing at
Moruga on the south coast. Despite an initial skirmish with the local tribes,
Columbus's sailors considered them the friendliest in the Caribbean islands.
This didn't suit the Spanish **slave traders** who followed hot on Columbus's
heels; despite protests from Spanish priests such as Bartolomeo de las Casas,
they gleefully exaggerated the Caribs' occasional ritual **cannibalism** to justify
enslaving them.

The first permanent **Spanish settlers** came to Trinidad in 1592, where they
built the small town of San José – present-day St Joseph in the north of the
island – complete with governor's residence, *cabildo* (council chamber) and
church. Although the fledgling capital was sacked in 1595 by **Sir Walter
Raleigh** as he headed for South America in search of El Dorado, it was quickly rebuilt, and the colony survived, despite its vulnerability to foreign attacks
and pirate raids, growing tobacco and cocoa for export to Europe. In 1687,
Capuchin monks arrived from Spain, setting up several **missions** around the
island. Alongside the proselytizing, the missions were also a means to control
the Amerindians through the *encomienda* labour system, a kind of semi-slavery
in which the Indians were forced to work on plantations and build more
churches.

To evade this threat to their way of life, some Amerindians moved to the rainforested interior. Others **rebelled**: in 1699, a group of Amerindians killed three
Capuchin friars at San Rafael. The reprisals were savage, as Spanish troops
slaughtered hundreds of Amerindians in the ensuing **Arena Massacre**.
Amerindians were further threatened by European diseases such as smallpox,
to which they had no resistance. Consequently, by the end of the eighteenth
century, some three hundred years after Columbus's arrival, the indigenous
population had been all but wiped out.

# The arrival of the Africans and the French

Despite all the depredations they visited upon its original inhabitants, the Spanish ultimately had neither the desire nor the resources to develop the island, treating it as little more than a convenient watering-hole en route to the riches of South America. The governors of Trinidad were left to do as they pleased – illegal trading of goods and slaves was commonplace – and due to its poor defences, the island suffered repeated attacks from French, Dutch and English **pirates**. When Don Pedro de la Moneda arrived from Spain to take up the governorship in 1757, he found his St Joseph residence practically in ruins, and decamped to Port of Spain.

After centuries of indifference, it eventually became clear to the Spanish government that if it didn't develop this neglected colony, somebody else would. In 1783 Spain issued the **Cedula of Population**, a decree designed to encourage fellow Catholics, **French planters** suffering Protestant discrimination in British Grenada and Martinique, to settle in Trinidad. The amount of land they were allocated depended on the number of slaves they brought with them. Immigrants of mixed European/African race (termed "coloured" by the Spanish) who brought slaves could also receive land (though only half as much as their white counterparts), thus opening the way for the development of a property-owning coloured middle class.

To implement this policy, Spain despatched a new governor, **José Maria Chacon**, in 1784. The economy flourished under his energetic administration, and people of French and African descent came to dominate the population. The island's culture also became increasingly French: it was during this period that **Carnival** was introduced, the French language created a local patois, and a society based on aristocratic principles of birth and connections developed.

As the repercussions of the **French Revolution** gave rise to civil and international wars throughout the West Indies, many more French – both republicans and royalists – sought refuge in neutral Trinidad. To Chacon's alarm, they brought their ideological conflicts with them. Along with the French came more coloureds, many with republican sympathies. Worried, the governor reported to Madrid that some of the newcomers' radical ideas were encouraging the slaves to "dream of liberty and equality".

# The British take over

The British, who already controlled much of the Caribbean, seized on the pretext that the island had become a nest of republicans and "bad people of all descriptions", despatching an invasion fleet under **Sir Ralph Abercromby** in 1797. The island had few defences: just five ships compared to the British force of eighteen, and only two thousand soldiers – many of whom had deserted – against seven thousand. The Spanish surrendered with hardly a shot fired, scuttling their own ships in Chaguaramas harbour, and Chacon was recalled to Spain in disgrace. It has been argued that, as a staunch royalist, he may have deliberately offered little resistance, preferring Spain's monarchist British enemies to her republican French allies.

The terms of defeat offered by Abercromby were lenient; residents could retain their property and Spanish law would remain in force. His choice of governor, **Thomas Picton**, was less fortunate. Left in charge of the island with near absolute powers, this harsh military officer soon instituted a **reign of terror**, deporting and executing suspected subversives on the flimsiest evidence – frequently confessions obtained under **torture**. Slaves and freed coloureds – whom he regarded as dangerous republicans – bore the brunt of this oppression. Followers of **African religious traditions** were persecuted especially harshly; those suspected of practising obeah were hauled before a tribunal, and if found guilty were whipped, hanged, mutilated or burned to death. By 1802, Picton's activities had become an embarrassment to the British government, then facing an influential anti-slavery lobby at home, and he was demoted.

Trinidad presented the British government with a unique administrative conundrum. Other Caribbean islands such as Barbados were governed by colonial assemblies, but that was scarcely an option in Trinidad. Any such assembly would inevitably be dominated by planters, who would never agree to share power with free coloureds, even though many of the latter were substantial property owners, and thus difficult to exclude from government under British law. The island therefore remained a **crown colony**, governed by French and Spanish law, with directions issued straight from the colonial office in London.

Various policies were tested in an attempt to curb the abuses of slavery, but these did little apart from infuriating the planters. Slaves were still treated harshly, with over a third of them having died clearing the rainforests to make way for plantations. The slaves resisted by organizing secret societies with their own militias, and attempted several rebellions. One such society, led by a powerful obeah man known as **King Samson**, was discovered and crushed at Christmas in 1805.

The British officially abolished the slave trade in 1807, but the planters' need for labour meant that slave smuggling continued. Even after the **Act of Emancipation** in 1834, the freed slaves were required to serve as apprentices for a further six years, and remained tied to their owners since the latter provided their living quarters. When the apprenticeship system was abolished in 1838, many former slaves moved to urban areas. As few labourers could be found to work on the estates, field wages in Trinidad consequently rose to become the highest in the Caribbean.

# The Indians arrive

The increased wages were not sufficient to make up for the labour shortage, however, so the British government sanctioned the immigration of **indentured labourers from India**. In May 1845 the first 225 arrived from Calcutta aboard the *Fatel Rozack*. By 1917, when the indenture system finally came to an end, some 145,000 Indians, mainly from Calcutta, had come to T&T. Fleeing from poverty and the increasingly harsh British rule in India, the immigrants had to sign contracts to work on the plantations for five years in return for their passage home at the end of that period. In 1854 the period of indenture was extended to ten years, and after 1895 the Indian immigrants had to pay a proportion of the cost of their return passage.

Though the system of indentured labour was better regulated and monitored than slavery, the working and living conditions of labourers and slaves were practically indistinguishable. Labourers lived in single-room **barrack houses**, unsanitary conditions meant that disease was rife, and the shortage of women immigrants heightened feelings of jealousy and possessiveness, resulting in many crimes of passion and domestic violence. The plantation owners failed to honour pledges on wages and working conditions, while breaches of contract by the labourers were treated as criminal offences punishable by imprisonment.

Many labourers did not return to India, but instead accepted land in lieu of their passage home. Known then and today as "East Indians" to differentiate them from the "West Indians", they formed the lowest rung of society, working in the agricultural sector scorned by the Afro-Caribbeans because of its link with slavery. They became a tight-knit community, maintaining many of their own traditions; a privilege that was (and still is) resented by many of the descendants of African slaves, who had been forbidden to practise their religion and culture. The white ruling class also looked down upon them, seeing the mainly Hindu immigrants as heathens and barbarians who worshipped false idols and ate with their hands; East Indian children were even considered illegitimate as Muslim and Hindu marriages were not recognized until 1945. Many of these children remained uneducated – the schools were either Catholic or Presbyterian, and parents feared that their children would be converted.

Yet despite their persecution, the Indian indentured labourers contributed greatly to Trinidad's developing national identity. Just as the Europeans had brought Carnival, which was taken up and enriched by former slaves, Indians introduced their own festivities and culture. The Muslims introduced **Hosay**, the Hindus brought **Diwali**, and Indian food, such as roti and curry, became staples for all Trinidadians.

# Other immigrants

Further adding to T&T's ethnic mix were immigrants from many other parts of the world. Several companies of **black American soldiers** who had supported Britain in its 1812 war against the US were given grants of land in southern Trinidad, where they founded villages named after the units in which they had served. After emancipation other immigrants, mainly freed slaves from other **Caribbean islands**, were attracted to Trinidad by the high wages. **Africans** liberated by the British Navy on anti-slave patrols settled in urban areas, becoming craftsmen and construction workers, establishing strong communities that maintained their own cultural institutions and heritage. The first **Chinese immigrants** arrived in Trinidad in 1853 as part of another attempt by the government to meet the continuing labour shortage on the plantations. The plan failed on account of the high transport costs and an appalling mortality rate among the immigrants; those who survived tended to become shopkeepers, and their descendants today constitute a small but visible minority. **Portuguese** labourers were also brought to the country in the mid-1800s, but the practice was short-lived as the employment of Europeans in manual work was seen as a threat to the established racial hierarchy.

Except for a handful of **Jews** who settled in Trinidad during World War II, the last group of immigrants to join the island's melting pot were the **Syrians** who came in 1913, seeking refuge from religious persecution in the Lebanon. Though they only account for 0.1 percent of the country's population, their dominance of the cloth trade has given them a high profile. They form a tight-knit community, disapproving of intermarriage and often sending for spouses from their native land.

# The people get organized

Through the nineteenth century, Trinidadian society remained deeply stratified on the basis of race and class, with the white planters firmly at the top of the heap. In the 1880s and 1890s, however, reform movements began to challenge the status quo. An improved national **education system** and an enlarged franchise inspired the formation of political lobbying groups linked to the international labour movement. The **Trinidad Workingmen's Association** (TWA) – which had close links to the **British Labour Party** – and the **East Indian National Association** were both established in 1897; while the **Pan African Association** and the **Ratepayers' Association** were formed in 1901. Dominated by black, coloured and Indian professionals, these organizations lobbied the British Colonial Office for an elected governing body for the island.

In 1899, Britain made ailing **Tobago** a ward of Trinidad, though the larger island itself still had no effective form of self-government. Resentment came to a head over the introduction of new **water rates**, and in 1903 a protest meeting in Port of Spain's Woodford Square erupted into a **riot**, in which eighteen people were shot dead by the police, and the Red House – seat of the colonial government – was burned to the ground. Although Joseph Chamberlain, the British Secretary of State for the Colonies, finally agreed in 1913 to an **elected assembly** for Trinidad and Tobago (albeit one with very limited powers), it was still more than ten years before the first Legislative Council convened in the rebuilt Red House.

Trinidad's burgeoning **oil industry** and the aftermath of **World War I** further politicized the populace. High inflation during this time led to strikes, resulting in increased cooperation between Africans and Indians, while fuel was added to the fire by black **West Indian regiments** who returned from the Great War with stories of discrimination at the hands of the British they had been fighting to defend. The **East Indian Destitute League**, established in 1916 and supported by the National Congress, which was then fighting for independence in India, fought to abolish indentureship. A 1919 **dockyard strike** erupted into violence, and the government, alarmed by the anger and unity of the population, called in British troops to restore order. Even with the continual government crackdowns, the tide had finally turned, with socialism, national independence and the concept of black consciousness then being promoted in Jamaica by Marcus Garvey, now firmly planted in the public mind.

In 1925, the TWA president **Arthur Cipriani** was elected to the new legislative council. A white French Creole who had fought with the British West Indians in the war, Cipriani campaigned hard for workers' rights and secured some important concessions, including compensation for industrial injuries. His essentially reformist politics had little effect on the underlying balance of power, however; wages were actually falling, malnutrition was widespread, living conditions grim and industrial accidents appallingly common. As the world economy nosedived into the **Great Depression** of the 1930s, Cipriani soon found himself outflanked by a new generation of radicals.

In 1932, after trade unions became legal, strikes broke out across the country. The oil workers soon found a charismatic leader in **Uriah Butler**, who broke away from the TWA to found the **British Empire Workers** in 1935. Black nationalism became popular after the failure of the west that same year to defend Ethiopia from Mussolini, while Indian race consciousness was heightened after the visit of several cultural leaders from their homeland.

One of the most influential groups of Trinidadian black intellectuals formed around the *Beacon*, a stridently anti-colonial, anti-government and anti-Catholic literary and political magazine that was published from 1931 to 1934, exploring issues of West Indian identity and attempting to instil a sense of pride among Afro-Trinidadians. In its regular "India section", Indo-Trinidadians wrote of their situation and the struggle for independence in India. Many of its contributors – who included Albert Gomes, C.L.R. James, Alfred Mendes and R.A.C. de Boisseiere – went on to become leading politicians.

# The transition to Independence

World War II was an important precursor to Trinidad and Tobago's eventual independence. During this period the country's socio-economic character changed due to the presence of the **US military**, who had leased Chaguaramas, the Bocas islands and Waller Field in 1941 to provide a base for their Caribbean fleet. The Americans improved Trinidad's infrastructure and exposed the population to high-level technology for the first time. The **high wages** they were prepared to pay for the construction of buildings and roads lured workers from the agricultural sector and ensured the decline of many estates. The Americans' racial attitudes, cruder than the more subtle racism of the British, and the aura of easy money that attracted many Trinidadian women, soon caused much of the populace to resent their presence and further increased the desire for independence.

In 1945 **universal suffrage** was granted to all those over the age of 21, though there were still property and income restrictions for those who wanted to stand as candidates for the legislature. Both the 1946 and 1950 elections were won by political parties linked to the trade unions. Britain, meanwhile, was not prepared to hand over total control while radical labour politics dominated the political arena.

In January 1956, a group of black intellectuals formed the **People's National Movement** (PNM) under the leadership of the Oxford-educated historian **Dr Eric Williams**. The party's black nationalist policies, and the charismatic leadership and immense intellectual authority of "the Doctor", soon gained widespread support among a population tired of colonial government and the divisions within the labour movement. The PNM's only serious opposition was from the **People's Democratic Party** (PDP), supported primarily by rural Hindus.

After a controversial campaign that raised racial tension by portraying the PDP as reactionary Hindus, the PNM won the most seats in the **September 1956** election. Though they lacked an outright majority the Colonial Office allowed them to form a government. The PNM remained in power for the next thirty years, with Williams as prime minister until his death in 1981.

Many Caribbean leaders saw a **federation of West Indian islands** as the way forward for the region, and at first Williams was an enthusiastic proponent of the idea. With British support, it was decided that Trinidad should be the capital, and in 1958 a federal government was elected, with the Barbadian premier Grantley Adams as prime minister. But political rivalries and the reluctance of the larger islands to subsidize the smaller ones resulted in a watered-down federation with no tax-raising powers. When Jamaica voted to leave the federation in September 1961, Williams announced that "one from ten leaves nought," after which Trinidad followed suit. In May 1962 the federation was officially dissolved.

Though the PNM adopted a radical stance during the early 1960s under the influence of Marxist intellectual C.L.R. James, persuading the US military to leave the country in 1961 and campaigning vigorously for independence, the party's essentially corporatist nationalism attempted to unite capital and labour, despite their conflicting economic interests. With the labour movement in disarray, politics split along racial lines, with government the preserve of Afro-Caribbeans, the opposition that of East Indians.

**Independence** was finally granted in 1962 as Britain eagerly rid itself of its last colonies. After the PNM created a new constitution without consulting the opposition PDP, the country seemed to be heading towards civil war; only a last-minute compromise by the PNM pulled it back from the brink. As the 1960s progessed, disillusionment began to seep through Trinidadian society. Independence, it seemed, had done little to change the colonial structure of society.

# Protest, wealth and disillusionment

The late 1960s were marked by repeated industrial unrest. The **Black Power** movement, which had already had a profound impact on the United States, caught the imagination of many disaffected Trinis. In 1970 its supporters launched a wave of marches, protests and **wildcat strikes** that shook Trinidad to the core. Businesses and banks were bombed, and when the police shot dead a young Black Power member named **Basil Davis**, 60,000 people took to the streets for his funeral. The government declared a state of emergency; an **army mutiny** in Chaguaramas was only quashed when coastguard vessels prevented the soldiers from marching on Port of Spain by shelling the main road; and rumours abounded that a bloody coup had been averted and plans had been discovered for mass executions of "enemies of the people".

The crisis proved cathartic. Many whites had fled the country; those who remained could no longer expect the deference to which they had been accustomed, while the government encouraged locals to be trained for jobs previously occupied by expatriates. During this time, the PNM owed its survival in office less to any strength of its own, than to the divisions in the opposition. "We are winning by default," PNM minister Hector McLean observed drily.

By the start of the 1970s, when Trinidad was practically bankrupt, vast reserves of **oil** were discovered off the east coast just as the world was sliding into the oil crisis of 1974, and the country found itself swimming in money overnight. Ambitious public projects were undertaken and the country settled back to enjoy the boom years. But this sudden wealth had its down side. People got used to the easy life, productivity fell, agriculture dwindled, inefficiency, bribery (locally known as "bobol") and corruption clogged the system.

When oil prices fell in the 1980s, the economy went into recession, unemployment rose sharply and inflation soared. Williams died in office in 1981, a disillusioned man with his policies in ruins; his former finance minister **George Chambers** took over the reins. As the population became increasingly dissatisfied, the opposition parties started to unify. In 1986, PNM was ousted, for the first time in Trinidad's post-Independence history, by the

**National Alliance for Reconstruction** (NAR), led by the Tobagonian **A.N.R. Robinson**, who had resigned from Williams' government in 1970.

The NAR tried to resolve some of the more pressing problems facing the country, but within a year the government was breaking up into factions. Harsh economic measures, including **devaluation** of the TT dollar and a stringent IMF-inspired recovery programme, were widely seen as undemocratic and beneficial only to the rich. In 1990, the **Jamaat-al-Muslimeen** – a revolutionary Muslim organization – attempted to overthrow the government, holding Robinson and several of his cabinet hostage. Though the coup was crushed and Robinson released after a six-day siege, the government's authority was irreparably undermined, and the following year the PNM returned to power under the leadership of **Patrick Manning**.

Over the next five years, the PNM stabilized the economy and paid off the IMF, helped by increased oil revenues during the Gulf War. The 1995 election split the country down the middle, with the PNM and the Indo-Trinidadian **United National Congress** (UNC) both winning exactly seventeen seats. The two representatives of the NAR held the balance of power; they used it to support the UNC, making **Basdeo Panday**, the leader of the sugar workers' union, the country's first East Indian prime minister. Although the 2000 election returned the UNC to power with nineteen seats, Panday's government was to last only ten months, as the following October, three UNC parliamentarians defected to the opposition. After much political squabbling, new elections in October 2002 returned the PNM to power, with Manning confirmed as prime minister.

# Current issues

One of the PNM administration's first acts after its election in 2002 was to introduce legislation aimed at tackling the recent rise in **crime**, particularly the abduction of important business people. Until the 1970s the country was virtually crime-free, and by international standards crime is still low; Trinidad had just 115 reported murders in 2000, compared to 800 in Jamaica, a country with twice the population. But for Trinbagonians – used to leaving their doors unlocked at night – the emergence of "bandits" has given rise to crime paranoia, with somewhat sensationalized accounts splashed across the newspapers daily. **Domestic violence** is a major problem in the country, where the culture is predominantly macho and it's widely held that physical threats in relationships are natural.

Neither has T&T completely escaped the heightened worldwide fear of **terrorism** since the September 11, 2001, attacks in the US and the subsequent wars in Afghanistan and Iraq. In January 2003, the *Sunday Express* newspaper reported that an unidentified radical Muslim group was operating a chemical weapons factory on the island and claimed the group had threatened to attack US and British visitors to the country. This rather alarmist story led to travel warnings being issued by the US and British governments and the cancellation of some cruise-ship stopovers, but, not surprisingly, no terrorist attacks took place.

**Corruption** also continues to be a cause for concern, with recent actions of both Manning and Panday called into question. In the former's case, the appointment of Manning's wife, Hazel, as Minister of Education prompted accusations of nepotism, while Panday was officially charged in September 2002 with fraud in connection with his failure to declare a large deposit made to his wife's bank account in the UK while he was still in office.

Though Trinidad and Tobago is promoted as a rainbow nation – its national anthem includes the phrase "every creed and race finds an equal place" – **race** remains an underlying issue. While certainly a subtler problem than in Europe or America, big business is still dominated by the minority of white Trinis. In addition, the continued rise of the Indo-Trinidadian population's numbers and influence often arouses anxiety and resentment among the Afro-Caribbeans, whom they now slightly outnumber.

By international standards, however, Trinidad and Tobago is a model of racial harmony. It can also boast the most **stable economy** in the Caribbean; GDP has grown steadily since 1994, while unemployment (10 percent in 2002) and the level of external debt have declined. Although oil continues to be an important source of revenue, the country is transitioning from an oil-based to a natural gas-based economy; indeed, T&T is already the fifth largest exporter of liquefied natural gas in the world. The income generated from oil and gas is increasingly being used to develop other sectors, including manufacturing, finance, services and tourism. Meanwhile, a joint government and private sector initiative, **Vision 2020**, aims to achieve developed nation status for T&T by 2020 through improvements in areas such as health, the environment, telecommunications and social services.

This does not mean that life is easy for the majority: high-tech malls co-exist with board shacks where inhabitants live without electricity or running water, the social security system is minimal and many can't afford health care. But compared with the rest of the Caribbean, Trinidad and Tobago is making progress, and its future holds some promise for a more even spread of wealth.

# Carnival

T&T's most **popular export** and main **tourist attraction**, Carnival originated in southern Europe with the Roman feast of **Saturnalia**, a midwinter celebration of birth and renewal, and the inversion of the norm. It developed during the Middle Ages into the **Feast of Fools**, in which the pretensions of the Catholic Church were scabrously mocked. The Church, unsurprisingly, did its best to suppress the festival, but in the long run assimilation proved more effective, and Carnival was incorporated into the Catholic faith as a final binge (carne vale – "farewell to flesh") before the fasting period of Lent. Most Carnivals staged around the world today were established by Trinis and are based on the Trinidadian model – often even importing costumes and skilled craftsmen from T&T to ensure creativity and authenticity.

## Carnival comes to Trinidad

Introduced to Trinidad by **French planters** in the late eighteenth century, Carnival was initially the preserve of the white Creole establishment. Celebrated in the three days prior to Ash Wednesday, it was a comparatively decorous affair in which the gentry made house-to-house visits to attend masqued balls. The Carnival principle of inversion allowed the white ruling class a brief fictive escape from the "cares" of power and respectability: the men would dress as "negres jardins" (field labourers), the women as "mulatresses", representing their slaves or their husbands' mulatto mistresses.

The slaves also celebrated Carnival, in semi-secret, on the plantations; after **emancipation** in 1834, the ex-slaves took their own Carnival procession onto the streets in bands, protected by groups of *batonniers* or stick men. The revellers' costumes often satirized the affectations and eccentricities of their former masters with men dressing as fashionable planters' wives with large breasts and posterior. A number of characters drew on West African traditions and folklore, especially a little demon known as **jab jab** and the stilt-walking **moko jumbie**. The parade was enlivened by the use of **percussion instruments** and the introduction of **canboulay**, a procession of flambeaux carriers celebrating the former plantation workers' newfound freedom from the difficult and dangerous task of saving burning cane fields – the name is derived from the French *canes brulées*, or burning cane.

### Satire and civil disobedience

Disapproving of what they saw as the "desecration" of the Sabbath by the first day of Carnival, the British authorities decreed in 1843 that the festivities could not begin until Monday morning. Since no time was specified, the Carnivalgoers started celebrating on the stroke of midnight – the origin of the wild procession known as **Jouvert** that begins Carnival today. Many of the masquerades acted out in the street processions took the form of trenchant **satires** of the colonial government, and in 1846 the authorities attempted to ban revellers wearing masks. Carnival found defenders in unexpected quarters, however: the French planters, keen to defend their own traditions in the face of increasing Anglicization, and the coloured middle class, whose desire for respectability kept them aloof from Carnival itself but who saw attempts to control it as an assertion of white domination.

Carnival continued to provide an outlet for irreverence and satire through the nineteenth century, with outrageous parodies of British **sailors** stationed on the island, as well as characters representing underworld archetypes: **jamettes** (prostitutes) and **jamets** ("sweetmen", or kept lovers), and the transvestite **pissenlets** (literally "wet-the-bed"). Bands organized **drumming** and **kalenda** (stickfighting), which is thought to have originated in the use of bamboo sticks to fight fires in the cane fields. None of this went down too well with the colonial administrators from Victorian Britain, and in 1877 **Captain Baker**, the island's police chief, began a campaign to tame Carnival. When British soldiers attempted to intercept a group of masqueraders in 1881, a riot broke out. Undeterred, the authorities went on to prohibit the jamets and pissenlets on the grounds of their lewdness. African-style drumming was banned in 1884, while canboulay and stickfighting – seen respectively as a fire hazard and an incitement to violence – were outlawed a year later under the **Peace Preservation Act**.

# Carnival becomes respectable

Carnival was not so easily quashed, however, and a more sedate masquerade took to the streets in the following years. Social protest was channelled into the emerging labour movement (see p.325), and Carnival became an officially tolerated safety valve for social pressures, with the coloured middle class soon joining in. During the 1890s, Carnival became increasingly organized and socially acceptable with the introduction of a **competition** for best band by Port of Spain merchant and city councillor Ignatius Bodu – fondly remembered as today's masqueraders as Papa Bodi. Over the course of the twentieth century, practically every aspect of Carnival became the subject of a competition. In 1921, the calypsonian Chieftain Douglas opened the first organized calypso tent to preview the songs that would be heard in the forthcoming Carnival (see p.341 for more on calypso); the tents proliferated, and as they became established venues, the canvas tents gave way to permanent structures (though the name remains – see p.343).

During **World War II**, Carnival was suspended by the colonial government as a possible threat to public order, and when it returned on VE Day, 1945, it marched to the sound of a different drum – the **steel pan** fashioned from oil drums brought to the island by the US military. As the national independence movement gained momentum, Carnival flourished right alongside. Recognizing its importance to Trinidad's cultural identity and sense of nationhood, Eric Williams's newly elected nationalist party established the **National Carnival Commission** in 1957 to organize and promote the festivities, and set up the competition in which a Calypso King is crowned.

Since then, Carnival has continued to reflect the state of Trinidadian society and politics. In 1970, as the Black Power movement gained widespread support, many of the masquerades explicitly addressed the topics of racism and white control of the economy. And as women have come to take a more prominent role in the islands' public life, they have become increasingly involved in Carnival, now making up the majority of the masqueraders. While Carnival has become socially-conscious and more a celebration of Trinidadian identity and nationhood, its world-famous mas makers don't shy away from tackling ambitious or controversial themes.

# Carnival today

To the eye of an uneducated onlooker, the two days of Trinidad and Tobago's explosive Carnival might appear to be a chaotic spectacle of revellers, costumes, sound systems and street dancing. However, underpinning the whole event is an order and structure that is the culmination of year-long preparations.

It's said that **preparations** for the next Carnival begin as soon as the event itself is over on Ash Wednesday, with participants deconstructing their performances and discussing plans for the following year. The real countdown to Carnival begins in late autumn, however, when the more organized mas bands hold launches for their Carnival designs – usually huge parties where costumes are displayed and the first revellers sign up. Once Christmas is out of the way, things get serious. Mas band launches become ever-more frequent, the big steel bands open up their yards for visitors to watch practice sessions, calypsonians perform their Carnival compositions in the "tents" that spring up in Port of Spain and each weekend features a bewildering choice of pre-Carnival fetes.

With the soca monarch and Panorama competitions out of the way, Carnival begins in earnest on the Sunday before the main event, with a fabulous parade of traditional "ol mas" characters at Port of Spain's Victoria Square. Come the evening, the **Dimanche Gras** competition is held – this is where the **King and Queen of the Bands** and the all-important **Calypso Monarch** are crowned. Carnival then officially starts at 4am on the Monday morning with **Jouvert**, or dirty mass, when participants dress in macabre or satirical home-made costumes, or join a mud band and smear themselves with mud, grease or paint before taking to the streets in an anarchical expression of Carnival's darker side. This wild party lasts into the first daylight hours of **Carnival Monday**, when spectators are advised to wear old clothes and leave their inhibitions at home, as revellers will delight in rubbing themselves up against each other and getting everyone as dirty as possible. Once the bacchanal of Jouvert has dispersed, the first parade begins by 9pm, when the mas bands take to the streets accompanied either by steel pan bands or monstrous trucks bearing columns of speakers.

Both in Trinidad's Port of Spain and Tobago's Scarborough there are set routes for bands to follow, along which, at certain points, panels of judges wait to mark each one. The main "stages" and judging points, where each band struts as much of its stuff as possible, is the Queens Park Savannah (also known as the Big Yard) in Port of Spain and Scarborough's Market Square. Those who still have any energy left when Monday's parade is over will attend **Monday Night Mas** – an ongoing party with DJs that lasts throughout the night.

Tuesday is Carnival's big day, the culmination of all the hard work, competitions and preparations that have been in motion since the beginning of January. This is when the bands dress in full costume and parade the streets as loudly and as proudly as they can, all competing for the much coveted **Band of the Year** title.

Though the actual **construction** of each band's costumes is becoming increasingly specialized and skilled, commercialism and changing fashions have, sadly, led to the loss of many traditional Carnival characters as more and more mas camps turn to **bikini mas**, reducing their costumes to sequins, glitter and feathers attached to a basic bikini. A handful of designers are making a determined effort to preserve the link to Carnival's historic roots. Jason Griffith and his Sailor band used to ensure that **sailors** were still seen in the Carnival procession, "D" Midas Associates still produce costumes made by **traditional** methods, and Peter Minshall (see box, p.119) has ensured the survival of

## Essential Carnival vocabulary

**Bands** These are not musical bands, but a large collection of costumed masquer-aders.

**Chipping** Slow, shuffling walk with a rhythm dictated by the music from trucks and steel bands during Carnival.

**Dimanche Gras** A big event on the Sunday before Carnival Monday at which the winners of most of the Carnival competitions are decided.

**Fete** A large open-air party or concert – of which there are many during the run-up to Carnival.

**Jump up** To dance in the parade for a while – before **falling out** when you've had enough.

**Mas** Short for masquerade.

**Mas camp** The headquarters of Carnival bands, where costumes are made and reg-istrations to be part of a band are taken.

**Make mas** To make a Carnival costume.

**Ol' mas** Traditional Carnival characters such as jab jabs and sailors.

**Play mas** To join a Carnival band and take part.

**Road march** The calypso or soca song played the most during Carnival.

**Wining** The grinding of your hips into another's – be prepared to wine, and be wined to, at any point during Carnival.

characters such as **moko jumbies** in the performance section of his band Callaloo.

Carnival's **Las' Lap** kicks in at dusk on Carnival Tuesday when everything becomes just a bit more frantic as the last hours of the event are made the most of, until midnight strikes and one year's Carnival officially ends and the count down to next year's begins.

For **more on Carnival**, including a calendar of events, see p.47; for mas camps see p.94; and for panyards see box, p.101.

# Taking part

Almost ten percent of T&T's population actively participates in Carnival and the best way for any visitor to truly understand this enduring, celebratory form of Trinbagonian self identity is to join in and play mas. Anyone wanting to join a band should visit one of the many mas camps to register; some bands allow you to register on their websites. Port of Spain has dozens of camps, of which the main ones are: Barbarossa (☎628 6008, @www.barbarossaintl.com) and Legends (☎622 7466, @www.legendscarnival.com), both based in Woodbrook, Poison (☎632 3989, @www.poison.co.tt) based in Petit Valley and Peter Minshall's Callaloo (☎634 4491, @www.callaloo.co.tt) in Chaguaramas. Or simply ask around either of the islands and you'll soon find your way into a band. Even if you don't want to play mas, a visit to a mas camp is a fascinating experience – here you can witness the creation of these famous fantastic costumes and enjoy the buzz and excitement of Carnival in the making.

**Virtual Carnival**
Anyone who can't be in Trinidad and Tobago to witness Carnival in person, can now check out real-time internet Carnival coverage, for a fee, on TIDCO's website: @www.visitTNT.com

# Religion

Trinis sometimes joke that God must be from T&T, and it's easy to see why; deep faith and a laid-back attitude mean that while outsiders fret and panic, locals tend to sit back calmly and wait with a belief that "God will solve all problems."

In this profoundly spiritual republic, most people hold some kind of religious conviction. Schoolchildren receive routine religious instruction and most grow up making weekly visits to the church, temple or mosque. Adults are equally devout, with most people affiliated with one faith or another.

Trinbagonian religion represents a polyglot of faiths as cosmopolitan as the population. Spain's long period of rule in Trinidad gave the **Catholic Church** a head start over other religions, and it retains the largest number of believers at 29.4 percent of the population. Most Indians remain **Hindu**, and devotees of that faith make up 23.8 percent of Trinidad's population. **Anglicans** account for 10.9 percent, **Muslims** 5.8 percent, **Presbyterians** 3.4 percent and the remaining 26.7 percent are a mix of Pentecostals, Seventh Day Adventists, Moravians, Spiritual Baptists and followers of the Church of God and Yoruba **Orisha** faiths.

# Indian religions

Brought to Trinidad by indentured Indian workers in the nineteenth century, **Hinduism** represents T&T's largest religious denomination after Catholicism. Though you'd hardly believe it, judging by the proliferation of grandiose mosques, **Islam** actually has a much smaller worship base. For the most part, Muslim religious practice has changed little since arriving in T&T, save for the festival of **Hosay**, which has grown from a rather sombre affair to a Carnival-esque party in which people of all denominations take part – much to the consternation of the Shiite faithful, who feel that the drinking and revelry depreciates the festival's solemn origins. For more on Islam in T&T, visit ⓦ www.islam.org.tt.

## Hinduism in Trinidad

Centred upon the worship of multiple deities rather than a single god (see box, opposite), the central tenets of Hinduism include **dharma**, the laws of duty and order in the universe and society, while one's position in life is determined by the eternal cause-and-effect repercussions of **karma**. Though the indentured workers all worshipped under the banner of Hinduism, their wide-ranging geographical and social origins reflected the huge **differences** in religious practice and status in India, and as they settled into their new life in Trinidad, they created a hybrid Hinduism that's unique to the island.

One of the main differences between Hinduism in Trinidad and in India is the lack of a **caste system** in T&T. The strong friendships forged during the passage – which gave rise to the term *jihaji bhai* ("ship brother") – transcended differences in social status, and many new-found friends chose to settle together and work the same plantations. Slowly, the caste system was eroded; only the priestly Brahman caste, whose **pundits** officiate at religious rites, has survived in Trinidad.

## Some Hindu deities

**Shiva** The God of creation and destruction, all-powerful Shiva (alongside Vishnu) rides his faithful bull Nandi, and is often depicted with several faces, each with a third eye in the middle of the forehead, and his hair wreathed with snakes.

**Vishnu** Blue-skinned, four-armed Vishnu holds a conch, discus, lotus and mace, and is often depicted in the coils of a large snake. He has manifested himself on earth nine times; his tenth visit as Kalki will bring deliverance to the pure and destruction to the wicked.

**Durga** This fierce female goddess is Shiva's consort. She wears a garland of skulls about her neck, blood drips from her mouth, and in her ten arms she holds various weapons and the head of a demon.

**Ganesh** Red-skinned Ganesh, the elephant God, sits chubby and benign astride a lotus or throne, holding a water lily, conch, discus and a club or bowl of sweets. The deity of learning and literature, he is the author of the 100,000-stanza philosophical poem, the *Mahabharata*.

**Lakshmi** The goddess of light and prosperity, Lakshmi is associated with Diwali festivities. She sits on a lotus flower and embodies beauty, grace and charm. Her form varies depending on the incarnation of her consort Vishnu.

**Saraswati** Taking her name from a sacred Indian river, the goddess of purification, fertility, music and eloquence sits on a water lily or peacock and plays a sitar or lute. She is also the inventor of writing.

**Hanuman** Depicted as a large monkey bearing a mace, Hanuman is a demon-fighter, the God of acrobats and wrestlers, and the inventor of Sanskrit grammar.

**Rituals** have also been modified. Whereas in India, prayers for blessing – called **pujas** – are lengthy processes, each with a specific meaning and directed toward a particular deity, in Trinidad several *pujas* are often combined, with several deities involved. Everyone who takes part must be ceremonially cleansed, and the list of articles necessary for a *puja* is long: oils, herbs, spices, ghee, incense, flowers, pictures (*murtis*) of the deity to be honoured, a bamboo flag pole and a **jhandi** (prayer flag) of the deity's assigned colour. Once the pundit arrives, he arranges the items and utters mantras that invoke the deity. The pole is then anointed and the flag raised, and all those present are considered blessed.

Daily Hindu rites in T&T include lighting **deyas**, reciting **mantras** and **throwing jal** (water); the latter is done by a designated child, who rises in the morning before the rest of the household and pours petal-laden water from a brass **lotah** near to a tulsi bush – a strain of basil that's planted in most Hindu gardens. Other Indian traditions that have acquired a Trini slant are the celebrations that now accompany the Phagwa and Diwali festivities (see p.189).

For more on the Hindu faith in Trinidad, visit the excellent site run by pundit Bhadase Maharaj, which has features on festivals, deities and Hindu practices: @www.trinihindu.faithweb.com.

# African religions

Brought to the island by enslaved blacks and further popularized by free Africans who arrived during the nineteenth century, T&T's **African religions** centre upon the acceptance of a synthesis between the spiritual and temporal worlds. This belief in mystical powers – spirits or gods – which organize and animate the material universe is categorized in Western terms as "**animist**". The two main sects – **Spiritual Baptists** and the more secretive **Shango** or **Orisha** – are widespread, with a particular concentration in Tobago. In both creeds – and also in **obeah**, which has a significant following in T&T – spirits are seen to have a distinct influence upon the living and must therefore be (depending on the situation) respected, pacified, praised, worshipped or feared through ritual dances, chants, drumbeats, offerings, prayer and superstitions.

## Spiritual Baptists

More overtly Christian than Orisha, the **Spiritual Baptist** faith surfaced during the late nineteenth century, brought to the island by black Americans. Then known as **Shouter Baptists** because of their propensity for loud and demonstrative worship, the sect was frowned upon by the British, who banned membership through the **Shouters Prohibition Ordinance** of 1917. **Shouter Baptist Liberation Day**, March 30, commemorates the abolition of this law in 1951 after years of campaigning. The day is still celebrated with ceremonies all over T&T, and a convention at the Queen's Park Savannah in Port of Spain.

Spiritual Baptists ground their beliefs in the Bible and worship the **Holy Trinity** of the Father, the Son and the Holy Ghost as three separate entities. They are well organized, and have their own specially designed churches (unlike the more common sheds), with pews for the congregation, an altar from which the leader or priest preaches, and a **centre pole** decorated with flowers, jugs of water and candles to harness and attract the spirits. The characteristic white robes and colourful headwraps worn by followers (which signify their dedication to a particular saint or spirit) are a notable part of the Trinbago Sunday scenery, when you'll occasionally see bands of Baptists ringing their bells and chanting hymns in public. **Baptism**, where white-clad converts are ritually dipped into a body of moving water (usually the sea), is also commonly seen.

Lasting between three and six hours, **services** usually involve purification rituals designed to cast out **jumbies** (evil spirits) that might be lurking in the church: lighted candles are placed in front of doors and windows, incense is lit, brass bells are rung and perfumed water strewn about. Bible readings precede the chants and handclapping, both of which intensify as **spirit manifestations** are brought about by a kind of hyperventilation known as **adoption**. Spirit possession – **catching the power** – is accompanied by bell-ringing and chanting called **trumpeting the spirit**, the origin of the "shouter" tag. Those who catch the power may grunt, gesticulate, speak in tongues or relay the counsel of the spirits in plain English, usually sharing their power by touching each of the assembled members.

## Orisha

A Yoruba religion driven underground during British rule, **Orisha** (also Orisa or Shango) remains a somewhat clandestine cult. The faith centres upon worship of several deities called "orishas", which are honoured through drumming, dancing, chanting and animal sacrifices. Each orisha's personality is described in stories that reveal their activities on earth, with each assigned an individual drumbeat, colour, day of the week, favourite food and liquor, sacrificial animal (usually a chicken or goat) and an association with a Christian saint; this last tradition allowed Orisha worship to be syncretized with Christian festivals when the faith was outlawed.

The patron orisha of Trinidad and Tobago, **Shango**, is one of the faith's most powerful deities. The god of thunder, fire, war and drumming, Shango carries an axe, his colours are red and white, his patron St Barbara, and his favoured day Saturday (sometimes Friday). Equally respected is **Ogun**, Shango's brother and another war orisha, who represents blacksmiths and iron, but there are hosts of others, and each member of the faith is aligned with an individual god through a spirit possession when they first enter the cult.

Orisha worship takes place in a **palais**, an open space sheltered from the elements by a galvanized roof and decorated with the symbols of individual orishas – daggers, cutlasses, hammers, jugs of water and ritual items such as olive oil for anointing, and offerings of flowers, fruit and foods. Known as **feasts**, most ceremonies take place over several days, and begin with the specialized drum patterns that summon Ogun. Drumming, dancing, chanting and hyperventilation encourage possession of devotees by various orishas, while sacrifices may be performed to honour the spirits that descend.

---

### Jumbies in Trini folklore

**Douens** The malevolent spirits of unbaptized children, these genderless waifs have backward-facing feet and hide their featureless faces beneath a wide-brimmed straw hat. They lurk in places where real children play; superstitious parents never call their child's name in the open, lest the douens remember it and lure the child away.

**Jackalantern** A mysterious light that misleads night-time travellers, luring them deep into the bush before vanishing.

**La Diablesse** An attractive female devil, La Diablesse (pronounced "jablesse") wears the floppy hat and flowing gown of French colonial times, and lures men (particularly unfaithful husbands) deep into the forest, never to return. At fetes, her frenzied dancing outshines the other women and attracts the men. The only way to distinguish her is by her feet; one is normal, the other a cloven hoof. She can only be avoided by wearing one's clothes inside out.

**La Gahou** Also known as lugarhoo, this spirit feeds on fresh blood. Iron chains slung about its body rattle and drag along the ground, and its sheaf of sticks functions as a whip; it can alter its form (usually becoming a jackass or dog) as well as changing size from minute to monstrous. A pair of scissors opened to resemble a cross and a Bible placed at the head of the bed will force the hungry beast to revert to its human form.

**Mama D'Leau** Spirit and protector of rivers and lakes, Mama D'Leau (pronounced "mama glow") sits naked at the edge of running water, incessantly combing her long hair. Beneath the water, she has the lower body of a snake, which she uses to pull any man who comes along to a watery death. To escape Mama D'Leau, you must remove your left shoe and walk home backwards.

**Papa Bois** Tall and strong, his hair entwined with leaves, Papa Bois is the guardian of the trees, birds and animals that live in the forests. He imitates animal calls, leading hunters deep into the bush to become hopelessly lost. Papa Bois is assisted by douens, who lead him to animal traps so that he can release the captives.

**Phantom** The keeper of the roads, this impossibly tall jumbie is visible only from the waist down, as his torso and head are hidden in the trees. He uses his long legs to straddle roads, stopping travellers and crushing them to death if they attempt to pass.

**Soucouyant** This female vampire lives in villages as a reclusive old woman. At night, she sheds her skin to travel the country in the form of a ball of fire searching for victims, her skin kept in an overturned mortar bowl until her return at daybreak. She can only be stopped by dousing the skin in salt, which prevents her from re-entering it, or dropping piles of rice in homes and at crossroads; she is compelled to pick them up one by one until sunrise brings about her discovery.

# Obeah

A retention of African animist traditions, **obeah** (from the Ashanti term *obay-foi*, meaning witchcraft or magic) is the belief in a spiritual power that can influence events in the temporal world, curing disease, providing good fortune or wreaking revenge. Though dismissed by most as mumbo–jumbo, obeah still has some followers, particularly in Tobago and in rural areas of Trinidad, where **blue bottles** (the local brand of milk of magnesia is commonly used) are placed over front doors or in gardens to ward off the evil spirits known as **jumbies** (see box. p.337).

Other obeah superstitions include scrubbing the home with pumpkin leaves to drive out evil forces, avoiding sweeping the home after 6pm (doing so brushes away good luck), and entering the house backwards if you come home at midnight to avoid bringing in evil spirits. The **evil eye**, usually called **maljo** (*mal yeux*), is a widely believed concept; bad luck is commonly blamed on someone having "set maljo" on the recipient, and people wear red and black jumbie beads to fend it off.

Believers occasionally resort to hiring the services of an **obeah man** (or woman), also known as a bush doctor or herbalist, and an **ojhaman** or **seer-man** in the Indian community. Usually, the practitioner's extensive knowledge of natural medicines is the main reason for a consultation, and a variety of ailments are still successfully treated with bush baths, teas and decoctions of herbs, barks, leaves and roots (see box, below). Spiritual and physical problems are often viewed as part of the same thing; arthritis, for example, indicates that a curse has been placed on the sufferer.

In special circumstances, such as unrequited love, loss of an object or a string of bad luck, the obeah man may be paid to invoke or dispel a curse, which is done through a ritual to bring on the desired effect – called "**working obeah**" – that is reversible only by a more powerful obeah man. Most obeah men and

## Traditional herbal medicine

One of the most widely practised aspects of the traditional African belief system known as **obeah** is herbal medicine. From boiling up bois cano leaves for a cold or bois bande bark and ruction root to revive a flagging libido, many Trinbagonians make use of **herbal medicine**, and most know the uses of the common plants, herbs, roots and barks that make up the materia medica of what's called **bush**. Concoctions are usually brewed into a **tea** and drunk or infused into the skin through a **bush bath**, and the curative power of the remedies is said to be for spiritual as well as physical health, getting rid of "blight" or maljo, the evil eye. Herbs must be picked during certain phases of the moon to ensure their effectiveness.

During the plantation era, every slave community had its **herbalist**, who doled out concoctions for every kind of ailment and presided over births long before Western midwifery was available, prescribing remedies to ease the pain of childbirth and see-ing the mother through the week-long "lying in" period, when special tonics were administered.

Elements of these traditions remain strong in Trinbagonian attitudes to health, par-ticularly in the customs of **cooling** and **purging**, which clean the blood and purify the system. After a dose of cooling herbs such as wild senna, caraili, mauby or paw-paw bark, comes a purge of aloes or castor oil, a monthly ritual that has whole fam-ilies queuing up outside the bathroom door as the medicine takes effect. Other pop-ular remedies include lemon grass, black sage, shandelay and Christmas bush for **colds**, zebapik, chadon beni and fever or carpenter grass for **temperatures**, lime or St John's bush for **itching**, and soursop and ti Marie leaves for **insomnia**.

women today are hardly sinister characters cooking up bubbling potions under a full moon, but instead respected figures dispensing herbal medicines to rural communities.

# Rastafari

Developed in Jamaica, **Rastafari** – particularly the well-organized, egalitarian **Twelve Tribes of Israel** sect, who have branches in both islands – has become increasingly popular in recent years, attracting a very visible local congregation. Believers and nonbelievers flock to reggae parties (known here as **nyabinghis**), "Jah" has become interchangeable with "God" in popular vocabulary, particularly among the youth, and the red, gold and green colours of the faith are everywhere.

With a mission of spreading love and unity, Rastafarians believe that Ethiopia's **Haile Selassie** is God or **Jah**, the 225th incarnation of King Solomon and a latter-day Christ. A second tenet is **repatriation** of all believers to the spiritual home of Africa and away from **Babylon**, the oppressive, corrupt society of the Western world and all that it represents.

Rastafarians live according to their interpretations of biblical readings; Proverb 15:17 "Better is a dinner of herbs where love is, than a stalled ox and hatred therewith" directs their **ital** (natural and unprocessed) diet; no salt in cooking, no meat and few dairy products. Alcohol, cigarettes and chemical stimulants are also prohibited, though many Rastas see no problem with the odd drink or cigarette. **Ganja** (marijuana) is taken to aid meditations or used at prayer meetings; "He causeth the grass to grow for the cattle, and the herb for the service of man" (Psalm 104:14). **Dreadlocks** are directed by a loose interpretation of Leviticus 21:5; "They shall not make baldness upon their head, neither shall they shave off the corner of their beard", which Rastas read as meaning they should not tamper with their hair at all.

# Music

Trinbagonian music is some of the most exciting, entertaining and thought-provoking in the Caribbean. Most local people display a healthy dedication to their national musics: the down-tempo, lyrically based calypso (more traditionally known as kaiso); the faster, more contemporary sounding, dance-oriented soca, in all its manifestations; and steel pan, that lilting tinkle that's synonymous with the region.

Most people here have a direct connection with the industry as well, whether by entering the annual round of amateur calypso competitions to be crowned National Flour Mills or *Trinidad Guardian* **Calypso King** or **Queen**, or by **beating iron** in the rhythm sections that spring up seemingly out of nowhere at the slightest hint of a celebration. Everyone's a critic, too, as a multitude of aficionados analyse the calypsos and soca hits released for Carnival season, when the professionals are pitted against each other in the **Calypso**, **Soca** and **Chutney Soca Monarch** competitions and pannists take over the Savannah in the quest for the **Panorama** title.

However, T&T's musical spectrum is far wider than just soca and calypso: at Christmas, you'll also hear the Spanish guitars and nasal crooning of **parang**, while East Indian festivals such as Hosay and Phagwa take place to the sound of frenetic **tassa** drumming, and all forms of Indian music are put on show at the **Mastana Bahar** talent contest. Jamaican dancehall reggae – called **dub** – is popular among the youth, and has been fused with calypso-style political lyrics and hip-hop beats to create **rapso**, the republic's newest and most exciting genre.

## Parang

Likely a result of the influence of either Spanish missionaries or of Venezuelan cocoa workers, **parang**, traditionally a Christmas music, is one of the last vestiges of Spanish influence on the islands. During the festive season, which starts in October and ends with Epiphany (Jan 6), groups of roving players – called **parranderos** – descend on private households to perform **aguinaldos**; these are sentimental Spanish songs accompanied by rapid, Mediterranean-style strums on four-stringed instruments, usually **guitar**, **mandolin** and **cuatros**, with violin, box bass, tambourines, maracas and other percussion instruments providing backup.

Parang's Spanish **lyrics** can be romantic or humorous, though many are devoted to **religious** themes such as the exploits of saints and the birth of Jesus. Whatever the lyric, the music is always infused with a sense of joyous celebration, and the festivities are enhanced by the consumption of Spanish-derived dishes such as pastelles, arepas, pelau and strong draughts of rum or poncha crema, a spirit-laced eggnog.

Though the parang tradition has waned a little in recent years, it still remains strong in communities dominated by people of Spanish and Amerindian ancestry, such as Santa Cruz, San Raphael or St Joseph. At Lopinot (see p.157), site caretaker and master parrandero Martin Gomez is usually willing to give a demonstration at any time of the year. Leading performers include the Queen of Parang, Daisy Voisin, the Lara Brothers, Los Ninos de Mundos, Sharlene Flores, Marcia Miranda and Scrunter. In recent years, soca-parang – a fusion of parang, soca and calypso with English – has gone some way to revitalize the art form.

# Calypso to soca

The heart of T&T's music scene and one of its greatest cultural exports, **calypso** represents far more than catchy melodies and witty lyrics for the average Trinbagonian. Nearly everyone here is an expert scholar of the genre, capable of using the most obscure quote to illustrate an argument or make a moral point as well as singing along to classic compositions without skipping a single nuance. Trinbagonians analyse calypsos endlessly until the messages in each year's crop become ingrained in the national consciousness. The "poor people's newspaper", calypso has addressed every phase of T&T's development, commenting on shifts in society and attitudes towards love, sex, marriage, masculinity, race and religion.

While many non-Trinidadians equate the genre with the glib Caribbean clichés of Jamaican Harry Belafonte's *Banana Boat Song* or *Island in the Sun*, to its home audience, calypso has always been their most accessible form of **social commentary**. Calypsonians use double entendre and allegory to make points that would get a politician arrested for libel, and it's widely believed that Eric Williams's PNM government would not have enjoyed thirty years in power without the support of the beloved calypsonian Mighty Sparrow. Recognizing the revolutionary potential of the "people's music", one of the first actions of 1990 coup leader Abu Bakr was to establish a television station given over exclusively to replays of political calypsos critical of the government.

Calypso developed from the songs of praise and derision performed in Africa by travelling troubadours known as **griots**. First known as **cariso** or **kaiso**, calypso as we know it first emerged on the plantations during the 1700s, where slaves used song as a means of covert communication as well as a rhythmic accompaniment to their back-breaking work. Cariso was also a form of entertainment for the planters; notorious Diego Martin estate owner Pierre Begorrat could be tempered only by the sweet verses of **Gros Jean**, his personal **chantuelle**, as these nascent calypsonians were known.

After emancipation, when the chantuelles were finally able to express themselves as free men, they entertained Carnival revellers with insurgent and satirical quips. However, the British found these uninhibited displays unsettling and associated calypso with vulgarity and **civil disobedience**, a stigma that remained for many years. Clashes between revellers and colonial officers, as well as objections from the upper classes to "obscenity" in lyrics, led to the prohibition of African drumming in 1884. In the absence of drums, musicians were forced to be inventive, and created the **tamboo bamboo** – tuned sticks of bamboo beaten on the ground to give a variety of percussive notes – to provide a legal rhythm for their mas and calypso.

## Calypso's golden era

By the beginning of the twentieth century, calypso had entered a period of rapid evolution: English replaced French patois, and brass and string instruments took over from the basic rhythms of the tamboo bamboo. Armed with suitably boastful sobriquets, calypsonians such as **Atilla the Hun**, **Growling Tiger**, **Lord Invader**, **Lord Melody** and **Chieftain Douglas** refined their art and turned professional, performing for paying audiences at makeshift venues in downtown Port of Spain. Known as **tents**, these are still the best places to hear calypso at its most authentic (see p.343). Though veiled in metaphor and double entendre, much of the early material was as risqué and contro-

**versial** as it is today; sex, religion, race and satirical portrayals of public figures were the meat of calypsos that usually included the patois disclaimer "**sans humanité**" – "without mercy".

During the 1930s, calypso also found an overseas audience, largely through the efforts of white appropriators such as Paul Whiteman, whose "Sly Mongoose" had been a huge US hit in the 1920s. However, local singers – including Atilla and Roaring Lion – took trips to the US to record, and the genre gradually gained a level of social acceptance. Nevertheless, the colonial government still had a vested interest in controlling what they perceived to be subversive lyrics, and the 1934 Theatre and Dance Halls Ordinance enabled the **censorship** of so-called offensive compositions and the outright **prohibition** of pieces deemed particularly seditious. Any calypso seen to undermine British rule (or champion black culture) was unceremoniously banned. Calypsonians were required to submit their compositions for government inspection before public performance, and officers stationed in the tents ensured that songs met with British approval. It should come as no surprise that pieces from this time, which are still sung today, are often anti-colonial and anti-European.

During World War II, calypso got another boost through the support of **American troops** stationed at Chaguaramas. Entertainment-hungry soldiers responded enthusiastically to calypso-based nightclub floor shows and the tents were packed to the rafters, the lyrics now accompanied by sophisticated **brass bands**. Calypso's success overseas undermined British suppression, and the genre flourished, though the soldiers' preference for comedy and frivolity over politics or picong (private jokes that went over the head of a foreign audience) led to a trivialization of the lyrics. However, the brawling, fornicating habits of the soldiers did not go unnoticed, and calypsonians documented the morally bereft Port of Spain society during American occupation. Lord Invader's infamously cynical smash hit *Rum and Coca Cola* (see p.116) gave calypso international acclaim, ironically through an Andrews Sisters cover which sold five million copies in the US. Denied a share of the profits, Invader successfully sued.

Dominated by **Mighty Sparrow** (Ⓦwww.mightysparrow.com) and the inimitable late **Lord Kitchener**, calypso grew in popularity throughout the 1950s and 1960s. Tourists descended on T&T to experience this latest craze first-hand and the tents went from strength to strength, with new venues springing up each year. In 1956, Dr Eric Williams's newly elected PNM government created the **Calypso King** competition, and Sparrow swept to victory with the classic *Jean and Dinah*, which gloried in the fact that local women would have to fall back on Trini men now that US soldiers had departed. Crowned monarch so many times that he was eventually barred from competition and given the special title of "Calypso King of the World", Sparrow continued to overshadow his competitors, and calypso lyrics settled into two strands: praise or picong for the "Doctor", and salacious references to love and sex.

Though Independence in 1962 saw calypsonians infusing their lyrics with optimism, by the late 1960s, a new radical politics shook Trinidad, and militant lyricists such as **Valentino**, **Black Stalin** and **Mighty Chalkdust** delivered incisive commentaries on post-colonial society. But despite some innovations – **Calypso Rose** became the first female "king" in 1978, and the competition was renamed **Calypso Monarch** – the 1970s turned out to be a decade of stagnation for calypso. As the anti-establishment, pro-black themes of Jamaican roots reggae held sway over Caribbean musical tastes and sensibilities, calypso lyrics sank to an all-time low of banality.

People still wanted something lively to jump up to on the road and in the fetes, though, and from the early 1980s **soca** (see p.344) began to overshadow its parent during Carnival season. While soca took care of the nation's need to "wine and grind and have a good time", calypso was allowed the breathing space to return to its roots. The genre received a massive creative boost in the middle of the decade through the sensitive, thoughtful work of a single artist, **David Rudder** (📟www.davidrudder.co.tt). An accountant and session singer who worked with brass band Charlie's Roots, Rudder burst onto the scene in 1986, securing an unheard-of triple victory in the Young King, Calypso Monarch and Road March competitions with his beautiful, down-tempo *Bahia Girl*.

Rudder's victory sent shock waves through the calypso community. Previously, a budding calypsonian would only have dared to compete after a rigorous apprenticeship as a solo artist in the tents, earning the tacit blessing of the handful of established artists who dominate the Monarch competition. Rudder had no such patronage, and hadn't bothered to acquire a fanciful sobriquet or a wardrobe of sequinned stage clothes, either. Though he placed second in Calypso Monarch the following year, Rudder subsequently decided not to compete again, on the grounds that he preferred making music to winning prizes. It was a revolutionary and contentious gesture in a genre that tends to concentrate all its energy in capturing the attention of the Savannah judges and sticking to well-known formulas. David Rudder has continued to release some of T&T's most original and thought-provoking compositions. Widely considered Trinidad's answer to Bob Marley, Rudder is also one of the few Trini singers to be embraced internationally while maintaining the support of his home audience.

Today, each year's competition has its own intrigues and excitement. In 2002, a North American film crew caught the action as Gypsy, returning to calypso after a brief foray into mainstream politics, took on Lord Relator and Lord Superior. Their heated exchanges make up only a small part of the 2003 documentary **Calypso Dreams**, which featured performances and interviews with the likes of Ras Shorty I, Sparrow, Calypso Rose and Singing Sandra, and was narrated by David Rudder and Chalkdust.

## Competitions and tents

**Kaiso** (the older term for calypso is preferred by purists) continues to underpin the soca scene. In the **tents** that provide a practice run for the Monarch competition, an older crowd of enthusiasts disentangle the metaphors and squeal at the jokes that are often unintelligible without a good knowledge of Trinbago affairs and gossip. Most artists concentrate on two numbers during the season, usually one with a political slant and another with a more lighthearted theme, be it picong or sex. Whether they get to perform them both is up to the audience; after the first few verses, kaisonians leave the stage, returning only if the claps and catcalls are deemed loud enough to bring them back on.

These days, the most established tents have a permanent location and a roster of well-known artists supplemented by the year's crop of promising newcomers; lineups change annually, and the lists below are not definitive. Traditional kaiso is best heard at **Calypso Revue**, the former home of Lord Kitchener, where the stalwart line-up usually includes Cro Cro, Ronnie McIntosh, Pink Panther and Sugar Aloes. **Kaiso House** is equally good, with Shadow topping a bill of Iwer George, Singing Sandra, Singing Sonia and Brother Resistance. A break from the norm, Nikki Crosby and Errol Fabian's **Maljo Kaiso** is a humorous cabaret-type performance, in which calypsonians' tunes are intermingled with skits – it's one of the best to attend if you're a first-timer, as the visual edge gives you more of a chance of keeping up with the jokes. **Yangatang**, marshalled by corrosively funny MC Sprangalang, also features lots of humour alongside the calypso. Those looking for the big, old names of calypso should head to **House of Stars**, which features the likes of Black Stalin, Calypso Rose, Gypsy, Iwer George, Sparrow and Denyse Plummer. **Spektakula Forum** is one of the best attended tents, with MCs Tommy Joseph and Donna Hadad and regulars such as Scrunter, Chalkdust, Crazy and Gypsy, as well as the year's most popular soca artists. Most of the tents also participate in **clashes**, where kaisonians attempt to outwit each other with improvised material. (For addresses and practical information on the tents, see the Carnival calendar, p.108–109.)

## Soca

Most attribute the birth of **soca** to the late calypsonian **Lord Shorty** (later Ras Shorty I after he converted to Rastafarianism), who died in 2000. Distressed at the moribund state of calypso in the 1970s, which was then playing second fiddle to reggae, he made a conscious decision to breathe new life into the genre. He added Indian instruments, as well as a souped-up rhythmic structure that created an infinitely more danceable form that fitted in with the popularity of disco; when he unveiled his song *Indrani* in 1973, it took T&T by storm. Shorty wanted what he called **sokah** to reflect the soul of calypso, to deal with love and romance as well as the joys of feting, but his legacy is a party music, best heard during Carnival.

From January 1 until Carnival, soca artists release their new material in massive outdoor launch parties; one of the biggest is Crosby's launch, held outside the record shop in St James. Once released, the material does the rounds of the Carnival **fetes**, which whip the loyal listeners into a frenzy and provide a swift induction into soca culture; soon, everyone knows what to do when commanded to "wave yuh rag" or show that they know which dance step accompanies each song. Alongside piped soca from the DJs, fetes usually have a live show consisting of **brass bands** such as Blue Ventures, Question or Charlie's Roots backing the year's most successful soca artists.

Since Blue Boy's *Soca Baptist* became the Road March (the most heavily played tune as mas bands pass judging points on the Carnival route) of 1980, soca has dominated Carnival and become the music of choice among a nation of professional feters, sustained by more than 400 new releases per year. In 1994, the soca/calypso dichotomy was officially recognized when a separate **Soca Monarch** competition was set up. The climax of the soca madness that envelops pre-Carnival Trinidad, Soca Monarch has surpassed its parent event in terms of crowd numbers; it was won for several years running by **Super Blue**, the new name adopted by Blue Boy after he conquered cocaine addiction, and other recent holders of the title include calypsonian Shadow, who brought a welcome dose of traditionalism back to what had become a rather puerile "jump-and-wine" winners list. Bunji Garlin and Iwer George have each held the title since they shared it in 2002. The **Road March** title has now become more or less a soca domain, and is often taken by **Xtatik**, a loose collective headed by heart-throb and expert winer **Machel Montano** (⊛www.machelmontano.com), and recently, Fay Anne Lyons, Super Blue's daughter, won with *Display*, making her only the third woman to have won the title.

Alongside a multitude of home-grown acts such as Destra Garcia, Rupee, Sanelle Dempster, KMC, Tony Prescott, Anselm Douglas, Iwer George and

Traffik, soca's main names also include a strong contingent from **Barbados**; acts such as TC or Alison Hinds' incredibly popular band **Square One** travel over for the season to headline at fetes. Successful soca (and calypso) artists are fostered in most eastern Caribbean islands, while Arrow, the man behind the world's most overplayed soca hit *Hot, Hot, Hot*, actually hails from Montserrat.

## Chutney soca

East Indians have given soca their own slant through **chutney**, which mixes sparse, fast soca beats with sitars and thumping dholak drums. Sung in a mixture of Hindi and English, lyrics tend toward the lighthearted, and chutney fetes – attended predominantly by young East Indians – have become a showcase for sensual dance steps that combine athletic wining with the delicate arm and hand movements of classical Indian dance. However, many older Hindus dislike chutney, finding the overtly sexual dancing and sometimes risqué lyrics distasteful.

Established in 1996, the **National Chutney Soca Monarch** (Ⓦwww.southex.co.tt/chutney) competition is the annual focus for chutney artists, and the finals (usually held at Skinner Park in San Fernando) now attract up to 20,000 enthusiasts. Chutney vocalists to look out for include the smooth **Rikki Jai** (usual winner of the Chutney Monarch competition), Heeralal Rampartap, Sonny Mann and Drupatee Ramgoonai; the late Sundar Popo also recorded some classic chutney tunes. Chutney has also influenced the conventional soca industry, with white calypsonian Denise Plummer still flirting with the form, as does Machel Montano.

# Steel pan

Said to be the only new acoustic instrument of the twentieth century, the **steel pan** evolved from the Trinbagonian propensity for using available materials as percussion instruments. During the Carnivals of the 1930s, **tamboo bamboo**-led kalinda music was supplied by bands of young men from deprived areas such as Port of Spain's Laventille and Belmont, who were unanimously viewed as "**bad johns**" or thugs by the more fortunate. With names such as Desperadoes and Invaders, these loosely organized bands supplemented the tamboo with "**rhythm sections**", beating steel rods against anything from brake drums and buckets to dustbin lids to satisfy the urge for rhythm.

It was only a matter of time before someone realized that discarded saucepans or biscuit tins – and later the **oil drums** brought over by US troops – could be hammered into concave sections that produced rough notes; these early raw materials explain why steel drums are known as **pans**. Depending upon who you believe, the first pan was played at some point in the late 1930s, either by **Winston Spree Simon** of the John John band (now Carib Tokyo), who tapped out *Mary Had a Little Lamb*, or **Neville Jules** of Hell Yard (now Trinidad All Stars) who managed the basic chords of a calypso called *Whoopsin, Whoopsin*.

By the end of the war, experimentation with basic pans had produced up to fourteen notes, and the 1946 victory Carnival was dominated by the ringing of steel bands. However, the associations of **violence** lingered, and the **pan-yards** that sprang up throughout the East–West Corridor were widely viewed – probably quite correctly – as seething dens of iniquity. Feuds were common, and in 1950 a bloody **pitched battle** between Invaders and Tokyo had Carnival revellers running for cover. Calypsonian Blakie documented the clash: "It was bacchanal/Fifty Carnival/Fight for so, with Invaders and Tokyo/When the two bands clash/Mamayoe, if yuh see cutlass/Never me again/To jump in a steelband in Port of Spain."

However, the violence tailed off after this and the movement gained respectability (and respect) as the music became more polished and complex. Soon, bands of up to 200 pannists played a sophisticated repertoire of classical pieces as well as calypso, and the nation's dedication to pan began in earnest. In 1950, the **T&T Steelband Association** (now **Pan Trinbago**; ⓦwww.pantrinbago.co.tt) was established to promote and coordinate the movement, setting up a round of competitions that eventually led to the first annual **Panorama** tournament in 1963; twenty-odd years later, the steel pan was officially declared the national instrument by then-PM Patrick Manning.

These days, the panyard calendar revolves around Panorama, a hugely popular affair that involves almost all of T&T's steel bands and attracts around 25,000 people to Port of Spain's Savannah stage, renamed in local vernacular as the "**Big Yard**" during the event. To qualify for the event, bands from the **regional zones** compete at regional venues; the Port of Spain Savannah for the north, the Orange Grove Savannah in Tacarigua for the east, Skinner Park in San Fernando for central and south, and Shaw Park, Scarborough for Tobago. The bands that get the highest number of points qualify for the **preliminaries**, which are held a couple of weeks before Carnival (for more on Panorama, see p.109, and on panyards, p.101). Other pan events include the October **World Steel Band Festival**, where bands from all over the world beat classical and calypso music pieces, while pan does sweet justice to jazz at **Pan Ramajay** in May, and at the **Pan Jazz Festival** in November (for details of these events, see "Basics" p.47).

## The steel band

Transforming a dirty old oil drum into a shiny, playable **steel pan** demands skill and experience, and the **craftsmen's** job is further complicated by the poor quality steel used to make most drums. Surprisingly, empty steel drums are not that easy to come by, and shortages are common; in 1997, Pan Trinbago resorted to importing from Venezuela.

Once the raw material is secured, the drum begins its metamorphosis. All pans other than the bass must first be **cut** to size, and a five-pound sledge-hammer is used to beat the unopened end into a convex shape. The pan is then **heated** over a wood fire; oil is used to **temper** the metal, and a coating of **chrome** gives a better surface and a shiny finish. The **tuner** then takes over, marking the notes and beating them out with a hammer and chisel, an extremely specialized process that's usually achieved with the help of a keyboard. A finished pan will sell for around **TT$2500**.

In contemporary bands, different types of pan produce a variation of tones. The main melody is held by the **tenor** or **soprano** pan, which has the largest range of notes. **Guitar** and **cello pans** provide the background harmonies, and the booming **bass pan** underpins it all. However, no steel band would be complete without its rhythm section or **engine room**, as the percussion section is known. In addition to a conventional drum kit, cow bells, shakers and scrapers, there is the **iron**, assorted bits of metal beaten with iron rods – an old brake drum produces just the right metallic clank. Known as **iron men**, the percussionists have to be pretty burly in order to keep up the repetitive beat for hours on end.

Each band is led by an **arranger**, who will adapt music from a variety of sources for the steel band. Though some arrangers work with more than one band, there are several long-standing relationships: Jit Samaroo and Renegades, Len "Boogsie" Sharp and Phase II Pan Groove, Pelham Goddard and Exodus. Though most bands used to play it safe and enter Panorama with calypsos familiar to audience and judges alike, original compositions have become popular since 1987, when Phase II won with a Boogsie Sharp original, *Dis Feeling Nice*. Lord Kitchener was a master composer of pan music, and since his death many bands have entered his compositions for Panorama.

Most contemporary steel bands are comprised of between 50 and 200 volunteer pannists, who play one or two harmonic pans; with up to six instruments, bass pannists have to be pretty dextrous, twisting around to reach the right notes. A steel band is based at a **panyard**, usually a semi-open practice space where instruments are stored. As the band needs to be mobile, pans are housed in welded metal structures with wheels, plank floors and a galvanized canopy which can be pushed along by supporters; some bands also use flat-bed trucks to move through the streets. **Pan round the neck** bands are usually smaller, comprising 50 or so players who carry their instruments with a strap around the neck.

# Reggae

After the bacchanal of Carnival, the nation gives up soca and calypso for Lent, and you'll find it difficult to pick up anything other than **reggae** or religious music on the radio. **Dub** to Trinbagonians, **reggae** has made massive inroads among the youth, who favour the "conscious" music of local, Rasta-oriented artists such as Capleton, Sizzla and Buju Banton as well as more upfront and lewd material from Jamaica. DJ families such as **Matsimela** and **Black Stone** play at large indoor parties, and their broadcasts are some of the most popular in T&T radio. Reggae has also lent its influence to soca, with many artists employing the vocal style (and the language and accent) or experimenting with the self-explanatory sub-genre of **ragga soca**. The most popular ragga soca performer is **Bunji Garlin**, "the girls dem darlin" (@www.triniweb.com/bunji), who thrills the ladies and bigs up the blokes with his smooth Trini-Jamaican cocktail.

# Rapso

Born out of the Black Power movement and labour strife of the early 1970s, rapso is far from a derivation of American rap. Indeed, it's another Trinbagonian form which is a politically conscious fusion of African-style drum beats, soca melodies and spoken calypso-esque vocals infused with the militancy of American rap. Early lyrics were said to have been created during strikes and chanted on picket lines, but the genre's originator is generally considered to be **Lancelot "Kebu" Layne** who released *Blow Away* in 1970 and *Get Off My Radio* in 1971. In 1976, Cheryl Byron, the "Mother of Rapso", became the first rapso artist to perform in a calypso tent, while Brother Resistance emerged as the "Father of Rapso" in the 1980s. Resistance has since emerged as the most popular rapso artist and has even written a seminal book on the art form (see p.358). Rapso's popularity has increased with the emergence of new artists in the 1990s, and still represents the freshest section of Trinbago music, evolving in tempo and style each year. Artists such as Resistance, Ataklan, Black Lyrics and Kindred write poetic, haunting lyrics that centre upon black empowerment and resistance to oppression; as Brother Resistance states, "rapso is the power of the word in the rhythm of the word." The proselytizing is always backed up by the stinging, drum-dominated rhythms that have earned a huge youth following; Ataklan's reggae-influenced, dance-oriented tracks are essential plays at Carnival fetes, while 3 Canal remain the movement's most popular proponents. **Rapso month**, held at venues across Port of Spain in April or May, is a great opportunity to hear the rising stars of this newest expression of T&T's seemingly endless musical fertility; for more on events surrounding the festival, contact Rituals Records (☎625 3262, ⓦwww.ritualsmusic.com).

# Flora and fauna

Joined to the South American mainland during the Ice Age when sea levels were lower, Trinidad and Tobago only became separate entities when movements of the Caribbean tectonic plates submerged the Orinoco Delta some 10,000 years ago. The islands owe their immense environmental diversity to this period of attachment, which has left them with many South American plants, animals and birds, as well as the flora and fauna found elsewhere in the Caribbean. Few places of relative size harbour such variety.

A wide range of **habitats** supports the wildlife; **Tobago** boasts the oldest **protected rainforest** in the Western Hemisphere along its main ridge of mountains, as well as **marshes** and **lagoons** in the western tip, a network of ornate offshore **reefs** and the **bird sanctuaries** of Little Tobago and the St Giles islands. In **Trinidad**, the rich **wetlands** at Nariva Swamp support several plant and animal species found nowhere else in T&T, while Caroni Swamp offers easy access to **mangroves** and their inhabitants. The dry, treeless prairie at Aripo – the island's only remaining true **savannah** plain – sustains unusual plants and orchids as well as bird life. Trinidad's hills are afforded some government protection, and contain three state reserves: the **Northern Range Sanctuary**, the **Valencia Wildlife Sanctuary** in the northeast and the **Trinity Hills Wildlife Sanctuary** in the southeast. However, with only a handful of game wardens and forest rangers to defend the forests, and the industrial wasteland of the west coast constantly encroaching on virgin land, the island's wildlife is under constant threat. For more on the T&T environment, visit the **website** of Environment Tobago (⑩www.scsoft.de/et/et2.nsf) or the Trinidad and Tobago Field Naturalists Club (⑩www.wow.net/ttfnc); the Environmental Management Authority's site is also worth a browse (⑩www.ema.co.tt).

# Trees and shrubs

Although T&T's **woodlands** are disappearing at a significant rate, they still make up around 40 percent of the country's total land area. Several different forest types are found on the islands, including thick, warm and wet **evergreen** and **deciduous** woodlands. Higher elevations see **montane** forest – wet and cool with plenty of epiphytic growth – with the stubby 2-metre canopy of **elfin** forest occupying only the highest mountain peaks.

About **350 species** of tree grow in T&T, including the exotically named pink bark, gustacare, crapaud, saltfishwood, sardine, purpleheart, bloodwood, hairy cutlet and naked Indian. The main forest trees are **mora**, **teak**, **mahogany**, **cedar**, **cypre**, **Caribbean pine** and **balata**; the latter produces a milky latex used to coat golf balls. Immediately noticeable, the **bois cano** has large, deeply lobed leaves that dry into a distinctive claw shape; and the mighty 40-metre **silk cotton** or kapok tree (its fruits contain the cotton-like kapok) boasts an impressive girth of buttressed roots spreading elegantly to meet the ground – Amerindians used entire trees for their dug-out pirogues. The spreading branches of the **samaan** are often employed to shade cocoa and coffee, while the **banyan** looks more like a collection of interweaved vines than a tree, as its boughs produce aerial roots that form secondary trunks when they reach the ground. The **tree fern's** diamond-patterned trunk and top-heavy crown of fern-like leaves lend a primeval aspect to high altitude forests.

## Ornamental trees

A host of **ornamental** trees turn T&T's forests into a patchwork of colour during the dry months (Dec–May), when the intense orange-red flowers of the mountain **immortelle** compete with two varieties of **poui**, which shed their leaves to make way for cascades of dusky pink or bright yellow blossoms. The **cassia** also produces prolific cascades of deep yellow or pink flowers. Covering a flat, wide-spreading crown, the deep red **flamboyant** or poinciana flowers bloom in August as well as April; during the dry season, half-metre pods full of rattling seeds dangle from the leafless branches.

Flowering sporadically throughout the year, the 15-metre **African tulip** or "flame of the forest" produces clusters of deep red blooms along outer branches; unopened buds in the centre of the flower are sometimes used as natural water pistols, as they contain a pouch of water which spurts out at speed when pressure is applied. Creating patches of mauve throughout Trinidad's forests, the crown of the **crepe myrtle** is usually smothered with blooms, while **bauhinia** or orchid tree and **jacaranda** add to the purple hues.

## Fruit trees

Among the huge variety of **fruit trees**, the most easily recognizable is the **mango**, with its rounded, dense crown of long, leathery leaves over a short trunk. Diminutive, twisty-branched **guava** trees grow wild throughout the islands; crack open one of its green-skinned, pink-fleshed fruit and you're sure to see a squirming contingent of small white worms. **Banana** plants are not trees in the strict botanical sense; their huge, tattered leaves grow from a central stem made up of overlapping leaf bases. Covered by large purple bracts, the flowers hang from the main stem and eventually develop into the fruit. **Plantain** trees are similar, with larger, less tattered leaves and bigger, more robust fruit. Equally easy to recognize, **pawpaw** (papaya) has a long hollow stem with large splayed leaves and fruit at the top. The fruit of **West Indian cherry** trees are bright red when ripe; they look similar to their temperate counterparts, but are much more sour. An excellent source of vitamin C, they are sweetened and juiced.

Still grown in groves for export, **cocoa** is easily identifiable by its lichen-smothered trunk, dark green shiny leaves and 20-centimetre ridged oval pods that grow from the trunk and turn from light green to brown, yellow, orange or purple when ripe. Covered with a sweet white gloop, the beans inside can be sucked when raw, but are usually dried and roasted to make cocoa powder. **Cashew** trees, with their strongly veined oval leaves, are common; the familiar nut pokes out of the bottom of a sweet-tasting, pear-shaped red fruit, whose shell produces an oily liquid that is a skin irritant. With dark, evergreen leaves, **nutmeg** trees produce a peach-like fruit that encases the nut, itself covered with a bright red network of mace.

The lifeblood of many a craft vendor, the fruits of the **calabash** tree grow to more than 35 centimetres in diameter and are traditionally halved and hollowed out to make bowls. Tall and compound-leaved, the **tamarind** tree bears a 10-centimetre brown pod; when ripe, the inner seeds are surrounded by an acidic pulp that's used to make tamarind balls, drinks and as a seasoning. Employed as a vegetable but classified as a fruit, **breadfruit** was brought to the Caribbean by Captain Bligh aboard the *HMS Providence* as food for plantation slaves. With spreading branches decorated by large serrated leaves, the spherical fruits are lime-green and pockmarked. Its close cousin is the chataigne or **breadnut**, a similar tree with smaller, spiky fruits that are eaten roasted.

## Coastal trees and palms

Trinidad's swamps of red, black and white **mangrove** trees, with their dense tangle of aerial roots, help protect coastal communities from hurricane surges, filter sediments that smother reefs and provide a nursery for fish and crustaceans.

Among the most common seashore plants is the **Indian almond**, with its symmetrical branches; the nuts can be eaten once the outer pods turn brown, though they don't taste like conventional almonds. On exposed shores, the **sea grape** lies low and twisted, but in less windswept conditions it's wide and spreading, and can attain a height of 15 metres. The flat, round leaves are distinctively veined and turn a deep red as they mature. Once they've turned purple, the grapes are edible if a little sour. Definitely one to avoid, the **manchineel** tree also grows to about 15 metres with a wide spreading canopy dotted with indistinct green fruits and flowers, all of which are extremely **poisonous** – even standing below a manchineel during rain incurs blistering from washed-down sap.

Commercial plantations on both islands have made the **coconut** T&T's most prevalent palm. It's an incredibly versatile tree; the water and meat are consumed fresh at the jelly stage, while the flesh of older coconuts is grated and used in baking or immersed in water and strained to produce the coconut milk that flavours a thousand local dishes. Coconut oil is used in soap, cosmetics and cooking, while the leaf fronds thatch roofs and make hats or floor mats, the husks are used to make floor buffers and pieces of hard shell are made into jewellery and cups.

There are many varieties of **ornamental palm**: often used to mark out driveways, the 30-metre **royal palm** is classically shaped with bushy fronds and a grey, ruler-straight trunk with a green section near to the top. Similar but even taller at an average of 40 metres, the **cabbage palm** has thicker, messier looking fronds. Squat and dominated by its spiky leaves, the **cocorite** is one of the most common forest palms. The ultimate in tropical splendour, the **traveller's palm** is actually a member of the banana family – the name refers to mini-ponds at the base of the trunk that provide a convenient water source. Fronds fan out from the base in an enormous peacock's tail shape as high as 10 metres.

# Plants and flowers

Of T&T's various **wild plants**, some notable specimens include the **jumbie bead vine**, which produces shiny red and black poisonous seeds used in craft items and as good luck charms; they are said to ward off evil spirits, and a bead kept in a purse will keep it filled with money. A variety of mimosa with scratchy stems, **ti Marie** grows prolifically throughout the islands, and resembles a miniature bracken. It's also known as "the sensitive plant" for its ability to curl back its leaves at the slightest touch.

The largest of the epiphytes that grow along tree branches, electricity wires and any available surface is the **wild pine bromeliad**, a spiky-leafed relative of the pineapple that produces a battered-looking red flower. These "air plants" are not parasites – they draw their nutrients from the mineral-rich rainforest atmosphere – but host trees have been known to collapse under the weight of several of them. Ten-litre water reserves trapped between the leaves provide a habitat for insects and frogs. Other epiphytes include 200 different species of **orchids**, many of them so small that you'll need a magnifying glass to appreciate them. These chancers grow on living or dead plant or tree matter and in lowland savannahs such as Aripo in eastern Trinidad. In the lowland forests, both the **monkey throat** and the pendulous **jack spaniard** with its trailing wasp-like petals are particularly distinctive, while the common **lamb's tail** grows horizontally from large trees, and has attractive maroon-flecked green petals with a white and pink stamen.

T&T's most eye-catching flora, however, are the 2300 varieties of **flowering plant** which provide beds, borders and hedges with a splash of colour, and you'll often see several varieties of multicoloured **croton** leaves in between the blooms. The national flower is the **chaconia**, a wild poinsettia which grows throughout the local forests, but the ubiquitous **bougainvillea** is the most spectacular ornamental, its red, white, orange and pink papery bracts spilling out into intensely coloured clumps. Distinguishable by its protruding pollen-tipped stamen, **hibiscus** takes on an abundance of hues and shapes; the lacy **coral hibiscus** has clusters of tiny curling red petals and a red frill at the end of the stamen, while the popular **Mexican creeper** provides a clambering shower of delicate pink or white. A dark-leafed shrub with clusters of small red flowers, **ixora** is another popular ornamental that flowers throughout the year.

Flamboyant **tropical flowers** are grown commercially in T&T and also flourish in the wild. Brush-like **ginger lilies** are one of the most common exotics; the deep pink or red bracts hide the insignificant true flower, and the shiny, banana-like leaves are used in flower arrangements. A close relative, the **torch ginger's** deep crimson cluster of thick waxy petals makes an impressively showy head. However, the queen of local exotics – and the symbol of the PNM political party – are the 40 vividly coloured varieties of **balisier**, all members of the heliconia family, which include the aptly named **lobster claw** and the red, yellow and green **hanging heliconia**, which looks like a series of fish hanging from a rod. Equally prevalent are the artificial-looking **anthuriums**, a shiny, heart-shaped red, pink or white bract with a long penile stem or spadix protruding from the centre. The flashy **bird of paradise**, a blue and purple flower that resembles a bird's head graced by a deep orange crest, is rarer.

# Fauna

With more than 100 species of **mammal** roaming the forests and flats (not including T&T's 50,000-plus goats), hunting remains a popular pastime and wild meat is consumed with gusto whenever available. Most hunters go after the most common varieties; aside from the burgeoning populations of **red squirrel**, the smallest quarry is the herbivorous **agouti**, a brown, rabbit-sized rodent that looks like a long-legged guinea pig and feeds on fruits and leaves, and its larger relative the **lappe** or **paca**, which has longer legs and a pattern of stripes and spots on its fur. Equally desirable for the pot is the **manicou** or opossum, an unattractive cat-sized marsupial with a rat-like tail and a long snout that forages for scraps and carrion. The nine-banded **tatoo** or armadillo is increasingly rare, as is the brown-coloured **red brocket deer** (extinct in Tobago) and the **quenk**, an aggressive wild hog with small sharp tusks that eats roots, bulbs and occasionally snakes. Another threatened species, the metre-long **ocelot** wildcat, or tiger cat, has been extensively hunted for its beautiful spotted pelt.

**Otters** live in and around the Madamas and Paria rivers in Trinidad, but shy away from humans. Trinidad's cutest water-dwelling mammal, the herbivorous **West Indian manatee** or sea cow grows up to four metres long and can live for 50 years. However, the destruction of its swampland habitat by development and by drainage for agriculture has decimated local populations, with less than a hundred still living in the protected Nariva Swamp.

The islands' largest **monkey** colonies also live in Nariva; with red-furred, hulking frames and a bulbous, bearded larynx, troops of up to fifteen **red howlers** defend their territory with the eerie, deafening roars that prompted their name. Smaller but extremely intelligent, **weeping capuchin** monkeys live in the tree-tops in troops of up to twenty, and are able to use basic tools to crack open nuts as well as occasionally expressing their irritation at human intrusions by raining down a volley of sticks on curious heads. Around 60 species of **bat** inhabit T&T's forests and caves, most living on a diet of insects, fruit, nectar and pollen. The two notable exceptions are the **vampire bat**, which prefers a more gruesome food source, creeping up on sleeping livestock and drinking their blood, and the **frog-eating bat**, which distinguishes between poisonous and edible species by listening to mating calls.

## Reptiles and amphibians

The largest of the 70 species of **reptile** is an endemic sub-species of the **spectacled caiman**, a 3-metre alligator with an elongated snout that inhabits swamps, rivers and dams, and feeds on fish and birds. Among the 47 different **snakes**, only four are venomous. With the girth of a man's arm and a length of up to 3 metres, the **fer-de-lance** is particularly aggressive, and is identifiable by its pointed head, yellow underside and chin, and orange/brown triangular markings. The **bushmaster** is slightly longer (up to 4 metres) with a burnt orange skin distinctly patterned by dark brown diamonds with smaller diamonds of orange within. Its venom can be lethal to the young, old or infirm, but most people manage to get the antidote in time. For advice on dealing with snake bites, see "Health", p.25. Both snakes are known as mapepire (pronounced "mah-pee-pee") and inhabit forest areas. The two varieties of poisonous **coral snake**, the common and large coral snake, are smaller, rarer and less aggressive; they're easy to spot, with black skin and red and white rings around the body.

Known as macajuel (pronounced *makka*-well), **boa constrictors** – including **anacondas** – are T&T's largest snakes, and can grow up to a fearsome 10 metres in length. Most are patterned with brown diamonds that provide camouflage. They are not venomous, but can easily crush a large mammal in their powerful coils.

Among more than 20 species of **lizard** are **geckos**, usually referred to as zandolie or ground lizards. The **twenty-four-hour lizard** gets its name from a local myth which warns that if you disturb one, it will attach itself to your body and remain there for 24 hours – at the end of which you die. The bright green, spiky-backed, herbivorous **iguana** is a favourite delicacy, especially if it's carrying eggs; unsurprisingly, it spends most of its time hiding from human captors in leafy treetops. The metre-long, dark brown **matte lizard** relies on speed to stay out of the cooking pot, raising itself onto its hind legs to accelerate to 11kph in two seconds.

T&T's most common **amphibian** is the **crapaud** (pronounced "crappo"), a warty, hand-sized frog with a loud, booming croak. Another frog, the

## Leatherback turtles

Weighing up to 700kg and measuring three to four metres across, **leatherback turtles** have undergone few evolutionary alterations in their 150-million-year history. Named for the soft, leathery texture of their ridged, blue-grey **carapace** (which is more like a skin than a shell, and bleeds if cut), leatherbacks spend most of the year in cool temperate waters gorging on jellyfish, often eating twice their body weight per day. However, during the **egg laying season** (March–July; the best months for seeing turtles are April, May and June), females swim thousands of miles, returning to the beach of their birth to lay their own eggs in the sand, a fascinating, moving two-hour process that takes place under the cover of night.

Choosing a spot above the water line, the turtle excavates a metre-deep **egg chamber** with her muscular back flippers, her body heaving with the effort and her eyes dripping mucous tears to protect against grains of sand. A trance-like state takes over during the laying of around 100 soft-skinned white eggs, about the same size as a chicken's. After filling in the nest and compacting the sand, leatherbacks may make several decoy nests with their powerful front flippers to confuse predators. The process over, the leatherback drags herself back to the water.

Leatherbacks often return to the same beach up to ten times per season – a necessary repetition, as only 60 percent of all eggs laid will mature into hatchlings – many are dug up by dogs or poachers – and only one or two of these will become fully-grown turtles. **Hatchlings** usually emerge from the sand about sixty days later and make a moon-guided dash for the sea. Many are eaten by dogs, birds and fish; these days, any that manage to emerge during the day are herded into groups by wardens until darkness provides a little more safety.

### Turtle-watching

You can see leatherback egg laying at Grande Riviere, Matura and Fishing Pond in Trinidad or Parlatuvier, Stone Haven Bay, Bloody Bay and Turtle Bay in Tobago. Trinidad's turtle beaches are **protected areas** during the laying season, and you need a **permit** to enter after dark; these cost TT$5 and are available from the Forestry Division at Long Circular Road in Port of Spain (☎622 4521, 3217 or 5214) and in San Fernando (☎657 7256), or the District Revenue Office in Sangre Grande (☎668 3835). Note that no permits are required to visit turtle nesting sites in Tobago. The services of a Forestry Division guide will cost an additional US$10. Alternatively, you can call Nature Seekers (☎668 7337), who patrol Matura Beach during the laying season and offer sensitive and informative **turtle-watching trips**. GREAT (Grande Riviere Environmental Awareness Trust) at Grand Riviere offer the same service; although the group is younger and not as well organized, the beach is smaller and you have a greater chance of seeing several turtles. Both of the above groups arrange permits. If you don't have transport to get you to a laying beach, contact one of the tour operators listed on p.53, most of which offer turtle-watching excursions. In Tobago, several hotels along the Mount Irvine coast organize turtle-watching trips, including the *Seahorse Inn* (☎639 0686). During your observations, make sure to stay 15 metres away and refrain from shining bright lights or taking flash photos until turtles have started laying; before this point, turtles are easily distracted and may return to the sea.

**colostethus**, provides a night-time chorus reminiscent of a demented guinea pig. Trinidad's only endemic amphibian, the **golden tree frog**, lives on the epiphytic plants that cling to the rainforest trees of the island's two highest mountains, El Tucuche and El Cerro del Aripo. In addition to the land turtle, or **morocoy**, five species of **sea turtle** lay their eggs on local beaches: the green turtle, the olive ridley, the hawksbill (illegally poached for its tortoise-shell), the loggerhead and – rarest and largest of them all – the giant leatherback (see box, this page).

## Birds

With more than 430 recorded types of **birds**, Trinidad and Tobago ranks among the world's top ten in terms of numbers of species, and offers the best **bird-watching** in the Caribbean (see "Basics", p.50). The **national birds** are the **scarlet ibis** (Trinidad) and the **cocorico** (Tobago), both of which adorn the republic's coat of arms; the latter is paradoxically classified as vermin. A native of Venezuela and best seen at the Caroni Swamp, the scarlet ibis typifies the eye-catching colours of local species, while the golden-brown, pheasant-like cocorico has a fleshy, bright red turkey-style wattle at its throat and a rau-cous call.

The sugar-water feeders at most hotels are a great way to see smaller birds at close quarters. Before Trinidad got its European name, the Amerindians called it **Ieri**, the land of the hummingbird. There are fifteen different species of these brightly coloured miniatures in T&T, of which the most frequently seen are the **copper-rumped hummingbird** and the **white-necked jacobin**, both with fabulous iridescent feathers The most unusual hummer is the 6-cen-timetre **tufted coquette**, Trinidad's smallest bird and the third smallest in the world, with a red and yellow body, dark wings and a pretty red crest.

Both jet-black, the blunt-beaked **smooth-billed ani** and the shiny **cowbird** with a sharper beak and beady yellow eyes are the local equivalent of pigeons. The audacious 10-centimetre black and yellow **bananaquit** is supposed to subsist on nectar, but has become a frequent visitor to hotel breakfast tables, dipping its sharp little beak into fruits and sweet preserves. Seen wherever there are cattle, **white egrets** roost on ruminating rumps in a mutually rewarding relationship that provides the egret with a constant supply of insects and the cow some relief from bloodsuckers.

In the forests and flats, frequently sighted birds include **white-bearded man-akins**, which perform intricate courtship displays in designated areas known as **leks** (several other species also use leks), several intensely coloured **woodpeck-ers**, **antbirds**, **trogons** and **tanagers** – the palm tanager is a cool olive with black flecks on its wings, while the bay-headed variety is a brilliant emerald with a russet head. Various **honeycreepers** display dazzling hues of turquoise and black; the purple variety's near-black feathers only show purple in the sunshine.

Of larger birds, common varieties include multicoloured **toucans**, **parrots**, **yellow orioles** and **giant cowbirds**, as well as the crow-like **crested oropendola**, black with a yellow tail, cream beak, beady blue eyes, a truly exotic call and a marvellous way of building nests: metre-long, teardrop-shaped constructions of dry grass that hang in groups from tree boughs. Though it can be hard to spot the **bearded bellbird**, you'll certainly hear its penetrating "bok, bok" call in the hill forests. Birds of prey include the **peregrine falcon**, as well as several **kites** and **hawks**, including the **ornate hawk-eagle**, the largest of the lot. The ubiquitous **vultures** – called corbeaux – perform a nec-essary, if unsavoury, function by devouring dead animals.

## Oilbirds

Squat, mottled brown and whiskered, **oilbirds** have the honour of being the world's only nocturnal fruit-eating birds, and Trinidad supports eight breeding colonies. Spending the daylight hours inside their caves, oilbirds are unusually gregarious; up to forty birds will huddle on a single ledge, squawking and picking through each others' feathers for parasites. Mature birds venture into the open only at night, using sonar to assist their manoeuvres through the forests in search of palm, laurel and camphor fruits, often travelling as far as 120km from the colony in each foray. Fruits are swallowed whole and the seeds regurgitated, and in-flight consumption is an important agent of reforestation.

Oilbirds rear one **brood** of young each year, laying between two and four eggs over several days in nests constructed from regurgitated, cement-like matter that rapidly turns the snowy-white clutch a dirty brown. Both parents share the 32-day incubation, after which the blind, featherless fledglings emerge, remaining immobile for up to three weeks and feeding on partially digested fruit pulp. Development is slow; a patchy cover of downy feathers grows after 21 days, and young birds do not fledge until they are 100 to 120 days old.

A young oilbird weighs twice as much as a mature one, due to the high **fat content** that gave rise to the name. The Amerindians and Capuchin monks used to boil the fledglings down for their oil, which they then used to fuel cooking fires and make flambeaux. The Amerindians also called the oilbird guacharo, "the one who wails and mourns", on account of the rasps, screams, squawks and snarls that make up its call; an eerie sound that also inspired the bird's French patois sobriquet, diablotin – devil bird.

Tobago sustains a few species not seen regularly in Trinidad, such as the **red-crowned woodpecker**, **rufous–tailed jacamar** and the **white-tailed sabrewing**. The smaller island is also the best place to see **blue-crowned mot-mots** (locally called king of the woods), with deep orange breasts, green-blue heads and long flowing tail feathers. Offshore of both islands, **boobies** and **brown pelicans** trawl for fish, the latter being the only pelican to dive from great heights into the sea, scooping up its quarry in its large pouched bill. However, if a **frigate bird** is around, smaller sea birds often lose their catch, as the frigate feeds on stolen goods snatched from the beak of more efficient fishers.

## Insects and spiders

With 92 varieties of **mosquito** in T&T, and far too many kinds of **cockroach** (ranging from 7-centimetre dark brown pests to the rare albino variety), you could be forgiven for doing your best to disregard the rest of the country's invertebrate life, but many species are vital to the local ecosystems. More than 600 varieties of **butterfly** flit between local flowers, ranging from the 2-centimetre crimson–and–black red devil to the commonly seen bright blue 7-centimetre emperor and the cocoa mort bleu, brown and mauve with eye-like spots on the wings.

Armies of black, brown or red bachac or **leaf-cutting ants**, with almost triangular heads and sharp, sizeable pincers, are divided into ranks. Large workers trim entire shrubs into coin-sized pieces and carry them on their backs to the nest, while smaller workers fend off any potential predators. The leaf-pieces are then shredded and chewed into compost for the cultivation of the fungus that feeds the colony. A single nest may discard as much as 20 cubic metres of waste material in five years, banking it up over the subterranean colony, which houses up to 2.5 million ants. Living in equally complex societies that can number one billion, **termites** attach their large, irregular earthen nests to the sides of trees.

Aside from the spindly-limbed specimens that inhabit interior corners, the largest common **spiders** are black and red and about 8 centimetres long, spinning the classic hexagonal trap. More unusual is the **trapdoor spider**, which conceals its forest-floor burrow with a hinged doorway, springing out to drag passing prey into the hole. Ten species of **tarantula** range from a delicately hued violet and brown to hairy and black, and can measure between 8 and 15 centimetres including the legs. Apart from a bird-eating variety, most are nocturnal insect hunters that construct their basic, messy-looking web tunnels on grassy banks or in dead wood.

## Marine life

Sediment flows from the Orinoco River have prevented the build-up of extensive **reefs** around Trinidad, but off Tobago, where visibility ranges from 12 to 50 metres, are some of the Caribbean's richest and most pristine reefs. Among the sixty or so **coral** varieties are rotund brains, patterned with furrowed trenches, branching umber elkhorn and staghorn, stalagmite-like pillar coral and cool green star coral. Extremely striking are the groups of intricate soft coral sea plumes, sea whips and purple sea fans, while brilliant yellow anemones and red, brown, purple and green sponges provide a splash of colour, some growing up to three feet in diameter. **Caribbean spiny lobsters** and green or spotted **moray eels** lurk in the crevices between corals – if provoked, the eels can inflict a nasty bite.

Sand flats and seagrass fields between the reefs host spiny black **sea urchins**; the spines of round **white urchins** are too short to puncture skin. Long, thin and off-white, **sea cucumbers** sift through the sea floor to feed on deposited nutrients, while **starfish** and **queen conch** snails move slowly along the seagrass blades, vacuuming up organisms that live there.

The reefs harbour a huge variety of multicoloured tropical **fish**, including parrot fish, electric blue creole wrasse, queen and French angel fish, striped grunts and spiny puffer fish – which balloon in size if threatened – as well as tarpon and trigger fish. Giant seven-metre **manta rays** are best seen around Speyside in Tobago (see p.309); you'll also encounter smaller eagle, spotted and Atlantic torpedo rays, and southern stingrays. **Dolphins** and **porpoises** are common, and docile, fifteen-metre **whale sharks** are occasional visitors, feeding on plankton and small fish. Other **large fish** include reef, tiger and nurse **sharks**, grouper, dolphin (the fish not the mammal), kingfish (wahoo), tuna, blackjack, marlin, blue cavalli, sailfish, bonita and barracuda.

# Books

T he following books should, for the most part, be readily available in the US, UK and/or T&T. Where a book is only published in one country we have specified which. It is also worth visiting the library in Port of Spain – many local authors whose work is unavailable abroad are well represented in its West Indian section. If you are staying for more than a couple of weeks, you can fill out a form, pay a TT$20 refundable deposit and borrow books. In Tobago the library in its temporary location on Signal Hill will lend books to visitors for TT$10 per book. Books that are especially recommended are marked with a ⊠ .

## Fiction and poetry

**Michael Anthony** *Cricket in the Road and Other Stories* (Heinemann, UK). An anthology of short stories evoking the atmosphere and lifestyle of Trinidad. Concise, thought-provoking pieces, rich in description. His novel *In the Heat of the Day* (Heinemann, UK) is centred on the industrial unrest that led to the 1903 water riots, while *The Year in San Fernando* (Heinemann, UK) is an acute portrayal of San Fernando in the 1940s, seen through the eyes of a teenage boy on a year's sojourn from his village home.

**Robert Antoni** *My Grandmother's Erotic Folk Tales* (Faber & Faber). Outlandish – though not very erotic – tales of life on Caribbean island Corpus Christi (aka Trinidad), under US military occupation during World War II, as told by a saucy 97-year-old to her grandson. Wonderfully evocative of wartime Trinidad.

**Kevin Baldeosingh** *The Autobiography of Paras P* (Heinemann, UK). Biting satirical novel, with plenty of implicit references to society figures. Extremely funny.

**Valerie Belgrave** *Ti Marie* (Heinemann, UK). A romantic, passionate novel set in the late eighteenth century when Britain and Spain were fighting for control of Trinidad – a Caribbean *Gone with*

*the Wind*, but far more intelligent and historically accurate.

**Dionne Brand** *In Another Place, Not Here* (Vintage, Canada). A sensuous tale of the relationship between two women, set in Canada and Trinidad.

**Brother Resistance** *Rapso Explosion* (Karia Press, UK). An excellent introduction to rapso poetry compiled by the father of the art form. These politically conscious poems describe the fears, hopes, dreams and lives of Trinidad's youth in contemporary Trini dialect.

**Roslyn Carrington** *A Thirst for Rain* (Kensington). Love story set in the St Ann's foothills, centred around food seller Myra and her relationship with saga boy Slim, ex-stickfighter Jacob and teenage daughter Odile, with some fabulous descriptions of Port of Spain.

**Leroy Clarke** *Douens* (Karaele, US). A book of unusual, intriguing drawings and poems that draw on Trinidadian folklore to explore issues of identity and conscience.

**Lynn Joseph** Author of numerous children's books about Trinidad, including *Jump Up Time: A Trinidad Carnival Story* (Harper Childrens, USA), the tale of two sisters, one of whom is competing to be a Carnival Queen.

⊠ **Earl Lovelace** *The Dragon Can't Dance* (Andre Deutsch,

UK) is a passionate examination of the motivation behind Carnival – if you only read one book about Trinidad, this should be it. In *The Wine of Astonishment* (Heinemann, UK), Lovelace highlights the persecution of the Spiritual Baptists, while in *The Schoolmaster* (Heinemann, UK), a powerful and superbly handled allegory of colonialism, a repected schoolmaster abuses his position of power in an isolated and ill-informed country village.

**Alfred Mendes** *Black Fauns* (New Beacon, UK). An interesting and amusing book about the mainly female inhabitants of a barrack yard in the 1930s. As they attempt to cope with poverty, ambition and betrayal they reveal the sense of community that made barrack yard living bearable. The cleverly plotted *Pitch Lake* (New Beacon, UK) highlights the snobbery, racism and insecurity of a young middle-class Portuguese man that eventually lead to his moral, spiritual and physical downfall.

**Sharlow Mohammed** *The Promise* (Sharlow, T&T). A powerful and evocative account of the experiences of the Indian indentured labourers. *When Gods were Slaves* (Sharlow, T&T) follows the fate of Anyika – the name means endurance – from his happy life in an African village through the trials of slavery in Trinidad.

**Shani Mootoo** *Cereus Blooms at Midnight* (Granta, UK). This Irish-Trinidadian-Canadian author's ambitious first novel deals with the relationship between an old woman dying in a Caribbean nursing home and her young gay nurse.

**Pamela Mordecai and Betty Wilson** (eds); *Her True True Name* (Heinemann, UK). Collection of short stories by women writers from the Caribbean. The T&T section includes work from Dionne Brand, Rosa Guy, Marion Patrick-Jones and Merle Hodge.

**Shiva Naipaul** *Beyond the Dragon's Mouth* (Hamish Hamilton, UK) blends journalistic and fictional anecdotes of the author's travels from Port of Spain to London, Liverpool, Hull, Iran and Surinam. *The Chip-Chip Gatherers* (Hamish Hamilton, UK) is a darkly funny tale of the machinations of the one rich man in a poor rural community. His novel *Fireflies* (Hamish Hamilton, UK) chronicles with empathy and ironic humour the moral, financial and spiritual decline of a rich and influential Indo-Trinidadian family.

★ **V.S. Naipaul** *A House for Mr Biswas* (Penguin, US/UK). Mr Biswas – a newspaper journalist trapped by poverty into living with his domineering in-laws – struggles to establish his own identity. *In a Free State* (Penguin), a collection of five tales that won the Booker Prize in 1971, explores people's changing roles and attitudes when transplanted from their homelands, while the stories in *Miguel Street* (Andre Deutsch, UK Penguin) paint a picture of community life in Trinidad seen through the eyes of a small boy. *The Middle Passage* (Penguin) – the first of the travel books that have dominated Naipaul's later output – looks at the effects of colonialism on five societies in the Caribbean and South America.

**Elizabeth Nunez** A powerful Trinidad-born author whose moving novels include *The Limbo Silence* (Seal Press, USA), the tale of a Trinidadian girl's efforts to integrate into an all white school in Wisconsin during the civil rights movement while longing for her homeland; and *Bruised Hibiscus* (Seal Press, USA), set in a small Trinidadian village, the murder of a white woman reunites two childhood friends who are forced to relive memories of witnessing abuse by white plantation owners.

**Marion Patrick-Jones** *J'Ouvert Morning* (Columbus Publishers,

T&T). A novel spanning three generations of ordinary Trinidadians, detailing their lives and tribulations from the melodramatic to the mundane.

**Lawrence Scott** Established Trinidadian author and winner of the Commonwealth Writers Prize in 1999. His books include *Ballad for the New World and Other Stories* (Heinemann, UK). A clever collection of short stories evoking pre-Independence Trinidad and the experiences of a white boy growing up in the colony, with ironic humour and sensitivity. And, more recently, *Night Calypso* (Allison & Busby, UK), set on the island of El Caracol, off the coast of Trinidad, when it was a leper colony in 1935; the novel revolves around the troubled life of orphan Theo who goes to live with the island's doctor.

## Trinbagonian literature

It is scarcely surprising that with their diverse cultural heritage, opaque dialect and witty, imaginative use of language, the people of Trinidad and Tobago have developed a rich literary heritage, producing a stable of world-class writers far out of proportion to the size of the country. This unique literary tradition emerged in the 1930s with the publication of the *Beacon*, a radical journal that ran from 1931 to 1934. Featuring poetry and short stories by young Trinidadian writers and intellectuals such as **C.L.R. James** and **Alfred Mendes**, the magazine fostered the development of **"yard literature"**, social realist stories such as Mendes's *Black Fauns*, describing the experiences of poorer Trinidadians.

**Trinbagonian** literature flourished after World War II with the emergence of a new generation of novelists. **Samuel Selvon's** wryly humorous novels chronicle both the experience of growing up in Trinidad and the trials and tribulations of an emigrant in London, while those of **Earl Lovelace** are a lyrical celebration of Trinidadian life and culture, its "shacks that leap out of the red dirt and stone, thin like smoke, fragile like kite paper balancing on their rickety pillars as broomsticks on the edge of a juggler's nose" (*The Dragon Can't Dance*).

The late 1950s saw the appearance of Trinidad's most internationally acclaimed novelist, **V.S. Naipaul**. The son of a journalist, Naipaul grew up in Chaguanas and Port of Spain, winning a scholarship in 1950 to study English at Oxford University. He wrote his first book, *The Mystic Masseur* (1957), at the age of 23 while working for the BBC Caribbean Service in London. It was his fourth, *A House for Mr Biswas*, that made his name in 1961. Drawing on the experiences of his father, the novel explores the frustration and claustrophobia of an ambitious intellectual in a colonial society. Naipaul's ironic treatment of the snobbery, corruption and small-mindedness of Trinidadian life has earned him an ambivalent reputation in his homeland. His brother **Shiva Naipaul** also garnered substantial literary acclaim with books such as *Fireflies* (1970) and *Beyond the Dragon's Mouth* (1984), before his sudden death of a heart attack at the age of forty in 1985.

Trinidad's best-known poet, the Nobel Prize-winner **Derek Walcott**, was actually born in St Lucia, but lived in Port of Spain for decades, establishing the Trinidad Theatre Workshop there (see p.85). An accomplished and prolific lyric poet, Walcott draws on the Elizabethan tradition, using both traditional rhyme and metre and free verse to explore issues of exile and identity and evoke the rich, heady atmosphere of the Caribbean.

Other **T&T poets** to look out for are Cecil Herbert, Errol Hill, Barnabos Romon-Fortune, E.M. Roach, H.M. Telemaque, Leroy Clarke, Krishna Samaroo, Wayne Brown and Kevin Baldeosingh. **Women poets** are numerous but hard to find published; perhaps the best anthology is *Washer Woman Hangs Her Poems in the Sun*, which touches on subjects ranging from the mundane to the supernatural, providing endless insights into the Trinbago mentality.

Samuel Selvon *A Brighter Sun* (Longman Drumbeat, UK). An evocative and amusing story of an Indo-Trinidadian young man learning the responsibilities of adult life during the upheavals of World War II. *The Lonely Londoners* (Longman, UK) is a witty account of a group of West Indian immigrants adjusting to the cold climate, racism and big-city life of 1950s London. Its sequel, *Moses Ascending* (Heinemann, UK), is an ironic tale of an apathetic Trinidadian's experience of the Black Power movement and race relations in 1970s London.

**Eintou Pearl Springer** *Moving Into the Light* (Ian Randle Publishing, Jamaica), *Out of the Shadows* (Karia Press, UK). Two outstanding collections of passionate poems from T&T's most prominent female performance poet.

★ **Derek Walcott** *Omeros* (Farrar, Straus, Giroux/Faber). An extraordinary tour de force that draws on Homer's *Odyssey* to produce a vast Caribbean epic of the dispossessed. Many of the works in Walcott's *Collected Poems 1948–1984* (Farrar, Straus, Giroux/Faber) evoke the sights and sounds of Trinidad, including the famous "Laventille", dedicated to V.S. Naipaul.

**Margaret Watts** (ed) *Washer Woman Hangs Her Poems in the Sun* (Ferguson, T&T). An anthology of modern women poets from Trinidad and Tobago, full of marvellous pieces tackling everything from Carnival to Caribbean men.

# History and current affairs

**Michael Anthony** *First in Trinidad* (Paria, T&T) An over-detailed account of the first appearances in Trinidad of everything from the postal service to Carnival; his *The Making of Port of Spain* (Caribbean Publications, T&T) and *Towns and Villages* (Circle Press, T&T) will tell you everything you could ever want to know about the capital and many of the villages.

**B. Bereton** *A History of Modern Trinidad 1783–1962* (Heinemann, US/UK) The most comprehensive book on the island's history.

**James Ferguson** *Eastern Caribbean in Focus* (Latin America Bureau, UK). Overview of the history, culture, economics and societies of the eastern Caribbean.

**C.R. Ottley** *Spanish Trinidad* (Longman, UK). An exhaustive account of Trinidad's history from 1498 to 1797. *The Story of Tobago* (Longman, UK) is an engaging account of Tobago's history from the Caribs to Hurricane Flora in 1963.

★ **M.S. Ramesar** *Survivors of Another Crossing* (University of the West Indies Press, T&T). An excellent, informative book with photographs recording the experiences of the indentured Indians from 1845 to the 1930s.

**Selwyn Ryan** *Revolution and Reaction*, *The Disillusioned Electorate* and *The Muslimeen Grab for Power* (all University of the West Indies Press, T&T). Three excellent accounts of recent T&T history: the first covers the Black Power years, the slump of the 1970s and the subsequent oil boom; the second deals with the economic downturn of the late 1980s, the disintegration of the PNM and the rise and rapid fall of the NAR; while the third analyses the causes and impact of the 1990 coup attempt.

**E. Williams** *History of the Peoples of Trinidad and Tobago* (A&B Distributors, US). Before becoming T&T's first prime minister, Williams was a respected academic and expert on Caribbean history; his book gives an excellent background to the development of the islands.

# Trini life and culture

★ **Funso Aiyejina** (ed) *Self-Portraits* (University of the West Indies, WI). Originally published in the T&T Review between 1995 and 2001, this is an absorbing collection of interviews with a dozen contemporary West Indian writers and critics, including one of Trinidad's finest – Earl Lovelace.

**Gerard A. Besson** (ed) *Trinidad Carnival* (Paria, T&T). Reproduction of Caribbean Quarterly's 1956 Carnival edition, this collection of pieces from eminent Trinidadian academics and musicologists is sometimes a little heavy, but has fascinating accounts of the development of Carnival from the nineteenth century to the 1950s.

**Adrian Bird** *Trinidad Sweet* (Inprint, T&T). If you ignore the occasional sexist comment this book provides an excellent and detailed insight into Trinidadian culture, mentality and the island. Full of anecdotes, humorous observations and fascinating titbits.

**Hunter Davies** *A Walk around the West Indies* (Trafalgar Square, US/Orion, UK). Personal travelogue of luxury holidays in the islands, with an interesting chapter on Tobago, but more useful for the perspective it puts on T&T in comparison to the rest of the region (though Trinidad is ignored and branded somewhat dangerous).

**Dave DeWitt and Mary Jane Willan** *Callaloo, Calypso and Carnival* (Crossing Press, US). Lively and informative cookbook-cum-travel guide, with accounts of T&T, calypso, Carnival, culinary and wider history, and including all the classic recipes, from pelau to black cake.

**Patrick Leigh Fermor** *The Traveller's Tree* (Penguin, UK). Written in the late 1940s, this classic account of a Caribbean tour has an interesting section on Trinidad, describing Port of Spain with an eagle eye and analysing the island's history, as well as its music and the "saga boy" fashions of the time.

**Martin Haynes** *Trinidad and Tobago Dialect* (self-published, T&T). Hard to find out of Trinidad but well worth it; Trini patois divided up into themes; "jorts" (food) "t'reads" (clothes) and "fete-in" (partying) as well as some beautiful sayings, old wives' tales and proverbs.

**Errol Hill** *The Trinidad Carnival: Mandate for a National Theatre* (New Beacon Books). The definitive guide for anyone seeking to understand the background of Trinidad's Carnival from the beginning of masquerade rituals to the development of a contemporary spectacle.

**James T. Houk** *Spirits, Blood & Drums: The Orisha Religion in Trinidad and Tobago* (Temple University Press, USA). An anthropological study of the Caribbean religion of Orisha.

**C.L.R. James** *Beyond a Boundary* (Duke University Press/Random House). Autobiographical book on cricket and life in Trinidad in the 1920s.

**Amryl Johnson** *Sequins for a Ragged Hem* (Virago, UK). Intense and personal portrayal of Trinidad, Tobago and other Caribbean islands.

**Paul Keens-Douglas** *Lal Shop* (Keensdee, T&T). A collection of anecdotes written for the author's *Sunday Express* column "Is Town Say So". Each piece is a random reproduction of classic "ol' talk", with titles such as "Yu ever stop to wonder how calypsonians get dey name?" or "Dat boil corn sufferin' from real malnutrition". Difficult to get hold of out of T&T, this engaging slice of rum shop banter written in patois gives a good picture of local sensibilities.

★ **Luise Kimme** *Chachalaca* (self-published, T&T). Evocative, intense snippets of Tobago life lovingly – and idiosyncratically – described in German and English by emigrant sculptor Kimme. Available from her studio in Tobago (see p.277). Two books on her work are also available; *Halcyon Days* and *Resurrection to Dance* (Prospect Press T&T).

**John Newel Lewis** *Ajoupa* (self-published, T&T, o/p). A marvellously idiosyncratic and enthusiastic account of the unique architecture of Trinidad and Tobago, illustrated by the author's superb line drawings.

**Dr Hollis Liverpool** *Rituals, Power & Rebellion: The Carnival Tradition in Trinidad and Tobago 1793–1962* (Frontline Distribution, USA). A comprehensive account of the African peoples' contribution to the development of Trinidad and Tobago's Carnival; the author is also known as the Calypso King, Mighty Chalkdust.

**Zenga Longmore** *Tap-Taps to Trinidad* (Hodder & Stoughton, UK). Caribbean travelogue with an excellent T&T account, during which the author is at the mercy of her tyrannical Trini aunt.

**Peter Manuel** *Caribbean Currents* (Latin America Bureau, UK). Excellent, well-researched account of the Caribbean music scene with a strong T&T section that details the development of soca and calypso as well as Indian music and culture.

★ **Peter Mason** *Bacchanal! Carnival, Calypso and the Popular Culture of Trinidad* (Temple University Press/Latin America Bureau). Packed with interviews with calypsonians and costume designers, this is the most up-to-date and informative book on Trinidad's Carnival.

**Olga Mavrogordato** *Voices in the Street* (Inprint, T&T). Detailing the history of some of the many old buildings around Port of Spain.

**John Mendes** *Cote Ce, Cote La* (self-published, T&T). The original dictionary of Trinbagonian words, with sections on Carnival and proverbs and drawings by Carnival designer Wayne Berkley. Widely available on the islands.

**Noel Norton** *Another Look at Trinidad and Tobago* (Calaloux Publications, USA). A glossy book of beautiful photographs from this Trini photographer, capturing the people and landscapes of T&T with accompanying text by Geoffrey MacLean.

**Raymond Quevedo** *Atilla's Kaiso* (University of the West Indies Press, T&T). Written by veteran kaisonian Atilla the Hun shortly before his death, this provides a true insider's view of the development of calypso as well as the lyrics of some of his best compositions.

**Louis Regis** *The Political Calypso: True Opposition in Trinidad and Tobago* (University of Florida Press, USA). A discussion of political calypso in national life, which looks at the relationship between the calypsonian and the politician.

**Lystra St John** *Remedies and Recipes of my Ancestry* (self-published, T&T). A materia medica of Trinbago bush medicine with sections on supernatural illness, remedy and ailment lists, botanical and local names for herbs and a selection of African and Trinbagonian recipes.

**Stephen Stuempfle** *The Steelband Movement: The Forging of a National Art in Trinidad and Tobago* (University of Pennsylvania Press, USA). Traces the history of steel pans from the 1930s to the present day, including the cultural impact of this new music form.

**Keith Warner** *The Trinidad Calypso* (Heinemann, UK). Excellent history of calypso.

**Peter van Koningsbruggen** *Trinidad Carnival: Quest for a National Identity* (Macmillan, UK). An excellent examination of attitudes surrounding Carnival and its socio-economic impact on Trinidad.

**Steve Vertovec** *Hindu Trinidad* (Macmillan, UK). Concise academic review of Hindu religion and culture in Trinidad, with an excess of facts and figures.

# Natural history

★ **Richard Ffrench** *A Guide to the Birds of Trinidad and Tobago* (Macmillan, UK). Definitive guide to T&T's bird life, including information on habitat, habits, appearance and calls as well as a description of the islands' natural history and environment. The pocket-sized version with pictures and descriptions of 83 common species is handy for travellers.

★ **Julian Kenny** *Native Orchids of the Eastern Caribbean* (Macmillan, UK). Beautifully illustrated orchid guide with special emphasis on Trinidad's orchids, written by a professor at the University of the West Indies.

**Julian Kenny** *Views From the Ridge* (Prospect Press T&T). Supported by the Guardian Life Wildlife Fund, this thoughtful product of 50 years exploring T&T's natural ecosystems is a beautifully illustrated strong appeal for sustainability.

**G.W. Lennox & S.A. Seddon** *Flowers of the Caribbean; Fruits and Vegetables of the Caribbean; Trees of the Caribbean* (all Macmillan, UK). Slim and handy reference volumes with glossy, sharp colour pictures and concise accounts.

**John C. Murphy** *Amphibians & Reptiles of Trinidad and Tobago* (Krieger Publishing, USA). A comprehensive guide to the 130 species and sub-species of T&T's herpetofauna.

**V.C. Quesnel & T. Francis Farrell** *Native Trees of Trinidad and Tobago* (T&T Field Naturalists' Club, T&T). Detailed descriptions of 58 trees, including botanical descriptions, colour photographs and notes on ecology and usage.

# Guidebooks

**Comeau, Guy, Hesterman and Hill** *T&T Field Naturalists' Club Trail Guide* (T&T Field Naturalists' Club, T&T). Definitive guide to hiking trails in Trinidad and Tobago with detailed descriptions, lengths and sketch maps. Useful sections on local geology and preparing for a hike but difficult to get hold of, though a new edition is in production.

**Richard Ffrench and Peter Bacon** *Nature Trails of Trinidad* (SM Publications, T&T). Easy to use, up-to-date guide to hikes in Trinidad.

**William L. Murphy** *Birder's Guide to Trinidad and Tobago* (Peregrine Enterprises, USA). Complete information on finding birds in T&T.

**Kathleen O'Donnell and Harry Pefkaros** *Adventure Guide to Trinidad and Tobago* (Hunter, US). Not very adventurous, and the hand-drawn maps are terrible, but the highly personal style makes for some interesting observations.

**Elizabeth Saft** (ed) *Insight Guide to Trinidad and Tobago* (APA, UK). Lavishly illustrated and full of good contextual information written by local experts, if a little thin on practicalities.

# Language

# Language

# Language

T&T's rich and varied vocabulary stems both from the republic's tumultuous history and from a love of wordplay. Amerindians, the Spanish and the French have all left their mark in the names of towns and villages around the country such as Arima, Sangre Grande and Pierreville. In isolated villages such as Paramin in Trinidad, French Creole (or patois) is still a working means of communication for village elders. Meanwhile, Spanish surfaces in parang lyrics, and Hindi is still spoken in Indian communities.

The nation's diverse ethnic mix has also influenced **Creole English**; Trinis will say "its making hot" as the French would say "Il fait chaud". Terms such as *pomme cythere* (golden apple) and *dou dou* (sweetheart, from the French *doux doux*) are commonplace, and French patois phrases are still part of the vernacular; *tout bagai* and *toute monde* are catch-alls meaning "everything". Hindi words, such as *dougla* and *aloo* (potato), have also entered the language.

The language of T&T is often oblique and allusive. **Double entendres** – possibly a legacy of slavery, when people had to watch what they said – are common, especially in **calypsos** as a means of voicing political criticism to avoid libel actions. Nicknames, such as "Silver Fox" for former prime minister Basdeo Panday, are often used, and if you are not well versed in local slang you'll need a Trini interpreter to appreciate the subtleties of the songs.

Other idiosyncrasies include a habit of using the part to refer to the whole, calling an arm a hand, or a leg a foot – when someone breaks their arm, for example, they'll say "meh han break". People will also describe the afternoon as evening – it's common to be greeted with "good evening" at 3pm, while "goodnight" is used as a greeting. "Local" is used to refer to the country as a whole, everywhere else is "outside" or "in foreign".

## Trini expressions

**Cockroach have no right in fowl party** Don't involve yourself in situations where you are unwelcome or out of place.

**Crab in a barrel** Futile backstabbing, from the way crabs will pull one another down in their attempts to escape from a barrel, so that none succeeds.

**Crapaud smoke your pipe** You are in big trouble.

**De fruit doh fall far from de tree** Children often turn out like their parents.

**Every bread have it cheese** Everyone, no matter how ugly, will find his or her matching partner.

**Get cage before yuh ketch bird** Before you can ensnare a woman, you need a house to put her in.

**If you play with dog, you must get fleas** Hanging out with lowlifes will eventually rub off on you.

**Like yuh went to school in August and yuh best subject was recess** A description of someone who is not too intelligent.

**Man plans, God laughs** It doesn't matter what you plan to do, it never turns out that way.

**Now yuh cookin' with gas** When you finally understand something; getting the picture.

**Out de lite** Turn off the light.

When opening a bottle of rum, a capful is thrown onto the ground "for the spirits/ancestors".

In memory of the dead, on the day of their wake, the street where the deceased lived is lined with candles on the pavement.

Trinis avoid walking on concrete manhole covers, not out of superstition but from a well-founded fear that they will collapse.

On hearing T&T's national anthem, all Trinis come to a direct halt and stand silently to attention – you are expected to do the same.

Meals are rarely eaten together in families unless it is a special occasion; usually a pot with food is left on the stove for each individual to dip into when necessary.

Trinis go everywhere with their "rags" – a facecloth or bandanna to wipe sweat, wave in a fete or place over their head as night falls – this is done to prevent any moisture in the air from possibly causing a head cold (a common Trini belief).

If it starts to rain, Trinis stop – waiting under shop awnings for the shower to pass. "It was raining" is a valid excuse for being late, even for a job interview.

All Trinis peel their oranges in the same way, using a knife in a circular motion from top to bottom, leaving the pith intact.

Expect a Trini goodbye to take half an hour from the point that they say they are leaving. If you're waiting for a lift, patience is essential while the goodbyes are done slowly and diplomatically to ensure no one is left out and a good vibe is kept.

**When cock get teeth** Pigs might fly.
**You've got size** You've put on weight.
**Yuh cyar play sailor an' fraid power** If you're going to be controversial you have to accept the consequences.
**Zandolie fin' yuh hole** Disparaging advice meaning know your place and stick to it.

# Glossary

**Abir** Pink dye thrown around by (and amongst) participants of the Hindu Phagwa festival.

**Ajoupa** Amerindian building with a palm-thatch roof and walls of clay and cow manure.

**All fours** Popular card game, often played for money.

**Babash** An illegal, extremely potent bootleg white rum, also called bush rum and mountain dew.

**Bacchanal** A rowdy event or social commotion, or just general scandal.

**Bachac** Large, black-brown leaf-cutting ant, which gives a nasty bite.

**Bad head** Being drunk or having a hangover.

**Bad John** Man of violent or criminal reputation, now a bit outdated.

**Bamsie** Bottom; backside.

**Bandit** A thief or mugger.

**Bareback** When a man is naked from the waist up. Also unprotected sex.

**Bashment** A big party, as in "de bashment fete for 98", or something very good.

**Bath suit** Swim suit.

**Beastly** Used to describe an extremely cold beer.

**Beat pan** To play the steel pan.

**Big truck** Large bottom, usually a woman's.

**Big up** To promote yourself and give thanks to others.

**Big yard** Trinidad's largest panyard; the Savannah at Panorama time.

**Bill it** To roll a joint.

**Block** A specific area, as in "he cool, he's from meh block"; also a liming spot for local youths, as in "mih see Harrison by de block las' night", and a place where weed is sold on the street.

**Blue food** Root vegetables such as dasheen or tannia.

**Blues** The TT$100 dollar bill.

**Blunt** A marijuana joint.

**Bobo** Cut, graze or scab.

**Bobol** Corruption, embezzlement.

**Boldfaced** Being pushy or demanding.

**Boo** No good, worthless, usually used in reference to low-grade weed.

**Bow** To engage in oral sex.

**Brabadap** Loud or uncouth person.

**Brands** Name-brand clothing, usually sportswear.

**Brass band** The bands that back live acts at fetes; traditionally, soca and calypso songs hinge on a repeated brass refrain.

**Break a lime** To leave when a lime is in full swing, causing others to think about leaving, and often used to guilt-trip the person who wants to leave.

**Brethren** Friends.

**Brush** Sexual intercourse.

**Buller** Derogative term for a gay man.

**Bump** To get a light from someone else's cigarette.

**Bumper** Another word for backside, usually a woman's. Of Jamaican origin. (See also "big truck".)

**Bush** Generic term for forests and undeveloped countryside, as in "me doh trust de bush, not at all". Also medicinal herbs; a "bush bath", "bush tea".

**Buss** To do something; eg to "buss a lime". Also bust, broken.

**Cascadura** Scaly black fish with folklore behind it; if you eat it, you're destined to end your days in Trinidad.

**Charged** Inebriated; drunk.

**Chinee** Person of Chinese descent.

**Chip-chip** Mollusc found on Trinidad's beaches; see **pacro**.

**Commesse** Confusion, controversy.

**Cook up/cook out** Food prepared in one pot, usually outside.

**Coolie** Derogatory term for someone of Indian descent.

**Creole** A broad term describing a person of mixed European and African descent born in T&T. Also classic Caribbean food, such as callaloo and coo-coo.

**Cut eye** A nasty look, also a "bad eye".

**Cutlass** Machete.

**Darkers** Sunglasses.

**Dotish** Stupid, ridiculous looking. Sometimes "doltishness" as well.

**Dou dou** Sweetheart.

**Dougla** Person of mixed Indian and African parentage.

**Ease up** To slacken, as in "ease up yuh mout'" (be quiet).

**East Indian** A person of Indian descent.

**Ent** Coined by Ronnie McIntosh's song of the same name, used at the end of a statement to mean "is that not so" or "that's true isn't it?"

**Enviggle** To persuade someone against their better judgement to do something.

**Fatigue** Witty repartee.

**Fete** A large, open-air party or concert; the biggest fetes are held around Carnival time.

**Feting** Attending fetes, partying.

**Flambeaux** A flaming torch made by filling a glass bottle with kerosene and lighting the cloth wick. Used by oyster salesmen to advertise their wares.

**Flask** A half bottle of rum.

**Flex** To let loose or party intensively, also a mode of behaviour, as in "I does flex positively".

**Flim** Film, movie.

**Free up** Relax, let go.

**Fresh water yankee** Mocking term for Trinbagonians who use foreign mannerisms picked up during short trips to the US.

**Friending** Having a sexual relationship with someone.

**Frizzle-fowl** Breed of chicken with rumpled feathers that make it look like it's been dragged through a hedge backwards.

**Fronting** Pretentious, false behaviour put on in order to impress others.

**Funk** The end of a weed joint, attached to a cigarette to make it last a little longer and give a subtle added high.

**Gallery** Verandah or porch where you can sit outside.

**Get on bad** To dance and jump up with abandon at a fete.

**Goin' down** Making a serious commitment in a relationship.

**Ground provisions** Root vegetable tubers (yam, dasheen etc), also just "provisions".

**Gyal** Girl, young woman.

**Hard wuk** Rough and passionate sex; wuk (work) is a general term for sex.

**Hops** Bread rolls, usually eaten as "hops an' ham".

**Horning** Two-timing, being unfaithful to your partner.

**Horrors** Lots of problems, bad vibes caused by anger.

**Ignorant** Quick to take offence, antagonistic.

**Ital** Rastafarian term meaning natural or pure, often used to refer to meatless food cooked with little salt.

**Jackspaniard** Large, aggressive hornet-like wasp which delivers a vicious sting; also called a jep.

**Jamette** Woman of questionable morals; also known as a jagabat.

**Jammin'** Working hard.

**Jumbie** Spirit or ghost, also a night person; "boy, you does favour a jumbie calling meh at this time in night."

**Jump-up** Frenetic partying or a frenetic party.

**Kaiso** Old-time word for calypso music, still frequently used in the calypso tents.

**Ketch it** To get high on marijuana.

**Lackeray** Gossiping.

**Laginiappe** Pronounced "lan-nyap", a little extra, a bonus.

**Las' lap** Final parade of revellers on Carnival Tuesday before the abstinence of Lent begins.

**Licks** To lash or hit someone.

**Lickser** Person who gets free things through sly methods, used with a tone of admiration.

**Lime** To socialize with friends on the street, in a bar, in a person's house, by a river, anywhere. T&T's favourite pastime.

**Lock off** Maintain a low profile for a while.

**Lyrics** Flirtatious sweet talk, usually from a man to a woman.

**Maaga** Skinny, slim.

**Macafouchette** Leftovers from a meal

**Macco** A busybody prying into other people's business.

**Macco man** Derogatory term for an effeminate and gossipy man.

**Make style** Show off

**Maljo** Evil eye.

**Malkadi** Epilepsy. Having a fit.

**Mamaguy** To fool someone with smart talk, making false promises.

**Mampy** Fat woman.

**Mauvais langue** Damaging gossip.

**Melongene** Aubergine, eggplant. Also called by its Indian name *baigan*.

**Mess up** Spoil a good time.

**Nannie** Indian term for a woman's private parts.

**Navel string** Placenta, buried by the superstitious under a fruiting mango tree to ensure a prosperous life. Also used to denote someone's roots or a place they frequent, as in "yuh navel string eh buried in Carnival fete yuh know".

**Ol' talk** Idle chatter.

**One time** Immediately, now.

**Outside man/woman** A person with whom

you are committing adultery.

**Pacro** Sea barnacle cooked up into "pacro water", a thin fishy broth said to have aphrodisiac qualities.

**Pan** The steel drum as a musical instrument.

**Panyard** Headquarters of steel pan bands.

**Pappy show** From puppet show, meaning nonsense, something inconsequential and ridiculous.

**Parlour** Small grocery store.

**Pelt** To throw.

**Petit carem** Dry spell in the middle of the rainy season, usually in September.

**Picong** The tradition of making fun of someone through an exchange of witty comments.

**Piper** Crack user.

**Pitch oil** Kerosene.

**Plam plam** Vagina.

**Planasse** To hit someone with the flat part of a machete.

**Pot hound** Skinny mongrel dog.

**Pressure** General term for stress or problems, as in "it real pressure, man".

**Prim** To be high on marijuana.

**Provision ground** Vegetable garden.

**Puja** Indian prayer or offering to the gods.

**Pum pum** Vagina. Pum pum shorts are tight hot pants.

**Puncheon** High proof rum.

**Raggamuffin** Borrowed from Jamaican slang, in T&T this describes a young, streetwise person.

**Ras** Dreadlocks or a person with them.

**Real** Plenty.

**Reds** Someone of African descent but with a light skin colour, also known as high brown.

**Respect** Used as a greeting especially between Rastafarians.

**Safe** A multi-faceted term mainly used as an affirmation meaning all will be OK.

**Saga boy** Flashy dresser.

**Salt fish** Salted cod, as well as a crude euphemism for a woman's vagina.

**Scheups** A sign of irritation, disapproval or derision also known as kissing or sucking the teeth. Dating back to the 1800s, this common sound in Trinidadian conversation came from the French planters who used it as a way of undermining the authority of the new British rulers.

**Scruntin'** Penniless, broke.

**Sea bath** To go for a swim in the sea.

**Semi demi** Something unexpected, a little bit of magic.

**Sensie** Marijuana, short for sensimilla.

**Sketel** Usually a woman who sleeps around,

but can also be used for a man.

**Slackness** Impolite, crude and low-down behaviour.

**Sound system** A crew of DJs operating the decks and providing the huge speaker boxes at fetes and parties.

**Spranger** Crack user, petty thief or volatile person.

**Storm** Getting into a fete without paying by climbing over the fence, sweet-talking the doorman, etc.

**Stupidness** The preferred term to describe ridiculous, slack, time-consuming actions or behaviour.

**Sweetman** A man who is financially supported by a woman.

**Swizzle stick** A whisk used for stirring callaloo or juicing fruits to make punch.

**Tabanca** The depression caused by the ending of a love affair. In extreme states, "tabantruck".

**Tan-ta-na** Excitement, confusion.

**Tanty** Aunt or a person who is like an aunt.

**Tapia** Hut made with thatch and mud walls.

**Ting** A thing, woman or a euphemism for all kinds of eventualities – "tings a gwan".

**Tobago love** Disguising your feelings for a loved one, possibly due to finding it difficult to express your emotions.

**Torshont** (pronounced "torshore") A loofah.

**Totie** Penis; the title of Errol Fabian's 1998 calypso *Ato Tea Party* was a play on the word; all those named in the song were strenuous in their efforts to deny that they wanted to taste some of "Ato tea" (Ato Bolden is Trinbago's most celebrated athlete).

**Trace** A road or street that once was or still is a dirt track.

**Travel** Using public transport.

**Vex** Angry or annoyed.

**Vex money** Extra money to take out with you, in case you have an argument with your partner and have to pay your own way home.

**Wapie** A card game.

**Wassi** Lewd, uninhibited behaviour and dancing at fetes; wining down to the ground.

**We is we** You are among friends.

**Wine** To dance by rotating hips and bottom in an erotic manner. Your "wining bone" is what allows you to move with suitable sensuality.

**Wrapping paper** Cigarette paper used for rolling joints.

**Wutless** Worthless, no good.

**Yampie** Matter that collects at the corner of the eyes after sleep.

**Yard fowl** Chickens raised in someone's backyard.

**Zaboca** Avocado.

**Zig zag** Altering your opinions to fit the circumstances.

# ...music & reference

Trinidad & Tobago

**Africa & Middle East**
Cape Town
Egypt
The Gambia
Jordan
Kenya
Marrakesh
   DIRECTIONS
Morocco
South Africa, Lesotho
   & Swaziland
Syria
Tanzania
Tunisia
West Africa
Zanzibar
Zimbabwe

**Travel Theme guides**
First-Time Around the
   World
First-Time Asia
First-Time Europe
First-Time Latin
   America
Skiing & Snowboarding
   in North America
Travel Online
Travel Health
Walks in London & SE
   England
Women Travel

**Restaurant guides**
French Hotels &
   Restaurants
London
New York
San Francisco

**Maps**
Algarve
Amsterdam
Andalucia & Costa del Sol
Argentina

Athens
Australia
Baja California
Barcelona
Berlin
Boston
Brittany
Brussels
Chicago
Crete
Croatia
Cuba
Cyprus
Czech Republic
Dominican Republic
Dubai & UAE
Dublin
Egypt
Florence & Siena
Frankfurt
Greece
Guatemala & Belize
Iceland
Ireland
Kenya
Lisbon
London
Los Angeles
Madrid
Mexico
Miami & Key West
Morocco
New York City
New Zealand
Northern Spain
Paris
Peru
Portugal
Prague
Rome
San Francisco
Sicily
South Africa
South India
Sri Lanka
Tenerife
Thailand

Toronto
Trinidad & Tobago
Tuscany
Venice
Washington DC
Yucatán Peninsula

**Dictionary Phrasebooks**
Czech
Dutch
Egyptian Arabic
EuropeanLanguages
   (Czech, French, German,
   Greek, Italian,
   Portuguese, Spanish)
French
German
Greek
Hindi & Urdu
Hungarian
Indonesian
Italian
Japanese
Mandarin Chinese
Mexican Spanish
Polish
Portuguese
Russian
Spanish
Swahili
Thai
Turkish
Vietnamese

**Music Guides**
The Beatles
Bob Dylan
Cult Pop
Classical Music
Country Music
Elvis
Hip Hop
House
Irish Music
Jazz
Music USA

Opera
Reggae
Rock
Techno
World Music (2 vols)

**History Guides**
China
Egypt
England
France
India
Islam
Italy
Spain
USA

**Reference Guides**
Books for Teenagers
Children's Books, 0–5
Children's Books, 5–11
Cult Fiction
Cult Football
Cult Movies
Cult TV
Ethical Shopping
Formula 1
The iPod, iTunes &
   Music Online
The Internet
Internet Radio
James Bond
Kids' Movies
Lord of the Rings
Muhammed Ali
Man Utd
Personal Computers
Pregnancy & Birth
Shakespeare
Superheroes
Unexplained
   Phenomena
The Universe
Videogaming
Weather
Website Directory

**Also! More than 120 Rough Guide music CDs are available from all good book and record stores. Listen in at www.worldmusic.net**